New Perspectives on Asset Price Bubbles

To my great colleague
Bill Ziemba

With warmest regards

Lassos Malliaris

Chicago, January 5, 2012

New Perspectives on Asset Price Bubbles: Theory, Evidence, and Policy

EDITED BY DOUGLAS D. EVANOFF,
GEORGE G. KAUFMAN, AND
A. G. MALLIARIS

OXFORD
UNIVERSITY PRESS

OXFORD

UNIVERSITY PRESS

Oxford University Press, Inc., publishes works that further
Oxford University's objective of excellence
in research, scholarship, and education.

Oxford   New York
Auckland   Cape Town   Dar es Salaam   Hong Kong   Karachi
Kuala Lumpur   Madrid   Melbourne   Mexico City   Nairobi
New Delhi   Shanghai   Taipei   Toronto

With offices in
Argentina   Austria   Brazil   Chile   Czech Republic   France   Greece
Guatemala   Hungary   Italy   Japan   Poland   Portugal   Singapore
South Korea   Switzerland   Thailand   Turkey   Ukraine   Vietnam

Published by Oxford University Press, Inc.
198 Madison Avenue, New York, New York 10016
www.oup.com

Library of Congress Cataloging-in-Publication Data

New perspectives on asset price bubbles : theory, evidence and policy / edited by
Douglas D. Evanoff, George G. Kaufman and A.G. Malliaris.
    p. cm.
Includes bibliographical references and index.
ISBN 978-0-19-984440-1 (pbk. : alk. paper) — ISBN 978-0-19-984433-3 (cloth : alk. paper)
1. Stocks—Prices.   2. Securities—Prices.   3. Capital market.   4. Financial crises.
5. Monetary policy.   I. Evanoff, Douglas Darrell, 1951-   II. Kaufman, George G.
III. Malliaris, A. G.
HG4636.N49 2012
338.5'42—dc23   2011029596

9 8 7 6 5 4 3 2 1
Printed in the United States of America
on acid-free paper

CONTENTS

ACKNOWLEDGMENTS

The editors are grateful to the CME Group Foundation for financial support to organize at Loyola University Chicago a conference titled "New Perspectives on Asset Price Bubbles: Theory, Evidence and Policy." They acknowledge official University support from Abol Jalilvand, Dean of the Business School at Loyola University Chicago; Don Schwartz, Director of the Risk Management Center at Loyola University Chicago; and Susan Phillips, Administrative Assistant, Department of Finance. For assistance with the organization and administration of the conference they thank Graduate Scholars Pooja Agrawal, Eunmi Choi, April Heitz, Joseph Rizzi, and Brian Whelan.

The editors thank the authors Franklin Allen, Gary Gorton, Takeo Hoshi, Anil Kashyap, Ben Bernanke, Mark Gertler, Claudio Borio, Jose Scheinkman, and Wei Xiong for the seminal articles in asset bubble research featured in this volume. They also thank the publishers of the journals where these original contributions appeared for permission to reproduce them. Special thanks are also given to the European Central Bank and the Federal Reserve Bank of Kansas City for allowing the authors of research presented at these institutions' conferences to include their papers in this volume.

Special thanks also go to contributors of new articles presented at the conference or submitted in the days following the conference, all aimed at updating the state of asset bubble research in light of the financial upheaval over the past few years. Contributors include Gadi Barlevy, Andrew Filardo, Kenneth Kuttner, Viral Acharya, Hassan Naqvi, Werner De Bondt, William Poole, Ben Friedman, Lawrence Christiano, Cosmin Ilut, Roberto Motto, Massimo Rostagno, John Geanakoplos, Tassos Malliaris, Bob Chirinko, and Huntley Schaller.

Finally, the editors are grateful for the valuable guidance during the preparation of this book from Terry Vaughn, Executive Editor; Catherine Rae, Economics Editor; and the staff at Oxford University Press.

CONTRIBUTORS

Viral Acharya

Viral V. Acharya is the C.V. Starr Professor of Economics in the Department of Finance at New York University's Stern School of Business, and research associate at the National Bureau of Economic Research. Prior to joining NYU, Acharya was a professor of finance and academic director of the Private Equity Institute at the London Business School, research affiliate of the Center for Economic Policy Research, and an academic advisor to the Bank of England. He was a Senior Houblon-Normal Research Fellow at the Bank of England in the summer of 2008.

Acharya's research interests are in the regulation of banks and financial institutions, corporate finance, credit risk and valuation of corporate debt, and asset. He has published widely in leading professional journals.

Acharya has a Bachelor of Technology in computer science and engineering from the Indian Institute of Technology (Mumbai) and a Ph.D. in finance from New York University.

Franklin Allen

Franklin Allen is the Nippon Life Professor of Finance and Economics at the Wharton School at the University of Pennsylvania and co-director of the Wharton Financial Institutions Center. He was formerly Vice Dean and Director of Wharton doctoral programs.

Allen has served in various editorial capacities at several leading academic journals in finance and economics. A frequent winner of Wharton teaching awards, Allen's research has focused on corporate finance, asset pricing, and the economics of information. He is a past president of the American Finance Association, the Financial Management Association, the Western Finance Association, the Society for Financial Studies, and the Financial Intermediation Research Society.

Allen received a B.A. from University of East Anglia, and M.Phil. and a Ph.D. in economics from the University of Oxford.

Gadi Barlevy

Gadi Barlevy is a senior economist and research advisor at the Federal Reserve Bank of Chicago, where he conducts research on labor economics, economic fluctuations, economic growth, financial economics, and information economics. Prior to joining the Chicago Fed, Barlevy was an assistant professor of economics at Northwestern University and a visiting professor of economics at Tel Aviv University. He has published widely in leading academic journals, serves as coeditor at *Theoretical Economics*, and previously served as coeditor at the *Review of Economic Dynamics* and as an associate editor at the *European Economic Review*.

Barlevy received a B.A. from the University of California at Berkeley and a Ph.D. in economics from Harvard University.

Ben Bernanke

Ben Bernanke is the Chairman of the Board of Governors of the Federal Reserve System. Before his appointment as Chairman in 2006, Bernanke was Chairman of the President's Council of Economic Advisers from June 2005 to January 2006 and had been a member of the Board of Governors from 2002 to 2005.

Before his public service, Bernanke was Howard Harrison and Gabrielle Snyder Breck Professor of Economics and Public Affairs and Chairman of the economics department at Princeton University. He previously had been the class of 1926 Professor of Economics at Princeton and an associate professor of economics at Stanford. He has also been a visiting professor at New York University and the Massachusetts Institute of Technology and was Director of the Monetary Economics Program at the National Bureau of Economic Research, a Fellow of the Econometrics Society, and editor of the *American Economic Review*.

Bernanke has a B.A. in economics from Harvard University and a Ph.D. in economics from the Massachusetts Institute of Technology.

Claudio Borio

Claudio Borio is Head of the Research and Policy Analysis Section of the Monetary and Economic Department at the Bank for International Settlements (BIS). At the BIS, he also served as Head of the Secretariats for the Committee on the Global Financial System and for the Gold and Foreign Exchange Committee. Borio previously worked as an economist at the OECD and as a lecturer and research fellow at Oxford University. Borio has published extensively on numerous issues in finance including on the relationship between asset prices and financial and monetary stability, monetary policy, and financial supervision and regulation. He is an associate editor of a number of academic journals including the *Journal of Financial Stability*.

Borio has a B.A., an M.Phil. and a D.Phil. in economics from Oxford University.

Robert Chirinko

Robert Chirinko is a professor in the Finance Department at the University of Illinois at Chicago and a research fellow at the Center for Economic Studies in Munich, Germany. His research focuses on financial markets, capital formation, corporate governance and finance, and tax policy. He previously held faculty positions at Cornell University, Emory University, and the University of Chicago, and visiting positions at Stanford University, the University of Munich, the Federal Reserve Bank of Kansas City, and the University of Illinois at Urbana/Champaign.

Chirinko has received the Outstanding Doctoral Dissertation Award (shared with L. Summers) from the National Tax Association, the James L. Barr Memorial Award in Public Economics, and the Vernon Award from the Association for Public Policy Analysis and Management. During fall 2006, he was a Houblon-Norman/George Senior Fellow at the Bank of England.

Chirinko has a B.A. in economics from the University of Pennsylvania, and an M.A. and Ph.D. in economics from Northwestern University.

Lawrence J. Christiano

Lawrence Christiano is the Alfred W. Chase Professor of Business Institutions in the economics department of Northwestern. He is also a consultant to the Federal Reserve Banks of Chicago, Cleveland, and Minneapolis, and a research associate at the National Bureau of Economic Research. Prior to his appointment at Northwestern, Christiano worked at the Federal Reserve Bank of Minneapolis and was a professor at the University of Chicago. Christiano's research has been focused primarily on the problem of determining how the government's monetary and fiscal instruments ought to respond to shocks over the business cycle. He published widely and has been an associate editor for many leading academic journals, including the *Journal of Money, Credit and Banking, American Economic Review, Journal of Economic Theory, and Review of Economics and Statistics*.

Christiano has a B.A. in history and economics and an M.A. in economics from the University of Minnesota, an M.S. in econometrics from the London School of Economics, and a Ph.D. in economics from Columbia University.

Werner F. M. De Bondt

Werner F. M. De Bondt is a professor of finance and Director of the Richard H. Driehaus Center for Behavioral Finance at De Paul University in Chicago. Previously he was the Frank Graner Professor of Investment Management at the University of Wisconsin, Madison. De Bondt has also been a visiting professor at universities in Belgium, the Netherlands, Switzerland, Sweden, and at Cornell University.

De Bondt studies the psychology of investors and financial markets. He is one of the founders of the field of behavioral finance. He has examined key concepts of bounded rationality, for example, people's tendency to exaggerate the true impact of new information, their bent toward wishful thinking, and their biased perceptions of risk. De Bondt's research articles have appeared in major academic journals.

De Bondt has an M.B.A. from Louvain University in Belgium and an M.P.A. and Ph.D. in Business Administration from Cornell University.

Douglas Evanoff

Douglas Evanoff is vice president and senior research advisor for banking issues in the economic research department at the Federal Reserve Bank of Chicago. His research interests include consumer credit issues, mortgage markets, bank cost and merger analysis, and financial regulation. His research has been published in leading academic journals, including the *American Economic Review, Journal of Financial Economics, and Journal of Money, Credit and Banking*, among others. He has also edited a number of books addressing issues associated with financial institutions.

Evanoff serves as chairman of the Chicago Fed's annual Conference on Bank Structure and Competition. Prior to joining the Chicago Fed, he was a lecturer in finance at Southern Illinois University and an assistant professor at St. Cloud State University. Evanoff has a B.A. from Western Kentucky University, an M.A. from the University of New Orleans, and a Ph.D. in economics from Southern Illinois University.

Andrew Filardo

Andrew Filardo is Head of Economics for Asia and the Pacific at the Bank for International Settlements office in Hong Kong. He initially joined the BIS as a senior economist in Basel and then transferred to the Hong Kong office.

Prior to joining the BIS, Filardo served on the staff of the Council of Economic Advisers. He also was a visiting scholar at the Bank of England and Bank of Canada and was an assistant vice president and economist at the Federal Reserve Bank of Kansas City. He has authored articles on business cycles, asset prices, monetary policy, globalization, and the inflation process. Filardo received his Ph.D. from the University of Chicago.

Benjamin M. Friedman

Benjamin Friedman is the William Joseph Maier Professor of Political Economy and formerly Chairman of the Department of Economics at Harvard University. Friedman has written extensively on economic policy, and, in particular, on the role of the financial markets in shaping how monetary and fiscal policies affect overall economic activity. He is the author and/or editor of more than 10 books, as well as the author of more than 100 articles on monetary economics, macroeconomics, and monetary and fiscal policy. He is also a frequent contributor to publications reaching a broader audience, including *The New York Review of Books*. He has served as director of financial markets and monetary economics research at the National Bureau of Economic Research. Before joining the Harvard faculty, he worked at Morgan Stanley.

Friedman received the A.B., A.M., and Ph.D. degrees in economics from Harvard University. He also received a M.Sc. degree in economics and politics from King's College, Cambridge, where he studied as a Marshall Scholar.

John Geanakoplos

John Geanakoplos is the James Tobin Professor of Economics at Yale University. He was Director of the Cowles Foundation for Research in Economics from 1996 to 2005. Geanakoplos was a cofounder and is codirector of the Hellenic Studies Program at Yale. He was elected a fellow of the Econometric Society and the American Academy of Arts and Sciences. He was awarded the Samuelson Prize in 1999 and the first Bodossaki Prize in economics in 1994 (for the best economist of Greek heritage under 40). He was a visiting professor at the University of California at Berkeley, Churchill College, Cambridge, the University of Pennsylvania, Harvard, Stanford, and MIT. From 1990 to 1994 he was a Managing Director and Head of Fixed Income Research at Kidder, Peabody & Co.

Geanakoplos received a B.A. in Mathematics from Yale University and an M.A. in mathematics and a Ph.D. in economics from Harvard University.

Mark Gertler

Mark Gertler is the Henry and Lucy Moses Professor of Economics at New York University and a Research Associate at the National Bureau of Economic Research. He previously taught at Cornell University and the University of Wisconsin and was a visiting professor at Princeton, Columbia, Yale, and MIT. Gertler also serves as an academic consultant for the Federal Reserve Bank of New York and is a co-editor of the *American Economic Review*. He was formerly chairman of the economics department at NYU and also was a director of the C.V. Starr Center for Applied Research. Gertler is a Fellow of the Econometric Society, a Guggenheim Fellow, and a Fellow of the American Academy of Arts and Sciences.

Gertler received a B.A. from University of Wisconsin and a Ph.D. from Stanford University.

Gary Gorton

Gary Gorton is the Frederick Frank Class of 1954 Professor of Management and Finance at the Yale School of Management and is a research associate at the National Bureau of Economic Research. Previously, Gorton was the Robert Morris Professor of Banking and Finance at the Wharton School of the University of Pennsylvania and taught at the Graduate School of Business of the University of Chicago. In 1994, he was the Houblon-Norman Fellow at the Bank of England. His research has been published in numerous leading journals, including the *American Economic Review, Review of Economic Studies, Review of Financial Studies, Journal of Economic Theory, Journal of Political Economy, Journal of Finance, Journal of Monetary Economics, Journal of Business*, and *Journal of Money, Credit and Banking*.

Gorton received a B.A. from Oberlin College and masters degrees in economics and Chinese studies from the University of Michigan, University of Rochester, and Cleveland State University and a Ph.D. in economics from the University of Rochester.

Takeo Hoshi

Takeo Hoshi is the Pacific Economic Cooperation Professor in International Economic Relations at the School of International Relations and Pacific Studies (IR/PS) and Department of Economics at the University of California at San Diego. He is also a research associate at the National Bureau of Economic Research and at the Tokyo Center for Economic Research. Hoshi served as Associate Dean of (IR/PS) from 2003 to 2005 and Acting Dean from August through December 2006 and February through August 2009.

Hoshi is the inaugural recipient of the 2006 Enjoji Jiro Memorial Prize, which is given by *Nihon Keizai Shimbun-sha* (Japanese equivalent of the *Wall Street Journal*) and the recipient of 2005 JEA-Nakahara Prize, which is awarded every year by the Japanese Economic Association to a Japanese economist with international recognition under the age of 45. He has been a visiting scholar at the Bank of Japan Institute for Monetary and Economic Studies and has been the editor in chief of the *Journal of the Japanese and International Economies* since 1999.

Hoshi has a B.A. from Tokyo University and a Ph.D. from MIT.

Cosmin Ilut

Cosmin Ilut is an assistant professor of economics at Duke University. His research focuses on macroeconomics, international finance, asset pricing, and the economics of information. He has authored and coauthored several working papers on monetary policy.

Ilut has a B.A. in economics from Babes-Bolyai University (Romania), an M.A. in economics from Central European University (Hungary), and a Ph.D. in economics from Northwestern University.

Anil K. Kashyap

Anil Kashyap is the Edward Eagle Brown Professor of Economics and Finance and Richard N. Rosett Faculty Fellow at the University of Chicago Booth School of Business. He is also a consultant to the Federal Reserve Bank of Chicago and serves as a member of the Economic Advisory Panel of the Federal Reserve Bank of New York and as a Research Associate at the National Bureau of Economic Research, where he is as co-organizer of the NBER's Working Group on the Japanese Economy and of the NBER's Working Group on the Functioning of Financial Firms and Resolution of Their Distress. He is also an advisor to the Government of Japan, is on the Congressional Budget Office's Panel of Economic Advisers, and serves on the Board of Directors of the Bank of Italy's Einuadi Institute of Economics and Finance. His research has won numerous awards, including a Sloan Research Fellowship, the Nikkei Prize for Excellent Books in Economic Sciences, and a Senior Houblon-Norman Fellowship at the Bank of England. Prior to joining the Chicago Booth faculty in 1991, Kashyap was an economist at the Board of Governors of the Federal Reserve System.

Kashyap has a B.A. from the University of California at Davis and a Ph.D. in economics from the Massachusetts Institute of Technology.

George Kaufman

George Kaufman is the John Smith Professor of Finance and Economics at Loyola University Chicago. Previously, he was the John Rogers Professor of Banking at the University of Oregon and a senior economist at the Federal Reserve Bank of Chicago. He was also a visiting professor at Stanford, University of California at Berkley, and Southern California University. He is past president of the Western Finance Association, Midwest Finance Association, and International Banking, Economic, and Finance Association and served on the board of directors of the American Finance Association. He is coeditor of the *Journal of Financial Stability* and was an associate editor of a number of journals, including the *Journal of Financial and Quantitative Analysis* and the *Journal of Money, Credit and Banking*.

Kaufman received a B.A. from Oberlin College, an M.A. from the University of Michigan, and a Ph.D. in economics from the University of Iowa.

Kenneth N. Kuttner

Kenneth Kuttner is a professor of economics at Williams College and a research associate at the National Bureau of Economic Research. Prior to joining the Williams faculty, Professor Kuttner was the Danforth-Lewis Professor of Economics at Oberlin College and served as an economist at the Federal Reserve banks of New York and Chicago. He was also a visiting professor at Columbia University and the University of Wisconsin. Kuttner is associate editor of the *Journal of Money, Credit and Banking*.

Kuttner has an A.B. degree from the University of California at Berkeley and an M.A. and Ph.D. in economics from Harvard University.

A. G. Malliaris

Anastasios G. (Tassos) Malliaris is the Walter F. Mullady Sr. Professor of Economics and Finance in the School of Business Administration at Loyola University Chicago. He has published widely in the areas of quantitative analysis in economics and the economics of asset price bubbles. He is a coeditor of the *Journal of Economic Asymmetries* and associate editor of *Multinational Finance* and *European Research Studies*. Malliaris is President of the Multinational Finance Society and Past-President of the North American Economic and Finance Association and the Athenian Policy Forum.

Malliaris has a B.A. in economics from the Athens University of Economics and Business, a Ph.D. in economics from the University of Oklahoma, and a Ph.D. in mathematics from the University of Chicago.

Roberto Motto

Roberto Motto is Adviser in the Monetary Policy Strategy Division at the European Central Bank. He has been working at the European Central Bank since 2000, taking up different functions. He specializes in monetary, macroeconomic, and financial issues and time series analysis. He has published in the *Journal of Applied Econometrics*, the *Journal of Money, Credit and Banking*, and the *Journal of Economic Dynamics and Control*, and has written several working papers. He holds a Ph.D. in Economics from the University of York.

Hassan Naqvi

Hassan Naqvi is an assistant professor of finance at the National University of Singapore. Before this, he was a research assistant at the Financial Markets Group of the London School of Economics and a lecturer in economics at the

University College of Lahore (India). His research interests include banking, corporate finance, and international finance. He has published a number of articles and chapters in books.

Naqvi has a B.S. in economics from University of London, an M.S. in finance and economics from the London School of Economics, and a MPhil and a Ph. D. in finance from the London School of Economics.

William Poole

William Poole is a senior fellow at the Cato Institute and a Distinguished Scholar in Residence at the University of Delaware. Prior to joining Cato, Poole was the President and Chief Executive Officer of the Federal Reserve Bank of St. Louis and served on the Federal Open Market Committee. He had previously served as member of the President's Council of Economic Advisers. Poole has also served as the Herbert H. Goldberger Professor of Economics at Brown University, a professor of finance at Johns Hopkins University, a senior economist at the Board of Governors of the Federal Reserve System in Washington, and a visiting professor at Erasmus University (Netherlands). He has published widely on current monetary and regulatory policy issues.

Poole has an A.B. degree from Swarthmore College and M.B.A and Ph.D. degrees from the University of Chicago. Swathmore honored him with a Doctor of Law degree in 1989.

Massimo Rostagno

Massimo Rostagno is the Head of the Monetary Policy Strategy Division of the ECB's Directorate General Economics. Before joining the European Central Bank in 1998, he was a research economist at the Banca d'Italia and later desk Economist in the European Department of the IMF. He has written on the political economy of fiscal policy, on the reform of social security, on the history and theory of monetary standards, and on monetary economics in general. He has published in the *Quarterly Journal of Economics*, *Journal of Money, Credit and Banking*, and *Journal of Economic Dynamics and Control* and contributed to several other publications.

Huntley Schaller

Huntley Schaller is a Professor of Economics at Carleton College. He has been a visiting professor at Princeton University, MIT, and the Institute for Advanced Studies in Vienna. His research has focused primarily on the interaction between the real and financial sides of the economy, focusing on investment, asset prices, the stock market, financial market imperfections, monetary policy, corporate governance, acquisitions, bubbles, and the effect of taxes. His work has been widely published, including in the *American Economic Review*, the *Journal of Monetary Economics*, the *Journal of Financial Economics*, the *Review of Economics and Statistics*, the *Journal of Money, Credit and Banking*, the *Journal of Economic Dynamics and Control*, and the *Canadian Journal of Economics*.

Schaller has a B.A. from McGill University and his Ph.D. from MIT.

José A. Scheinkman

José Scheinkman is the Theodore A. Wells '29 Professor of Economics at Princeton University. Previously, Scheinkman was the Alvin H. Baum Distinguished Service Professor and Chairman of the Department of Economics at the University of Chicago. He also was a visiting professor at Collège de France and Princeton University, and is a research associate at the National Bureau of Economic Research. He was coeditor of the *Journal of Political Economy* and associate editor of the *Journal of Economic Theory*. He has served as a consultant to the Financial Strategies Group of Goldman, Sachs & Co. and is a founder and partner of Axiom Investments.

Scheinkman is a member of the National Academy of Sciences, a Fellow of the American Academy of Arts and Sciences, a Fellow of the Econometric Society, was awarded a John Simon Guggenheim Memorial Fellowship, and received a *docteur honoris causa* from the Université Paris-Dauphine.

Scheinkman has a B.A. from the Federal University of Rio de Janeiro, an M.S. from the Institute for Mathematics (Brazil), and an M.A. and Ph.D. from the University of Rochester.

Wei Xiong

Wei Xiong is a professor of economics at Princeton University. Before holding this position, he was a visiting professor of finance at Northwestern University and an assistant professor of economics at Princeton University. He is also a research associate at the National Bureau of Economic Research. He is a finance editor of *Management Science* and previously was associate editor of the *Review of Finance*. Xiong has numerous publications, including articles in the *Journal of Finance*, *Journal of Financial Economics*, and *Journal of Political Economy*.

Xiong has a B.S. in physics from the University of Science and Technology of China, an M.A. from Columbia University, and a Ph.D. in finance from Duke University.

INTRODUCTION

CHAPTER 1

New Perspectives on Asset Price Bubbles

AN OVERVIEW[1]

Douglas D. Evanoff,
George G. Kaufman, and
A. G. Malliaris

The primary purpose of this book is to critically reexamine the profession's understanding of asset price bubbles in light of the major financial crisis of 2007–2009. It is well known that asset bubbles have occurred in the past, with the October 1929 stock market crash as perhaps the most demonstrative example. However, the remarkable positive performance of the U.S. economy from 1945 to 2006, and, in particular, during the Great Moderation of 1984 to 2006, suggested to the economics profession and monetary policymakers that asset bubbles could be effectively ignored with little real adverse economic impact. For example, the October 1987 one-day U.S. stock market crash of 20% did not seriously impact the real economy. Likewise, the bursting of the Internet bubble in 2000, when the NASDAQ dropped by 70% from its level of about 4,500 in early 2000 to 1,500 in April 2002, contributed only to an eight-month mild recession from March to November, 2001.

In contrast to these mild real economic consequences of asset bubbles bursting, both the Great Crash of 1929, which was followed by a severe economic depression, and the crash of the Japanese stock and real estate markets that led to the so-called "lost decade" in Japan should have reminded us that the severity of the spillover from asset bubbles bursting should not be underestimated.

The recent financial crisis of 2007–2009, which was followed by the "Great Recession" lasting 18 months from December 2007 to June 2009, has triggered a debate about what we really know about asset price bubbles and how (and whether) they can be managed in the public interest.

There are various components to this debate. For example, the efficient markets hypothesis views extraordinary movements in asset prices as a consequence of significant changes in information about fundamentals. This approach to asset pricing downplays the need to consider asset bubbles as a source of financial instability. It is also inconsistent with Greenspan's famous "irrational exuberance" explanation that implied that asset prices may be driven by something other than fundamentals.

Additionally, there is limited consensus as to what causes asset bubbles, and why some deflate on their own while others continue to grow. There is also disagreement on what triggers a bubble to burst, and whether we can accurately anticipate the associated risks and their potential damage to the real economy. Further, there is disagreement as to whether there are specific policy measures that central banks can and should take to respond to asset bubbles to limit their potential damage.

The Greenspan-Bernanke Federal Reserve followed an asymmetric approach to bubble management. This approach advocated no associated monetary policy action during the bubble formation and growth, but a speedy response in the form of a liquidity injection and reduction in market rates when the bubble burst to reduce the potential loss of output and employment. This approach was supported by considerable academic research and appeared to work well until September 2008, when the financial system came close to a meltdown.

The significant adverse consequences of the recent financial crisis have intensified the policy debate and encouraged theoretical modeling and empirical testing of asset price bubbles and their potentially considerable adverse economic impact. In particular, the financial crisis of 2007–2009 has prompted Fed chairman Bernanke to encourage an "open mind" in reconsidering the role of central banks in addressing asset prices as well as the optimal regulatory framework for anchoring prudential policies (Bernanke 2010). Other Fed officials have also reconsidered appropriate policy responses to asset price bubbles in light of the recent crisis (Kohn 2008, Yellen 2009, and Dudley 2010). Malliaris (2012) comprehensively examines the views of central bankers on bubble management both prior to and after the crisis.

As a result, there has been a wide-spread reevaluation of appropriate policy tools for addressing asset bubbles. Central banks have a rather limited toolset to implement their mandates of price stability and, in the United States, maximum employment. What tools other than macrostability policies are available to address asset bubble formation? Is there a potential role for macroprudential regulation? Finally, to the extent that the development of asset bubbles go beyond rationality, behavioral finance may be critical in our understanding of booms and busts.

This volume is the result of the conference "New Perspectives on Asset Price Bubbles: Theory, Evidence and Policy" organized by the editors of this book at Loyola University Chicago on April 8, 2011, and funded by the Chicago Mercantile Group Foundation. The core purpose of the conference was to contrast traditional and newer views on appropriate policy responses to asset bubbles in light of lessons learned from the recent financial crisis. Five previously published classic papers that were thought to represent the orthodox thinking about asset bubbles prior to the crisis were selected by the editors after consultation with numerous colleagues. As the basis for the conference, five distinguished economists were then invited to write original papers evaluating the accuracy of the analysis in the "classic" papers, challenging the orthodox thinking, and providing new insights. This book includes both the five classic papers and the five papers presented at the conference evaluating the original contributions. Additionally, other leading scholars were asked to contribute their analyses on issues related to bubbles. Lastly, conference keynote lectures by Benjamin Friedman and William Poole round out the volume.

This overview essay by the editors highlights the main strands of inquiry on asset bubbles in both the previously published classic papers and the responding new papers. We present the fundamental results reached in these papers, along with a fresh evaluation of their relevance in guiding policymakers during the global financial crisis. This overview identifies new lessons to be learned from the recent crisis about the significance of asset bubbles and appropriate policy responses. It also emphasizes our current inadequacies in certain areas for determining optimal policy.

The first paper by Allen and Gorton (1993) raises the critical question: Are stock prices determined by fundamentals or can "bubbles" exist? They carefully develop a detailed analytical model and show that the existence of bubbles is consistent with rational behavior. This "existence" result was not fully appreciated at the time either by the profession or by central bankers, who often doubted the existence of bubbles. Barlevy (2012) reviews the contribution of Allen and Gorton, discusses the state of theoretical models of asset price bubbles, and evaluates the lessons learned from the financial crisis. He expresses some frustration with the gap between the theoretical work on asset bubbles and the apparent change in views coming out of the financial crisis about the appropriate policy response. Little in the theoretical literature supports the contention that intervention is appropriate. He concludes that theoretical models of bubbles have not adequately addressed welfare considerations and thus are unable to offer convincing analytical guidance to central banks as to whether an economy is better off with, or without, a bubble. Ideally, an asset price bubble model can be developed to address such welfare considerations.

Among the various types of asset bubbles, stock market and housing bubbles are historically of major interest to central banks. Other bubbles such as exchange rate, oil, gold, and other commodities are of lesser concern. Ex ante, it is difficult to predict if a stock market or housing bubble will keep growing until it abruptly bursts on its own with a loud bang, or will quietly deflate on its own without much impact. While it is too early to fully evaluate the costs to the U.S. and global real economies of the bursting of the dual bubbles in housing and stock markets in recent years, the evidence from Japan is not encouraging. Hoshi and Kashyap (2000) discuss in detail the Japanese banking crisis that prevailed for most of the decade of the 1990s, following the abrupt crashing of both the Japanese stock and real estate markets. Filardo (2012) agrees with the Hoshi and Kashyap assessment of the Japanese crisis, but argues that being aware of the causes of past crises was not sufficient to protect the Asia-Pacific economies from the more recent crisis.

He underscores the broader perspective that the global financial system needs to be strengthened and that the spillovers of the international financial crisis to Asia and the Pacific presented daunting policy challenges for the central bankers in the region. Among other groups, the G20, the Financial Stability Board, the Basel Committee on Bank Supervision, and the Committee on the Global Financial System continue to address these challenges.

In their seminal paper, Bernanke and Gertler (1999) expand the financial accelerator model by incorporating exogenous bubbles in asset prices. An asset bubble affects real activity via the wealth effect on consumption and firms' financial decisions via appreciations of assets on the balance sheet. Stochastic simulations lead the authors to conclude that central banks should view price stability and financial stability as highly complementary and central bank policies should not respond to changes in asset prices, except insofar as they signal changes in expected goods and services inflation. This paper offered the intellectual foundation for the asymmetric approach to asset bubbles, also called the "Jackson Hole Consensus." Kuttner (2012) offers a detailed assessment of the Bernanke and Gertler results in view of the financial crisis. He presents two, now uncontroversial, lessons from the financial crisis that challenge the Gertler-Bernanke results. First, macroeconomic stability and price stability do not guarantee financial stability. Second, because the bursting of an asset bubble can wreak havoc on the real macroeconomy, the central bank's financial stability mandate should not be taken lightly. At issue, obviously, are how the bubble is identified and what policy tools are used to address it: interest rate policy or macroprudential supervision and regulation?

Borio (2003) addresses the financial instability that results from an asset bubble bursting. He argues that in order to improve the safeguards against financial instability, it is important to move beyond microprudential regulation and account for the cross-firm interconnections and externalities created when financial institutions encounter problems. One needs to address the potential spillover effects that can adversely affect general market conditions, other financial institutions, and ultimately the real sector of the economy. He stresses the need to strengthen the macroprudential framework for financial supervision and regulation. Acharya and Naqvi (2012) examine how the banking sector may contribute to the formation of asset price bubbles when there is access to abundant liquidity. Excess liquidity encourages lenders to be overaggressive lenders and to underprice risk in hopes that revenues from loan growth will more than offset any losses from the aggressive behavior. Thus asset bubbles are more likely to be formed by excess liquidity. They conclude that central banks and macroprudential supervision and regulations should lean against liquidity.

Scheinkman and Xiong (2003) observe that episodes of asset price bubbles are characterized by high trading volume and high price volatility. They develop a behavioral-based model of asset price bubbles, assuming short-sale constraints. An asset buyer may be willing to pay a price above fundamentals because, in addition to the asset the buyer acquires, she also obtains an option to sell the asset to other traders who may have more optimistic beliefs. De Bondt (2012) reviews the Scheinkman and Xiong paper and offers a detailed overview of behavioral finance from the perspective of asset bubbles. He challenges the idea that pure fundamentals and rationality drive decision-making and pricing and emphasizes the need to more fully incorporate behavioral issues into decision-making models.

The two keynote speakers present their views about asset price bubbles and the recent financial crisis. Friedman (2012) observes that the recent financial crisis clearly challenges the assumption of rationality employed in many of the analyses and the efficiency of the financial system to optimally allocate capital. Poole (2012) stresses that the large literature on asset bubbles has not incorporated the results from control theory from the 1960s and the rational expectations literature from the 1970s and proceeds to outline a new synthesis.

Christiano, Ilut, Motto, and Rostagno (2010) use historical data and model simulations for 18 boom periods in the United States to challenge some of the traditional views on appropriate monetary policy. They show that if inflation is low during stock market bubbles, an interest rate rule that narrowly targets inflation actually destabilizes asset markets and the macroeconomy. The authors note that economic historians have documented that in every stock market bubble in the last 200 years in the United States, excluding the Civil War and World Wars I and II, asset price bubbles occurred during years of low inflation. A logical consequence of this empirical fact is that by setting interest rates to target low inflation, the central bank is actually setting real rates below the natural rate, thus fueling a bubble. Therefore one can make the argument that a central bank that follows an asymmetric response to asset bubbles actually encourages an asset price bubble in its growing phase. This challenges the conventional wisdom of the Jackson Hole Consensus. To reduce volatility in asset prices and the real economy, Christiano, Ilut, Motto, and Rostagno propose including credit growth in the interest rate targeting rule.

Geanakoplos (2012) describes his ideas on leverage as a major cause of bubbles. He gives four reasons why the most recent leverage cycle was worse than previous cycles. First, leverage reached levels never seen before in previous cycles. Second, there was a double leverage cycle: in securities on the repo market and in real estate in the mortgage market. These cycles fed off each other and as security prices fell, leverage collapsed along with the housing mortgage market. Third, credit default swaps (CDSs) played an enormous role in the recent crisis, and had been absent from previous cycles. CDSs helped optimists leverage at the end of the boom, but most importantly they provided an opportunity for pessimists to leverage, and so made the crash come much earlier than it would have without them. Lastly, because leverage got so high and prices fell so far, a much larger number of people and businesses ended up underwater than in earlier cycles.

Malliaris (2012) reexamines the main arguments of whether or not monetary policy should respond to asset bubbles. The question of how the central bank should respond to an asset bubble can be reformulated in two ways. First, how does the central bank respond while an asset bubble is growing, and second, how does it respond after the bubble bursts? There has been strong agreement among economists that a central bank should respond to the bursting of a bubble by aggressively decreasing the Fed funds rate to minimize the adverse impact of financial instability on the real economy. However, there is no clear answer to the question of how the central bank should respond to an asset bubble before it bursts. If there is evidence that the asset price bubble is contributing to goods inflation, then there is general agreement that the central bank should respond. But what if prices remain stable? We noted earlier that Bernanke and Gertler argued that the central bank should not respond to the bubble prior to its bursting, while others believe that it should try to target the bubble or at least lean against it to avoid, or at least minimize, future financial instability. Malliaris concludes that the high costs associated with the 2007–2009 financial crisis undermined the Bernanke and Gertler, or Jackson Hole Consensus, position. The new central bank policy paradigm seems to have shifted toward "leaning against bubbles" and giving due consideration to alternative tools other than interest rate policy tools.

However, even if one accepts Malliaris' new paradigm, there is still a significant gap between being willing to consider alternative policy tools to address bubbles and deciding on the most appropriate policy response. This is probably the area in which our knowledge is most lacking. There is little justification in the existing theoretical literature for such intervention (e.g., see Barlevy 2012) and little empirical evidence on the effectiveness of alternative tools. Moreover, neither policymakers nor supervisory staffs have shown an enhanced ability to identify something as an asset bubble that may eventually burst. Similarly, it is not obvious that policymakers would know how best to deflate or manage a bubble even if they were successful at identifying it. These are the two most daunting challenges for financial researchers: determining effective means to identify asset bubbles and determining the most effective and appropriate response to manage the bubble once it is identified.

Finally, Chirinko and Schaller (2012) emphasize the distortive impact of asset bubbles on efficient capital allocation, irrespective of whether they burst, by studying whether bubbles lead to overinvestment. A fundamental function of the stock market is the efficient allocation of capital to its most productive uses. The efficiency of the stock market was initially called into question by events in the late 1990s, when some observers believed that stock market overvaluation—that is, a bubble—led to overinvestment. The overinvestment story predicts that firms with high stock prices and poor investment opportunities should have discount rates consistently below the market rate. Their empirical work finds support for the overinvestment hypothesis, consistent with a misallocation of resources during bubbles.

In conclusion, the major financial crisis of 2007–2009 appears to have been caused by several interrelated factors. In this volume, we investigate one such factor: the bursting of the housing bubble. But the papers included cannot do full justice to the subject. Nor are they the final word on the subject. We hope that the reader will find numerous useful ideas and suggestions in these papers for further research. Below is an initial list to excite the reader:

- How can theoretical models of asset pricing be modified to address welfare implications for bursting or not bursting bubbles?
- How can central banks ex ante judge the potential mopping-up costs of not addressing asset bubbles?
- Why did the Great Moderation bring macroeconomic stability, but not financial stability?
- Under what conditions does the financial system allocate capital efficiently? Do asset bubbles distort the allocative efficiency of the financial system? How significant is the distortion?
- How can behavioral finance enrich asset price bubble modeling?
- Does inflation targeting distort the natural rate of interest and destabilize asset markets?
- How have recent financial innovations impacted leverage and liquidity?
- Now that domestic and global financial stabilities have been elevated as macroeconomic goals, how can prudential supervision and regulation best achieve these goals?
- With the policy action proposed by the Jackson Hole Consensus having been shown to be extremely costly, what additional information is needed to allow policymakers to know ex ante that leaning against a bubble is optimal policy?

Notes

1. The views expressed are those of the authors and may not reflect those of the Federal Reserve Bank of Chicago or the Federal Reserve System.

References

Acharya, Viral V., and Hassan Naqvi. 2012. "Bank Liquidity and Bubbles: Why Central Banks Should Lean against Liquidity." In this volume.

Allen, Franklin, and Gary Gorton. 1993. "Churning Bubbles." *Review of Economic Studies* 60, 813–836. Reprinted in this volume.

Barlevy, Gadi. 2012. "Rethinking Theoretical Models of Bubbles: Reflections Inspired by the Financial Crisis and Allen and Gorton's Paper, 'Churning Bubbles'." In this volume.

Bernanke, Ben S. (2010). "Monetary Policy and the Housing Bubble." Speech at the annual meeting of the American Economic Association, Atlanta, January.

Bernanke, Ben, and Mark Gertler. 1999. "Monetary Policy and Asset Price Volatility." *Economic Review of the Federal Reserve Bank of Kansas City,* 4th Quarter, 17–51. Reprinted in this volume.

Borio, Claudio. 2003. "Towards a Macroprudential Framework for Financial Supervision and Regulation?" *CESifo Economic Studies* 49, 181–216. Reprinted in this volume.

Chirinko, Robert S., and Huntley Schaller. 2012. "Do Bubbles Lead to Overinvestment? A Revealed Preference Approach." In this volume.

Christiano, Lawrence J., Cosmin Ilut, Roberto Motto, and Massimo Rostagno. 2010. "Monetary Policy and Stock Market Booms." in *Macroeconomic Challenges: The Decade Ahead*, Federal Reserve Bank of Kansas City. Reprinted in this volume.

De Bondt, Werner. 2012. "Asset Bubbles: Insights from Behavioral Finance." In this volume.

Dudley, W. C. 2010. "Asset Bubbles and the Implications for Central Bank Policy." Remarks given at the Economic Club of New York, April 7.

Filardo, Andrew. 2012. "The Impact of the International Financial Crisis on Asia and the Pacific: Highlighting Monetary Policy Challenges from an Asset Price Bubble Perspective." In this volume.

Friedman, Benjamin M. 2012. "Struggling to Escape from 'Assumption 14.'" In this volume.

Geanakoplos, John. 2011. " Leverage and Bubbles: The Need to Manage the Leverage Cycle." in *Approaches to Monetary Policy Revisited—Lessons from the Crisis*, edited by Marek Jarociński, Frank Smets, and Christian. In this volume.

Hoshi, Takeo, and Anil Kashyap. 2000. "The Japanese Banking Crisis: Where Did It Come From and How Will It End?" *NBER Macroeconomics Annual*, 129–201. Reprinted in this volume.

Kohn, D. L. 2008. "Monetary Policy and Asset Prices Revisited." Presented to the 26th Annual Monetary Policy Conference of the Cato Institute, Washington, DC, November 19.

Kuttner, Kenneth N. 2012. "Monetary Policy and Asset Price Volatility: Should We Refill the Bernanke-Gertler Prescription?" In this volume.

Malliaris, A. G. 2012. "Asset Price Bubbles and Central Bank Policies: The Crash of the 'Jackson Hole Consensus'." In this volume.

Poole, William. 2012. "An Old Perspective on Asset Price Bubbles Policy." In this volume.

Scheinkman, José A., and Wei Xiong. 2003. "Overconfidence and Speculative Bubbles." *Journal of Political Economy* 111, 1183–1219. Reprinted in this volume.

Yellen, Janet. 2009. "A Minsky Meltdown: Lessons for Central Bankers." Presented to the 18th Annual Hyman Minsky Conference of the State of the U.S. and World Economies—*Meeting the Challenges of the Financial Crisis*, April 16.

BUBBLES: THEORY AND EVIDENCE

CHAPTER 2

Churning Bubbles

Franklin Allen and Gary Gorton

1. Introduction

There has been a long and continuing debate on the determinants of stock prices. One view is that these prices reflect economic fundamentals; that is, a firm's stock price equals the present discounted value of its dividends. Another view is that stock prices are "bubbles" and deviate from their fundamentals.[1] As an empirical matter, there is currently no consensus on which of these views is correct?[2]

Historically, the possibility that stock prices are bubbles was raised by a number of extreme incidents. Perhaps the most well known of these is the South Sea bubble. During the first half of 1720 the stock price of the British South Sea Company rose by over 700% ; during the last half of 1720 the price fell back to about 50% above its value at the start of the year (see Neal 1990, 111). A similar rise and sudden decline occurred in the stock price of John Law's Mississippi Land Company in France. Both episodes were precursors of the stock market crashes of subsequent centuries of which October 1929 and October 1987 are perhaps the most famous. While it is by no means clear that these events constitute evidence of bubbles, they were important in that many of them led to regulation. For example, the South Sea bubble caused the British Parliament to pass the South Sea Act, which effectively eliminated the stock market as a source of funds for over a century. In the United States, the Great Crash of 1929 led to the creation of the SEC and the introduction of numerous regulations, many of which are still in force.

In an important contribution, Tirole (1982) argues that in a discrete-time finite-horizon setting stock prices cannot deviate from fundamentals unless traders are irrational or myopic.[3] He makes three important arguments in ruling out finite bubbles. First, with a discrete and finite number of points in time a bubble would never get started because it would "unravel." To see this let the final date in the economy be T. Then at date T − 1 an agent would not buy the asset at a price above the discounted value of its payoff at T because he would incur a loss if he did so. Therefore, the bubble cannot exist at T − 1. Similarly, by backward induction it follows that a bubble cannot exist at any point in time. Secondly, if the probability of being able to sell the asset tends to zero as the horizon approaches then traders can only be induced to hold the stock by a price path that goes to infinity. Because there is finite wealth, there must be a date at which the (real) price path necessary to support the bubble would exceed the total available wealth in the economy. At . that date the bubble would crash, but then at the date before that no other trader would buy the asset. Again by backward induction the bubble cannot get started. Finally, without insurance motives for trading not all of the finite number of traders can rationally expect to benefit since they know that the bubble is a zero-sum game. If traders are risk averse, some must be strictly worse off since they bear risk and not everybody can have a positive expected return.

Tirole's (1982) results exemplify the difficulties of constructing theories which are based on conventional assumptions and which are consistent with bubbles. These difficult ties have led some authors to abandon the traditional neoclassical assumption of rational behavior. One example is Shiller (1984) who models stock prices as being subject to "fads." Another is DeLong, Shleifer, Summers, and Waldmann (1990) who assume that some traders continue to hold beliefs even after it becomes clear these are rejected by the data. These irrational traders are consistently overly optimistic (or overly pessimistic) and take larger positions than they would if they were rational. This means they bear more risk than is optimal but their wealth is not driven to zero. They therefore persistently cause stock prices to deviate from their fundamentals.[4]

The model presented below takes a different approach. We assume all agents are rational but they populate an imperfect world which is characterized by asymmetric information. In particular, there is an agency problem between investors and portfolio managers which is similar to that originally identified by Jensen and Meckling (1976) between bondholders and equityholders. In the corporate finance literature the analysis of agency relationships is now commonplace and their implications for firms' investment decisions are well known. It is widely accepted that asymmetric information can lead to firms making inefficient investment decisions.

One of the most significant changes in the structure of capital markets over the last four decades has been the growth of institutional investors. In many countries, a significant fraction of the wealth held in stocks is now invested indirectly through financial intermediaries. For example, in the United States 45% of the value of equities quoted on stock markets was held by institutional investors in 1991.[5] In contrast, institutional investors held only 6.5% of shares in 1952 (see Goldsmith 1971, 78).

Despite this importance of intermediaries, the implications of agency relationships between investors and portfolio managers for asset pricing have not been fully investigated. It is argued below that one of the manifestations of asymmetric information in this context is that asset prices can deviate from their fundamental values and be subject to bubbles. In our model some of the portfolio managers' trades are not motivated by changes in information, liquidity shocks, or risk sharing. Instead they are churning their clients' portfolios in the hope of a speculative profit.

We assume there are two types of people who can obtain the qualifications necessary to become a portfolio manager. The first group, who are good portfolio managers, can each identify a number of undervalued firms and this allows them to make a higher return on the funds they invest than traders with no special information. We use a model related to that of Glosten and Milgrom (1985) to show how they accomplish this. Thus markets are not strong-form efficient but this is not inconsistent with rationality. The second group consists of bad portfolio managers who are unable to identify undervalued firms. Lenders cannot observe which type of portfolio manager they are entrusting their wealth to.

In Section 2 we focus on the actions of the bad portfolio managers. We assume that these portfolio managers, who have no wealth of their own, receive a proportion of the profits that they make so their payoff has the form of a call option; this is later shown to be an optimal contract. This type of compensation scheme, where the payment to the portfolio manager is a call option on the portfolio's incremental return, is widely used in practice in the investments industry (see, e.g., Kritzman 1987). In our model its important feature is that it can induce risk-loving behavior.

We show that the trading activity of these portfolio managers causes a bubble in the sense used by Harrison and Kreps (1978) and Tirole (1982). A bubble is defined to be a price path supported by the trading of agents who are "willing to pay more for [the security] than they would pay if obliged to hold it [to horizon]." We show that the bad portfolio managers strictly prefer to speculate in this sense.[6] This strict preference can occur because of the fact that there is an asymmetry in their incentives. If they lose the money entrusted to them they obtain nothing no matter how badly they do. If they do well they keep a proportion of what they make. They are therefore prepared to purchase securities which are trading above their fundamental provided there is some chance of a capital gain even though they know that there is a good chance they will lose their investors' money when the bubble crashes.

In Section 3 we consider the entire stock market, of which the bad portfolio managers are a part. In Section 3.1 we develop a model of how the good portfolio managers profitably trade on their information. In Section 3.2 we consider both groups of portfolio managers and demonstrate that the contract assumed in Section 2 is an optimal contract. It is not worthwhile for lenders to entrust their wealth to portfolio managers who they are sure will speculate. However, they cannot tell them apart from the good portfolio managers that can identify undervalued firms. Therefore, in equilibrium, the good managers subsidize the ones that speculate and lenders earn their opportunity cost.

The example presented in Sections 2 and 3 shows that bubbles can occur when funds are invested by portfolio managers and there is an agency problem. Since our results differ from those of Tirole, an important issue concerns the robustness of our example and its implications for theories of asset pricing. Section 4 discusses the critical elements of the example that lead to bubbles.

2. Speculative Bubbles

This section considers a stylized model of a stock market in which there are three traders. We assume that these traders have no wealth of their own but instead manage other people's wealth for them. They receive a proportion of any profits they make. It is shown in Section 3 that this contract can be optimal. Section 2.1 outlines the basic model.

The key issue is whether or not these traders perceive there to be some chance of a capital gain at all points in time. This depends on what they conjecture about the strategies of other traders. We consider a very stylized structure which makes traders' conjectures about other traders' actions very simple. In particular, we assume in Section 2.2 that traders leave the market when they "die" and that their "death" times are correlated in a particular way. This rationale for exiting from the market, and the correlation structure of these "death times," are clearly not meant to be taken literally but rather are devices for streamlining the model in order to focus on the theoretical issue of the existence of bubbles in a finite world. The main point is to develop a simple structure under which the logical sequence of conjectures traders go through will not lead to unraveling but to rational traders deciding to speculate. Having developed this structure we go on to briefly show, in Section 2.3, how the model can be extended to the case where a trader's exit from the market arises from an endogenous decision rather than being due to an exogenous event.

2.1. THE BASIC MODEL

The following assumptions detail the basic model.

Assumption A1. There are three traders called Persons 1, 2, and 3.

Assumption A2. The model lasts for one continuous period, beginning at $t = 0$ and ending at $t = 1$. Trades can occur at any time between 0 and 1.

Assumption A3. The traders consume just before they die, which occurs somewhere between 0 and 1.

Assumption A4. The agents' utility is an increasing function of consumption. They can be either risk neutral or risk averse. They have limited liability; there is no possibility of negative consumption.

Assumption A5. Person 1 dies at date t_1, which is drawn from a uniform distribution on $[0, 1)$. Person 2 dies at t_2 where

$$t_2 = t_1 + (1/3)(1 - t_1) \tag{1}$$

Person 3 dies at t_3 where

$$t_3 = t_1 + (2/3)(1 - t_1). \tag{2}$$

·*Assumption* A6. Agents learn their death times just in time to allow them to trade and consume before they die. Death is private information.

Assumption A7. There exists a firm with a certain payoff which for simplicity we normalize to zero. In other words the fundamental is zero. This is known to all traders. The firm issues one indivisible share. This share cannot be sold short.

Assumption A8. Person 1 is always endowed with the share. Person 1 knows his identity.

Assumption A9. Persons 2 and 3 are not endowed with any shares. They do not know their identities (i.e. whether they are going to die last) and assign equal weight to each of the two possibilities.

Assumption A10. Persons 2 and 3 have no wealth of their own. However, they are able to invest other people's wealth. They are to be thought of as portfolio managers. They have a fixed amount B (= 1 in illustrations) to invest. The amount π they repay to investors if the amount they have at the end is y, is:

$$\pi = B + \alpha(y - B) \text{ for } y \geqq B,$$
$$= y \text{ for } y < B, \tag{3}$$

where $0 \leqq \alpha \leqq 1$. (In illustrations it is assumed that $\alpha = 0.95$.) In effect, the payoff the portfolio managers receive is a call option. The accounting system is such that they cannot simply consume the money they borrow. They can only consume the fee that they are paid for managing the portfolio. It follows from (3) that this is a proportion $1 - \alpha$ of the profits that they make if these are positive and nothing if they are negative.

Assumption A11. The identity of the owner of the share is private information throughout.

Assumption A12. Trade occurs in the following way. All traders have the same expectations about prices *p(t)* at which trades will occur at time *t*. When a person decides to sell the share he contacts a broker who seeks out a buyer. He locates one or the other of the traders that remain in the market with equal probability. If he finds another trader then trade occurs at $p(t)^e$. If the seller cannot find a buyer this becomes public information and the price of the share falls to zero. For purposes of illustration we focus on

$$p(t)^e = t \text{ for } t \in [0, 1). \tag{4}$$

Assumption A13. When a trade occurs only parties to the trade observe the transaction.

Assumption A14. All agents know the structure of the model and the distributions of the random variables, but do not observe the particular realizations of random variables.

2.2. EXAMPLE OF A BUBBLE

The share considered has a fundamental of zero. It is clear that an equilibrium with $p(t)^e = 0$ exists where the share price reflects this fundamental. The question that we address is the following. Do there exist other price paths such that a rational agent is prepared to buy the share at a strictly positive price even though he knows the final payoff to the share is zero? The agency problem between investors and their portfolio managers is not sufficient by itself to provide a satisfactory theory of bubbles in asset prices. When the portfolio managers have a call option on the incremental value of the portfolio, they may be indifferent between buying and not buying a stock that is trading above its fundamental. If they are prepared to buy then bubbles may exist. However, a theory which critically depends on people's behavior when they are indifferent is not very satisfactory. We therefore develop a theory where portfolio managers in the group that cannot identify undervalued securities are strictly better off investing in stocks trading above their fundamental.

Our first result is:

Proposition 1. *When death times are unknown there exists a set of self-fulfilling beliefs such that two trades will always occur at a strictly positive price between date 0 and date 1 provided:*

(i) $0 < p(t)^e < B$ *for all* $t \in [0, 1)$;
(ii) $p'(t)^e > 0$ *for all* $t \in [0, 1)$.

To see why this holds, consider a numerical example where $t_1 = 0.1$ so that $t_2 = 0.4$ and $t_3 = 0.7$ (from (1) and (2)). As mentioned in the previous subsection, we also assume $p(t)^e = t$, $B = 1$, and $\alpha = 0.95$. For ease of exposition we start by describing a sequence of events, shown in Figure 2.1, without analyzing the traders' decisions. We

TRUE VALUES OF DEATH TIMES: $t_1 = 0.1$; $t_2 = 0.4$; $t_3 = 0.7$.

SEQUENCE OF EVENTS

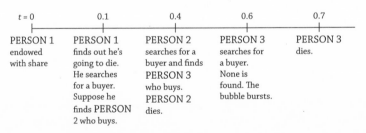

$t = 0$	0.1	0.4	0.6	0.7
PERSON 1 endowed with share	PERSON 1 finds out he's going to die. He searches for a buyer. Suppose he finds PERSON 2 who buys.	PERSON 2 searches for a buyer and finds PERSON 3 who buys. PERSON 2 dies.	PERSON 3 searches for a buyer. None is found. The bubble bursts.	PERSON 3 dies.

Figure 2.1 Example with unknown death times

then consider a set of beliefs and show that these support the decisions in Figure 2.1. Finally, we show that the beliefs are self-fulfilling.

At $t = 0$, Person 1 is endowed with the share. At $t = 0.1$, he finds out he is going to die and searches for a buyer, which is Person 2 or 3 with probability 0.5. For concreteness we assume he finds Person 2, who buys the share at a price of 0.1. At $t = 0.4$, just before he dies, Person 2 searches for a buyer and finds Person 3, who buys the share at a price of 0.4.[7] He makes a profit of $0.4 - 0.1 = 0.3$ and after repaying his investors consumes $(0.05)(0.3) = 0.015$. At $t = 0.6$ Person 3 searches for a buyer, but finds none. The bubble bursts and the price of the stock falls from 0.6 to zero. Finally, at $t = 0.7$ Person 3 dies.

At the time of his death, he has 0.6 remaining and so is only able to return this amount to his investors. He consumes nothing.

Consider the following set of beliefs. Given that $p'(t)^e > 0$, all agents believe that:

(a) if there is a prospective buyer alive (who has not already owned the stock) he will be prepared to buy the share when approached.

Agents who do not know their own identity believe that:

(b) any agent offering to sell at a date in the interval $0 \leqq t < 1/3$ is Person 1 selling at t_1 with probability 1; and
(c) any agent offering to sell at a date in the interval $1/3 \leqq t < 1$ is Person 1 selling at t_1 with probability 0.4 or Person 2 or 3 selling at t_2 with probability 0.6.

We demonstrate below that these beliefs support the sequence of actions in Figure 2.1 as an equilibrium and that they are self-fulfilling. Figure 2.2 outlines the sequence of the buyers' conjectures about the seller's identity discussed below.

First consider Person 1's decision. He knows from the structure of the model that for $0 \leqq t \leqq 1$ Person 2 and 3 will be alive. Thus from (a), Person 1 believes he can sell the share at any time until his death. Since the share price is increasing through time, it is optimal for Person 1 to hold the share until he has to sell it at his death time t_1. Thus at $t = 0.1$, Person 1 will search for a buyer. There is a 0.5 probability he will find Person 2 and 0.5 probability he will find Person 3. For concreteness we suppose that Person 2 is found.

Next consider Person 2's decision. From (b), he believes that the seller is Person 1. He can put himself in the place of Person 1 and by doing so deduce that Person 1's optimal strategy is to sell at Person 1's death time. He therefore knows that $t_1 = 0.1$ which implies that $t_2 = 0.4$. This means that he should not wait past $t = 0.4$ to sell the share since if he survives that date he will be the sole remaining trader; until that date there will definitely be another buyer. Since the price is increasing, he should sell at $t = 0.4$.

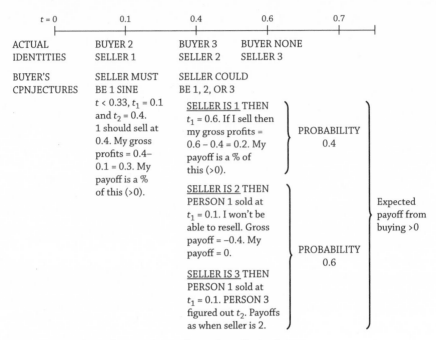

Figure 2.2 The buyer's conjectures about the seller's identity

Person 2 finds the remaining trader, Person 3, at $t = 0.4$. Consider Person 3's decision. Since he was not endowed with the share he knows he is Person 2 or 3, but does not know which. Since he is approached at $t = 0.4$ he does not know whether the seller is Person 1, 2, or 3. It follows from (c) that he believes there are two possibilities. There is a 0.4 probability that the seller is Person 1 in which case $t_1 = 0.4$. This implies that $t_2 = 0.6$ in which case from (c) the share could be sold at any date up to this point. We refer to this first possibility as state S to indicate the share can be sold again. He also believes there is a 0.6 probability that the seller is Person 2 or 3. In this case Person 1 must have sold it at $t_1 = 0.1$ and there will be no one for the trader to resell it to. We refer to this second possibility as state N to indicate that no resale is possible.

The payment schedule in (3) implies Person 3 cannot lose from buying the share and he can gain if he manages to resell it at a higher price. Since he attaches a 0.4 probability to there being another trader who he can resell the share to at a higher price, he is strictly better off purchasing the share. What is the optimal time for him to try to sell the share? If state N is the true state, then there is no other trader to sell the share to. This possibility therefore has no effect on his optimal selling time. If state S is the true state, then $t_1 = 0.4$ and $t_2 = 0.6$. Hence, since price is rising his optimal action is to search for a buyer at $t = 0.6$. In fact, in this example there is no other buyer to be found, so at $t = 0.6$ he realizes that he is Person 3 and the bubble crashes. At $t = 0.7$ Person 3 dies.

So far we have considered the case where $t_1 = 0.1$. It can be seen that for $0 \leqq t_1 \leqq 1/3$ the analysis is the same because only Person 1 can die in this interval. For $1/3 \leqq t_1 \leqq 1$ it can be seen that the beliefs (a) again make it optimal for Person 1 to sell at his death time. The difference here is that the identity of the seller in the first transaction will be unknown. The buyer's decision is then the same as Person 3's at $t = 0.4$ above; he cannot distinguish between states S and N and assigns probabilities of 0.4 and 0.6 to these, respectively. Any other transactions in the interval $1/3 \leqq t \leqq 1$ also have this feature so that the analysis of other possible cases is similar to that of the illustration.

Why are the beliefs (a), that when found a prospective buyer (who has not already owned the stock) will always purchase the share, correct in equilibrium? First, consider somebody who is approached after $t = 1/3$. A prospective purchaser will be better off buying provided he believes that there is some probability that he can resell the share. This depends on whether there is some probability he can locate a prospective buyer and this conjectured buyer believes that he can resell the share, and so on. From the point of view of any new buyer there is always a 0.4 probability of another willing buyer later. This chance of state S is independent of time. At any point a prospective buyer cannot distinguish between the seller being Person 1 or the seller being Person 2 or 3 and hence whether or not another buyer remains. As a buyer goes through the logical sequence of conjectures concerning whether he will be able to resell, he knows for certain that the share cannot be resold more than once. However, the person that he might sell to will think there is a 0.4 probability he will be able to resell and so on; as far as each buyer in the sequence is concerned there is always a possibility that the share can be resold once. This is true for an infinite sequence of conjectured buyers. No matter how close to $t = 1$ a sale were to occur, (1) and (2) together with $p'(t)^e > 0$ imply that there is always a 0.4 possibility of reselling the share at a profit so unraveling does not occur. For anybody approached before $t = 1/3$ the analysis is similar except there is a probability of 1 they can locate another willing buyer. Thus beliefs (a) are correct in equilibrium.

Why are beliefs (b) and (c) correct in equilibrium? It was argued above that Person 1 always sells at his death time t_1 and the person he sells to always sells at t_2. The unconditional distribution of $t1$ is uniform on $[0, 1)$ with density 1 and the unconditional distribution of t_2 implied by (1) is uniform on $[1/3, 1)$ with density $3/2$ as shown in Figure 2.3. Hence, the beliefs (b) that for $0 \leqq t_1 \leqq 1/3$, anybody selling the stock is Person 1 with probability 1 are correct. For $1/3 \leqq t_1 \leqq 1$ the probability the seller is Person 1 (i.e., state S) is $1 / (1 + 3/2) = 0.4$ and the probability the seller is Persons 2 or 3 (i.e., state N) is $(3/2) / (1 + 3/2) = 0.6$. Beliefs (c) are, therefore, also correct in equilibrium.

These arguments show that provided the expected price is always below B so that traders have enough resources to buy the share and provided the price path is rising, there will always be two trades at a strictly positive price. Thus Proposition 1 is demonstrated.

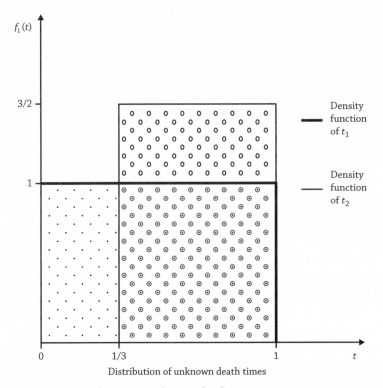

Figure 2.3 Distribution of unknown death times

Portfolio managers make at least two trades in the model presented. These trades are not motivated by changes in information, liquidity needs, or risk sharing. They arise solely from the incentives that portfolio managers are faced with. Even though the expected return to trading is negative, the payoff function for managers makes it worthwhile for them. They are churning their customers' accounts for their own benefit.

This is slightly different from the standard notion of churning where it is the prospect of commissions that causes managers to trade unnecessarily but the basic idea is similar; the cost is in terms of a negative (or lower than normal) expected return rather than an explicit commission. Agency problems lead to trades that are not in the investors' interests.

Why do our results differ from those of Tirole (1982)? We relax three of the assumptions that he makes. He assumed that time is discrete and there are a finite number of periods. In this case a bubble can never get started because it would unravel. If an asset's payoff at date T is known to be zero then at date $T-1$ nobody will buy it at a positive price. Similarly at date $T-2$ and so on so that the asset is always worthless. In our model time is continuous so that although there is a final date $t = 1$ there is no date corresponding to $T-1$; no matter how close to $t = 1$ it is always possible to resell the share before the final date. The unraveling argument is not applicable.

Tirole's second assumption is that the probability of being able to sell the security tends to zero as the horizon is approached. In order for a bubble to exist, the price must then tend to infinity. This is not possible because there is finite wealth; if the price path did go to infinity the amount needed to purchase the share would exceed the total wealth available in the economy. Again by backward induction the bubble cannot get started. In our model the probability of being able to sell the security does not tend to zero. No matter how close to $t = 1$ a trade occurs the probability of finding a subsequent buyer is 0.4. It is always optimal for the trader to hold the stock until the conjectured t_2. Without some correlation structure of this type, the chance of finding a buyer would fall toward zero and the price path would need to rise to infinity to induce the trader not to sell.

Tirole's third assumption is that investors do not have an insurance motive for trading. Given this, not all of the finite number of traders can expect to be better off ex ante since they know that the bubble is a zero-sum game. If they are risk averse some must be strictly worse off. In our model all the traders participating in the bubble are strictly better off ex ante. The reason is that they are investing with other people's money and their reward structure is such that they do not care about the magnitude of any losses they incur. The people who bear the losses ex post are the investors lending them the money. They are willing to lend because the traders are pooled with portfolio managers who can identify profitable investment opportunities; the good portfolio managers effectively subsidize these losses by paying a higher amount to lenders than they would have to in the absence of the bad portfolio managers. It is this aspect of our model which is the most crucial for our result that asset prices can deviate from their fundamentals. It is explained in Section 3.

2.3. EXTENSIONS

The purpose of most of the assumptions used in the previous section is to simplify the analysis. For example, having Person 1 endowed with the share limits the number of cases that need to be considered. It would also be possible to have the share randomly endowed. In that case neither Persons 1, 2, or 3 know their identity and the number of possible states of the world each agent must consider is significantly increased. However, the results do not change substantively.

The assumption that outlines the way in which trade occurs is an important one. Its role is essentially similar to that of the Walrasian auctioneer and price-taking in standard competitive models since it allows strategic aspects of traders' behavior to be ignored. Its purpose is again to simplify the nature of the conjectures that people make about what could have happened in the past.

The proposition indicates that any price path which is monotone increasing is an equilibrium. In addition the fundamental is of course also an equilibrium.

This multiplicity of equilibria is similar to that which arises in infinite-horizon overlapping-generations models. As in these cases one way of describing which equilibrium occurs is to associate each equilibrium with the outcome of an exogenous random event or "sunspot."

The analysis above has the feature that agents' decisions to leave the market are exogenous. As discussed in the introduction, "death" is not meant to be taken literally but rather is meant to represent any event that causes the trader to leave the market; for example, death could correspond to the timing of liquidity needs. Another possibility is that the decision to leave the market can be made endogenous, and the model correspondingly more realistic, by extending the basic model outlined above. In this subsection we sketch such an extension. Proofs are provided in Allen and Gorton (1988).

To endogenize the exit decision suppose that there is a possibility of bankruptcy in which case the security will pay off zero immediately. There is also assumed to be a level of wealth for each trader beyond which the marginal utility of consumption is so low that the rate at which their wealth is increasing is insufficient to compensate them for the risk of the firm going bankrupt so they sell and leave the market. In other words, for trader i:

$$u_i(C) = C \text{ for } C < C_i^*.$$
$$= C_i^* \text{ for } C \geq C_i^*. \tag{5}$$

For Person 1 the critical level of wealth C_i^* is drawn from a uniform distribution on $[0, 0.05)$. For Person 2

$$C_2^* = \beta (0.05 - C_1^*) \tag{6}$$

where β is the unobservable realization of a random variable distributed uniformly on $(0.0.5)$. For Person 3 it is also the case that

$$C_3^* = \beta (0.05 - C_1^*) \tag{7}$$

Agents learn their Ct at $t = 0$. The realizations are private information.

Note that if β were a constant, then knowledge of C_2^* would be sufficient to prevent bubbles because all other agents' C_i^*'s could be computed once some agent was approached to buy the security. An agent would then know how many other agents remained in the market and an unraveling argument would hold. But bubbles can exist if we suppose that there is another source of uncertainty, such as β, which reflects uncertainty about how the death times are linked. Even though each agent knows his own C_i^*, the second source of uncertainty, β, does not allow agents to infer the ordering of C_i^*'s and so the sequence of logical conjectures here is similar to the previous case. Because of the uncertainty induced by β, there is always a positive probability of another buyer. By specifying a set of beliefs corresponding to the probabilities induced by the distribution of death times given the distribution of β, it can be shown that bubbles exist. As before a buyer will be willing to buy because he rationally conjectures that all future buyers will also buy. (This is proved in Allen and Gorton 1988.)

It can readily be seen that for C in the relevant range $0 \leqq C \leqq 0.05$ a trader will sell the share when his wealth reaches C_i^*. This is because the utility from holding the share (assuming he is not the last person) is increasing when wealth is below C_i^* and decreasing when it is above. When trader i's wealth reaches C_i^* the effect is the same as dying in terms of his behavior: he sells and leaves the market. The formal arguments are similar since the structure of the C_i^*'s ($i = 1, 2, 3$) induces the same ordering of exits as was previously assumed by the structure of death times.

In the case sketched there is a dramatic change in traders' marginal utilities of consumption. In general this is not necessary. All that is required is that there is some critical consumption level such that the marginal utility of consumption is low enough that it is no longer worthwhile holding onto the security because there is a chance of bankruptcy. Hence, in principle, any standard utility function, $u(c)$, with a declining marginal utility of consumption can be consistent with bubbles provided the marginal utility of consumption falls to a low enough level. The assumption concerning the possibility that the security will be retired ensures that it is strictly optimal for the agents to sell the stock when they reach their critical consumption level.

An important feature of the case with standard utility functions is that the correlated structure of death times that was assumed previously is no longer critical. In the case considered, Persons 2 and 3 have identical utility functions but this is not essential. The critical consumption levels determine the period of time the traders hold the share; the ordering of times at which the traders leave is determined by the order in which they receive the share. The main thing that is important is that traders cannot identify whether or not they are the last person who is prepared to buy the share; it must always be possible that the person selling the share is the one that was endowed with it so that one other person remains to sell it to. Provided they always attach a positive probability to being able to resell they are strictly better off buying the share and bubbles can exist.

In the model analyzed in Sections 2.1 and 2.2 it was possible for buyers, between $0 \leqq y \leqq 1/3$ to be certain of making money since they were sure there would be a seller. However, this feature is due to the particular form of equations (1) and (2). It can be seen that in the version of the model in this section, where (1) and (2) are replaced by (6) and (7), there is never any time period in which buyers can be certain they will be able to sell the stock. Hence, the only people willing to trade in the market will be portfolio managers whose payoff is effectively a call option.

3. The Entire Stock Market

In the previous section we considered the three traders who trade the stock which experiences the bubble. These three people are strictly better off in expected utility terms from doing this compared to not doing anything, even when they are risk averse. Person 1 is endowed with the stock and is able to sell at a positive price. The traders who are not endowed with the stock, Persons 2 and 3, are also strictly better off. The reason for this is that the money they invest is not their own. They manage other people's money and keep a share of any of the profits they make. If they are unsuccessful they repay less than they were given to manage and are no worse off than if they had not managed other people's wealth. This implies, of course, that the lenders cannot make money or break even by lending to these portfolio managers alone. Why then would anybody be willing to lend to them? In this section we consider a more complete model of the stock market with asymmetric information, where it is optimal for people to lend to portfolio managers using the contract assumed in Assumption A10.

In the complete model consumers who wish to invest at date 0 invest their money with investment firms that hire portfolio managers. There are two types of portfolio managers. "Good" portfolio managers can identify a limited amount of undervalued securities. "Bad" portfolio managers have no superior information. Similarly to Glosten and Milgrom (1985) and a number of other papers, the informed good portfolio managers can profit by trading on their information at the expense of traders who have urgent needs to sell their securities.

We begin, in Section 3.1, by developing a simple model which explains how the good portfolio managers can profit from their superior information. Then, in Section 3.2, we consider optimal contractual arrangements between the investment firms, who cannot observe portfolio manager type, and the portfolio managers. We show that the optimal contract involves pooling. Thus, in equilibrium, the losses of the bad portfolio managers, who speculate in the bubble stock, are effectively subsidized by the good portfolio managers.

In Section 2 the payoffs to the security were known with certainty by everybody and the appropriate definition of a bubble was clear; if the security traded above its fundamental (the present value of its payoffs) this was said to be a bubble. With asymmetric information the notion of a bubble must be modified since investors with different information sets can have different views on a stock's fundamental. In this case one appropriate definition of a bubble is when the security trades at a price which is greater than the fundamental that is the highest out of all investors' information sets. The notion of a bubble used in Section 2 is then a special case of this definition where everybody has the same information about a particular security.

There are two types of people who acquire the necessary qualifications to become a portfolio manager. There are good portfolio managers, denoted by the subscript g, who can identify securities which are undervalued. The amount of stock they can identify as being undervalued costs B. The second type of person that attains the qualifications necessary to become a portfolio manager cannot identify undervalued securities. They can identify bubble securities, and find it optimal to speculate in these stocks, as described in Section 2. These managers are denoted by the subscript s. The lender cannot observe the type of the portfolio manager. In this case it may be possible for type s portfolio managers to obtain funds to speculate with even though in a full information world they would not be able to do so.

There are assumed to be two types of stocks: (i) asymmetric information stocks; and (ii) symmetric information stocks. Both good and bad portfolio managers can distinguish between these types of stock. However, only good portfolio managers can distinguish between overvalued and undervalued stocks and profit from this, as we explain below. Bad portfolio managers speculate in the symmetric information stocks and bubbles may exist in these. Figure 2.4 portrays the component parts of the entire stock market.

We assume that all agents are risk neutral and also add the following assumptions to the basic model.

Assumption A15. There is a group of lenders who are prepared to lend as much as investment firms require provided that on average their expected return is equal to their opportunity cost, which for simplicity is taken to be zero.[8]

Assumption A16. The good portfolio managers represent a proportion γ of those who manage portfolios and the bad portfolio managers who speculate represent a proportion $1 - \gamma$.

Assumption A17. There exist uninformed traders who experience life cycle or other events which result in a desire for immediate liquidity; these traders are referred to a liquidity sellers. As a result, amounts of stock worth S are sold at

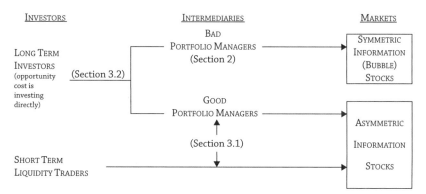

Figure 2.4 The entire stock market

various points in time. The liquidity sellers do this by approaching a broker who guarantees an immediate sale.

Assumption A18. There are a large number of uninformed traders who are willing to buy a stock if their expected return is equal to their opportunity cost of zero. For simplicity we assume that each uninformed buyer buys at most once.

Assumption A19. Good portfolio managers can spend their time identifying undervalued asymmetric information stocks. Bad portfolio managers cannot distinguish between undervalued and overvalued asymmetric information stocks. As an alternative to trading asymmetric information stocks, good and bad portfolio managers can spend their time identifying and trading symmetric information or bubble stocks.

Assumption A20. When amounts of stock worth S is offered for sale, good portfolio managers who have acquired information on the stock each have $B = 1$ available to invest; the total amount they have between them is B_g^*; and they behave competitively. Liquidity sellers needs are greater than the aggregate amount that good portfolio managers have available for investment, $S > B_g^*$.

Assumption A21. Good portfolio managers' information consists of knowledge that the payoff distribution of an asymmetric information stock at date 1 is either high, with realization H and mean EH, or low, with realization L and EL, where $EH > EL \geqq 0$. For a given security the probability that the payoff is high is $0 > \eta < 1$.

Assumption A22. It is not possible for a lender to observe whether the portfolio manager invests his money in a profitable investment, in an asymmetric information stock, or whether it is used for speculation. However, the final value of y is observable and can be contracted upon.

Assumption A23. Short sales are not possible for any security.

3.1. PROFITABLE TRADING WITH SUPERIOR INFORMATION

In this subsection we develop a model in which the good portfolio managers make profits by trading the asymmetric information stocks. These profits offset the losses made by the bad portfolio managers who speculate in the symmetric information stocks, which we term "bubble" stocks. The reason that good portfolio managers can make a profit is that there are liquidity sellers whose consumption needs are sufficiently urgent that they are forced to sell at a price below the expected value of the stock.

A common form of trading is a broker market in which sellers approach an intermediary and ask that securities be sold at the best possible price. The broker posts a price at which the securities are offered for sale. As in Glosten and Milgrom (1985), there is adverse selection and a zero-profit condition. In the event that orders are greater than the available quantity, the available amount is rationed pro rata; whether a stock is rationed or not does not become public information.

The broker understands that there may be informed traders buying the security so the posted price takes into account this adverse selection. Consequently, on the event of a trade the prices are "regret free."

At various points during the period liquidity traders offer securities for sale via their brokers. Good portfolio managers receive private information about the value of the securities offered for sale. Suppose a security is offered for sale. The unconditional value of the security is:

$$V = \eta\, EH + (1 - \eta)\, EL \tag{8}$$

Let P_S be the price posted by the broker at which the security will be sold.

In this setting we can prove the following proposition:

Proposition 2. *The posted price of an asymmetric information security, P_S, is lower than the unconditional expected value, V. Liquidity sellers receive less than the unconditional expected value, uninformed traders break even, and good portfolio managers make positive expected profits conditional on their information.*

To see these results, start by considering Assumption A17. According to this assumption liquidity sellers need to sell S/P_S of their shares immediately. Even if the good portfolio managers (who are informed) decide to purchase the stock, they do not have sufficient funds to satisfy all the sellers' needs since $B_g^* < S$. Thus, the uninformed liquidity buyers must also participate. The first issue is at what price the uninformed liquidity buyers will be willing to participate. Suppose the initially posted price was above the unconditional expected value of the share, $P_s > V$. The uninformed liquidity buyers would clearly be unwilling to buy and the liquidity sellers would not obtain the cash they need. Hence, it must be the case that $P_s \leq V$.

Next, suppose the posted price was equal to the unconditional expected value of the shares so $P_s = V_s$. At such a price, the good portfolio managers would buy B_g if the stock had true mean EH and so was undervalued. On the other hand if the stock had true mean EL and was overvalued, good portfolio managers would not submit any orders. (They would like to short sell the stock since it is overvalued but this is ruled out by Assumption A23.) In order for the broker to guarantee a sale of S on behalf of the liquidity sellers, irrespective of whether the stock has true mean EH or EL and hence whether informed traders bid, uninformed buyers must submit orders worth B_L such that $B_L \geq S$. At price P_s the expected profit of the uninformed buyers from submitting orders worth $B_L \geq S$ is:

$$\Gamma = \eta\left(\frac{B_L}{B_L + B_g}\right)\frac{S}{P_s}(EH - P_s) + (1 - \eta)\frac{S}{P_s}(EL - P_s). \tag{9}$$

The first term is their expected profit when the stock has true mean EH, which occurs with probability η. In this case both the informed and uninformed will submit orders and the stock will be rationed. The uninformed buyers get their pro rata share $B_L / (B_L + B_g)$ of S and make a profit of $(EH - P_S)$ on each share since the stock is priced at P_S. Similarly, the second term is their expected profit when the stock has true mean EL, which occurs with probability $(1 - \eta)$. The informed submit no orders so the uninformed get the entire S / P_s shares and make an expected loss of $(EL - P_S)$ on each share.

Since high-value stocks are rationed but low-value stocks are not, the uninformed receive a proportion of overvalued stocks which is greater than $(1 - \eta)$. As a result of this adverse selection their expected profit is negative when $P_s = V$. To see this formally note that when $P_s = V$, (9) can be written in the form:

$$\Gamma = \frac{S}{P_s}\left[-\eta\left(\frac{B_g}{B_g + B_L}\right)(EH - V)\right] < 0. \tag{10}$$

Hence uninformed buyers will not participate when $P_s = V$. This means brokers cannot guarantee liquidity sellers their cash and $P_s = V$ cannot be the equilibrium.

Finally, consider the case where the posted price is below the unconditional expected security values, $P_s < V$. Provided P_s is sufficiently below V to compensate for the adverse selection, uninformed buyers will be able to earn their opportunity cost of zero and will be willing to participate. Setting $\Gamma = 0$ in (9), solving for P_s, and using (8), gives the following value for the equilibrium price P_s^*:

$$P_s^* = V\frac{\left[1 - \eta\left(\dfrac{B_g}{B_L + B_g}\right)\left(\dfrac{EH}{V}\right)\right]}{\left[1 - \eta\left(\dfrac{B_g}{B_L + B_g}\right)\right]} < V. \tag{11}$$

In order to induce the uninformed liquidity buyers to participate, the initially posted price is below the unconditional expected value of the security.

It is immediate that at price P_s^* the liquidity sellers will receive less than the unconditional expected value of their stock and uninformed buyers will earn their opportunity cost of zero. This leaves the good portfolio managers. They will only bid for the stocks they know to have a high mean. They have an amount available and want this amount to be invested in the high mean stocks. They can anticipate, however, that these stocks will be rationed. They, therefore, bid for B_g / P_s^* where B_g solves $[Bg / (Bg + B_L)] S = B_s^*$ and their aggregate expected gross profits are: $EH (B_s^* / P_s^*) > 0$.

Since a good portfolio manager has funds $B = 1$ to start with, each buys $1 / P_s^*$ shares and has expected gross profits of $EH P_s^* > 0$. Thus the proposition is demonstrated.

The price and transactions volume are public information, but the extent of any rationing is not. This corresponds to the fact that in actual markets nonparticipating investors do not observe order imbalances. Consequently, if a stock which was rationed is sold again, the posted price must again be below the unconditional expected value to ensure the uninformed buyers participate.[9] This means that a good portfolio manager who purchased an undervalued stock would have to pay a liquidity premium to sell and they would not earn a profit on their private information. Good portfolio managers therefore have an incentive to hold the stock until date 1 and so will not find it worthwhile to speculate.

3.2. OPTIMAL CONTRACTS FOR PORTFOLIO MANAGERS

The next step in the analysis is to consider the contracts that investment firms use to hire portfolio managers. In order to do this we introduce the following assumptions.

Assumption A24. Investment firms cannot credibly precommit to keep on employing bad managers once they have been identified as bad.

Assumption A25. The investment firms operate in a competitive industry and so make zero expected profits.

Assumption A26. Good portfolio managers are in short supply.

Assumption A27. For ease of exposition we assume that the bad portfolio managers can identify a bubble stock with the price path and distribution of returns considered in Section 2.2. They each have a probability of $1/3$ of being Persons 1, 2, and 3. This implies that the probability distribution of their final gross return y (i.e., including the money they borrow initially), given that $B = 1$, is distributed as illustrated by the solid line in Figure 2.5. Person 1 makes a profit which is uniformly distributed between 0 and 1 so their gross profit is uniformly distributed between 1 and 2. Person 2's and Person 3's profit depends on whether or not they are found by Person 1 when he decides to sell the stock. If they are found they make a profit which is uniformly distributed between 0 and $1/3$ so that their gross return is uniformly distributed between 1 and $4/3$. If they are not found by Person 1 when he sells, they make a loss which is uniformly distributed between $1/3$ and 1 so their gross return is uniformly distributed between 0 and $2/3$.

Assumption A28. For undervalued asymmetric information stocks, the distribution of H is shown by the dashed line in Figure 2.5. For overvalued asymmetric information stocks $L = EL = 0.7$.

Assumption A29. The proportion of good stocks $\eta = 0.5$. The proportion of good portfolio managers $\gamma = 0.034$. The ratio $B_g / (B_L + B_g) = 0.1$.

Assumption A24, concerning the absence of precommitment, is important because it ensures a pooling equilibrium. Investment firms make a loss employing bad portfolio managers. Therefore, once they have identified a manager as bad, they will fire him. A precommitment to keep employing portfolio managers who have been identified as bad seems unrealistic since the investment firm can always find a reason to fire them, for example, they arrive to work late.[10]

Assumptions A25 and A26, that investment firms are in a competitive industry and good portfolio managers are in short supply, mean that good portfolio managers earn a rent from their ability. However, the fact that they are pooled with bad managers means that the amount they earn is less than if their ability could be identified and they did not have to subsidize the losses of the bad managers.

Assumptions A27 and A28 allow the analysis of Section 2 to be combined with the analysis of this section while maintaining tractability. In order to proceed it is necessary to derive the distribution of expected returns of the good portfolio managers.

Lemma 1. The gross profits of the good portfolio managers have the distribution shown by the dashed line in Figure 2.5.

The gross profits of a good portfolio manager are H/P_s^*. Using (11) and Assumptions A28 and A29 it can be shown that $P_s^* = 1$. Hence the distribution of the gross profits of a good portfolio manager is H and is also shown by the dashed line in Figure 2.5. The lemma is demonstrated.

The inability to precommit, Assumption A24, implies that bad portfolio managers will behave in exactly the same way as good ones during the job application

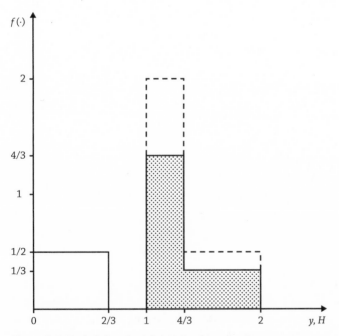

Figure 2.5 Probability distributions of returns by agent type

process no matter what contracts the firm offers; any contract which is attractive to good portfolio managers will also attract bad portfolio managers in the same proportions as they exist in the population. We start by considering this pooling equilibrium.

By Assumption A26, good portfolio managers are in short supply and by Assumption A25 investment firms are competitive. Consequently, good portfolio managers earn rents from their ability to identify over- and undervalued stocks. Ordinary uninformed investors can invest in securities directly and earn an expected return of zero, which is their opportunity cost. In order to be willing to lend to investment firms, ordinary investors must obtain an expected return of at least zero from them. To find the optimal contract, the good portfolio managers' expected earnings are maximized subject to ordinary investors obtaining their opportunity cost. Therefore, the optimal payment schedule must satisfy the following program:

$$\max \pi(y) \, E_g[y - \pi(y)] \tag{12}$$

subject to:

$$\gamma Eg \, \pi(y) + (1 - \gamma)Es\pi(y) \geqq B, \tag{13}$$

where E_g denotes the expectation operator with respect to the good portfolio managers' distribution of returns and E_s denotes the expectation operator with respect to the distribution for the bad portfolio managers that speculate. The constraint (13) ensures that lenders earn a return equal to their opportunity cost.

For bubbles to occur it is also necessary that the good portfolio managers prefer to invest in asymmetric information stocks and bad portfolio managers choose to speculate. It is possible to show the following.

Proposition 3. *Under the maintained assumptions, the contract with the linear repayment schedule*

$$\pi^*(y) = 1 + 0.95(y - 1) \text{ for } y \geqq 1,$$
$$= \text{ for } y < 1, \tag{14}$$

is such that lenders earn their opportunity cost and is an optimal contract. Good portfolio managers prefer to invest in the asymmetric information stocks and bad portfolio managers prefer to speculate in the bubble stocks, so bubbles can exist.

It can readily be verified using the numerical values in Assumption A29 that investors earn their opportunity cost. To see that the contract is optimal consider the first part of the schedule specified in (14). The good portfolio managers only produce outputs in this region. The expected revenue received from them is given by

$$\pi(y) = \int_1^{4/3} 2\pi(y)dy + \int_{4/3}^2 (1/2)\pi(y)dy. \tag{15}$$

For $y \geqq 1$ the expected revenue received from the bad portfolio managers is

$$E^1_s \pi(y) = \left(\frac{2}{3}\right) E_g \pi(y), \tag{16}$$

where the superscript 1 refers to the expectations taken over the range $y \geqq 1$. Hence, no matter what the form of the payment schedule $\pi(y)$ the amount of revenue raised from the bad portfolio managers is always 2/3 the amount raised from the good managers; altering the form of the payment schedule for $y \geqq 1$ does not enable any more to be extracted from the bad group. It follows that the first part of the schedule in the proposition is optimal.

The second part of the schedule for $y < 1$ is also optimal because only bad portfolio managers produce outputs which fall in this region. The good portfolio managers' utility is unaffected by the form of the payment schedule in this region and lowering the payment below y can only reduce the revenue raised from the bad portfolio managers. Thus, the second part of the payment schedule is optimal.[11]

Evaluating total expected revenue using Assumption A27 gives $E_g y = 1.333$. The expected earnings of a good portfolio manager if he invests in undervalued asymmetric information stocks are therefore $0.05(1.333 - 1) = 0.01667$. From (16), the expected earnings from speculating (irrespective of whether the portfolio manager is good or bad) are $(2/3)0.01667 = 0.01111$. Thus good portfolio managers prefer to invest in undervalued asymmetric information stocks because they earn more by using their information than by speculating in bubble stocks.

We now turn to the final part of the proposition that bad portfolio managers prefer to speculate. Since there is limited liability, bad portfolio managers can potentially make positive profits by "plunging" in an asymmetric information stock (i.e., investing everything in it). If it turns out to be a high-value stock, then positive profits are made. If it's a low-value stock the profits are negative but because of the form of (14) the portfolio manager's earnings are zero. Plunging is the best a bad portfolio manager can do investing in asymmetric information stocks; diversifying across asymmetric information stocks reduces the probability of obtaining a gross return above 1 and hence the managers' expected earnings given the form of their compensation contract.

A bad portfolio manager's expected earnings from plunging are therefore positive and in this case are given by $\eta(1 - \alpha)(EH/P_s^* - 1) = 0.5(0.0167) = 0.00833$. Since this is less than the expected earnings from speculating,

0.01111, bad portfolio managers prefer to speculate. Hence, the proposition is demonstrated.

3.3. DISCUSSION

The call option form of portfolio managers' compensation schemes creates the possibility of bubbles, as outlined in the analysis of Section 2. Bad portfolio managers will be willing to trade bubble securities at prices which are higher than the highest fundamental perceived by any of the traders. For example, suppose that one of the securities that is available is like that in Section 2 and it is known by all traders to have a payoff of zero with certainty. Thus all traders have the same information set with regard to this security and this is common knowledge. As in Section 2, the security can trade at a positive price so that there is a bubble. Even if groups have different beliefs about the fundamental of a security it will still be possible to show that bad portfolio managers will be willing to trade the stock at a price above the maximum. The call option feature of portfolio managers' compensation schemes means they can be willing to purchase a stock if there is some prospect of a capital gain even though they know with certainty that its price will fall below its current level at some point in the future. This means it would even be possible to use a definition of a bubble where the price must be above the highest possible payoff which is given positive probability by any investor and still obtain examples of a bubble.

In order to derive the proposition it was assumed that all agents are risk neutral. If agents are risk averse then the form of the optimal contract will not be the same as that in Proposition 3; risk sharing will become a factor. Nevertheless, the characteristics of the contract will usually be similar. It will be optimal to extract revenue from the bad portfolio managers by penalizing poor performance and rewarding good performance. Although the optimal contract may not have the exact form of a call option, it may often provide incentives for bad managers to speculate and go for large risky payoffs even when this is associated with poor average returns.

Assumption A24, about the absence of precommitment, ensured that only a pooling equilibrium existed. If investment firms can precommit to retain a manager even when they know he is bad and will not make profitable investments, then a pooling and a separating equilibrium may exist. The pooling equilibrium is the same as that described above. The separating equilibrium involves the investment firm offering a menu of contracts to separate the good managers from the bad. In a separating equilibrium, there are two payment schedules: one for the good managers, π_g, and one for the bad managers, π_b. These are chosen to maximize (12) subject to (13) and the constraints that the bad managers do not have a strict incentive to want to mimic the good managers and vice versa. Thus, the assumption of no precommitment plays an important role in the analysis since it ensures a pooling equilibrium.[12]

4. Robustness and Implications

The purpose of this paper has been to show that there exists a class of models different from those considered by Tirole (1982) where rational behavior is consistent with security price bubbles. The most important difference between our approach and Tirole's is that we assume investors hire portfolio managers to invest their wealth for them; the agency problem that arises between investors and managers because of the asymmetric information between them means that asset prices can deviate from their fundamentals.

We have demonstrated the existence of bubbles by considering an example. For tractability the assumptions made were very specific. This was necessary to enable a set of self-fulfilling beliefs that ensure existence of equilibrium to be identified. An important question concerns the robustness of this example. In other words how general is the class of models in which bubbles can arise? There are four elements of the example that appear crucial to the result:

1. At any point in time there must be an infinite number of trading possibilities before the horizon.
2. Agents must be unable to deduce whether or not they are the last person in the market.
3. Markets are inefficient so that there exists a group of portfolio managers that makes an above normal rate of return which allows the losses of the bad portfolio managers to be covered.
4. The agency relationship between investors and portfolio managers involves a compensation scheme for the managers which has the form of a call option and can induce risk-loving behavior.

We discuss each of these points in turn and then make some final comments.

Continuous time is an important feature of our model because it allows for an infinite number of trading possibilities even though the horizon of the model is finite. This alone does not allow bubbles to exist. In our model there are a finite number of agents, and Tirole (1982) showed that bubbles cannot exist in infinite-horizon models with a finite number of agents. Bubbles of the type considered in this paper require an infinite number of trading possibilities, but it is possible to reinterpret the model here as an infinite-horizon model with infinitely-lived agents.

The second point concerns the information that agents have. The factor that is critical for our result is that agents have an identification problem. In particular, they must not be able to deduce whether or not they are the last person. In the example presented, adding one piece of information allows traders to determine whether they are the last person. However, this does not mean that the result is not robust since adding an extra source of noise restored the original result, as shown in Section 2.3.

The third point relates to the assumption that securities markets are not strong-form efficient. There are a number of ways in which markets may not be strong-form efficient . We modeled this inefficiency by assuming the presence of some traders with urgent needs to trade, following Glosten and Milgrom (1985). All that is really required is some form of inefficiency where one group can outperform another. For example, a version of the Grossman and Stiglitz (1980) model where a group of traders has a comparative advantage at gathering information, will lead to similar results. The advantage of the approach taken here is that it allows bounded distributions to be used. Grossman and Stiglitz require normal distributions. Since these are unbounded they are inconsistent with finite wealth, which is an important component of our model.

The fourth point concerns the importance of a compensation scheme for portfolio managers that has the form of a call option and induces risk-loving behavior. In the examples above the bubbles can be thought of as a manifestation of the inefficiency resulting from this aspect of the agency relationship between investors and portfolio managers. This is the counterpart of the well-known result in the corporate finance literature that debt-financed firms may be willing to accept negative net present value investments (see, e.g., Jensen and Meckling 1976).

An important assumption of the analysis showing this type of compensation scheme is optimal is that the minimum payoff to portfolio managers is zero. This implies that they cannot be penalized at all. As in many models of agency relationships, if the agent can post his own capital to guarantee performance, the agency problem is mitigated and may disappear. For example, in the corporate finance context if firms can post enough collateral to guarantee the loan they will not have an incentive to undertake negative net present value projects. This solution is rarely feasible since firms usually cannot post collateral. Similarly, in many situations portfolio managers will not be able to post capital to guarantee their performance.

In practice, portfolio managers do not usually bond themselves in this way. For example, prior to 1985 in the United States the SEC prohibited investment fees from depending directly on the change in value of the portfolio. Typically, the fees for portfolio managers were based on assets under management. Thus, if a manager did well then his fees would increase because new investors would be attracted to invest under his direction. There were no payments from the manager to the investors if performance was bad. The worst that could happen as a result of poor manager performance was a zero fee (see Grinold and Rudd 1987). Since 1985 incentive fees have been permitted. Kritzman (1987) points out that in this case:

> Incentive fees are typically structured with two components—a base
> fee ... and a contingent fee, which allows the manager to share in the

incremental return relative to an established benchmark. The manager does not usually share in negative relative returns; that is, he does not pay his client when he underperforms the benchmark. This asymmetric structure essentially grants the money manager a call option on some fraction of incremental return. . . . It is possible that a manager will expose the portfolio to undue risk in the absence of any insights whatsoever. (21–22)

Thus, our modeling of the compensation scheme for portfolio managers as a call option, which is essential to the results in the model, tends to correspond to what is observed in practice. In addition, its possible inducement of risk-loving behavior is well-recognized.

In the introduction we mentioned early historical episodes of bubbles. In those days there were no mutual funds, of course. However, many people borrowed to invest since there were no margin requirements. For example, Neal (1990, 75–77) points out that much of the investment in the South Sea Company and Mississippi Land Company was with borrowed money. Borrowing is a special case of the repayment schedule we have modeled (in (3)) so that a similar analysis holds.

There are two further considerations with regard to the agency relationship. The first concerns the available alternative investments. In the example of Section 3 it was shown that it was strictly better for the bad portfolio managers to invest in the bubble security than the alternatives. In general, this result will not hold if the alternatives are sufficiently attractive. However, given the call option feature of the compensation scheme it will hold in many situations. The second consideration concerns the effects of repeating the relationship. Often in agency models the effects of reputation mitigate the problem. In portfolio management it is not clear this occurs. Bad managers must consistently produce high returns in order to remain pooled with good managers. In order to achieve this they have to take risky positions. Thus the problem may be exacerbated rather than mitigated.

Any arguments concerning the generality of the example presented are clearly only speculative. The important issue for future research is to identify more precisely how general is the class of models where agency problems between investors and portfolio managers cause assets to be mispriced and bubbles to exist.

Notes

1. Camerer (1989) gives a survey of this literature.
2. The results of Leroy and Porter (1981), Shiller (1981), and Grossman and Shiller (1981), among others, suggest that stock prices deviate from market fundamentals. Those who have challenged the methodology adopted include Flavin (1983), Kleidon (1986a, 1986b), and Marsh and Merton (1986). West (1988) provides a survey of this and related controversies. Price paths that deviate from fundamentals have also been observed in experimental settings (see Smith, Suchanek, and Williams 1988).
3. In infinite-horizon models, rational bubbles have appeared as explanations for the existence of fiat money starting with Samuelson (1958). Important contributions were subsequently made

by Wallace (1980), Blanchard (1979), Blanchard and Watson (1982), and Tirole (1985), among others. Although these theories can explain a number of features of bubbles, they are not entirely satisfactory explanations of the phenomena the empirical literature on stock prices has been concerned with. Some of these models require that prices grow slower than the expected growth rate of the aggregate wealth of the economy. There is no explanation of how bubbles get started or of why they crash since starting and stopping are taken as exogenous in these types of models. Diba and Grossman (1988) have argued there is no possibility that price bubbles can crash and restart.

4. See Camerer (1989) for other examples.

5. This information was privately communicated to us by NASDAQ.

6. For an alternative definition and approach to bubbles see Gilles and Leroy (1992).

7. Strictly speaking to avoid "openness" problems, Person 2 sells at "0.4^-." A person who dies at $t_2 = 0.4$ learns it at "0.4" and death occurs at "0.4^+." Trade is not permitted at date "0.4." For ease of exposition, these complexities are omitted in our subsequent discussion.

8. The inclusion of investment firms is not necessary for the results obtained. It would be equivalent if investors were to contract directly with portfolio managers. The investment firms are included for expositional reasons to make clear the phenomenon that is of interest. When investors are risk averse or there are transaction costs of contracting, investment firms play an important economic role in pooling the risk associated with portfolio managers and reducing the transaction costs of contracting.

9. The uninformed traders that participated initially will know if there was rationing and therefore whether the stock is undervalued. By Assumption A18, however, uninformed buyers buy at most once. Allowing them to buy repeatedly could be incorporated but would increase the complexity without adding any insights.

10. It is important to note that this inability to precommit to keep on employing bad portfolio managers is not inconsistent with the ability to write contracts where people are ensured of being paid for working as portfolio managers. Once a performance contract has been signed, and the job completed, third parties have little difficulty enforcing the terms. Thus, portfolio managers can be assured of payment because their ex post performance is verifiable. If a person were to be fired after they had done the work they would still have to be paid.

11. The optimal contract is not unique. For $y \geq 1$, (16) implies many schedules are possible. For $y < 1$, any schedule ensuring all revenue is paid to the investors is optimal.

12. In some circumstances a partially pooling equilibrium may exist. This would involve investment firms offering two contracts. The first would attract good portfolio managers and the second would attract both types with the good types randomizing between the two. In the first the good would not be subsidizing the bad so to obtain indifference it would be necessary that $B < 1$. Since there is partial pooling there would still be the possibility of bubbles since the bad managers in the pooled group would act as in Section 2. Also, since the expected return to the lenders per unit invested would be higher for the contract with the restricted B, precommitment would again be necessary.

References

Allen, F. and G. Gorton. 1988. "Rational Finite Bubbles." University of Pennsylvania, Rodney L. White Working Paper No. 41–88.

Blanchard, O. 1979. "Speculative Bubbles, Crashes and Rational Expectations." *Economic Letters* 3, 387–389.

Blanchard, O. and M. Watson. 1982. "Bubbles, Rational Expectations, and Financial Markets." In P. Wachtel, ed., *Crises in the Economic and Financial Structure* Lexington, MA: Lexington Books.

Camerer, C. 1989. "Bubbles and Fads in Asset Prices: A Review of Theory and Evidence." *Journal of Economic Surveys* 3, 3–41.

DeLong, J., A. Shleifer, L. Summers, and R. Waldman. 1990. "Noise Trader Risk in Financial Markets." *Journal of Political Economy* 98, 703–738.

Diba, B., and H. Grossman. 1988. "Rational Inflationary Bubbles." *Journal of Monetary Economics* 21, 35–46.

Flavin, M. 1983. "Excess Volatility in Financial Markets: A Reassessment of the Empirical Evidence." *Journal of Political Economy* 91, 929–956.

Gilles, C. and S. Leroy. 1992. "Bubbles and Charges." *International Economic Review* 33, 323–339.

Glosten, L. and P. Milgrom. 1985. "Bid, Ask and Transaction Prices in a Specialist Market with Heterogeneous Informed Traders." *Journal of Financial Economics* 14, 71–100.

Goldsmith, R. 1971. *Institutional Investor Study Report of the Securities and Exchange Commission: Supplementary Volume I.* House Document No. 92–64, part 6. 92nd Congress, First Session. Washington, DC: U.S. Government Printing Office.

Grinold, R. and A. Rudd. 1987. "Incentive Fees: Who Wins? Who Loses?" *Financial Analysts Journal* 43, 27–38.

Grossman, S., and R. Shiller. 1981, "The Determinants of the Variability of Stock Market Prices." *American Economic Review* 71, 222–227.

Grossman, S., and J. Stiglitz. 1980. "On the Impossibility of Informationally Efficient Markets." *American Economic Review* 70, 393–408.

Harrison, J., and D. Kreps. 1978. "Speculative Behavior in a Stock Market with Heterogeneous Expectations." *Quarterly Journal of Economics* 92, 323–336.

Jensen, M., and W. Meckling. 1976. "Theory of the Firm: Managerial Behavior, Agency Costs and Ownership Structure." *Journal of Financial Economics* 3, 305–360.

Kleidon, A. 1986a. "Bias in Small Sample Tests of Stock Price Rationality." *Journal of Business* 59, 237–261.

———. 1986b. "Variance Bounds Tests and Stock Price Valuation Models." *Journal of Political Economy* 94, 953–1001.

Kritzman, M. 1987. "Incentive Fees: Some Problems and Some Solutions." *Financial Analysts Journal* 43, 21–26.

Leroy, S., and R. Porter. 1981. "The Present Value Relation: Tests Based on Implied Variance Bounds." *Econometrica* 49, 555–574.

Marsh, T., and R. Merton. 1986. "Dividend Variability and Variance Bounds Tests for Rationality of Stock Prices." *American Economic Review* 76, 483–498.

Neal, L. 1990. *The Rise of Financial Capitalism: International Capital Markets in the Age of Reason.* Cambridge: Cambridge University Press.

Samuelson, P. 1958. "An Exact Consumption-Loan Model of Interest with or without the Social Contrivance of Money." *Journal of Political Economy* 66, 467–482.

Shiller, R. 1981. "Do Stock Prices Move Too Much to Be Justified by Subsequent Changes in Dividends?" *American Economic Review* 71, 421–436.

———. 1984. "Stock Prices and Social Dynamics." *Brookings Papers on Economic Activity* 2, 457–498.

Smith, V., G. Suchanek, and A. Williams. 1988. "Bubbles, Crashes, and Endogenous Expectations in Experimental Spot Asset Markets." *Econometrica* 56, 1119–1151.

Tirole, J. 1982. "On the Possibility of Speculation under Rational Expectations." *Econometrica* 50, 1163–1181.

———. 1985. "Asset Bubbles and Overlapping Generations." *Econometrica* 53, 1499–1528.

Wallace, N. 1980. "The Overlapping Generations Model of Fiat Money." In J. Karaken and N. Wallace, eds., *Models of Monetary Economies.* Minneapolis: Federal Reserve Bank of Minneapolis.

West, K. 1988. "Bubbles, Fads and Stock Price Volatility Tests: A Partial Evaluation." *Journal of Finance* 43, 639–656.

CHAPTER 3

Rethinking Theoretical Models of Bubbles

REFLECTIONS INSPIRED BY THE FINANCIAL CRISIS AND
ALLEN AND GORTON'S PAPER "CHURNING BUBBLES"[1]

■

Gadi Barlevy

Introduction

Three years have now passed since national U.S. house price indices began their precipitous decline. The chain of events associated with the recent housing crisis continues to reverberate today—not just in the housing market but in financial markets and the overall economy. At this point, we probably do not have enough perspective and hindsight to assess the full ramifications of this episode. Nevertheless, we can start asking whether and how this episode should change the way economists think about asset markets. Many observers have argued that the housing market experienced a classic asset price bubble. Thus, one way to begin an inquiry into the implications of the events of the past three years is to ask how they ought to shape economic models of bubbles in particular. This chapter tackles this topic.

Ordinarily, revising one's theoretical models given a particular episode involves two steps: (1) identifying several key stylized facts that emerge during the relevant episode and (2) figuring out what these facts reveal about the various theories that have been proposed for explaining this phenomenon. Thus, in contemplating how to revise theoretical models of bubbles, it is natural to ask the following questions: Are certain models more consistent with the relevant set of stylized facts? And should we modify the most suitable from within this class of models to accommodate facts that these models cannot yet capture? In the case of asset price bubbles, however, this standard approach seems to be of limited value. While there is a large body of work attempting to model the phenomenon of a bubble as defined by most economists—a deviation between the price at which an asset trades and its fundamental value—these models were largely viewed as unsatisfactory even before the most recent crisis. For example, Santos and Woodford (1997) argue that the bubbles produced in some of these models are special and fragile. In some models, the conditions necessary to sustain a bubble have been rejected empirically; see, for example, the work by Abel et al. (1989), which shows that dynamic inefficiency, a necessary condition for the existence of bubbles in certain models, has little empirical support. While not all models of bubbles require dynamic inefficiency for a bubble to emerge, many of the models that are not rejected by the evidence in Abel et al. (1989) turn out to be highly stylized, relying on a contrived or special set of assumptions, and whose main purpose is to demonstrate that bubbles are possible rather than to capture the main elements of historical episodes often cited as examples of bubbles. For example, the Allen and Gorton (1993) model reprinted in this volume stipulates 29 assumptions before showing that a bubble is possible in the framework it studies. As another example, Allen, Morris, and Postlewaite (1993) construct a bubble in a finite horizon setting, but require no less than 11 distinct states of the world to construct this example. Neither of the models developed in these papers, nor many of the other available models of bubbles, was meant to be particularly realistic or to capture the salient features of asset markets in the real world. Rather, their purpose was to show that bubbles can occur in equilibrium, even when agents are rational and trade in their own best interests. Confronting these models with evidence from yet another episode that many believe is an example of a bubble is therefore unlikely to be particularly illuminating.

What, then, can we learn from the recent crisis that will be useful for thinking about theoretical models of bubbles? I will argue that the recent episode serves to highlight a particular feature of most existing models of bubbles that does not seem to have attracted much attention or discussion before the most recent crisis—namely, the implications of these models for welfare. The reason the crisis draws attention to this feature is because the crisis led to a shift in attitude regarding the appropriate policy response to evidence of an incipient bubble in asset markets. Before the current crisis, the conventional view among policymakers was that central banks should only respond to asset prices to the extent that they affect expected inflation. This view is conveyed in the Bernanke and Gertler (1999) paper reprinted in this volume. According to this view, if asset prices were to collapse and the implied fall in wealth were to depress economic activity, central banks should stand by and provide additional liquidity, just as they should if economic activity were depressed for other reasons. But the severity of the recent financial crisis has convinced many that central banks cannot simply stand by as asset prices start rising, and that some form of intervention—either regulatory or monetary in nature—is warranted. This view is most clearly expressed in various speeches given by members of the Federal Open Market Committee in 2009 and is, to varying degrees, also reflected in the chapters in this book written as follow-ups to the original Bernanke and Gertler (1999) paper.[2] In order to properly gauge when and how central banks should intervene in the face of a potential asset price bubble, we would like to have models of bubbles to guide our thinking. But the fact is that few of the existing models of bubbles found in the literature imply that bursting a bubble will make society as a whole better off, and a few imply exactly the opposite. The crisis thus exposes an important challenge for future theoretical work on bubbles—namely, to see if there is a way to rationalize the emerging view that argues for suppressing bubbles as an appropriate direction for policy.

This chapter is organized as follows. I begin by providing a precise definition of a bubble as the phenomenon that models ought to capture. I then turn to the question of why some of the more commonly used models of bubbles thus defined suggest that asset price bubbles are good. This discussion draws heavily on Barlevy (2007). Next, I consider examples of models in which bubbles do not make all agents better off. These models illustrate that even when bubbles do not make society as a whole better off, it does not typically follow that bursting an existing bubble is Pareto improving. Instead, eliminating bubbles may make some agents better off, but at the same time makes others worse off. The Allen and Gorton (1993) model reprinted in this volume that partly inspires this chapter turns out to have the same implication. However, I argue that this model could potentially be modified so that bursting bubbles might be a desirable policy goal. That said, the argument for why bursting a bubble can make society better off does not correspond to what those who advocate more intervention by central banks in response to a bubble seem to have in mind. Nevertheless, I argue that agency models along the lines laid out by Allen and Gorton in their paper contain some of the key features that speak to these issues. Thus, these models may ultimately prove useful for exploring whether we can capture the intuition about bubbles some policymakers have drawn from the crisis.

Defining a Bubble

Let me be clear about what I mean when I refer to a bubble. In the popular press, the term "bubble" is often used to describe a situation in which the price of an asset has increased significantly in a short period of time and is therefore suspected of being vulnerable to an equally rapid price collapse. Academics have occasionally used this definition as well. For example, Kindleberger (1996) defines a bubble as "an upward price movement over an extended range that then implodes" (13). However, most economists find this definition problematic. Aside from the fact that it is inherently imprecise given it is not clear how much the price of an asset must rise or how quickly in order for the asset to qualify as a bubble, large price swings sometimes occur naturally and benignly in response to shifts in supply and demand. For example, new fashion accessories that gain and lose popularity can exhibit similar price swings. However, many economists would view such price swings as a welcome and desirable outcome rather than a cause for concern, since they signal to producers which products are in high demand. Unlike the popular press, the vast majority of economists tend to reserve the term bubble for the case where the price of an asset increases at such a rapid rate that it seems implausible that this increase reflects changes in the underlying worth of the asset (and thus as a signal of its value). That is, the distinguishing feature of a bubble as most economists use the term is that changes in the price of the asset are not believed to signal changes in the true nature of the object being priced. Economists have therefore sought to define bubbles in a way that distinguishes them from objects whose prices fluctuate because of cyclical changes in their inherent desirability; some economists—for example, Camerer (1989)—have taken to calling the latter objects "fads."

To capture the idea that a bubble corresponds to an asset whose price misrepresents its true worth, economists have proposed defining a bubble as any asset whose price differs from the "fundamental" value of the asset.[3] The fundamental value is in turn defined as the expected value of all dividends the asset yields over its lifetime, properly discounted to reflect the present-day value of dividends paid at future dates. Intuitively, an asset is a claim to a stream of future payments. Hence, the value of an asset derives from the fact that it offers resources, in the form of dividends, to the various people who will own the asset over time. If the price of the asset differs from this value, it can be legitimately viewed as mispriced, since the price does not reflect the true value from creating such an asset on the collective behalf of all future owners of the asset. In many cases, the fundamental value of the asset is a pretty straightforward concept. However, there are some circumstances in which it is not possible to properly assign a unique fundamental value to an asset. For example, traders may have different information about dividends, or they may discount the future at different rates, so each will assign a different fundamental value to the asset. Allen, Morris, and Postlewaite (1993) discuss these issues in more detail, and argue that in some cases it might still be possible to describe an asset as overvalued in these contexts.

Note that this definition of a bubble does not presuppose either a run-up in the price of the asset or an eventual collapse; it only stipulates that the asset does not reflect its intrinsic worth. However, a rapid increase in the price of an asset may be an indication that an asset is overvalued if there are no concurrently large changes in the dividends or information about future dividends. Hence, in practice the way economists define a bubble may be consistent with empirical episodes often described as bubbles by noneconomists. This definition also allows an asset to remain overpriced forever, although in principle the price is always vulnerable to collapse because there is essentially nothing that justifies its high price. The point is that economists distinguish an asset as a bubble not by what actually happens to the price of the asset but by what *could* happen to it.

When Can Bubbles Arise?

To understand why many existing models of bubbles do not imply that driving down the price of an overvalued asset makes society as a whole better off, and might in fact make it worse off, it is important to understand why bubbles can arise in the first place. A good starting point to organize this discussion is to start with the opposite question, namely, under what conditions bubbles cannot arise. Tirole (1982) provided a particular set of conditions under which bubbles can be ruled out.[4] The conditions he laid out are as follows. First, there are only finitely many traders, although they can each potentially trade infinitely many times. Second, all traders are rational, and this is common knowledge among all traders. That is, traders are not only rational, but they know that the traders they interact with are rational, the traders they interact with know that they too are interacting with rational traders, and so on. Third, all traders initially agree on what states of the world are possible and share a common prior distribution over the likelihood of these states. This assumption does not rule out that traders may be subsequently exposed to disparate information that on their own would lead them to have very different views about the likelihood of different states of the world. However, since traders know that other traders started with the same priors and were exposed to different information, they would interpret disagreements with other traders not as an opportunity to exploit traders who think differently from them, but as evidence that other traders receive different information that should also be taken into account.[5] Tirole's fourth assumption is that all resources are allocated efficiently across agents before the commencement of trade between the agents.

Tirole (1982) showed that under these assumptions, asset bubbles could not arise. The intuition for this result is as follows. The assumption that the initial allocation of resources is efficient implies no mutually advantageous trades are possible between the agents. As a result, any investor who agrees to buy an overvalued asset must believe that his trading strategy will benefit him at the expense of the remaining traders. In particular, he must expect to gain at their expense by selling them a claim to a stream of dividends for more than it is worth. When there are only finitely many traders, these beliefs cannot all simultaneously be true: If everybody who buys the overvalued asset expects to benefit at the expense of all other traders, there won't be any traders left from whom to actually benefit. The argument is analogous to why the children in Garrison Keillor's fictional town of Lake Wobegon cannot all be above average as its residents claim, since deviations from the average have to sum up to zero. In a similar fashion, not all traders can expect to gain at the expense of all remaining traders taken together, since the net expected gains of all traders together have to sum up to zero.

For bubbles to occur, then, at least one of Tirole's (1982) assumptions must be violated.[6] Which of these conditions do existing models of bubbles do away with? To answer this question, it will help to divide models of bubbles into three broad classes of theories, and discuss which are the key assumptions that are violated in each group.[7] The first and earliest models of bubbles are overlapping generations models—for example, Allais (1947), Samuelson (1958), Diamond (1965), and Tirole (1985). The central feature of these models is that individuals earn the bulk of their income when they are young and would like to save some of their earnings to consume when they are old. One way for agents to save is to purchase assets when young that they can sell when old to the next cohort of young people looking to save. In some cases, even inherently worthless assets that pay no dividends can trade at a positive price because young agents always expect to sell them to the next cohort of young agents at a price that makes buying such assets an attractive way to save. These cases are associated with a bubble as defined earlier in this chapter, since they imply assets trade above their fundamental value of zero.

These models all violate Tirole's (1982) first assumption that there must be only finitely many traders. Indeed, this feature is essential for sustaining the bubble, since each young person always believes he can sell the asset when he is old to a new young person. With only finitely many traders, the last young person to buy the asset would realize he would have no one to sell the asset to, so the asset would be worthless to him as a savings instrument and he would have no incentive to buy it. But then the whole argument for why a bubble is sustainable unravels, since the young person before him would also refuse to buy the asset, knowing he would have no one to sell the asset to. Proceeding by this logic, no agent would ever pay a positive price for the asset. Thus, generating a bubble in these models requires there to be infinitely many agents. However, in many of these overlapping generations models, it is also true that bubbles can occur if and only if the economy is dynamically inefficient in the absence of a bubble, violating Tirole's (1982) fourth assumption. In particular, dynamic inefficiency implies that agents in the economy can achieve mutual gains by agreeing to a scheme of intergenerational transfers in which each period's young give resources to the old in exchange for getting resources when they turn old from the young of the next generation. Strictly speaking, violating the fourth assumption is not essential, and there are examples of overlapping generations models where bubbles occur even when the economy is dynamically efficient. But in practice, many of the models of bubbles in overlapping generations environments violate two of Tirole's (1982) assumptions—namely, a finite number of traders and an environment where the allocation of resources prior to trade is efficient.

A second class of models of bubbles captures the notion that agents who trade in assets are trying to profit at the expense of other traders in the market. That is, agents buy assets they know to be overvalued with the expectation that they will be able to sell them for a capital gain to someone else who doesn't realize how much the asset is truly worth. One early model along these lines was developed by Harrison and Kreps (1978), who assume traders have disjoint prior beliefs about the possible states of the world.[8] This violates Tirole's (1982) third assumption that traders begin with common prior beliefs, and as such implies that agents view disagreements with other agents as a chance to profit at the other party's expense rather than as a reason to doubt and update their own beliefs. A closely related set of models, known as "greater fool" models, was subsequently developed by Allen, Morris, and Postlewaite (1993) and Conlon (2004). In these models, agents once again buy assets that they believe they can sell to others at a profit, although the mechanics of the model are somewhat different. In particular, agents buy an asset that they know is overvalued but that they believe other agents may not know with certainty is overvalued. As Allen, Morris, and Postlewaite (1993) note explicitly, these models do not require that agents have disjoint priors. Instead, allowing agents to maintain different beliefs turns out to be important in these models only insofar as it creates a reason for agents to trade. Any feature that would generate trade could similarly lead to a bubble. As is well known, differences in beliefs are isomorphic to differences in marginal utility across agents. Under the latter interpretation, agents have common prior beliefs, but differences in their marginal utility imply they would like to trade the assets in some states of the world, violating Tirole's (1982) fourth assumption that resources are already allocated efficiently. Hence, these types of models can be viewed as violating either the assumption of common prior beliefs or the assumption that resources are allocated efficiently before agents can trade.

The final class of models of bubbles is known as agency theories of bubbles. This class encompasses the model presented in the Allen and Gorton (1993) paper reprinted in this volume, as well as models in work by Allen and Gale (2000) and Barlevy (2008). In these models, traders who buy overvalued assets buy them not with their own funds, but with funds secured from others. Hence, traders are effectively acting as agents of those who endow them with funds. Depending on the nature of the contract between the principal providing the funding and the agent who purchases the asset, a trader who buys the asset may value the asset differently from its inherent value, since the trader may not bear all of the losses if the trade proves to be unprofitable. As a result, it will be possible for assets to trade at a price that deviates from their underlying fundamentals. Of course, this requires that the principals who fund these traders agree to finance these trades in the first place. Since creditors incur a loss from such traders, they would try to avoid them if they could. To be willing to fund such traders, creditors must not be able to distinguish between these speculators and other agents who wish to secure funding for productive purposes that lenders would be happy to fund. The fact that some agents need to secure funds for productive purposes implies the initial allocation of resources prior to trading must not have been efficient, since lending is necessary to achieve these gains. Hence, these models once again violate Tirole's (1982) fourth assumption that resources are allocated efficiently prior to trade.

In sum, in many existing models of bubbles, an explicit or implicit assumption needed to sustain a bubble in equilibrium is that resources are allocated inefficiently prior to trade. This fact is useful for understanding why existing models do not necessarily imply that bursting bubbles is Pareto improving or even desirable. In particular, it evokes a well-known result in economic theory known as the "theory of the second best" (a term coined by Lipsey and Lancaster, 1956–57). This theory argues that policies that would be undesirable when markets are efficient can be desirable when they are inefficient. The classic example of this theory involves distortionary taxation. One way to ensure efficiency is to ensure that no goods are taxed in a distortionary way. But suppose that among a set of goods with identical costs of production, all but one is already subject to a distortionary tax. Since all goods are equally costly to produce, efficiency would dictate that their relative prices be the same. Hence, it would be preferable to introduce a distortionary tax on the remaining good to match all other goods, even though taxes are inherently distortionary. By the same token, although it might be desirable for an asset to reflect its fundamental value in an efficient economy, it is not obvious that this would be desirable in an economy that is already inefficient. It might even be possible that driving the price of the asset to its fundamental value will be bad for social welfare. Given that most existing models of bubbles essentially involve economies that are already distorted along some dimension, it should not be too surprising that what may intuitively seem like a desirable policy turns out to be undesirable.

Socially Desirable Bubbles

The clearest demonstration that bursting a bubble can make society worse off rather than better off comes from overlapping generations models of bubbles. Consider the Diamond (1965) model of an overlapping generations economy with accumulable capital. The model can be summarized as follows. In each period, a new cohort of individuals is born, who will live for two periods. Agents who are born in date t derive utility from consumption when young, c_t^y, and when old, c_{t+1}^o, according to a utility function $u\left(c_t^y, c_{t+1}^o\right)$. They are endowed with one unit of labor when young. The size of each cohort is normalized to one, so the aggregate endowment of labor is equal to 1. Output can be produced from labor and capital according to the following production technology

$$Y_t = F\left(K_t, (1 + g)^t L_t\right),$$

where $F\left(\cdot\right)$ is a concave function that is homogeneous of degree 1, K_t denotes the total stock of capital at date t, L_t denotes the aggregate amount of labor employed in production, and $g \geq 0$ denotes the rate of labor-augmenting technological progress. That is, although the total amount of labor workers that can supply each period is constant given all cohorts are assumed to be of equal size, workers become more productive over time and each cohort's labor endowment yields more effective labor than previous cohorts. Given the assumptions on $F\left(\cdot\right)$, I can rewrite output as

$$Y_t = (1 + g)^t L_t f\left(k_t\right),$$

where $k_t = K_t / (1 + g)^t L_t$ is the ratio of capital to effective labor. Firms can hire capital and labor in competitive markets. In equilibrium, firms will employ these factors optimally, so we can obtain equilibrium prices from the firm's first order conditions. Assuming for simplicity that capital does not depreciate, the rental rate on capital is given by

$$r_t = f'(k_t),$$

while the price of a unit of effective labor is given by

$$w_t = f(k_t) - f'(k_t) k_t.$$

Agents when young earn w_t. Given certain assumptions on the utility function $u(\cdot)$, the young would like to save part of their income w_t to consume when they are old. One way to do this is to buy capital when they are young, which they can rent out to firms when they turn old and then sell off to the next cohort of young. Under fairly weak conditions, this economy converges to a steady state in which k_t tends to be a constant value k^*, while output Y_t and capital K_t grow at rate g. Note that so far, buying capital is the only way the young are allowed to save for old age. In particular, there are no other assets agents can trade, and so k^* denotes the steady-state ratio of capital to effective labor in the absence of any bubble.

Following Diamond (1965), I next introduce an additional way for agents to save in the model, namely, inherently worthless pieces of paper that agents can buy when young and sell when old. Diamond interpreted these pieces of paper as government debt. However, they can equally be viewed as claims on an asset that pays no dividend. Let b_t denote the total value of these claims at date t. Then agents who buy the asset at date t earn a return b_{t+1} / b_t on the asset when they sell it at date $t + 1$. If this rate compares favorably to the return on capital, they would be willing to save using this asset. If $b_t > 0$, these pieces of paper qualify as bubbles given the definition provided earlier: They provide no dividends, so their fundamental value is zero, and yet they trade at a positive market price. Whether a bubble can exist in this economy thus amounts to whether there exists an equilibrium in which b_t is positive.

Diamond (1965) showed that a necessary condition for a bubble is if the growth rate g was at least as large as $f'(k^*)$, which recall is just the interest rate associated with the steady state when there is no bubble. The intuition for this result is as follows. Since individuals always have the option to save using capital, an equilibrium in which they hold both capital and intrinsically worthless assets requires that the two forms of saving yield the same return.[9] Since saving using capital yields a return of $1 + r_t$, that is, the profits from renting out capital and then selling it to the young, this implies that the value of the intrinsically worthless asset must grow at rate r_t, that is,

$$b_{t+1} = (1 + r_t)b_t.$$

Since the price of a unit of effective labor $w = f(k^*) - f'(k^*)k^*$ is also constant at steady state, the income each young cohort earns will grow at rate g in the long run, commensurate with the growth in labor productivity. Since the young must be able to afford to buy the asset, their income cannot consistently grow at a slower rate than the bubble. But this implies that

$$g \geq r^* = f'(k).$$

However, as is well known, the case where $g > f'(k^*)$ implies the economy is dynamically inefficient. That is, agents are accumulating too much capital, and all agents could be made better off if instead of investing resources in capital, the young would allocate some of these resources to augmenting the consumption of the current old in each period. Since a bubble diverts resources away from capital accumulation, it serves a positive purpose. In fact, one can show that the equilibrium in which there is a bubble that grows at rate g is Pareto efficient. Bursting the bubble will therefore always make at least some agents worse off. The policy implications of this model are thus precisely the opposite of the lesson many appear to have drawn from the recent crisis: Rather than intervening to offset the bubble, policymakers should ensure bubbles persist. Should a bubble burst, it would be best to create a new bubble.[10]

Non-Welfare-Improving Bubbles

Although the standard overlapping generations model tends to imply bubbles are good, this feature is not true of all models of bubbles or even of all overlapping generations models of bubbles. This shouldn't be surprising: The theory of the second best only states that correcting one distortion in an economy with other distortions need not raise welfare. It does not imply that correcting a distortion will necessarily lower welfare. I now discuss several models in which bubbles do not promote social welfare as in the Diamond (1965) model described in the previous section. However, these models again turn out to be of limited value for capturing the emerging view among policymakers on the necessity of intervention against bubbles, since these models still imply that bursting a bubble cannot improve welfare in a Pareto sense, that is, make society as a whole better off. The Allen and Gorton (1993) model reprinted in this volume, which I discuss in further detail later, turns out to be one example of such a model. But I begin my discussion with two examples based on modifications of the overlapping generations model described previously. Both of these modifications involve a similar point, namely, that the existence of a bubble requires that the economy grow at a rate that exceeds the market rate of return, while dynamic inefficiency requires that the growth rate exceed the social rate of return on investment.

In the standard model, the market rate of return and the social return on investment are the same. But if there is some distortion that drives a wedge between the two rates of return, as will be the case in the two models I describe, a bubble can emerge even without dynamic inefficiency.

The first model I consider was developed by Grossman and Yanagawa (1993).[11] They modify the production structure of the overlapping generations model described in the previous section so that labor productivity grows not at an exogenous rate but at a rate that depends on endogenous capital accumulation. In particular, suppose production takes place at multiple firms, and let k_{it} and l_{it} denote the capital and labor employed by firm i. The production function for each firm is assumed equal to

$$y_{it} = F\,(k_{it},\, K_t \cdot l_{it}),$$

where K_t denotes aggregate capital. Thus, labor at each firm becomes more productive the larger the aggregate capital stock. This specification is inspired by the work of Romer (1986), who interprets capital as knowledge that can spill over to firms beyond the original firm that acquired the knowledge. This specification has two implications. First, the growth rate of labor productivity is now determined endogenously rather than exogenously. Second, and more importantly for our purposes, it implies capital accumulation involves a positive externality, since when firms choose how much capital to invest in, they will not take into account that their capital accumulation benefits other firms. This implies the economy as a whole will underaccumulate capital. As a result, a bubble can occur even when there is too little capital: A necessary condition for a bubble is that the economy grows faster than the private rate of return, but now this no longer implies there is too much capital accumulation. Since a bubble still serves to crowd out capital given that young individuals saving for retirement hold part of their wealth in the bubble asset instead of capital, the presence of a bubble will make future generations distinctly worse off by depriving them of capital and leaving them less productive than they could have been.

At first, this model might seem to offer a case for policy intervention in response to a bubble, since bursting a bubble allows resources to be redirected toward accumulating productive capital as opposed to merely bidding up the value of some nonproductive asset. But as Grossman and Yanagawa (1993) point out, this intervention is in fact not Pareto improving. The intuition is as follows. The only way that bursting a bubble gives rise to more capital is if the resources that would have otherwise been used to produce consumption goods for today's old are redirected to the production of capital. The old will thus be worse off, unless we divert some resources used to produce consumption goods for today's young. But today's young will not benefit from any additional capital that would be created, since the capital will only be deployed when they are old, leaving their labor productivity unchanged. Hence, today's young will be worse off, unless they are compensated when they are older with an offer of more consumption goods, which would have to be taken from that generation's young. Grossman and Yanagawa (1993) show that this scheme amounts to an intergenerational transfer scheme, and would simply re-create the original bubble. Hence, the only way to make sure today's old are not harmed by bursting the bubble is to create a new bubble, which would crowd out capital accumulation just as the original bubble did. Policy intervention to stem a bubble can lead to greater capital accumulation that would be beneficial in the long run, but only by making some of today's agents strictly worse off. Hence, the model does not imply that bursting a bubble is desirable for society as a whole. Since political economy considerations tend to favor policies that benefit current generations, this would suggest policymakers ought to be averse to acting against a bubble if one emerged.

A second example of a model in which bubbles do not necessarily raise welfare comes from a recent paper by Farhi and Tirole (2011). Their model also builds on the original overlapping generations structure in the previous section, but with two modifications. First, instead of allowing the young to save by accumulating capital, the young can save by lending to other agents who need resources for production. More precisely, agents in their model live for three periods rather than two. They are endowed with resources when young—analogous to the agents who receive a labor endowment when young in the Diamond (1965) model—and when they reach middle age they can operate a production project that uses resources they put in plus any additional resources they borrow to produce output that they receive when they turn old. However, there is a friction that limits the amount borrowers can pledge to repay, so the return a lender earns will be less than the social rate of return from production. Farhi and Tirole (2011) then add an intrinsically useless asset that agents can trade. The young can therefore save in at least two ways: 1) by lending to middle-aged agents who will repay them when they turn old and the lender reaches middle age and 2) by purchasing an intrinsically worthless asset.

Second, Farhi and Tirole (2011) introduce still another way for agents to save, namely, to buy nonaccumulable assets available in fixed supply that yield a positive stream of dividends. In principle, there is no reason to focus on the possibility that bubbles arise on the intrinsically worthless assets as opposed to the assets available in fixed supply. But introducing these assets explicitly helps convey an important point. In particular, the presence of a bubble still drives equilibrium interest rates up, just as in the original Diamond (1965) model, and hence drives down the price of the asset available in fixed supply. Owners of the asset available in fixed supply will therefore be made worse off by the presence of a bubble. But just as in the Grossman and Yanagawa (1993) framework, this does not imply that intervening to burst a bubble will make society as a whole better off, since those who own the bubble will be made worse off. Once again, this model does not provide a good foundation for why intervening to stem a bubble once it arises would be socially desirable. Rather, it shows that bursting a bubble can potentially make some—but not all—agents better off.

Agency Models of Bubbles

I now turn to agency models of bubbles, which include the Allen and Gorton (1993) paper included in this volume. As I noted earlier, these models also imply that bursting a bubble can only make some but not all agents better off, just as in the Grossman and Yanagawa (1993) and Farhi and Tirole (2011) models. However, with agency models there may be a simple way to modify the model so that bursting a bubble could potentially generate a Pareto improvement. To the best of my knowledge, this point has not been made before, and is certainly not in Allen and Gorton's original paper. If it is true, this would suggest that there may be a coherent framework in which intervening to burst a bubble can be justi-fied, in line with the emerging view that central banks should be ready to inter-vene if they suspect a bubble is present in asset markets. However, as I discuss later, it is less clear whether the modification I conjecture captures the reasons for why policymakers appear to be gravitating toward this view.

I begin by examining the welfare implications of the Allen and Gorton (1993) model. To understand the welfare implications of the bubble that emerges in this model, it is important to first understand why the model gives rise to a bubble, something that is not entirely easy given the model is quite elaborate and relies on a large number of assumptions.[12] Essentially, a bubble can occur because under the contract traders enter into in equilibrium, they have an incentive to buy an asset for more than its inherent value (zero in the model) as a way to place a bet at someone else's expense on whether they will find another trader to sell the asset to. In particular, they stand to earn a profit if they find another trader but incur no loss if they do not. Creditors agree to fund such agents because they cannot distinguish between those who are gambling with the funds they receive and other productive agents who are profitable to fund. Allen and Gorton (1993) model the latter as agents who can spot undervalued assets, but what the latter agents do that makes them productive is not essential. In equilibrium, creditors offer the same contract to both types, and they earn enough profits from prof-itable agents to offset their losses from those who gamble with the funds they receive.[13] Hence, bubbles can occur because speculators bid up the price of assets to above their fundamental value given they can shift their losses onto those who fund them, and the latter shift their expected losses onto agents with profitable opportunities that require funding. The bubble thus redistributes resources from those with profit opportunities to those without. Since agents who provide fund-ing would always like to finance profitable investors, eliminating speculation will make profitable traders better off by the same amount it makes speculators worse off. The latter simply profit at the expense of the former. To put it another way, if all agents in the model—profitable traders, speculators, and creditors—had to remit their earnings to a representative household, the income of the household would be the same whether there was a bubble or not. Eliminating bubbles would therefore not make the representative household either better off or worse off.

So far, this result seems to mirror the results for modified versions of the over-lapping generations model discussed in the previous section—that is, eliminating a bubble will make some people better off and some people worse off, but does not make all agents better off. However, agency models of bubbles offer some hope that, if properly modified, they might imply that bursting a bubble can make all agents better off. In particular, suppose the agents who gamble at the expense of those who fund them had an outside opportunity to engage in production. As long as the return on their investment was small, they would prefer to engage in speculation and earn rents at the expense of the agents who fund them. Society, in contrast, would prefer for these agents to engage in production, which yields positive surplus, rather than gambling at the expense of others, which yields no surplus for society as a whole. Eliminating a bubble may thus increase the total amount of resources available to society, and allow for a redistribution that keeps all agents at least as well off as they were under the bubble. One needs to confirm that this is indeed possible, unlike in the Grossman and Yanagawa (1993) model, where the timing of when agents need to be compensated makes it impossible to both reallocate resources and make all agents better off. This confirmation requires a more formal analysis than I conduct here, but a priori it seems possible that a modified version of the Allen and Gorton (1993) framework could imply that bursting a bubble is Pareto improving.

It should be noted that while modifying agency models of bubbles this way may imply that agents are collectively better off in a world where the bubble is elimi-nated relative to the market equilibrium in which a bubble exists, the argument that policy intervention against a bubble is desirable would depend on how the bubble is eliminated. In particular, capturing the gains from eliminating a bubble requires that agents who previously engaged in profitable activities continue to do so and that agents who previously engaged in speculation shift to socially profitable pro-duction. Whether this occurs depends on how policymakers eliminate the bubble. For example, an intervention that hampers the functioning of the market for funds or raises the cost of securing funds can eliminate bubbles, but only at the cost of preventing profitable agents from securing funds for their activities. In that case, it is no longer obvious that intervention would make society better off. By contrast, if profitable activities require an input that is not complementary with speculation, subsidizing this input may raise welfare by drawing more agents to this activity rather than speculation without discouraging the agents who were already willing to engage in profitable production when a bubble exists.[14] Further analysis along these lines is needed before we can gauge whether the misallocation of resources that can arise in models with agency problems ultimately justifies policy intervention.

Why Do Policymakers Want Intervention?

In the previous section, I proposed one scenario under which there may be a rea-son for policymakers to intervene against bubbles. Still, it is not obvious that a model along these lines would capture the concerns that have led to the shift in thinking about policy toward bubbles. In particular, the speeches by policymakers cited earlier argue that policymakers may want to intervene against bubbles not because of a concern about resource misallocation while asset prices are rising, but to avoid future crises and recessions of similar magnitude to the recent crisis, which they believe was caused by a bubble in the housing market. That is, these speeches emphasize the large cost of waiting to clean up, not the consequences of distortions that occur along the way as asset prices are rising.

Policymakers appear to have reconsidered the previous conventional wisdom about how they should act when facing possible bubbles because of two main concerns. The first is that if a bubble is sustained by credit emanating from the financial sector, then losses incurred by the financial sector once the bubble bursts can threaten the stability of the financial system. The second is that the bursting of a bubble can trigger a severe contraction in output—either indirectly, by harming the financial sector, or directly, if the collapse in asset values impairs the balance sheets of firms and makes it more difficult for them to secure additional funding even when the financial system may be unaffected by the bubble's collapse. In both cases, the implicit justification for intervention involves the damage that may arise when the bubble bursts and asset prices fall. Inherent in this view is some presumption that stemming a bubble early on, before it has a chance to grow more, ought to minimize the extent of the damage when asset prices fall.

Capturing these notions with a formal model represents a challenge, at least given existing models of bubbles. Consider first the concern about threats bubbles pose to the financial system. The Allen and Gorton (1993) model touches on the issue of losses to lenders, since the whole point of the model is that bubbles are associated with risk-shifting whereby agents who secure funds from creditors transfer their losses from unsuccessful speculation onto their creditors. At first, this might seem encouraging. However, an essential point of the model is that creditors would not fund speculators in the first place if they didn't expect to cover their losses from loans to unprofitable agents with gains from loans to profitable agents. Indeed, lenders in the model make zero expected profits, and the losses they anticipate on unsuccessful speculators who hold the asset when the bubble bursts should be balanced by the profits they earn in the meantime from profitable borrowers. While it may be possible to generate the result that creditors do realize losses in some states of the world within this class of models, the point remains that lenders in these models typically have incentive to minimize their exposure to such losses, especially if financial intermediation turns valuable when a bubble bursts so that creditors who survive stand to earn high profits from providing their services. This could potentially mitigate the scope of these models to generate large and costly losses to the financial system. Understanding the implications of such models may necessitate explicitly incorporating the cost of disruptions to financial intermediation and their implications for the incentives of lenders to guard themselves against risks—features that are missing from current models that emphasize agency costs as a source of bubbles.

Another important insight that comes out of the Allen and Gorton (1993) model is that when assets trade hands between agents who are all financed externally, bursting the bubble may not be effective in curtailing losses to the lending sector as a whole. In particular, their model posits that assets are initially owned by agents who have full claim to the asset and then the assets are sold to an agent financed by an outsider investor, who in turn sells it to yet another agent financed by an outside investor. Suppose the central bank moves to stem the bubble after the first trade, on the grounds that it wants to deflate the bubble before it grows. This intervention would prevent the second agent from buying the asset, and keep losses from being incurred by the investor who funds that agent. But bursting the bubble would make the first agent unable to repay the investor who financed him originally; that investor would incur a loss that he would not have incurred otherwise. Although the losses to the second creditor would be larger than the losses the first creditor incurs as a result of central bank intervention, this is in part because these losses correspond to profits the first creditor earns at their expense. In the aggregate, it is not obvious whether moving to burst a bubble early on improves the net position of lenders as a whole, especially if trade in assets is largely confined to agents who are leveraged.

Next, consider the threat that the bursting of a bubble poses to economic activity. To the extent this threat arises because of instability to the financial system, the same issues described previously would make it a challenge to capture this aspect with existing models. But a fall in asset prices could arguably upset economic activity directly rather than through the financial system. For example, to the extent that assets serve firms as collateral for borrowing, a collapse in asset values may make it difficult for firms to borrow, limiting their ability to produce.[15] Once again, the case for policy intervention early on when the bubble is still small can be challenging to capture. In particular, the fact that a collapse in asset values hurts firms would suggest that bursting the bubble early might also impair firms' balance sheets. Indeed, a plausible argument can be made that the role of policy in this case is to prevent a bubble from bursting rather than to prick it early on, a point that Kocherlakota (2009) makes explicitly. However, there might be ways to modify the model so that bursting the bubble early might be better than bursting it later. One channel would be if what mattered for production was not the level of the value of the collateral but the change in this value. such as models in which agents are constrained only in response to a surprise shock that forces them to adjust their balance sheets. One example is the model by Jermann and Quadrini (2009), in which a shock to the amount firms can borrow forces short-term readjustment but has no effect in the long run because firms can shift from debt into equity. Another possible channel would maintain the assumption that firms can only borrow against the value of their collateral, but the more overvalued the asset is before it crashes, the more undervalued it will become once the bubble bursts. That is, asset prices overshoot when they crash, to an extent that depends on how overvalued the asset was to begin with.

Allen and Gale (2004) raise this possibility, observing that in practice asset price collapses appear to be associated with liquidity crises and fire sales, during which assets seem to trade below their fundamental value. But no existing model of bubbles offers a theoretical argument for why more overvaluation on the way up should be associated with greater undervaluation after the crash. We therefore remain far from being able to capture the intuition that seems to be guiding policymakers as they reevaluate the appropriate policy response in the face of a potential asset price bubble.

Conclusion

Most of the existing literature on bubbles has focused on demonstrating that under certain conditions, it will be possible for an asset to trade at a price that differs from its fundamental value. Given this restricted purpose, there is little that happened during the most recent crisis that would help us to discriminate among existing models that were never really designed to match a broad set of facts associated with episodes many accept as examples of bubbles. The more relevant lesson to draw from the crisis is that given the shift in conventional wisdom on what constitutes an appropriate policy response toward bubbles, there is a wide gap between the implications of existing models of bubbles and the emerging view that policymakers should intervene against bubbles if and when they emerge. This is because few, if any, of the existing models imply that policy intervention is warranted when a bubble emerges, and some imply that bubbles are desirable. Even in models where bubbles are not inherently desirable, bursting them need not make society as a whole better off. While I sketch out ways to possibly modify existing models so that bubbles are Pareto inferior, the case they offer for intervention is distinct from the expressed views of policymakers, who seem to have in mind some notion that letting a bubble grow can exacerbate the damage if and when a bubble eventually bursts. Moreover, how a policy deflates a bubble can matter for whether such an intervention is desirable, and we have few models that explore this issue.

That said, agency models along the lines of the Allen and Gorton (1993) model may offer a useful starting point for exploring whether and when the emerging view on intervening against bubbles is appropriate. These models contain several key elements that one would like for exploring these issues. First, there is a direct link between bubbles to credit or, more generally, a market for funds. Second, these models imply that a bubble emerges because speculators can shift some of the risk they are exposed to onto those who fund them. Thus, these models already embody the notion that speculative activity exposes lenders to potential losses. Although few papers have adapted the Allen and Gorton (1993) model, presumably because it is so highly stylized, subsequent work such as Allen and Gale (2000) offers simpler models that are based on the same basic idea. The latter model has already been adapted to analyze empirically relevant questions. For example, Barlevy and Fisher (2010) use an agency model to explore the housing market, and show that under plausible restrictions bubbles can emerge in this market, even though lenders can observe what borrowers are doing and which property they are using as collateral. Dubecq, Mojon, and Ragot (2009) use an agency model to explore what happens when agents are uncertain about regulatory policy. Future work may reveal this class of models to be equally useful for investigating other issues the recent crisis has brought to the fore.

Notes

1. This paper reflects the author's own views and not the views of the Federal Reserve Bank of Chicago or the Federal Reserve System.
2. For examples of speeches on the appropriate policy response to bubbles, see Dudley (2009), Stern (2009), and Yellen (2009).
3. Much of my discussion will focus on the case where the price exceeds the fundamental value of an asset, sometimes known as a "positive" bubble. This is the scenario policymakers seem to have in mind when they argue that central banks should stand ready to lean against rising asset prices. This is not to deny that "negative" bubbles, in which the price of the asset lies below its fundamental value, aren't also interesting. Although I focus on positive bubbles in most of my discussion, toward the end of my discussion I return to a point in Allen and Gale (2004) that one reason to worry about positive bubbles is that they may lead to negative bubbles when they burst.
4. Milgrom and Stokey (1982) contemporaneously derived similar conditions under which no speculation would occur, meaning that traders would not enter into trades in the hope of profiting at the expense of other traders.
5. For a discussion on the merits and validity of the assumption of common prior beliefs, see Morris (1995).
6. In addition to violating one of Tirole's (1982) assumptions, a necessary condition for a bubble to occur is that there be some limitation on the short selling of the assets on which bubbles emerge. In particular, since a bubble is worth more than the present discounted value of the dividends it yields, agents can make arbitrage profits by shorting the bubble and then using the proceeds they earn to pay out dividends, pocketing the amount left over as profit. If people were free to short the asset, the threat of infinite supply would ensure the price of an asset could never exceed its fundamental value, thus precluding the possibility of a bubble. Since Tirole focused on deriving conditions under which bubbles don't occur rather than the conditions in which they do, this assumption does not play a role in his analysis.
7. My survey of the literature on models of bubbles is necessarily partial. For example, I do not discuss behavioral models of bubbles, some of which violate Tirole's restriction that all agents be rational. Some of these behavioral approaches are discussed elsewhere in this book. I also ignore models such as Abreu and Brunnermeier (2003) that model the collapse of a bubble but treat the emergence of the bubble in the first place as exogenous.
8. The paper by Scheinkman and Xiong (2003), which is reprinted in this volume, builds on the original Harrison and Kreps (1978) framework, but treats the different priors of the agents as the result of behavioral forces such as overconfidence.
9. This follows because in the model the returns on capital and the bubble are both assumed riskless. The analysis is more complicated, but similar in spirit, if we allow either to be risky. See Weil (1987) for an analysis of the case where the return on the bubble asset is risky but the return on capital is not, and Abel et al. (1989) for an analysis of the case where the return on capital is risky.

10. Although the overlapping generations model runs counter to the notion that overvalued assets are undesirable, it does capture a notion many would find compelling, namely, that the bursting of a bubble is a distinctly unwelcome event that makes society worse off. This point is particularly emphasized in Kocherlakota (2009), who develops a related model in which agents have an incentive to save, although not for life-cycle reasons as in the original overlapping generation models. In his model, the bubble again serves a useful purpose, and its collapse leads to disintermediation and a fall in output, phenomena that do not arise in overlapping generations models.

11. Similar models were independently proposed by Saint-Paul (1992) and King and Ferguson (1993).

12. Indeed, there seems to be some confusion about which features of the Allen and Gorton (1993) model are essential for generating a bubble. For example, Camerer (1989) cites an early version of the paper and attributes the bubble to a lack of common knowledge about how many traders will arrive in the future. Faust (1989) attributes the bubble in the model to the fact that the model assumes continuous time, implying the model is essentially an overlapping generations model reworked to a finite horizon but with continuous time and thus infinitely many trading opportunities. Tirole (2006, 8) cites as important the fact that agents in the model have short horizons.

13. This raises the question of why creditors design contracts in a way that allows agents to earn profits at their expense. Allen and Gorton (1993) focus on an equilibrium in which all creditors offer a contract that creates this opportunity as part of a coordination failure. That is, creditors could shift to collectively offering a different contract that discourages speculation—such as a simple debt contract—but no single creditor has any incentive to unilaterally offer a different contract. This result may seem fragile. However, this result is due to some idiosyncratic features of the Allen and Gorton framework, such as the fact that the asset is intrinsically worthless. If instead the asset had some value that was stochastic, as in Allen and Gale (2000), coordinating on a debt contract would no longer work to prevent a bubble from occurring.

14. This scenario is inspired by Arnott, Greenwald, and Stiglitz (1994), who discuss when economic outcomes in an economy plagued with information frictions may be constrained inefficient. In particular, they argue that subsidizing a complementary input is one example where intervention is warranted.

15. On the link between asset prices and economic activity, see Kiyotaki and Moore (1997).

References

Abel, Andrew, Greg Mankiw, Lawrence Summers, and Richard Zeckhauser. 1989. "Assessing Dynamic Efficiency: Theory and Evidence." *Review of Economic Studies* 56(1), 1–19.

Abreu, Dilip, and Markus Brunnermeier. 2003. "Bubbles and Crashes." *Econometrica* 71, 173–204.

Allais, Maurice. 1947. *Economie et Interet*. Paris: Imprimerie Nationale.

Allen, Franklin, and Douglas Gale. 2000. "Bubbles and Crises." *Economic Journal* 110, 236–255.

———. 2004. "Asset Price Bubbles and Monetary Policy." In Meghnad Desai and Yahia Said, eds., *Global Governance and Financial Crises*. New York: Routledge.

Allen, Franklin, and Gary Gorton. 1993. "Churning Bubbles." *Review of Economic Studies* 60(4), 813–836.Allen, Franklin, Stephen Morris, and Andrew Postlewaite. 1993. "Finite Bubbles with Short Sales Constraints and Asymmetric Information." *Journal of Economic Theory* 61, 206–229.

Arnott, Richard, Bruce Greenwald, and Joseph Stiglitz. 1994. "Information and Economic Efficiency." *Information Economics and Policy* 6(1), 77–88.

Barlevy, Gadi. 2007. "Economic Theory and Asset Bubbles." *Economic Perspectives*, Federal Reserve Bank of Chicago, Third Quarter, 44–59.

————. 2008. "A Leverage-Based Model of Speculative Bubbles." Federal Reserve Bank of Chicago Working Paper WP-08–01.

Barlevy, Gadi, and Jonas Fisher. 2010. "Mortgage Choices and Housing Speculation." Federal Reserve Bank of Chicago Working Paper WP-10–12.

Bernanke, Ben, and Mark Gertler. 1999. "Monetary Policy and Asset Price Volatility." *New Challenges for Monetary Policy: A Symposium*. Kansas City, MO: Federal Reserve Bank of Kansas City. Reprinted in this volume.Camerer, Colin. 1989. "Bubbles and Fads in Asset Prices." *Journal of Economic Surveys* 3(1), 3–41.

Conlon, John. 2004. "Simple Finite Horizon Bubbles Robust to Higher Order Knowledge." *Econometrica* 72, 927–936.

Diamond, Peter. 1965. "National Debt in a Neoclassical Growth Model." *American Economic Review* 55, 1126–1150.

Dubecq, Simon, Benoit Mojon, and Xavier Ragot. 2009. "Fuzzy Capital Requirements, Risk-Shifting and the Risk Taking Channel of Monetary Policy." Banque de France Working Paper No. 254.

Dudley, William. 2009. "Lessons Learned from the Financial Crisis." Speech delivered to the Eighth Annual BIS Conference, Basel, Switzerland, June 26. http://www.newyorkfed.org/newsevents/speeches/2009/dud090702.html

Farhi, Emmanuel, and Jean Tirole. 2011. "Bubbly Liquidity." IDEI Working Paper, February (revised version of 2009 working paper 577).

Faust, Jon. 1989. "Supernovas in Monetary Theory: Does the Ultimate Sunspot Rule Out Money?" *American Economic Review* 79, 872–881.

Grossman, Gene, and Noriyuki Yanagawa. 1993. "Asset Bubbles and Endogenous Growth." *Journal of Monetary Economics* 31, 3–19.

Harrison, J. Michael, and David Kreps. 1978. "Speculative Investor Behavior in a Stock Market with Heterogeneous Expectations." *Quarterly Journal of Economics* 92, 323–336.

Jermann, Urban, and Vincenzo Quadrini. 2009. "Macroeconomic Effects of Financial Shocks." National Bureau of Economic Research Working Paper No. 15338.

Kindleberger, Charles. 1996. *Manias, Panics, and Crashes: A History of Financial Crises*. New York: John Wiley & Sons.

King, Ian, and Don Ferguson. 1993. "Dynamic Inefficiency, Endogenous Growth, and Ponzi Games." *Journal of Monetary Economics* 32, 79–104.

Kiyotaki, Nobuhiro, and John Moore. 1997. "Credit Cycles." *Journal of Political Economy* 105, 211–248.

Kocherlakota, Narayana. 2009. "Bursting Bubbles: Consequences and Cures." University of Minnesota working paper.

Lipsey, R., and Kelvin Lancaster. 1956–1957. "The General Theory of the Second Best." *Review of Economic Studies* 24(1), 11–32.

Milgrom, Paul, and Nancy Stokey. 1982. "Information, Trade, and Common Knowledge." *Journal of Economic Theory* 26, 17–27.

Morris, Stephen. 1995. "The Common Prior Assumption in Economic Theory." *Economics and Philosophy*, 11, 227–253.

Romer, Paul. 1986. "Increasing Returns and Long-run Growth." *Journal of Political Economy* 94, 1002–1037.

Saint-Paul, Gilles. 1992. "Fiscal Policy in an Endogenous Growth Model." *Quarterly Journal of Economics* 107, 1243–1259.

Samuelson, Paul. 1958. "An Exact Consumption-Loan Model of Interest with or without the Social Contrivance of Money." *Journal of Political Economy* 66, 467–482.

Santos, Manuel, and Michael Woodford. 1997. "Rational Asset Pricing Bubbles." *Econometrica* 65, 19–57.

Scheinkman, José, and Wei Xiong. 2003. "Overconfidence and Speculative Bubbles," *Journal of Political Economy* 111, 1183–1219.

Stern, Gary. 2009. "Remarks to Helena Business Leaders." Speech delivered in Helena, Montana, July 9. http://www.minneapolisfed.org/news_events/pres/Stern07-09-09.cfm

Tirole, Jean. 1982. "On the Possibility of Speculation under Rational Expectations." *Econometrica* 50, 1163–1182.

———. 1985. "Asset Bubbles and Overlapping Generations." *Econometrica* 53, November, pp. 1499–1528.

———. 2006. *The Theory of Corporate Finance*. Princeton, NJ: Princeton University Press.

Weil, Philippe. 1987. "Confidence and the Real Value of Money in an Overlapping Generations Economy." *Quarterly Journal of Economics* 102, 1–22.

Yellen, Janet. 2009. "A Minsky Meltdown: Lessons for Central Bankers." Speech delivered to the 18th Annual Hyman P. Minsky Conference on the State of the U.S. and World Economies, April 16. http://www.frbsf.org/news/speeches/2009/0416.html.

CONSEQUENCES
OF BUBBLES BURSTING

CHAPTER 4

The Japanese Banking Crisis

WHERE DID IT COME FROM AND HOW WILL IT END?

Takeo Hoshi and Anil Kashyap

1. Introduction*

Japan's financial system is in the midst of a major transformation. One driving force is deregulation. The reform program that has come to be known as the *Japanese Big Bang* represents the conclusion of a deregulation process that began more than 20 years ago. By the time the Big Bang is complete, in 2001, banks, security firms, and insurance companies will face a level playing field on which unfettered competition can occur. At that time, Japanese financial markets will be at least as liberalized as the U.S. markets.

A second (and we will argue related) driving factor is the current huge financial crisis. As of September 1998, the estimates of bad loans in Japan remain at 7% of GDP (see Section 4 below for further details). This crisis has included the first significant bank failures since the end of the U.S. occupation of Japan. In policy circles, the banking problems are widely identified as one of the key factors for the poor performance of the Japanese economy over the last couple of years.[1] A growing academic literature suggests that the problems in the banking sector are now creating a serious drag on the economy's ability to recover.[2]

The Japanese government during the 1990s has taken a number of steps to address the financial problems. Starting with the loan purchasing program set up in early 1993, followed by the establishment of banks to buy out failed credit cooperatives and the *jusen,* and culminating in the reforms that reorganized the supervision authority for banks and earmarked over ¥60 trillion for bank reorganization and capitalization, there have been a nearly continuous set of attempts to fix the banking problem.[3]

In the latest attempt, the Long-Term Credit Bank of Japan (LTCB) and Nippon Credit Bank (NCB) were nationalized in late 1998, and three regional banks were put under receivership in the first half of 1999. Their balance sheets are supposed to be cleaned up so that they can be sold. Meanwhile, in March 1999, 15 large banks applied for a capital injection and received ¥7.4592 trillion of public funds. These banks are also required to carry out restructuring plans that will include eliminating 20,000 workers, closing 10% of their branches, and increasing profits by 50% over the next four years.[4] Nevertheless, critics, including the U.S. Treasury, have argued that these steps have been inadequate.[5] In the latter half of 1999, two more regional banks were shut down and ¥260 billion of public funds were injected to recapitalize four other regional banks. As of this writing there is still widespread pessimism about whether the banks have turned the corner.

We believe that a recurring problem with the Japanese government's attempts to overcome the crisis has been the lack of a clear vision for the future of the Japanese banking system. For instance, the debate that culminated in the passage of the Financial Reconstruction Bill in the fall of 1998 was drawn out because the ruling Liberal Democratic Party (LDP) and the major opposition party (the Democrats) haggled over two competing plans. On the surface, the negotiation seemed to center on what should happen to the Long-Term Credit Bank, which had been rumored to be insolvent for almost four months. At a deeper level, however, the two plans represented competing views about the current condition of the Japanese banking system.

LDP leaders believed that the major banks could not be allowed to fail. To them, the biggest problem with the Japanese banks was they were not strong enough to support (supposedly) healthy customers. Thus, the desired solution was to inject public funds into the major banks as they did in March 1998, to prevent a credit crunch. In the event of a failure, protecting solvent borrowers, by transferring the failed bank's business to a bridge bank, was given the highest priority.

The Democrats argued instead that giving public funds to the weak banks was a waste of taxpayers' money. Weak banks should be nationalized and restructured. Through this process, the Japanese banking sector would reemerge smaller but healthier.

In the end the LDP and the Democrats reached a compromise and passed the Financial Reconstruction Act. This law allows the newly created Financial Reconstruction Commission to choose between nationalization and a bridge bank scheme when a bank fails. However, shortly thereafter, over the objections of the Democrats, the LDP also formed a coalition with the Liberal Party and managed to pass the Prompt Recapitalization Act to help recapitalize supposedly healthy banks.[6]

Thus, the struggle in the Diet during the fall of 1998 amounted to a battle over whether the Japanese banking sector has too little capital or whether Japan is currently overbanked. To settle this issue one needs to ask what the banking sector will look like once the current crisis is over and the deregulation is complete. This question has attracted little attention. For instance, although there is now some discussion of how many large banks might be viable, aside from Moody's (1999) and Japan Economic Research Center (1997) (which we discuss in detail below) we are unaware of any attempts to determine how many *assets* will remain in the banking sector.[7]

More importantly, the mergers and closures that have occurred thus far (including the fall 1999 megamergers) have not reduced capacity in the industry. If the overbanking hypothesis is correct, these adjustments alone will probably not help. Similarly, the March 1999 capital injection required the 15 banks that received funds to reduce their general administrative expenses by ¥300 billion, but at the same time to increase loans to prevent a so-called "credit crunch." We believe that one needs a clear vision of the future of the industry to evaluate this situation.

One of the primary contributions of this paper is an attempt to make some educated guesses about the future size of the industry. We hope that by providing these estimates we can inform the debate over how much assistance it is reasonable to provide now. We believe that it is impossible to determine the appropriate level of resources to earmark for rescuing the existing banks without taking a position on what role the banks will play in the post–Big Bang economy.

To answer this question about the future, it is necessary to review the recent history of the financial system. In particular, we need to know how the Japanese banking system got into so much trouble. Having determined the cause of the current trouble we can then ask what will have to occur in order for the banks to get out of trouble. Based on our diagnosis, we can then assess what the financial system, particularly the banking system, will look like once the crisis is over.

The story that emerges from our investigation points to the nature of the deregulation leading up to the Big Bang as playing a major role in the banking crisis. During the Japanese high-growth era, usually dated from the mid-1950s through the mid-1970s, the financial system was regulated to steer both savers and borrowers toward banks. As growth slowed in the mid-1970s a gradual deregulation process started. By the late 1980s this deregulation had eliminated many of the restrictions regarding large corporations' options for financing. During the 1980s these key bank clients began sharply reducing their dependence on bank financing. By the 1990s large Japanese firms' financing patterns had begun to look very similar to those of the large U.S. firms.

Meanwhile, innovation and the deregulation of the restriction on households' investment moved much more slowly. Most Japanese savings into the late 1990s continued to flow into banks. The banks therefore remained large but had to search for new lending opportunities. (The same type of argument is emphasized by Gorton and Rosen [1995] in their discussion of the U.S. banking crisis.) The new lines of business that they entered turned out badly.

We conclude that the lopsided nature of the financial deregulation, combined with maturing of the Japanese economy and slow growth starting in the mid-1970s, created a disequilibrium situation that has lasted to date. To eliminate the disequilibrium, further deregulation of the financial system will be inevitable. Once the deregulation is complete, the Japanese allocation of savings and the investment financing patterns will move further toward the patterns seen in the United States. We show this will imply a substantial decline in the prominence of the banks.

To paint this picture we divide the discussion into five parts. First, we review the regulatory conditions that prevailed prior to the Big Bang, focusing on the banking regulation that has governed the system over the last two decades. We argue that the regulation in Japan and the United States is converging and that the United States provides a sensible benchmark to use in forecasting what might happen in Japan. Section 3 provides some empirical support for this proposition. We show how past deregulation in Japan has altered firms' borrowing patterns and banks' activities. In Section 4 we describe the current state of the banking industry. This brief section aims to clarify some common misperceptions about the current crisis and explain why there are so many different estimates of its scope. In Section 5, we look ahead and ask how much lending will be required if Japanese firms' borrowing patterns move closer to those seen in the United States. Our calculations suggest that this will imply a sizable contraction in the traditional banking sector. Finally, in the conclusion we briefly discuss several scenarios for the transition between the current system and the eventual system.

2. Financial Regulation in Japan

To understand the current conditions and to put the current rules in context it is necessary to review briefly some background information. Until the 1920s, the Japanese banking system was characterized by free competition with little regulation. The Bank Act of 1890, for instance, set no minimum capital level for banks. A series of banking crises in the 1920s, especially the banking panic of 1927, led the Japanese government to change completely its attitude toward regulating banks, and tight regulation of the banking sector began. Government regulation and control of the financial system intensified under the wartime economy.

This pattern continued during the U.S. occupation of Japan. Indeed, some reform measures implemented during the occupation, such as the Glass-Steagall-style strict separation of commercial and investment banking, helped perpetuate the government's strong role in the financial sector. The financial system was also highly segmented. The regulatory framework that was completed during the occupation period stayed more or less in place until the mid-1970s.[8]

During the high-growth era from 1955 through 1973, banks dominated the financial system. Bond markets were repressed, and equity issuance was relatively uncommon.[9] In the 1970s this all began to change.

One big change was slower aggregate growth. Up until this time household savings were mostly channeled through banks to finance business investment. With lower growth the corporate funding requirements fell. The success of the Japanese economy in the rapid-economic-growth period also helped the corporations accumulate internal funds. This intensified the decline in the borrowing requirements of the companies.

A third feature of the economy in the 1970s was that the government began to run sizable deficits. The deficits arose because of a combination of slower growth in tax revenue, a policy decision to engage in deficit spending to try to spur the economy, and an expansion of the Social Security system. To finance the deficits, the government significantly ramped up its bond issuance.

2.1. CHANGES AFFECTING SAVERS

The increase in the government-bond issues changed the financial system. Previously, the limited amounts of debt that were issued were sold almost exclusively to financial institutions. The coupon rates were low, but the banks and other buyers tolerated this because the total amount issued was small and other government regulation was protecting them from competition. Moreover, it was customary for the Bank of Japan to periodically buy up the government bonds from the financial institutions as a way to keep money-supply growth in line with aggregate growth. But the soaring debt issuance would have impaired the banks' profitability if they had been forced to absorb all the low-yielding government bonds.

Thus, the Ministry of Finance was compelled to open a secondary market for government bonds in 1977, and to start issuing some bonds through public auctions in 1978. The opening of the secondary market for government bonds, combined with accumulation of financial wealth by households during the rapid economic growth of the 1960s and the early 1970s, increased the demand for bonds. Moreover, many of the restrictions in the bond markets that had been put in place to ration funds during the high-growth era now started to look out of date.

The expansion of the secondary market for government bonds undermined the interest-rate controls that had been a prominent feature of the postwar financial system. Since the government bonds were now traded at market prices, investors were able to stay away from the other financial assets, such as deposits, whose interest rates were set at artificially low levels. Thus, opening up the government-bond market led to the liberalization of interest rates in many other markets. For example, interest rates in the interbank lending market, the *tegata* market, and the *gensaki* market were all freed from any regulation by the late 1970s.[10] All the other interest rates except deposit rates were fully liberalized by the end of the 1980s. Starting with large deposit accounts, the deposit rates were gradually decontrolled during the 1980s and the 1990s, and were completely unrestricted by April 1993.

In addition to the interest-rate deregulation, there were several other steps that gave savers better options. Money-market mutual funds slowly began to appear, and investing in other new instruments such as commercial paper eventually became possible. However, there was a lag between the time when bond financing and commercial-paper issuance became commonplace and when savers could easily hold these securities. A summary of the major changes is contained in Table 4.1. The key conclusion from this table is that options for savers *gradually* changed and many restrictions survived into the late 1990s. As we will see, these changes lagged the changes that benefited borrowers and in several respects were not nearly as dramatic.

2.2. CHANGES AFFECTING BORROWERS

Probably the biggest development for borrowers was the emergence of vibrant bond markets both at home and abroad. In the domestic market, until the mid-1970s firms seeking to issue bonds had to secure approval from a body known as the Bond Issuance Committee. This group determined not only who would be allowed to issue bonds but also how much each issuer could raise. Firms seeking to issue bonds had to satisfy a set of financial conditions relating to size, profitability, and dividend payments. In addition, bonds had to be issued with collateral.

The first step toward liberalization came in 1975 when the Bond Issuance Committee adopted a policy of honoring the requested amount of bond issues by every company. The collateral requirements also became gradually less important. In 1979, unsecured straight bonds and unsecured convertible bonds were permitted, but the bond issue criteria were so stringent that only two companies (Toyota Auto and Matsushita Electric) were qualified to issue. The criteria for unsecured bonds were gradually relaxed during the 1980s.

Several of the key developments played out in international markets. This first became possible because of the reform of the Foreign Exchange and Trade Control Act in 1980. Foreign exchange transactions, which were "forbidden in principle" under the old rule, were made "free unless expressly prohibited." The internationalization was further advanced in 1984 by the abolition of the "real demand principle," which required foreign exchange transactions to be backed by "real" demand for foreign exchange, such as foreign trade. Following the suggestions in the Yen-Dollar Commission report, the euro market was substantially deregulated and the Tokyo offshore market was opened in 1986.

The foreign bond markets were attractive for Japanese firms because they made it possible to bypass the Bond Issuance Committee.[11] Perhaps most importantly, no collateral was required in foreign markets. This led to high levels of issuance in foreign markets. Warrant bonds, which were introduced in 1981 and allowed the holders to have an option to buy shares at a prespecified price during a certain period, were a leading example. Throughout the 1980s many warrant bonds were issued outside Japan, even though these securities did not prove to be very popular in the domestic market.

Liberalization also proceeded in the domestic market. By 1987 the domestic commercial-paper market was created, giving firms another nonbank source of funding. By the late 1980s firms began to be able to avoid the bond issuance criteria if they were rated. Finally in 1996 all rules regarding bond issues were lifted.

Table 4.1 **Significant Events Affecting the Choices Available to Japanese Savers**

1979	Negotiable CD market set up.
1981	Maturity-designated time deposits introduced (up to 3 years.); new type of loan trust fund (called "big") accounts introduced by trust banks.
1982	Money-market dealers allowed to begin buying bills; securities companies banned from selling foreign-currency zero-coupon Euro bonds to residents (ban lifted subject to certain restrictions in February 1983).
1983	Banks start over-the-counter sale of government bonds to the general public; government-bond time deposit account introduced; mediumterm government-bond time deposit account introduced; postal insurance system permitted to invest in foreign bonds; banks authorized to sell long-term government bonds and medium-term government bonds over the counter.
1984	Short-term Euro-yen loans to residents liberalized; domestic trade in CDs and CPs issued abroad permitted.
1985	Initial relaxation of time-deposit rates (for deposits over 1 billion yen) and money-market certificate (MMC) rates (interest-rate ceiling of 0.75% below weekly average newly issued CD rate); bankers' acceptance market created.
1986	Treasury bill auction begins.
1987	Freely determined interest rates permitted for time deposit accounts over ¥100 million.
1988	Postal savings system allowed to progressively increase foreign investments and to diversify domestic investments (no longer obligated to place all its funds with the Trust Fund Bureau).
1989	Introduction of small-lot MMCs (minimum lot ¥3 million); unregulated interest rates for time deposits over ¥10 million.
1990	Interest-rate ceilings for money-market certificates removed; residents allowed to hold deposits of up to ¥30 million with banks overseas without prior authorization.
1991	Unregulated interest rates for time deposits over ¥3 million; pension funds and investment trusts allowed to buy securitized corporate loans.
1992	Securities houses allowed to offer money-market funds (minimum deposit of ¥1 million provided that more than half of such funds are invested in securities).
1993	All time-deposit rate ceilings removed.
1994	All major interest-rate restriction have been removed.
1997	Security houses allowed to handle consumer payments for their clients; restriction on minimum sales unit of commodity funds removed.
1998	OTC sales of investment trusts by banks and insurance companies.
1999	Liberalization of brokerage commissions for stock trading.

Sources: Takeda and Turner (1992); Ministry of Finance, *Banking Bureau Annual Report,* various issues; Ministry of Finance, *Securities Bureau Annual Report,* various issues.

Over this period regulations regarding stock markets were also changed. Listing requirements were eased, and commissions were eventually deregulated. These changes made equity issuance more attractive, although initial public offerings were typically more underpriced in Japan than elsewhere (see Jenkinson 1990).

The key changes regarding the opening up of capital markets are collected in Table 4.2. Comparing this table and the previous one shows that the financing options for bank borrowers opened up much faster than the options for savers. As we document below, by the end of the 1980s many of the banks' traditional clients had already migrated to cheaper bond financing. One striking statistic is that during the decade the number of firms permitted to issue unsecured domestic bonds grew from two to over 500.

The third leg of deregulation dealt with changes in bank powers. The major changes are shown in Table 4.3. We draw three important lessons from the list. First, bank powers were expanded very slowly and gradually. While the banks' main borrowers were able to get quickly into the bond market, the banks had their hands tied in many respects. For instance, securitizing loans was not even possible until 1990. Second, many new types of businesses, particularly fee-generating activities, did not become available until relatively recently. For example, through 1998 Japanese banks were still prohibited from collecting fees by offering loan commitments. Thus, banks in Japan were essentially forced to continue to try to make money through conventional deposit-taking and loan-making during the 1980s. [Gorton and Rosen (1995) point out that similar problems were present in the United States. Furthermore, the absence of an active takeover market for banks likely exacerbated the problems in both countries.] Finally, even up until the end of 1990s there were significant barriers which continued to keep investment banking and commercial banking separated in Japan.

The culmination of the deregulation is the Big Bang.[12] When the government first proposed the program in the fall of 1996, it was heralded as drive to make Japanese financial markets "free, fair and global." As we describe more completely below, the result will be that banks, insurance companies, and securities dealers will be able to compete directly.

2.3. COMPARISONS WITH THE UNITED STATES

As we look ahead we see these changes pushing the Japanese financial system to become more similar to the U.S. system. In fact, ever since the U.S. occupation of Japan there has been a certain degree of similarity between the financial systems in the two countries. A key reason for the similarity is that Article 65 of the Securities and Exchange Act was passed in March 1947 with the intent of mimicking the U.S. Bank Act of 1933 (Glass-Steagall). Both laws mandated a separation of investment and commercial banking. This separation has constituted a defining feature that differentiates the two financial systems from those in Europe and has shaped the evolution of both systems.

Table 4.2 **Significant Events in the Liberalization of Capital Markets**

1975	Bond issuance committee begins to honor requested amounts for firms that pass the criteria.
1976	Official recognition of *gensaki* (repurchase agreement) transactions.
1977	First issue of 5-year government bonds; first issue of Euro-yen bonds by a nonresident; secondary trading of government bonds permitted.
1978	First issue of medium-term coupon government bond (the first to be issued by auction; 3-year bonds on this occasion, followed by 2-year bonds in June 1979 and 4-year bonds in June 1980).
1979	Unsecured straight bonds and unsecured convertible bonds permitted.
1980	Foreign Exchange and Trade Control Act amended so "free unless prohibited" replaces "forbidden in principle."
1981	Warrant bonds introduced.
1982	Criteria for the issuance of unsecured bonds by Japanese residents in overseas market clarified.
1983	Eligibility standards for issuing unsecured convertible bonds relaxed.
1984	"Real demand rule" for foreign exchange lifted; swap agreements and hedging of forward foreign-exchange transactions allowed; collateral requirement for nonresident issue of Euro-yen bonds dropped; freer issuance of yen-dominated CDs in Japan; standards for issuing *samurai bonds*[a] by private companies eased.
1985	First unsecured straight corporate bond issued; bond futures introduced; first *shogun bond*[b] issue; first Euro-yen straight bond issued.
1986	The credit rating system in the qualification standard fully introduced for Euro-yen bonds issued by nonresidents; floating-rate notes and currency conversion bonds introduced for Euro–yen issued by residents; first issue of short-term government bonds (TB); public issue of 20-year government bonds; Japan offshore market opened (minimum deposit ¥100 million; minimum time 2 days).
1987	Introduction of credit rating system in the qualification standards for Euro-yen bond issues by residents; packaged stock futures market established on the Osaka Stock Exchange, ending a ban introduced in 1945; commercial-paper market created.
1988	Restrictions on samurai CP issues by nonresidents relaxed.
1989	Tokyo International Financial Futures Exchange established; rating criteria for bond issuance added.
1990	Accounting criteria for bond issuance removed.

(continued)

Table 4.2 **(continued)**

1992	Bond issuance restrictions eased: more companies allowed to issue bonds overseas, and restraints on samurai bonds relaxed.
1995	Deregulation on OTC (JASDAQ) market, creating a new market to facilitate fundraising for start-ups.
1996	All bond issuance restrictions removed.
1998	Introduction of medium-term notes; relaxation of rules governing asset-backed securities.

Sources: See Table 4.1.

[a] Yen-dominated public bonds which are issued in Japan by non-Japanese residents.

[b] Foreign-currency-denominated bonds issued in Japan by nonresidents.

Table 4.3 **Significant Events Relating to the Range of Permissible Activities for Banks**

1979	Banks permitted to issue and deal in CDs; banks permitted to introduce short-term *impact loans* (foreign-currency loans to residents) subject to certain conditions.
1980	Foreign exchange banks allowed to make medium- and long-term impact loans.
1982	Japanese banks permitted to lend yen overseas on a long-term basis to borrowers of their choice (earlier priority system for overseas yen lending is abolished).
1983	Banks start over-the-counter sale of government bonds to the general public; banks authorized to affiliate with mortgage securities companies.
1984	Securities licenses granted to subsidiaries/affiliates of some foreign banks with branches in Japan (equity stakes limited to 50%); permission for foreign and Japanese banks to issue Euro-yen CDs with maturities of 6 months or less; banks allowed to deal on their own account in public bonds.
1985	Foreign banks allowed to enter trust banking business; banks began trading in bond futures; medium and long-term Euro-yen loans to nonresidents liberalized.
1986	City banks authorized to issue long-term mortgage bonds; banks' overseas subsidiaries authorized to underwrite and deal in CP issues abroad.
1987	Banks allowed to engage in private placement of bond issues; banks begin underwriting and trading in the domestic CP market; banks allowed to deal in foreign financial futures.
1988	Banks allowed to securitize home loans.

(continued)

Table 4.3 **(continued)**

1989	Banks begin brokering government-bond futures; banks allowed to securitize loans to local governments.
1990	Banks allowed to securitize loans to corporations; banks allowed to enter the pension trust business through their investment advisory companies.
1992	Financial System Reform Bill passes the Diet, allowing banks to set up subsidiaries to enter the securities business (effective April 1993).
1993	Three-bureaus agreement ends, allowing banks to be lead underwriters in foreign bond issues; IBJ, LTCB, Norin Chukin Bank, Sumitomo Trust, and Mitsubishi Trust establish their subsidiary security firms.
1994	Major city banks establish their subsidiary security firms.
1998	Ban on financial holding companies lifted.
1999	Banks, trust banks, and securities houses can enter each other's markets; banks allowed to issue straight bonds.
2001	Banks and securities houses will be allowed to enter the insurance business.

Sources: See Table 4.1.

In what follows, we argue that not only has the evolution been similar, but the banks in the two countries are going to become even more similar in the future.

The Japanese banks have traditionally been more successful than the U.S. banks in their attempts to participate in investment banking. For instance, the banks were able to play the role of trustee of collateral in the bond underwriting process in Japan, while they were mostly shut out in the United States. Similarly, Japanese banks were able to take limited equity positions in the firms to which they were lending. However, as Dale (1992) points out, like the U.S. banks, the Japanese banks were "excluded from market-making in and the public distribution of corporate securities." This constraint kept the Japanese banks from becoming full-fledged, German-style universal banks. Instead the Japanese financial system, like the U.S. system, was fragmented, with banks, insurance firms, and securities firms each maturing while facing little direct competition from each other.

Within the banking system in each country there was further segmentation. In the United States, cross-border branching was restricted until recently so that banks could not compete on a nationwide basis. Similarly, in Japan, competition between city banks, trust banks, regional banks, long-term credit banks, and other small banks such as credit unions has traditionally been restricted by legal measures and administrative guidance by the Ministry of Finance.

Beyond the segmentation, there are further similarities in the ways that the bank powers in the two countries changed over time. In both countries, the drive by the commercial banks to reenter investment banking has taken more than 50 years. During this period the deregulation process has been slow and incremental. In the United States, for example, banks were allowed to enter investment banking through subsidiaries only in 1987, as regulators began to reinterpret Section 20 of the banking laws, which prohibits banks from having affiliates that are "principally engaged" in nonbanking activity. Over time the permissible fraction of bank income accruing from the so-called "Section 20 subsidiaries" has slowly risen.

In Japan, the financial system reform in 1993 made it possible for banks to enter the securities business through subsidiaries, but the actual establishment of bank-owned securities subsidiaries was only gradually permitted over the next couple of years. The range of securities services that these subsidiaries can provide is still limited, but the limitations will be incrementally removed between now and 2001.

Importantly, as banking deregulation proceeded in Japan, there was discussion over whether a shift toward permitting universal banking would be desirable. In March 1989 the Ministry of Finance convened an advisory group dubbed the Second Financial System Committee of the Financial System Research Council. This group described five possible routes toward permitting more integration of commercial and investment banking: separated subsidiaries, multifunctional subsidiaries, holding companies, universal banks, and a piecemeal approach (Second Financial System Committee 1989). According to the committee, "the sight of banks pushing out in every direction in pursuit of high returns, even at high risk, might shake people's faith in them." Thus, the committee recommended against a universal banking approach. Ultimately, in 1993, the separated-subsidiary approach was adopted. Later, in 1997, relaxation of Section 9 of the Anti-Monopoly Act made it possible to establish a financial holding company.

As the turn of the century approaches, firms trying to offer one-stop financial shopping are facing fewer and fewer barriers in both countries. In Japan, as a result of the Big Bang, it is already possible to create a holding company that can span the securities and insurance industries. By April 2001 it will be possible to bring banking into the same holding company. In the United States legislation to repeal Glass-Steagall was finally passed, allowing the banking, securities underwriting, and insurance businesses to be integrated. Thus, in the near future the regulatory conditions in the two countries will be very similar.

Once the deregulation in both countries is complete, a transition featuring competition among entrenched securities firms, insurance companies, and banks will begin. In the previous version of this paper, Hoshi and Kashyap (1999b), we tabulated all the major alliances in the Japanese financial services industry that were announced in 1998 and early 1999. This very long list of tie-ups suggests that a scramble is already under way to provide much broader services than have been available in the past, and that the same sort of tie-ups are occurring in the United States and in Japan. Finally, the list also shows that foreign institutions are aggressively entering the Japanese market.

Collectively these patterns suggest that banks in the two countries are going to face the same types of competitive pressures and will have some sort of options available to respond to the pressures. Although the Japanese banks start from a much weaker capital position than the U.S. banks, it is hard to see why the bank activities in the two countries will not become similar.

3. An Empirical Look at the Fallout from the Deregulation

To support our contention that Big Bang is going to push the financial system in Japan to look more like the U.S. system, we examine several pieces of evidence. For organizational purposes it is convenient to separate the discussion into the responses of the borrowers, savers, and lenders. We will see that the behavior of large and small borrowers turns out to be quite different. On the bank side we will distinguish between the portfolio adjustments that were made and the new business opportunities that were missed. For the savers we will see that the deregulation prior to the Big Bang has not made a big difference.

Throughout most of our discussion we will emphasize the importance of regulatory shifts. This choice does not mean that we doubt the importance of other factors such as macroeconomic conditions. In fact, it is quite reasonable to assume that the deregulation may have contributed to the fast growth of lending in the late 1980s that preceded the long recession of the 1990s. However, for the purposes of looking ahead we do not believe that it is necessary to separately identify the role of macroeconomic factors. Our basic point is that the past deregulation did have some independent effects and that based on the responses to past deregulation it is reasonable to expect that the Big Bang will have a large effect as well. Thus, our empirical work is aimed at showing that regulatory shifts have clear, independent influences on borrowers, savers, and banks.[13]

3.1. THE RESPONSE OF BORROWERS TO FINANCIAL-MARKET DEREGULATION

It is widely recognized that part of the reason why banks in Japan got into trouble is that they lost many of their best borrowers in a very short period of time.[14] As mentioned earlier, between 1983 and 1989 the Japanese bond market blossomed, permitting many internationally known companies to tap the public debt markets for the first time. While this story is well known, we are unaware of any attempts to compare the bank dependence of large Japanese and U.S. firms before and after the deregulation. We provide evidence that the Japanese deregulation has permitted the largest Japanese firms to become almost as independent of banks as their U.S. counterparts.

A major challenge in conducting this investigation is the limited availability of comprehensive data on bank borrowing by firms. In Japan there are essentially two types of data that can be used. For exchangetraded firms, the corporate financial statements that are publicly available generally break out bank borrowing. This means that for these (typically) large firms one can get fairly good data. As an example, the Japan Development Bank Database provides this type of information on over 2,000 firms for 1997.

To learn anything about unlisted companies one must rely on survey data. The most comprehensive survey that we know of on this topic is conducted by the Ministry of Finance and published in the *Hojin Kigyo Kiho* (*Quarterly Report of Incorporated Enterprise Statistics*). The cross-sectional coverage of these data is excellent. All nonfinancial corporations with book capital of ¥1 billion ($8.33 million using the exchange rate of 120 ¥/$) are included in the survey.[15] The remaining (small corporations) are randomly sampled with sampling factors that depend on their size. Only very tiny firms (those with less than ¥10 million in capital) are completely excluded. We believe that the survey is sufficiently comprehensive that it essentially sidesteps the selection problems associated with using listed data.[16]

The main drawback with the survey information is that data for firms with similar amounts of capital are aggregated, so that no firm-level statistics are accessible. Unfortunately, all the size thresholds used in the MOF data are based on *nominal* thresholds, so that over time (as the price level rises) firms drift into the upper grouping, even if their size measured in constant prices is unchanging. We discuss the effect of this limitation in the places where we believe it might be important.

In our analysis we focus on the ratio of (the book value of) bank debt to (the book value of) total assets as the basic measure of the importance of bank financing. We scale by assets to eliminate pure size differences.[17] Below we also show some results which distinguish among different industries. The industry comparisons can be motivated in many ways, including as an attempt to correct for industry-level differences in risk and collateralizability of assets.

Table 4.4 shows the ratio of the bank debt to total assets based on the MOP data for different-sized Japanese firms over time. The data pertain to the second quarter of each year between 1980 and 1998. In addition to showing data for all industries, the table also displays separate series for manufacturing, wholesale and retail trade, and all other firms. The largest firms which are separately identified in the sample are those with a book value of equity greater than ¥1 billion in current prices. In the second quarter of 1998 the 5,363 firms in this category had average assets of ¥112 billion.[18]

The table reveals a consistent pattern of large Japanese firms scaling back their bank borrowing. The shift has been most pronounced among manufacturing firms, where the ratio of bank debt to assets has dropped by almost 50%. Moreover, the shift was effectively complete by 1990––since then the ratio has been roughly constant. This timing suggests that the banks lost many of their traditional clients soon after the opening up of the bond market.

There was also a substantial drop in bank dependence for the trade firms. In publicly available versions of the survey all trade firms are shown together, but the

Table 4.4 Hojin Kigyo Tokei Data on the Ratio of Bank Debt to Assets for Japanese Firms (large firms have book value of equity greater than 1 billion yen)

Year	All Industries		Manufacturing		Wholesale and retail		Other	
	Large firms	Small firms	Large firms	Small firms	Large firms	Small firms	Large firms	Small firms
1978	0.3786	0.3332	0.3654	0.3294	0.3818	0.2929	0.4007	0.3847
1979	0.3587	0.3282	0.3372	0.3009	0.3689	0.2897	0.3890	0.3984
1980	0.3431	0.3214	0.3181	0.2860	0.3486	0.2892	0.3833	0.3908
1981	0.3484	0.3329	0.3193	0.2954	0.3628	0.3015	0.3886	0.4048
1982	0.3473	0.3649	0.3122	0.3081	0.3650	0.3109	0.3947	0.4833
1983	0.3513	0.3600	0.3041	0.3178	0.3847	0.3059	0.4073	0.4433
1984	0.3420	0.3634	0.2806	0.3230	0.3762	0.3113	0.4197	0.4487
1985	0.3219	0.3754	0.2577	0.3257	0.3755	0.3184	0.3853	0.4705
1986	0.3281	0.3884	0.2560	0.3417	0.3910	0.3341	0.3938	0.4721
1987	0.3304	0.4039	0.2487	0.3613	0.3992	0.3373	0.4011	0.4912

Year								
1988	0.3202	0.4161	0.2179	0.3436	0.3865	0.3604	0.4050	0.5040
1989	0.3022	0.4311	0.1819	0.3438	0.3605	0.3543	0.4069	0.5364
1990	0.2901	0.4130	0.1614	0.3438	0.3106	0.3475	0.4174	0.4933
1991	0.2907	0.4225	0.1584	0.3350	0.3176	0.3367	0.4158	0.5225
1992	0.2867	0.4147	0.1645	0.3537	0.3092	0.3443	0.3971	0.4899
1993	0.2934	0.4342	0.1786	0.3837	0.3049	0.3621	0.3981	0.5033
1994	0.2925	0.4346	0.1800	0.3783	0.3145	0.3953	0.3915	0.4878
1995	0.2846	0.4317	0.1756	0.3878	0.2995	0.3891	0.3826	0.4827
1996	0.2797	0.4336	0.1658	0.3641	0.2857	0.3682	0.3850	0.5081
1997	0.2732	0.4224	0.1595	0.3653	0.2827	0.3775	0.3801	0.4773
1998	0.2761	0.4257	0.1647	0.3527	0.2876	0.3978	0.3796	0.4773

Note: The survey includes all the corporations with book capital of ¥1 billion ($8.3 million using the exchange rate of 120 ¥/$) in all nonfinancial industries. The rest (small corporations) are randomly sampled with sampling factors depending on their sizes. The average value of assets for the large firms is ¥112 billion ($934 million) in 1998. There were 5,363 large firms and 1,161,179 small firms in the 1998 survey. The firms in the "other" category are all those which are not in manufacturing, wholesale trade, or retail trade.

Source: Ministry of Finance, Hojin Kigyo Tokei.

Ministry of Finance provided us with unpublished data for selected years which allow us to separate wholesale trade companies from the retail trade companies. From the unpublished data we learned that the drop in bank dependence is more pronounced for retail trade firms than for wholesale trade firms. For instance, between 1980 and 1998 the large retail trade companies cut their bank-debt-to-asset ratio from 0.35 to 0.26, while the wholesale firms cut theirs from 0.35 to 0.30. Table 4.4 also indicates that remaining large firms hardly changed their bank borrowing.

To explore the effect of the nominal thresholds we also looked at other data for listed firms. In Table 4.5 we report analogous statistics in which we define large firms to have real assets (measured in 1990 prices) to be greater than ¥120 billion ($1 billion). Using this consistent size definition, the manufacturing firms show an even more pronounced shift away from bank debt. The larger drop is partly expected, since the nominal size thresholds in the MOF survey data will cause some smaller firms (which are presumably more bank-dependent) to drift into the large-firm category over time.

The third and fourth columns in Table 4.5 show the patterns for large, listed wholesale and retail firms. The retail firms show the same general pattern as the manufacturing firms, although the drop in bank dependence is less pronounced. For the listed wholesale trade firms the bank-debt-to-asset ratio drifted up noticeably in the 1980s, before beginning to decline in the 1990s. This nonmonotonic decline can be traced to the behavior of the nine large general trading firms and is not representative of other wholesaling companies. The trend disappears when these nine firms are omitted, and the aforementioned unpublished MOF data showed a slight overall drop in bank dependence.[19] The final column in the table shows that the remaining large listed firms have also cut their bank borrowing.

The two tables together show a clear pattern of rapid adjustment by the large firms (except for possibly a few wholesale trade companies). Notice in Table 4.5 that for all the sectors where bank dependence was falling, the bank-debt-to-asset ratios in 1990 and 1998 were about the same, so that in fact much of the adjustment had occurred before the onset of slow aggregate growth.

In contrast, among the small firms there has been no clear reduction in bank dependence. Indeed, Table 4.4 shows that in each of the major sectors the smaller firms have become somewhat more bank-dependent as the deregulation has progressed, although in manufacturing and in the "other" sector small firms' bank dependence is below the peaks that occurred in the late 1980s and early 1990s. As we discuss below, we believe that some of these patterns are attributable to the fact that the banks themselves did not shrink much as the deregulation proceeded.

One question raised by these patterns is what they imply for the future of relationship financing in Japan. The data in Tables 4.4 and 4.5 clearly show that even before the Big Bang had taken place, the large Japanese firms had cut their bank dependence. Tight dependence of large firms on their banks was probably the most unusual aspect of the Japanese financial system.[20] A growing literature

Table 4.5 **Ratio of Bank Debts to Assets for Publicly Traded Japanese firms (large firms are defined to have book value of assets > ¥120 billion at 1990 prices)**

Year	Manufacturing	Wholesale	Retail	Nonmanufacturing excluding wholesale and Retail
1970	0.3621	0.3006	0.3019	0.3605
1971	0.3655	0.3207	0.3153	0.3620
1972	0.3891	0.3438	0.3486	0.3848
1973	0.3758	0.3590	0.3919	0.3961
1974	0.3388	0.3170	0.4367	0.3864
1975	0.3606	0.3513	0.4371	0.3860
1976	0.3809	0.3804	0.4378	0.3912
1977	0.3712	0.3902	0.4022	0.3863
1978	0.3650	0.4121	0.3640	0.3796
1979	0.3471	0.3970	0.3180	0.3691
1980	0.3157	0.3641	0.2922	0.3677
1981	0.3043	0.3745	0.3046	0.3595
1982	0.2970	0.3665	0.3142	0.3688
1983	0.2949	0.3989	0.3369	0.3788
1984	0.2736	0.4050	0.3239	0.3813
1985	0.2446	0.4003	0.3122	0.3793
1986	0.2380	0.4348	0.2975	0.3173
1987	0.2316	0.4503	0.2600	0.3107
1988	0.2031	0.4800	0.2134	0.3069
1989	0.1654	0.5242	0.1900	0.2976
1990	0.1269	0.5079	0.1726	0.2745
1991	0.1333	0.4784	0.1820	0.2757
1992	0.1386	0.4884	0.1830	0.2806
1993	0.1452	0.4983	0.1986	0.2755
1994	0.1496	0.4865	0.1915	0.2861

(continued)

Table 4.5 (continued)

Year	Manufacturing	Wholesale	Retail	Nonmanufacturing excluding wholesale and Retail
1995	0.1431	0.4768	0.2042	0.2878
1996	0.1311	0.4523	0.1943	0.2850
1997	0.1256	0.4311	0.1841	0.2899

Source: Authors' calculations using the Japan Development Bank Database of companies listed on the major Japanese stock exchanges.

(e.g., Petersen and Rajan 1994; Berger and Udell 1995) shows that relationship financing for small firms is quite prevalent also outside of Japan. It appears that any relationship financing that will continue in Japan will be more like what is observed elsewhere in the world.

To put the size of the shift in behavior of the large firms in perspective, we offer a comparison with financing patterns in the United States. This effort is complicated because of the absence of completely comparable data for the United States. Contrary to the conventions followed in Japan, there are no standard sources that provide firm-level information on firms' bank borrowing. U.S. firms do sometimes identify bank lending in the footnotes to their financial statements, but databases such as Compustat do not report such information. So we cannot report data which would be comparable to Table 4.5.

The only broad-based U.S. data on bank borrowing patterns come from a survey conducted by the Census Bureau called the Quarterly Financial Report for Manufacturing, Mining, and Trade Corporations (QFR).[21] The QFR contains the financial statistics for corporations aggregated by industry and by size. Like the MOF survey, the size thresholds are based on nominal thresholds, although the QFR size cutoffs are based on assets rather than capital. The coverage of the QFR for manufacturing industries is outstanding. All the corporations with total assets of $250 million and over are included in the survey. Smaller firms are randomly sampled with sampling factors ranging from 1/2 to 1/160, depending on their sizes.

Unfortunately the QFR coverage beyond manufacturing is quite limited. For firms in three industries (mining, wholesale trade, and retail trade) all the corporations with total assets $250 million and over are included, but small corporations are intentionally excluded. Since 1988 the definition of "small" has been set so that no corporations with total assets under $50 million are included; previously, between 1981 and 1987, this threshold has been $25 million in current prices. This prevents us from examining the financing pattern of small firms outside manufacturing. Moreover, for industries that are not covered by the QFR (transportation, communication, services, construction, etc.), we cannot get data even for large firms.

It is fairly straightforward to find a breakpoint in the QFR data that can be compared with the *Hojin Kigyo Tokei Kiho* data described in Table 4.4. Recall from Table 4.4 that the average asset size of the large Japanese firms was $934 million in 1998. According to QFR for 1998, the average size of total assets for manufacturing corporations with assets $10 million or above was $1,020 million. Thus, it appears that "large" firms in Table 4.4 are roughly comparable to QFR data for firms with total assets of $10 million.

Table 4.6 shows data on the bank-debt-to-asset reported in the QFR from 1979 through 1997. Columns 2 through 4 show data on all manufacturing firms and then on large and small manufacturing firms respectively. We draw three conclusions from this part of the table. First, and most importantly, the time-series variation in bank dependence in the U.S. data is much less noticeable than in the Japanese data. Second, for the large firms there has been a slight upward drift in the bank-debt-to-asset ratio. Consequently the bank dependence of the U.S. and Japanese large firms is much closer now than in the 1980s—we explore this further below. Third, the small manufacturing firms in the two countries do not seem to be converging in their borrowing behavior. The small U.S. manufacturing firms have held steady with a ratio of bank debt to assets between 16% and 19%. In contrast, the small Japanese firms' ratio has crept up from about 29% to 35%.[22]

The remainder of Table 4.6 provides information on borrowing patterns by wholesale and retail trade firms. Interpreting these figures requires some care, since the universe of firms included in the sample has changed greatly across the years—see the footnotes to the table for details. Despite these changes, it seems safe to conclude that very large nonmanufacturing firms in the United States are still much less bank-dependent than similar firms in Japan.

One potential concern with Table 4.6 is that the nominal size thresholds may be responsible for some of drift upward in the large manufacturing firms' bank dependence. Unfortunately, we were unable to obtain any unpublished data from the U.S. Census Bureau to check this directly. However, based on the checks which we were able to perform using published data, this does not seem likely to be too much of an issue. For instance, it is possible to study manufacturing firms with more than $1 billion in assets. Within this sample, the firms which drift into the category should already be quite large and have a low level of bank dependence. This sample of firms shows the same basic patterns as in Table 4.6: bank dependence rises in the late 1980s and then falls in the 1990s, but remains at a higher level than in 1980.

Comparing Tables 4.4 and 4.6, we find that the bank dependence of the large Japanese firms has become closer to that of comparable-sized U.S. firms, particularly in manufacturing industries. The convergence, however, still looks incomplete. One possible reason for this may be cross-country differences in the

Table 4.6 Quarterly Financial Reports Data on the Ratio of Bank Debt to Assets for U.S. Firms (large manufacturing firms are defined as having nominal assets> $10 million)

Year (4th quarter)	All manufacturing	Large manufacturing	Small manufacturing	Wholesale	Retail	All industries
1979	0.0660	0.0550	0.1642	0.1777	0.1255	0.0919
1980	0.0680	0.0575	0.1688	0.1882	0.1206	0.0937
1981	0.0665	0.0568	0.1676	0.1844	0.0637	0.0850
1982	0.0712	0.0617	0.1695	0.2383	0.0546	0.0829
1983	0.0644	0.0542	0.1710	0.2028	0.0524	0.0746
1984	0.0754	0.0652	0.1860	0.1995	0.0553	0.0839
1985	0.0731	0.0632	0.1867	0.1825	0.0681	0.0820
1986	0.0796	0.0714	0.1878	0.1773	0.0797	0.0882
1987	0.0830	0.0751	0.1892	0.1865	0.0922	0.0932
1988	0.0950	0.0875	0.2045	0.1886	0.1296	0.1064
1989	0.1004	0.0944	0.1988	0.1937	0.1434	0.1130

(continued)

Table 4.6 (continued)

Year (4th quarter)	All manufacturing	Large manufacturing	Small manufacturing	Wholesale	Retail	All industries
1990	0.1032	0.0976	0.2009	0.1868	0.1417	0.1146
1991	0.0954	0.0899	0.1954	0.1771	0.1287	0.1064
1992	0.0924	0.0875	0.1831	0.1786	0.0968	0.1007
1993	0.0863	0.0814	0.1771	0.1671	0.0916	0.0945
1994	0.0850	0.0798	0.1868	0.1676	0.0932	0.0940
1995	0.0862	0.0809	0.1934	0.1703	0.0993	0.0961
1996	0.0834	0.0782	0.1910	0.1623	0.1026	0.0932
1997	0.0877	0.0834	0.1794	0.1513	0.1089	0.0966

Note: For manufacturing firms all corporations with total assets of $250 million and over are included in this survey. Smaller manufacturing firms are randomly sampled with sampling factors ranging from 1/2 to 1/160, depending on their sizes. We define large firms to be those with nominal assets greater than $10 million. The sampling rules governing the inclusion of wholesale and retail trade firms have changed over time. In the 1979 and 1980 surveys, the rules for these sectors were the same as those for manufacturing. From 1981 to 1987, only firms with assets above $25 million were included. From 1988 on, firms had to have assets above $50 million to be included.

Source: Quarterly Financial Report for Manufacturing, Mining, and Trade Corporations (QFR) produced by Bureau of Census.

industrial structure. Average bank-debt-toasset ratios vary considerably across industries. For instance, in the 1998 MOF data shown in Table 4.4, the range of bank-debt-to-asset ratios varies between 0.09 and 0.42 across manufacturing industries (using two-digit SIC codes to identify industries).

This type of variation is not surprising, given the differences in riskiness and collateral of different industries. Such variation will probably persist even after the Big Bang. Therefore one would only expect convergence in the bank-debt-to-asset ratio for the entire manufacturing sector if the asset distribution across industries were the same in both countries. This suggests that it is advisable to study the borrowing patterns at the two-digit industry level (or finer).

One problem with looking to industry-level data is that there is less detail on the size distribution of firms within industries. The published QFR data only show separate information for firms with assets above and below $25 million. The published Quarterly Report of Incorporate Enterprise Statistics includes no information on different-sized firms in each industry. By getting unpublished data from Japan we were able to make some very rough comparisons.[23] The Japanese data cover firms with capital above ¥1 billion, so there is a slight size mismatch in the comparison.[24] The overlap in industrial classification definitions allows us to match 14 industries (food; textiles; pulp and paper; printing and publishing; chemicals; petroleum and coal products; stone, clay, and glass; iron and steel; nonferrous metals; fabricated metal products; machinery; electrical and electronic machinery; transportation equipment; and precision machinery).

Table 4.7 reports information on how large Japanese firms' bank dependence has compared with U.S. firms' bank dependence over time. For the Japanese firms we show the bank-debt-to-asset ratio in 1980 and 1998. Since there is no noticeable trend in the U.S. data, we report only the 1998 levels for the U.S. industries— using other years or an average of several years made no difference in what follows. The last two columns of the table show the difference for each of 14 industries in two periods. In 1980, the difference was diffusely distributed between 0 and 0.56. For the industry average the difference was 0.197. The table shows that by 1998 the distribution had become much more concentrated around zero. By 1998, for 10 out of 14 industries, the Japanese bank debt ratios are within 10 percentage points of the U.S. ratios. Moreover, for these 10 industries the distribution of differences in bank dependence is more symmetric, with three of the 10 Japanese industries appearing less bank-dependent than their U.S. counterparts.

Interestingly, the four industries where convergence has not occurred (pulp and paper, nonferrous metals, petroleum, and iron and steel) are all cases where a significant portion of the Japanese firms have performed poorly.[25] We believe that for these depressed industries the effects of deregulation are likely being masked by the poor profitability of the firms; going to public debt markets is always hard for financially troubled firms. Overall we read the industry-level comparisons as further suggesting that large Japanese and U.S. manufacturing firms have become fairly similar in their bank dependence.

Table 4.7 **Industry-Level Comparisons of Bank-Debt-to-Total-Assets Ratio for Large U.S. and Japanese Manufacturing Firms**

Industry	U.S. 1998	Japan 1980	Japan 1998	Japan 1980 minus U.S. 1998	Japan 1998 minus U.S. 1998
Food	0.1216	0.1925	0.1369	0.0709	0.0153
Textiles	0.2014	0.3828	0.2465	0.1814	0.0451
Pulp and paper	0.1167	0.4372	0.3535	0.3205	0.2368
Printing and publishing	0.0860	0.0808	0.0852	-0.0052	-0.0008
Chemicals	0.0758	0.3145	0.1649	0.2387	0.0891
Petroleum and coal	0.0240	0.5836	0.4168	0.5596	0.3928
Stone, glass, and clay	0.1531	0.3708	0.1941	0.2177	0.0410
Iron and steel	0.1138	0.3924	0.2647	0.2786	0.1509
Nonferrous metals	0.0726	0.4458	0.3599	0.3732	0.2873
Metal products	0.1788	0.3150	0.1738	0.1362	-0.0050
Machinery	0.0725	0.2415	0.1568	0.1690	0.0843
Electronic machinery	0.0497	0.1542	0.0919	0.1045	0.0422
Transportation durables	0.0393	0.1479	0.1096	0.1086	0.0703
Precision machinery	0.1551	0.1647	0.1020	0.0096	-0.0531
Average	0.1043	0.3017	0.2040	0.1974	0.0997

Note: Large U.S. firms are defined as those having assets > $25 million.

Source: See text.

Table 4.8 **Industry-Level Comparisons of the Ratio of Bank Debt to Total Assets for Small U.S. and Japanese Manufacturing Firms**

Industry	U.S. 1998	Japan 1980	Japan 1998	Japan 1980 minus U.S. 1998	Japan 1998 minus U.S. 1998
Food	0.2637	0.3945	0.4877	0.1308	0.2240
Textiles	0.1971	0.3300	0.3460	0.1329	0.1489
Pulp and paper	0.2334	0.2591	0.3910	0.0257	0.1576
Printing and publishing	0.1958	0.3115	0.2600	0.1157	0.0642
Chemicals	0.1775	0.2095	0.2874	0.0320	0.1099
Petroleum and coal	0.1763	0.3917	0.2576	0.2154	0.0813
Stone, glass, and clay	0.2246	0.3068	0.4302	0.0822	0.2056
Iron and steel	0.1910	0.2818	0.4137	0.0908	0.2227
Nonferrous metals	0.1977	0.2727	0.4078	0.0750	0.2101
Metal products	0.1814	0.2720	0.4000	0.0906	0.2186
Machinery	0.1865	0.2622	0.3671	0.0757	0.1806
Electronic machinery	0.1771	0.2390	0.2632	0.0619	0.0861
Transportation durables	0.1795	0.2504	0.3271	0.0709	0.1476
Precision machinery	0.1295	0.2039	0.3236	0.0744	0.1941
Average	0.1937	0.2847	0.3545	0.0910	0.1608

Note: Small U.S. firms are defined as those having assets < $25 million.

Source: See text.

Table 4.8 shows a comparable set of industry differences for small manufacturing firms. The contrast with the previous table is striking. For the small firms there is no sign of convergence, and if anything the differences are larger than in 1980. However, the differences were even larger in 1993, so the relative gap is now closing. Nevertheless, there is still a long way to go.

3.2. SAVERS' RESPONSE TO THE DEREGULATION

An obvious question is why the small and large borrowers fared so differently. We believe that the key to understanding the difference comes from looking at the behavior of the banks' depositors. Japanese households have historically held the dominant part of their financial assets in bank deposits. The conventional explanation for this (e.g., Hamada and Horiuchi 1987) was the relatively low overall level of financial assets held by the households along with the high transactions costs of operating in immature capital markets. Table 4.9, which shows the ratios of bank deposits to GDP for G7 countries, suggests that at the onset of deregulation in 1983 Japan had far more bank deposits (relative to GDP) than any of the other G7 countries. The total deposit-to-GDP ratio in Japan stood at 1.58, more than double the ratio for Italy, the next highest country.

The table also shows that by 1996 the picture had hardly changed. Japan still looks anomalous in its deposit/GDP ratio. Figure 4.1 shows yearly data for the city banks and confirms that there were no unusual breaks in the pattern and that even the large commercial banks were gaining deposits (relative to GDP) in the last two decades. The fact that deposits at the city banks account for only about 10% of the deposits recorded in the IMF data is one way of seeing the importance of postal savings accounts. As we discuss below, forecasts of the future of the banking system need to be conditioned on what will happen to the postal savings accounts.

Why didn't the Japanese savers prune their bank deposits? One answer is that the deposit-to-GDP ratio may not tell the complete story. The last column in Table 4.9 shows that the ratio of deposits to *wealth* fell from 67% in 1983 to 62% in 1996. So from the households' perspective they did cut back slightly on their use of banks. Nevertheless, there does seem to be a puzzle as to why the banking reliance remained so strong, particularly since there were so many steps taken to liberalize financial markets during this time.

We believe that there were several features of the deregulation process that kept savers from pulling their money out of the banks. First, the deregulation process was very slow in allowing individual investors easy direct access to capital markets. For example, participating directly in the stock market remained expensive for individuals until very recently. Up until April 1998, commissions on trades as large as ¥50 million were still fixed and regulated. Only in October 1999 were all commissions fully deregulated. Similarly, a range of activities including stock options trading by individuals, over-the-counter trading of equity-related derivatives, and trading nonlisted stocks through securities firms were prohibited until December 1998. So prior to the Big Bang it was very costly for individual investors to participate in capital markets directly.

But the limited direct access only partially explains individuals' strong attachments to bank deposits. One obvious question is why investment trusts (which have existed for many years) didn't draw money away from banks. Here again regulation was important. Until 1998, investment trusts in Japan were limited to contract-type funds, and company-type funds (i.e., U.S.-style mutual funds) were not allowed. Furthermore, any investment trust had to be sold to more than 50 investors, precluding the possibility of establishing funds specialized for a few rich investors, like many hedge funds, vulture funds, and LBO funds in the United States.

Table 4.9 **Ratios of Bank Deposits to GDP for Selected Years, G7 Countries**

Country	Year	(Demand deposits)/ GDP[a]	(Time deposits)/ GDP[b]	(Total deposits)/ GDP[c]	(Nonbank deposits)/ GDP[b, c]	Addendum: (total deposits)/wealth[d]
Canada	1983	0.09	0.55	0.63	0.58	0.35
	1996	0.17	0.62	0.79	0.75	0.33
France	1983	0.18	0.43	0.61	0.46	0.57
	1996	0.20	0.45	0.65	0.68	0.36
Germany	1983	0.11	0.40	0.50	0.72	0.55
	1996	0.18	0.42	0.60	0.93	0.43
Italy	1983	0.31	0.36	0.67	0.59	0.35
	1996	0.27	0.25	0.52	0.51	0.33
Japan	1983	0.21	1.36	1.58	1.50	0.67
	1996	0.28	1.78	2.06	1.43	0.62
U.K.	1983	0.10	0.25	0.35	0.85	N/A
	1996	N/A	1.06	1.06	0.91	N/A
U.S.	1983	0.11	0.46	0.57	0.74	0.25
	1996	0.11	0.31	0.42	0.50	0.16

[a] International Financial Statistics, International Monetary Fund. This information includes all institutions that accept deposits, not only commercial banks.
[b] Bank Profitability: Financial Statements of Banks, Statistical Supplement, Organisation for Economic Co-operation and Development, several issues.
[c] For United Kingdom the data correspond to 1984. For United Kingdom and Japan, nonbank deposits include interbank deposits.
[d] Financial Accounts of OECD Countries, Organisation for Economic Cooperation and Development, several issues.

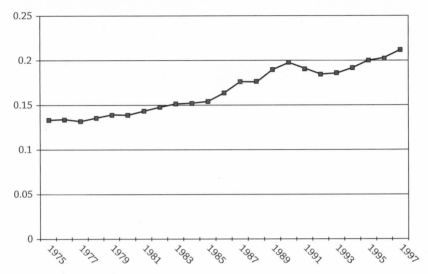

Figure 4.1 Households' deposits at city banks relative to GDP, 1975–1997.
Source: Bank of Japan, *Economic Statistics Annual*, various issues

More importantly, entry into the investment trust business was limited by other regulations. This protection muted some of the incentives to improve the returns on investment trusts. Since almost all the investment trust companies were subsidiaries of securities companies, they were often interested in churning all the accounts they managed to collect the high commissions for their parents. Consequently the investment trusts had a poor track record, generally underperforming market indices by large margins (Cai, Chan, and Yamada 1996; Ohmura and Kawakita 1992, chapter 7; Yonezawa and Maru 1984, 31).

Other financial services companies were barred from offering investment trusts until the 1990s. But even in the 1990s, when the entry barriers finally started to be removed, the investment trust companies were still required to get government approval each time they set up a new investment trust fund. The restriction remained until December 1998 and stifled competition in introducing innovative products.[26]

We believe these factors together significantly limited the options of savers and led them to keep much of their money in the banks. Notice that our explanation does not emphasize any attempts by banks to attract funds to take advantage of their deposit insurance guarantees. This does not imply that we completely dismiss the moral-hazard stories that have been emphasized by others (e.g., Cargill, Hutchison, and Ito 1997; Hutchison 1998). Rather, we believe that our complementary explanation stressing the limited degree to which savings options were deregulated has been overlooked.

Of course, one might still wonder who ended up buying all the bonds that the companies issued. Figure 4.2 shows the distribution of bond purchases during

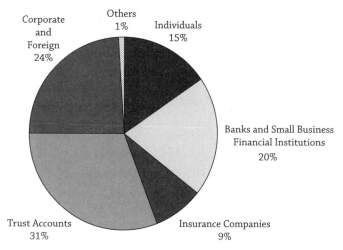

Figure 4.2 Bond purchases by sector, 1981–1990. Source: Flow-of-funds accounts; see text for details

the 1980s.[27] Consistent with our account, direct individuals' purchases were relatively small. Given the aforementioned impediments, we do not find this surprising. Instead, it appears that various types of financial institutions (most notably insurance companies, commercial banks, and trust banks) were major purchasers, along with corporations and foreigners.[28]

We draw two further conclusions from this reading of the evidence. First, the Big Bang is likely to be more important in generating new options for savers than for borrowers, who by 1990 had already gained important alternatives to bank financing. Second, we believe that the historical record gives us little quantitative guidance as to how the households will respond to the Big Bang. It is clear that the banks will face significant new competition for funds, but there is too little evidence for us to make any strong predictions about which competitors will be the most threatening to the banks. Banks themselves are now allowed to sell investment trusts over their counters (since December 1998). This means that when we make our projections about the future size of the banking industry, our calculations will not rely on any specific assumptions about the future supply of funds to the industry. Instead, as a plausibility check we will see what our forecasts imply about future changes in household portfolio decisions.

3.3. BANKS' RESPONSES TO THE DEREGULATION

Our account of the savings behavior suggests that banks had a bit of a windfall in that they were able to hold on to many of their deposits despite the deregulation. But the windfall was not big enough to offset the adverse fallout from deregulation, and by the end of the 1990s the banks were in bad shape. While our story clearly gets the timing of events right, it may not correctly characterize the causation. For instance, one alternative explanation is that the Japanese banks are suffering now purely because of the poor performance of the overall Japanese economy in the 1990s. While we believe that macro conditions played an important role in shaping the fate of the industry, the question we care about is whether macro factors were all that mattered. To assess this question we offer several pieces of evidence.

The starting point for our exploration is to see how the banks responded under the constraints of the prevailing regulations. As mentioned above, Japanese banks prior to the Big Bang were not really able to move into the nontraditional areas of banking that many of the other global banks have pursued. To gauge the significance of these restrictions we compare the recent profitability and income sources for large U.S. and Japanese banks.

Table 4.10 shows data on the U.S. banks. Unfortunately, the regulatory reports from which these data are compiled do not directly provide information on revenue sources by line of business. As a crude measure of the income from nontraditional activities one can look at noninterest income. The table shows that noninterest income (relative to total income) has doubled since the early 1980s. This ratio has climbed steadily, and most banking experts use these figures to argue that U.S. banks are successfully pushing into new lines of business.

The table also shows that U.S. bank profitability at the end of 1990s is at near-record levels. The U.S. banks successfully rebounded from their very poor performance in the late 1980s. The initial recovery may have been partly due to luck, because the steep U.S. yield curve made it very easy for banks to make money by taking in deposits and investing them in government securities. However, even as the U.S. yield curve has flattened out, U.S. bank profits have remained high, and during this time the percentage of noninterest income has continued to grow.

Table 4.11 shows similar data for large Japanese banks. Perhaps surprisingly, they have about the same fraction of revenue coming from fee-based activities in the late 1990s as in the early 1980s. Although during the 1990s the banks have made a lower fraction of income from interest receipts, most of the decline has been due to an increase in capital gains realized by selling securities.[29] Put differently, the total of interest income and "other" income has hardly changed in Japan. The table also shows how profitability (measured by either return on assets or return on equity) has deteriorated in the 1990s (even more so than the U.S. banks in the late 1980s). Interestingly, the raw ROA levels (shown in the third-to-last column) are typically higher than the adjusted ROA levels, which omit gains and losses from securities sales (and are shown in the last column).[30] Thus, it appears that the banks have tried to mask some of the performance deterioration by realizing capital gains on securities holdings.

While the Japanese banks have yet to expand much into nontraditional lines of business, they did reorganize their traditional lending patterns. Figure 4.3 shows

Table 4.10 **Profitability and Noninterest Income: Major U.S. Banks, 1976–1996**

Year	Noninterest income[a]	ROA[b]	ROE[c]
1976	0.1053	0.0055	0.0919
1977	0.1024	0.0058	0.1013
1978	0.0967	0.0062	0.1106
1979	0.1377	0.0065	0.1185
1980	0.1294	0.0049	0.0889
1981	0.1171	0.0036	0.0297
1982	0.1271	0.0041	0.0481
1983	0.1431	0.0049	0.0634
1984	0.1093	0.0055	0.0759
1985	0.1325	0.0071	0.1287
1986	0.1448	0.0065	0.1040
1987	0.1506	0.0003	−0.0135
1988	0.1513	0.0071	0.1468
1989	0.1472	0.0041	−0.1150
1990	0.1527	0.0023	0.0534
1991	0.1864	0.0056	0.0783
1992	0.2213	0.0104	0.1384
1993	0.2465	0.0131	0.1684
1994	0.2373	0.0127	0.1691
1995	0.2246	0.0128	0.1645
1996	0.2535	0.0146	0.1670

Note: Data are taken from the December call report for each year. Each entry is the average over the top 1% institutions (according to total assets) of the ratio for the year. All the variable names in the footnotes are extracted from the instructions for submitting call reports, 1976–1996.

[a] Mean ratio of noninterest income to total income. Before 1984, noninterest income is computed as total income (riad4000) minus interest income (the sum of riad4000, riad4020, riad4025, riad4063, riad4065, and riad4115). From 1984 onward, there is a specific item that keeps track of noninterest income (riad4107). Thus, from 1984 onward, we define noninterest income as riad4000 minus riad4107.

[b] Mean return on assets, computed as net income (riad4340) divided by total assets (rcfd2170).

[c] Mean return on equity, computed as net income (riad4340) divided by total equity capital (rcfd3210).

Table 4.11 **Interest Income, Fee Income, Return on Assets, and Return on Equity for Japanese City Banks**

Year	RINT[a]	RLINT[b]	RFEE[c]	ROCUR[d]	ROA[e]	ROE[f]	AROA[g]
1976	0.9317	0.7152	0.0359	0.0024	NA	NA	NA
1977	0.9314	0.6980	0.0375	0.0028	0.0013	0.0528	0.0028
1978	0.8967	0.6385	0.0415	0.0047	0.0012	0.0476	0.0026
1979	0.8965	0.5876	0.0451	0.0031	0.0012	0.0484	0.0026
1980	0.8987	0.5568	0.0347	0.0025	0.0007	0.0300	0.0013
1981	0.9292	0.5760	0.0286	0.0019	0.0009	0.0425	0.0017
1982	0.9320	0.5163	0.0298	0.0015	0.0022	0.1094	0.0047
1983	0.9388	0.5192	0.0308	0.0014	0.0020	0.1030	0.0047
1984	0.9362	0.5482	0.0323	0.0015	0.0024	0.1297	0.0053
1985	0.9380	0.5091	0.0288	0.0014	0.0023	0.1190	0.0051
1986	0.9236	0.5541	0.0319	0.0018	0.0022	0.1213	0.0044
1987	0.8965	0.5301	0.0337	0.0030	0.0026	0.1341	0.0059
1988	0.8463	0.4764	0.0323	0.0036	0.0030	0.1541	0.0070
1989	0.8338	0.4867	0.0310	0.0940	0.0036	0.1617	0.0031
1990	0.8690	0.4894	0.0267	0.0696	0.0027	0.1073	0.0009
1991	0.9075	0.5857	0.0236	0.0364	0.0019	0.0683	0.0014
1992	0.9103	0.6213	0.0242	0.0424	0.0014	0.0465	0.0022
1993	0.9205	0.6091	0.0313	0.0153	0.0008	0.0248	0.0023
1994	0.8482	0.5324	0.0355	0.0651	0.0007	0.0212	−0.0012
1995	0.8011	0.4679	0.0361	0.1224	−0.0002	−0.0046	−0.0045
1996	0.8074	0.3906	0.0363	0.0867	−0.0042	−0.1171	−0.0077
1997	0.7916	0.3710	0.0410	0.1188	−0.0001	−0.0040	−0.0024

Note: Data are from the Nikkei Database for the accounting year ending in March of each year.

[a] Proportion of interest income in the current income.

[b] Proportion of interest income on loans in the current income.

[c] Proportion of fee income in the current income.

[d] Proportion of the other current income, including realized capital gains on securities.

[e] After-tax net income divided by total assets from March of the previous year.

[f] After-tax net income divided by total capital (capital plus reserves) from March of the previous year.

[g] Adjusted ROA: (current-profits less gains from sales of the securities + losses from sales from the securities + losses from revaluation of securities) / (total assets from March of the previous year).

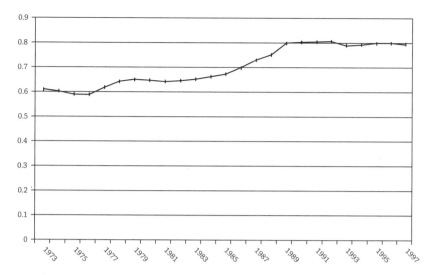

Figure 4.3 Proportion of loans to small enterprises, 1973–1997. Source: Bank of Japan, *Economic Statistics Annual*, various issues.

the proportion of bank loans to small enterprises.[31] The graph shows a dramatic increase in small business lending in the 1980s. As the banks started to lose their large customers to capital markets, they went after small firms. Most observers agree that previously the banks had not had close ties to many of these smaller borrowers. We return to this point below.

Figure 4.4 shows a second aspect of the banks' portfolio shift: increasing loans to the real estate industry. The proportion of loans to the real estate industry started to soar in the beginning of 1980s and soon surpassed the previous peak, which had occurred during the Japanese Archipelago rebuilding boom of 1972–1973. By the early 1990s, the proportion of loans to the real estate industry by banks had doubled from its level in the early 1980s.

A third change in the banks' behavior, which has been emphasized by Peek and Rosengren (1997a, 1997b), was a noticeable increase in foreign lending. As they explain, in some cases this lending was done through separately capitalized subsidiaries so that not all the loans would show up on the parent bank's balance sheets. Peek and Rosengren's analysis shows that the foreign activity has dramatically slowed in the 1990s.

One way to evaluate the portfolio shifts and performance is to see if they might have represented a natural response to the underlying economic conditions. After all, land prices were soaring in the late 1980s, so perhaps the shift into property-based lending was simply in keeping with past practices. To explore how much of the banks' performance might be attributable to basic economic conditions, we ran several regressions.

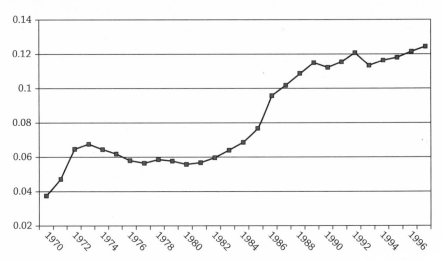

Figure 4.4 Proportion of loans to the real estate industry, 1970–1997.
Source: Bank of Japan, *Economic Statistics Annual*, various issues.

Figure 4.5 City banks' adjusted ROA, 1956–1997. Note: Raw ROA has been adjusted
for gains and losses due to sale or revaluation of equity holdings. Source: Ministry of
Finance, *Banking Bureau Annual Report*, various issues, and Nikkei Database.

The dependent variable for the regressions is the adjusted return on assets
(AROA) for city banks, which is shown in the last column of Table 4.11. As a
robustness check we also tried the same regressions using the raw ROA series
and found the same basic patterns. The adjusted ROA series is graphed in Figure
4.5. The figure shows that Japanese bank performance slowly declined from the
mid-1950s through the 1980s and then sharply deteriorated in the 1990s.

To determine the role of deregulation on performance one would like to include a proxy for deregulation in a full-blown model of bank profitability. Unfortunately, we lack not only a compelling theoretical model that makes tight predictions about the exact determinants of (adjusted) ROA, but also convincing proxies for the impact of deregulation. Given these limitations, we take the indirect and admittedly ad hoc approach of looking only to see whether the dynamics for ROA changed following deregulation. Operationally our strategy amounts to checking whether there is a stable relation between ROA and standard macroeconomic variables before and after 1983 (the date at which we argue the deregulation of the bond market began in earnest). Thus, our modest goal is to provide evidence against a story that posits that macro factors can *fully* explain the banks' performance after the onset of deregulation.

We considered interest rates, land prices, stock prices, and GDP growth to be the baseline set of macroeconomic variables that could be plausibly justified as determinants of ROA. Intuitively, these variables allow for monetary policy, collateral, and general economic conditions to drive bank performance. Because we had just under 30 years of data and did not have much guidance about how many lags to allow for in the regressions, we did almost no experimenting with other variables. The one exception was inflation, which we measured using the GDP deflator; we found no independent effect of controlling for inflation.

Data limitations largely drove our choices of the specific proxies used in the regressions. In particular, the call rate (which measures the price of overnight credit between banks) is the only consistent interest-rate series that is available from the 1950s onward. We take the difference between the nominal call rate and the current year's inflation to form our real call-rate series.[32] ROA has been adjusted for gains and losses due to sale or revaluation of equity holdings.

Similarly, the only consistent land price data come from a semiannual survey conducted by the Japan Real Estate Research Institute. One survey covers all land prices nationwide, and the other pertains to land prices in the six major metropolitan areas. The logarithmic differences in both series (again subtracting inflation) are graphed in Figure 4.6. This graph also shows the logarithmic difference of the TOPIX stock return index and inflation.

The figure shows three important things. First, the stock return series is much more volatile than either land price series. Large swings in stock prices routinely occurred throughout the period. Second, large changes in the relative price of land also had happened several times prior to the late 1980s. Furthermore, the land price changes were not always coincident with the swings in stock prices. This is important because it means that we have some hope of identifying the econometric connection between land prices, stock prices, and bank profits. Finally, the figure also shows that the choice of which land price series to use could be potentially important. The late 1980s land price run-up was concentrated in the major cities.

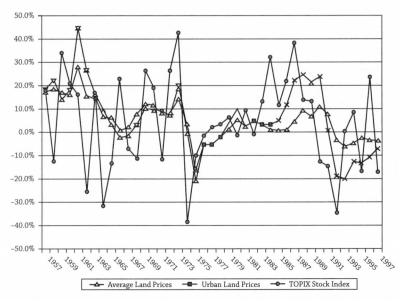

Figure 4.6 Percentage real change in land and stock prices, 1957–1997. Note: All nominal data are converted to constant prices using the GDP deflator.
Source: Japan Real Estate Research Institute and Tokyo Stock Exchange.

Two representative regression specifications among those we tried are shown in Table 4.12. One key issue is how to account for the long-term decline in profitability documented in Figure 4.5. In the first pair of regressions (which differ only in which land price is used) we include a time trend in addition to the macroeconomic variables. We draw two conclusions from these regressions. First, and not surprisingly, the time trend is the most important variable in the equation. Second, aside from stock prices, which are of borderline importance, most of the macro variables appear to have no correlation with bank profitability.

The next two columns repeat the first specification except that a lagged dependent variable is added. The addition of the lagged dependent variable marginally improves the R^2 and wipes out the explanatory power of the time trend. The t-statistics of several of the macro variables rise, but the tests on the statistical significance of the sum of the coefficients, shown at the bottom of the table, continue to indicate that only the stock price coefficients are likely to be different from zero. This same pattern turned up in all of the variations that we tried that included lagged dependent variables. From this we conclude that prior to the mid-1980s there was at best a loose link between macro variables and bank profitability.

For both specifications we then checked how they fit after 1983. Figures 4.7 and 4.8 compare the actual values and fitted values for the regression

Table 4.12 **Regressions Relating Banks' Return on Assets and Macroeconomic Variables (dependent variable is city banks' adjusted return on assets; sample period is 1957–1983)**

Variable	Coefficient and (t-statistic)			
	Regression 1	2	3	4
Intercept	0.01138	0.01182	0.00337	0.00413
	(5.833)	(5.951)	(0.990)	(1.122)
Time trend	−0.00026	−0.00028	−0.00009	−0.00010
	(−3.645)	(−4.039)	(−0.982)	(−1.018)
Real GDP growth	−0.00377	−0.00359	−0.00255	−0.00020
	(−0.331)	(−0.295)	(−0.263)	(−0.018)
Real GDP growth ($t-1$)	0.00479	0.00343	0.01993	0.01432
	(0.456)	(0.359)	(1.893)	(1.495)
Log change in real average land price	−0.00584	–	−0.01355	–
	(−0.761)	–	(−1.906)	–
Log change in real average land price (t − 1)	0.00646	–	0.00861	–
	(1.281)	–	(1.981)	–
Log change in real urban land price	–	−0.00299	–	−0.00634
	–	(−0.654)	–	(−1.487)
Log change in real urban land price (t − 1)	–	0.00241	–	0.00369
	–	(0.671)	–	(1.149)
Real call rate	0.00620	0.00501	0.01547	0.01166
	(0.518)	(0.423)	(1.442)	(1.080)
Real call rate (t − 1)	−0.00862	−0.00983	−0.00495	−0.00725
	(−0.971)	(−1.039)	(−0.648)	(−0.864)
ROA (t − 1)	–	–	0.53427	0.48948
	–	–	(2.693)	(2.375)
Log change in real equity prices	0.00370	0.00362	0.00392	0.00343
	(2.088)	(2.159)	(2.608)	(2.319)
Log change in real equity prices (t − 1)	0.00248	0.00273	0.00201	0.00191
	(0.973)	(1.089)	(0.928)	(0.857)
R^2	0.8259	0.8144	0.8826	0.8651

(continued)

Table 4.12 (continued)

| Variable | Coefficient and (t-statistic) | | | |
	Regression 1	*2*	*3*	*4*
GDP growth	0.9432	0.9916	0.2135	0.3381
Land prices	0.9274	0.8858	0.4271	0.4743
Interest rates	0.8467	0.6896	0.3743	0.6972
Equity prices	0.1113	0.0820	0.0756	0.0994
p-values from tests for the equality of coefficients after 1984				
	0.0149	0.0241	0.0298	0.0658

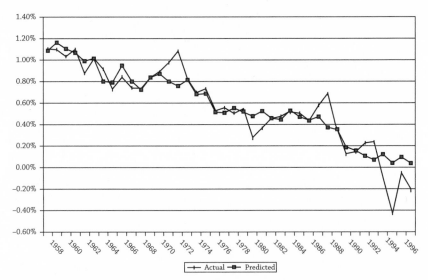

Figure 4.7 Actual versus predicted adjusted ROA for city banks (without the lagged dependent variable). Source: Authors' calculations using regression coefficients from regression 1 in Table 4.12.

specification including average land prices (regressions 1 and 3 in the table). Importantly, the fitted values are one-step-ahead forecasts, so the actual values of the right-hand variables are being used in forming these predictions. By taking this approach rather than going with a full dynamic simulation we are giving the prediction equation its best chance at explaining the postderegulation events.

Our main conclusion from the figures is that the macro variables lead to an underprediction of bank ROA in the late 1980s and an overprediction in the 1990s. This is most clearly seen in Figure 4.7 (which shows the results when there is no lagged dependent variable), but even in Figure 4.8, where the lagged dependent variable keeps the forecasts more closely on track, the 1988 and 1989 peaks are underestimated and the last few years of the sample are overestimated. This evidence leads us to doubt stories which argue that the formation of the bubble and its bursting can *fully* explain the banks' performance over the last 15 years.

An alternative way to judge the stability of the models is to check for a structural break in the coefficients. Having only 15 years of data in the deregulated era led us to suspect that this type of test would have very little power. Nevertheless, the tests for structural breaks shown in the bottom half of the table indicate that none of the four equations is stable across the two regimes. In each case we can decisively reject the hypothesis of no change in the coefficients. In addition to being statistically different across the two periods, the differences also appear to be large in terms of their economic implications. For instance, many of the coefficients reverse their signs and the magnitude of the coefficient on lagged dependent variable also moves noticeably. Overall the tests for coefficient stability also confirm the inability of a set of stable macro correlations to explain the recent ROA data.

While we view this evidence as suggestive, we recognize that there are clear limitations to how hard we can lean on the lack of a well-fitting time-series model for bank profitability. Our preferred interpretation of the Table 4.12 results is

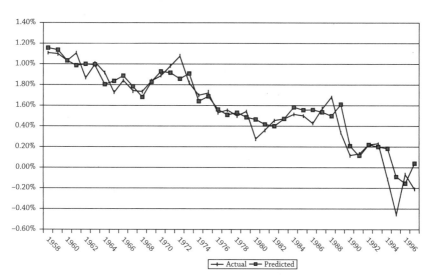

Figure 4.8 Actual versus predicted adjusted ROA for city banks.
Source: Authors' calculations using regression coefficients from regression 3 in Table 4.12.

that the deregulation pushed the banks to alter their business practices so that their exposure to macroeconomic factors changed. But it is also possible that we have simply failed to control for the correct macro factors and that the poor specification of our model is masking the truth.

We believe a stronger test of the importance of deregulation can be conducted by looking at cross-bank differences in performance. If our story emphasizing the role of deregulation is correct, then those banks which relied more heavily on loans to customers who obtained access to capital markets should have underperformed after deregulation. To test this hypothesis we check whether bank performance in the postderegulation period is negatively correlated with the bank's preregulation dependence on bank loans to traditional customers.

In this analysis we continue to date the start of the deregulation period as fiscal year 1983. Our performance measure is again return on assets corrected for the gains and losses from stock sales and the revaluation of stock holdings. To measure postderegulation performance we use a time average of this variable. Time averaging allows us to avoid being too dependent on correctly specifying the exact dates of the adjustment period. However, it could also mean that we are including observations when the response to deregulation had yet to begin or was already complete. To guard against this possibility we consider two different averaging intervals. We first use the average return for 1991–1997. We then also use the average for 1984–1997 so that we pick up both the boom in the late 1980s and the stagnation in the 1990s.

We consider two types of predergulation bank characteristics that could influence the postderegulation performance. One factor is a bank's reliance on income from traditional activities. We expect banks intensive in traditional activities to have fared (relatively) badly in the deregulation environment. As a proxy we use the proportion of current income coming from interest on loans. If this proportion is high, it indicates that the bank's performance was relatively dependent on traditional activities at the onset of the reforms.

A second factor relates to the bank's customer base at the onset of deregulation. Ideally we would like to know which banks had many customers that were eligible to shift to bond financing. Unfortunately, data on the external financing options for the bank customers are not available. We were able to collect information on the proportion of loans made to listed firms and the proportion of loans made to manufacturing firms. Given that the listed firms are typically large and are required to release audited information on their performance, we think this is a fairly good proxy. We expect the banks that had a higher exposure to listed firms to have been at more risk of losing customers to the capital markets. We also know that the size-based standards of the bond issuance rules made it easier for manufacturing firms to go to the capital markets in the 1980s. Thus, we also expect the banks that had more clients in the manufacturing industry to have also been more likely to lose customers.

All the data except for the listed company loan shares come from Nikkei database on bank balance sheets and income statements. The data on the loan shares were collected from Keizai Chosakai's annual publication *Kin'yu Kikan no Toyushi*. The sample for the regressions includes 10 city banks, 3 long-term credit banks, 6 trust banks, 64 regional banks, and 60 second-tier regional banks.[33]

Table 4.13 shows the estimation results. Each column reports the coefficient estimates and their *t*-statistics for a different regression model. We draw several conclusions from this table. First, the proportion of interest on loans in the current income in 1983 is significantly negatively correlated with the postderegulation performance. The correlation seems to be robust, as it turned up in all the specifications that we considered. Second, the proportion of loans to listed firms is also negatively correlated with postderegulation performance, although the statistical significance of the coefficient is marginal when the average for whole postderegulation period (1984–1997) is used.[34] Finally, the proportion of loans to manufacturing industry in 1983 is also significantly negatively correlated with the postderegulation performance. We read these results as saying the firms that were more at risk because of the deregulation did seem to underperform after 1983.

Returning to the big picture, there are several ways to interpret the differences in the paths taken by the U.S. and Japanese banks. One interpretation is that the Japanese banks had a different vision of the future of the industry and pursued that vision. For instance, maybe the strong Japanese growth in the late 1980s led the banks to assess the profitability of various strategic options differently than U.S. banks (which were trying to recover from the bad loans they had extended in Latin America). We believe the regression evidence in the last two tables casts some doubt on this explanation, but perhaps a more complicated story involving incorrect future beliefs could explain the performance data. In this case, the fact the Japanese strategy may not have worked out is more of an accident than anything that was caused by the regulatory regime.

A second reading of the evidence is that the Japanese banks were constrained by the regulation from taking the path of the U.S. banks. Since many fee-generating lines of business were not available, the banks chose to move into property-related lending and lending more to small firms, perhaps knowing that this involved taking on more risk.[35] This was not the only option for the banks. When large customers started to leave bank financing, the banks could have started buying government bonds and other securities instead of lending to new customers. We know now both that this strategy looked relatively attractive and that few, if any, banks in Japan followed it. Regardless of what one decides about the rationality of the banks' responses, it seems clear that banks would never have chosen to search for new lines of business if their large customers had not shifted their financing patterns in response to the deregulation. In this sense, the regulatory mix seems to have mattered, and one interpretation of our findings is that the poor performance was partially due to the deregulation.

Table 4.13 Cross-Section Regressions Relating Postderegulation Return on Assets with Prederegulation Bank Characteristics

Independent Variable	Dependent Variable Is Adjusted Return on Assets, 1991–1997				Dependent variable is adjusted return on assets, 1984–1997			
	Model 1	Model 2	Model 3	Model 4	Model 5	Model 6	Model 7	Model 8
City-bank dummy	0.00281 (1.165)	0.00042 (0.385)	0.00129 (0.942)	0.01114 (3.875)	0.00619 (3.432)	0.00246 (3.139)	0.00245 (2.604)	0.01034 (4.797)
Long-term credit dummy	0.00076 (0.269)	-0.00232 (-1.395)	0.00094 (0.353)	0.01181 (3.103)	0.00508 (2.413)	0.00066 (0.593)	0.00157 (0.933)	0.01041 (3.804)
Trust-bank dummy	-0.00155 (-1.002)	-0.00204 (-1.756)	0.01426 (2.410)	0.02019 (3.230)	0.00478 (4.277)	0.00317 (3.995)	0.00914 (2.206)	0.01448 (3.235)
Regional-bank I dummy	0.00904 (3.064)	0.00490 (7.003)	0.00375 (11.154)	0.01544 (5.319)	0.01065 (4.667)	0.00532 (10.306)	0.00460 (18.479)	0.01396 (5.994)
Regional-bank II dummy	0.00948 (2.863)	0.00407 (7.527)	0.00272 (10.591)	0.01526 (4.802)	0.01100 (4.342)	0.00462 (10.635)	0.00388 (19.752)	0.01399 (5.538)

	(1)	(2)	(3)	(4)	(5)	(6)	(7)	(8)
1983 interest on loans relative to current income	-0.00898 (-2.092)			-0.01463 (-3.658)	-0.00927 (-2.833)			-0.01203 (-3.824)
1983 fraction of loans to manufacturing firms		-0.00828 (-2.882)		-0.00637 (-2.420)		-0.00434 (-2.078)		-0.00408 (-2.107)
1983 fraction of loans to publicly traded firms			-0.01589 (-3.165)	-0.01579 (-3.040)			-0.00612 (-1.719)	-0.00670 (-1.747)
Adjusted R²	.479	.498	.509	.548	.345	.332	.326	.387

Note: Dependent variable: return on assets adjusted for gains and losses of stock sales averaged over either 1991–1997 or 1984–1997.

Mean of dependent variable: 0.001901 (average for 1991–1997); 0.003931 (average for 1984–1997).

Independent variables are measured for accounting year ending in the March of 1983. The 143 observations include data for 10 city banks, three long-term credit banks, six trust banks (excluding Nippon Trust), 64 regional banks, and 60 second-tier regional banks. Each column shows coefficient estimates for a separate regression model. Numbers in the parentheses below coefficients are t-statistics, calculated using a heteroskedastic consistent covariance matrix following White (1980).

For the purposes of looking ahead, it may not matter whether we can separate these two alternatives. At this point the Japanese banks remain among the
largest in the world, yet they are now among the least profitable. Moreover, the
approach of sticking to traditional banking and focusing on new, smaller customers has failed. As Hoshi and Kashyap (1999b) show, foreign firms and nonbank
financial firms are moving quickly to compete with banks for funds. It seems reasonable to conclude that the Japanese banks are going to be pushed by all of these
considerations to shift their strategy and become more like U.S. banks. But the
current conditions of the industry may place some constraints on which options
are achievable. Thus, before making any forecasts, we briefly review the current
conditions of the banks.

4. The Bad-Loans Problem

While it is widely recognized that Japanese banks are in bad shape, there appears
to be little consensus on the magnitude of the problems. For instance, in early
February 1999 a top Ministry of Finance official (Eisuke Sakakibara) was quoted
as saying that the financial crisis would be over within a matter of weeks. At
the time private-sector analysts were arguing that conditions were deteriorating
and that bold new steps were needed. Such conflicting opinions have been common for the last several years.

One problem plaguing the entire discussion is that there is no common standard for what people mean when they refer to "bad loans." One reason for this
ambiguity is that the standards for determining which loans the banks identify as
being at risk on their financial statements have varied over time. A second problem
is that numbers from the bank balance sheets are only one of three types of estimates which are sometimes used to identify loans that are at risk. Unfortunately,
these three types of estimates are not even intended to measure the same thing,
and for each approach there are judgmental decisions that can swing the numbers considerably. As we now show, these considerations explain why, to a casual
observer, there have been such divergent claims about the scope of the banking
crisis in Japan. After having clarified the size of the problem, we then discuss its
implications for the future.

4.1. ESTIMATES BASED ON DATA FROM BANKS' FINANCIAL
STATEMENTS

Remarkably, Japanese banks did not disclose anything about the extent of their
problem loans prior to 1993. This lack of disclosure made it impossible to say
very much about the condition of the banks. Since 1993 the banks have included
footnotes on their financial statements that classify loans according to the
health of the borrowers. The decisions about which loans should be identified in

the footnotes have been made by the Japanese Bankers Association (Zenginkyo). Importantly, these voluntarily disclosed data are not supposed to take account of differences in the chances the different loans might be repaid (say because of differences in the collateral associated with the loans). For example, if a borrower files for bankruptcy, all the loans made to the borrower are treated equivalently.

Table 4.14 shows these voluntarily disclosed data for 1993 through 1998. The first half of the table shows information for major banks (city banks, trust banks, and long-term credit banks), and the second part shows the comparable number for all banks (major banks plus regional banks). From March 1993 to September 1995, the statistics covered only the loans to failed enterprises and the loans for which no payments had been made for at least six months. Thus, the figures did not include any restructured loans. Moreover, regional banks did not have to disclose (and many chose not to disclose) the loans with suspended payments. Under this reporting convention the amount of bad loans fluctuated around ¥12 trillion (roughly 3.5% of total loans) for major banks and ¥13.5 trillion (roughly 2.5% of total loans) for all banks.

For the major banks, intermittent data on loan write-offs are available for this period from the website of the Financial Supervisory Agency. These data, shown in the third column of the table, indicate that write-offs were quite low in these first couple of years of the banking crisis. The fourth and seventh columns of the table show that during this period the banks were also slow in increasing the amount of funds set aside to cover the bad loans. Although provisioning was increasing, the loan loss reserves were never sufficient to cover the expected losses. For instance, as of September 1995, the loan loss reserves covered only 52% of bad loans for major banks (and 60% for all banks). Analysts in the private sector repeatedly argued that the reported data grossly understated the true extent of the problems. For example, Ohara (1996) argued that as of March 1995 the bad loans for the major banks were more likely to be as large as ¥75 trillion, once all the restructured loans and future liabilities of the affiliated nonbanks were properly accounted.

Starting with the accounting data released in March 1996, a couple of changes were made. First, the regional banks were now instructed to classify any loans with suspended payments as bad. More importantly, the bad-loan definition was expanded to include loans for which the interest rates were cut to levels below the Bank of Japan discount rate at the time of the concession. These changes led to a sharp jump in the reported figures (with the totals rising to ¥20 trillion for major banks and almost ¥27 trillion for all banks). At the same time the amount of write-offs jumped.

The accounting data released in the following March included another change in definition, as loans to enterprises undergoing creditor-assisted restructuring were now included. Although the definition was expanded, the amount of bad loans declined slightly (to ¥18 trillion for major banks and ¥24 trillion for all

Table 4.14 Problem Loan Statistics for Japanese Banks: 1993–1998 (billion yen)

Date	Major banks			All banks		
	Bad loans	Cumulative write-offs[a]	Special reserves for loan losses	Bad loans	Cumulative write-offs[a]	Special reserves for loan losses
March 1993	11,730	424	3,699	12,685	N/A	4,876
September 1993	12,662	N/A	3,875	13,732	N/A	5,128
March 1994	12,472	2,514	4,547	13,659	N/A	5,967
September 1994	12,198	N/A	4,798	13,439	N/A	6,327
March 1995	11,637	5,322	5,537	12,961	N/A	7,305
September 1995	11,969	N/A	6,173	13,421	N/A	8,047
March 1996	20,357	10,812	10,345	26,831	11,602	13,469
September 1996	18,846	N/A	9,508	24,383	N/A	12,035
March 1997	18,447	14,488	9,388	23,987	15,918	12,299
September 1997	17,890	N/A	10,330	23,896	N/A	13,685
March 1998	21,978	17,988	13,601	29,758	19,911	17,815

September 1998	22,008	18,653	12,457	30,078	19,630	16,932
March 1999	20,250	22,256	9,258	29,627	24,620	14,797

Note: Definitions of bad loans: From March 1993 to September 1995, for major banks, loans whose payment had been suspended for 6 months or more; for regional banks, only loans for failed enterprises. From March, 1996 to September 1996, loans for failed enterprises, loans whose payment had been suspended for 6 months or more, and loans with interest rates lowered below the BOJ discount rate at the time of the rate cut. From March 1997 to September 1997, loans for failed enterprises, loans whose payment had been suspended for 6 months or more, loans with interest rates lowered below the BOJ discount rate at the time of the rate cut, and loans for enterprises under restructuring. For March 1998, loans for failed enterprises, loans whose payment had been suspended for 3 months or more, and loans with relaxed conditions.

Coverage: From March 1993 to September 1995, the numbers are for 21 major banks (11 city banks, 7 trust banks, 3 long-term credit banks) and 151 banks in all (64 regional banks and 66 second-tier regional banks in addition to the major banks). Hyogo Bank, which was closed in 1995 and reopened with a new name (Midori Bank) and organization, is not included in the numbers for March 1996 and later. The merger between Mitsubishi Bank and Bank of Tokyo in April 1996 (to form Mitsubishi Bank of Tokyo) reduced the number of city banks by one. Taiheiyo Bank (later Wakashio Bank) and Hanwa Bank failed in 1996 and dropped out of the sample, starting in March 1997. Hokkaido Takushoku Bank, one of the major banks, failed in 1997 and dropped out of the sample in March 1998. Tokuyo City, Kyoto Kyoei, Naniwa, and Fukutoku dropped out of the sample in September 1998. In March 1999, Long-Term Credit Bank, Nippon Credit Bank, Kokumin, Koufuku, and Tokyo Sowa were eliminated from the coverage. As a result of these changes, the sample for March 1999 covers 17 major banks (9 city banks, 7 trust banks, and 1 long-term credit bank), as well as 121 other banks (64 regional and 57 second-tier regional banks) for a total of 138 banks.

ª Cumulative direct write-offs (which include losses on sales of loans to other entities such as the CCPC and losses on support to other financial institutions) (billion yen).

Sources: Federation of Bankers Associations of Japan, Analysis of Financial Statements of All Banks, *various issues. Federation of Bankers Associations of Japan,* Analysts of Interim Financial Statements of All Banks, *various issues. Financial Supervisory Agency (FSA), "The Status of Risk Management Loans Held by All Banks in Japan (as of the end of September, 1998)," press release, January 22, 1999 and FSA, "The Status of Risk Management Loans Held by All Banks in Japan (as of the end of March 1999)," press release, July 23, 1999.*

banks). The amount of loan loss reserves also declined by ¥1 trillion for major banks and by ¥1.2 trillion for all banks. One contributing factor to the declines was an acceleration in the actual write-offs (which remove bad assets from the balance sheets). A second factor that probably helped was the brief recovery of the Japanese economy in 1996.

In March 1998, the definition of bad loans was once again expanded. The new definition, which remains in place at this writing, identifies bad loans (now called "risk management credits") as loans to failed enterprises, loans whose interest payments have been suspended for three months or more, and loans with concessions (which cover loans with reduced interest rates and loans to corporations under reorganization). This expansion of the definition and the deterioration in the economy in 1997 sharply increased the stock of bad loans. Thus, as of March 1999, despite continued write-offs and removal of many banks which failed over the last couple of years, the official amount of bad loans for the major banks (all banks) stood at ¥20 trillion (¥30 trillion).[36] Overall, the bad-loan numbers quoted on the bank financial statements still tend to be low, since the banks need not identify loans to firms that are in trouble but where no restructuring or missed payments have yet been recorded.

4.2. ESTIMATES BASED ON SUPERVISORY GUIDELINES

For supervisory purposes, the regulators have always been aware of this problem, so the Bank of Japan and Ministry of Finance (and now the Financial Supervisory Authority [FSA]) have focused on the chances that a loan will be collected. This means that both the condition of the borrower and the quality of collateral are relevant. Accordingly, loans to the same borrower can be classified into different categories if they are secured by different collateral and hence offer different expected levels of repayment. The coverage of assets which are considered is also slightly broader than the voluntarily disclosed data, since this assessment includes loanlike items such as securities loaned in addition to conventional loans.

Under this scheme, which is also used by U.S. regulators, loans are classified into four categories. Category 4 includes the loans that are noncollectable or of no value. These are the unsecured portions of loans made to failed firms. Category 3 is the set of loans that are seriously doubtful with regard to their ultimate collection. These include loans to bankrupt (or nearly bankrupt) companies that are secured, but where the market value of collateral is well below the book value. In practice these loans are expected to return little or nothing, unless the value of the collateral increases dramatically. The FSA describes Category 2 loans as "credits subject to specific risk management." These loans are not yet judged to be uncollectible but are deemed to require attention; the popular press sometimes refers to the Category 2 loans as being in the "gray zone." Category 2 loans are sometimes further classified to separate those loans that require "special attention" from the others. For example, the Financial Reconstruction Commission's guideline on provisioning for nonperforming loans suggests two different provisioning ratios for these two subcategories. Finally, Category 1 covers the remaining loans whose repayment is not supposed to be in any doubt.

Because of the large number of Category 2 loans (which are mostly excluded from the numbers shown on the bank financial statements), this classification scheme generally produces much larger estimates of problem loans. In 1998, the government started to publish aggregate statistics on loans sorted according to these criteria. The banks' own assessments are reported in the top panel of Table 4.15. In December 1998 the FSA released its own estimates for the major banks (as of March 1998, based on their 1998 on-site examinations). These figures are shown in the bottom panel of the table. The FSA data suggest that the major banks in Japan had ¥57.4 trillion of bad loans (or 14% of total loans) as of March 1998.

Converting these figures into the expected cost of cleaning up the bank balance sheets requires two more assumptions. First, one has to decide whether the supervisors have correctly identified all the problem loans at the banks. It is generally agreed that the banks' self-reporting has been fairly optimistic. For example, when Nippon Credit Bank (NCB) was nationalized, the FSA announced that it had problem loans of more than ¥3.7 trillion; NCB's own assessment put the losses at roughly ¥3.2 trillion. The same kind of underreporting was uncovered when the Long-Term Credit Bank (LTCB) was nationalized. Comparing the top and bottom panels in Table 4.15 shows that the FSA believed that the major banks had failed to identify roughly ¥7 trillion of risky loans. In April 1999, the FSA issued new guidelines that included detailed instructions on how to classify loans.

A second problem is determining the fraction of the Category 2 and Category 3 loans that will ultimately be lost. A study by the Supervision Department of the Bank of Japan (1997) found that 17% of Category 2 loans and 75% of Category 3 loans identified in 1993 became uncollectable within three years. Although the sample size used in the BOJ study was very small, the numbers provide an upper bound on the recovery rates for Category 2 and Category 3 of 83% and 25% respectively. Assuming that the Category 4 loans are worthless, but that Category 2 loans do return ¥83 against every ¥100 owed and that Category 3 loans return ¥25 per ¥100, the data in Table 4.15 imply that the total expected loss amounts to ¥14.78 trillion (which is about 3% of GDP or 3.5% of total loans).

Some private-sector analysts find this calculation very optimistic, because the calculation is based on the amount of problem loans reported by banks and FSA, and the figures in BOJ study overestimate the true recovery rates for problem loans. For example, Ohara (1998) estimates that the amount of bad loans at the major banks to be ¥73.4 trillion as of March 1998. Assuming a 25% recovery rate for the risk management loans and 62.5% recovery rate for the remaining bad loans, she arrives at ¥35 trillion (7% of GDP) as the estimated loss. Fiorillo (1999) estimated, as of February 1999, the size of loans for the major banks that will eventually be uncollectable to be ¥38 trillion, or 7.6% of GDP.[37] These estimates

Table 4.15 **Distribution of Loans by Supervisory Classification, Banks' 1998 Self-Reported Data[a]**

		Loans (billion yen)				
Sample	*Date*	*Category 1*	*2*	*3*	*4*	*Total loans*
Major banks	Mar. 1998	371,607	45,157	4,808	125	421,697
All banks	Mar. 1998	544,814	65,488	6,065	130	616,495
Major banks	Sept. 1998	354,629	45,537	5,697	77	405,940
All banks	Sept. 1998	524,980	66,078	6,863	86	598,007

March 1998 Data for 19 major banks as determined by FSA audits[b]

Loans (billion yen)				
Category 1	*2*	*3*	*4*	*Total Loans*
364,332	48,971	7,756	637	421,696

There are four loan categories used by bank supervisors. Category 4 includes the loans that are noncollectable or of no value. Category 3 is the set of loans that are seriously doubtful with regard to their ultimate collection. In practice these loans are also expected to return nothing. Category 2 loans are "credits subject to specific management risk." These loans are not yet judged to be uncollectable but are deemed to require special attention. Category 1 covers the remaining loans, whose repayment is not supposed to be in any doubt. (See text for further details.)

[a] Source: Financial Supervisory Agency, "The Status of Risk Management Loans Held by All Banks in Japan (as of the end of September, 1998)," press release, January 22, 1999. The figures include loans of Long-Term Credit Bank and Nippon Credit Bank, but exclude those of Hokkaido Takushoku Bank, Tokuyo City Bank, Kyoto Kyoei Bank, Naniwa Bank, Fukutoku Bank, and Midori Bank.

[b] Source: Financial Supervisory Agency website (www.fsa.go.jp), published in December 1998. Note that these figures include loans of the Long-Term Credit Bank and Nippon Credit Bank.

suggest (plausibly to us) that many more loans will have to be written off than have been disposed of so far.

4.3. ESTIMATES BASED ON THE DISCLOSURES MANDATED BY THE FINANCIAL RECONSTRUCTION ACT

Since April 1999 another set of bad-loan estimates have been floating around. Section 7 of the Financial Reconstruction Act (FRA) requires each bank to report bad loans (as described below) to the Financial Reconstruction Commission and to publish the data. Unfortunately, the FRA definition of bad loans falls in between the two previously described definitions. In particular, the FRA highlights loans to failed enterprises and de facto failed enterprises, loans to near-bankrupt companies, loans whose interest payments have been suspended for more than three months, and loans with concessions. Essentially this means that the FRA definition includes the Category 3 and 4 loans according to the supervisory definition, but not all of the Category 2 loans. Instead the FRA definition focuses only on any remaining loans that would be counted in the banks' voluntarily disclosed data.

Given this reporting convention, the FRA estimates should be expected to lie in between the two prior sets of estimates. In the first round of disclosure, which covered the conditions as of March 1999, the amount of bad loans at all banks was ¥34 trillion. Based on data from the websites of the FSA and FRC, this was about ¥4 trillion larger than voluntarily disclosed data, but far lower than the ¥64 trillion estimated by the supervisors. This is about ¥6 trillion larger than the voluntarily disclosed data, but far below the supervisory estimates (Fiorillo 1999). For a further discussion of how the various sets of estimates compare see Iwahara, Okina, Kanemoto, and Narisawa (1999).

Overall, we conclude that there are three key considerations that must be kept in mind when evaluating different estimates of the size of the bad-loan problem. First, and most importantly, one must check whether the data are based on assessments of the collectability of loans or are taken from the bank financial statements. Second, assuming that most people will want the collection-based estimates, it is necessary to determine whether the data have been self-reported by the banks or are based on supervisors' (or private-sector analysts') estimates. Finally, it is imperative to be clear about what assumptions are being used regarding the fraction of the gray-zone loans that will be collected.

To help put the Japanese bad-loans problem in perspective, Table 4.16 shows the size of banking crises in other developed countries over the last two decades (see Corbett 1999b, for a more comprehensive comparison). Clearly the Japanese crisis is much larger than the U.S. savings-and-loan crisis, and thus a full bailout would require significantly more resources than were deployed in the U.S. rescue.

Discussions of what to do about a bailout are further clouded by the fact that the government is already running a large deficit (estimated to be more than 6% of GDP by the IMF, 1998b). On top of this, Japan faces a significant upcoming Social Security problem. This has led the government to try to rein in the deficits. For instance, the Fiscal Structural Reform Act passed in November 1997 required the government to bring the deficit below 3% of GDP by fiscal year 2003. The weakness of the economy led the government to first push back the goal by two years in May 1998 and then eventually suspend the Act completely in December 1998. There is still strong sentiment, however, within the government for trying to begin cutting the deficit as soon as possible.

We draw two conclusions from this assessment. First, the fiscal concerns suggest it is important to focus on the amount of funds that would be needed to keep a large enough banking sector in place to serve borrowers once the crisis is over and the deregulation has taken hold. By looking ahead, one can try to determine

Table 4.16 **Review of Selected Countries' Banking Problems, 1980–1996**

Country	Period	Nonperforming loans[a]	Fiscal cost[b]	Comments
Argentina	1980–1982	9%	4%	37% of state-owned banks were nonperforming. Failed
	1989–1990	27%	N/A	banks held 40% of financial system assets.
	1995	N/A	N/A	45 of 205 institutions were closed or merged.
Australia	1989–1992	6%	1.90%	
Chile	1981–1987	16%	19%	8 banks intervened in 1981 (33% of outstanding loans, 11 in 1982–1983 (45% of outstanding loans).
Colombia	1982–1985	15%	5%	
Czech Rep.	1991–present	38%	12%	
Finland	1991–1994	13%	8%	Liquidity crisis in 1991.
France	1991–1995	9%	1%	
Indonesia	1992–1995	25%	2%	Nonperforming loans concentrated in state-owned banks.
Italy	1990–1995	10%	N/A	
South Korea	Mid-1980s	7%	N/A	
Malaysia	1985–1988	32%	5%	Loans loss equivalent to 1.4% of GDP.

		a	b	
Mexico	1982	N/A	N/A	Banking system nationalized.
	1994–present	12%	6%	
Niger	1983–present	50%	N/A	
Norway	1987–1993	6%	3%	
Philippines	1981–1987	30%	13%	
Sweden	1990–1993	18%	4%	
United States	1980–1992	4%	2%	1,142 S&L institutions and 1,395 banks were closed.
Uruguay	1981–1985	59%	31%	
Venezuela	1994–present	N/A	17%	

Sources: IMF (1998c) and Lindgren, Garcia, and Saal (1996).

[a]Estimated at peak of the crisis, as percentage of total loans.

[b]Estmated as percentage of annual GDP during the restructuring period.

the minimum amount of public money that will be needed. We can then compare the minimum estimates with the various proposals that have been made.

Second, in assessing the options that the banks have in developing new strategies it is important to allow for their weak capital positions. The flip side of the problems documented in Tables 4.14 and 4.15 is that the Japanese banks have very low levels of capital and are likely to have trouble raising much money in the capital markets in the short run. For instance, Moody's rating agency gives most of the major Japanese banks a financial strength rating of E or E+ (the two lowest ratings on their scale). Such banks are expected to "require periodic outside support." As a consequence the banks are unlikely to be able to purchase other large firms in order to acquire expertise. Similarly, bankruptcy seems like a real risk that would become more imminent if they were to undertake any large investments that have long payback periods. With this in mind, we sketch one scenario for the future of the Japanese banking sector.

5. Quantifying the Impending Shrinkage of the Japanese Banking Sector

The evidence presented in Section 3 suggests that large Japanese manufacturing companies have already reduced their reliance on banks to about the level of bank dependence observed in the United States. If our conjecture that other firms will soon be following this lead is correct, it is natural to ask what that might imply for the future of Japanese banks. The purpose of this section is to explore this question quantitatively.

5.1. MAINTAINED ASSUMPTIONS AND CAVEATS

Before diving into the calculation it is important to recognize several caveats about the exercise. First, our approach should be thought of as only calibrating the eventual size of a possible reduction in loan demand. We will explore several different assumptions about potential shifts, but all of our scenarios will take years to play out, so that the numbers that follow can at best be thought of as medium-run forecasts. We discuss the timing issues further in the next section.

Second, we are implicitly assuming that loan demand will drive the size of banks. Although we believe this is the most reasonable assumption to make, it could fail for a variety of reasons. For instance, depositors may continue to stuff their money into the banks even after all the Big Bang reforms are complete. For the most part we have also ignored the presence of the huge Japanese postal savings system (PSS). But there is a continuing debate about whether the PSS should be reformed. It is easy to imagine PSS reforms that wind up pushing large savings flows back toward the banks. We will briefly discuss the plausibility of the size of the implied adjustment in deposits after we present our findings.

Another risk of basing our forecasts on loan demand is the possibility that the banks could shed loans but pick up enough new lines of business so that they would not have to shrink.[38] Given that the Japanese banks currently have very little expertise outside of traditional banking and limited capital to buy such expertise, this scenario may seem unlikely right now. However, if some of these banks end up being sold to foreign financial services firms, it becomes much more realistic. In view of the rapidly changing competitive landscape of the Japanese financial services industry, we view this as a genuine possibility.

A third complication is that, because we focus on the bank-debt-to-asset ratio, one must take a stand on what will happen to the growth of corporate assets in order to draw any conclusions about the level of bank lending. Put differently, if corporate assets are growing, then forecasts of a declining bank-debt-to-asset ratio need not imply that the level of bank loans will fall. However, there are several pieces of evidence which suggest that an assumption of zero growth of corporate assets is a reasonable forecast for Japanese firms over the medium run.

One consideration is the recent evidence on asset growth. The Hojin Kigyo Tokei data suggest that total assets for all industries grew only at 1.7% a year from 1993 to 1998. Since new firms are added to the survey each year, the number in fact overstates the true growth rate of corporate assets. If this trend were to continue, then asset growth would be sufficiently low not to matter much for our purposes.

Another factor, which has been emphasized by the Japan Economic Research Center (1997), is that Japanese corporations are expected to begin reducing their financial assets (especially low-return liquid assets) as their financial management skills improve. The dwindling of the banks' practice of requiring compensating balances, together with the winding down of cross-shareholdings, will further contribute to the reduction of financial assets. Thus, even if a business-cycle recovery leads Japanese corporations to start increasing their fixed assets, declining financial assets will be a significant offsetting factor. For these reasons we believe that a reasonable benchmark is to translate any forecast declines in the bank-debt-to-asset ratio into one-for-one declines in bank lending.

Finally, we also recognize that this whole exercise ignores the potential general equilibrium feedbacks that could occur with large changes in intermediation. Partly this is out of necessity, since building a full model of the financial sector is not yet possible. However, this strategy can be partially justified if we maintain that the economic role of banks is tied to loan generation, particularly to smaller firms, and that for most other activities banks are redundant. Under this view, if the banks were to hold onto customers that might otherwise go to the capital market, the banks would have to match the capital-market rates. As these rates are increasingly determined by global forces, our assumption does not seem very unreasonable.

Keeping in mind all these caveats, we now explore what would happen if all Japanese corporations followed the lead of the large manufacturing firms that have already moved toward U.S. levels of bank dependence.[39] Since we want to consider several scenarios, we start by describing and defending the two basic assumptions that are common to all projections. After discussing these premises we outline the different scenarios that we consider.

The first key assumption is that loan demand for large and small firms can be aggregated within sectors. Thus, for each sector we treat all large firms and all small firms identically. We do not necessarily treat large firms and small firms symmetrically within or across sectors. Our main justification for this approach is the evidence in Table 4.6 regarding the relative stability of the bank borrowing patterns exhibited by the U.S. firms.

Our second key assumption involves the choice of sectors to be analyzed. The only really reliable data that we have for the United States pertain to manufacturing. We also have some information for large firms in the wholesale and retail trade sectors. In all of our projections we model these three sectors separately, in some cases making finer assumptions about what is happening within manufacturing. Unfortunately, this means that we have no U.S. data to guide us for other industries. For this reason we aggregate the remaining Japanese industries into an "other" category.

5.2. IMPLICATIONS OF U.S. BORROWING PATTERNS FOR JAPANESE LOAN DEMAND

There are three basic inputs into the forecasts that we report. The first piece of information is the 1998 total amounts of borrowing done by large and small firms across our four sectors of the Japanese economy. These numbers come from the *Hojin Kigyo Tokei,* and we follow the convention from Table 4.4 of defining large firms to have a book value of capital above ¥1 billion. The second element in the calculation is the initial observed levels of bank dependence for the large and small firms in the different sectors. These numbers can also be computed directly using the unpublished data we obtained.

Table 4.17 shows the 1998 distribution of bank borrowing and bank dependence for Japanese firms. Table 4.4 has already shown the noticeable differences in large- and small-firm bank dependence across sectors. We draw three further conclusions from Table 4.17. First, the "other" category covers over half of the bank borrowing done by firms in the sample. Since we have no representative data for these firms in the United States, this means that a significant portion of our forecast will be based purely on imputations for what might happen to this large, unmodeled segment of borrowers.

Second, the table shows that Japanese banks are already serving primarily small borrowers. Adding up loans made to small firms across all four sectors reveals that small borrowers receive about 64% of the bank credit tracked in the *Hojin Kigyo Tokei.* One check on the plausibility of our forecasts will be to see if they imply reasonable splits between the aggregate amount of large- and small-firm borrowing.

Table 4.17 **Distribution of the 1998 Quantity of Bank Borrowing and the Ratio of Bank Debt to Assets for Japanese Firms**

Sample A	Total bank borrowing (trillion yen)	Ratio of bank debt to assets	Fraction of category borrowing by small firms
All firms, all industries	445	0.3567	0.6432
Large firms, all industries	159	0.2761	
Small firms, all industries	286	0.4257	
All firms, manufacturing	92	0.2372	0.5738
Large firms, manufacturing	39	0.1647	
Small firms, manufacturing	53	0.3527	
All firms, wholesale trade	65	0.3392	0.7160
Large firms, wholesale trade	19	0.3027	
Small firms, wholesale trade	46	0.3562	
All firms, retail trade	41	0.4110	0.8193
Large firms, retail trade	7	0.2559	
Small firms, retail trade	34	0.4746	
All firms, other industriesb	247	0.4348	0.6207
Large firms, other industries	94	0.3796	
Small firms, other industries	153	0.4773	

Source: Ministry of Finance, *Hojin Kigyo Tokei.*

[a] Large firms are those that have book value of equity greater than ¥1 billion.

[b] All those which are not in manufacturing, wholesale trade, or retail trade.

Lastly, the table also indirectly shows the comprehensive coverage of the *Hojin Kigyo Tokei*. According to balance-sheet information for all banks, total lending should be about ¥450 trillion as of March 1998.[40] The coverage in our sample is ¥445 trillion. The close match actually masks two differences. One is that the survey includes borrowing from financial institutions such as credit unions that are not counted as banks. However, the survey also excludes borrowing done by truly tiny firms and individuals. It appears these two differences largely cancel.

The final ingredient needed for our forecasts is the assumed level of bank dependence that will prevail in the new steady state. Wherever possible we try to pin down these figures using the U.S. experience. Based on the QFR data from Table 4.6, we can get benchmarks for large and small manufacturing firms, large retail firms, and large wholesale firms. In fact, for the manufacturing sector we can do better and get two-digit-level data for the 14 industries. However, we have no solid data for the borrowing by U.S. firms in the "other" industries and therefore try several very different ways of calibrating the changes for these firms.

Since each hypothesized steady state requires eight assumptions about the bank-debt-to-asset ratios (two types of firms in four sectors), there are endless simulation possibilities. To simplify the reporting, we focus on three different variations that we believe should bound the implied adjustments. Each of these variations amounts to setting a switch that pins down two or more of the eight bank-debt-to-asset ratios.

The first set of alternatives involves differing assumptions about the behavior of Japanese manufacturing firms. Our simplest assumption is that the large and the small firms' bank dependences in Japan converge to the same levels that hold for the typical large and small manufacturing firms in the United States. We call this case the *simple manufacturing assumption*. This assumption ignores the differences in industrial composition between the two countries. Therefore, we repeat the calculations assuming instead that large and small Japanese firms' bank dependences converge on an industry-by-industry basis to the U.S. levels. Here we have data for 14 industries (shown in Tables 4.7 and 4.8), and we form a fifteenth category for the remaining firms. Although we conduct the calculations at the industry level, the results are aggregated back to the total manufacturing level for reporting purposes. We denote this second case as the *industry-adjusted manufacturing assumption*.

A second pair of assumptions relates to the treatment of small firms in the wholesale and retail sectors. Although the QFR gives us some data on U.S. borrowing propensities for large firms, there are no QFR data for small firms in these sectors. The only available data that we know of describing small-firm borrowing patterns in the United States are in the 1993 National Survey of Small Business Finances (NSSBF). This survey, conducted for the Board of Governors of the Federal Reserve System and the U.S. Small Business Administration, covers a nationally representative sample of very small businesses.[41]

Petersen and Rajan (1994) have analyzed these data and were kind enough to provide us with some simple tabulations of the ratio of bank debt to assets for these firms. These tabulations suggest that for the NSSBF the total debt ratio was between 0.18 and 0.24 for the sector groupings that we are analyzing (on an asset-weighted basis). We also learned that banks supply about half of all loans to these firms. However, there are two factors that make us hesitant to rely completely on these numbers in our simulations. One concern is that the firms in the NSSBF are very small. For instance, the top decile of firms in this sample includes firms with as little as $2.3 million in assets. The "small" Japanese firms that we are studying appear to be about 10 times bigger in terms of average assets.

Second, we know that bank borrowing becomes more important once firms grow. For instance, within the NSSBF sample, both the fraction of firms with any debt and the fraction of firms' debt owed to banks rise with firm size. Thus, we suspect that U.S. firms which would be comparable in size to our sample of Japanese firms would be more bank dependent in their financing than are the NSSBF firms. Nevertheless, it seems to us unlikely that this growth effect would be strong enough to push the firms' bank-debt-to-asset ratio much beyond 35% (which is the upper end of the range for the total debt-to-asset ratio in the NSSBF).

With these numbers as a reference we consider two different scenarios for the small trade firms. The first approach plays off of the small-firm-to-large-firm borrowing ratio that is observed in U.S. manufacturing. We apply this ratio to the level of the QFR for large firms in each sector to get a target level of small firms in each sector. We describe this assumption as identifying small trade firms' bank dependence using U.S. manufacturing data. Given the data in Table 4.6, we can see that this will imply bank-debt-to-asset ratios of about 0.23 and 0.32 for small retail and wholesale firms respectively.

Are these numbers reasonable? In the NSSBF sample they are 0.24 and 0.20, respectively. Using the figures from Table 4.6, this suggests that the ratio of the NSSBF levels of bank dependence to the levels found for large retailers and wholesalers is in line with the approximately 2:1 ratio found in U.S. manufacturing. Thus, we believe that unless the NSSBF data significantly understate small firms' bank dependence, assuming the small and large firms' differences are about the same (in ratio terms) across sectors seems plausible.

Our second approach exploits the fact that we can observe both small and large firms' borrowing patterns for the Japanese trade firms. In this case we get the steady-state target level of small-firm borrowing for wholesalers by multiplying the ratio of small-firm to large-firm bank dependence of wholesalers in Japan by the level of bank dependence for large U.S. wholesalers. In essence this assumes that both large and small Japanese wholesalers will adjust by the same *percentage*. We carry out the same calculations for retailers, and describe this assumption as identifying small trade firms' bank dependence using existing Japanese borrowing patterns. Using these assumptions, the target levels of bank dependence are 0.20 and 0.18 for small retail and wholesale firms respectively. These targets are both below the levels found in the NSSBF and thus are likely to lead us to overstate the decline in bank dependence.

Our third and last set of cases involves the assumptions about the levels of bank dependence for the other industries such as transportation, communications, services, and construction, where we have absolutely no QFR data. Based on the Japanese data shown in Table 4.17, we can see that as of 1998 these firms are more bank-dependent than the wholesale and retail firms. However, these firms also have more of their bank borrowing being done by large firms than is the case for either wholesalers or retailers. Considering both these factors, we use the average proportional adjustment done by the wholesale and retail trade firms to come up with the required adjustment for the large and small firms in the other category. More specifically, we assume that the ratio of the target level to the current level of bank dependence for large (small) "other" firms is equal to the weighted average of the target-to-current ratio for large (small) firms in wholesale and retail trade industries. In the NSSBF data the *level* of bank dependence for other sector firms is close to the level of bank dependence for trade firms. Thus, for small firms this assumption (which does not force the levels to converge) seems conservative.

Given the amount of guesswork involved constructing this benchmark, we consider a second refinement in which we assume these other firms only adjust half as much as the similar-sized average trade firm. We describe this refinement as *halfway convergence* to distinguish it from the first case above, which is called *full convergence*. Halfway convergence is an attempt to trade off our ignorance about how the large firms in this sector are financed against the presumption that capital-market financing is likely to displace at least some bank lending.

We summarize the pairs of alternatives and introduce some shorthand notation for describing them in Table 4.18. Since the three alternatives are mutually exclusive, we have eight total cases to consider. By comparing the scenarios where two of the three factors are held constant, we will be able to take "derivatives" to determine which of the convergence assumptions are most powerful. Below, as a sensitivity check, we also explore what happens if we do not assume that the large Japanese firms in wholesale and retail trade go all the way to the levels seen in the United States.

Table 4.19 compares the eight alternative steady states for future loan demand with the current levels of borrowing by Japanese firms. We draw five main conclusions from the calculations. First and most importantly, under all the scenarios we explore, *the U.S. benchmark implies a large impending decline in loan demand by Japanese firms.* The smallest hypothesized contraction suggests a decline of more than 25% in bank-loan demand. Even recognizing that these calculations refer to medium-term adjustments, we find the implied drops to be quite large. We discuss the transitional implications of this kind of shift in the concluding section.

Second, the forecasts all seem reasonable in their implications for the steady-state customer mix of the Japanese banks. The various scenarios all imply that small firms will account for between 62% and 72% of bank borrowing. These ranges seem to be plausible, and since this ratio was calculated endogenously, we find this to be a reassuring check on the methodology and our assumptions.

The other three conclusions concern which of the different assumptions appear to be quantitatively important. The different treatment for manufacturing firms does not appear to matter much. Holding constant our other assumption about the nonmanufacturing firms, the decision to take account of interindustry variation in manufacturing borrowing patterns only changes the implied level

Table 4.18 **Alternative Assumptions Regarding Loan Demand Used for Calculating Steady Loan Amounts**

Sector(s) directly affected	Shorthand name	Brief description
Manufacturing	Simple manufacturing convergence	Large and small Japanese manufacturing firms' bank fdependence converges to U.S. levels.
Manufacturing	Industry-adjusted manufacturing convergence	Within each of 15 anufacturing industries, large and small Japanese firms' bank dependence converges to the U.S. levels.
Wholesale and retail trade	Small trade firms' borrowing based on U.S. manufacturing	The ratio of bank dependence between U.S. large and small manufacturing is imposed to infer the target level of borrowing for small trade firms.
Wholesale and retail trade	Small trade firms' borrowing based on current Japanese patterns	The existing ratio of bank dependence between large and small firms within each sector is imposed to infer the target level of borrowing for small firms in each sector.
Other industries	Full convergence	Target levels for these firms are set to deliver an equal percentage adjustment in bank dependence for similar-sized trade firms.
Other industries	Halfway convergence	Target levels for these firms are set to deliver an equal percentage adjustment in bank dependence for similar-sized trade firms.

of borrowing by about 0.1%. The implied percentages of aggregate borrowing by small firms also do not move very much across these two assumptions.

In contrast, the other two assumptions make a big difference. These two assumptions interact, since the target levels assumed for the small trade firms also help determine the target level of borrowing by small firms in the other category. Whether or not the "other" firms adjust all the way or just halfway accounts for at least an 11-percentage-point difference in the total projected level of borrowing. Similarly, the two alternatives for the target levels of borrowing by small trade firms lead to an estimated difference of at least seven percentage points. As predicted, the benchmark based on the patterns in U.S. manufacturing produces smaller declines. Overall, the large size of these effects suggests that further work to narrow the uncertainty over which assumptions to rely upon is needed.

5.3. PLAUSIBILITY CHECKS FOR THE IMPLIED SHRINKAGE IN THE JAPANESE BANKING SECTOR

Given the large magnitudes of the projected decline in lending, one would like to see if there are other implications of this forecast that can be verified or alternative assumptions might overturn the prediction. We briefly describe three plausibility checks that we have conducted.

Our first test is to see whether the sectoral implications for drops in loan demand are credible. Implicit in all the estimates shown in Table 4.19 is the assumption that firms in the trade sector fully converge to the levels of bank dependence in the United States. Given the sizable existing gaps between large firms' bank dependence in the two countries documented in Tables 4.4 and 4.6, this is a fairly strong assumption. Indeed, one might also question whether it

Table 4.19 **Implied Reductions in Lending for Japanese Banks, Assuming U.S. Borrowing Patterns**

Assumption for manufacturing firms	Assumption for target of small trade firms	Assumption for target level in other industries	Implied decrease in lending	Fraction of total lending to small firms
Simple convergence	Based on U.S. manufacturing	Full convergence	41.5%	70.6%
		Half convergence	29.8%	67.4%
	Based on current Japanese patterns	Full convergence	52.4%	63.8%
		Half convergence	37.5%	63.4%
Industry-adjusted convergence	Based on U.S. manufacturing	Full convergence	41.6%	71.3%
		Half convergence	29.9%	68.0%
	Based on current Japanese patterns	Full convergence	52.5%	64.7%
		Half convergence	37.5%	64.1%

Note: Calculations assume that Japanese firms' borrowing patterns move toward U.S. levels. Benchmarks for the United States are taken from QFR for the 2nd quarter of 1998. For categories where the QFR data are not sufficient, the assumptions shown in columns 2 and 3 are used. These assumptions are described fully in the text and briefly in Table 4.18.

is prudent to forecast that bank dependence among small manufacturing firms will converge.

To address these concerns we conducted another set of simulations that presume far less convergence than is built into our baseline scenario. In these simulations, we maintained that only large manufacturing firms would fully converge to the same level of bank dependence. For all the remaining firms, Japanese firms were posited to move halfway toward the level of bank dependence that is observed in the United States. We view these assumptions as being extremely conservative, and yet they still imply reductions in the bank-debt-to-asset ratio between 22% and 29% (depending on which of the various assumptions are used to pin down the target levels for the small trade and other firms).

From Table 4.17 one can see why a reduction of at least 20% seems inevitable. The key observation is that the 1998 borrowing patterns in Japan do not involve much bank credit going to large trade firms. So varying their bank dependence does not have much aggregate effect. But about 42% of total bank lending is going to small firms in retail trade and other industries which have very high bank-debt-to-asset ratios. Even modest adjustments by these firms, combined with a continued decline in bank borrowing by the numerous large manufacturing firms, will generate a large decline in the bank-debt-to-asset ratio.

A second plausibility check involves exploring what our forecast will imply for depositors. The evidence in Section 3 suggested that in the past Japanese individuals have not abandoned the banks. One obvious question is whether our medium-term forecast implies incredible shifts in the behavior of depositors.

Figure 4.9 shows how (as of June 1998) Japanese households allocated their ¥1,200 trillion of financial assets. As we pointed out in Table 4.9, the Japanese households historically have heavily relied on deposits. Figure 4.9 indicates that currently 59% of household financial assets are in cash and deposits (including postal savings). A 30% rate of shrinkage for bank loans translates into ¥133 trillion reduction (using 1998 second-quarter data from *Quarterly Report of Incorporated Enterprise Statistics*). If we consider an extreme case, then deposits at these institutions also must fall by 30%. This would reduce the total amount of cash and deposits (including postal savings) by 18%, and its proportion in total financial wealth would fall to 48%. In the deposit-to-GDP ratio we would also expect a decline of 18%, which would reduce the ratio to 1.69.

Looking at Table 4.9, we note that a deposit-to-GDP ratio of 1.69 would still be higher than what is found in any of the other industrialized countries shown in the table. The prediction that the proportion of cash and deposits in the household financial assets will decline to 48% is also plausible—this would still leave Japan with more deposits relative to wealth than other G7 countries. Similarly, the Japan Economic Research Center (JERC) (1997) forecast that the proportion of cash and deposits in household financial assets will decline to 45% by 2010 and to 35% by 2020.

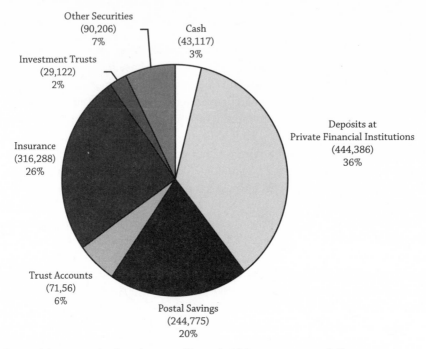

Figure 4.9 June 1998 distribution of households' savings across different instruments. Total wealth is ¥1,239,710 billion. (Category totals in billions of yen are shown in parentheses.). Source: Flow-of-funds accounts.

Their forecast is premised on a massive shift of household assets from deposits to investment trusts, which they see growing from their current level of 2.3% to 9.1% by 2010 and to 20% by 2020. In our scenario, if we assume all the decline in household deposits is matched by an increase in investment trusts, then we would expect the share of investment trusts to increase to 13%. Thus, our scenario also implies a huge boom for investment trusts.

There are many other analysts who forecast similar gains for investment trusts. For instance, Naito (1999) argues that because of a 1998 change in regulation, investment trusts are the most appealing financial product for households. The 1998 change allowed "company-based" investment trusts, which are closer to U.S. mutual funds than are "contract-based" investment trusts, which have existed in Japan throughout the postwar period. Perhaps more importantly, the change allowed banks and insurance companies to sell investment trusts at their counters starting in December 1998. According to the *Nihon Keizai Shinbum* (November 12, 1999), the amount of investment trusts purchased through banks and insurance companies through October 1999 was already ¥2.4 trillion. The total amount of investment trusts outstanding also had increased to ¥53 trillion. Given these considerations, we do not find the implications of forecasts for bank deposits to be implausible.

Finally, we ask whether there are any methods one might use to estimate the future size of the banking sector that do not rely on assumptions about loan demand. Moody's (1999) offers a prediction based on profitability. It argues that a reasonable benchmark is to assume that Japanese banks will need to have the same ratio of tangible equity to assets as is found in other countries.[42] Moody's estimates that as of March 1999 Japanese banks have a tangible-equity-to-asset ratio of 4.2%, while large U.S. banks have a ratio of around 6.5%. Assuming that equity issuance is not possible, this leads Moody's to forecast a reduction of over ¥100 trillion in risk-weighted assets to reach the U.S. level.[43] As they note, in the short run this can be done partially by securitizing loans. But ultimately this seems like another way to arrive at the conclusion that a large contraction in the sector is needed.

An alternative prediction is available from a long-term forecast published by the Japan Economic Research Center (1997). The JERC forecasts the levels of financial assets and liabilities for each sector identified by Bank of Japan flow-of-funds statistics. Although they do not reveal detailed assumptions behind their forecasts, some of their predictions are based on assumptions very similar to ours. For instance, they assume the Japanese corporate financing patterns will move toward the U.S. model. Looking at their forecasts for the market values of financial assets and liabilities, we find that their prediction implies that the bank-debt-to-asset ratio for the corporate sector will decline from 0.4461 in 1995 to 0.2395 by 2020. Since they use the market values, the numbers are not directly comparable to our numbers, but the magnitude of the decline in the bank-debt ratio (46% in 25 years) is as large as what our analysis implies.

Because they assume rather high rates of growth in assets (3.3% per year for 25 years), they forecast the level of bank loans to rise from ¥555 trillion in 1995 to ¥675 trillion in 2020 (0.76% growth per year). Assuming a more reasonable growth rate for assets, their prediction would imply a reduction in the absolute level of loans. For example, if the assets grew only at 1.5% per year, then bank loans would be projected to decline to ¥432 trillion by 2020, a 22% drop.

6. Conclusions

We have argued that the disequilibrium created by the gradual and lopsided deregulation in the Japanese financial system played an important role in the current banking crisis. The deregulation allowed large bank customers to quickly shift from bank financing to capital-market funding. Meanwhile, the deregulation did relatively little for savers, so banks continued to attract deposits. However, the deregulation of bank powers also was slow and gradual. This meant that if the banks were to keep lending they would need to seek out new customers. The banks did take on many new small customers. They also expanded their real estate lending. Ultimately these bets proved to be unprofitable.

In support of this story, we present a variety of evidence. One finding is that the banks' performance was worse in the 1990s than would be predicted just on the basis of macroeconomic conditions. Similarly, across banks, we find that the banks that were most at risk for losing customers to the capital markets performed worse than others. Both these results suggest the importance of the deregulation. We also document that large Japanese firms (particularly in manufacturing) are now almost as independent of bank financing as comparable U.S. firms.

We argue that once the Big Bang financial deregulation is complete, even the relatively small firms will start following the route already taken by the large firms by cutting their dependence on bank loans. By assuming other firms' financing patterns will also converge to the U.S. patterns, we calculated how much the Japanese banking sector must shrink in the steady state. Uniformly, the scenarios that we examined imply a massive contraction in the size of the traditional banking business in Japan.

While there are many reasons why one might quibble with the details of the calculations in Table 4.19, we think they at least provide a reasonable benchmark. To overturn the basic thrust of the calculations, one must argue that the basic U.S. benchmark is inappropriate. We believe we have made a compelling case that for the large firms the benchmark is reasonable. For the small firms, we concede that there is much more guesswork involved. But, even if we take our most conservative scenario where full convergence in bank dependence is only assumed for large manufacturing firms and all remaining firms move halfway toward the U.S. levels, we still end up projecting more than a 20% decline in loan demand. This forecast is comparable to the one Moody's (1999) arrived at by making quite different assumptions.

What would a 20% decline imply for the configuration of the banking sector? There are many possible ways that this could shake out. However, given the current debate over how much public money should be used to prop up the banks, one natural question to ask is how many weak banks would have to completely exit to eliminate the excess capacity in the industry. To pursue this, we took the ranking of 142 Japanese banks as of September 1998, put forward in the March 1999 issue of *Kin'yu Business,* and calculated the share of loans for each bank.[44] This allows us to examine how many banks must exit so that the cumulative shrinkage in loans is sufficient to bring the system to its new steady state.

We find that a 20% reduction in lending requires a complete exit of the lowest-rated 45 banks of a total of 142 banks. These include Long-Term Credit Bank (LTCB) and Nippon Credit Bank (NCB), which were nationalized in late 1998, and the regional banks that were put into receivership in the first half of 1999. Perhaps more importantly, this set of 45 banks would include three of the 15 major banks (Daiwa, Tokai, and Chuo Trust) that received a government capital injection in March 1999. If we consider a 30% shrinkage, which is closer to the average of the Table 4.19 estimates, the number of weak banks that would have to be eliminated jumps to 69, including three more (Yokohama, Asahi, and Toyo

Trust) of the 15 banks which received government money. Even if the relatively healthy banks can somehow be convinced to cut back on some of their lending, it is hard to escape the conclusion that any transition looks like it will involve the exit of a number of major banks.

Because any assessment of banks' health is somewhat subjective, we also looked at the Moody's Investor Service (1999) rankings. They estimate the "financial strength" of 51 Japanese banks. Their ratings range from B (Shizuoka Bank) to E (10 banks including LTCB and NCB). Moody's assessment differs from the *Kin'yu Business* ranking in that it focuses on solvency and looks at not only obligations of the parent but also those of supported subsidiaries. Nonetheless, the *Kin'yu Business* ranking and Moody's rating identify very similar sets of weak banks. For example, 10 of the 45 lowest-ranked banks in *Kin'yu Business* are rated by Moody's, and of those eight have the lowest rating (E) and the other two are the next lowest rating (E+), Among *Kin'yu Business's* 69 worst banks, 15 are rated by Moody's, and of those nine have E and the other six have E+. Thus, the weakest banks in the *Kin'yu Business* ranking are also rated very low by Moody's.

Given this overlap, it is therefore not surprising that if we base our exit forecasts on the Moody's data we get a very similar picture. If we assume that 10 banks with E ratings will disappear, their cumulative loans amount to 11.5% of total loans in the banking sector. Three of 15 banks (Daiwa, Chuo Trust, and Mitsui Trust) that have received capital injections are included in this group. If all the banks with E ratings and E+ ratings were to exit, their cumulative loans would be 49% of total loans, suggesting a much bigger contraction than we expect. However, included in the set of E and E+ banks are 13 of the 15 banks that received government money, so it still seems like a nontrivial fraction of these banks may be redundant.

How long will it take for such a shift in the Japanese banking to be completed? The speed of adjustment will primarily depend on three factors: how fast corporations adjust their financing, how fast households shift their funds out of bank deposits, and how fast the banking industry is reorganized. The previous experience suggests that the adjustment by corporate borrowers will be fairly quick. Although the restrictions on corporate financing options were only gradually loosened, many firms adjusted quickly and most completed their adjustments in less than 10 years. The deregulation of the remaining restrictions on corporate financing will be rapid. Thus, we expect the adjustment on the corporate finance side to be complete well within 10 years.

How fast will the households move? Because the most significant elements of the liberalization of savers' options have started only very recently, this question is much harder to answer. As we saw above, the dependence on deposits by Japanese households starts from such a high level that even a modest change toward the patterns observed in other OECD economies would be sufficient to support our forecast. We believe that a modest shift can take place in 10 years, but there is a considerable amount of uncertainty in this conjecture.

Finally, the shrinkage of bank loans will imply a substantial exit in the banking industry unless Japanese banks shift away from traditional banking business very aggressively. The speed of such a reorganization obviously depends on the government's policy stance toward bank failures. As we saw in Section 4, the Japanese government seems finally to have begun addressing the bad-loan problem. The next step will require more closures of insolvent banks. If the current tough stance of the FSA and the FRC continues, the days of the convoy system of rescues will be over.

Nevertheless, once the restructuring begins in earnest, we imagine that it will take several years for the doomed banks to exit. Importantly, the mergers among the largest banks in the fall of 1999 are not the kind of restructuring we have in mind, unless contrary to the initial descriptions of these alliances, they facilitate reductions in assets that would not otherwise be possible. Combinations of organizations that do not promote downsizing are likely to be counterproductive. A particularly salient benchmark is Hokkaido Takushoku, which, although it has been dead for more than two years, still has most of its assets in the banking system. Our forecasts require that the assets of a failed institution be disposed of, not merely moved into other banks. The Hokkaido Takushoku experience suggests that the reorganization could take years, although we see no reason to expect it to take more than a decade. Thus, overall, we expect the transition to the new steady state to be fairly complete by the end of the next decade.

Notes

* This article was originally published in *NBER Macroeconomics Annual, 14, 2000.* It is reprinted with permission of the original publisher with only minor alternations to adhere to the style of Oxford University Press. Kashap's work was supported through a grant from the National Science Foundation to the National Bureau of Economic Research. Hoshi's work was supported by a grant from Tokyo Center for Economic Research. The views expressed in this paper do not necessarily reflect those of the Federal Reserve Bank of Chicago or the Federal Reserve System.

1. For example, both the International Monetary Fund (IMF) (1998a) and the Organisation for Economic Co-operation and Development (OECD 1998) country reports on Japan for 1998 point to the banking problems as a key factor in causing the post-November 1997 slowdown in growth. The Japanese government's 1998 Economic White Paper also identifies problems in the financial sector an important factor in prolonging the recession (Economic Planning Agency 1998).

2. For instance, Bayoumi (1998) finds that fluctuations in asset prices played an important role in recent Japanese business cycles and that the shocks were mostly transmitted through bank lending. Without associated changes in bank loans, asset price fluctuations would not have affected the real economy very much, he argues. Likewise, Ogawa and Kitasaka (1998) report that small firms were especially hard hit by the decline in bank loans in the 1990s and that small- and large-firm investment differentials have emerged as the slow growth has continued. Motonishi and Yoshikawa (1998) find that the index of (firms' perception of) banks' willingness to lend (loose or tight) in BOJ's *Tankan* survey worsened substantially from late 1997 and contributed to slow growth, especially at small firms. Finally, Woo (1998) argues that since 1997 there has been a marked shift in bank-loan supply that has contributed to the weak growth in 1997 and 1998.

3. For a discussion of the loan purchasing program by the Cooperative Credit Corporation see Packer (1998). For a review of the *jusen* problems see Milhaupt and Miller (1997).

4. For more details on the restructuring plans, see Choy (1999). Individual restructuring plans in Japanese can be downloaded from the Financial Reconstruction Commission website (www.frc.go.jp).

5. For instance, Lawrence Summers, while he was U.S. Deputy Secretary of the Treasury, was reported to have suggested to Hakuo Yanagisawa, chairman of the Financial Reconstruction Committee, that another round of capital injections may be necessary *(Nikkei Net Interactive,* February 26, 1999.)

6. See Fukao (1999) for a summary and an analysis of the two laws, and Corbett (1999a) for a more complete history of the policies leading up to the fall 1998 legislation.

7. For example, Atkinson (1998) argues that there will be only two to four major banks in Japan. We believe it is more important to focus on the size of the sector than on the number of banks.

8. See Patrick (1967, 1971, 1972) and Hoshi and Kashyap (2004) for further details.

9. For instance, Patrick (1972) examined financial intermediation in this period and found that the "capital issue markets played a relatively minor role" (112).

10. In a *gensaki* transaction, a seller sells a security to a buyer with an agreement to repurchase the same security at a certain price on a certain future date. The *gensaki* market is open to all corporations. In a *tegata* transaction, a seller sells a bill before its maturity to a buyer at a discount. The *tegata* market is restricted to financial institutions.

11. However, some self-regulation by the security houses continued, so that firms in the 1980s were still forced to satisfy versions of the bond issuance criteria in order to be able to issue debt abroad. Although Japanese banks technically could underwrite foreign bond issues by Japanese corporations through the banks' foreign subsidiaries, the three-bureaus agreement of 1975 suggested that banks should "pay due respect to the experience gained by and the mandate given to the Japanese securities firms" (Rosenbluth 1989, 152). In practice, the three-bureaus agreement has been interpreted to prohibit subsidiaries of Japanese banks from becoming the lead underwriters of bond issues by Japanese corporations. Thus the Japanese banks did not have much say about the self-regulation of foreign bond issues.

12. There are many good summaries of the provisions of the Big Bang. Two recent guides are Craig (1998) and Toyama (1998).

13. There are several studies that focus on drawing a more comprehensive picture of what caused the current banking problem in Japan. Cargill, Hutchison, and Ito (1997) list both macroeconomic conditions generated by loose monetary policy in the late 1980s and reduced corporate dependence on bank financing, on which we focus, as contributing factors to the problem. They also list other factors such as government deposit guarantees and regulatory forbearance. Cargill (1999) gives a similarly comprehensive list. By estimating some cross-section regressions, Ueda (1999) confirms the importance of both macroeconomic conditions and financial deregulation in bringing about the banking problem.

14. For instance, see Cargill, Hutchison, and Ito (1997), Cargill (1999), Ueda (1999), Lincoln (1998), Hutchison (1998), and Hoshi and Kashyap (2004).

15. In what follows we use this exchange rate. We use GDP deflators when it is necessary to convert nominal amounts into real amounts.

16. For example, the 1997 fourth-quarter survey was sent to 23,475 firms, and the response rate was over 80% (19,007).

17. This ratio can also be thought of as the product of the bank-debt-to-total-debt ratio and the total-debt-to-total-asset ratio. This decomposition distinguishes the total amount of leverage from the sources of financing for borrowers. For our purposes we believe this distinction is not very helpful, since the banks presumably care about their total lending. To a first approximation it probably does not matter if they are losing business over the kind of long periods that we are studying because of overall deleveraging as opposed to more competition from other funding sources. We also checked that using book-value data would not paint a misleading picture. A quick comparison of data on national income accounts in Japan and the United States suggested that the gap between the current value of assets (the analogue to market value) and

the historical value was similar in the two countries. Thus, we see no obvious biases from using book-value data for both countries.

18. Of the 5,363 large firms, 2,192 were in manufacturing, 941 were in trade (wholesale or retail), and the remaining 2,230 were in other industries. There were 1,161,179 small firms in the 1998 survey; with 232,313 in manufacturing, 363,707 in trade, and 565,159 in the other industries.

19. The nine companies in question are Mitsui Bussan, Itochu, Kanematsu, Sumitomo and Company, Tomen, Nissho Iwai, Nichimen, Marubeni, and Mitsubishi and Company. When they are excluded, the ratio of bank debt to assets is much lower in most years (e.g., 0.248 in 1998 as opposed to 0.431), and in 1998 it is slightly lower than in the early 1970s. We have heard several anecdotes suggesting that this discrepancy arises because the large trading companies took on considerable bank debt in the 1980s in order to set up subsidiaries to enter the real estate business.

20. See Aoki and Patrick (1994) for a comprehensive study of the tight dependence of Japanese firms on banks. There is no contradiction in saying that the past relationships for the large firms may have been valuable but were not sustained after deregulation. This will be the case if, as capital markets improved, the costs of being tied to the banks was rising. See Hoshi and Kashyap (2004) for further discussion on this point.

21. See Gertler and Gilchrist (1994) for more discussion of the QFR.

22. Toward the end of the 1990s, however, the bank dependence of the small Japanese manufacturing firms did decline. We expect this pattern to continue after the Big Bang.

23. We thank Itsuko Takemura for providing these data.

24. The ¥1billion cutoff is closer to a $10 million cutoff. However, using the published data on all manufacturing firms, we verified that the firms with between $10 and $25 million in assets are of limited importance. Thus, we believe that the size mismatch is not likely to mislead us about the general trends in bank dependence in the two countries.

25. We thank Bob Uriu for pointing this out.

26. When a career official at the Ministry of Finance was arrested on corruption charges, the most important favor that he supposedly provided to the security firms was quickly approving the prospectuses of new investment funds that they proposed (*Nihon Keizai Shimbun*, March 6, 1998, evening edition).

27. These statistics are built up from flow-of-funds data that show owners of domestically issued corporate bonds including convertibles and warrant bonds. The corporate bonds held by government financial institutions are excluded from the total to isolate the corporate bonds held by the private sector. Since the privatization of NTT in 1985 and JR in 1987 reclassified their bonds from public bonds to corporate bonds, the number includes NTT (JR) bonds that were issued before 1985 (1987) and had not been retired as of the end of 1990 in addition to the net purchases of corporate bonds.

28. At the aggregate level corporate borrowing was rising, since the large firms were tapping the bond markets and the smaller firms were increasing their bank borrowing. The savings that were funding this seem to have previously been going toward financing the government deficit, which was falling in the late 1980s.

29. This shows the practice referred to as *fukumi keiei*, hidden asset management. The Japanese banks and large firms often hold shares which were purchased long ago and therefore have unrealized capital gains. These firms sometimes try to smooth their earnings by selling the shares when operating profits are low. Table 4.11 shows this clearly. To protect their cross-shareholding the sellers often buy back the shares after realizing the capital gains.

30. The corrected return on assets is calculated as (current profits-gains from sales of stocks and other securities + losses from sales of stocks and other securities + losses from devaluation of stock holdings) / (total assets at the beginning of the period).

31. These data are taken from the *Bank of Japan Economic Statistics Monthly*. The small firms here are defined to be those that are not large according to the Bank of Japan definition: large firms are those firms which have more than ¥100 million in equity and more than 300 regular

employees. The definition of small firms here roughly corresponds to that in the other tables in this paper.

32. Using instead the nominal call rate along with a separate inflation variable made no difference in what follows.

33. Nippon Trust and Banking was excluded from the analysis because its return on assets is dramatically lower than all the other banks in the sample for the 1990s. Including this bank noticeably changes the results, especially the ones concerning the effect of loans to listed firms. There are some other trust banks and long-term credit banks that experienced very low return on assets for the 1990s, but none of them individually influences the regression results in any significant way. When we ran the same set of regressions excluding all trust banks and long-term credit banks, we obtained qualitatively similar results.

34. One problem with using listed firms is that we do not know if they in fact qualified to issue bonds. For some of the smaller listed firms the bias in the bond issuance rules may have been a problem.

35. At least ex post, property lending was risky. For example, four major banks (Sanwa, Sumitomo, Dai-ichi Kangyo, and Tokyo-Mitsubishi) published data showing nonperforming loans broken out by the industry. For these banks, between 16% and 40% of total nonperforming loans are to the real estate sector, and for all the banks besides Dai-ichi Kangyo this is the leading sector for nonperforming loans.

36. See the footnotes to Table 4.14 for a complete list of when various banks were dropped from the official statistics.

37. Private-sector analysts also point out that there are probably large losses in financial institutions besides the banks.

38. There are also factors that push in the other direction. For instance, these calculations ignore the possibility of foreign lenders taking away business from the Japanese banks.

39. The whole exercise is very much in the spirit of Rajan and Zingales (1998).

40. This figure excludes overdrafts. We believe that excluding overdrafts makes sense because such commitment lending is unlikely to be affected by the Big Bang. See Kashyap, Rajan, and Stein (1999) for theoretical support for this argument and empirical evidence showing that even in the United States the commitment business is dominated by banks.

41. The target population is all for-profit, nonfinancial, nonfarm business enterprises that had fewer than 500 employees and were in operation as of year-end 1992. The public data set contains 4,637 firms and describes all the loans each firm has as of year-end 1992, as well as the institutions that these loans came from.

42. The ratio they consider is Tier 1 capital (as defined by the Basle banking accord) minus state capital minus preferred securities, divided by risk-weighted assets (see Moody's 1999, 24, for details).

43. Loans are roughly ¥450 trillion, so if the reduction were made entirely by cutting loans, this would imply a 22.2% decline.

44. They rank ordinary banks (city banks and regional banks) and trust banks separately by looking at size (measured by the average amount of funds), profitability (measured by business-profits-to-asset ratio and interest margin), efficiency (measured by expense ratio and interest income per employee), and solvency (measured by capital ratio, nonperforming-loan ratio, provision ratio for nonperforming loans, and market-to-book ratio of securities holdings). In order to combine two separate rankings, we reranked city banks, trust banks, and a long-term credit bank (Industrial Bank of Japan) using eight of the nine indicators used by *Kin'yu Business*. The last indicator (market-to-book ratio of securities holdings) was not easily available. We established the rankings of trust banks and IBJ in the list of ordinary banks by comparing them with city banks included in the list. For example, we rank Sumitomo Trust after DKB (ranked 12 in *Kin'yu Business*) and before Fuji (ranked 28), since Sumitomo Trust is located more or less between DKB and Fuji according to the indicators we are looking at. Finally, we added the two banks that were nationalized in late 1998, Long-Term Credit Bank of Japan and Nippon Credit Bank, at the bottom of the ranking.

References

Aoki, M., and H. Patrick. 1994. *The Japanese Main Bank System: Its Relevance for Developing and Transforming Economies*. New York: Oxford University Press.

Atkinson, D. 1998. "Nihon ni oote ginko ha 2–4 ko shika hitsuyo denai" (Japan needs no more than 2–4 major banks). Goldman Sachs Investment Research.

Bank of Japan, Bank Supervision Department. 1997. "Sin'yo risuku kanri no koudo-ka ni muketa jiko satei no katsuyo ni tsuite" (Using self-examination to improve credit risk management). *Nihon Ginko Geppo*, October, 1–16.

Bayoumi, T. 1998. "The Morning After: Explaining the Slowdown in Japanese Growth in the 1990s." International Monetary Fund, working paper.

Berger, A., and G. Udell. 1995. "Lines of Credit and Relationship Lending in Small Firm Finance." *Journal of Business* 68, 351–381.

Cai, J., K. C. Chan, and T. Yamada. 1996. "The Performance of Japanese Mutual Funds." Columbia University, Center on Japanese Economy and Business, Working Paper 107.

Cargill, T. 1999. "What Caused the Current Banking Crisis?" University of Nevada, Reno. Manuscript.

Cargill, T., M. M. Hutchison, and T. Ito. 1997. *The Political Economy of Japanese Monetary Policy*. Cambridge, MA: MIT Press.

Choy, J. 1999. "Japan's Banking Industry: The 'Convoy' Disperses in Stormy Seas." Japan Economic Institute Report 10A.

Corbett, J. 1999a. "Crisis, What Crisis? The Policy Response to Japan's Banking Crisis." In C. Freedman, ed., *Why Did Japan Stumble? Causes and Cures*. Northhampton, MA: Edward Elgar.

———. 1999b "Japan's Banking Crisis in International Perspective." In M. Aoki and G. Saxonhouse, eds., *Finance, Government, and Competitiveness*. Oxford: Oxford University Press.

Craig, V. 1998. "Financial Deregulation in Japan." *FDIC Banking Review* 11(3), 1–12.

Dale, R. 1992. *International Banking Deregulation: The Great Banking Experiment*. Malden, MA: Blackwell Publishers.

Economic Planning Agency. 1998. *Keizai Hakusho* (Economic white paper).

Fiorillo, J. 1999. Private correspondence.

Fukao, M. 1999. "Re-capitalizing Japan's Banks: The Functions and Problems of the Financial Revitalization Act and the Bank Recapitalization Act." Keio University. Manuscript.

Gertler, M., and S. Gilchrist. 1994. "Monetary Policy, Business Cycles, and the Behavior of Small Manufacturing Firms." *Quarterly Journal of Economics* 59, 309–340.

Gorton, G., and R. Rosen 1995. "Corporate Control, Portfolio Choice, and the Decline of Banking." *Journal of Finance* 50, 1377–1420.

Hamada, K., and A. Horiuchi. 1987. "The Political Economy of Financial Markets." In K. Yamamura and Y. Yasuba, eds., *The Political Economy of Japan*, vol. 1, *The Domestic Transformation*. Stanford, CA: Stanford University Press.

Hoshi, T., and A. Kashyap. 2004. *Corporate Financing and Governance in Japan: The Road to the Future*. Cambridge, MA: MIT Press.

———. 1999b. "The Japanese Banking Crisis: Where Did It Come From and How Will It End?" National Bureau of Economic Research Working Paper No. 7520.

Hutchison, M. 1998. "Are All Banking Crises Alike? University of California, Santa Cruz, working paper.

International Monetary Fund (IMF). 1998a. "Japan Selected Issues." International Monetary Fund Staff Country Report 98/113.

———. 1998b. *International Financial Statistics*. Washington, DC: International Monetary Fund.

———. 1998c. *World Economic Outlook May 1998*. Washington, DC: International Monetary Fund.

Iwahara, S., Y. Okina, Y. Kanemoto, and K. Narisawa. 1999. "Kin'yu kikan no furyo saiken no jittai to hatan shori sukiimu" (The reality of bad loans at financial institutions and schemes to deal with failures). *Jurist* (Tokyo) 1151, 10–36.

Japan Economic Research Center. 1997. *2020 nen no Nihon no Kin'yu* (Japanese finance in 2020). (Tokyo) Japan Economic Research Center.

Jenkinson, T. J. 1990. "Initial Public Offerings in the United Kingdom, the United States and Japan." *Journal of the Japanese and International Economies* 3(4), 428–449.

Kashyap, A., R. Rajan, and J. Stein. 1999. "Banks as Liquidity Providers: An Explanation for the Coexistence of Lending and Deposit-Taking." National Bureau of Economic Research Working Paper No. 6962.

Lincoln, E. 1998. "Japan's Financial Problems." *Brookings Papers on Economic Activity* 2, 347–385.

Lindgren, C.-J., G. Garcia, and M. I. Saal. 1996. *Bank Soundness and Macroeconomic Policy.* Washington, DC: International Monetary Fund.

Milhaupt, C. J., and G. P. Miller 1997. "Cooperation, Conflict, and Convergence in Japanese Finance: Evidence from the 'Jusen' Problem." *Law and Policy in International Business* 29, 1–78.

Moody's Investors Service. 1999. *Moody's Banking System Outlook.*

Motonishi, T., and H. Yoshikawa. 1998. "Causes of the Long Stagnation of Japan during the 1990s: Financial or Real." Tokyo University, working paper.

Naito, K. 1999. "Nihon-ban Big Bang ni yotte toujousuru kin'yu shohin no kojin kin'yu shisan unyo he no eikyo" (The impact of new financial products introduced by the Japanese Big Bang on financial investments by individuals). Fuji Research Institute Research Paper.

Ogawa, K., and S. Kitasaka. 1998. "Bank Lending in Japan: Its Determinants and Macroeconomic Implications." Osaka University, working paper.

Ohara, Y. 1996. "Japan's Banking: The Darkest Hour before Dawn. The Future Is in the Hands of MoF." Columbia University, Center on Japanese Economy and Business, Working Paper 127.

———. 1998. *Ginko Sector One Point* (Banking sector one point). (Tokyo) SBC Warburg.

Ohmura, K., and H. Kawakita 1992. *Zeminaru Nihon no Kabushiki Shijo* (Seminar Japanese stock markets). Tokyo: Toyo Keizai Shinpo-sha.

Organisation for Economic Co-operation and Development. 1998. *OECD Economic Surveys 1998: Japan.* Paris: OECD.

Packer, F. 1998. "The Disposal of Bad Loans in Japan: The Case of CCPC." Federal Reserve Bank of New York. Manuscript.

Patrick, H. T. 1967. "Japan, 1868–1914." In R. Cameron, O. Crisp, H. T. Patrick, and R. Tilly, eds., *Banking in the Early Stages of Industrialization.* New York: Oxford University Press.

———. 1971. "The Economic Muddle of the 1920s." In J. W. Morley, ed., *Dilemmas of Growth in Prewar Japan.* Princeton, NJ: Princeton University Press.

———.1972. "Finance, Capital Markets and Economic Growth in Japan." In A. W. Sametz, ed., *Financial Development and Economic Growth.* New York: New York University Press.

Peek, J., and E. Rosengren. 1997a. "The International Transmission of Financial Shocks: The Case of Japan." *American Economic Review* 87, 495–505.

———. 1997b. "Collateral Damage: Effects of the Japanese Real Estate Collapse on Credit Availability and Real Activity in the United States." Federal Reserve Bank of Boston Working Paper 97–95.

Petersen, M., and R. Rajan. 1994. "The Benefits of Firm-Creditor Relationships: Evidence from Small Business Data." *Journal of Finance* 49, 3–37.

Rajan, R., and L. Zingales. 1998. "Financial Dependence and Growth." *American Economic Review* 88, 559–586.

Rosenbluth, F. M. 1989. *Financial Politics in Contemporary Japan.* Ithaca, NY: Cornell University Press.

Second Financial System Committee of the Financial System Research Council. 1989. Interim Report on "a New Japanese Financial System." English translation by the Federation of Bankers Associations of Japan.

Takeda, M., and P. Turner. 1992. "The Liberalisation of Japan's Financial Markets: Some Major Themes." Bank of International Settlements, working paper.

Toyama, H. 1998. "The Monetary Regulatory and Competitive Implications of the Restructuring of the Japanese Banking Industry." Bank of Japan, working paper.

Ueda, K. 1999. "Causes of the Japanese Banking Instability in the 1990s." Bank of Japan. Manuscript.

White, Halbert. 1980. "A Heteroskedasticity-Consistent Covariance Matrix Estimator and a Direct Test for Heteroskedasticity." *Econometrica* 48, 817–838.

Woo, D. 1998. "In Search of 'Capital Crunch': Supply Factors behind the Credit Slowdown in Japan." International Monetary Fund, working paper.

CHAPTER 5

The Impact of the International Financial Crisis on Asia and the Pacific

HIGHLIGHTING MONETARY POLICY CHALLENGES FROM A NEGATIVE ASSET PRICE BUBBLE PERSPECTIVE

Andrew Filardo

1. Introduction

The international financial crisis of the late 2000s has revived interest in asset price bubble research. For some, the event confirmed the enduring relevance of studying asset price bubbles in our economies. For others, it was a realization that asset price bubbles are of much greater significance than previously thought.

The financial and policy preconditions that foster "frothy" asset prices which characterize bubbles have been the focus of considerable attention. While doubtless important, it is not the only aspect that requires greater understanding. We also need to develop a better understanding of the whole life-cycle of asset price bubbles, from their origins, to their expansion and spread, the inevitable collapse, and the aftermath that has to be cleaned up. It is increasingly recognized that researchers must not treat bubbles as one-off, exogenous events. The challenge is to develop a more holistic approach, and then build into our policy models endogenous bubble behavior. Such behavior may indeed be rare but nonetheless has its origins in a number of avoidable factors, not least being some combination of financial fragility, flawed policy frameworks, and poor risk management decisions.

This paper contributes to our understanding of asset price bubbles by looking at assets when they are severely underpriced, i.e., when there are negative asset price bubbles. Generally, negative asset price bubbles are an underrepresented protagonist in most crisis stories, and this has certainly been the case in the recent international financial crisis. The particular illustration for this paper comes from an examination of the financial market spillovers from the West to Asia and the Pacific.

Where did the spillovers come from and how will the crisis end?[1] While there are many different ways to conceptualize the spillovers, this paper will show how cross-border spillovers led to the severe underpricing of various types of assets in Asia and the Pacific. And, just as the policy response to the bursting of the dot-com bubble in the United States may have contributed to the housing problems in the 2000s, there are concerns that accommodative monetary policy in response to the negative asset price bubble and associated macroeconomic fallout may be laying the foundation for a round of positive asset price bubbles.

The paper begins with a brief discussion of a negative asset price bubble and a narrative of the international financial crisis in Asia and the Pacific. Prior to September 2008, the international financial crisis had had a limited impact on Asia-Pacific markets. To be sure there were periods of unusual stress but, by and large, the region was more focused on macroeconomic policy issues throughout much of the year. That all changed in late 2008 as the region, despite its strong economic and financial fundamentals, entered what was to become a sharp V-shaped business cycle. Through the lens of a negative asset price bubble perspective, this paper helps to shed new light on the unusual dynamics as well as the policy trade-offs faced during the crisis and afterward. Asia and the Pacific economies are particularly useful "laboratories" to examine these phenomena because of the diverse economic, financial, and policy frameworks in place.

The paper also presents a simple model of endogenous asset price bubbles to clarify some of the policy issues. The model assumes there are two regions of the world that are susceptible to domestic asset price bubbles. This type of model emphasizes the highly persistent nature of financial shocks associated with boom-bust dynamics and the potential spillovers across geographic borders. An asset price bubble in one economy can influence the likelihood of an asset price bubble in the other economy. Possibly most important, the actions of the policymaker in one region can affect not only the occurrence of a bubble in its domestic market but also the occurrence of a bubble in the other region. This type of model also elevates the importance of tail risk considerations for policymakers, opening up consideration of more complex monetary policy trade-offs than in conventional macroeconomic models.

The paper then explores the implications, combining both the narrative from the crisis and the implications of the theoretical model to understand better the regional policy trade-offs that occurred during the international financial crisis. In addition to emphasizing the critical importance of having strong economic and financial fundamentals going into a crisis period, it also highlights the value of monetary policymakers adopting state-dependent policy frameworks. During normal times, monetary policy focused on price stability makes sense. During crisis times, the priorities of a central bank may need to be adjusted by putting more weight on financial stability than on short-term inflation stability. This comes down to placing more weight on tail risks when making policy decisions. Practically, this means that short-term deviations from (implicit and explicit) inflation targets may be appropriate, if not optimal, when coming out of a crisis.

The paper proceeds as follows. Section 2 lays out the basic intuition of a negative asset price bubble. Section 3 reviews the Asia-Pacific experience during the recent international financial crisis, highlighting aspects of this new bubble perspective. Section 4 then presents a simple international monetary policy model with negative asset price bubbles to explore the theoretical channels of spillovers and the policy trade-offs. Section 5 describes results. Section 6 draws on the historical narrative and theoretical findings to evaluate the policy implications. Section 7 offers some conclusions.

2. Conceptualizing Negative Bubbles

An asset price bubble can be thought of as the gap between an asset price's valuation and its theoretical value based on fundamentals. Positive asset price bubbles arise when market prices exceed the fundamental value and, analogously, negative ones when market prices fall below the fundamental value.[2]

While this symmetry is appealing, the dynamics of positive and negative asset price bubbles are likely to be asymmetric. Positive price bubbles, be they in equities, housing, foreign exchange, or other widely held assets, are generally thought to inflate gradually over time.[3] The main driver is typically assumed to be overconfidence that manifests itself in elevated risk appetite (technically, less risk aversion) and overly optimistic expectations of future earnings. While the prices are misaligned with longer-term fundamentals, the origin of big bubbles often corresponds to periods of history when innovations, real or financial, foster an environment of unbridled optimism about the future. And, they can be egged on when policymakers and other influential institutions and people rally support along the way by arguing that this time it is different. In such a situation, optimism breeds more optimism until significant doubts surface about the sustainability of the upward trend in asset prices. The break in confidence, even something that, in retrospect, might seem relatively minor, signals the beginning of the tumble in asset prices as the bubble bursts. Macroeconomically relevant bubbles are those that, when they collapse, have severe consequences for the real economy.

Negative asset price bubbles, in contrast, would seem to come in a wider variety of types. On the one hand, negative asset price bubbles can develop and burst in a way analogous to positive asset price bubbles, as irrational beliefs permeate an economy; for the negative asset price bubbles it would be irrational pessimism. One can envision this bubble process building over time slowly, as pessimism and risk aversion breed further pessimism and risk aversion. Over time asset prices would underperform historical norms and the overpricing of risk would eventually raise the attractiveness of the assets as an investment. Ultimately, economic and financial fundamentals reassert themselves, confidence returns, and the negative bubble deflates—it could deflate either with a pop or with a fizzle.

On the other hand, negative asset price bubbles could start more dramatically. In this case, a sudden negative overreaction to current events leads to a significant and immediate underpricing of risk. The wave of pessimism could also initiate deleveraging of the financial system and equally wrenching adjustments to household and corporate balance sheets. In such circumstances, it may be hard to rule out the possibility that the process could be remarkably persistent and unusually nonlinear. If medium-term fundamentals were sound initially, it opens up the possibility that strong policy actions would be effective in stemming the downward spiral and effecting a more rapid recovery than would otherwise be the case.

Modeling these dynamics is not without challenges. The slow, persistent decline in confidence can be modeled as a gradual expansion of a negative asset price bubble. The growth and collapse could be captured by a time-varying Markov process, as has been done for positive asset price bubbles.[4] However, a sharp initial decline in asset prices associated with a collapse in confidence may require additional modeling. One approach is to think of the sharp decline in asset prices as a one-off shock which then ripples through the system. This could set off a more generalized pall of pessimism that then leads to further declines, which can be modeled as a mixture of random shocks and a time-varying Markov process. These options will be explored below.

This more asymmetric version of the negative asset price bubble appears well suited to addressing international financial market spillovers similar to the type seen during the international financial crisis in Asia. As described further in more detail in the next section, Asia had a strong set of economic and financial fundamentals going into the crisis. This, however, was not sufficient to protect Asia from the virulence of the pessimism emanating out of the West. The break in confidence was initially sharp, then it worsened as the financial pessimism morphed into a macroeconomic crisis before experiencing a rapid macro-financial recovery.

3. Asia and the Spillovers from the International Financial Crisis

The notion of a negative asset price bubble is a useful lens through which to analyze the spillovers to Asia during the international financial crisis, the dynamics of the recovery and, possibly most important, the policy trade-offs faced by policymakers in the region.[5] To fully appreciate the relevance of this perspective, it is useful to review the timeline and impacts of the crisis on Asia.

To be sure, economies in the region were affected by the international financial crisis in different ways. Some saw a sharp contraction in output while others experienced a growth cycle recession (Figure 5.1). At the risk of oversimplifying the complexities of such a large, diverse region, this paper argues

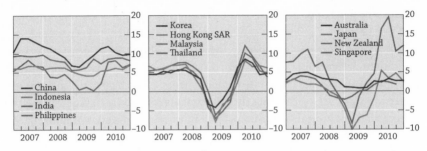

Figure 5.1 Real GDP growth (In percent).
Source: National data.

that the chronology of the crisis in Asia and the Pacific can be succinctly characterized in five phases: (1) the initial headwinds blowing from the West, (2) the tsunami, (3) the immediate aftermath, (4) the recovery, and (5) the long road to full normalization.[6]

THE HEADWINDS, MID-2007 TO MID-2008

The initial cracks in the financial system of the West had a relatively limited impact on the economies in Asia during this phase of the international finance crisis.[7] In the run-up to the crisis, it is important to remember that global financial markets were robust and credit growth was strong. The pricing problems that developed early in the crisis were largely limited to certain classes of risky assets, as exemplified by the difficulties at BNP Paribus and later at Bear Stearns. There were also stresses in interbank markets in some advanced economies that led to large, temporary liquidity injections that were needed to restore more orderly financial conditions in some economies. Relative to what was to follow, these rumblings paled in comparison—economically and financially—to the seismic event that occurred in September 2008.

In Asia, the direct spillovers at this time were relatively modest financially and did not significantly alter the macroeconomic trajectories for output and inflation. The Asian exposures to the so-called toxic assets were rather modest. But the region was not immune from the more generalized decline in risk appetites of global investors. Low-grade borrowers in India, Indonesia, and the Philippines lost access to markets for a while. And even high-grade borrowers faced much higher financing rates, which was a burden for those economies with large external financing needs. Equity prices came off highs achieved late in 2007 (Figure 5.2).

All in all, however, the impact of these financial headwinds on the prospects for economic growth in Asian economies was modest. GDP growth forecasts were still seeing 4%–5% growth in 2008 and 2009, despite these financial rumblings. Strong Asian growth at the time fed increasingly popular views that

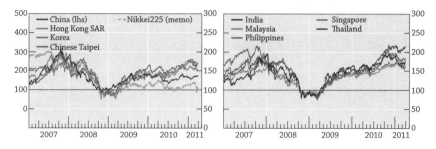

Figure 5.2 Equity prices in Asia[1].
[1]In local currency. December 2008 = 100.

the region had become sufficiently resilient to shocks from the rest of the world that it could be characterized as effectively decoupling from the West. One manifestation of this was heavy U.S. dollar borrowing, as expectations of domestic currency appreciation (or at least stability) remained in place in many economies but especially in Korea. While this view would eventually be discredited in the next phase of the crisis, the robust economic activity in 2007 and 2008 contributed to concerns of overheating and price stability. Rising inflation pressures in Asia came from global energy and food prices, which also helped to insulate commodity-producing economies from the financial headwinds from the West.

Monetary policy throughout much of the region was being tightened during this phase, especially in India and Indonesia, where inflation rates reached double digits. Japan was a stark exception as it kept its policy rate at 0.5%, as its incipient recovery after a very long period of subpar performance seemed particularly vulnerable to the adverse developments in North America and Europe. Malaysia also kept policy rates relatively low as it expressed concerns about the downside tail risks that were brewing on the other side of the Pacific Ocean. New Zealand lowered its policy rates in part because of the slowing of the economy but also the rising term premium on its borrowing.

It is also important to note the performance of banks in the run-up to this phase of the international financial crisis. Asia-Pacific banks weathered this period rather well, continuing to report earnings and experiencing only minor losses. Capital adequacy ratios remained high throughout the period, nonperforming loans were low, and loan-to-deposit ratios were at a comfortable level as global wholesale funding markets experienced stress (Figure 5.3). In part, the health and resilience of Asia-Pacific banking systems stemmed from the relatively traditional bank business models. On the liability side, the banks rely heavily on retail deposits; Australia, Korea, and New Zealand, though, relied on wholesale funding more extensively than the others. On the asset side, banks generally used the traditional originate and hold approach, and investments in complex financial instruments remained limited.

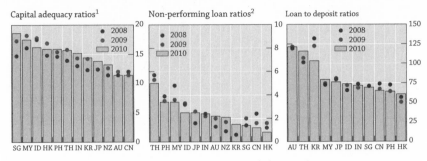

Figure 5.3 Soundness of banking sector in Asia and the Pacific. In percent.
AU = Australia; CN = China; HK = Hong Kong SAR; IN = India; ID = Indonesia;
JP = Japan; KR = Korea; MY = Malaysia; NZ = New Zealand; PH = Philippines;
SG = Singapore; TH = Thailand.
[1]Total capital as a percentage of total risk-weighted assets.
[2]Definitions may vary across countries.
Sources: Bloomberg; CEIC; IMF; national data.

In part, the Asian banking model reflected the relatively conservative regulatory regime developed in the 2000s, in light of the lessons learned during the Asian financial crisis of the late 1990s. During that crisis, the weak banking regulatory systems led to financial system weaknesses that resulted in a dramatic reversal in fortunes. Crises in Asia and elsewhere also served as a backdrop for this approach by both the regulators and the regulated. Naturally, regulators took a relatively conservative approach toward financial stability issues. Maybe more important, the regulated sector also took a conservative approach toward risk management, generally adopting practices that provided a high degree of resilience during the recent international financial crisis.

Asia and the Pacific also learned important lessons from their 1990s crisis about the value of fiscal discipline and the value of possessing a war chest of foreign reserves, just in case. Fiscal authorities strengthened their policy frameworks in the 2000s, leaving them with considerable fiscal room for maneuver at the time of the international financial crisis. Fiscal surpluses were the rule rather than the exception and government debt was relatively low on an international standard; Japan was a notable exception to this trend.

The region had accumulated massive quantities of foreign reserves throughout the decade. Early on, central banks and finance ministries focused on building buffer stocks motivated primarily by achieving reserve adequacy levels using various metrics (e.g., reserves as a share of GDP, as a share of three months of imports, and of one year of short-term debt). Later in the decade, prolonged exchange rate intervention, which added further to reserves holdings, was largely a by-product of the exchange rate regime. As economies in the region resisted nominal exchange rate pressures, foreign reserves reached unprecedented levels. Some of these reserves and forward FX positions that were built before 2007 helped protect the region from credit rating downgrades as the headwinds from the West picked up. And some economies used the stock of reserves to help provide dollar liquidity and stabilize their currencies.

THE FINANCIAL TSUNAMI, LATE 2008

Despite the strong economic and financial fundamentals in Asia and the Pacific, the region was not immune from the sharp intensification of the international financial crisis after the collapse of Lehman Brothers in September 2008. The arrival of the financial tsunami to the shores of Asia-Pacific was fast and occurred with unprecedented intensity. The initial impact was felt in the financial markets as market confidence and risk appetite collapsed. Asia-Pacific equity indexes fell sharply at the end of 2008, even after prices drifted down from the highs in 2007 through most of the year. Housing prices also faced downward pressures.

Possibly more revealing was the sharp spike in sovereign CDS spreads in the region (Figure 5.4). Indonesia, Korea and the Philippines experienced the worst of it. But all were affected to varying degrees. The iTraxx Asia ex Japan spread jumped from around 150 to 600 briefly, before settling to around 400. The iTraxx Japan did not jump as high initially but then rose to the 500–600 range.

The skyrocketing CDS spreads represented massive reassessments of risks. Research by Kim, Loretan, and Remolona (2010) found that most of the increase was due to changes in risk appetite, rather than changes in the underlying expected default rates. This provides solid evidence that in Asia and the Pacific overpricing of risk is an important factor. Moreover, the change in risk appetite had consequences for the real economy. Along with a rapid reversal of commodity prices, there was a multiplication of the downside risks to the economic outlook,

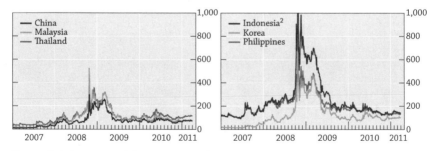

Figure 5.4 Sovereign debt CDS premia[1].

[1]CMA 5-Year Credit Default Swap premia; in basis points.

[2]Indonesia's premia exceeded 1000 on December 22, 2008, reaching a peak of 1256.7 on December 23, 2008.

and genuine concerns about the consequences for financial stability in the region became evident.

These developments also highlighted the nature of the spillovers of the international financial crisis to Asia and the Pacific. To be sure, part of it could be blamed on deteriorating prospects for economic growth and earnings through trade channels. But a more substantial part was due to a massive wave of investor pessimism that led to an abrupt swing in the mispricing of risk: from a large underpricing of risk before the crisis to a significant overpricing of risks after the Lehman bankruptcy (Figure 5.5). In other words, a large negative asset price bubble spilled over to the region.

One interesting feature of the international financial crisis was the severe disruption in international, especially U.S.-dollar-denominated, money and capital markets. The disruptions raised financing costs faced by borrowers in Asia and the Pacific, which intensified the impact of the break in confidence. Huge gross U.S.-dollar-denominated exposures in economies such as Korea proved very costly as Asian currencies depreciated. The disruptions happened in three ways: by directly reducing the availability of offshore credit to Asia-Pacific residents; by increasing demand from nonresidents to borrow in Asia-Pacific markets; and by leading market-makers to scale back their activities.

With respect to the curtailment of offshore credit, the initial consequences were modest (Figure 5.6). The small size and covered nature of most Asia-Pacific countries' short-term foreign liabilities limited funding problems. During normal times, Asia-Pacific firms did not have large U.S. dollar borrowing requirements, as many were able to meet their requirements from export revenues and some held foreign currency assets which more or less matched the maturity of their foreign currency liabilities. For example, in Malaysia, Thailand, and the Philippines, interbank liabilities were typically matched by short-term foreign currency assets, such as trade finance. In Australia and New Zealand, foreign currency liabilities

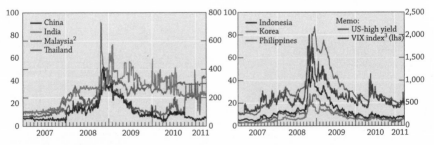

Figure 5.5 Bond spreads[1].

[1]Over benchmark U.S. Treasury bonds; in basis points.

[2]Malaysia's bond spread exceeded 600 on October 23, 2008, reaching a peak of 730.7 bps on the same day.

3Implied volatility of U.S. equities.

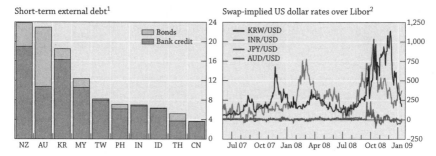

Figure 5.6 Foreign currency funding pressures. AU = Australia; CN = China; ID = Indonesia; IN = India; KR = Korea; MY = Malaysia; NZ = New Zealand; PH = Philippines; TH = Thailand; TW = Chinese Taipei.

[1]External liabilities with a remaining maturity of one year or less, as a percentage of GDP; at end-September 2008. Bonds refer to foreign currency debt securities outstanding; bank credit refers to consolidated international claims of BIS reporting banks.

[2]Spreads between U.S. dollar interbank rates implied by covered interest parity and three-month U.S. dollar Libor, in basis points; implied rates are calculated from forward and spot exchange rates against the U.S. dollar and local onshore interbank rates.

Source: Bloomberg; Datastream; BIS calculations.

were systematically swapped into local currency, and local banks shifted funding to local sources when offshore markets no longer offered attractive financing on a swap-covered basis.

However, the freezing-up of short-term markets for U.S. dollars in September and October 2008 had serious repercussions for Asia and the Pacific. The drying up of offshore credit, at the same time exports were collapsing, forced firms needing to refinance dollar-denominated debts and derivative exposures to sell local currency assets and to seek U.S. dollar borrowing from locals. Banks in India and Korea offered exceptionally high interest rates in October 2008 to raise U.S. dollars from local sources. In other Asia-Pacific markets, including Australian dollar and yen markets, demand for U.S. dollars led to some stress, but not severely so. A second way in which the disruptions in U.S. dollar markets caused local financing conditions to tighten was that nonresidents sought to tap Asia-Pacific markets and swap the proceeds for U.S. dollars or other foreign currencies, pushing up local yields and credit spreads in the process. Third, international banks responded to the difficulties that they themselves faced in securing financing by scaling back their activities. As a result, Asia-Pacific securities became more expensive to trade. International banks were important dealers not only for foreign currency securities issued by Asia-Pacific borrowers but also for local securities and derivatives. Their retrenchment caused transaction costs to increase and liquidity to drop for a wide range of instruments.

The U.S. dollar squeeze was addressed in part by the ample foreign exchange reserves that Asian economies had amassed in the previous decade. Furthermore, the liquidity assistance in foreign currency provided by the swap facility with the Federal Reserve was a game changer. The actual amount of support was helpful in addressing local banking needs as well as regional needs, more generally, as the U.S. dollars were circulated in the region. In addition, the swap lines provided a signaling effect that was significant in calming market jitters.[8] The knowledge that the Federal Reserve stood ready to provide emergency funds was potentially more important than the massive war chests of international reserves. Australia, Japan, and Korea drew on the swap lines, while New Zealand and Singapore did not.

Policymakers in the region responded to this changing financial environment with alacrity. Even though the complete set of data would not be available for months, there was no doubt that Asia and the Pacific were facing a sharp intensification of the crisis coming from the North Atlantic. The policy response was swift and deliberate.

On the policy side, monetary policy interest rates were cut across the board and some were deep (Figure 5.7). New Zealand started with relatively high policy rates and cut 325 basis points. A number of economies cut their reserve requirements. Massive emergency fiscal stimulus plans were announced. With trade collapsing, in part because of the expected drying up of trade finance, special trade finance programs were announced. This liquidity squeeze in various markets complicated the monetary transmission mechanism; local currency liquidity supports

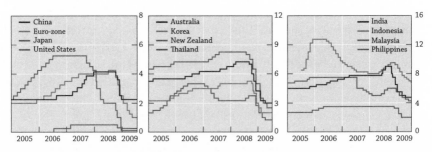

Figure 5.7 Monetary policy rates[1]. In percent.

[1]Policy target rates or their proxies. For China, household saving deposits one-year rate; for the euro area, ECB minimum bid refinancing one-week rate; for Japan, BoJ target rate; for the United States, fed funds rate; for Australia, RBA cash target rate; for Korea, overnight call rate target before March 7, 2008, one-week BOK Base Rate thereafter; for New Zealand, official cash daily rate; for Thailand, 14-day repo rate before January 17, 2007, one-day repo thereafter; for India, RBI repo cutoff yield; for Indonesia, BI reference interest rate; for Malaysia, overnight policy rate; for the Philippines, overnight reserve repurchase agreement RRP daily rate.

Source: Bloomberg.

were provided, including extending maturities of the borrowing and broadening of collateral eligibility for the borrowing.

THE IMMEDIATE AFTERMATH, LATE 2008 TO EARLY 2009

By late 2008, it became increasingly evident to policymakers that this financial tsunami had hit the shores of Asia and the Pacific and was quickly morphing into a full-blown macroeconomic meltdown (Figure 5.8). Exports fell sharply, with the small open economies being severely hit. Industrial production was collapsing as inventories liquidation accelerated the descent. At the time, it was not clear just where the bottom of the cycle would finally end up. As GDP contracted in most of the Asia-Pacific economies, the prospects for growth in 2009 and 2010 were also marked down significantly. Hong Kong, Japan, Singapore, and Thailand were the hardest hit economies, with real GDP falling by more that 9%. All this shows just how potent the spillover channels were.

There were some silver linings in the dark clouds. The stability of the renminbi against the dollar—when other Asian currencies fell—brought about a real effective exchange rate appreciation in China. China, India, and Indonesia—the three largest emerging market economies in Asia—were able to grow above 5%. This helped to support economic activity throughout the region owing to the extensive regional supply chains. And the aggregate demand sustained relatively high commodity prices, which was important for the commodity-exporting economies.

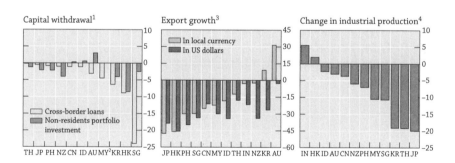

Figure 5.8 Crisis impact on capital flows, exports, and industrial production in Asia. AU = Australia; CN = China; HK = Hong Kong SAR; ID = Indonesia; IN = India; JP = Japan; KR = Korea; MY = Malaysia; NZ = New Zealand; PH = Philippines; SG = Singapore; TH = Thailand.

[1]Q4 2008 data for cross-border loans and 2008 annual data for nonresident portfolio investment (gross flow), both as a percentage of 2008 GDP.

[2]Data on nonresident portfolio investment not available.

[3]January–February 2009 over January–February 2008.

[4]December 2008 over June 2008; percentage change.

Source: IMF; CEIC; Datastream; IMF; national data; BIS.

Moreover, the ability of these three large Asian economies to weather the storm laid the foundation for the eventual global recovery. One lesson from the crisis was that those economies most vulnerable to a shock to external demand suffered heavily. The large economies with substantial domestic demand sectors and limited financial linkages globally weathered the storm relatively better than the small open economies.

The credit crunch in the region compounded the macroeconomic decline. International banks retreated from the region, leaving fewer lenders, at the same time that risk appetite fell. Those economies with less highly-rated financial systems suffered more as risk spreads ballooned, and as a consequence borrowers faced much higher external funding costs. Cross-border capital outflows aggravated the situation for those economies with fairly liquid and open equity markets, such as Korea. The retreat of international banks also precipitated cross-border banking outflows, especially in the financial centers of Hong Kong and Singapore.

One of the big surprises was the vulnerability of trade finance during the crisis. Trade credit in Asia-Pacific is typically denominated in U.S. dollars and is short term in nature; hence, it is thought of as being low-risk. However, as dollar liquidity dried up at the height of the crisis, and the FX swap market became dysfunctional, exporters found it difficult to roll over this form of credit. Domestic and regional banks partially filled the gap left by the international banks, and new guarantees from governments and international agencies helped too.

In the end, however, the containment of the downside risks can be attributed in large part to the confidence-restoring actions of the governments in the region. In addition to further easing of monetary policy, large supplementary fiscal packages were arranged, in some cases complementing earlier packages (Figure 5.9). China's multiyear spending initiatives eventually rose to between

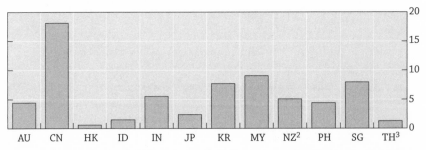

Figure 5.9 Announced size of fiscal stimulus relative to 2008 GDP[1]. In percent. For an explanation of the economy abbreviations, see Figure 5.8.

[1]Data up to April 2009; some announced stimulus plans may be spread over multiple years.

[2]2007 GDP number used as a denominator.

[3]Not including infrastructure spending plans of THB 1.43 trillion over the 2010–12 period.

Source: IMF; Reuters News; UNESCAP.

10% and 15% of GDP. The median size of the packages in the region was about 5% of GDP.

A range of unconventional policy actions complemented the conventional macroeconomic tools. They included liquidity assistance in local currency, lending of foreign exchange, expansion of blanket deposit insurance, guarantees of nondeposit liabilities, bank capital injections, short-sale restrictions, relaxation of the mark-to-market rules, and the purchase of assets. Explicit and implicit government guarantees also helped to restore the rather fragile confidence during this period. As market fears receded and counterparty risks diminished, market sentiment turned around and became buoyant by March 2009. As mentioned above, foreign liquidity availability played a critical role in calming markets, especially when they became concerned about adequate U.S. dollar liquidity. The large foreign reserve positions in the region released during the crisis augmented the Fed's bilateral swap arrangements in several key Asian economies. The renewed interest in ensuring foreign reserve adequacy in the future prompted the expansion of intraregional bilateral swap arrangements and spurred progress toward the $120 billion multilateral reserve pooling arrangement under the Chiang Mai Initiative.

THE V-SHAPED RECOVERY (SPRING 2009 AND BEYOND)

By early spring 2009, the region showed incipient signs that it was turning the corner. Regional financial markets rallied, reflecting substantially diminished headwinds. Economic activity started to pick up in various parts of the region. While the hardest hit economies experienced a classic V-shaped recovery, this pattern was in no way certain during early 2009. The speed of the recovery was subject to considerable uncertainties about both the durability and the breadth of the recovery. One view that received considerable attention at the time was that Asia-Pacific economies could not fully recover until major export destinations in North America and Europe had substantially improved prospects. With little evidence of a sustained turnaround in the major advanced economies, a rapid recovery seemed doubtful, especially because of the lingering financial system stresses and of debt-ladened balance sheets of the banks, the shadow banking system, households, and governments. Despite concerns about the major advanced economies, the region did rebound.

By late 2009, however, the success in the region shifted the balance of risks from the downside to the risk of overheating. At the time, accommodative monetary policy remained largely in place as much of the fiscal stimulus continued. Financial markets were on the mend. Another issue that arose during this time for policymakers in the region was that of capital flows. Capital flows returned to Asia and the Pacific, with varying intensities across time and economies. Most broad categories of cross-border flows were picking up. These included foreign direct investment, bond and equity portfolio flows, and cross-border bank lending. A number of factors were in play in the region, not least being the prospects for a leading role in the global recovery and the need to tighten monetary policy before the major advanced economies and the other emerging market economies did so. One complicating factor was the flare-up in sovereign debt concerns in Europe during 2010. This sent a wave of pessimism across the globe, with global risk aversion reversing course for a while. Early on, regional asset prices were impacted in a manner consistent with the higher correlation of global financial markets (Figure 5.10). By year-end, however, investors appeared to be fairly discriminating, geographically, in their appetite for risk; Asia-Pacific fundamentals were sound and risk spreads reflected this.

Against this backdrop, monetary policymakers faced difficult trade-offs. On the one hand, higher policy rates tended to draw in more capital inflows as international interest rate differentials widened. And, for those resisting currency appreciation, this meant a buildup of one-sided currency bets and carry trade dynamics. On the other hand, low policy rates and the associated prolonged accommodative monetary policy were thought to contribute to asset price bubbles. The evidence during this period supported these concerns. Asia-Pacific equity prices rose rapidly above precrisis highs, and property prices in particular jurisdictions saw meteoric rises that raised concerns about bubbles. This was particularly the case in Hong Kong, Singapore, and certain cities in China. The reluctance to rely on policy interest rates saw policymakers experimenting with the use of administrative measures such as capital controls and macroprudential tools to rein in capital flow pressures and rapid credit expansion.

LONG ROAD TO FULL NORMALIZATION, 2010 TO PRESENT

As noted above, the stance of monetary policy in Asia and the Pacific remained accommodative long after the recovery began. Indeed, by measures of the real policy interest rate, the stance of monetary policy was extremely loose

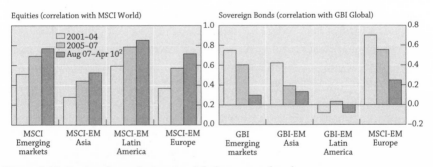

Figure 5.10 Regional correlations in global asset markets[1].

[1]Calculated on daily returns in U.S. dollars.

[2]Period of increased global market volatility.

Source: Datastream; JPMorgan Chase; MSCI Barra.

Figure 5.11 Monetary policy, credit growth housing prices, and inflation in Asia.

[1]Policy target rates or their proxies corrected by forward- and backward-looking inflation component (equally weighted 12-month backward-looking CPI inflation and 12-month forward-looking consensus expectations); average of China, Hong Kong SAR, India, Indonesia, Korea, Malaysia, Philippines, and Thailand.

[2]Annual change; average of China, Hong Kong SAR, India, Indonesia, Korea, Malaysia, Philippines, Singapore and Thailand.

[3]End 2005 = 100; average of China, Hong Kong SAR, Indonesia, Korea, Malaysia, Singapore, and Thailand.

Source: CEIC, IMF IFS, national data.

(Figure 5.11). One concern is that central banks in the region were keeping policy rates too low for too long. The pickup in inflation and the reemergence of asset price bubbles all support this conclusion. Going forward, this view would suggest that the inflation fight will be quite difficult. With inflation having picked up, a sharp increase in nominal policy interest rates will be required to raise real policy rates sufficiently to rein in inflationary pressures. If too disruptive, the monetary policy reaction could precipitate a dramatic slowdown and open up another set of daunting policy challenges. This view would argue that, just as in the past, monetary policy that is too procyclical leads to boom-bust dynamics, with respect to goods and services prices as well as asset prices.

In contrast, when looking at the situation through the lens of a negative asset price bubble perspective, the performance of monetary policy in the region takes on a more positive evaluation. This alternative view maintains that the accommodative monetary policy was the appropriate response to the enduring downside risks associated with fragile confidence. Despite nearly two years of recovery, concerns persist that Asia-Pacific economies are susceptible to considerable risks as long as prospects of a sustained recovery in the West remain shaky. Moreover, sovereign risk concerns in Europe and balance sheet adjustments—for governments, corporations, and households—in the West, more generally, represent significant tail risks clouding an otherwise fairly bright outlook in Asia and the Pacific (excluding Japan) over the medium term.

This perspective would argue that monetary authorities in the region have been justified in keeping monetary policy accommodative. The easy policies have helped to boost confidence and so deepen and broaden the recovery—providing resilience in case of another negative shock. But if the tail risks do not materialize, inflation will rise. Such an ex post increase in inflation, however, is just a reflection of the risk management approach to monetary policy. Policy based on a risk management approach to the range of risks facing monetary authorities actually helps to ensure that the risks do not materialize ex post—so this should not be viewed as a policy failure. In other words, it would be incorrect to evaluate the performance of Asia-Pacific central banks by inflation performance alone—as some advocates of inflation targeting might suggest. Rather, the performance should be assessed on how well the monetary authorities balanced the risks in an ex ante sense.

Full recovery in Asia-Pacific economies and the normalization of the stance of monetary policy is not likely until the global economy is on a more sure footing. In the meanwhile, as the economic and financial tail risks fade, it is important for the policy stance to adjust accordingly. The role of tail risks in policy settings is illustrated in the next section of the paper.

4. The Model

One striking feature of the recovery in Asia-Pacific has been the persistence of very stimulative monetary policy in the region. Nominal policy interest rates were slashed during the height of the financial crisis. The policy response was not only meant to address the deterioration in the economic and financial prospects but also to address the multiplication of the downside tail risks that arose. More recently, there is a question about whether monetary policy should have been so accommodative for so long. To understand this motivation, we need to focus on the economics of tail risks. From a theoretical point of view, however, conventional linear quadratic monetary policy models generally assign no special importance to tail risks. As a consequence, this class of models is not particularly useful in addressing the dominant policy concerns of the past few years in Asia and the Pacific. Tail risks are all the more relevant in policymaking because of the weakness of conventional forecasting models in capturing sudden, sharp downward movements in macroeconomic activity.[9] This section adopts a less conventional framework to cast a brighter light on the challenges.

This section lays out an international monetary policy model that attempts to capture this unconventional dynamic. At the heart of the model is a negative asset price bubble which, when it develops, can put the economies into a tailspin. At the same time, recognizing this possibility, hypothetical monetary authorities in the regions have incentives not only to smooth inflation and output fluctuations but also to influence the size of the downside tail risks. The details of the model and solution methods are presented in the appendix for the interested reader.

This international monetary policy model has a relatively simple structure, extended from early modeling efforts by Filardo (2006). The model comprises three key blocks of equations: the macro block, the asset price block, and the monetary policy block for two countries or regions.

THE MACRO BLOCK—A TWO-REGION SETUP

The macro block specifies the output and the inflation dynamics for two regions of the world. This includes an IS equation and a PC equation for each economy (one economy is called the US and the other is called A):

Region US

$(IS_{US})\quad y_{t,US} = -\gamma_{US}\, r_{t-1,US} + \theta_{US}\, y_{t-1,US} + \varphi_{US}(\pi_{AP,t-1,US} - \pi_{t-1,US}) + \varepsilon_{t,US}$

$(PC_{US})\quad \pi_{t,US} = \pi_{t-1,US} + \alpha_{US}\, y_{t-1,US} + \beta_{US}\, \pi_{B,t-1,US} + \eta_{t,US}$

Region A

$(IS_A)\quad y_{t,A} = -\gamma_A r_{t-1,A} + \theta_A\, y_{t-1,A} + \theta_{A,US} y_{t-1,US} + \varphi_A(\pi_{AP,t-1,A} - \pi_{t-1,A}) + \varepsilon_{t,.}$

$(PC_A)\quad \pi_{t,A} = \pi_{t-1,A} + \alpha_A\, y_{t-1,A} + \beta_A\, \pi_{B,t-1,A} + \eta_{t,A}$.

The IS equations describe the evolution of output in the two regions. For region US, output is a function of the lagged policy rate (r), lagged output (y), the lagged real asset price return ($\pi_{AP,t-1,US} - \pi_{t-1,US}$), and a random error term. For region A, the equation is similar, except that it includes a feedback term from US output to region A. It is assumed that the US is a large region and that A is a relatively small region, in the sense that output developments in the US affect A but developments in A do not directly affect US.

The PC equations describe the evolution of goods and services price inflation in the two regions. The structure of this inflation equation is assumed to be symmetric across the two regions. Inflation is a function of past inflation, lagged output, the growth rate of the asset price bubble, and a random error term. The growth in the asset price bubble appears in the equations to capture the cross-country experience that consumer price inflation tends to go up less than would be expected during an asset price boom and goes down less than expected in an asset price collapse.

THE ASSET PRICE BLOCK

The asset price block describes the evolution of asset price returns in the two regions, $\pi_{AP,US}$ and $\pi_{AP,A}$. Asset price returns in each region are assumed to be composed of a part driven by fundamentals, e.g. $\pi_{F,US}$ for the US, and a part driven by a domestic asset price bubble, for example, $\pi_{B,US}$ for the US. In general, total asset price returns in each region can be described by the following identity: $\pi_{AP,k} = \pi_{F,k} + \pi_{B,k}, for\, k = \{US, A\}$.

The fundamental component of asset prices in each region is modeled in the following way:

$$(F_{US}) \quad \pi_{F,t,US} = \pi_{t-1,US} + \lambda y_{t-1,US} + \xi_{t,US} + \Lambda_{t,US}$$
$$(B_{US}) \quad \pi_{B,t,US} = \zeta_t(y_{t-1,US}, r_{t-1,US})$$

$$(F_A) \quad \pi_{F,t,A} = \pi_{t-1,A} + \lambda y_{t-1,A} + \xi_{t,A} + \Lambda_{t,A}$$
$$(B_A) \quad \pi_{B,t,A} = \zeta_t(y_{t-1,A}, r_{t-1,A})$$

The F and B equations describe the evolution of the fundamental and bubble components of asset prices, respectively. Fundamental asset price returns are assumed to be determined by domestic inflation and output conditions in each region. On the fundamental side, nominal asset returns vary positively with inflation and output.

The bubbles will follow an endogenous Markovian process, where the transition probabilities are functions of the state of the economy (y) and the stance of monetary policy (r). For example, a strong macroeconomic position and easy monetary policy raise the probability that a positive asset price bubble will develop; conversely, cyclical weakness and tight monetary policy raise the probability of a negative asset price bubble. The details about the asset price error terms and the bubble components will be described in more detail below.

MORE ON THE ASYMMETRIC BUBBLE SPECIFICATION

While positive asset price bubbles are thought to rise gradually over time and then collapse, the evolution of negative asset price bubbles can be more complex. For example, a negative asset price bubble can start with a large, downward collapse. One way to model this is to specify the Λ_t as a Poisson distribution; in other words, $\Lambda_t \sim Pois(\lambda)$, where λ is the expected number of asset price collapses over a period of time.

Alternatively, the negative asset price bubble can build over time in a symmetric manner as with a positive asset price bubble. In this case, the bubble component can be thought of a three-state bubble. This would account for the possibility of a positive asset price bubble, a no-bubble state, and a negative bubble state.

$$I_{t,US} = \begin{cases} 1, & +bubble \\ 0, & no\ bubble \\ -1, & -bubble \end{cases}$$

$$I_{t,A} = \begin{cases} 1, & +bubble \\ 0, & no\ bubble \\ -1, & -bubble \end{cases}$$

This state variables, $I_{t,US}$ and $I_{t,A}$, have time-varying Markovian probabilities governing the transitions:

$$P(I_{t,k} \mid I_{t-1,k}, X_{t-1,k}) = \begin{pmatrix} p_{-1,-1}(X_{t-1,k}) & p_{-1,0}(X_{t-1,k}) & 0 \\ p_{0,-1}(X_{t-1,k}) & p_{0,0}(X_{t-1,k}) & p_{0,1}(X_{t-1,k}) \\ 0 & p_{1,0}(X_{t-1,k}) & p_{1,1}(X_{t-1,k}) \end{pmatrix} \text{ for } k = \{US, A\}.$$

This asymmetric negative bubble specification offers a useful approach to model the asset price dynamics in Asia-Pacific economies in response to the financial crisis in the West. The initial collapse of asset prices in Asia-Pacific economies could be thought of as having worked through two key channels. First, it had implications for the macroeconomy by lowering output. Second, it had implications for the persistence of a negative bubble. By lowering output, the transition probabilities of remaining in a negative asset price bubble increased.

THE MONETARY POLICY BLOCK

Given the structure of the macroeconomy and asset prices, the monetary authority's challenge is fairly standard: to choose a policy rate in order to minimize the weighted average of the variance of output, inflation, and the change in interest rates. The monetary authority's loss function is

$$L = L_{US} + L_A \text{, where}$$
$$L_k = var(y_k) + \mu_{\pi,k} \, var(\pi_k) + \mu_{r,k} \, var(r_k - r_{-1,k}) \quad k = \{US, A\}.$$

In this paper, we will limit the search of the function to the class of linear feedback rules of the form $r_{t,k} = a_{y,k} y_{t,k} + a_{\pi,k} \pi_{t,k} + a_{F,k} \pi_{F,t,k} + a_{B,k} \pi_{B,t,k} + a_{D,k} D_{t,k}$, $k = \{US, A\}$, where D is the duration of the bubble. These extended Taylor rules include a conventional response to output and inflation. They also include a response to the fundamental component of asset prices. The more controversial aspect of this monetary policy response is the response to the bubble component. The hypothetical monetary authority can respond to the expansion of the bubbles and to the size of the bubble, which is proxied by the length of the bubbles. Succinctly described, the hypothetical monetary authority solves the following optimization problem,

$$\underset{\{a_{y,US}, a_{\pi,US}, a_{F,US}, a_{B,US}, a_{D,US}, a_{y,A}, a_{\pi,A}, a_{F,A}, a_{B,A}, a_{D,A}\}}{\operatorname{argmin}} L$$

subject to the law of motion of the economy described in the macro and asset price blocks of the model.

5. Results

The results from the model highlight some of the theoretical monetary policy trade-offs that Asia-Pacific central banks faced as the spillovers from the international financial crisis in the West reached their shores. Using the two-region model, six simulations are highlighted. These simulations assume that the underlying economic environment is susceptible to both positive and negative bubbles. The hypothetical monetary authorities choose to respond to economic and financial developments using linear Taylor-type rules.

The first set of simulations corresponds to conventional measures of Taylor-type rules that do not take bubbles into account. There are two practical ways to think about these simulations. First, one can think of a monetary authority that has not experienced bubbles and estimates a Taylor rule in nonbubble periods, and then sticks to this rule when bubbles arrive. Second, the monetary authority thinks of bubbles that it has seen in the past as one-off events and hence does not consider them to be a systemic feature of the monetary policy environment. In a sense, the monetary authority estimates a Taylor rule, abstracting from past periods of bubbles.

The second set of simulations corresponds to an environment in which monetary authorities use extended Taylor-type rules that take bubbles into account. In this case, bubbles are thought to be a regular part of the policy environment, just as inflation and output are. As a consequence, the monetary authority estimates the influence of the bubble environment when choosing its optimal response parameters.[10]

Conventional Taylor rule—responding to output and inflation. In these simulations (models 1 and 4 in Table 5.1), the monetary authorities in the two regions respond only to output and inflation. Model 4 assumes the existence of bubbles and reflects this dependence in the estimated parameters.

In general, the monetary authorities respond more aggressively to output when there are bubbles. In part, the monetary authorities in a bubble environment understand that bubbles are procyclical and therefore lean against the channel of influence of bubbles on output. And in part the additional response reflects the channel of influence that the monetary authorities have on the time-varying transition probabilities of the bubble. In the case of negative asset price bubbles and subpar output growth, the monetary authorities would want to ease more aggressively than in the case where their actions did not influence the likelihood of bubbles. One can interpret this bubble dimension of the monetary policy response as an attempt to alter the tail risk probabilities in monetary policy. In other words, monetary authorities try to alter the probabilities of undesirable outcomes.

From a technical point of view, the asymmetry in the inflation responses between the US monetary authority and the A monetary authority reflects the

Table 5.1 **Extended Taylor rule parameters**

	Estimated assuming no bubbles and responding to			Estimated assuming bubbles and responding to		
	(1) y, π	*(2)* y, π, π_{AP}	*(3)* y, π, π_F	*(4)* y, π	*(5)* y, π, π_{AP}	*(6)* $y, \pi, \pi_F, \pi_B, \pi_D$
$a_{y, US}$	.44	.50	.50	.70	.76	.69
$a_{\pi, US}$	1.48	1.26	1.27	1.32	1.13	.72
$a_{F, US}$		.30	.30		.22	.36
$a_{B, US}$		.30			.22	.12
$a_{D, US}$						.11
$a_{y, A}$	.46	.51	.51	.68	.73	.67
$a_{\pi, A}$	1.55	1.50	1.53	1.71	1.43	1.43
$a_{F, A}$		.31	.31		.21	.08
$a_{B, A}$		.31			.21	.17
$a_{D, A}$						.03
Loss function gain (normalized by L in Model 1)						
Total L	–	7%	5%	5%	16%	17%

asymmetry in the macroeconomic block; it is assumed that output developments in region US affect economic activity in region A but not vice versa. As the final line in the table shows, taking account of a bubble-prone environment in estimating the optimal policy response parameters yields a 5% improvement in the loss function.

Responding to asset prices. In models 2 and 5, the monetary authorities respond not only to output and inflation but also asset price returns. However, monetary authorities are not assumed to be able to distinguish fundamental movements in asset prices from bubble movements. As a consequence, they respond to total asset price variability (i.e., the estimated coefficient on the fundamental and bubble components of asset prices constrained to be equal).

In these models, the monetary authorities respond positively to asset price movements. As asset prices rise, the monetary authorities raise interest rates more than in the more conventional Taylor rule specification. Conversely, as asset prices collapse, the monetary authorities cut policy rates. The differences in the coefficients between model 2 and model 5 are instructive about the nature of the policy responses. In model 5, the asset price coefficient is less than the coefficient on model 2. This might be read to suggest that the monetary authority responds to asset price developments less in the bubble environment than when it assumes a no-bubble environment. This difference alone could lead to faulty inferences about how to respond to asset prices. Note, too, the coefficient on output rises in model 5. One way to interpret these differences is that responding to the bubble and fundamental asset prices in the same way leads to suboptimal responses. For example, in model 6, the optimal parameter on the bubble is less than that on the fundamental component. Moreover, in the case (model 5) where you cannot distinguish the bubble and the fundamental changes in asset prices, responding to y more aggressively than in model 2 underscores the implicit incentives associated with responding to the determinants of the bubble.

The ability of the monetary authority to respond to asset price returns improves the loss function by 7% in the case where the model was estimated without bubbles and 16% in the case where the full model was estimated.

Extended Taylor rule where the central bank can observe bubbles. In this case, the monetary authorities understand that positive and negative bubbles may arise over time and can observe them. As expected, monetary authorities further improve the loss function. The benefit of this extra flexibility to respond to bubbles yields modest gains. Figure 5.12 shows the results of the optimal monetary policy as the weight on inflation in the monetary authorities' preferences is varied. In this setup, most of the gains arise from a reduction in the variance of output.

These results underscore the basic thesis of this paper. Monetary authorities should lean against tail risks (in this case represented by the likelihood of asset price bubbles) as they arise and should actively try to influence them so as to smooth output and inflation on average over the cycle. As the prospect for asset price bubbles arise, monetary authorities should ease monetary policy and maintain that easy stance until the tail risks recede.

These potential gains may be exaggerated. In practice, monetary authorities have very limited ability to observe small, emerging bubbles that will eventually

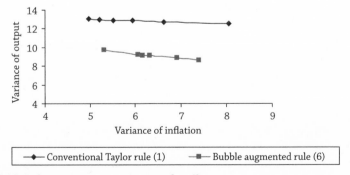

Figure 5.12 Inflation-output variance trade-off

develop into large, macroeconomically significant bubbles. In the model, they are able to respond early and with confidence as bubbles develop. Less problematic is the call for monetary authorities to respond to large asset price bubbles. Yes, they are also difficult to identify with a high level of confidence but they are somewhat easier to identify especially when they are correlated with prolonged credit expansion. Overall, these simulations have to be interpreted with care.

6. Policy Implications

The experience of Asia and the Pacific during the international financial crisis offers various lessons about the dynamics of asset price bubbles and their policy challenges. Before exploring the monetary policy challenges in some detail, it is important to briefly highlight some fiscal, foreign exchange reserve and general financial stability implications.

On the fiscal side, strong medium-term fiscal frameworks gave policymakers the ability to respond aggressively to crises. Instead of the fiscal situation raising the specter of fiscal dominance, skyrocketing sovereign risks and propelling the crisis forward, sound fiscal policies acted as an effective shock absorber. Now that the crisis is over and the acute need for stimulative fiscal packages has waned, the region can focus on restoring, and in some cases strengthening, the fiscal position of its economies. Indeed, for some central banks worried about economic overheating and rising inflation pressures, somewhat restrictive fiscal policy offers the benefits of slowing the growth of aggregate demand and of having less of an enticement effect on foreign capital flows than boosting policy interest rates.

On the foreign reserves side, the experience of the past 15 years has illustrated rather dramatically the importance of having an adequate war chest of reserves. Large reserve holdings are not without their costs, however. Carry costs of reserves can be very expensive, especially in low credit-rated jurisdictions. The accumulation of reserves may also lead to financial stability concerns. It is important to recognize that the size and form of the local currency liabilities that are the counterpart to foreign currency reserves may have major implications for the domestic financial system. If the reserve accumulation is sterilized by using reserve requirements, this policy tool acts as a tax on the regulated banking system and therefore may distort its growth, and drive financial services into the unregulated shadow banking system. If the issuance of central bank bills is used, prolonged reserve accumulations leave the banking system in emerging markets saddled with lazy assets that may increase the procyclicality of the financial system as banks search for yield. And, as we have seen in Latin America, as economies eschew foreign exchange rate smoothing via managing foreign exchange reserves, the private sector develops hedging devices that spur on financial deepening. Indeed, resisting exchange rate appreciation for too long and keeping the exchange rate too stable encourages borrowing in foreign currency by the private sector that has in the past been an important source of economic and financial instability.

The international financial crisis also underscores the broader perspective that the global financial system needs to be strengthened and made more resilient. Efforts at the G20, the Financial Stability Board, the Basel Committee on Bank Supervision, and the Committee on the Global Financial System, just to name a few key players, have been critical to achieving this aim. It is now important that the new principles and guidelines are implemented as part of a new framework for financial stability, not only in the economies that were most directly affected by the crisis, but by all, as there are considerable benefits from the new thinking.

MONETARY POLICY IMPLICATIONS

The spillovers of the international financial crisis to Asia and the Pacific have naturally presented daunting policy challenges for the central banks in the region. And there were valuable lessons that were learned. For example, the conventional wisdom prior to the crisis emphasized the importance of price stability as the primary objective of monetary policy. In the postcrisis period, there is a greater appreciation of the role that central banks also can play in helping to secure financial stability.

With respect to the bursting of asset price bubbles, we learned that monetary authorities are likely to respond in an asymmetric way. A hallmark of the precrisis conventional view of monetary policy was that central banks should act gradually on the way up the policy rate cycle, as well as on the way down. But the crisis revealed that a bursting bubble generates considerable downside risks to output, inflation, and the normal operation of the financial system. As a consequence, central bankers may need to respond aggressively, not gradually; by slashing policy rates, not by measured reductions over time; by communicating clearly the relevance of tail risks in the policy decisions, not by dwelling on the mean of the forecasts for inflation and output. In other words, the monetary policy strategy needs to be proactive and state-contingent.

In the case of negative bubbles, monetary authorities have to be wary of the fragility of private-sector confidence. When financial markets and investors are jittery about the future, prices of assets can become volatile. Such uncertainty will reduce substitutability across asset classes—and lead to significant mispricing. Overpricing of risk can raise the cost of borrowing, and the ensuing volatility in these costs can adversely affect the monetary transmission mechanism. As history has shown, monetary policy actions may be needed not only to counter the financial headwinds but also to restore confidence. And, even in the case where there is little evidence of a negative bubble, the mere possibility of a negative bubble may call for aggressive action from central banks in the form of a more accommodative stance on monetary policy than would otherwise be the case.

This bubble perspective suggests that monetary policy frameworks may need to formally incorporate state-contingent features. During normal periods, monetary authorities would generally adopt one strategy that relies more heavily on the role of stable market expectations. During periods of stress, monetary authorities may need to adopt more proactive policies.

In addition, there is a need for more research into the types of policy tools that would be most effective during periods of stress. During normal times, policy interest rates and flexible exchange rate regimes provide an effective environment in which monetary authorities operate. During periods of stress, however, there may be roles for quantitative tools of monetary policy. This is because of the reduced substitutability across assets and the impairment of the monetary transmission mechanism. The effectiveness of the specific tools will depend on the way in which the stress affects assets of differing riskiness and maturity. In emerging market economies, stress conditions may call for greater reliance on reserve requirements, liquidity facilities, and the asset composition of central bank balance sheets. The international financial crisis and its aftermath underscore the importance of having a better understanding of the relationship between interest rate policy tools and the wide range of quantitative tools available to monetary authorities.

Finally, as this paper has emphasized, these policy concerns arise in economies subject to domestically driven bubbles and also in economies subject to spillovers from other economies. Clearly, strengthening fundamentals—monetary, fiscal, and the financial system—are all important. Developing strategies to address spillovers is also important—just in case. And market confidence that an economy has a robust policy framework in place to counter periods of stress may by itself help insulate economies from the spillovers from ever reaching their shores. Such considerations may be rather important today as the long fight against the tail risks associated with a negative asset price bubble appears to be laying the foundation for frothy asset markets in Asia and the Pacific.

7. Conclusions

This paper argues for a more systematic exploration of the nexus of asset price bubbles and monetary policy. In contrast to the past literature, this paper focuses on the potential spillovers of a negative asset price bubble from one economy or set of economies to others. One key lesson from the crisis is that no matter how strong an economy's fundamentals are, and no matter how resilient it is to domestic economic and financial shocks, economic and financial globalization have opened up potent international transmission channels.

These policy challenges are difficult to model. The attempt to do so in this paper has yielded some encouraging results. The unconventional negative spillovers in the model are modeled by a negative asset price bubble, that is, macroeconomically significant asset prices that significantly undershoot values implied by medium-term fundamentals. This is modeled as a negative asset price bubble that represents a change in asset prices of greater persistence and nonlinearity than standard error processes in optimal monetary policy models. Despite this added complexity, the model can be solved and the policy implications analyzed.

The results highlight the role of tail risks in calibrating the monetary policy trade-offs facing central banks. These tail risks, of course, may not materialize and raise questions ex post about the policy responses in the aftermath of a financial crisis. However, it is important to evaluate central bank performance in this environment by the ex ante conditions. For flexible inflation-targeting central banks, this distinction may be particularly important at this policy juncture. The optimal monetary policy in this model suggests that central banks trade off the costs of higher inflation with the costs of prematurely withdrawing stimulus bolstering the normal operation of their financial markets.

In economies where this tail risk is significant, a short-term overshoot of inflation should be seen as part and parcel of an optimal monetary policy response, and not as a policy mistake. In other words, narrow inflation targeting is not optimal in the current policy setting. Moreover, the more elaborate trade-offs implied by the model could create communication complications for those central banks with flexible inflation-targeting regimes that have, in the past, convinced the public that medium-term inflation deviations from target, not accompanied by observable supply or demand shocks, were a yardstick for a central bank's performance.

Appendix

The calibration of the model is as follows:

Macroeconomic Block

$$\gamma_{US} = 0.2, \theta_{US} = 0.6 \text{ and } \varphi_{US} = 0.4;$$
$$\gamma_A = 0.2, \theta_A = 0.6, \ \theta_A^{US} = 0.3 \text{ and } \varphi_A = 0.4.$$
$$\alpha_{US} = 0.15 \text{ and } \beta_{US} = -0.04; \alpha_A = 0.15 \text{ and } \beta_A = -0.04$$

The two error terms, $\varepsilon_{t,US} \sim N(0,\sigma_{\varepsilon,US}^2); \varepsilon_{t,A} \sim N(0,\sigma_{\varepsilon,A}^2)$ and $\eta_{t,US} \sim N(0,\sigma_{\eta,US}^2);$ $\eta_{t,A} \sim N(0,\sigma_{\eta,A}^2)$, are assumed to be random variables with i.i.d. normal distributions with known variances $\sigma_{\varepsilon,US}^2 = 1.1$ and $\sigma_{\eta,US}^2 = 0.5; \sigma_{\varepsilon,A}^2 = 1.1$ and $\sigma_{\eta,A}^2 = 0.5$.

Asset Price Block

FUNDAMENTAL COMPONENT

The parameter on lagged output, λ_{US} and λ_A, is assumed to be 0.2 each and the error terms $v_{t,US} \sim N(0,\sigma^2_{v,US})$ and $v_{t,A} \sim N(0,\sigma^2_{v,A})$ are assumed to be random variables with an i.i.d. standard normal distribution with known variances $\sigma^2_{v,US} = 1.0$ and $\sigma^2_{v,A} = 1.0$.

BUBBLE COMPONENT

These state variables tracking the bubbles in each region, $I_{t,US}$ and $I_{t,A}$, have time-varying Markov probabilities governing the transitions:

$$P(I_{t,k} \mid I_{t-1,k}, X_{t-1,k}) = \begin{pmatrix} p_{-1,-1}(X_{t-1,k}) & p_{-1,0}(X_{t-1,k}) & 0 \\ p_{0,-1}(X_{t-1,k}) & p_{0,0}(X_{t-1,k}) & p_{0,1}(X_{t-1,k}) \\ 0 & p_{1,0}(X_{t-1,k}) & p_{1,1}(X_{t-1,k}) \end{pmatrix} \text{ for } k = \{US,A\}.$$

The corresponding multinomial probability distribution for $\zeta_{t,k}$ for k = {US,A} is

$$\pi_{B,t,k} = \zeta_{t,k} = \begin{cases} \theta_{p,k} & with\,probability\ p_{1,1}(\tilde{X}_{t-1,k}),\ given\,s_{t-1,k} = 1 \\ -\theta_{p,k}\tau_{t-1,k} & with\,probability\ 1 - p_{1,1}(\tilde{X}_{t-1,k}),\ given\,s_{t-1,k} = 1 \\ \theta_{p,k} & with\,probability\ p_{0,1}(\tilde{X}_{t-1,k}),\ given\,s_{t-1,k} = 0 \\ 0 & with\,probability\ p_{0,0}(\tilde{X}_{t-1,k}),\ given\,s_{t-1,k} = 0 \\ \theta_{n,k} & with\,probability\ p_{0,-1}(\tilde{X}_{t-1,k}),\ given\,s_{t-1,k} = 0 \\ \theta_{n,k} & with\,probability\ p_{-1,-1}(\tilde{X}_{t-1,k}),\ given\,s_{t-1,k} = -1 \\ -\theta_n\tau_{t-1,k} & with\,probability\ 1 - p_{-1,-1}(\tilde{X}_{t-1,k}),\ given\,s_{t-1,k} = -1 \end{cases},$$

where $\theta_{p,k}$ and $\theta_{n,k}$ represent the rate at which the bubble grows in the positive and negative bubble states, $\tau_{t-1,k}$ tracks the duration of the bubble phase, and $\tilde{X}_{t-1,k} = (y_{t-1,k}, r_{t-1,k})$. The bubble is parameterized so that $(\theta_{p,k} = 0.9, \theta_{n,k} = 0.9)$. The general specification of the time-varying transition probabilities is

$$P_{i,j,k} = G\left(\frac{\exp(\mu_{0,I_{t-1,k}} + \mu_{I_{t-1,k}}\tilde{X}_{t-1,k})}{1 + \exp(\mu_{0,I_{t-1},k} + \mu_{I_{t-1},k}\tilde{X}_{t-1,k})} \right) \text{ for } k = \{US,A\},$$

with the following parameterization:

$$P_{0,0,k} = 0.96 - 1.92 \times \left| \frac{\exp(0.5y_{t-1,k})}{1 + \exp(0.5y_{t-1,k})} - 0.5 \right|, \quad P_{0,1,k} = (1 - P_{0,0,k}) \times \frac{\exp(y_{t-1,k})}{1 + \exp(y_{t-1,k})},$$

$$P_{0,-1,k} = 1 - P_{0,0,k} - P_{0,1,k} \qquad \text{for } k = \{US,A\}.$$

The transition probabilities for the positive-bubble and negative-bubble states are

Version 1: $P_{1,1,US} = P_{-1,-1,US} = \exp(2.5)/(1+\exp(2.5))$ and

$$P_{1,1,A} = P_{-1,-1,A} = \exp(2.5)/(1+\exp(2.5)).$$

Version 2:

$$P_{1,1,US} = \frac{\exp(2.5+1.1y_{t-1,US}-0.4r_{t-1,US}-0.1\tau_{t-1,US})}{1+\exp(2.5+1.1y_{t-1,US}-0.4r_{t-1,US}-0.1\tau_{t-1,US})}, \; P_{1,0,US}=1-P_{1,1,US}$$

$$P_{-1,-1,US} = \frac{\exp(2.5-1.1y_{t-1,US}+0.4r_{t-1,US}-0.1\tau_{t-1,US})}{1+\exp(2.5-1.1y_{t-1,US}+0.4r_{t-1,US}-0.1\tau_{t-1,US})}, \; P_{-1,0,US}=1-P_{-1,-1,US}.$$

$$P_{1,1,A} = \frac{\exp(2.5+1.1y_{t-1,A}-0.4r_{t-1,A}-0.1\tau_{t-1,A})}{1+\exp(2.5+1.1y_{t-1,A}-0.4r_{t-1,A}-0.1\tau_{t-1,A})}, \; P_{1,0,A}=1-P_{1,1,A}$$

$$P_{-1,-1,A} = \frac{\exp(2.5-1.1y_{t-1,A}+0.4r_{t-1,A}-0.1\tau_{t-1,A})}{1+\exp(2.5-1.1y_{t-1,A}+0.4r_{t-1,A}-0.1\tau_{t-1,A})}, \; P_{-1,0,A}=1-P_{-1,-1,A}$$

Version 3:

$$P_{1,1,US} = \frac{\exp(2.5+1.1y_{t-1,US}-0.4r_{t-1,US}-0.1\tau_{t-1,US}+0.1\tau_{t-1,A})}{1+\exp(2.5+1.1y_{t-1,US}-0.4r_{t-1,US}-0.1\tau_{t-1,US}+0.1\tau_{t-1,A})}, \; P_{1,0,US}=1-P_{1,1,US}:$$

$$P_{-1,-1,US} = \frac{\exp(2.5-1.1y_{t-1,US}+0.4r_{t-1,US}-0.1\tau_{t-1,US}+0.1\tau_{t-1,A})}{1+\exp(2.5-1.1y_{t-1,US}+0.4r_{t-1,US}-0.1\tau_{t-1,US}+0.1\tau_{t-1,A})},$$

$$P_{-1,0,US} = 1-P_{-1,-1,US}.$$

$$P_{1,1,A} = \frac{\exp(2.5+1.1y_{t-1,A}-0.4r_{t-1,A}-0.1\tau_{t-1,A}+0.1\tau_{t-1,US})}{1+\exp(2.5+1.1y_{t-1,A}-0.4r_{t-1,A}-0.1\tau_{t-1,A}+0.1\tau_{t-1US})}, \; P_{1,0,A}=1-P_{1,1,A},$$

$$P_{-1,-1,A} = \frac{\exp(2.5-1.1y_{t-1,A}+0.4r_{t-1,A}-0.1\tau_{t-1,A}+0.1\tau_{t-1,US})}{1+\exp(2.5-1.1y_{t-1,A}+0.4r_{t-1,A}-0.1\tau_{t-1,US})}, \; P_{-1,0,A}=1-P_{-1,-1,A}.$$

MONETARY POLICY

The parameters of the loss function $(\mu_{\pi,k}, \mu_{r,k})$ for k = {US,A} are listed in the tables.

SOLUTION METHODS

The model is solved by simulating the shock processes and minimizing the monetary authorities loss function. Details are given in Filardo (2006).

Notes

1. We borrow these questions from the classic paper on the Japanese banking crisis by Hoshi and Kashyap (2000, 2004). While the questions are the same, the answers will be rather different. In the case of Japan, the crisis remained largely contained in the country and had its origin in the deep-seated problems of the Japanese banking system. In the case of the international financial crisis in Asia and the Pacific, the origin, dynamics, and geographic scope are much different. Even though Asia-Pacific economies learned the lessons of the Japanese experience, they could not escape the consequences of a different type of asset price bubble. This Asia-Pacific story will be told in this paper.
2. There is of course a long literature on bubbles from both historical and theoretical perspectives. See Shiller (1999, 2000) and Kindleberger (2000) for a broad historical perspective. This paper adopts the notion of irrational asset price bubbles (Meltzer, 2003), in contrast to their more mathematically rigorous cousins of the class of rational bubbles (Blanchard and Watson, 1982). The pragmatic policy perspective is consistent with that of Allen and Gale (1999) and Blanchard (2000).
3. See Detken and Smets (2004) and IMF (2009) for a general discussion of empirical asset price booms and busts. For housing price boom issues in particular, see Borio and McGuire (2004), Case and Shiller (2003), Himmelberg, Mayer and Sinai (2005) and Smith and Smith (2006).
4. See Filardo (2001, 2003a&b, 2006), for example.
5. The literature on asset prices bubbles and monetary policy has generally focused on the implications of positive asset price bubbles. These studies include Berger et al (2007) Bernanke and Gertler (1999, 2001), Bordo and Jeanne (2002), Borio and Lowe (2002, 2003), Borio and White (2003), Cecchetti et al (2000, 2003), Disyatat (2010), Gruen and Plumb (2005), Kent and Lowe (1997), and White (2006).
6. For greater detail, see Filardo et al. (2010).
7. Hoshi and Kashyap (2000) are particularly prescient in pointing out the parallels between the regulatory history of Japan and the United States, even if at the time they did not see that the similar pathologies in Japan's regulatory history were lurking under the surface and eventually would assert themselves in the United States. In a nutshell, they point out that weak underlying financial systems, despite apparent profitability during the good times, raise fundamental risks of crises with debilitating and prolonged macroeconomic consequences. Moreover, they highlight the tendency for deregulation and policy economy issues to metastasize over time, resulting in financial institutions seeking new lending opportunities without necessarily fully understanding—or the regulatory agencies recognizing—the risk exposures being created. Indeed, the newness of the financial environment as deregulation proceeds can lead to powerful incentives during the good times to overestimate the profitability of adopted strategies and underestimate the risk. See Gorton (2010) and Rajan (2010) for reflections on how perverse incentives in the U.S. financial system led to the international financial crisis. However, it is important to note that these perverse financial incentives were either absent or more muted in Asia and the Pacific, suggesting that Hoshi and Kashyap's brand of analysis sheds a bright light on the region's experience. Asia and the Pacific economies had adopted fairly conservative regulatory practices, reflecting lessons learned from the Japanese and Asian financial crisis experiences. While Asia and the Pacific were not immune to the powerful shock emanating from the West during the recent crisis, the speed at which these economies bounced back is a testament to the enduring applicability of the underlying financial analysis.
8. See Baba and Shim (2011) for a detailed analysis of the Korean case.

9. In particular, Andersen (1997) notes that financial variables are useful in tracking forecast errors (ex post) in bad times but not so helpful in good times. This asymmetry may justify stronger policy reactions to financial asset declines than increases (Turner, 2010).

10. Since all the right-hand-side variables of the rule are endogenous, even a conventional specification of a Taylor rule (i.e., responding to inflation and output) will yield different estimated coefficients when bubbles are assumed than when no bubbles are assumed.

References

Allen, F., and G. Gale. 1999. "Bubbles, Crises, and Policy." *Oxford Review of Economic Policy* 15 (3), 9–18.

Andersen, P. (1997). "Forecast Errors and Financial Developments." BIS Working Papers, No. 61, November.

Baba, N., and I. Shim. 2011. "Dislocations in the Won-Dollar Swap Markets during the Crisis of 2007–09." BIS Working Papers No. 344, April.

Berger, W., F. Kissmer, and H. Wagner. 2007. "Monetary Policy and Asset Prices: More Bad News for 'Benign Neglect.'" *International Finance* 10 (1), Spring, 1–20.

Bernanke, B., and M. Gertler. 1999. "Monetary Policy and Asset Price Volatility." In *New Challenges for Monetary Policy: A Symposium*. Kansas City, MO: Federal Reserve Bank of Kansas City. Reprinted in this volume.

———. 2001. "Should Central Banks Respond to Movements in Asset Prices?" *American Economic Review* 91 (2), May, 253–257.

Blanchard, O. 2000. "Bubbles, Liquidity Traps and Monetary Policy." In A. Posen and R. Mikitani, eds., *Japan's Financial Crisis*. Washington, DC: International Institute of Economics, 185–193.

Blanchard, O., and M. Watson. 1982. "Bubbles, Rational Expectations and Financial Markets." In P. Wachtel, ed., *Crises in the Economic and Financial Structure*. Lexington, MA: Lexington Books, 295–315.

Bordo, M., and O. Jeanne. 2002. "Boom-Busts in Asset Prices, Economic Instability, and Monetary Policy." NBER Working Paper No. 8966.

Borio, C., and P. Lowe. 2002. "Asset Prices, Financial and Monetary Stability: Exploring the Nexus." Paper presented at the BIS Conference "Changes in Risk Through Time: Measurement and Policy Options." BIS Working Papers No. 114.

———. 2003. "Imbalances or 'Bubbles'? Implications for Monetary and Financial Stability." In W. Hunter, G. Kaufman, and M. Pomerleano, eds., *Asset Price Bubbles: The Implications for Monetary, Regulatory, and International Policies*. Cambridge, MA: MIT Press, 247–270.

Borio, C., and P. McGuire. 2004. "Twin Peaks in Equity and Housing Prices." *BIS Quarterly Review*, March, 79–93.

Borio, C., and W. White. 2003. "Whither Monetary and Financial Stability? The Implications of Evolving Policy Regimes." In *Monetary Policy and Uncertainty: Adapting to a Changing Economy*. Kansas City, MO: Federal Reserve Bank of Kansas City, 131–211.

Case, K., and R. Shiller. 2003. "Is There a Bubble in the Housing Market? An Analysis." *Brookings Papers on Economic Activity* 2, 299–362.

Cecchetti, S., H. Genberg, J. Lipsky, and S. Wadhwani. 2000. "Asset Prices and Monetary Policy." Report prepared for the conference "Central Banks and Asset Prices," organized by the International Centre for Monetary and Banking Studies, Geneva, May.

Cecchetti, S., H. Genberg, and S. Wadhwani. 2003. "Asset Prices in a Flexible Inflation Targeting Framework." In W. Hunter, G. Kaufman, and M. Pomerleano, eds., *Asset Price Bubbles: The Implications for Monetary, Regulatory, and International Policies*. Cambridge, MA: MIT Press, 427–444.

Detken, C., and F. Smets. 2004. "Asset Price Booms and Monetary Policy." In H. Siebert, ed., *Macroeconomic Policies in the World Economy*. Berlin: Springer.

Disyatat, P. 2010. "Inflation Targeting, Asset Prices and Financial Imbalances: Conceptualizing the Debate." *Journal of Financial Stability* 6 (3), 145–155.

Filardo A. 2001. "Should Monetary Policy Respond to Asset Price Bubbles? Some Experimental Results." In G. Kaufman, ed., *Asset Price Bubbles: Implications for Monetary and Regulatory Policies*, Amsterdam: Elsevier Science, 99–124.

———. 2003a. "Monetary Policy and Asset Price Bubbles: Calibrating the Monetary Policy Tradeoffs." BIS working paper presented at the Bank of Korea Conference on Monetary Policy and Asset Prices, October 30.

———. 2003b. "Should Monetary Authorities Prick Asset Price Bubbles?" BIS working paper, December.

———. 2006. "Asset Price Bubbles and Monetary Policy: A Multivariate Extension." BIS, working paper, November.

Filardo, A., J. George, M. Loretan, G. Ma, A. Munro, I. Shim, P. Wooldridge, J. Yetman, and H. Zhu. 2010. "The International Financial Crisis: Timeline, Impact and Policy Responses in Asia and the Pacific." *BIS Papers* 52, 21–82.

Gorton, G. 2010. *Slapped by the Invisible Hand: The Panic of 2007*. New York: Oxford University Press.

Gruen, D., M. Plumb, and A. Stone. 2005. "How Should Monetary Policy Respond to Asset Price Bubbles?" *International Journal of Central Banking* 1(3), 1–33.

Himmelberg, C., C. Mayer, and T. Sinai. 2005. "Assessing High House Prices: Bubbles, Fundamentals and Misperceptions." *Journal of Economic Perspectives* 19 (4), 67–92.

Hoshi, T., and A. Kashyap. 2000. "The Japanese Banking Crisis: Where Did It Come From and How Will It End?" *NBER Macroeconomics Annual 1999*. National Bureau of Economic Research, Inc., 129–212.

———. 2004. "Japan's Financial Crisis and Economic Stagnation." *Journal of Economic Perspectives*, Winter, 3–26.

International Monetary Fund. 2009. "Lessons for Monetary Policy from Asset Price Fluctuations." *World Economic Outlook*, October, 93–120.

Kent, C., and P. Lowe. 1997. "Asset-Price Bubbles and Monetary Policy." Reserve Bank of Australia Research Discussion Papers No. 9709, December.

Kim, D., M. Loretan, and E. Remolona. 2010. "Contagion and Risk Premia in the Amplification of Crisis: Evidence from Asian Names in the Global CDS Market." *BIS Papers* 52, 318–339.

Kindleberger, C. 2000. *Manias, Panics and Crashes*. 4th ed. Cambridge: Cambridge University Press.

Meltzer, A. 2003. "Rational and Nonrational Bubbles," In W. Hunter, G. Kaufman, and M. Pomerleano, eds., *Asset Price Bubbles: The Implications for Monetary, Regulatory, and International Policies*. Cambridge, MA: MIT Press, 23–34.

Rajan, R. 2010. *Fault Lines: How Hidden Fractures Still Threaten the World Economy*. Princeton, NJ: Princeton University Press.

Shiller, R. 1999. "From Efficient Markets to Behavioral Finance." *Journal of Economic Perspectives* 17 (1), Winter, 83–104.

———. 2000. *Irrational Exuberance*. Princeton, NJ: Princeton University Press.

Smith, M., and G. Smith. 2006. "Bubble, Bubble, Where's the Housing Bubble?" *Brookings Papers on Economic Activity* 37 (1), March, 1–68.

Turner, P. 2010. "Central Banks and the Financial Crisis." *BIS Papers* 51, 21–25.

White, W. 2006. "Is Price Stability Enough?" BIS Working Papers No. 205, April.

BUBBLES AND MONETARY POLICY

CHAPTER 6

Monetary Policy and Asset Price Volatility

Ben Bernanke and Mark Gertler

During the past 20 years, the world's major central banks have been largely successful at bringing inflation under control. Although it is premature to suggest that inflation is no longer an issue of great concern, it is quite conceivable that the next battles facing central bankers will lie on a different front. One development that has already concentrated the minds of policymakers is an apparent increase in financial instability, of which one important dimension is increased volatility of asset prices. Borio, Kennedy, and Prowse (1994), among others, document the emergence of major boom-bust cycles in the prices of equity and real estate in a number of industrialized countries during the 1980s. Notable examples include the United States, Japan, the United Kingdom, the Netherlands, Sweden, and Finland.

Associated with the "bust" part of the asset price cycle in many of these cases were significant contractions in real economic activity. For example, many economists attribute at least some part of the 1990 recession (and the slow recovery) in the United States to the preceding decline in commercial real estate prices, which weakened the capital positions of banks and the balance sheets of corporate borrowers (Bernanke and Lown 1991). More recently, of course, we have seen asset price crashes in East Asia and Latin America, along with continued stagnation of stock and land prices in Japan, all of which have been associated with poor economic performance. With these experiences in mind, some observers have viewed the remarkable rise of the past few years in U.S. stock prices, and to a lesser extent in real estate prices, as an ominous development. Of course, as of this writing, whether the U.S. stock market boom will be sustained or will end in tears is anybody's guess.

In this paper we address the question of how central bankers ought to respond to asset price volatility, in the context of an overall strategy for monetary policy. To be clear, we agree that monetary policy is not by itself a sufficient tool to contain the potentially damaging effects of booms and busts in asset prices. Well-designed and transparent legal and accounting systems, a sound regulatory structure that helps to limit the risk exposure of banks and corporations, and prudent fiscal policies that help instill public confidence in economic fundamentals, are all vital components of an overall strategy to insulate the economy from financial disturbances. However, our reading of history is that asset price crashes have done sustained damage to the economy only in cases when monetary policy remained unresponsive or actively reinforced deflationary pressures. This observation is our justification for focusing on monetary policy here.

The principal argument of the paper is easily stated. Our view is that, in the context of short-term monetary policy management, central banks should view price stability and financial stability as highly complementary and mutually consistent objectives, to be pursued within a unified policy framework. In particular, we believe that the best policy framework for attaining both objectives is a regime of flexible inflation-targeting, either of the implicit form now practiced in the United States or of the more explicit and transparent type that has been adopted in many other countries. (We prefer the latter, for reasons explained briefly at the conclusion of the paper.)

The inflation-targeting approach dictates that central banks should adjust monetary policy actively and preemptively to offset incipient inflationary or deflationary pressures. Importantly, for present purposes, it also implies that policy should *not* respond to changes in asset prices, except insofar as they signal changes in expected inflation. Trying to stabilize asset prices per se is problematic for a variety of reasons, not the least of which is that it is nearly impossible to know for sure whether a given change in asset values results from fundamental factors, nonfundamental factors, or both. By focusing on the inflationary or deflationary pressures generated by asset price movements, a central bank effectively responds to the toxic side effects of asset booms and busts without getting into the business of deciding what is a fundamental and what is not. It also avoids the historically relevant risk that a bubble, once "pricked," can easily degenerate into a panic. Finally, because inflation targeting both helps to provide stable macroeconomic conditions and also implies that interest rates will tend to rise during (inflationary) asset price booms and fall during (deflationary) asset price busts, this approach may reduce the potential for financial panics to arise in the first place.

The remainder of the paper is organized as follows. We begin in Section 1 with an informal summary of our views on how asset prices interact with the real economy and of the associated implications for monetary policy. To address these issues more formally, Sections 2 and 2 present some illustrative policy simulations derived from a small-scale macroeconomic model that features an explicit role for financial conditions in determining real activity. We move from theory to practice in Section 4, in which we briefly examine the recent performance of monetary policy in the United States and Japan, both of which have experienced asset price volatility. Section 5 concludes with some discussion of additional issues. The appendix provides more details of the simulation model employed in Sections 2 and 3.

1. Asset Prices, the Economy, and Monetary Policy: An Overview

Asset prices, including, in particular, the prices of equities and real estate, are remarkably variable. And although we must not lose sight of the fact that ultimately asset prices are endogenous variables, there are periods when asset values seem all but disconnected from the current state of the economy. As we noted in the introduction, during the past two decades economies across the globe have experienced large boom-bust cycles in the prices of various assets, including equities, commercial real estate, residential housing, and others.

Should fluctuations in asset prices be of concern to policymakers? In the economist's usual benchmark case, a world of efficient capital markets and without regulatory distortions, movements in asset prices simply reflect changes in underlying economic fundamentals. Under these circumstances, central bankers would have no reason to concern themselves with asset price volatility per se. Asset prices would be of interest only to the extent that they provide useful information about the state of the economy.

Matters change, however, if two conditions are met. The first is that "nonfundamental" factors sometime underlie asset market volatility. The second is that changes in asset prices unrelated to fundamental factors have potentially significant impacts on the rest of the economy. If these two conditions are satisfied, then asset price volatility becomes, to some degree, an independent source of economic instability, of which policymakers should take account.

That both of these conditions hold seems plausible to us, though there is room for disagreement on either count. We briefly discuss each in turn.

As potential sources of "nonfundamental" fluctuations in asset prices, at least two possibilities have been suggested: poor regulatory practice and imperfect rationality on the part of investors ("market psychology"). Regarding the former, Borio and others present evidence for the view that financial reforms that dramatically increased access to credit by firms and households contributed to asset price booms in the 1980s in Scandinavia, Japan, the Netherlands, the United Kingdom, and elsewhere. Financial liberalizations in developing countries that have opened the gates for capital inflows from abroad have also been associated in some cases with sharply rising asset values, along with booms in consumption and lending.

But aren't liberalizations a good thing? It depends. As Allen and Gale (2000) and others have emphasized, problems arise when financial liberalizations are not well coordinated with the regulatory safety net (for example, deposit insurance and lender-of-last-resort commitments). If liberalization gives additional powers to private lenders and borrowers while retaining government guarantees of liabilities, excessive risk-taking and speculation will follow, leading, in many cases, to asset price booms. Ultimately, however, unsound financial conditions are exposed and lending and asset prices collapse. This scenario seems to characterize reasonably well the banking crises recently experienced in a number of countries, including the United States and Japan, as well as some of the recent crises in East Asia and Latin America.

The other possible source of nonfundamental movements in asset prices that has received much attention is irrational behavior by investors, for example, herd behavior, excessive optimism, or short-termism. There is, of course, a large amount of literature on bubbles, fads, and the like. This literature has gained a measure of credence because of the great difficulty of explaining the observed level of financial volatility by models based solely on economic fundamentals (see, for example, the recent survey by Campbell, 1999). Advocates of bubbles would probably be forced to admit that it is difficult or impossible to identify any particular episode conclusively as a bubble, even after the fact.[1] Nevertheless, episodes of "irrational exuberance" in financial markets are certainly a logical possibility, and one about which at least some central bankers are evidently concerned. With this concern as motivation, we present simulations of the economic effects of bubbles and of alternative policy responses to bubbles in Section 3.

The second necessary condition for asset price volatility to be of concern to policymakers is that booms and busts in asset markets have important effects on the real economy. Although the two-way causality between the economy and asset prices makes it difficult to obtain sharp estimates of the real effects of changes in asset prices, the historical experience—from the Great Depression of the 1930s to the most recent epidemic of crises—is supportive of the view that large asset price fluctuations can have important effects on the economy.

What are the mechanisms? One much-cited possibility is that changes in asset prices affect consumption spending via their effects on household wealth. We are not inclined to place a heavy weight on this channel, however. Empirical studies (for example, Ludvigson and Steindel 1999; Parker 1998) have not found a strong or reliable connection between stock market wealth and consumption, for example. This result is, perhaps, not too surprising, as much of the stock owned by households is held in pension accounts, implying that changes in stock values have relatively little direct impact on spendable cash.

Our own view is that the quantitatively most important connections between asset prices and the real economy operate through aspects of what in earlier work we have called the "balance-sheet channel."[2] The world in which we live, as opposed to the one envisioned by the benchmark neoclassical model, is one in which credit markets are not frictionless; that is, problems of information, incentives, and enforcement are pervasive. Because of these problems, credit can be extended more freely and at lower cost to borrowers who already have strong financial positions (hence, Ambrose Bierce's definition of a banker as someone who lends you an umbrella when the sun is shining and wants it back when it starts to rain).

A key implication of the existence of credit-market frictions is that cash flows and the condition of balance sheets are important determinants of agents' ability to borrow and lend. Research suggests that the effects of asset price changes on the economy are transmitted to a very significant extent through their effects on the balance sheets of households, firms, and financial intermediaries (see, for example, Bernanke, Gertler, and Gilchrist 1999; Bernanke and Gertler 1995). For example, firms or households may use assets they hold as collateral when borrowing, in order to ameliorate information and incentive problems that would otherwise interfere with credit extension. Under such circumstances, a decline in asset values (for example, a fall in home equity values) reduces available collateral, leads to an unplanned increase in leverage on the part of borrowers, and impedes potential borrowers' access to credit. Financial intermediaries, which must maintain an adequate ratio of capital to assets, can be deterred from lending, or induced to shift the composition of loans away from bank-dependent sectors such as small business, by declines in the values of the assets they hold.

Deteriorating balance sheets and reduced credit flows operate primarily on spending and aggregate demand in the short run, although in the longer run they may also affect aggregate supply by inhibiting capital formation and reducing working capital. There also are likely to be significant feedback and magnification effects. First, declining sales and employment imply continuing weakening of cash flows and, hence, further declines in spending. Bernanke, Gertler, and Gilchrist (1996) refer to this magnification effect as the "financial accelerator" (see Bernanke and Gertler 1989 for an early formalization). Second, there may also be feedback to asset prices, as declining spending and income, together with forced asset sales, lead to further decreases in asset values. This "debt-deflation" mechanism, first described by Irving Fisher (1933), has been modeled formally by Bernanke and Gertler (1989), Kiyotaki and Moore (1997), and Bernanke, Gertler, and Gilchrist (1999).

A large amount of literature has studied the macroeconomic implications of credit-market frictions, both theoretically and empirically.[3] We have reviewed that body of research on several occasions and will not attempt to do so here. We note, however, that in general this perspective has proved quite useful for interpreting a number of historical episodes, including the Great Depression (Bernanke 1983; Bernanke and James 1991), the deep Scandinavian recession of the 1980s, the "credit crunch" episode of 1990–1991 in the United States (Bernanke and Lown 1991), and the protracted weakness of the Japanese economy in the 1990s. A number of observers (Mishkin 1997; Aghion, Bacchetta, and Banerjee 1999; Krugman 1999) also have used this framework to make sense of the fact that, contrary to conventional wisdom, exchange-rate devaluations have appeared to be contractionary in a number of the developing countries that experienced financial crises in recent years. The explanation is tied to the fact that—beguiled by sometimes large interest differentials between loans made in foreign and domestic currencies—banks and corporations in these countries made liberal use of unhedged, foreign-currency-denominated debt. The large devaluations that subsequently occurred raised the domestic-currency value of these debts, wreaking havoc with bank and corporate balance sheets and inducing financial distress and major dislocations in credit, employment, and supplier relationships.

Beyond providing a mechanism via which nonfundamental movements in asset prices may disrupt the economy, a key implication of the credit-market-frictions perspective is that the magnitude of the effects of asset price fluctuations on the economy will depend strongly on *initial* financial conditions. By the term, we mean primarily the initial state of household, firm, and intermediary balance sheets.[4] In particular, the theory predicts a highly nonlinear effect of asset prices on spending (Bernanke and Gertler 1989). Thus, if balance sheets are initially strong, with low leverage and strong cash flows, then even rather large declines in asset prices are unlikely to push households and firms into the region of financial distress, in which normal access to credit is jeopardized, or to lead to severe capital problems for banks. Put another way, the extent to which an asset price contraction weakens private-sector balance sheets depends on the degree and sectoral distribution of initial risk exposure.

The current (1999) U.S. economy is, we conjecture, a case in point. After many years of expansion, strong profits in both the corporate and banking sectors, and enormous increases in the values of equities and other assets, U.S. balance sheets are in excellent condition. A correction in the stock market of, say, 25% would, no doubt, slow the economy, but our guess is that the effects would be relatively transitory, particularly if monetary policy responds appropriately. In contrast, a 25% decline in Japanese stock prices, given the parlous condition of its financial system and its seeming inability to implement a coherent stabilization policy, would (we expect) create grave and long-lasting problems for that economy.

If we believe that asset price swings can occur for nonfundamental reasons, and that these swings—either through balance-sheet effects or some other channel—have the potential to destabilize the real economy, then what are the implications for monetary policy? As suggested in the introduction, our view is that central banks can and should treat price stability and financial stability as consistent and mutually reinforcing objectives. In practice, we believe, this is best accomplished by adopting a strategy of flexible inflation targeting.[5]

What is flexible inflation targeting? Although specific practices differ, broadly speaking, a regime of inflation targeting has three characteristics. First, as the name suggests, under inflation targeting, monetary policy is committed to achieving a specific level of inflation in the long run, and long-run price stability is designated the "overriding" or "primary" long-run goal of policy. Importantly, inflation targeters are concerned that inflation not be too low as well as that it not be too high; avoidance of deflation is as important as (or perhaps even more important than) avoidance of high inflation. Second, within the constraints imposed by the long-run inflation objective, the central bank has some flexibility in the short run to pursue other objectives, including output stabilization—hence, the nomenclature "flexible inflation targeting."[6] Third, inflation targeting is generally characterized by substantial openness and transparency on the part of monetary policymakers, including, for example, the issuance of regular reports on the inflation situation and open public discussion of policy options and plans.

Our characterization of Federal Reserve policy in recent years is that it meets the first two parts of the definition of inflation targeting (see Section 4 for econometric support of this view) but not the third; that is, the Fed practices "implicit" rather than "explicit" inflation targeting. Bernanke and others (1999) argue that the Fed ought to take the next step and adopt explicit inflation-targeting. For most of the present paper, however, we make no distinction between implicit and explicit inflation-targeting; we return to the issue briefly in the conclusion.

For our purposes here, the main advantage of flexible inflation targeting is that it provides a unified framework both for making monetary policy in normal times, and for preventing and ameliorating the effects of financial crises. In particular, a key advantage of the inflation-targeting framework is that it induces policymakers to automatically adjust interest rates in a stabilizing direction in the face of asset price instability or other financial disturbances. The logic is straightforward; since asset price increases stimulate aggregate demand and asset price declines reduce it, the strong focus of inflation targeters on stabilizing aggregate demand will result in "leaning against the wind"—raising interest rates as asset prices rise and reducing them when they fall. This automatic response not only stabilizes the economy but it is likely to be stabilizing for financial markets themselves for several reasons. First, macroeconomic stability, particularly the absence of inflation or deflation, is itself calming to financial markets.[7] Second, the central bank's easing in the face of asset price declines should help to insulate balance sheets to some degree, reducing the economy's vulnerability to further adverse shocks. And, finally, if financial-market participants expect the central bank to behave in this countercyclical manner, raising interest rates when asset price increases threaten to overheat the economy and vice versa, it is possible that overreactions in asset prices arising from market psychology and other nonfundamental forces might be moderated.

The logic of inflation targeting also implies that central banks should ignore movements in stock prices that do not appear to be generating inflationary or deflationary pressures. We concede that forecasting the aggregate demand effects of asset price movements may not always be an easy task. However, it is certainly easier than, first, attempting to distinguish between fundamental and nonfundamental fluctuations in asset prices and, second, attempting to surgically "prick" the bubble without doing collateral damage to financial markets or the economy. We explore the implications of alternative policy responses to asset price fluctuations in greater detail in the next two sections.

2. Monetary Policy in the Presence of Asset Price Bubbles: A Quantitative Model

To make the discussion of Section 1 more concrete, we will present some model-based simulations of the performance of alternative monetary rules in the presence of bubbles in asset prices. To do this, we extend a small-scale macroeconomic model developed by Bernanke, Gertler, and Gilchrist (1999), henceforth BGG. For the most part, the BGG model is a standard dynamic new Keynesian model, modified to allow for financial accelerator effects, as described in the previous section. Our principal extension of the BGG model here is to allow for exogenous bubbles in asset prices.

In this section, we first provide an informal overview of the BGG model and then describe how we modify the model to allow for bubbles in asset prices. The equations of the complete model are given in the appendix.[8] (Readers who are not interested in any of this background material may wish to skip directly to the simulation results in Section 3.)

THE BGG MODEL

As noted, the foundation of the BGG model is a standard dynamic new Keynesian framework. The most important sectors are a household sector and a business sector. Households are infinitely lived; they work, consume, and save. Business firms are owned by entrepreneurs who have finite expected life.[9] There is also a government that manages fiscal and monetary policy.

Firms own the stock of physical capital, financing the acquisition of capital through internally generated funds (primarily revenues from production and capital gains on assets) and by borrowing from the public. With their accumulated capital plus hired labor, firms produce output, which may be used for consumption, investment, or government purchases. There is no foreign sector.

Following Taylor (1980), Calvo (1983), and others, BGG assume the existence of staggered nominal price setting. The resulting "stickiness" in prices allows monetary policy to have real effects on the economy. Optimization and forward-looking behavior are assumed throughout; the single exception is the Phillips curve relationship, in which inflation expectations are modeled as being formed by a combination of forward- and backward-looking behavior.[10] This modification increases the persistence of the inflation process, allowing a closer fit to the data.

The BGG model differs from this standard dynamic new Keynesian framework primarily in assuming the existence of credit-market frictions, that is, problems of information, incentives, and enforcement in credit relationships. The presence of these frictions gives rise to a "financial accelerator" that affects output dynamics. In particular, in the BGG model, credit-market frictions make uncollateralized external finance more expensive than internal finance. This premium for external finance affects the overall cost of capital and, thus, the real investment decisions of firms. The external finance premium depends inversely on the financial condition of potential borrowers. For example, a borrowing firm with more internal equity can offer more collateral to lenders. Thus, procyclical movements in the financial condition of potential borrowers translate into countercyclical movements in the premium for external finance, which, in turn, magnify investment and output fluctuations in the BGG model (the financial accelerator).

Consider, for example, a shock to the economy that improves fundamentals, such as a technological breakthrough. This shock will have direct effects on output, employment, and the like. In the BGG model, however, there are also indirect effects of the shock, arising from the associated increase in asset prices. Higher asset prices improve balance sheets, reducing the external finance premium and further stimulating investment spending. The increase in investment may also lead to further increases in asset prices and cash flows, inducing additional feedback effects on spending. Thus, the financial accelerator enhances the effects of primitive shocks to the economy.

The financial accelerator mechanism also has potentially important implications for the workings of monetary policy. As in conventional frameworks, the existence of nominal rigidities gives the central bank in the BGG model some control over the short-term real interest rate. However, beyond the usual neoclassical channels through which the real interest rate affects spending, in the BGG model there is an additional effect that arises from the impact of interest rates on borrower balance sheets. For example, a reduction in the real interest rate (a policy easing) raises asset prices, improving the financial condition of borrowers and reducing the external finance premium. The reduction in the premium provides additional stimulus for investment. BGG find the extra "kick" provided by this mechanism to be important for explaining the quantitative effects of monetary policy. Note also that, to the extent that financial crises are associated with deteriorating private-sector balance sheets, the BGG framework implies that monetary policy has a direct means of calming such crises.

The BGG model assumes that only fundamentals drive asset prices, so that the financial accelerator serves to amplify only fundamental shocks, such as shocks to productivity or spending. Our extension of the BGG framework in this paper allows for the possibility that nonfundamental factors affect asset prices, which, in turn, affect the real economy via the financial accelerator.

ADDING EXOGENOUS ASSET PRICE BUBBLES

The fundamental value of capital is the present value of the dividends the capital is expected to generate. Formally, define the fundamental value of depreciable capital in period t, Q_t as:

$$Q_t = E_t \sum_{i=0}^{\infty} [(1-\delta)^i D_{t+1+i} / \prod_{j=0}^{i} R^q_{t+1+j}$$

$$= E_t\{[D_{t+1} + (1-\delta)Q_{t+1}] / R^q_{t+1}\}, \qquad (2.1)$$

where E_t indicates the expectation as of period t, δ is the physical depreciation rate of capital, D_{t+i} are dividends, and R_{t+1} is the relevant stochastic gross discount rate at t for dividends received in period $t + 1$.

As noted, our principal modification of the BGG model is to allow for the possibility that observed equity prices differ persistently from fundamental values, for example, because of "bubbles" or "fads."[11] We use the term "bubble" here loosely to denote temporary deviations of asset prices from fundamental values, due, for example, to liquidity trading or to waves of optimism or pessimism.[12]

The key new assumption is that the market price of capital, S_t, may differ from capital's fundamental value, Q_t. A bubble exists whenever $S_t - Q_t \neq 0$. We assume that if a bubble exists at date t, it persists with probability p and grows as follows:[13]

$$S_{t+1} - Q_{t+1} = \frac{a}{p}(S_t - Qt)R^q_{t+1},\qquad (2.2)$$

with $p < a < 1$. If the bubble crashes, with probability $1 - p$, then

$$S_{t+1} = -Q_{t+1} = 0. \qquad (2.3)$$

Note that, because $a/p > 1$, the bubble will grow until such time as it bursts. For simplicity, we assume that if a bubble crashes it is not expected to reemerge. These assumptions imply that the expected part of the bubble follows the process

$$E_t\left(\frac{S_{t+1} - Q_{t+1}}{R^q_{t+1}}\right) = a(S_t - Q_t). \qquad (2.4)$$

Because the parameter a is restricted to be less than unity, the discounted value of the bubble converges to zero over time, with the rate governed by the value of a.[14] That is, bubbles are not expected to last forever.

Using (2.1) and (2.4) we can derive an expression for the evolution of the stock price, inclusive of the bubble:

$$S_t = E_t\{[D_{t+1} + (1 + \delta)S_{t+1}]/R^s_{t+1}\}, \qquad (2.5)$$

where the return on stocks, R^s_{t+1}, is related to the fundamental return on capital, R^q_{t+1}, by

$$R^s_{t+1} = R^q_{t+1}\left[b + (1 - b)\frac{Q_t}{S_t}\right]. \qquad (2.6)$$
$$\text{and } b \equiv a(1 - \delta).$$

Equation (2.6) shows that, in the presence of bubbles, the expected return on stocks will differ from the return implied by fundamentals. If there is a positive bubble, $S_t/Q_t > 1$, the expected return on stocks will be below the fundamental return, and vice versa if there is a negative bubble, $S_t/Q_t < 1$. However, if the bubble persists (does not "pop") a series of supranormal returns will be observed. This process seems to us to provide a reasonable description of speculative swings in the stock market.

The bubble affects real activity in the extended model in two ways. First, there is a wealth effect on consumption. Following estimates of the wealth effect presented in Ludvigson and Steindel (1999), we parameterize the model so that these effects are relatively modest (about four cents of consumption spending for each extra dollar of stock market wealth). Second, because the quality of firms' balance sheets depends on the market values of their assets rather than the fundamental values, a bubble in asset prices affects firms' financial positions and, thus, the premium for external finance.

Although bubbles in the stock market affect balance sheets and, thus, the cost of capital, we continue to assume that—conditional on the cost of capital—firms make investments based on fundamental considerations, such as net present value, rather than on valuations of capital including the bubble. This assumption rules out the arbitrage of building new capital and selling it at the market price *cum* bubble (or, equivalently, issuing new shares to finance new capital). This assumption is theoretically justifiable, for example, by the lemons premium associated with new equity issues, and also seems empirically realistic; see, for example, Bond and Cummins (1999).

In summary, the main change effected by our extension of the BGG framework is to allow nonfundamental movements in asset prices to influence real activity. Although the source of the shock may differ, however, the main link between changes in asset prices and the real economy remains the financial accelerator, as in the BGG model.

3. The Impact of Asset Price Fluctuations under Alternative Monetary Policy Rules

In this section we use the extended BGG model to simulate the effects of asset price bubbles and related shocks, such as innovations to the risk spread, on the economy. Our goal is to explore what types of policy rules are best at moderating the disruptive effects of asset market disturbances. To foreshadow the results, we find that a policy rule that is actively focused on stabilizing inflation seems to work well, and that this result is reasonably robust across different scenarios.

As a baseline, we assume that the central bank follows a simple forward-looking policy rule of the form

$$r^n_t = r^{-n} + \beta E_t \, \pi_{t+1}, \tag{3.1}$$

where r^n_t is the nominal instrument interest rate controlled by the central bank, r^{-n} is the steady-state value of the nominal interest rate, and $E_t \, \pi_{t+1}$ is the rate of inflation expected in the next model "period." We will always assume $\beta > 1$, so that the central bank responds to a one-percentage-point increase in expected inflation by raising the nominal interest rate by more than one percentage point. This ensures that the real interest rate increases in the face of rising expected inflation, so that policy is stabilizing.

The policy rule given by equation (3.1) differs from the conventional Taylor rule in at least two ways.[15] First, policy is assumed to respond to anticipations of inflation rather than past values of inflation. Clarida, Gali, and Gertler (1998, 2000) show that forward-looking reaction functions are empirically descriptive of the behavior of the major central banks since 1979. See also the estimates presented in the next section of this paper. The second difference from the standard Taylor rule is that equation (3.1) omits the usual output gap term. We do this primarily for simplicity and to reduce the number of dimensions along which the simulations must be varied. There are a number of rationales for this omission that are worth brief mention, however. First, for shocks that primarily affect aggregate demand, such as shocks to asset prices, rules of the form (3.1) and rules that include an output gap term will be essentially equivalent in their effects. Second, as we will see in the next section, empirical estimates of the responsiveness of central banks to the output gap conditional on expected inflation are often rather small. Finally, assuming for simulation purposes that the central bank can actually observe the output gap with precision probably overstates the case in reality. By leaving out this term we avoid the issue of how accurately the central bank can estimate the gap.

Although we do not include the output gap in the policy rule (3.1), because of our focus on asset price fluctuations, we do consider a variant of (3.1) that allows the central bank to respond to changes in stock prices. Specifically, as an alternative to (3.1), we assume that the instrument rate responds to the once-lagged log level of the stock price, relative to its steady-state value:

$$r^n_t = r^{-n} + \beta E_t\, \pi_{t+1} + \xi \log\left(\frac{S_{t-1}}{S}\right). \tag{3.2}$$

Alternative interpretations of policy rules like (3.2) are discussed in the next section.

We conducted a variety of simulation experiments, of which we here report an illustrative sampling. We begin with simulations of the effects of a stock market bubble that begins with an exogenous one percentage point increase in stock prices (above fundamentals). We parameterize equation (2.4), which governs the bubble process, so that the nonfundamental component of the stock price roughly doubles each period, as long as the bubble persists.[16] The bubble is assumed to last for five periods and then burst.[17] Just before the collapse, the nonfundamental component is worth about 16% of the initial steady-state fundamental value.

Asset bubbles with policy responding only to inflation. Figure 6.1 illustrates the simulated responses of the economy[18] to the bubble under two policy rules of the form (3.1): an "inflation accommodating" policy for which β + 1.01 and a more aggressive "inflation targeting" policy for which β + 2.0.[19]

As Figure 6.1 shows, under the accommodating policy, the bubble stimulates aggregate demand, leading the economy to "overheat." Inflation and output rise sharply. The rise in stock prices stimulates spending and output both through the balance-sheet effects described earlier (notice the decline in the external finance premium in the figure, which stimulates borrowing) and through wealth effects on consumption (which are the relatively less important quantitatively). When the bubble bursts, there is a corresponding collapse in firms' net worth. The resulting deterioration in credit markets is reflected in a sharp increase in the external finance premium (the spread between firms' borrowing rates and the safe rate) and a rapid fall in output. The decline in output after the bursting of the bubble is greater than the initial expansion, although the "integral" of output over the episode is positive. In the absence of further shocks, output does not continue to spiral downward but stabilizes at a level just below the initial level of output. Below we consider scenarios in which the collapse of a bubble is followed by a financial panic (a negative bubble), which causes the economy to deteriorate further.

In contrast to the accommodative policy, Figure 6.1 shows that the more aggressive "inflation targeting" policy greatly moderates the effects of the bubble. Although policy is assumed not to respond directly to the stock market per se, under the more aggressive rule, interest rates are known by the public to be highly responsive to the incipient inflationary pressures created by the bubble. The expectation that interest rates will rise if output and inflation rise is sufficient both to dampen the response of overall asset prices to the bubble and to stabilize output and inflation—even though, ex post, interest rates are not required to move by as much as in the accommodative policy.

Asset bubbles with a policy response to stock prices. Figure 6.2 shows simulation results analogous to those in Figure 6.1, except that now the central bank is allowed to respond directly to stock prices as well as to expected inflation. We set the parameter EQUA in equation (3.2) equal to 0.1, implying that (for constant expected inflation) a 10-percentage-point rise in the stock market leads to a one-percentage-point rise in the instrument rate. Of course, the full response of the short-term rate to a stock market appreciation is greater than that, because policy also responds to the change in expected inflation induced by a bubble.[20]

Figure 6.2 shows that the effect of allowing policy to respond to stock prices depends greatly on whether policy is assumed to be accommodating or aggressive with respect to expected inflation. Under the accommodating policy $\beta = 1.01$, allowing a response to stock prices produces a perverse outcome. The expectation by the public that rates will rise in the wake of the bubble pushes down the fundamental component of stock prices, even though overall stock prices (inclusive of the bubble component) rise. Somewhat counterintuitively, the rise in rates and the decline in fundamental values actually more than offset the stimulative

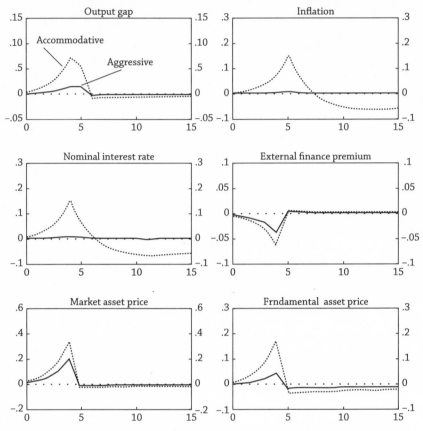

Figure 6.1 Effects of an asset bubble when monetary policy responds only to expected inflation. Note: The panels of the figure show simulated responses of selected variables to a positive innovation to the bubble process in period zero equal to 1% of the steady-state fundamental price. The ex ante probability that the bubble will burst in any period is 0.5. We assume a realization in which the bubble bursts in period 5. The solid lines show responses under an aggressive monetary policy, $r_t^n = 2.0E_t\pi_{t+1}$. The dashed lines show responses under an accommodative policy, $r_t^n = 1.01E_t\pi_{t+1}$.

effects of the bubble, leading output and inflation to decline—an example of the possible "collateral" damage to the economy that may occur when the central bank responds to stock prices. The result that the economy actually contracts, though a robust one in our simulations, may rely too heavily on sophisticated forward-looking behavior on the part of private-sector investors to be entirely plausible as a realistic description of the actual economy. However, the general point here is, we think, a valid one—namely, that a monetary policy regime that focuses on asset prices rather than on macroeconomic fundamentals may well be actively destabilizing. The problem is that the central bank is targeting the wrong indicator.

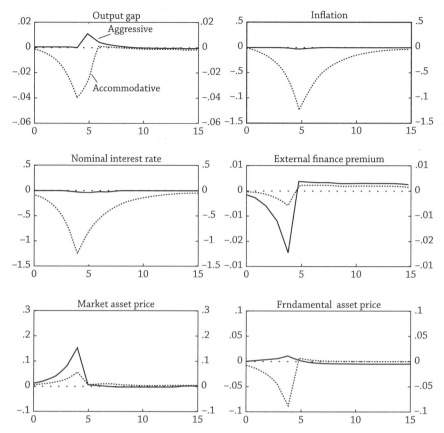

Figure 6.2 Effects of an asset bubble when monetary policy responds to stock prices as well as to expected inflation Note: The panels of the figure show simulated responses of selected variables to a positive innovation to the bubble process, under the same assumptions as in Figure 6.1. The solid lines show responses under an aggressive monetary policy, $r_t^n = 2.0E_t\pi_{t+1}+0.1s_{t-1}$. The dashed lines show responses under an accommodative policy, $r_t^n = 1.01E_t\pi_{t+1}+0.1s_{t-1}$.

Under the aggressive policy β = 2.0, in contrast, allowing policy to respond to the stock price does little to alter the dynamic responses of the economy. Evidently, the active component of the monetary rule, which strongly adjusts the real rate to offset movements in expected inflation, compensates for perverse effects generated by the response of policy to stock prices.

To recapitulate, the lesson that we take from Figure 6.2 is that it can be quite dangerous for policy simultaneously to respond to stock prices and to accommodate inflation. However, when policy acts aggressively to stabilize expected inflation, whether policy also responds independently to stock prices is not of great consequence.

As an alternative metric for evaluating policy responses to bubbles, we also computed the unconditional variances of output and inflation under the four different policy scenarios (accommodative versus nonaccommodative on inflation, responding to stock prices versus not responding). We considered bubbles lasting one, two, and three periods, weighting them in the population according to their relative likelihood of being realized (conditional on a bubble starting). The left panel of Table 6.1 reports the results. The table shows that a policy of focusing aggressively on inflation and ignoring stock prices does best by a significant margin, achieving the lowest unconditional variance of both output and inflation.[21]

Asset bubble then asset bust. So far in the simulations we have assumed that, after the collapse of the bubble, asset prices are again governed solely by fundamentals. With this assumption we tend to find that a stock-price crash wipes out the output gains from the bubble but not much more. There is only a slight overreaction in the decline in output.[22]

An alternative scenario, which may be of the greatest concern to policymakers, is that the collapse of a bubble might damage investor confidence sufficiently to set off a panic in financial markets. We model this possibility in a simple way by assuming that the crash of the bubble sets off a negative bubble in stock prices (an undervaluation) that is exactly symmetric with the positive bubble that preceded it. This panic is unanticipated by investors before it happens. If we maintain the assumption that the initial positive bubble lasts five periods before popping, then this alternative scenario implies a 10-period "boom-bust" scenario.

Figure 6.3 shows simulation results under the accommodative ($\beta = 1.01$) and aggressive ($\beta = 2.0$) policy rules, and assuming no direct response of policy to stock price movements ($\xi = 0$). The positive bubble followed by the negative

Table 6.1 **Variability of Output Gap and Inflation under Different Policy Rules**

	Bubble shock		Technology shock	
	Output gap	Inflation	Output gap	Inflation
Policy rule:				
$r_t^n = 1.01\, E_t \pi_{t+1}$	2.221	9.676	1.409	17.975
$r_t^n = 2.0\, E_t \pi_{t+1}$	1.471	.119	.103	.231
$r_t^n = 1.01\, E_t \pi_{t+1} + 0.1 s_{t-1}$	5.908	120.032	.987	39.855
$r_t^n = 2.0\, E_t \pi_{t+1} + 0.1 s_{t-1}$	1.518	1.556	.132	.767

Note: Shown are the unconditional variances of the output gap and inflation under different policy rules, for bubble shocks and technology shocks. A new bubble starts every period, and its size is randomly drawn from a standard normal distribution. The probability that a bubble will last one, two, or three periods is, respectively, 0.5/0.875, 0.25/0.875, and 0.25/0.875, reflecting the relative probabilities of each duration when p = 0.5. Technology shocks are permanent and are randomly drawn from a standard normal distribution.

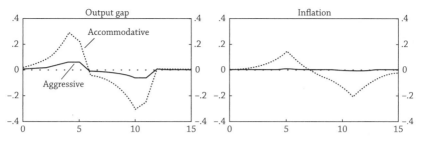

Figure 6.3 Effects of an asset boom followed by an asset bust. Note: Same exercise as in Figure 6.1, except that the positive bubble shock is followed by a symmetric negative bubble shock that lasts from periods 6 through 10. Monetary policy responds only to expected inflation.

bubble sets off an oscillation in both financial markets and the general economy. However, the magnitude of the oscillation depends critically on the type of monetary policy employed. Under the accommodative policy the cycle is large, whereas the more aggressive policy significantly dampens the oscillation. By strongly targeting expected inflation, monetary policy stabilizes aggregate demand and, thus, greatly reduces the economic effects of the volatility in stock prices. Note that in the experiment we assume that the negative asset bubble arises after the initial crash, regardless of the policy environment. However, if there is some connection between market psychology and fundamentals (for example, markets overreact to movements in fundamentals), and if financial market participants perceive policy has been effective in stabilizing fundamentals, then perhaps the panic might not arise in the first place. Put differently, an added benefit of the aggressive policy, not accounted for in our simulations, might be to reduce the overall likelihood of the follow-on panic.

Implications of reduced leverage. As we mentioned earlier, in a model with a financial accelerator, the impact of the bubble on real activity also depends on initial financial conditions, such as the degree of leverage among borrowers. Figure 6.4 explores the impact of a lower steady-state leverage ratio, 25% instead of 50% as in the baseline scenario. The figure shows that a reduction in leverage significantly moderates the cycle. Besides its reaffirmation of the superiority of inflation-focused monetary policy, this simulation also suggests a rationale for regulatory and tax policies that discourage excessive leverage.

Asset price fluctuations arising from a mixture of fundamental and nonfundamental sources. We saw in Figure 6.2 that allowing monetary policy to respond to asset prices can be destabilizing, particularly if policy is accommodative of inflation. The costs of targeting asset prices are probably greater in practice than suggested by the bubble scenario of Figure 6.2, because it is quite difficult or impossible for the central bank to discern whether changes in asset prices reflect fundamental forces, nonfundamental forces, or a combination of both. To the extent that asset price movements reflect fundamental forces, they should be accommodated

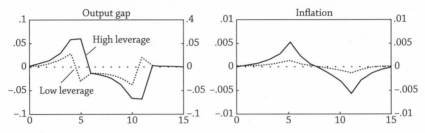

Figure 6.4 Effects of leverage on responses to an asset price boom and bust.
Note: Same exercise as in Figure 6.3, comparison of high steady-state leverage (ratio of net worth to capital of 0.5, as in baseline simulations) and low steady-state leverage (net worth to capital ratio of 0.75). Monetary policy is assumed to target expected inflation aggressively.

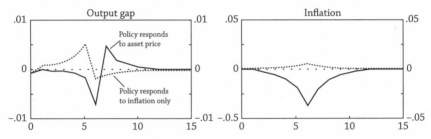

Figure 6.5 Responses to stock-price increases based on a mixture of fundamental and nonfundamental forces. Note: The figure shows the simulated responses of selected variables to a permanent 1% increase in productivity followed by a five-period positive bubble. Monetary policy is aggressive in targeting inflation. The solid line shows responses when policy responds to the lagged stock prices as well as expected inflation; the dashed line shows responses when policy responds to expected inflation only.

rather than resisted. Attempts to "stabilize" asset prices in that case are directly counterproductive.

To illustrate these issues, we consider a scenario in which improvements in productivity generate a rise in market fundamentals, as well as increasing potential output. However, a euphoric response to the fundamental boom also sets off a bubble. Specifically, we suppose that there is a 1% permanent increase in productivity that is followed one period later by the inception of a stock-price bubble, which we again assume lasts for five periods. Figure 6.5 shows the results, comparing an aggressive inflation stabilization policy with one that also allows for responses to stock prices. As the figure shows, in this scenario, tightening policy in response to the increase in asset prices prevents output from rising by the amount of the increase in potential output. In other words, responding to the rise in asset prices has the undesirable effect of temporarily stifling the beneficial impact of the technology boom.

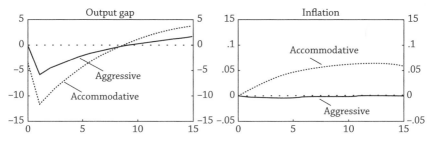

Figure 6.6 Effects of a rise in the external finance premium. Note: Shown are responses to an exogenous 50-basis-point rise in the premium for external finance, with autoregressive coefficient 0.9. Monetary policy responds only to expected inflation. The dashed lines show variable responses under accommodative monetary policy; the solid lines show responses under aggressive monetary policy.

We explore the issue a bit further by calculating the unconditional variability of the output gap (output minus potential output) under the four different policy scenarios, assuming in this case that only a productivity shock has buffeted the economy.[23] The right panel of Table 6.1 reports the results. As with the case of bubble shocks, the results indicate that the policy that responds aggressively to inflation and does not target stock prices works best.

A shock to the external finance premium. The last scenario we consider is a disruption of financial markets that temporarily tightens credit conditions. A real-world example is the default on Russian bonds in the fall of 1998 that induced significant capital losses for key bank creditors and drove up premiums on long-term corporate bonds.[24] The analogue in our model is a shock that drives up the premium for external finance, holding constant firm balance-sheet positions. Formally this can be modeled as a decline in the efficiency of the financial intermediation process (see Bernanke, Gertler, and Gilchrist 1999). Figure 6.6 shows the responses of output and inflation to an exogenous 50-basis-point rise in the external finance premium, under both the aggressive and accommodative policy rules (it is assumed here that policy does not respond to asset prices). The figure shows clearly that the aggressive policy response works best. We believe that this experiment helps to provide a rationale for the Fed's intervention in the fall of 1998. Basically, because the rise in the spread observed at that time had a potentially deflationary effect on the economy, it was appropriate to ease policy in response.

4. Estimated Reaction Functions for the Federal Reserve and the Bank of Japan

Section 3 considered the stabilizing properties of various hypothetical interest rate rules for central banks. These experiments raise the question of what rules (reaction functions) best describe the actual practice of contemporary central banks. In practice, do central banks react to forecasts of inflation and the output gap in a stabilizing manner? And do they react to stock prices implied by the pursuit of output and inflation stabilization? In this section we apply the methods of Clarida, Gertler, and Gali (1998, 2000), henceforth CGG, to estimate forward-looking reaction functions for the Federal Reserve and the Bank of Japan for the period since 1979. To preview the results, we find that the Fed has largely followed our advice over the past two decades, reacting in a strongly stabilizing manner to changes in the inflation forecast and the expected output gap but, for the most part, not reacting to changes in stock prices (except to the extent that they contain information about inflation and output). The record of the Bank of Japan is less satisfactory by our estimates. We find that easy monetary policy in Japan actively fueled the increase in stock prices during the 1987–1989 period. After the stock market crashed in 1990, Japanese monetary policy appeared to make some attempt to support stock prices but failed to react sufficiently aggressively to the declining rate of inflation. Consequently, Japanese monetary policy was too tight from late 1992 at least until the beginning of 1996. To some extent, it should be noted, these problems reflected the very slow rate of adjustment of nominal interest rates in the face of changing macroeconomic conditions.

CGG's approach, which we follow here, is to estimate forward-looking reaction functions of the form

$$r_t^* = \bar{r} + \beta E_t \, (\pi_{t+12} - \pi^*)$$

$$+ \gamma E_t \, (y_t - y_t^*) + \xi E_t z_t, \qquad (4.1)$$

where r_t^* is the targeted value of the nominal instrument rate (the federal funds rate for the United States, the call rate for Japan); $\bar{r}$ is the long-run equilibrium nominal rate; $Et(\pi_{t+12} - \pi^*)$ is the expected deviation of inflation from its target rate over the next 12 months; $E_t \, (y_t - y_t^*)$ is the contemporaneous value of the output gap, conditional on information available to the central bank at time t; and [equa in text] represents other variables that may affect the target interest rate. We expect the parameters β and γ to be positive. CGG point out that stabilization of inflation further requires $\beta > 1$, that is, for the real interest rate to rise when expected inflation rises, the nominal interest rate must be raised by more than the increase in expected inflation. In practice, values of β for central banks with significant emphasis on inflation stabilization are estimated to be closer to 2.0. Values less than 1.3 or so indicate a weak commitment to inflation stabilization (at these values of β the real interest rate moves relatively little in response to changes in expected inflation). Because of unmodeled motives for interest-rate smoothing, adjustment of the actual nominal interest rate toward its target may be gradual. CGG allow for this by assuming a partial adjustment mechanism, for example,

$$r_t = (1 - \rho)\, r_t^* + \rho\, r_t^* + \rho\, r_{t-1} + v_t$$

where r_t is the actual nominal interest rate and $p \notin [0,1)$ captures r_t^* the degree of interest-rate smoothing. Below, we follow CGG in assuming a first-order partial adjustment mechanism, as in equation (4.2), for Japan and a second-order partial adjustment mechanism for the United States. To estimate the reaction function implied by equations (4.1) and (4.2), CGG replace the expectations of variables in equation (4.1) with actual realized values of the variables, then apply an instrumental variables methodology,
using as instruments only variables known at time $t - 1$ or earlier. Under the assumption of rational expectations, expectational errors will be uncorrelated with the instruments, so that the IV procedure produces consistent estimates of the reaction function parameters.[25]

Estimation results are shown in Table 6.2 for the Federal Reserve and Table 6.3 for the Bank of Japan. Following CGG, we begin the U.S. sample period in 1979:10, the date of the Volcker Japan. Following CGG, we begin the U.S. sample period in 1979:10, the date of the Volcker regime shift, and the Japanese sample period in 1979:4, a period CGG refer to as one of "significant financial deregulation." The end

Table 6.2 **Federal Reserve Reaction Functions**

	β	γ	ρ_1	ρ_2	ξ	π^*
Baseline[a]	1.60	.14	1.27	−.34	–	2.88
	(.15)	(.04)	(.02)	(.02)		
Adding stock returns[b]	1.71	0.20	1.27	−.33	−.082[c]	2.79
	(.23)	(.07)	(.02)	(.02)	(.37)	

Note: The dependent variable is the federal funds rate. The output gap is measured as the residuals from a regression of industrial production on time and time squared for the period 1960:1–1998:12. Estimates are by GMM with correction for MA(12) autocorrelation. The optimal weighting matrix is obtained from first-step 2SLS parameter estimates. χ^2 tests for overidentifying restrictions are easily passed ($p > 0.95$) in all specifications.

[a] The instrument set includes a constant, plus lags 1–6, 9, and 12 of log-differenced commodity prices (Dow-Jones), log-differenced CPI, log-differenced output gap, and the federal funds rate.

[b] The instrument set is the same as above plus lags 1–6 of the log-differenced change in stock prices.

[c] Sum of the coefficients on lags 0–5 inclusive of the log-differenced change in stock prices. The reported standard error is for the sum of the coefficients. The p-value for the hypothesis that all six coefficients are equal to zero is 0.021.

Table 6.3 **Bank of Japan Reaction Functions**

	β	γ	ρ_1	ξ	π^*
Baseline[a]	2.21	.20	.95	–	1.73
	(.23)	(.05)	(.006)		
Adding stock returns[b]	2.25	.21	.95	–.006[c]	1.88
	(.29)	(.05)	(.006)	(.099)	
Sample period: 79:04–97:12					
Baseline[a]	2.00	.33	.95	–	2.12
	(.22)	(.11)	(.006)		
Adding stock returns[b]	1.85	.39	.96	–0.286[c]	1.59
		(.11)	(.004)	(.111)	
Sample period: 79:489:6					
Baseline1	1.12	.30	.94	–	-3.39
	(.15)	(.02)	(.004)		
Adding stock returns2	1.24	.30	.95	.1883	-1.56
	(.13)	(.02)	(.003)	(.035)	
Sample period: 89:07 - 97:12					

Notes: The dependent variable is the call rate. The output gap is measured as the residuals (forecast errors, after 1989:6) from a regression of industrial production on time and time squared for the period 1968:1–1989:6. Estimates are by GMM with correction for MA(12) autocorrelation. The optimal weighting matrix is obtained from first-step 2SLS parameter estimates. χ^2 tests for overidentifying restrictions are easily passed ($p > 0.95$) in all specifications.

[a] The instrument set includes a constant, plus lags 1–6, 9, and 12 of log-differenced commodity prices (IMF), log-differenced CPI, log-differenced output gap, log-differenced real yen-dollar exchange rate, and the call rate.

[b] The instrument set is the same as above plus lags 1–6 of the log-differenced change in stock prices.

[c] Sum of the coefficients on lags 0–5 inclusive of the log-differenced change in stock prices. The reported standard error is for the sum of the coefficients. The p-value for the hypothesis that all six coefficients are equal to zero is 0.020 for the full sample, 0.000 for both the 1979:4–1989:06 and 1989:7–1997:12 subsamples.

date in each case is 1997:12 (our data end in 1998:12 but we must allow for the fact that one year of future price change is included on the right-hand side).[26] We also look at two subsamples for Japan, the periods before and after 1989:6. It was at the end of 1989 that increases in Bank of Japan interest rates were followed by the collapse of stock prices and land values. For each country and sample period, the tables report two specifications. As in CGG, the baseline specification shows the response of the target for the instrument interest rate to the expected output gap and expected inflation. The second, alternative specification adds to the reaction function the current value and five lags of the log-difference of an index of the stock market (the S&P 500 for the United States and the TOPIX index for Japan). To help control for simultaneity bias, we instrument for the contemporaneous log-difference in the stock market index. In particular, we add lags 1 through 6 of the log-difference of the stock market index to our list of instruments (see note 20). Note, therefore, that in these estimates, the responses of policy to stock market returns arising from the predictive power of stock returns for output and inflation are fully accounted for. Any estimated response of policy to stock returns must therefore be over and above the part due to the predictive power of stock returns.

There are two ways to think about the addition of stock market returns to the reaction function. The first is to interpret it literally as saying that monetary policy is reacting directly to stock prices, as well as to the output gap and expected inflation. The second is to treat the addition of stock returns as a general specification test that reveals whether monetary policy is pursuing other objectives besides stabilization of output and expected inflation. To the extent that policy has other objectives, and there is information about these objectives in the stock market, then we would expect to see stock returns enter the central bank's reaction function with a statistically significant coefficient. For the United States, the estimates of the baseline reaction function (first line of Table 6.2) indicate that during the full sample period the Fed responded reasonably strongly to changes in forecasted inflation ($\beta = 1.60$). It also reacted in a stabilizing manner to forecasts of the output gap ($\gamma = 1.14$). Both parameter estimates are highly statistically significant. The CGG procedure also permits estimation of the implied target rate of inflation. For the United States, the estimated target inflation rate for the full period is 2.88% per year. Figure 6.7 shows that the actual and fitted values of the federal funds rate are very close for the full sample period.[27]

In the results reported in the second line of Table 6.2, we allow for the possibility that the Fed responded to stock market returns (or to information contained in stock market returns) independently of their implication for forecasts of inflation and the output gap. The estimated response of the funds rate to stock returns, –0.08, is relatively small, the "wrong" sign (if we think of the Fed as being tempted to try to stabilize stock prices), and statistically insignificant. Other parameter estimates are largely unchanged from the baseline specification. The force of these estimates is that, consistent with the advice we give in this paper, the Fed has focused its attention on expected inflation and the output gap and has neither actively sought to stabilize stock prices nor reacted to information in stock returns other than that useful for forecasting the output gap and inflation To help put the Fed's behavior into its historical context, Figure 6.8 shows the actual value and the estimated target value of the federal funds rate for the period January 1984 to the present. The target value differs

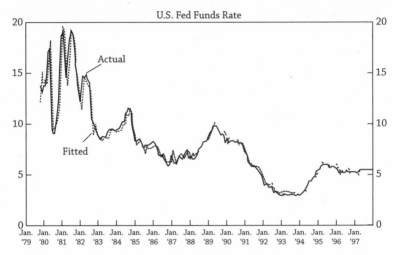

Figure 6.7 Actual and fitted values of the U.S. federal funds rate. Note: The figure shows actual and fitted values of the U.S. federal funds rate, with fitted values derived from a model that accommodates lagged adjustment of the actual rate to the target rate.

Figure 6.8 Actual and target values of the U.S. federal funds rate. Note: The figure shows actual and fitted values of the U.S. federal funds rate, with fitted values derived from a model that accommodates lagged adjustment of the actual rate to the target rate.

from the fitted value in that the latter incorporates the interest-rate smooth-ing parameters and the former implicitly sets these to zero, that is, the target value is the interest rate given by equation (4.1). For this figure, the target value at each date is calculated assuming that the Fed had perfect knowledge of the current output gap and inflation over the next year. We do this in order to con-centrate on intentional deviations of policy from the average reaction function, as opposed to deviations driven primarily by forecast errors. Because the target value abstracts from the interest-rate smoothing motive, there is a tendency for the actual rate to lag somewhat behind the target. Nevertheless, Figure 6.8 suggests that the Fed's actual choice of short-term rates followed target rates reasonably closely.

There are, however, three periods of deviation of the actual Fed funds rate from the target rate in Figure 6.8 that deserve comment. First, as was much remarked at the time, the Fed did not ease policy in 1985–1987, even though a sharp decline in oil prices reduced inflation during those years.[28] The view expressed by some contemporary observers was that the Fed made a conscious decision in 1986 to enjoy the beneficial supply shock in the form of a lower inflation rate rather than real economic expansion. However, it is also likely that much of the decline in inflation in 1986 was unanticipated, contrary to the perfect foresight assumption made in constructing the figure. If true, this would account for much of the deviation of actual rates from target in 1985.

Second, the Fed kept rates somewhat below target in the aftermath of the 1987 stock market crash. Again, forecasting errors may account for this deviation. The Fed was concerned at the time that the depressing effects of the crash would be larger than, in fact, they turned out to be.

Finally, and most interesting to us, the Fed kept the funds rate significantly below target from late 1991 until the beginning of 1995. This was a period of slow recovery from the 1990–1991 recession, which Fed officials argued was caused by financial "headwinds," such as excessive corporate leverage and bank capital problems. We interpret the 1991–1995 easing as being consistent with our advice, in that the Fed was concerned about financial conditions not for themselves but primarily for their implications for the macroeconomy.[29] In the event, though, it appears that the Fed eased by more than necessary in this period.[30]

We turn now to the case of Japan. For the entire sample period, estimates of the Bank of Japan's reaction function (Table 6.3) look qualitatively similar to those found for the Fed. For the whole 1979–1997 period, we estimate that the Bank of Japan responded actively to both expected inflation ($\beta = 2.21$) and to the output gap ($\gamma = 1.60$). The equation also fits the data quite well (Figure 6.9).[31] However, inspection of the data suggests two very different economic and policy regimes during this period: the so-called "bubble economy" of the 1980s, during which the economy and asset prices boomed, and the period since 1990 during which asset prices have collapsed and the economy has been extremely weak. Accordingly, and keeping in mind the problems inherent in estimation based on small samples, we reestimated the Bank of Japan's reaction function for the period before and after 1989:6. The date was chosen to separate the periods before and after the accession of Governor Mieno, who instigated a significant policy tightening at the end of 1989.

Table 6.3 shows that, for the first half of the sample period, the Bank of Japan remained committed to stabilization of inflation ($\beta = 2.00$) in the baseline

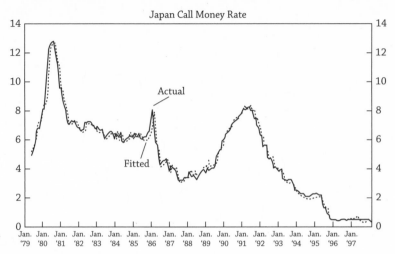

Figure 6.9 Actual and fitted values of the Japanese call money rate. Note: Comparison of the actual and fitted values of the Japanese call money rate, analogous to Figure 6.7.

specification, $\beta = 1.60$ (in the specification including stock returns). However, the specification including stock returns also shows that, wittingly or unwittingly, the Bank of Japan was also strongly reinforcing the asset price explosion. The estimated reaction of the Japanese call rate to stock returns during the past six months is -0.286 in the first half of the sample, with a standard error of 0.111. This says that each 10% increase in stock prices was associated with a 286-basis-point *decline* in the call rate—a number too large to be taken seriously, but an indication that policy was destabilizing toward the stock market prior to 1989. As noted, we do not necessarily interpret these results as saying that the Bank was actively attempting to raise stock prices. But it does seem that the Bank was pursuing objectives other than output and inflation stabilization (exchange rates?) which led it to ease excessively, and the stock market reflected that ease.[32]

For the second half of the sample, the results are much different. As the bottom third of Table 6.3 indicates, after 1989 the Bank of Japan greatly weakened its commitment to inflation stabilization ($\beta = 1.12$ in the baseline stabilization). We interpret the low estimated value of β, together with the negative estimated values of the inflation target, as indicating that the Bank was not actively resisting the powerful deflationary forces of this period. However, our estimates suggest that the Bank may have been attempting to stabilize the stock market, or some other factor proxied by the stock market; the estimated reaction of the call rate to stock market returns switches from the large negative value in the earlier subsample to a large and highly significant positive value ($\xi = 0.118$). From the perspective of the arguments advanced in this paper, the Bank of Japan would have done better to focus instead on stabilizing the inflation rate (in this case, preventing the plunge into deflation) than in responding to other factors.

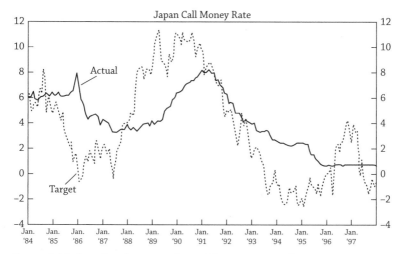

Figure 6.10 Actual and target values of the Japanese call money rate. Note: The figure shows actual and fitted values of the Japanese call money rate, analogous to Figure 6.8.

Again, a picture helps to provide historical context. In analogy to Figure 6.8, Figure 6.10 shows the actual call money rate and the estimated target rate in Japan after 1984. In this case, unlike in Figure 6.8, we calculate the target rate using the reaction function estimated for the pre-1989:7 sample, without stock returns. This reaction function seems the right one to use as a benchmark because it implies strongly stabilizing monetary policy, as suggested by the simulations in the previous section. Thus, the target rate for the post-1989 period in Figure 6.10 indicates what policy would have been if the earlier policies had been continued, with no attention paid to stock returns (except as forecasters of the output gap and inflation).

The results are, again, quite interesting. The target rate in Japan changed sharply during several episodes, and—possibly as a result of an excessive attachment to interest-rate smoothing—the actual call rate lagged far behind. Figure 6.10 suggests that policy was, on the whole, rather tight in Japan during the 1985–1987 period, despite the easing that followed the Plaza Agreement of September 1985. From 1987 to 1989, however, Japan faced strong inflationary pressures (including rocketing asset prices and rapid real growth), to which the Bank of Japan responded extremely slowly.[33] No doubt, it is this period that is responsible for our estimated result that monetary policy actively destabilized the stock market in the pre-1990 period.

Rates began to rise sharply following the appointment of Governor Mieno in December 1989, and continued to rise until the spring of 1991. The rate increase was undertaken with the intention of curbing the stock market and—like many other attempts to prick market bubbles, including the U.S. boom in 1929—the attempt was too successful for the good of the economy. Asset prices collapsed; and because Japan's financial arrangements were particularly sensitive to asset values (we would argue), the real economy collapsed as well.

Our estimates of the Bank of Japan's reaction function for the second half of the sample suggest two countervailing forces. On one hand, there was now some attempt to stabilize the stock market, or some factor proxied by the stock market, by cutting rates as the market fell. On the other hand, the Bank of Japan's commitment to stabilizing inflation (here, resisting deflation) seems to have become much weaker. The net effect was policy that was significantly too tight, at least until the beginning of 1996.[34]

We do not want to overstate the conclusions that can be drawn from this short comparison of U.S. and Japanese monetary policy since the mid-1980s. The comparative experience is at least suggestive, however, that focusing on the traditional goals of monetary policy—the output gap and expected inflation—is the more effective means of avoiding extended swings in asset prices and the resulting damage to the economy.

5. Conclusion

In order to explore the issue of how monetary policy should respond to variability in asset prices, we incorporated nonfundamental movements in asset prices into a dynamic macroeconomic framework. To a first approximation at least, we believe that our framework captures the main concerns that policymakers have about possible bubbles in asset prices. In particular, in our model, a large positive bubble exposes the economy to the risk of a sharp market correction, with adverse effects on aggregate demand and economic activity. In the absence of an appropriate policy response, the resulting economic contraction could be quite large. A severe market drop in our model also weakens balance sheets, induces financial distress, leads to further declines in asset prices, and widens spreads in bond markets. Although our framework omits some of the microeconomic details of episodes of stress (for example, nonprice credit rationing, reduced liquidity of financial markets), and, hence, is silent about certain types of lender-of-last-resort interventions that the central bank might undertake, we believe that these omissions are unlikely to affect our central conclusions about aggregate stabilization policy.[35]

The principal conclusion of this paper has been stated several times. In brief, it is that flexible inflation-targeting provides an effective, unified framework for achieving both general macroeconomic stability and financial stability. Given a strong commitment to stabilizing expected inflation, it is neither necessary nor desirable for monetary policy to respond to changes in asset prices, except to the extent that they help to forecast inflationary or deflationary pressures.

A couple of additional issues deserve very brief comment. First, our implicit focus in this paper has been on large industrial economies such as the United States and Japan. However, many of the recent financial crises around the world have occurred in small open economies, with international capital flows and attacks on the currency playing major roles. What lessons does our analysis bear for these countries?

More work would need to be done to extend our model to the open-economy case, and to include other sources of financial crisis, such as speculative attacks on the currency and bank runs. Such an extension would be worthwhile, we believe, because it seems to us that balance-sheet effects of the type captured in the BGG model have played an important role in propagating the effects of financial crises through the real economy. Although we have not yet done such an extension, one likely conclusion from such an exercise seems obvious enough and important enough to be worth stating now; that is: The logic of our approach suggests strongly that fixed exchange rates, as maintained by many of the countries recently hit by financial crises, are highly undesirable in a financially fragile environment.

The key problem with an exchange-rate peg is that its defense generally requires movements in interest rates that are perverse, relative to the objective of containing a financial crisis. In particular, the large increases in interest rates necessary to avert devaluation during a currency crisis exacerbate financial crises both directly, by depressing asset prices, reducing corporate profits, and putting pressure on banks, and also indirectly, by slowing current and expected rates of economic activity. In addition, fixed-exchange-rate regimes severely limit the short-run discretion of the central bank, either to assist the financial system (for example, through lender-of-last-resort activities) or to correct short-term imbalances in the economy.

Indeed, the record of fixed-exchange regimes in regard to the incidence and severity of financial crises is notoriously bad.[36] During the Great Depression currency crises (possible, of course, only if the exchange rate is fixed), banking panics, and stock market crashes frequently occurred together. Indeed, to the best of our knowledge, every one of the dozens of major banking panics of that era occurred in a country that was attempting to defend a fixed rate (its gold parity). For the postwar period, in a study spanning the 1970s through the 1990s, Kaminsky and Reinhart (1999) document that banking and currency crises frequently occurred together and appeared to be mutually reinforcing. The strong observed association between fixed exchange rates and financial crises appears to be weakened only under two conditions: First, if international capital flows are highly regulated and restricted, as was the case, for example, during the Bretton Woods era; or second, if the international monetary system is cooperatively managed by the major central banks, as was arguably the case during the classical gold standard of the late nineteenth century (Eichengreen 1992). Neither of these conditions prevails today.

So, what should small open economies do? Our analysis suggests that, if possible, they adopt flexible inflation targeting as part of a broad reform package that includes improved financial regulation and fiscal reform.[37] (Brazil has recently proposed a plan along these lines.)

The last part of the recommendation bears emphasis: Change in the monetary regime alone, without support from the regulatory and fiscal arms of government, is not likely to be sufficient. Moreover, we recognize that successful implementation of inflation targeting requires both ample political support from the government and a certain amount of institutional development, for example, the existence of adequate price indexes (see Eichengreen et al. 1999). With these caveats, we recommend that small open economies head in an inflation-targeting direction. Note that, along with providing enhanced macroeconomic and financial stability, a commitment to an inflation-targeting approach by a small open economy could well deliver greater long-run stability of the nominal exchange rate than a regime that attempts to fix the exchange rate but suffers frequent forced devaluations.

A second broad issue not yet addressed here concerns the difference between implicit inflation-targeting, of the type practiced by the Greenspan Fed, and explicit inflation-targeting, which involves considerable additional transparency and communication with the public. It is evident from recent U.S. experience that implicit inflation-targeting can give good results, and, indeed, our simulations help to show why a strong focus on stabilizing expected inflation promotes overall macroeconomic and financial stability. We, nevertheless, believe that the United States would benefit from a move to explicit inflation-targeting, for at least two reasons (see Bernanke and others 1999, for further discussion). First, making inflation targeting explicit would serve the important goal of ensuring continuity in monetary policy, or at least of increasing the likelihood that future policy would take the same general approach as recent policy has taken. In particular, if the inflation-targeting regime were made explicit, the transition from the current chairman to the next one would create less anxiety in financial markets and for the economy than otherwise. Second, transparency enhances the stabilizing properties of forward-looking policies. In particular, in the simulations reported in this paper we implicitly assumed transparency of policy, in that private-sector actors were assumed to know the policy rule. The results might be very different if, for example, we assumed that private agents thought the central bank was following the accommodative rule when, in fact, it was following the more aggressive inflation-targeting policy. Likewise, much of the stabilizing effect of our recommended policy arises because investors expect the central bank to raise interest rates when rising asset prices threaten to overheat the economy, and vice versa if declining asset prices threaten to induce an economic contraction. From the standpoint of maintaining both macroeconomic and financial stability in the future, the desirability of increased transparency in U.S. monetary policymaking is a topic deserving of close attention in the Fed's planning.

Appendix

EQUATIONS OF THE SIMULATION MODEL

The model used for simulations in Section 3 is given and briefly described below. To conserve space, we do not review the individual and firm optimization problems that underlie the behavioral equations and, instead, refer the reader to Bernanke, Gertler, and Gilchrist (1999) for details. What we present here is the log-linearized versions of the model equations that were used in the simulations. Except for the addition of an exogenous bubble in the asset price, the model is essentially the same as in BGG. The only other significant differences are that we use Gali and Gertler's (1999) variant of the new Keynesian Phillips curve and that we calibrate the wealth effects on consumption to match the evidence presented by Ludvigson and Steindel (1999).

Throughout, we follow the convention of writing steady-state levels of the variables in upper case and log-deviations from the steady state in lower case. Greek letters and lowercase Roman letters without subscripts denote fixed parameters, and subscripts denote time periods. The expectation given information known as of period [equa in text] of the value of variable χ in period is written $E_x\chi_r$.

Aggregate Demand

$$y_t = \frac{C}{Y}c_t + \frac{C^e}{Y}c_t^e + \frac{I}{Y}i_t + \frac{G}{Y}g_t \tag{A.1}$$

$$c_t = -\sigma r_t + Etc_{t+1} \tag{A.2}$$

$$c_t^e = s_t + k_{t+1} \tag{A.3}$$

$$E_t q_{t+1} = \varphi(i_{t+1} - k_{t+1}) \tag{A.4}$$

Equation (A.1) is the log-linearized version of the national income identity. We distinguish between consumption of households, C, and consumption of entrepreneurs/firm-owners, C^e; otherwise the notation is standard. (A.2) is the usual Euler condition for household consumption. (A.3) embodies the assumption that changes in entrepreneurial consumption are proportional to changes in stock values; in the simulations we normalize entrepreneurs' net worth so that the elasticity of entrepreneurial consumption to stock market wealth is about 0.04, as suggested by estimates in Ludvigson and Steindel (1999). (A.4) relates investment to the fundamental value of capital, embodying a one-period delay for planning new investment.

Returns to Stocks and Capital

$$s_t - q_t = \frac{(1-\delta)}{bR^q} E_t(s_{t+1} - \dot{q}_{t+1}). \tag{A.5}$$

$$r_t^q = (1-\vartheta)(mc_t + y_t - k_t) + \vartheta q_t - q_{t-1}. \tag{A.6}$$

$$r_t^q = (1-\vartheta)(mc_t + y_t - k_t) + \vartheta s_t - s_{t-1}. \tag{A.7}$$

$$E_t r_{t+1}^q - (1-b)(s_t - q_t). \tag{A.8}$$

$$E_t r_{t+1}^s = r_t - \psi(nt - st - k_{t+1}). \tag{A.9}$$

Equation (A.5) describes the expected evolution of the bubble, cf. (2.4) and recall $a \equiv b/(1-\delta)$. Note that the realized value of the bubble, conditional on not bursting, is defined by

$$s_{t+1} - q_{t+1} = \frac{R^q}{P(1-\delta)}(s_t - q_t).$$

Equation (A.6) defines the fundamental return to capital as the sum of the current return to capital and the increase in fundamental value, where mc is the marginal cost of production (equal to the inverse of the markup) and

$$\vartheta = (1-\delta)/\left(\frac{\alpha Y}{K} + 1 - \delta\right),$$

where α is capital's share. (A.7) defines the returns to stocks analogously. (A.8) shows that the relationship between the stock return and the fundamental return depends on the presence of the bubble; cf. (2.6). Equation (A.9) links the spread between safe returns and stock returns to firm leverage, where n is the log-deviation of firms' internal equity from its steady-state value.

Aggregate Supply

$$y_t = z_t + \alpha kt + (1-\alpha)l_t. \tag{A.10}$$

$$yt - l_t m_{ct} - c_t = (\chi - 1)l_t. \tag{A.11}$$

$$E_t - 1\,\pi_t = \kappa\,mc_t + \theta_f\,E_t\pi_{t+1}. \tag{A.12}$$

$$+\,\theta b\pi_{t-1}.$$

Equation (A.10) is a Cobb-Douglas production function, where z is the log-deviation of total factor productivity from its steady-state value and l is labor input. (A.11) is the first-order condition for households' labor-leisure decision, where χ is a parameter of the utility function (we assume log utility so that the coefficient on consumption in (A.11) is one). (A.12) describes the evolution of inflation when prices are changed stochastically as in Calvo (1983) and a subset of firms use rule-of-thumb pricing as in Gali and Gertler (1999). If $\theta_f = 1$ and $\theta_b = 0$ then (A.12) is the fully rational, forward-looking version of the Phillips curve with exogenously sticky prices. Allowing $\theta_b > 1$ introduces a backward-looking element and, hence, additional inertia into the inflation process.

Evolution of State Variables and Shock Processes

$$k_{t+1} = \delta i_t + (1 - \delta) + (1 - \delta)k_t. \tag{A.13}$$

$$n_t = R^q [\frac{K}{N}(r_t^s - E_{t-1}r_t^s) + \frac{(1 - \tau R^k)}{\tau}y_t + n_{t-1}]. \tag{A.14}$$

$$g_t = \rho_g g_{t-1} + \varepsilon_t^g. \tag{A.15}$$

$$z_t = \rho_z z_{t-1} + \varepsilon_t^g. \tag{A.16}$$

Equations (A.13) and (A.14) describe the evolution of the two state variables of the capital and internal equity, respectively. τ is the probability that a given firm survives into the next period. Equations (A.15) and (A.16) state that government spending and total factor productivity follow first-order autoregressive processes.

Monetary Policy Rule and Interest-Rate Determination

$$r_t^n = \overline{r}^n + \beta E_t \pi_{t+1}. \tag{A.17}$$

$$r_t = r_t^n - E_t \pi_{t+1}. \tag{A.18}$$

(A.17) is one example of an interest-rate rule for monetary policy; cf. equation (3.1). (A.18) defines the real interest rate.

Key parameter values include

$$\frac{G}{Y} = 0.2, \frac{N}{K} = 0.5, \frac{C}{Y} = 0.04, \sigma = 1.0,$$

$\delta = 0.025$ per quarter, $\alpha = 0.98$, $\beta = 0.99$, $b = 0.98(1 - .025)$, $\alpha = 0.33$, $\Psi = 0.05$, $\varphi = 0.25$, $\kappa = 0.086$, $\theta_f = 0.5$, $\theta_b = 0.5$, $\tau = 0.95$, $\chi = 13.3$.

Any parameters not reported are as in BGG.

Notes

1. As we show in the context of our simulation model below, even when a bubble is present, the market price can still be expressed as a discounted stream of cash flows, though with a discount rate that differs from the fundamental rate. In particular, periods in which the market price is above the fundamental are also periods in which the implied discount rate is below the true fundamental rate, and vice versa. Because the "fundamental discount rate" is not directly observable, it is, in general, impossible to know whether there is a nonfundamental component to the current stock price.

2. To be clear, for the analysis that follows it is only necessary that nonfundamental movements in asset prices affect aggregate demand. In other work we have found that, to explain the observed volatility of output, it is necessary to have a balance-sheet channel supplementing the traditional wealth effect.

3. For relevant surveys see Bernanke and Gertler (1995), Hubbard (1997), Gilchrist and Himmelberg (1998), and Bernanke, Gertler and Gilchrist (1999).

4. We implicitly include in this definition any institutional and regulatory structure that may affect private-sector risk exposure. For example, both U.S. and Japanese banks hold real estate (or make loans with real estate as collateral), but by law only Japanese banks are allowed to hold equities. This apparently incidental difference has strong implications for the likely effects of a stock-price collapse on bank capital and bank lending in the two countries, as indeed we have seen in Japan in the past few years.

5. Inflation targeting has been adopted in recent years by a substantial number of industrialized and developing countries, including (among many others) the United Kingdom, Sweden, Canada, New Zealand, Chile, and most recently Brazil. An extensive literature has developed on the early experience with this approach; see, for example, Goodhart and Viñals (1994), Haldane (1995), Leiderman and Svensson (1995), Bernanke and Mishkin (1997), and Bernanke et al. (1999) for comparative analyses.

6. Inflation targeting has been castigated in some quarters as a policy of "inflation nutters," to use Mervyn King's descriptive phrase. This criticism is simply incorrect, however. As Lars Svensson (1997, 1999) has shown, inflation targeting is completely consistent with a conventional quadratic central-bank loss function that places arbitrary weights on the output gap and inflation; in other words, inflation targeting in no way precludes significant attention to conventional stabilization objectives. So what then is new? One important advantage is that an inflation-targeting framework makes explicit (for both policymakers and the public) the simple fact that monetary-policy actions that expand output and employment, but which also leave the inflation rate higher than it was initially, do not necessarily increase social welfare on net. Instead, account must also be taken of the future losses in output and employment that will be necessary to bring inflation back to its initial level; or, alternatively, of the various distortions and reductions in long-term economic growth associated with a permanent increase in inflation. By enforcing the requirement that any sequence of policy actions be consistent with the long-run inflation target (a sort of nominal anchor requirement), the inflation-targeting framework eliminates the upward inflation ratchet that proved so costly in many countries in the 1960s, 1970s, and early 1980s.

7. Note that even theories that stress the self-fulfilling nature of crisis expectations (e.g., Obstfeld 1994) usually imply that such expectations can only arise if fundamentals are relatively weak.

8. Interested readers are referred to Bernanke, Gertler, and Gilchrist (1999) for additional detail.

9. Finite lives are a metaphor for the entry and exit of firms and the associated turnover in credit markets. The assumption of finite lives also prevents the business sector from ever reaching a steady state in which it is entirely self-financing.

10. Specifically, we use a variant of Calvo's (1983) staggered price setting model developed by Gali and Gertler (forthcoming) that allows a subset of firms to use rule-of-thumb pricing behavior. The resulting aggregate supply equation is similar in spirit to the "sticky inflation" model of Fuhrer and Moore (1995).

11. We also make some smaller changes that are important for the simulations we want to do, such as calibrating a realistic effect of changes in asset prices on consumption.

12. We do not attempt to rationalize why investors do not arbitrage the difference between the market and fundamental returns. To our knowledge, any theory of bubbles based on market psychology relies on some arbitrary assumption along these lines. This point also applies to the so-called rational bubbles of Blanchard and Watson (1982). We do not use Blanchard-Watson rational bubbles in this paper because their nonstationarity creates technical problems in our framework.

13. By treating the probability that the bubble bursts as exogenous, we rule out the possibility that monetary policy can surgically prick the bubble. Although it is certainly possible to endogenize this probability, so little is known about the effects of policy actions on market psychology that any modification along these lines would necessarily be ad hoc. Note that it is nevertheless the case in our framework that asset prices will be highly sensitive to monetary policy, since policy can affect the fundamental component. Thus, the empirical observation that asset prices react strongly to monetary policy actions is not direct evidence against the exogeneity assumption made here.

14. Note that $a = 1$ corresponds to the so-called rational bubble described in Blanchard and Watson (1982). Hence, our bubble specification can be made arbitrarily close to a rational bubble by the assumption that a is close to 1.

15. Note also that the rule given by (3.1) abstracts from an interest-rate smoothing motive, which appears to be important empirically; again see Clarida, Gali, and Gertler (1998) and the estimates in the next section. Ignoring this aspect of policy makes the simulation results presented below look somewhat less realistic (because policy reacts "too quickly" to changes in the economy) but does not affect the qualitative nature of the results.

16. We assume $p = 0.5$ and $a = 0.98$.

17. To be clear, agents in the model know only the ex ante stochastic process for the bubble and not the time that it will burst.

18. All simulations are reported as deviations from the steady state.

19. We consider the accommodating policy not because it is a realistic alternative, but rather to underscore the point that the impact of a bubble is highly sensitive to the response of monetary policy.

20. Note that we assume that policy responds to the (observable) level of stock prices, not the (unobservable) level of the bubble, which seems realistic. That distinction is not important in the present exercise but will become important in scenarios in which the central bank is uncertain about the source of the appreciation in stock prices.

21. Under the usual assumption that social welfare depends on the output gap and inflation, we can, therefore, unambiguously conclude that the inflation-targeting rule maximizes welfare.

22. The model does not include raw-material or finished-goods inventories. Inclusion of inventory stocks in the model would likely increase the downward reaction by adding an endogenous inventory cycle.

23. That is, for simplicity here we do not include a confounding bubble shock. The welfare comparisons would not be affected by including a bubble shock.

24. For evidence that general credit conditions tightened at this time, see Gertler and Lown (1999).

25. More specifically, CGG apply a GMM estimator with a correction for the moving average error induced by overlapping forecasts (see their endnote 11 for details). Our estimation procedure follows the CGG method very closely, with minor differences described below. In particular, we follow CGG in using as instruments a constant, and lags 1–6, 9, and 12 of log-differenced commodity price index, the log-differenced CPI, the log-differenced output gap, and the instrument interest rate. For Japan, lags 1–6, 9, and 12 of the real yen-dollar exchange rate are also included as instruments. For the commodity price index, we use slightly different series from CGG, specifically, an IMF series for Japan and the Dow-Jones commodity price index for the United States. In auxiliary regressions, discussed below, we also use lags 1 to 6 of the log-difference of the stock-price index (TOPIX in Japan and the S&P 500 for the United States).

Following CGG, we construct the output gap for the United States as the residuals of a regression of industrial production on a constant, time, and time squared, for the sample period 1960:1 through 1998:12. Because we believe that Japan has been well below potential output since about 1990, the output gap variable we construct for Japan is based on a quadratic trend for industrial production based on data beginning in 1968:1 and ending in 1989:6. Through 1989:6 the Japanese output gap is measured as the residual from this regression; subsequently it is equated to actual output less the extrapolated quadratic trend value of output. We thank Richard Clarida for providing the estimation programs.

26. Estimates (not shown) from samples ending in 1994:12, the end date used by CGG, closely replicated their results.

27. The fitted values assume that expected inflation and the expected output gap are the realized values. They are thus comparable to the target values reported in Figure 6.8; see below.

28. Kozicki (1999) observes, however, that this gap is greatly reduced if a core inflation measure is used in the estimation of the Fed's reaction function.

29. Kozicki (1999) makes a similar observation and provides support for her contention with the following revealing quote from Chairman Greenspan:

In the spring of 1989, we began to ease monetary conditions as we observed the consequence of balance-sheet strains resulting from increased debt, along with significant weakness in the collateral underlying that debt. Households and businesses became much more reluctant to borrow and spend and lenders to extend credit—a phenomenon often referred to as the "credit crunch." In an endeavor to defuse these financial strains we moved short-term rates lower in a long series of steps that ended in the late summer of 1992, and we held them at unusually low levels through the end of 1993—both absolutely and, importantly, relative to inflation. (Testimony of June 22, 1994)

30. An alternative interpretation, which is consistent with our general approach, is that financial conditions in certain key sectors and regions were sufficiently bad—e.g., bank capital positions well below regulatory minima—that the impact of small interest-rate changes on the economy was reduced. A reduction in the policy multiplier would justify more aggressive Fed policies during this period.

Our sample period does not include the episode of fall 1998, when the Fed reacted to increased quality spreads in the bond market by easing. Again, this action seems justifiable to us, in that the widening spreads could well have been interpreted as predicting a slowdown in the general economy.

31. The fitted values again assume perfect foresight by the central bank for inflation and the output gap.

32. Note that it would not be correct to argue that stock prices matter because of their predictive power for the output gap and inflation. We include stock returns in the information sets for forecasting these variables, thereby controlling for the predictive power of stock returns.

33. Figure 6.10 suggests that the Bank of Japan should have raised its key interest rate as high as 8% to 10% during 1987–1989, which some commentators at the conference thought would not have been politically feasible given that contemporaneous inflation (possibly as a result of exchange-rate appreciation) remained low. Our specific measure of the target rate is sensitive to our estimates of the size of the output gap in Japan at the time and is not to be treated as precise. What is striking about the period is not that the BOJ failed to tighten radically, but that it failed to tighten at all. In any case, for the record, we consider the failure to respond to deflationary pressures during 1992–1996 (see below) to be the most serious shortcoming of Japanese monetary policy during this period.

34. As can be seen in Figure 6.10, the target call rate went negative in 1993, out of the feasible range of the actual rate. Still, it was not until 1995 that the actual call rate went below 2.0%.

35. Further, to the extent that (say) collapse of the banking system would be deflationary, perhaps in a highly discontinuous way, it seems to us that lender-of-last-resort interventions are consistent with the philosophy of flexible inflation-targeting.

36. For an even broader indictment of fixed-exchange-rate regimes see Obstfeld and Rogoff (1995).

37. Dollarization or a currency union represent an alternative approach for small open economies that also avoids the instabilities of fixed exchange rates. These approaches have their own problems, however.

References

Aghion, Philippe, Philippe Bacchetta, and Abhijit Banerjee. 1999. "A Simple Model of Monetary Policy and Currency Crises." Manuscript, Massachusetts Institute of Technology.

Allen, Franklin, and Douglas Gale. 2000. "Bubble and Crises." *Economic Journal* 110, 236–255.

Bernanke, Ben S. 1983. "Non-monetary Effects of the Financial Crisis in the Propagation of the Great Depression." *American Economic Review* 73, 257–276.

Bernanke, Ben S., and Mark Gertler. 1995. "Inside the Black Box: The Credit Channel of Monetary Transmission." *Journal of Economic Perspectives* 9(4), 27–48.

———. 1989. "Agency Costs, Net Worth, and Business Fluctuations." *American Economic Review* 79, 14–31.

Bernanke, Ben S., Mark Gertler, and Simon Gilchrist. 1996. "The Financial Accelerator and the Flight to Quality." *Review of Economics and Statistics* 78(1), 1–15.<3m>. 1999. "The Financial Accelerator in a Quantitative Business Cycle Framework." In J. B. Taylor and M. Woodford, eds., *Handbook of Macroeconomics*. Amsterdam: North-Holland.

Bernanke, Ben S., and Harold James. 1991. "The Gold Standard, Deflation, and Financial Crisis in the Great Depression: An International Comparison." In R. G. Hubbard, ed., *Financial Markets and Financial Crises*. Chicago: University of Chicago Press for National Bureau of Economic Research.

Bernanke, Ben S., Thomas Laubach, Frederic S. Mishkin, and Adam Posen. 1999. *Inflation Targeting: Lessons from the International Experience*. Princeton, NJ: Princeton University Press.

Bernanke, Ben S., and Cara S. Lown. 1991. "The Credit Crunch." *Brookings Papers on Economic Activity* 2, 205–239.

Bernanke, Ben S., and Frederic S. Mishkin. 1997. "Inflation Targeting: A New Framework for Monetary Policy?" *Journal of Economic Perspectives* 11(2), 97–116.

Blanchard, Olivier, and Mark Watson. 1982. "Bubbles, Rational Expectations, and Financial Markets." In P. Wachtel, ed., *Crisis in the Economic and Financial Structure*. Lexington, MA: Lexington Books.

Bond, Stephen, and Jason Cummins. 1999. "Noisy Share Prices and Investment." Preliminary paper, Nuffield College and New York University, July.

Borio, C. E. V., N. Kennedy, and S. D. Prowse. 1994. "Exploring Aggregate Asset Price Fluctuations across Countries: Measurement, Determinants, and Monetary Policy Implications." Bank for International Settlements Economics Paper No. 40, April.

Calvo, Guillermo. 1983. "Staggered Prices in a Utility-Maximizing Framework." *Journal of Monetary Economics* 12, 383–398.

Campbell, John. 1999. "Asset Prices, Consumption, and the Business Cycle." In J. B. Taylor and M. Woodford, eds., *Handbook of Macroeconomics*. Amsterdam: North-Holland.

Clarida, Richard, Jordi Gali, and Mark Gertler. 1998. "Monetary Policy Rules in Practice: Some International Evidence." *European Economic Review*, June, 1033–1068.

———. 2000. "Monetary Policy Rules and Macroeconomic Stability: Evidence and Some Theory." *Quarterly Journal of Economics* 115, 147–180.

Eichengreen, Barry. 1992. *Golden Fetters: The Gold Standard and the Great Depression, 1919–1939*. New York: Oxford University Press.

Eichengreen, Barry, Paul Masson, Miguel Savastano, and Sunil Sharma. 1999. "Transition Strategies and Nominal Anchors on the Road to Greater Exchange-Rate Flexibility." Essays in International Finance no. 213, International Finance Section, Princeton University, April.

Fisher, Irving. 1933. "The Debt-Deflation Theory of Great Depressions." *Econometrica* 1, 337–357.

Fuhrer, Jeffrey C., and George R. Moore. 1995. "Inflation Persistence." *Quarterly Journal of Economics* 110(1), 127–160.

Gali, Jordi, and Mark Gertler. 1999. "Inflation Dynamics: A Structural Economics Analysis." *Journal of Monetary Economics* 44, 195–222.

Gertler, Mark, and Cara S. Lown. 1999. "The Information Content of the High Yield Bond Spread for the Business Cycle." Manuscript, Federal Reserve Bank of New York.

Gilchrist, Simon, and Charles Himmelberg. 1998. "Investment: Fundamentals and Finance." In B. Bernanke and J. Rotemberg, eds., *NBER Macroeconomics Annual*.

Goodhart, Charles A. E., and José Viñals. 1994. "Strategy and Tactics of Monetary Policy: Examples from Europe and the Antipodes." In Jeffrey Fuhrer, ed., *Goals, Guidelines, and Constraints for Monetary Policymakers*, Federal Reserve Bank of Boston Conference Series 38.

Haldane, Andrew G., ed. 1995. *Targeting Inflation*. London: Bank of England.

Hubbard, R. Glenn. 1997. "Financial Market Imperfections and Investment." National Bureau of Economic Research Working Paper No. 5996.

Kaminsky, Graciela, and Carmen Reinhart. 1999. "The Twin Crises: The Causes of Banking and Balance-of-Payments Problems." *American Economic Review* 89, 473–500.

Kiyotaki, Nobuhiro, and John Moore. 1997. "Credit Cycles." *Journal of Political Economy* 105, 211–248.

Kozicki, Sharon. 1999. "How Useful Are Taylor Rules for Monetary Policy?" Federal Reserve Bank of Kansas City, *Economic Review*, Second Quarter, 5–33.

Krugman, Paul. 1999. "Analytical Afterthoughts on the Asian Crisis." Manuscript, Massachusetts Institute of Technology.

Leiderman, Leonardo, and Lars E. O. Svensson, eds. 1995. *Inflation Targeting*. London: Centre for Economic Policy Research.

Ludvigson, Sydney, and Charles Steindel. 1999. "How Important Is the Stock Market Effect on Consumption?" Federal Reserve Bank of New York, *Economic Policy Review* 5(2), 29–52.

Mishkin, Frederic S. 1997. "The Causes and Propagation of Financial Instability: Lessons for Policymakers." In *Maintaining Financial Stability in a Global Economy: A Symposium*. Kansas City, MO: Federal Reserve Bank of Kansas City.

Obstfeld, Maurice. 1994. "The Logic of Currency Crises." Banque de France, *Cahiers Économiques et Monétaires* 43, 189–213.

Obstfeld, Maurice, and Kenneth Rogoff. 1995. "The Mirage of Fixed Exchange Rates." *Journal of Economic Perspectives* 9(4), 73–96.

Parker, Jonathan. 1998. "Spendthrift in America? On Two Decades of Decline in the U.S. Saving Rate." In B. Bernanke and J. Rotemberg, eds., *NBER Macroeconomics Annual*.

Svensson, Lars E. O. 1999. "Inflation Targeting as a Monetary Policy Rule." *Journal of Monetary Economics* 43, 607–654.

———. 1997. "Inflation Forecast Targeting: Implementing and Monitoring Inflation Targets." *European Economic Review* 41, 1111–1146.

Taylor, John B. 1980. "Aggregate Dynamics and Staggered Contracts." *Journal of Political Economy* 88, 1–24.

———. 1993. "Discretion versus Policy Rules in Practice." Carnegie-Rochester Conference Series on Public Policy, vol. 39, 195–214.

CHAPTER 7

Monetary Policy and Asset Price Volatility

SHOULD WE REFILL THE BERNANKE-GERTLER PRESCRIPTION?

Kenneth N. Kuttner

1. Introduction

Central banks have long struggled with the question of whether monetary policy should be used to dampen asset price booms. On June 29, 2005, for example, two years before the mid-2007 house price peak, members of the Federal Reserve's Federal Open Market Committee (FOMC) spent the afternoon debating the merits of a monetary policy response to the ongoing housing boom. Similar discussions took place during the great bull market of the mid-1990s amid growing concerns about unsustainably high stock prices. During the FOMC meeting of February 5, 1997, Alan Greenspan articulated the Fed's quandary of balancing financial and macroeconomic objectives when he remarked that "product prices alone should not be the sole criterion if we are going to maintain a stable, viable financial system," while adding:

> It is the real economy that matters. Finance is all very interesting and financial prices are quite important but only because they affect the real economy. Ultimately, that is what our charter is all about.[1]

New York Fed president Benjamin Strong grappled with exactly the same set of issues seventy years earlier during the stock market boom of the 1920s. Like Greenspan, Strong expressed misgivings about the stock market's lofty valuation, but lacking any tangible signs of product price inflation, resisted calls to tighten credit.[2]

Bernanke and Gertler's seminal article "Monetary Policy and Asset Price Volatility" (1999) has framed much of the recent debate on the appropriate monetary policy response to asset price fluctuations. Its influence stems from its precise definition of the problem, and from the clarity of its prescription: monetary policy should respond to the macroeconomic effects of asset price fluctuations, but not to the fluctuations themselves:

> The inflation-targeting approach dictates that central banks should adjust monetary policy actively and preemptively to offset incipient inflationary or deflationary pressures. Importantly, for present purposes, it also implies that policy should not respond to changes in asset prices, except insofar as they signal changes in expected inflation.[3]

While couched in terms of inflation targeting (IT), which Bernanke and Gertler viewed as a reasonable description of the Fed's policy framework, the conclusions apply broadly to any central bank seeking to minimize output and inflation volatility.

The 2007–2009 financial crisis has understandably led to a reconsideration of the Bernanke-Gertler (henceforth BG) conclusion. In hindsight, one cannot help but wonder whether a preemptive policy of rate hikes might not have attenuated the housing bubble. This paper's goal is to summarize and critically reexamine the BG policy prescription in light of recent events. It begins in Section 2 with a recapitulation of the main elements of the BG argument. Section 3 discusses the ways in which views on the BG recommendation have evolved in light of the financial crisis. Section 4 presents some new evidence on the relationship between interest rates and the behavior of stock and real estate prices in the years preceding the financial crisis. Section 5 concludes with an assessment of the BG recommendations, and the viability of alternative policy options.

2. A Review of the Bernanke-Gertler Analysis

The core of the BG argument is the proposition that "central banks should view price stability and financial stability as highly complementary and mutually consistent objectives."[4] This idea is neither new nor farfetched. Indeed, it would be hard to argue that macroeconomic instability is good for the financial system.

The deleterious effects of inflation volatility are well understood. Unanticipated inflation reduces the value of long-dated assets, diminishing the net worth of those assets' owners. As noted by Brumbaugh et al. (1987), among others, this phenomenon was a major contributor to the U.S. thrift crisis of the 1980s, in which high inflation and the accompanying high interest rates eroded mortgage lenders' capital base. Similarly, according to Fisher's (1933) debt-deflation theory, unanticipated deflation increases the real debt burden of debtors, creates financial distress, and amplifies economic downturns.[5]

These views have been echoed by Schwartz (1995), who observed that price instability, and the attendant variability in monetary policy, would lead to defaults:

> [Borrowers and lenders] evaluate the prospects of projects by extrapolating the prevailing price level or inflation rate. Borrowers default on loans not because they have misled uninformed lenders but because, subsequent to the initiation of the project, authorities have altered monetary policy in a contractionary direction. The original price level and inflation rates are no longer valid. The change in monetary policy makes rate-of-return calculations based on the yield of projects, based on the initial price assumptions of both lenders and borrowers, unrealizable.[6]

The historical record generally supports the contention that price volatility breeds financial crises. Bordo and Wheelock (1998), for example, examined historical data from the United States, the U.K., and Canada, in an investigation of what they termed the "Schwartz Hypothesis," after Schwartz (1995). Their main finding was that financial panics did tend to be associated with periods of high price volatility. This pattern is evident in Figure 7.1, which plots the level of consumer prices in Great Britain from the late eighteenth to the late nineteenth centuries. The major financial panics, marked by the vertical lines in the figure, often (but not always) follow periods of inflation, and precede episodes of deflation.

It is important to emphasize that factors other than price volatility are often responsible for financial crises. Bordo and Wheelock observed that a number

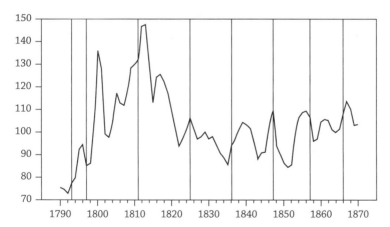

Figure 7.1 Retail prices and financial crises in the U.K., 1790–1870. Note: Data are from Officer (2010). Vertical lines mark the financial panics of 1793, 1797, 1811, 1825, 1836, 1847, 1857, and 1866.

of nineteenth- and early-twentieth-century U.S. banking panics occurred during periods of price stability. The same can be said of the British panics of 1793, 1836, and 1890. And indeed, the 2007–2009 financial crisis occurred in a global environment of low and stable inflation. The inescapable conclusion is that while macroeconomic and financial stability may be complementary, macroeconomic stability does not *guarantee* financial stability.[7]

2.1. A REVIEW OF THE BERNANKE-GERTLER MODEL

The BG analysis is based on what has become the canonical new Keynesian (NK) macro model with the usual spending ("IS") equation, a dynamic aggregate supply relationship, and a policy rule specifying the central bank's reaction to expected inflation and output. Because asset prices do not appear explicitly in the standard NK model, Bernanke and Gertler augment the model with wealth and "financial accelerator" effects. These provide channels through which asset market booms and busts affect aggregate spending: the former by affecting consumption spending, the latter by influencing the cost of external funds through collateral values.

Bubbles are modeled as realizations of an exogenous stochastic process. Each period, the bubble continues to grow with probability p, and bursts with probability $1 - p$. The stock price is the sum of the fundamental value, determined by the marginal product of capital, and the bubble term. Asset prices affect aggregate consumption through households' consumption spending, and firms' investment expenditures. Bubbles are therefore essentially another source of aggregate demand shocks, albeit one that follows a nonstandard statistical distribution.

It is also worth noting that in the BG framework, promoting financial stability has nothing to do with the prevention or attenuation of asset price bubbles, which are exogenous and unaffected by interest rates. Instead, the role of monetary policy is to mitigate bubbles' impact on aggregate demand: appropriately calibrated rate hikes will limit the expansionary effects of asset price rises, while rate cuts will cushion the blow when prices fall. This would be the appropriate policy response to any demand shock, of course. What turns this into a model of financial stability is the inclusion of the financial accelerator, which provides the primary mechanism through which asset prices affect aggregate demand.

Monetary policy is modeled as a policy rule of the form

$$r_t^n = \overline{r}^n + \beta E_t \pi_{t+1} + \xi S_{t-1} / S,$$

where S_{t-1}/S is the deviation of the stock price from its steady-state value, and r^n is the nominal interest rate. The paper considers only a limited range of values for the two reaction function parameters: β values of 1.01 and 2.0 are used to represent accommodative and aggressive reactions to inflation. The ξ stock price response is either zero or 0.1. The question of whether the central bank should respond to asset prices boils down to whether the policy rule with $\xi = 0.1$ performs better than the rule in which $\xi = 0$.

The quantitative criteria used to assess the policy rules' performance are the unconditional variances of output and inflation, which are obtained by simulating the model for alternative values of ξ and β. These criteria are consistent with the conventional quadratic loss function,

$$L = E_t \sum_{i=1}^{\infty} \delta^i [(\pi_{t+i} - \overline{\pi})^2 + \lambda(y_{t+i} - y^*)^2]. \tag{1}$$

where y is the log of real GDP, y^* is potential output, π is the inflation rate, $\overline{\pi}$ is the inflation target, δ is a discount factor, and λ is the weight attached to output fluctuations relative to deviations of the inflation rate from its target. This objective function, and in particular the λ parameter, is a useful way to evaluate the trade-offs between the potentially conflicting goals of output and inflation stability. BG's analysis of the alternative rules does not require using such an objective function, however. The reason is that, in their model, asset price bubbles create no trade-off between output and inflation volatility: stabilizing inflation also stabilizes output, and vice versa.[8]

A critical assumption underlying the use of an objective function like (1), or BG's simpler variance criterion, is that financial instability per se imposes no costs on the economy. Or to put it another way, financial crises affect economic well-being only to the extent that they create output or inflation volatility. The BG prescription of responding only to bubbles' impact on expected future inflation therefore follows naturally from the model structure, and the criterion used to evaluate alternative policy rules.

2.2. THE KEY BG RESULTS

The baseline BG results, which appear in Figure 7.2, are striking. By responding exclusively to expected inflation, monetary policy is able to stabilize inflation *and* output quite effectively, even in the presence of a bubble. With an aggressive

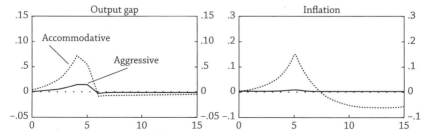

Figure 7.2 The BG response of output and inflation to a bubble shock, baseline case

response to inflation, the bubble causes only a mild increase in output, and the inflation rate remains virtually unchanged. It is important to emphasize that these results are obtained despite the fact that monetary policy is having no effect on the bubble itself, which is exogenous: stock prices continue to rise, stimulating spending through wealth and financial accelerator effects. The central bank is able to neutralize these effects almost completely with higher interest rates.

Equally striking is the absence of any discernible postcrash fallout. The bursting of the bubble removes the stimulus, but inflicts no collateral damage. Monetary policy then returns to a neutral policy stance, and the economy goes on as before. The only way to obtain a postbubble recession is to assume that positive bubbles are followed by *negative* bubbles, in which the asset price falls *below* the fundamental—but again, these aftereffects are easily combated by responding aggressively to expected inflation.[9]

Figure 7.3 shows what happens when the policy rule includes a response to the stock price. The performance is demonstrably worse than in the case of no stock price response, especially when monetary policy is accommodative with respect to inflation. Puzzlingly, output *falls* in the accommodative case, presumably because policy is overreacting to the bubble and sending the economy into a recession. Consequently, inflation declines sharply in this model simulation.

The logical conclusion is that a direct policy response to asset prices can actually increase output and inflation volatility. This holds even when bubbles are the only source of asset price fluctuations. The performance of the policy rule with $\xi > 0$ is even worse when asset price fluctuations are driven by fundamentals rather than bubble shocks. A policy response to asset prices is wholly counterproductive in this case, with the central bank tightening policy in a misguided effort to offset favorable technology shocks. The BG quantitative analysis therefore supports the "benign neglect" prescription: the monetary authority should ignore asset prices, except to the extent that they affect future inflation. Bursting bubbles may be bad for the economy, but they create no problems that cannot be solved with a few well-timed interest rate cuts.

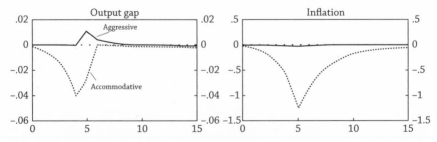

Figure 7.3 The BG response of output and inflation to a bubble shock, with stock price response

This rationale for a benign neglect policy is further buttressed by a number of practical concerns. One is the difficulty inherent in distinguishing bubbles from fundamentals-driven asset price fluctuations. Assets' prices are readily observable, but the fundamentals are not, at least not in real time. Bernanke (2002) cited Campbell and Shiller's (1998) bubble warning as an example of how even the best minds in finance can get it wrong—or at least sound the alarm prematurely. And Irving Fisher's ill-timed 1929 pronouncement that "stock prices are low" is surely the best-known example of the opposite error.[10] Consequently, there will inevitably be mistakes in both directions, with the central bank sometimes attempting to offset asset price appreciations that are based on fundamentals, and at other times failing to react to irrational exuberance.

A second problem pointed out by Bernanke (2002), and others, is that it is hard to burst bubbles safely. Empirical estimates of interest rates' influence on asset prices suggest that small interest rate hikes are unlikely to be effective. Sharp interest rate hikes, on the other hand, run the risk of causing a recession. Indeed, the prevailing view, as articulated in Friedman and Schwartz (1963), and others, blames the onset of the Great Depression on the Federal Reserve's misguided attempt to pop what it perceived to be a stock price bubble in 1928–1929.[11] Forty years earlier, the Bank of England's attempt to pop a speculative bubble at the end of 1889 itself precipitated a panic, and in the end it did not prevent the Barings crisis a few months later.[12] A third issue is that central bankers are justifiably loath to create the perception that they are passing judgment on the appropriate level of asset prices.

3. Evolving Views of the Bernanke-Gertler Prescription

Before the crisis, the question of whether monetary policy should respond to asset price fluctuations seemed to have been settled. The BG prescription of focusing exclusively on output and inflation forecasts had become the consensus view, and the policy worked well during the tech boom and bust earlier in the decade. And ex post, the Fed's response to the 1987 stock market crash, which focused on macro and financial damage control, has been interpreted as a successful application of the same policy.

Not surprisingly, the 2007–2009 financial crisis fractured that consensus, reigniting the long-standing debate on the appropriate response to asset prices and financial conditions more broadly. Leijonhufvud (2007) argued that central banks' neglect of asset price inflation is dangerous, on the grounds that expansionary monetary policy can create asset price inflation even as prices of goods and services remain stable. DeGrauwe (2007) concluded that "the subprime crisis shows that central banks cannot avoid taking responsibilities that include the prevention of bubbles and the supervision of all institutions that are in the business of creating credit and liquidity." Giavazzi and Giovannini (2010) went further, and suggested that IT actually undermined financial stability by creating a "low-interest-rate trap" that encouraged excessive risk taking and increased the likelihood of crises.

It is useful to distinguish three ways in which economists' views have evolved in response to the crisis. Some maintain is that in spite of the financial crisis, the BG prescription remains fundamentally sound. Others take issue with the BG findings narrowly, arguing that a more proactive, "leaning against the wind" policy response to asset prices (and financial conditions more broadly) can in fact contribute to macro stability. And some argue that financial stability should be a distinct policy objective, independent of output and inflation.

3.1. THE BG PRESCRIPTION IS FINE AS IS

One view, articulated by Ito (2010) and Svensson (2010), and others, argues for the retention of the BG prescription, and the IT framework associated with it. Adherents to this view accept the key premise that output and inflation volatility are the correct objectives, and share BG's interpretation of bubbles as exogenous demand shocks. They also emphasize the practical objections, summarized above, concerning the difficulty of discerning bubbles and safely deflating them.

This is not to say that financial stability should *not* be a policy objective. Instead, those who argue for retaining the BG prescription contend that monetary policy is the wrong tool for the job, and that the central bank (or whatever the relevant authority happens to be) should adopt more robust macroprudential regulatory policies. The availability of a second policy tool solves the Tinbergen (1952) problem of having more targets than instruments, and allows the monetary authority to focus exclusively on macroeconomic objectives. The question, as discussed below, is whether an effective financial stability tool is available.

3.2. THE BG PRESCRIPTION NEEDS ADJUSTMENT

A second view is that central banks should adopt a measured "leaning against the wind" strategy with respect to asset prices, or other measures of financial imbalances (e.g., leverage).[13] Prominent examples of papers advocating this approach include Cecchetti et al. (2000), Borio and Lowe (2002), Cecchetti et al. (2002), and Bordo and Jeanne (2002). While this view seems not (yet) to have been adopted by policymakers at the U.S. Federal Reserve, some within the International Monetary Fund are more open to the idea. In a recent issue of the *World Economic Outlook*, Fatás et al. (2009) suggested that monetary policy should at times take a more active role in countering financial imbalances: "The evidence ... does not support the idea that central banks should react automatically to changes in asset prices, still less that they should try to determine some appropriate level for asset prices. But they should examine what is driving asset price movements and be prepared to act in response."

Significantly, proponents of this strategy generally do not question the central bank's objective of minimizing output and inflation volatility, as embodied in equation (1). Instead, their view is that the best way to further macroeconomic stability involves a systematic response to financial imbalances. As noted by Svensson (2010), to the extent that the ultimate objective is output and inflation stabilization, leaning against the wind is perfectly consistent with flexible inflation targeting. In this case, asset prices would merely serve as leading indicators of future output and inflation, just as in the BG framework. Crockett (2003), Issing (2003), and Svensson (2010) acknowledged that the possibility of long-term fallout from a financial crisis may call for lengthening the inflation targeting horizon.

Drawing on the model of Kent and Lowe (1997), Cecchetti et al. (2000) and Cecchetti et al. (2002) made a case for leaning against the wind that represents more of a departure from the BG framework. Their insight was that if expected future inflation were to remain unaffected by a bubble, which it would if the bubble were not expected to persist very long, then reacting only to expected inflation would fail to prevent bubble-induced macroeconomic volatility.[14] Cecchetti et al. (2000) reported numerical simulations demonstrating that including an asset price term in the monetary authority's policy rule can, by offsetting the demand pressures created by unsustainable asset price increases, actually reduce inflation and output volatility.[15] Bernanke and Gertler (2001) took issue with the Cecchetti et al. (2000) conclusions, however, arguing that their analysis attributed to the monetary authority an unrealistic amount of information on the existence and duration of the bubble shock.

An important limitation of the BG analysis is that by assuming the asset price bubble to be exogenous, it rules out the possibility of monetary policy being able to affect financial stability *directly*. This necessarily limits the scope of monetary policy to responding to the fallout from asset price booms and busts, rather than directly going after the source of instability. Relaxing this assumption could therefore justify a more active response to asset prices, for example by using interest rate hikes to reduce the size of the bubble, and limit the damage caused by its subsequent collapse. The model of Kent and Lowe (1997) has this feature, and they showed that such a policy can, at least in principle, produce superior outcomes. This reasoning is consistent with that of Friedman and Schwartz, who chided the Federal Reserve for following a policy "which was too easy to break the speculative boom" in the years prior to 1928.[16]

Bean (2004) made a similar theoretical point in the context of a new Keynesian model, extended to include debt-financed capital accumulation and credit crunches. In that model, monetary policy did not affect the probability of a crunch, but it did influence the buildup of debt via its effects on the future output gap. Although Bean did not use the model to rationalize a response to asset prices per se, the model does suggest that optimal monetary policy should respond aggressively to expected future output, instead of focusing narrowly on inflationary pressures.

Another rationale for preemptive rate hikes recognizes the complications created by the zero lower bound (ZLB) on the nominal interest rate. Robinson and Stone (2006) made this point using a model in which bubbles stimulated aggregate demand, just as in the BG framework. However, they departed from BG in assuming that the central bank can reduce the expected duration of bubbles by raising the interest rate, and they also imposed the ZLB constraint on the policy rule. Their insight was that allowing a bubble to persist and grow increases the likelihood of a bust that would exceed the central bank's ability to offset it with a nonnegative interest rate. Consequently, if monetary policy can decrease the probability of the bubble's survival, central banks should react to asset price booms by raising interest rates, thus insuring against the undesirable ZLB outcome—even if it means accepting some additional near-term macroeconomic volatility.

3.3. THE BG PRESCRIPTION HAS DEEPER PROBLEMS

A third view is that monetary policy should respond to financial conditions *independently* of their impact on the output gap and inflation. Rationalizing such a response requires the plausible assumption that financial instability is costly for reasons other than the volatility it introduces in inflation and the output gap. Several different ways to model these costs have been proposed, all of which involve resource misallocation and the attendant economic inefficiencies.

Bordo and Jeanne (2002) argued that the effects of asset price bubbles, and their collapse, have effects that go beyond their impact on aggregate demand. Their specific focus is on the effects of collateral constraints on the productive sector. In their framework, the reversal of an asset price bubble is the equivalent of an adverse aggregate supply shock. Optimal monetary policy is therefore not just a matter of aggregate demand management. Instead, the appropriate policy response is to preempt asset price appreciation up to some point, but to revert to a more accommodative stance if the perceived probability of an improvement in fundamentals is high. Clearly, operationalizing such a nonlinear policy rule would present some serious challenges.

Like Bordo and Jeanne (2002), Dupor's (2002, 2005) model is one in which asset price bubbles create inefficiencies. His framework is one in which firms are not fully rational, and consequently mistake the bubble component of asset price movements for fluctuations in the fundamental value of capital. Bubbles can therefore lead to overinvestment, and distort consumption-leisure and consumption-investment decisions. Monetary policy can be used to offset these distortions by raising the interest rate when stock prices exceed their fundamental values. Naturally, this policy prescription requires that the monetary authority can observe stock price fundamentals.

Another approach is to include in the central bank's loss function a term involving financial distress.

$$L = E_t \sum_{i=1}^{\infty} \delta^i [(\pi_{t+i} - \overline{\pi})^2 + \lambda_y (y_{t+i} - y^*)^2 + \lambda_\Omega \Omega_{t+i}^2], \tag{2}$$

where the Ω term captures the welfare losses associated with financial crises. Woodford (2010) sketched a model with a welfare criterion of this form. The model's distinguishing feature is that it includes borrowers and savers rather than a single representative agent. Intermediation is required to equate the two agents' marginal utilities of consumption. Crisis-induced disruptions are costly because they create a marginal utility "gap" between the two consumers. The probability of entering a credit-constrained regime depends on the amount of leverage in the economy, which is in turn a function of monetary policy. The model's implication is that optimal policy involves balancing a crisis prevention objective against the conventional goals of output and inflation stabilization. While this can be interpreted as an extension of the flexible IT framework, it runs counter to the BG desideratum of responding to financial conditions only to the extent that they affect future output and inflation.

Expanding the objective function in this way requires that the central bank use interest rate policy to manage not only the trade-off between output and inflation, but also more subtle trade-offs between financial and macroeconomic objectives. Although these objectives may sometimes be aligned, inevitably instances will arise in which mitigating financial distortions will require accepting more output or inflation variability. Benjamin Strong recognized this dilemma when in 1925, pressed to quash rampant stock speculation, asked: "Must we accept parenthood for every economic development in the country? That is a hard thing for us to do. We would have a large family of children. Every time one of them misbehaved, we might have to spank them all."[17]

Practical challenges abound, and it may be unrealistic to think that central bankers have enough information to operationalize a policy based in the minimization of equation (2). Unlike inflation and output, there is no clear empirical counterpart to the Ω that appears in equation (2). Moreover, the models used to motivate a financial term in the objective function differ as the relevant variable. In Woodford's framework, leverage is the appropriate variable, but it remains to be seen how a meaningful aggregate gauge of leverage can be constructed, especially in a financial system where so much leverage is disguised as derivatives and concealed in off-balance-sheet transactions. In the Dupor and Bordo-Jeanne models, on the other hand, the central bank should respond to the deviations between the market and fundamental stock valuations, raising the perennial question of how such misalignments might be detected.

Another issue is determining the terms of the trade-off between inflation (or output) and the likelihood of a crisis. Implementing a targeting rule requires an estimate of the likely impact on Ω of a one-percentage-point reduction in the inflation rate—or alternatively, how much of a deviation from the macro objectives would be needed for a given reduction in the probability of a credit crunch. Also unknown is the magnitude of the impact of the policy interest rate on financial fragility. Conventional econometric methods can be used to estimate the impact of a 25-basis-point rate hike on real GDP at a given horizon. Estimating the marginal effects of interest rate changes on the likelihood of entering a credit constrained regime is a much more daunting task.

Communication and accountability are also serious concerns, particularly for inflation-targeting central banks. Because inflation and output are readily (if imperfectly) measured, it is straightforward to explain the central bank's monetary policy decisions in terms of the near-term trade-offs between the two. Moreover, the regular release of inflation and GDP data make it possible to hold policymakers accountable, with a modest time lag, for macroeconomic outcomes. It is not clear how these modes of communication and accountability would apply to a criterion as hard to measure as expected crisis-induced welfare losses, especially when crises occur irregularly, and at intervals measured in years.

3.4. TWO ADDITIONAL CONSIDERATIONS

Practical difficulties aside, it does not follow from the inclusion of the Ω term in the objective function that central banks should use monetary policy as a financial stability tool. That case rests on two additional arguments.

One is that other policy instruments for promoting financial stability are either unavailable or ineffective. If that were not the case, then those tools could be used to address financial imbalances, leaving the monetary authority free to concentrate on macroeconomic objectives. The question of these tools' efficacy is beyond the scope of this paper, but recent experience suggests that the U.S. financial system has evolved in ways that have rendered regulatory measures much less effective. A great deal of lending takes place by unregulated financial institutions like mortgage brokers, for example. And even those that are nominally subject to prudential regulation have successfully used mechanisms like structured investment vehicles (SIVs) and "repo 105" transactions to partially circumvent capital and liquidity requirements. The interest rate is the one policy tool that is difficult to evade.

The second argument one would have to make in order to justify a monetary policy response to financial conditions is that such a policy could actually *do* something to affect financial stability. This could happen in at least four different ways. First, contractionary policy could reduce either the size or duration of any bubble by restricting the volume of credit supplied. Second, tighter monetary policy could limit financial fragility by decreasing the demand for credit as in Bordo and Jeanne (2002) and Woodford (2010). Third, if low interest rates lead to excess risk-taking, as alleged by Borio and Zhu (2008) and Gambacorta (2009), then higher interest rates would discourage such risk taking while possibly dampening the bubble. Finally, higher interest rates could directly offset the sorts of distortions that arise in the Dupor (2002, 2005) model.

These channels' practical relevance is not well established, however. Part of the reason is that monetary policy is entirely absent from most bubble models, such as those of Allen and Gorton (1993) and Scheinkman and Xiong (2003). One that does include an explicit role for the central bank is Allen and Gale (2000), but it does so via the crude assumption that the central bank directly controls the supply of credit, up to a random shock realization. The assumption was justified on the grounds that the central bank controls the required reserve ratio and the supply of bank reserves, and these jointly determine the volume of credit available to investors.

While it may have been a reasonable characterization at some point in the past, this view of the link between monetary policy and credit supply is by now hopelessly dated. With the progressive reduction of the statutory required reserve ratio, and its further de facto reduction via the introduction of sweep accounts in the mid-1990s, reserves now constitute less than 1% of bank credit and deposits, as shown in Figure 7.4. Of course the level of banking system reserves would not matter if a reliable link existed between reserves and bank credit. This turns out not to be the case, however. The solid line in Figure 7.5 shows the logarithm of the ratio of bank loans to total reserves, interpretable as the log "loan multiplier," whose upward trend reflects the declining share of reserves in bank credit plotted in Figure 7.4. The dotted line shows the residual from the regression of the logarithm of total loans on a constant, a linear time trend, and the log of total reserves, which can be interpreted as the error from a cointegration relationship. Standard tests fail to reject the null of no cointegration, suggesting no stable long-run link exists between reserves and bank credit.

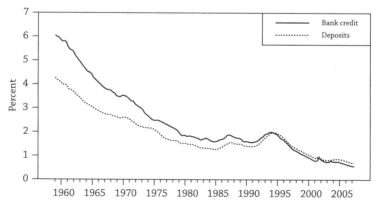

Figure 7.4 Total reserves as a percentage of deposits and bank credit, United States.
Note: Data are from the Federal Reserve's H.8 release.

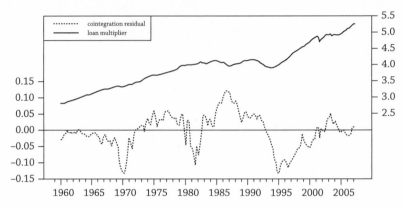

Figure 7.5 The loan multiplier and the loan-reserves cointegration residual, United States. Note: Data are from the Federal Reserve's H.8 release, and author's calculations.

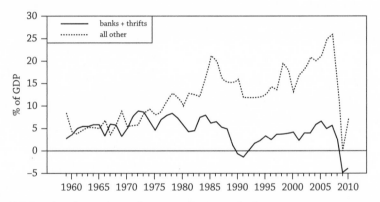

Figure 7.6 Lending by traditional intermediaries and others. Note: Data are from the Federal Reserve's Z.1 release. Shaded areas are NBER-designated recessions.

Moreover, as documented in Friedman and Kuttner (2010), policy rate changes by the U.S. Federal Reserve (and other major central banks as well) require virtually no changes in nonborrowed reserves, and hence will not meaningfully affect the aggregate size of the banking system's balance sheet. And in any case, banks' and thrifts' combined share of total credit has declined steadily from 45% in 1975 to only 18% in 2010. Expressed as a share of GDP, credit extended by institutions not subject to any reserve requirement surpassed lending by banks and thrifts in the early 1980s (Figure 7.6). Indeed, very little of the precrisis lending boom can be attributed to lending by traditional intermediaries. The inescapable conclusion is that changes in reserves or the required reserve ratio now affect only a small part of the financial system, and would therefore be unlikely to have a meaningful effect on credit supply.

4. Can Interest Rate Policy Dampen Asset Price Booms?

With conventional monetary policy exerting very little direct influence over the volume of bank credit, much less the quantity of total credit, the burden of checking imbalances falls entirely on interest rates. Specifically, interest rates would presumably affect individuals' and institutions' demand for assets and credit, with higher interest rates tending to reduce asset prices and restraining credit growth.[18] This section considers the issue of whether interest rates can either contribute to or attenuate asset price growth—a critical question if interest rate policy is to be used to promote financial stability.

4.1. EXISTING RESEARCH

Empirical research on the topic has failed to document a large impact of short-term interest rates on stock prices, much less any connection to bubbles or crises. Campbell (1991) and Campbell and Ammer (1993) decomposed the variance of stock prices into components attributable to interest rates, dividends, and the equity premium, and found that interest rate fluctuations contributed only 3% of the variance. Bernanke and Kuttner (2005) looked specifically at the response of stock prices to unanticipated changes in the federal funds rate. Their main finding was that a 100-basis-point surprise rate increase would lead to a stock market decline of roughly 5%.[19] This suggests that while monetary policy does have a quantitatively meaningful impact on the stock market, an extended campaign of rate hikes would be required to dampen a sustained, double-digit increase in equity prices like that experienced in the four years leading up to the crisis.

Given the role played by the real estate market in the 2007–2009 crisis, it is not surprising that a large number of recent papers have sought to document a relationship between interest rates and property prices. These studies' findings are generally inconclusive, however. The Ahearne et al. (2005) descriptive analysis suggests that low interest rates do tend to precede housing price peaks, with a lead of approximately one to three years. Using a vector autoregression (VAR) that included interest rates, credit, and money, Goodhart and Hofmann (2008) uncovered a "significant multidirectional link" between these variables and property prices, although the direction of causality was unclear. Focusing more narrowly in the impact of the federal funds rate, Dokko et al. (2009) found that deviations from the Taylor rule explained only a small portion of the precrisis rise in property prices. Jarociński and Smets (2008) reached similar conclusions using a Bayesian VAR. Using a dynamic factor model as an alternative to the VAR method, Del Negro and Otrok (2007) attributed a relatively small amount of variance to the aggregate national factor, suggesting a small role for interest rates. And using the Campbell (1991) decomposition, Campbell et al. (2009) found that interest rate fluctuations contributed very little to changes in real estate prices.

Finally, Glaeser et al. (2010) employed a user-cost model of house prices, and concluded that only a small portion of the pre-2007 rise in real estate prices was due to low interest rates.

4.2. A LOOK AT THE RECENT PRECRISIS EXPERIENCE

Discerning the impact of monetary policy on stock and property prices is not an easy task, in part because asset prices depend heavily on unobserved factors, such as risk premia and expectations. Ideally, one would run a randomized controlled trial in which different monetary policies (or policy rules) were assigned to different central banks, and observe the behavior of asset prices across countries. Lacking a controlled experiment, a highly imperfect alternative is to look across countries for a relationship between interest rates and stock and property prices during the period leading up to their peaks, which in most cases occurred in 2007 or 2008. If monetary policy were capable of moderating asset price booms, then one would expect to see those countries with higher short-term interest rates experiencing smaller asset price gains than those with lower interest rates.

To investigate this hypothesis, monthly data on stock prices, short-term policy interest rates, and consumer prices were obtained for 32 countries from the International Monetary Fund's International Financial Statistics database. The 32 countries included 12 from the euro area, seven noneuro developed countries, and 13 emerging market economies. Residential property prices were obtained from the Bank for International Settlements. These data are not consistently collected, however, and usable series were available for only 27 of the 32 countries. Quarterly or lower frequency data were interpolated to calculate monthly series. Although all are residential property prices, the specific coverage (e.g., single-family houses versus flats, new versus existing dwellings, etc.) varies across countries. The appendix contains additional information on the data.

Figure 7.7 shows the distribution of annualized real asset price growth over the four years leading up to the price peak. For equities, this occurred between May and November 2007, depending on the country. The peak dates for real estate prices were more dispersed: in the United States house prices peaked slightly before stock prices, while elsewhere (e.g., Greece and Italy) the decline did not commence until the end of 2008.[20] Stock price growth ranged from strong to spectacular over this period, with all but one of the countries in the sample enjoying real double-digit growth, many in excess of 20% per year. The average for developed economies is 20%, and 29% for emerging market economies. Property prices generally grew more slowly, averaging 5% per year in real terms for both sets of countries. Not surprisingly, Iceland holds the record for real estate exuberance, with an annual real growth rate over four years of 12%.

But before investigating the link between monetary policy and asset prices, it is useful to take a brief detour to characterize monetary policy over this period,

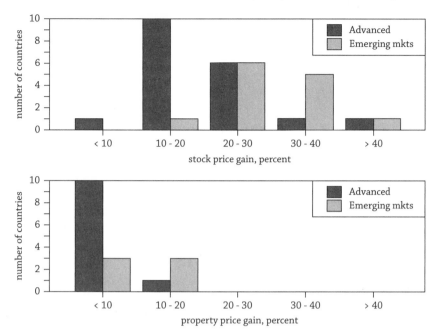

Figure 7.7 Distribution of real annualized stock and property price gains, four years prepeak

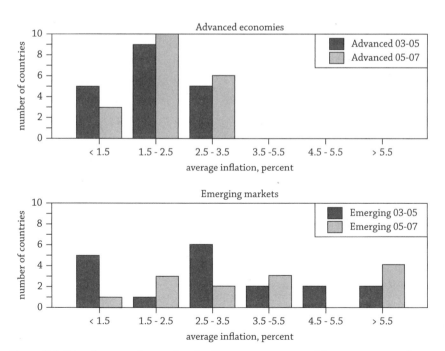

Figure 7.8 Distribution of annualized inflation rates, two and four years prepeak. Note: Consumer price data are from the IMF.

and in particular to assess the claim that central banks were too slow to raise interest rates in the face of rising asset prices. One way to do this is to estimate an equation to describe the degree to which the countries in the sample tended to respond to inflation, which, as shown in Figure 7.8, increased slightly over this
· period. The regression equation used is

$$r_i = \beta_0 + \beta_1 \pi_i + \beta_2 d_i^{em} + \varepsilon_i, \tag{3}$$

where r_i is the short-term nominal interest rate (monetary policy instrument or operational target) for country i, π_i is the inflation rate, and d_i^{em} is a dummy variable for emerging market economies. The interest and inflation rates are the averages for the two years prior to the stock market peak. Since its members share a common monetary policy, the euro area is treated as a single country, and the euro-area harmonized CPI is used to calculate the inflation rate. Naturally, it would be dangerous to interpret this equation as structural: over a two-year period, there is surely feedback from the interest rate to inflation, and the equation plainly omits other relevant determinants of the interest rate, such as the output gap.

The results from estimating equation (3) appear in Table 7.1. Reassuringly, countries with higher inflation tended to set higher nominal interest rates, and taken at face value the inflation coefficient of 2.34 suggests that the reaction is more than two-for-one. However the estimated parameters are heavily influenced by Turkey and Brazil, which had much higher inflation and interest rates than the other countries in the sample. Excluding these two observations, the point estimate falls to a more reasonable 1.34. The coefficient on the emerging market dummy suggests these central banks set slightly lower interest rates, conditional on a given level of inflation, but the difference is not statistically significant.

Table 7.1 The Cross-Country Relationship between Inflation and the Interest Rate

	Dependent variable = short-term nominal interest rate				
		Regressor			
	Intercept	Inflation	Emerging market	N	$\overline{R}^2$
Full sample	−1.15 (0.56)	2.35*** (4.02)	−0.30 (0.14)	21	0.468
Excluding Turkey & Brazil	1.21 (1.03)	1.32*** (3.43)	−0.70 (0.62)	19	0.374

Note: The numbers shown are the estimated coefficients in an OLS regression of the short-term nominal interest rate on the variables listed during the two years prior to the peak on the listed variables. Asterisks denote statistical significance: *** for 1%, ** for 5%, and * for 10%; t-statistics are in parentheses.

One issue with levels regressions like equation (3) is that the neutral interest rate may differ across countries, implying country-specific intercepts. One way around this is to look instead at the *change* in the interest rate over the year period, and to regress that on the corresponding change in the inflation rate,

$$\Delta r_i = \beta_0 + \beta_1 rr_i + \beta_2 \Delta \pi_i + \beta_3 d_i^{em} + \varepsilon_i, \tag{4}$$

where rr_i is the beginning-of-period real interest rate (the nominal rate minus the 12-month lagging inflation rate) and $\Delta \pi_i$ is the change in the inflation rate over the two-year period. The reason for including the real interest rate is to allow for a kind of error-correction mechanism: a negative value of β_1 would imply that countries with high initial levels of the real rate would reduce the nominal rate (or raise it more slowly) than those with low initial real rates.

Table 7.2 displays estimates of equation (4), both including and excluding Turkey and Brazil. With adjusted R-squareds of 0.388 (0.715 with Turkey and Brazil included), the equation captures the cross-country pattern of interest rate changes reasonably well. The positive intercept is consistent with a general trend toward higher interest rates over this period, and central banks raised the policy rate roughly one-for-one with the inflation rate. These patterns are evident in Figure 7.9, which depicts the evolution of real rates over this period. There is a

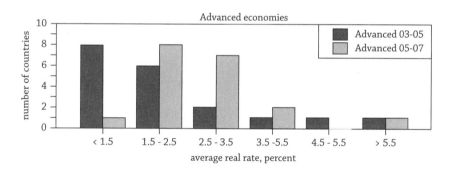

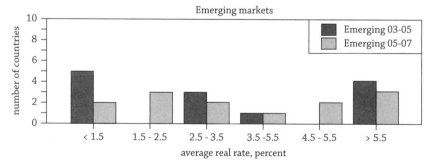

Figure 7.9 Distribution of real interest rate levels, two and four years prepeak. Note: Consumer price and interest rate data are from the IMF.

Table 7.2 **The Cross-Country Relationship between Inflation and Interest Rate Changes**

	Dependent variable = short-term nominal interest rate change					
	Regressor					
	Intercept	*Lagged real rate*	*Inflation change*	*Emerging market*	*N*	$\overline{R}^2$
Full sample	1.70*** (3.83)	−0.19*** (3.55)	1.10*** (4.02)	−0.33 (0.14)	21	0.715
Excluding Turkey & Brazil	1.75*** (5.08)	−0.22** (2.21)	1.00*** (3.94)	−0.70 (0.62)	19	0.388

Note: The numbers shown are the estimated coefficients in an OLS regression of the change in short-term nominal interest rate on the variables listed during the two years prior to the peak on the listed variables. Asterisks denote statistical significance: *** for 1%, ** for 5%, and * for 10%, *t*-statistics are in parentheses.

modest but pronounced rightward shift in the distribution for developed economies. Although the shift appears smaller for the emerging market economies, the coefficients on the emerging market dummies are statistically insignificant.

Together, the results in Tables 7.1 and 7.2 suggest that the 21 central banks in the sample collectively reacted appropriately to gradually rising price pressures in the two years to the crisis although with an estimated coefficient on inflation equal to or slightly greater than 1, one could argue that they could have responded more aggressively.

Having summarized central banks' interest rate policies over this period, the next question is whether these policies made any difference to the behavior of asset prices in their respective countries. Three alternative regression equations were used to address this question. The first expresses the annualized real percentage change in the asset price Δy_i (representing either equities or real estate) as a function of the average nominal interest rate and the average inflation rate during the two years leading up to the crisis, along with a dummy for euro-area countries and another for emerging market economies,

$$\Delta y_i = \beta_0 + \beta_1 r_i + \beta_2 \pi_i + \beta_3 d_i^{em} + \beta_3 d_i^{eu} + \eta_i. \tag{5}$$

A second specification replaces the levels of the interest and inflation rates with their changes,

$$\Delta y_i = \beta_0 + \beta_1 \Delta r_i + \beta_2 \Delta \pi_i + \beta_3 d_i^{em} + \beta_4 + d_i^{eu} \eta_i. \tag{6}$$

A third uses as regressors the real interest rate prevailing two years prior to the peak, rr_i and the estimated residual from equation (4), $\hat{\varepsilon}_i$ as a gauge of the degree to which (conditional on inflation) monetary policy was tighter or looser than average,

$$\Delta y_i = \beta_0 + \beta_1 rr_i + \beta_2 \widehat{\varepsilon}_i + \beta_3 d_i^{em} + \beta_4 d_i^{eu} + \eta_i. \tag{7}$$

It goes without saying that these regression equations could provide at best circumstantial evidence on how monetary policy affects asset prices. For one thing, there would be simultaneous equation bias if central banks responded to asset price appreciation with higher interest rates. But since this would result in a positive correlation between asset price growth and the interest rate, the net effect would be an upward bias in the (negative) interest rate coefficient(s). Similarly, the level of economic activity may affect asset prices and the interest rate (via a policy reaction function), but the regression does not include any variable that would capture this effect. This would also tend to reduce the likelihood of finding a significant negative coefficient on the interest rate.

None of the three equations is at all successful at explaining cross-country patterns in stock price movements. As shown in Table 7.3, the only statistically significant parameter estimates are the intercepts, and in the specification involving the real interest rate (specification 3) the coefficients on the emerging market dummies. The adjusted R-squareds are negative for two of the specifications, and

Table 7.3 **The Effect of Interest Rates on Stock Prices**

	Dependent variable = prepeak annualized stock price gain		
		Specification	
Regressor	(1)	(2)	(3)
Intercept	21.6***	21.6***	18.1***
	(4.0)	(4.6)	(4.2)
Euro area dummy	4.1	5.3	4.9*
	(0.7)	(1.0)	(0.9)
Emerging market dummy	9.9	7.1	7.2
	(1.7)	(1.3)	(1.3)
Average interest rate 2 years prepeak	0.46		
	(0.78)		
Average inflation 2 years prepeak	−2.15		
	(1.11)		
Interest rate change from 2 years prior		−2.39	
		(1.57)	
Inflation change from 2 years prior		4.85	
		(1.64)	
Real interest rate 2–4 years prepeak			0.31
			(0.70)

Table 7.3 **(Continued)**

	Dependent variable = prepeak annualized stock price gain		
		Specification	
Regressor	*(1)*	*(2)*	*(3)*
Adjusted R^2	−0.016	0.043	−0.001

Note: The numbers shown are the estimated coefficients in an OLS regression of the annualized percentage change in stock prices on the listed variables during the two years prior to the peak. Asterisks denote statistical significance: *** for 1%, ** for 5%, and * for 10%; t-statistics are in parentheses. The total number of usable observations is 32.

Table 7.4 **The Effect of Interest Rates on Property Prices**

Dependent variable = prepeak annualized property price gain			
		Specification	
Regressor	*(1)*	*(2)*	*(3)*
Intercept	9.2**	3.9	8.8***
	(2.1)	(1.3)	(3.1)
Euro area dummy	−3.7	−1.7	−5.9*
	(1.0)	(0.5)	(1.7)
Emerging market dummy	5.7	9.3**	4.9
	(1.2)	(2.2)	(1.4)
Average interest rate 2 years prepeak	−1.03		
	(1.43)		
Average inflation 2 years prepeak	0.32		
	(0.23)		
Interest rate change from 2 years prior		1.26	
		(0.93)	
Inflation change from 2 years prior		−2.82*	
		(1.74)	
Real interest rate 2–4 years prepeak			−1.93**
			(2.53)
Interest rate deviation from fitted rule			2.28
			(1.51)
Adjusted R^2	0.148	0.178	0.283

Note: The numbers shown are the estimated coefficients in an OLS regression of the annualized percentage change in property prices on the listed variables during the two years prior to the peak. Asterisks denote statistical significance: *** for 1%, ** for 5%, and * for 10%; t-statistics are in parentheses. The total number of usable observations is 27.

a paltry 0.04 for the equation involving the interest and inflation rate changes (specification 2). In this equation, the coefficients on the interest rate and inflation rate changes have signs (negative for the interest rate, positive for inflation) that are consistent with the hypothesis that tighter monetary policy reduces asset price appreciation. Unfortunately, they are not statistically significant, either individually or jointly.

The property price regressions fare slightly better than those for the stock price, but the results are also inconclusive. As shown in Table 7.4, other than the intercepts and those on the dummy variables, only two of the estimated coefficients are statistically significant at even the 10% level. The statistically significant –1.93 coefficient on the real interest rate in specification 3 suggests an inverse relationship between real interest rates and property prices. Quantitatively, the effect is modest, with a one-percentage-point increase in the real rate reducing the rate of appreciation by two percentage points. The marginally significant –2.82 coefficient on inflation in specification 2 has the wrong sign, however, as it suggests that lower real interest rates tend to depress property prices.

Taken together, these rough-and-ready regression results lend little support to the view that marginal interest rate adjustments can meaningfully dampen asset price bubbles, corroborating the Reinhart and Reinhart (2011) examination of the U.S. historical experience. The 21 central banks in the sample were not collectively "behind the curve" in responding to consumer price inflation, and yet most of the countries experienced spectacular stock price booms and many (though by no means all) saw sharply rising property prices. The observed cross-country differences in real interest rates are relatively small, however, and the estimates' imprecision may be due to the lack of variance in the independent variables. Bolder policy experiments—rate hikes of one or two percentage points—surely would have been more informative than the incremental adjustments that took place over this period. The search continues for a definitive link between interest rates and asset price bubbles.

5. Conclusions

Two lessons from the financial crisis of 2007–2009 are uncontroversial. One is that macroeconomic stability, and price stability in particular, does not guarantee financial stability. The second is that because the bursting of asset price bubbles can wreak havoc on the real economy, the central bank's financial stability objective should not be overlooked. The critical question is what, if anything, monetary policy should do to further that objective.

The Bernanke and Gertler (1999) monetary policy prescription is to treat the symptoms of financial instability by counteracting the effects of booms and busts on aggregate demand, rather than attempt to deflate the asset price bubbles that create the instability. The conclusion was based on a macro model with exogenous asset bubbles, and no welfare costs to financial instability other than its effects on output and inflation volatility. Model simulations demonstrated that varying the policy interest rate in response to asset price fluctuations would lead to more volatile output and inflation, even if the asset price fluctuations were known to be caused by bubbles.

The crisis has reopened the question of whether financial stability considerations should shape monetary policy. A case can be made for using monetary policy in such a capacity if it can in fact dampen asset price booms, and if bubbles impose economic costs that are not entirely reflected in output gaps and inflation fluctuations. The recent crisis has surely lent support to the proposition that financial crises create significant economic inefficiencies, such as the misallocation of resources to the construction of unsold houses, not to mention the costs associated with litigation and liquidation. These considerations could be used to justify moving away from the BG prescription and toward a policy intended to attenuate financial booms.

The results reported in this paper (and elsewhere) provide scant empirical support for the efficacy of modest monetary policy interventions in restraining asset price growth, however. Moreover, such a strategy would present a number of practical difficulties. One obstacle is the measurement of financial imbalances. Common gauges, such as asset prices and aggregate leverage, are imperfect indicators of the likelihood of a financial crisis. A second challenge is communication: it would not be easy to explain why tighter policy is imperative when price inflation is subdued. A third problem is judging the policy's success, since no amount of leaning against the wind will entirely prevent financial crises. Finally, the political economy dimension of the problem should not be overlooked. Given the disproportionate share of households' wealth held in the form of home equity, it would be dangerous for the Federal Reserve to try to dampen property price appreciation. The mere perception that the Fed was following such a policy would surely give rise to calls to curtail its independence.

Ultimately, the decision to deviate from the BG prescription may hinge on the availability of alternative, nonmonetary policies for dealing with financial system risk. Regulatory measures, and macroprudential regulation in particular, are clearly better suited than interest rate policy to the promotion of financial stability. The timidity of the financial reforms enacted in the United States thus far is not encouraging, however. Basel III may eventually introduce some macroprudential element into banking regulation, but its weakness is that it would apply only to banks. Monetary policy may be the only available tool for dealing with the markets and unregulated financial institutions that were at the epicenter of the 2007–2009 crisis in the United States. Lacking a viable alternative policy tool, it would not be surprising if some central banks chose to hedge their bets, and give greater weight to asset prices in the conduct of monetary policy.

Notes

1. From the transcript of the FOMC meeting of February 4–5, 1997, p. 103.
2. See Ahamed (2009), 276–277.
3. Bernanke and Gertler (1999, 18).
4. Bernanke and Gertler (1999, 18).
5. Cargill et al. (1997), among others, argued that the decline in prices prolonged Japan's banking crisis in the mid-2000s, and this is one reason why some economists, including Bernanke (2000), called on the Bank of Japan to adopt an inflation target.
6. Schwartz (1995, 24).
7. Issing (2003) made a similar point. Conversely, examining the experience of a number of countries, Posen (2003) concluded that a financial crisis is neither a necessary nor sufficient condition for the occurrence of deflation.
8. Blanchard (2004) referred to this property as a "divine coincidence."
9. Theoretical bubble models, like that of Allen and Gorton (1993), often appeal to short-selling constraints to limit investors' ability to bet against asset price declines. Since no such constraints exist for stock purchases, the theoretical basis for negative bubbles is less clear.
10. Or *was* it an error? McGrattan and Prescott (2004) argued that the stock market boom of the late 1920s was in fact justified by economic fundamentals. This illustrates the difficulty of identifying asset price bubbles, even with 70 years' worth of hindsight.
11. Bernanke (2002) includes a compact summary of these views.
12. See Kuttner (2010).
13. A vocal minority, including Roubini (2006), dismissed practical concerns about the detectability of bubbles and the dangers of trying to pop them, and argued for a much more aggressive policy response to asset prices. Posen (2006) offered a spirited rejoinder.
14. The same point may also apply to a situation in which the Phillips curve was very flat, or inflation expectations were firmly anchored by an inflation target.
15. In a related line of research, Akram et al. (2007) and Akram and Eitrheim (2008) simulated an econometric model of the Norwegian economy in an effort to assess the performance of monetary policy rules that included asset prices. They found that responding to debt growth can contribute to financial stability, but this is offset by the destabilizing effects of interest rate volatility. The general conclusion is the advisability of such a policy depends on the source of the shocks.
16. Friedman and Schwartz (1963, 290). There is some tension between this diagnosis and their contention that excessively contractionary monetary policy caused the Depression. Their argument is apparently that monetary policy was too loose before 1928 and too tight thereafter.
17. The passage is from a letter from Strong to New York Fed economist Carl Snyder, May 21, 1925, quoted in Ahamed (2009, 277).
18. This does not necessarily involve deflating or puncturing bubbles, of course. Leaving aside the possibility of bubbles, by shrinking the discount factor applied to future revenues, low interest rates increase the value of long-dated assets, *ceteris paribus*, while higher rates decrease those values.
19. Similar results were obtained by Rigobon and Sack (2003) and Gürkaynak et al. (2005).
20. In several of the European countries, such as Germany, real property prices were essentially flat over this period, and so the price increase would have been the same regardless of what peak date was chosen.

References

Ahamed, Liaquat. 2009. *Lords of Finance*. New York: Penguin.

Ahearne, Alan, John Ammer, Brian Doyle, Linda Kole, and Robert Martin. 2005. "House Prices and Monetary Policy: A Cross-Country Study." International Finance Discussion Paper 841, Board of Governors of the Federal Reserve System.

Akram, Q., Gunnar Bårdsen, and Kjersti-Gro Lindquist. 2007. "Pursuing Financial Stability under an Inflation-Targeting Regime." *Annals of Finance* 3, 131–153.

Akram, Q. Farooq, and Øyvind Eitrheim. 2008. "Flexible Inflation Targeting and Financial Stability: Is It Enough to Stabilize Inflation and Output?" *Journal of Banking and Finance* 32, 1242–1254.

Allen, Franklin, and Douglas Gale. 2000. "Bubbles and Crises." *Economic Journal* 110, 236–255.

Allen, Franklin, and Gary Gorton. 1993. "Churning Bubbles." *Review of Economic Studies* 60, 813–836. Reprinted in this volume.

Bean, Charles R. 2004. "Asset Prices, Financial Instability, and Monetary Policy." *American Economic Review* 94, 14–18.

Bernanke, Ben S. 2000. "Japanese Monetary Policy: A Case of Self-Induced Paralysis?" In Ryoichi Mikitani and Adam S. Posen, eds., *Japan's Financial Crisis and Its Parallels to U.S. Experience.* Washington, DC: Institute for International Economics.

———. 2002. "Asset Price 'Bubbles' and Monetary Policy." Speech delivered to the New York Chapter of the National Association for Business Economics, New York, October 15.

Bernanke, Ben S., and Mark Gertler. 1999. "Monetary Policy and Asset Price Volatility." In *New Challenges for Monetary Policy: A Symposium.* Kansas City, MO: Federal Reserve Bank of Kansas City. Reprinted in this volume.<3m>. 2001. "Should Central Banks Respond to Movements in Asset Prices?" *American Economic Review* 91, 253–257.

Bernanke, Ben S., and Kenneth N. Kuttner. 2005. "What Explains the Stock Market's Reaction to Federal Reserve Policy?" *Journal of Finance* 60, 1221–1258.

Blanchard, Olivier J. 2004. "Comments on 'Inflation Targeting in Transition Economies; Experience and Prospects,' by Jonas and Mishkin." In Ben S. Bernanke and Michael Woodford, eds., *The Inflation Targeting Debate.* Chicago: University of Chicago Press.

Bordo, Michael D., and Olivier Jeanne. 2002. "Monetary Policy and Asset Prices: Does 'Benign Neglect' Make Sense?" *International Finance* 5(2), 139–164.

Bordo, Michael D., and David C. Wheelock. 1998. "Price Stability and Financial Stability: The Historical Record." *Federal Reserve Bank of St. Louis Review,* September–October, 41–62.

Borio, Claudio, and Philip Lowe. 2002. "Asset Prices, Financial and Monetary Stability: Exploring the Nexus." Working Paper 114, Bank for International Settlements.

Borio, Claudio, and Haibin Zhu. 2008. "Capital Regulation, Risk-Taking and Monetary Policy: A Missing Link in the Transmission Mechanism?" Working Paper 268, Bank for International Settlements.

Brumbaugh, R. Dan, Jr., Andrew S. Carron, Dwight M. Jaffee, and William Poole. 1987. "Thrift Industry Crisis: Causes and Solutions." *Brookings Papers on Economic Activity,* 1987(2), 349–388.

Campbell, John Y. 1991. "A Variance Decomposition for Stock Returns." *Economic Journal* 101(405), 157–179.

Campbell, John Y., and John Ammer. 1993. "What Moves the Stock and Bond Markets? A Variance Decomposition for Long-Term Asset Returns." *Journal of Finance* 48, 3–37.

Campbell, John Y., and Robert J. Shiller. 1998. "Valuation Ratios and the Long-Run Stock Market Outlook." *Journal of Portfolio Management,* Winter, 11–26.

Campbell, Sean D., Morris A. Davis, Joshua Gallin, and Robert F. Martin. 2009. "What Moves Housing Markets: A Variance Decomposition of the Rent-Price Ratio." *Journal of Urban Economics* 66(2), 90–102.

Cargill, Thomas F., Michael M. Hutchison, and Takatoshi Ito. 1997. *The Political Economy of Japanese Monetary Policy.* Cambridge, MA: MIT Press.

Cecchetti, Stephen G., Hans Genberg, John Lipsky, and Sushil Wadhwani. 2000. *Asset Prices and Central Bank Policy.* Geneva: International Center for Monetary and Banking Studies.

Cecchetti, Stephen G., Hans Genberg, and Sushil Wadhwani. 2002. "Asset Prices in a Flexible Inflation Targeting Framework." In William C. Hunter, George G. Kaufman, and Michael Pomerleano, eds., *Asset Price Bubbles: Implications for Monetary, Regulatory, and International Policies.* Cambridge, MA: MIT Press.

Crockett, Andrew. 2003. "Central Banking under Test?" *BIS Papers* 18, 1–6.

DeGrauwe, Paul. 2007. "There Is More to Central Banking Than Inflation Targeting." November. http://www.voxeu.org/index.php?q=node/716.

Del Negro, Marco, and Christopher Otrok. 2007. "99 Luftballons: Monetary Policy and the House Price Boom across U.S. States." *Journal of Monetary Economics* 54, 1962–1985.

Dokko, Jane, Brian Doyle, Michael Kiley, Jinill Kim, Shane Sherlund, Jae Sim, and Skander Van den Heuvel. 2009. "Monetary Policy and the Housing Bubble." FEDS Working Paper 2009–2049, Board of Governors of the Federal Reserve System, December.

Dupor, Bill. 2002. "The Natural Rate of Q." *American Economic Review* 92, 96–101.

———. 2005. "Stabilizing Non-fundamental Asset Price Movements under Discretion and Limited Information." *Journal of Monetary Economics* 52, 727–747.

Fatás, Antonio, Prakash Kannan, Pau Rabanal, and Alasdair Scott. 2009. *World Economic Outlook, 2009*. Washington, DC: International Monetary Fund.

Fisher, Irving. 1933. "The Debt-Deflation Theory of Great Depressions." *Econometrica* 1, 337–357.

Friedman, Benjamin M., and Kenneth N. Kuttner. 2010. "Implementation of Monetary Policy: How Do Central Banks Set Interest Rates?" In Benjamin M. Friedman and Michael Woodford, eds., *Handbook of Monetary Economics*. New York: North-Holland.

Friedman, Milton, and Anna J Schwartz. 1963. *A Monetary History of the United States, 1867–1960*. Princeton, NJ: Princeton University Press.

Gambacorta, Leonardo. 2009. "Monetary Policy and the Risktaking Channel." *BIS Quarterly Review*, December, 43–53.

Giavazzi, Francesco, and Alberto Giovannini. 2010 "The Low-Interest-Rate Trap." July. http://www.voxeu.org/index.php?q=node/5309.

Glaeser, Edward L., Joshua D. Gottlieb, and Joseph Gyourko. 2010. "Can Cheap Credit Explain the Housing Boom?" National Bureau of Economic Research Working Paper No. 16230.

Goodhart, Charles, and Boris Hofmann. 2008. "House Prices, Money, Credit, and the Macroeconomy." *Oxford Review of Economic Policy* 24(1), 180–205.

Gürkaynak, Refet S., Brian P. Sack, and Eric T. Swanson. 2005. "Do Actions Speak Louder Than Words? The Response of Asset Prices to Monetary Policy Actions and Statements." *International Journal of Central Banking* 1(1), 55–93.

Issing, Otmar. 2003. "Monetary and Financial Stability: Is There a Trade-off?" *BIS Papers* 18, 16–23.

Ito, Takatoshi. 2010. "Monetary Policy and Financial Stability: Is Inflation Targeting Passé?" Working Paper 206, Asian Development Bank.

Jarociński, Marek, and Frank R. Smets. 2008. "House Prices and the Stance of Monetary Policy." *Federal Reserve Bank of St. Louis Review* 90, 339–365.

Kent, Christopher, and Philip Lowe. 1997. "Asset-Price Bubbles and Monetary Policy." Research Discussion Paper 9709, Reserve Bank of Australia.

Kuttner, Kenneth N. 2010. "Victorian Financial Crises and Their Implications for the Future." *Business Economics* 45(2), 102–109.

Leijonhufvud, Axel. 2007 (June). "The Perils of Inflation Targeting." http://www.voxeu.org/index.php?q=node/322.

McGrattan, Ellen R., and Edward C. Prescott. 2004. "The 1929 Stock Market: Irving Fisher Was Right." *International Economic Review* 45, 991–1009.

Officer, Lawrence H. 2010. "What Were the UK Earnings and Prices Then?" http://www.measuringworth.com/ukearncpi/.

Posen, Adam S. 2003. "It Takes More Than a Bubble to Become Japan." In Anthony Richards and T. J. C. Robinson, eds., *Asset Prices and Monetary Policy*. Sydney: Reserve Bank of Australia.

———. 2006. "Why Central Banks Should Not Burst Bubbles." *International Finance* 9, 109–124.

Reinhart, Carmen M., and Vincent Reinhart. 2011. "Pride Goes Before a Fall: Federal Reserve Policy and Asset Markets." National Bureau of Economic Research Working Paper No. 16815.

Rigobon, Roberto, and Brian Sack. 2003. "Measuring the Reaction of Monetary Policy to the Stock Market." *Quarterly Journal of Economics* 118, 639–670.

Robinson, Tim, and Andrew Stone. 2006. "Monetary Policy, Asset-Price Bubbles, and the Zero Lower Bound." In Takatoshi Ito and Andrew K. Rose, eds., *Monetary Policy with Very Low Inflation in the Pacific Rim*. Chicago: University of Chicago Press.

Roubini, Nouriel. 2006. "Why Central Banks Should Burst Bubbles." *International Finance* 9, 87–107.

Scheinkman, José A., and Wei Xiong. 2003. "Overconfidence and Speculative Bubbles." *Journal of Political Economy* 111, 1183–1220. Reprinted in this volume.

Schwartz, Anna J. 1995. "Why Financial Stability Depends on Price Stability." *Economic Affairs* 15(4), 21–25.

Svensson, Lars E. O. 2010. "Inflation Targeting." In Benjamin M. Friedman and Michael Woodford, eds., *Handbook of Monetary Economics*. New York: North-Holland.

Tinbergen, Jan. 1952. *On the Theory of Economic Policy*. Amsterdam: North-Holland.

Woodford, Michael. 2010. "Inflation Targeting and Financial Stability." Presentation at the conference "The Future of Monetary Policy," EIEF, Rome, September.

Data Appendix

The following table lists the countries included in the analysis, the months during which stock and property prices peaked, and the coverage and frequency of the property price statistics.

Peak month				
Country	*Stock*	*Property*	*Coverage*	*Freq.*
Australia	Oct. 2007	Mar. 2008	8 cities	Q
Austria	May 2007	Sept. 2007	Excluding Vienna	Q
Belgium	May 2007	Sept. 2008	Existing dwellings	Q
Brazil	Dec. 2007			
Canada	July 2007	May 2008	Existing dwellings	
Chile	Oct 2007			
Czech Republic	Oct. 2007	Sept. 2008	Existing flats	Q
Denmark	Oct. 2007	Sep.t 2007	Single family	Q
Estonia	July 2007	Jun 2007	All flats	Q
Finland	Oct. 2007	Jun 2008	Existing dwellings	Q
France	May 2007	Sept. 2008	Existing dwellings	M
Germany	June 2007	Dec. 2007	New W. Germany	A
Greece	Oct. 2007	Dec. 2008	Urban, excluding Athens	Q
Hungary	July 2007	June 2008	Existing Budapest	Q
Iceland	July 2007	Oct. 2007	Reykjavik	M

Peak month

Country	Stock	Property	Coverage	Freq.
Ireland	May 2007	Dec. 2006	All dwellings	Q
Israel	Oct. 2007	July 2007	Owner occupied	M
Italy	May 2007	Dec. 2008	All dwellings	H
Korea	Oct. 2007	Sept. 2008	All dwellings	M
Mexico	Oct. 2007			
Netherlands	July 2007	Aug. 2008	All dwellings	M
New Zealand	May 2007	Dec. 2007	All dwellings	Q
Norway	July 2007	June 2008	All dwellings	Q
Poland	July 2007			
Slovak Republic	Nov. 2007	June 2008	Existing dwellings	Q
Slovenia	Aug. 2007	Mar. 2008	Existing dwellings	Q
Spain	Oct. 2007	Mar. 2008	All dwellings	Q
Sweden	May 2007	Sept. 2008	Owner occupied	Q
Switzerland	May 2007	May 2007	1-family	Q
Turkey	Oct. 2007			
United Kingdom	June 2007	Aug. 2007	All dwellings	M
United States	July 2007	Mar. 2007	Existing 1-family	

BUBBLES AND MACROPRUDENTIAL REGULATION

CHAPTER 8

Towards a Macroprudential Framework for Financial Supervision and Regulation?

Claudio Borio

Words, like nature, half reveal and half conceal the soul within.

—Alfred, Lord Tennyson

When I use a word...it just means what I choose it to mean— neither more, nor less.

—Humpty Dumpty

1. Introduction[1]

Financial instability may not necessarily be here to stay. But it has been sufficiently prominent over the last couple of decades to rise, slowly but surely, to the top of the international policy agenda. The sizable economic costs of financial crises in industrial and emerging market countries could not be ignored.

Banking supervisors were used to a quiet life in the (largely) financially repressed systems that emerged in the postwar period. They have been much busier of late. Bankhaus Herstatt failed in 1974. Few could have imagined then that this would mark the beginning of a long journey in ever closer and wider international cooperation among prudential authorities. Now, some 30 years on, efforts to upgrade bank capital standards are grabbing the headlines worldwide. They have even become an issue in electoral campaigns.

These efforts are part of a broader challenge: strengthening the safeguards against financial instability. The basic question is how best this should be done.

The answer ultimately depends on how we think of financial instability, of its ultimate causes and implications. Events have forced many of us to go back to basics; to question assumptions we once took for granted. The debate has been rich and has furthered our understanding greatly. Even so, having lost some trusted "points of reference" we are still searching for new ones.

This essay will argue that we can get a bit closer to the right answers by exploring the implications of an ungainly word, increasingly used but still looking for a precise meaning. The word is "macroprudential." The thesis is that to improve further the lines of defense against financial instability we should strengthen the macroprudential orientation of the regulatory and supervisory framework.

In fact, the process is well under way. Friedman once said: "We are all Keynesians now."[2] One could equally well say: "We are all (to some extent) macroprudentialists now"—to coin another clumsy word. The shift in perspective has been remarkable over the last few years. And it is likely that it will continue.

We might be moving toward the right answers. But this essay will raise still more questions. The intention is to use the "macroprudential" perspective as a kind of looking glass, to put old issues into a new focus. Once that is done, however, more questions will emerge.

The outline of the essay is the following. Section 2 defines terms and concepts: what is meant by a "macroprudential" perspective? Section 3 will argue that this perspective is useful to understand financial instability. Section 4 moves from diagnosis to remedies, and argues that the macroprudential perspective can also be helpful in identifying broad sets of policy responses. Finally, some conclusions are drawn.

2. The Micro- and Macroprudential Dimensions Defined[3]

2.1 DEFINITIONS

Shades of gray are best appreciated when set against their two primitive components, black and white. Likewise, it is especially helpful to *define* the micro- and macroprudential perspectives in such a way as to sharpen the distinction between the two. So defined, by analogy with black and white, the macro- and microprudential souls would normally coexist in the more natural shades of gray of regulatory and supervisory arrangements.

As defined here, the macro and microprudential perspectives differ in terms of *objectives* and the *model* used to describe risk (Table 8.1).

Table 8.1 **The Macro- and Microprudential Perspectives Compared**

	Macroprudential	*Microprudential*
Proximate objective	Limit financial system-wide distress	Limit distress of individual institutions
Ultimate objective	Avoid output (GDP) costs	Consumer (investor/depositor) protection
Model of risk	(in part) Endogenous	Exogenous
Correlations and common exposures across institutions	Important	Irrelevant
Calibration of prudential controls	In terms of system-wide distress; top-down	In terms of risks of individual institutions; bottom-up

The *objective* of a macroprudential approach is to limit the risk of episodes of financial distress with significant losses in terms of the real output for the economy as a whole. That of the microprudential approach is to limit the risk of episodes of financial distress at individual institutions, regardless of their impact on the overall economy.

So defined, the objective of the macroprudential approach falls squarely within the macroeconomic tradition. That of its microprudential counterpart is best rationalized in terms of consumer (depositor or investor) protection.[4]

To highlight the distinction between the two, it is useful to draw an analogy with a portfolio of securities. For the moment, think of these as the financial institutions in an economy. Assume, further, that there is a (monotonically) increasing relationship between the losses on this portfolio and the costs to the real economy. The macroprudential approach would then care about the tail losses on the portfolio as a whole; its microprudential counterpart would care *equally* about the tail losses on *each* of the component securities.

The implications for the setting of prudential controls are straightforward. The macroprudential approach is top-down. It first sets the relevant threshold of acceptable tail losses for the portfolio as a whole. It then calibrates the prudential controls on the basis of the marginal contribution of each security to the relevant measure of portfolio risk. As portfolio allocation theory teaches us, correlations[5] across securities, and the distinction between systematic and idiosyncratic risk, are of the essence. By contrast, the microprudential approach is bottom-up. It sets prudential controls in relation to the risk of each individual security. The result for the overall portfolio arises *purely* as a consequence of aggregation. Correlations across securities are ignored.[6]

Next, consider the *model* used to describe risk. The macroprudential perspective assumes that risk is in part *endogenous* with respect to the behavior of the financial system; the microprudential approach assumes that it is *exogenous*.

The analogy can be helpful here too. In finance theory, we are used to thinking that the risk of a portfolio depends on some exogenous risk factors. The macroprudential approach assumes that these risk factors are in part endogenous with respect to the characteristics of the portfolio. By contrast, the microprudential approach assumes that risk can be taken as exogenous. In fact, its analysis is squarely in the tradition of partial equilibrium. The focus on the risk profile of individual securities (read institutions) justifies the choice.[7]

Moreover, since the macroprudential approach measures risk in terms of the dispersion of an economy's output, it also recognizes that the financial system has first-order effects on it. These effects are ignored in the microprudential perspective.

A microprudentialist would argue that for a financial system to be sound it is necessary and sufficient that each individual institution is sound. A macroprudentialist would take issue with this. To him, it would not be necessary: the output costs of financial stress at individual institutions, or even groups of institutions, banks or otherwise, need not be large enough. More subtly, he would not regard it as sufficient either. This would depend on *how* soundness was pursued. In his view, a macroprudential approach would have a better chance of securing financial stability and, thereby, of also making *individual* institutions safer. The approach could help in the identification of vulnerabilities and in designing appropriate policy responses.

As argued below, this has to do with the nature of financial instability, and hence with the role of risk perceptions and incentives. The endogeneity of risk comes into its own here. At this point, however, let's just pick an illustration that brings out the difference in perspectives most starkly.

By taking risk as exogenous, it would not be possible for a microprudentialist to conceive of situations in which what was rational, even compelling, for an individual institution could result in undesirable aggregate outcomes. A macroprudentialist would find this possibility natural. For example, it could make sense for a financial firm to tighten its risk limits and take a defensive stance in the face of higher risk. But if all did that, each of them could end up worse off. Tightening credit standards and liquidating positions could precipitate further financial stress and asset price declines. Risk would thereby increase.

2.2 FROM DEFINITIONS TO ACTUAL PRACTICES

How do current prudential frameworks compare against this stark macro-micro distinction? It is easy to see that the two souls coexist to varying degrees. Some differences may reflect historical and institutional aspects, including whether prudential powers are located with central banks or separate agencies. Others depend on whether we focus on objectives or on the means through which those objectives are pursued.

Take the *micro* elements first. Prudential standards are generally calibrated with respect to the risks incurred by individual institutions, the hallmark of a microprudential approach. The widespread use of peer group analysis in assessing risk is micro too. The benchmark here is the average performance of institutions, regardless of what this implies in the aggregate. And microprudential is also a certain reluctance to contemplate adjustments in standards or the intensity of supervision that would internalize macroeconomic consequences. Recall, for instance, the differences of opinion between the Federal Reserve and the Office of the Controller of the Currency in the United States during the "headwinds" of the early 1990s. At the time, the Fed was concerned about the implications for overall risk of a tightening of supervisory standards with respect to real estate exposures pursued by the other supervisory agency.

Next, consider the *macro* elements. Prudential authorities for banks often list among their objectives preventing systemic risk, even though the notion is vague enough to accommodate goals that could fall short of a macro approach: not all situations where systemic risk is invoked need involve potentially significant costs for the real economy. Likewise, it is not unusual for the intensity of supervision to be tailored to the size and complexity of institutions, which may match, by design or incidentally, their systemic significance. And the monitoring of risk goes well beyond peer group analysis. It routinely looks at aspects such as concentration of exposures across institutions and vulnerabilities to common shocks, like those associated with asset prices and sectoral, regional, or macroeconomic developments.

3. Financial Instability: From Micro to Macro

Which elements predominate is very much in the eye of the beholder. From a policy perspective, however, what matters is the balance between the two. Arguably, there are good reasons why we should strengthen further the macroprudential orientation of the framework.

At least three reasons spring to mind. First, in some important respects, the macroprudential objective actually subsumes the rationale for its microprudential counterpart. Second, as a result of a better balance between market and official discipline, strengthening the macroprudential orientation holds out the promise of better economic performance. Third, and more subtly, the nature of financial instability is such that a strict microprudential approach is less likely to deliver a safe and sound financial system. Take each in turn.

3.1 REASON 1: HIGH COSTS OF FINANCIAL INSTABILITY

The output costs of financial instability can be very large and their incidence widely felt. Even acknowledging measurement difficulties, studies indicate that the costs of banking crises can easily run into double digits of GDP.[8] Output and growth opportunities are forgone. Severe financial distress can numb the effectiveness of standard macroeconomic tools, such as monetary and fiscal policies. Among industrial countries, Japan vividly illustrates this point. And the very social fabric of society can come under strain. The experience in a number of emerging market countries is telling.

Put bluntly, if the microprudential objective is rationalized in terms of depositor protection, there is a sense in which its macroprudential counterpart subsumes it. For the macroprudential objective is couched in terms of the size of the losses incurred by economic agents, *regardless of which hat they happen to wear*. In particular, even in those cases where depositor protection schemes may insulate depositors from *direct* losses, they cannot spare them the indirect, and more insidious, pain of widespread financial distress as citizens of a country.

3.2 REASON 2: BALANCE BETWEEN MARKET AND POLICY-INDUCED DISCIPLINE

Since a microprudential approach seeks to limit the failure of *each* institution, regardless of its systemic consequences, it is arguably more likely to result in an overly protective regulatory and supervisory framework. Any failure, no matter how unimportant for the economy, could seriously damage the reputation of supervisors. The risk is that market forces may be stifled excessively. Resources can be misallocated and growth opportunities forgone. If taken too far, and underpinned by overly generous safety net arrangements, a microprudential approach could even undermine the very objective it is supposed to attain. It is well known that numbed incentives to monitor and limit risk can ultimately generate costly instability—the so-called moral hazard problem.[9]

This does not mean that depositor protection schemes are undesirable. Far from it. Limited schemes can act as effective precommitment mechanisms. By limiting the incidence of losses on the more vulnerable segments of society, they can relieve political economy pressures to "bail out" institutions.[10] By the same token, they can facilitate a more discriminating attitude toward the resolution of financial distress and thereby underpin a shift toward a macroprudential orientation. The point is that the pursuit of depositor protection objectives is best done through a combination of a macroprudential orientation and more targeted protection schemes.

3.3 REASON 3: NATURE OF FINANCIAL INSTABILITY

While a commonly held view of systemic risk suggests that financial stability can be secured through a microprudential approach, an analysis of the origin of financial crises with significant macroeconomic costs suggests that a macroprudential perspective is important. This analysis also reveals certain peculiar characteristics of risk perceptions that hold clues about possible policy responses. The distinction between the cross-sectional and time dimension of risk, especially system-wide risk, is crucial here. In addition, incentives play an important role. It is worth elaborating on these points in some detail.

Two Views of Systemic Risk

The commonly held view of systemic risk that limits the tension between the micro- and macroprudential perspectives combines three ingredients.[11] First, and most importantly, it tends to see widespread financial distress as arising primarily from the failure of *individual* institutions. The failure then spreads, through a variety of *contagion* mechanisms, to the financial system more generally. Interlinkages through balance sheets and overreactions driven by imperfect information are seen as key channels. Second, it tends to treat risk as endogenous in terms of the *amplification* mechanisms, but not with respect to the *original* shock, which is seen as exogenous. Third, this often goes hand in hand with a rather static view of instability. In other words, for a variety of reasons, the financial system is seen as initially vulnerable; suddenly, a shock occurs, which is then amplified by the endogenous response of market participants. There is no role for the factors underlying the *buildup* of the vulnerability in the first place. Finally, in many models, structurally *illiquid* portfolios are the key source of vulnerability and amplification. Liquid liabilities, and the threat of deposit runs, play a key role.

This view has an impeccable intellectual pedigree. Some of its more formal elements go back at least to the canonical model of systemic risk of Diamond and Dybvig (1983).[12] This view permeates much of the literature on systemic risk that focuses on domino effects, as exemplified in the well-known review article by Kaufman (1994). And it has also influenced much of the thinking in the policy community.[13]

There is little doubt that systemic risk *can* arise from processes of this kind. Failures that result from mismanagement at individual institutions are the most obvious examples. In this case, exposures through payment and settlement systems and the interbank market more generally are key channels of transmission.[14] Possible instances may include, for example, Herstatt, Drexel Burnham Lambert, BCCI, and Barings, just to quote a few. In these cases, idiosyncratic factors have the potential to become systemic through the web of contractual, informational, and psychological links that keeps the financial system together. By now, we understand these processes reasonably well.

But the significance of such instances pales in comparison with that of the cases where systemic risk arises primarily through *common exposures* to macroeconomic risk factors across institutions. It is this type of financial distress that carries the more significant and longer-lasting real costs. And it is this type that underlies most of the major crises experienced around the globe. By comparison with the canonical model of systemic risk, these processes are still poorly understood.

Financial crises of this type can differ in many respects. The precise configuration of vulnerabilities varies, including whether they are primarily located among private- or public-sector borrowers, the relative role of domestic and cross-border exposures, and the importance of foreign currency mismatches. The precise triggers and hence timing are essentially unpredictable. And the main forces behind the crises can either be domestic or foreign.

Even so, beyond these differences, behind many such episodes a fairly common, if highly stylized, pattern can be detected. Generally, there is first of all a buildup phase. This is normally characterized by booming economic conditions, benign risk assessments, a weakening of external financing constraints, notably access to credit, and buoyant asset prices (Figure 8.1).[15] The economy may be perceived as being on a permanently higher expansion path. This configuration promotes and masks the accumulation of real and financial imbalances; the system becomes overstretched. At some point, the process goes into reverse. The unpredictable trigger can reside either in the financial sphere (e.g., an asset price correction) or in the real economy (e.g., a spontaneous unwinding of an investment boom). If the system has failed to build up enough buffers and the contraction goes far enough, a financial crisis can erupt. Ex post, a financial cycle, closely intertwined with the business cycle, is evident.[16]

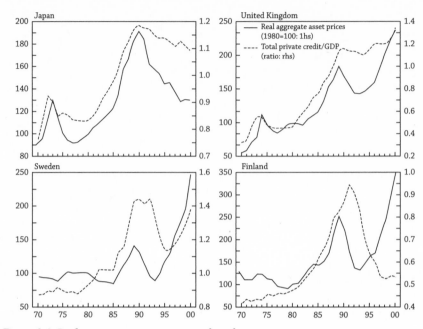

Figure 8.1 Real aggregate asset prices and credit. Note: The real aggregate asset price index is a weighted geometric mean of real share prices, real residential property prices, and real commercial property prices; the weights are based on net wealth data, and the deflators used are those of private consumption. *Source*: Private real estate associations (inter alia, Jones Lang LaSalle); national data; BIS estimates and calculations.

It is not difficult to detect elements of this kind behind many of the severe financial crises in industrial and emerging market countries since at least the 1980s.

These include several of the banking crises in Latin America in the 1980s and early 1990s, the crises in East Asia later in the decade, those in the Nordic countries in the late 1980s to early 1990s and the more prolonged one in Japan. Moreover, even if no major crisis broke out, countries such as the United States, the United Kingdom, and Australia also experienced strains in their financial systems in the early 1990s following similar patterns.

By comparison with many canonical models of systemic risk, three key differences stand out. First, it is not possible to understand the crises unless we understand how vulnerabilities *build up over time*. This requires an understanding of the mutually reinforcing *dynamic* interaction between the financial and the real economy, and not just in the unfolding of financial stress but, importantly, as risk builds up. What we need is a proper theory of business fluctuations that merges financial and real factors. The triggering shock is, in fact, the least interesting aspect of the story. The boom sows the seeds of the subsequent bust. To an important extent, risk is *endogenous*. Second, it is not so much contagion from individual failures but *common exposures* to the same risk factors that explain the crisis.[17] Third, much of the action is on the *asset side* of balance sheets as opposed to the liability side. It is on the asset side that the exposures build up and the underlying changes in valuation originate. The liability side can play a role primarily in the precise unfolding of the crisis, as it can affect the abruptness and virulence with which asset side adjustments are enforced. For instance, the foreign currency external financing constraint is critical for emerging market countries. But it is the deterioration in asset quality that fundamentally drives the process.[18] This is all the more so given the willingness to socialize losses in our time.[19]

The Role of Risk Perceptions

If we look at the genesis of the crises more closely we will find another curious feature. Indicators of *risk perceptions* tend to decline during the upswing and, in some cases, to be lowest close to the peak of the financial cycle. But this is precisely the point where, with hindsight at least, we can tell that risk was greatest. During the upswing, asset prices are buoyant, risk spreads narrow, and provisions decline. They clearly behave as if risk fell in booms and rose in recessions. And yet, there is a sense in which *risk rises in booms*, as imbalances build up, *and materializes in recessions*, as they unwind.[20]

This observation points to a fundamental distinction between the dimensions of risk. We all seem to be better equipped to measure the cross-sectional than the time dimension of risk. And we find it especially difficult to measure how the absolute level of systematic (system-wide) risk evolves over time.[21] It is no coincidence, for instance, that rating agencies pay particular attention to the relative riskiness of borrowers or instruments.[22] Nor, indeed, that much of the existing literature on the effectiveness of market discipline is of a cross-sectional nature.[23] By the same token, one could argue that the Achilles heel of markets may not be so much *indiscriminate* reactions to idiosyncratic problems but rather preventing the buildup of *generalized* overextension. This is why there is much mileage to be gained by focusing not so much on contagion but on common exposures.

The Role of Incentives

And risk measurement is only part of the story. Another important aspect has to do with *incentives*. The key problem here is the wedge between individual rationality and desirable aggregate outcomes. We are all very familiar with the arguments here. Notions such as "prisoner's dilemma," "coordination failures," and "herding" spring to mind.[24] Just a few specific examples: would it be reasonable to expect a bank manager to trade off a sure loss of market share in a boom against the distant hope of regaining it in a future potential slump? Or to adopt less procyclical measures of risk on the grounds that if others adopted them as well a crisis might be less likely? Or to fail to tighten credit standards or liquidate positions only because, if everyone else did the same, the depth of a recession could be mitigated? Policy responses will need to keep this tension in perspectives very much in mind.

Bounded Rationality and Distorting Government Intervention?

Thus, a combination of risk perceptions that fall short of a tall order and distorting incentive wedges seem to underlie much of the financial instability that we see. And importantly, it would not seem necessary to rely on either bounded rationality—appealing as this may be to careful observers of human nature—or misguided government intervention to explain the economic processes at work.

Ultimately, it might be possible convincingly to rationalize the observed instability by building rigorous frameworks starting from the inevitably imperfect and hence differential information that characterizes all human interactions. Consider just a few examples. Recent research indicates that rational departures of asset values from fundamentals can be sustained given short horizons of agents and differential information (lack of "common knowledge").[25] And those short horizons can be justified on the basis of contractual arrangements that reflect conflicting incentives and differential information between suppliers of funds, on the one hand, and users or managers of those funds, on the other ("principal/agent problems"). The same can be said of the asymmetric nature of booms and busts. For instance, short-selling constraints may make positive departures from fundamentals more likely than negative ones,[26] while the natural asymmetries linked to financing constraints and hence balance sheet weakness, together with capital overhangs, could explain the specific characteristics of the busts. And, of course, it is precisely imperfect information that can best explain the presence of such short-selling/financing constraints, notably reflecting concerns with counterparty/credit risk, and limits to arbitrage more generally.[27]

For much the same reason, there is a risk of attaching too high a weight to distorting government intervention as the root cause of financial instability. This is not to deny that, as already noted, the "moral hazard" problem associated with mispriced (explicit or implicit) government guarantees can unwittingly contribute, and often has contributed, to instability. After all, one of the objectives of strengthening the macroprudential orientation of the prudential framework is precisely to reduce the scope of such subsidies. Rather, the point is that both logically and historically the causes of financial instability *precede* government intervention. Logically, as noted, differential information and distorted incentives are sufficient to generate instability. Indeed, the original notion of moral hazard is linked to this more general imperfect information inherent in economic relationships. And historically, financial instability predates extensive government intervention in the economy.[28] In fact, it was the widespread financial instability of the interwar years that largely prompted the establishment of extensive safety nets and prudential frameworks.[29]

4. From Diagnosis to Remedies

So much for definitions and diagnosis. But what about policy responses? It is here that question marks find their preferred habitat. Given our state of knowledge, it is at best possible to sketch out broad directions for change rather than to identify concrete proposals.

In that spirit, what follows highlights a few key issues. In keeping with the previous analysis, it considers the cross-sectional and time dimensions of risk in turn, although much of the discussion focuses on the time dimension.

4.1 THE CROSS-SECTIONAL DIMENSION

Three specific questions stand out when considering the cross-sectional dimension of risk. What should be the scope of the prudential framework? How should standards be calibrated? What are the implications of size?

A macroprudential approach suggests that the *scope* of the prudential framework should be rather broad. The capacity to intermediate funds and allocate risks, thereby sustaining economic activity, is key (Tsatsaronis 2002). To varying degrees, all financial institutions perform this function. In fact, markets as well as institutions do so.[30] At the same time, it is still the case that certain institutions, because of their specific function, may be more relevant than others. For instance, the role of "banks" as suppliers of liquidity services of next-to-last resort implies that financial distress at these institutions may have larger macroeconomic costs. These characteristics would need to be taken into account too.

For practical purposes, a macroprudential perspective would thus suggest that in assessing vulnerabilities to financially induced macro stress the gaze should be cast widely. The perspective is also broadly consistent with the shift under way toward greater convergence in prudential standards across financial intermediaries.[31]

As regards *calibration*, at a high level of abstraction the main implication of a macroprudential approach is straightforward. The prudential standards should be calibrated with respect to the marginal contribution of an institution to system-wide macro risk. The approach would make an explicit distinction between the "systematic risk" (common exposure) charge and the "idiosyncratic risk" charge. The latter would be nonzero only to the extent that failure of the institution had macro stress effects, either directly or through knock-on channels.[32]

But how exactly can the decomposition between systematic and idiosyncratic risk be estimated? This is clearly an open question for research. For institutions whose securities are publicly traded, their prices could yield some, albeit noisy, information.[33] For others, balance sheet information, in terms of asset composition or performance, could provide some raw material. But it is too early to tell what the results of such a line of research might be. What we *can be* confident about is that as risk measurement techniques develop, the raw material for inference and aggregation will improve. The New Basel Capital Accord should play a key role in this respect.

The one area where measurement is less of a problem relates to the *size* of institutions. *Other things equal*, larger institutions have greater system-wide significance. As such, from a macroprudential perspective they would be subject to tighter prudential standards.[34] This is indeed consistent with the common practice of at least subjecting them to more frequent and intense supervision. But one could easily imagine going one step further. This could involve, for instance, higher capital requirements for any given level of institution-specific risk.[35] In principle, the strengthening of Pillar 2 under the New Capital Accord could be quite helpful here.

4.2 THE TIME DIMENSION

It is in the time dimension that the macroprudential perspective comes into its own, not least because of the endogeneity of risk. If the perspective is correct, then it stands to reason that cushions should be built up in upswings so as to be relied upon when the rough times arrive.[36] This would strengthen institutions' ability to weather deteriorating economic conditions, when access to external financing becomes more costly and constrained. Moreover, by leaning against the wind, it could reduce the amplitude of the financial cycle, thereby limiting the risk of financial distress in the first place. In other words, this strategy would add a welcome counterweight to the powerful procyclical[37] forces in the system.

The question is: how can this best be done? There are many aspects to this problem. What follows focuses only on four of them. First, how ambitious should we realistically be in seeking to improve risk measurement? Second, given the procyclicality in risk assessments, what could be the implications of the more risk-sensitive New Capital Accord? Third, to what extent can longer horizons help in mitigating biases in risk assessment and stabilizing the system? Finally, what is the appropriate division of labor between accounting and prudential norms?

Can the Measurement of Risk through Time Be Improved?
The choice of strategy to ensure that cushions are built up at the right time depends on views about how far it is realistically possible to improve on the measurement of the time dimension of risk. Consider two views, in increasing order of ambition.

The *first view* assumes that it is, in effect, fruitless to try to improve significantly on how risk is measured though time. Judgments about the profile of macro risk are too hard to make.[38] The poor record of forecasters is seen as evidence of this. At the same time, while it may be hard to tell whether the risk of a downturn is higher or lower, it is much easier to tell whether the current state of the economy is above or below previous average experience. The question then, for instance, is *not* whether the boom is sustainable or not, but, rather, whether the economy *is* in a boom.

On this basis, it is simply prudent to take advantage of the favorable conditions to build up cushions as a form of insurance, without *explicitly* taking a stance on the future evolution of the economy. Moreover, what is true for the economy's output is also true for other variables correlated with financial distress, such as asset prices and credit expansion.

Given the skepticism about the ability to measure changes in risk, this view tends to favor relatively simple rule-based adjustments. Many types of policy would seem to fall under this broad heading. One example is Goodhart and Danielsson's (2001) suggestion of relating various prudential norms to loan or asset price growth. Another, quite subtle, example is the loan provisioning rule recently introduced by the Spanish supervisory authorities (so-called "statistical provisions"). In this case, yearly provisioning expenses tend to be based on average loan loss experience over past business cycles.[39] More generally, conservative valuation principles, such as valuing assets at the lower of market or book value, could be seen as performing a similar function.

The main advantage of this family of policy options is their simplicity. In addition, once the rule is accepted, there is no issue of the authorities being seen as "outguessing" markets. This would make the rules easier to implement in comparison with discretionary adjustments in prudential tools based on measures of risk, with the authorities inevitably in the defensive against the manifested consensus of market participants. Finally, concerns with possible mistakes in the use of discretion or a limited "credit culture" among market participants would add to their appeal.

Their main disadvantage is that by *themselves* they would not do much to encourage conscious improvements in risk measurement. As a result, they would also tend to exacerbate incentives to arbitrage them away.[40] Depending on their specific features, they could also be seen as unduly intrusive and blunt. Some of them would clearly not be consistent with the search for a better balance between market and policy-induced discipline.

The *second view* argues that it is worth seeking to improve the way we measure risk through time. Statements about changes in risk may well be possible conditional on a richer information set. These could eventually form the basis for judgments about the risk of financially induced macro stress. These judgments in turn could underpin a more articulated policy response, including through discretionary measures. It is worth elaborating on this.

The current efforts to develop indicators of banking crises or, more generally, macroprudential indicators and assessments of financial system vulnerabilities belong to this family of responses. My own reading of the evidence is that we are still a long way from an adequate answer, but that the glass is half full.

Our own research at the BIS tends to confirm this. With Phil Lowe, we have recently begun to explore how far one could predict banking crises in both industrial and emerging market countries on the basis of a very parsimonious approach guided by the stylized features of the financial cycle.[41] We measured the performance of the indicators in terms of the noise-to-signal ratio, following the very useful toolkit applied to currency and banking crises by Kaminsky and Reinhart (1999). We did, however, make a few important modifications. First, we used ex ante information only, as required by policymakers. Second, we focused on cumulative processes, measured in terms of deviations of the key variables from ex ante recursive trends. This was supposed to capture the buildup of vulnerabilities. Third, we looked only at a very limited set of variables: private credit to GDP, real asset prices, and investment. Fourth, we calibrated the signal by considering the variables jointly, rather than on a univariate basis. Finally, we allowed for multiple horizons, in the conviction that the precise timing of a crisis is essentially unpredictable.

As a first go, the results were encouraging (Table 8.2). Over a three-year horizon, close to 60% of the crises could be predicted, and only one in almost 20 observations was incorrectly classified (crisis or noncrisis). Likewise, crying wolf too often, the usual problem, was far less of an issue here. A large part of the improvement resulted from the use of cumulative rather than marginal processes. The credit gap alone, for instance, clearly outperformed exceptionally high growth rates in credit. It could capture around 80% of the crises, with a comparatively low noise-to-signal ratio by the standards of the literature, although at the cost

Table 8.2 **Indicators of Banking Crises**

| Horizon[a] | Private-sector credit | | | | Joint credit (4% points) and real asset price[c] (40%) gaps[d] | |
| | Real credit growth (7%)[b] | | Credit gap[c] (4% points) | | | |
	Noise/ signal	% crises predicted	Noise/ signal	% crises predicted	Noise/ signal	% crises predicted
One-year	.54	74	.24	79	.13	42
Two-year	.43	87	.21	79	.08	53
Three-year	.39	89	.20	79	.06	55

Note: Based on a sample of 34 industrial and emerging market countries; annual data 1960–1999, including 38 crises.

[a] A signal is correct if a crisis takes place in any one of the years included in the horizon ahead (always including the current year). Noise is identified as mistaken predictions within the same horizon.

[b] Percentage annual growth rate.

[c] Equity prices only.

[d] A gap is measured as the percentage (point) deviation from an ex ante, recursively calculated Hodrick-Prescott filter. Credit is measured as a ratio to GDP.

of higher noise by comparison with the multivariate, joint calibration (one in six observations incorrectly classified).

We interpret these results as saying that it should be possible to form judgments about the buildup of vulnerabilities with a *reasonable* degree of comfort. After all, our preliminary analysis could be improved in several directions, in terms of both the definition of variables and techniques. Indeed, more recently in a follow-up study, we showed how the inclusion of a real exchange rate gap helps to improve the results in the case of emerging market countries (Borio and Lowe 2002b).[42] More generally, the literature on measuring indicators of pending financial macro stress is very much in its infancy.[43] And the information available to policymakers to form a judgment is much richer, and likely to improve over time.[44,45]

The above indicators could give some idea of the probability of distress; what about the other key variable, that is, the extent of possible losses given distress? Here, macro stress tests, conceptually analogous to their micro counterparts, could play a role. These would map assumed adverse changes in macro risk factors into losses in the financial system. In recent years, considerable work has been done in this area,[46] but, again, much more research is needed to develop acceptable methodologies.

One could then imagine a two-pronged approach. On the one hand, indicators of potential distress could be used to form a judgment about the probability of adverse outcome. These could be complemented by other, perhaps more traditional, measures of macroeconomic risks to the outlook. On the other hand, stress tests could be used to assess the likely damage of an adverse event. The indicators would add "bite" to the stress tests, which could otherwise be discounted too easily. The resulting information could then help to calibrate a prudential response or to adjust micro-based risk measures.

Such a top-down approach to risk measurement would likely reduce the procyclicality of current risk measurement methodologies. Indeed, a review of the methodologies would indicate that these either tend to ignore macroeconomic factors or, to the extent that they do not, may even incorporate them in a way that could exacerbate procyclical tendencies.

Given space constraints, it is only possible to illustrate the basic point here.[47]

Consider three types of methodology: those of rating agencies, banks' internal ratings, and full credit risk models.

By design, *rating agencies*' risk assessments tend to be comparatively less sensitive to the business cycle, although downgrades in particular do bunch up in recessions. One way of rationalizing this is that they pay special attention to relative risk. Another is to think of agencies as rating companies based on a standardized macro stress scenario, such as a "typical" recession.[48]

Banks' internal rating methodologies vary considerably across institutions. Available evidence is rather limited, but it generally points to a higher degree of procyclicality. This may result from a tendency to adjust credit risk perceptions assuming the continuation of current conditions and to focus on rather short horizons, more in line with the annual accounting cycle. For the quantification of risk, one year is quite common.[49]

Most quantitative credit risk models do not incorporate macro effects. The degree of procyclicality of the corresponding risk assessments arises from the use of rating agencies' and, above all, market inputs, notably share prices and credit spreads. Moreover, further developments of the models could actually *exacerbate* the procyclical properties. For instance, the models so far ignore the positive correlation between the probability of default and loss-given-default, which is at least in part associated with recessions.[50] As with internal ratings, one-year horizons are commonly used.

The New Basel Capital Accord and Procyclicality

This procyclicality in risk assessments has attracted considerable attention recently as a result of the proposed revision to the Capital Accord. In its search for greater risk sensitivity, the new Accord implies that, in contrast to previous arrangements, the minimum capital on a given portfolio will change alongside its perceived riskiness, whether measured by external or banks' own internal ratings. The Accord would then result in a much better measurement of cross-sectional or relative risk, as it was originally designed to do. But it might have unintended consequences with respect to the time dimension of risk.[51]

There is indeed some preliminary empirical evidence to suggest that minimum capital requirements will be more procyclical than under current arrangements. In particular, they could increase considerably in bad times. The size of the effect depends very much on the type of risk assessment methodology used and the option adopted. The available evidence, however, suggests that swings of the order of 30% in the course of a normal business cycle may be possible. As indicated by evidence from Mexico gathered by Segoviano and Lowe (2002), these could be greater in case of larger business cycle fluctuations accompanied by financial distress (Figure 8.2).[52]

Even so, regardless of what happens to the *minimum* requirements, the more important question is whether capital cushions as a *whole* and risk measurement generally will be more procyclical under the new Accord. Here, one can point to a number of factors that could alleviate or even fully offset the additional procyclical influences. Think of these factors as another instance of the famous "Lucas critique": behavior changes as the regime changes. The previous evidence may be partly misleading. There are at least two reasons for this.[53]

First, the Accord is helping to spread and "hardwire" a historic improvement in risk measurement and management culture. The level of the debate has risen immensely over the last couple of years. And awareness of the potential adverse implications of unduly procyclical risk assessments has risen pari passu, among both market participants and supervisors. More generally, better risk management means that problems can be identified and corrected earlier.

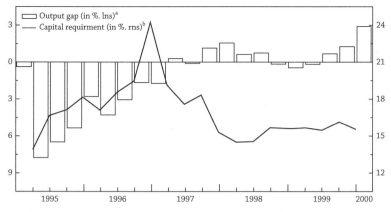

Figure 8.2 Mexican output gap and hypothetical IRB capital requirements.
[1.] Hodrick Prescott filter applied.
[2.] Based on a uniform internal rating system used by banks. The system has been devised by the supervisory authorities.
Source: Segoviano and Lowe (2002).

Second, Pillars 2 and 3 can underpin this shift. Greater disclosure means that markets may become less tolerant and more suspicious of risk assessments that move a lot over time and lead to substantial upgrades in good times. And supervisors, if they so wished, could rely on the strengthened supervisory review powers to induce greater prudence in risk assessments and/or an increase in capital cushions above the Pillar 1 minima. As advocated by the Basel Committee, stress-testing the credit exposures can be an invaluable tool here.

The bottom line is that we do not quite know the answer. At the same time, there are reasons for cautious optimism. We will need to watch developments closely. But in doing so, we should never lose sight of the fact that the positive contribution to financial stability of the new Accord goes well beyond its implications for procyclicality.

Longer Horizons and the Role of Maturity

Encouraging *longer horizons* for risk assessment could help to limit procyclicality. In particular, it stands to reason that the longer the horizon over which agents chart the future, the less likely it is that they could continue to anticipate the persistence of current conditions. In jargon, lengthening the assessment horizon is likely to strengthen any mean-reverting tendencies in risk perceptions and hence prudence. We know, for instance, that over longer horizons equity returns mean-revert while over shorter ones they show approximate random walk behavior.[54] Recall also the famous paper by Frankel and Froot (1990), which had found similar properties in foreign exchange traders' expectations.[55]

The *maturity* of credit exposures implicit in contracts is important here. The residual maturity determines the time horizon over which events could affect the value of the contract. Longer maturities therefore encourage longer assessment horizons. And they could arguably limit the risk of generalized withdrawal of funds or credit crunches at times of stress. Think, for example, of the risks implied by the short maturity of external debt in the case of emerging market countries. Here again, we see the tension between a micro- and a macroprudential approach. *Other things equal*, from the perspective of an individual institution, the longer the maturity of its exposure, the higher the credit risk faced. But for an economy in the aggregate, it is by no means clear that shorter maturities would reduce overall credit risk. What may make sense from the perspective of an individual institution may also have unintended consequences in the aggregate. The calibration of prudential standards would need to take these effects into account as well.[56]

Longer horizons may also be relevant for *capital* decisions. Conceptually, the risk quantification horizon for capital decisions corresponds to the time required to take remedial action, either by replenishing capital or shedding risk. A macroprudential perspective would explicitly incorporate the fact that, at times of generalized stress, remedial action would necessarily be harder and hence take longer, not least owing to the endogenous increase in risk from attempts to manage exposures. The one-year horizon adopted in current practices may well be too short. In fact, empirical evidence tends to support this conclusion.[57]

The Relationship between Accounting and Prudential Norms

These considerations point to the *broader relationship between* accounting valuations, on the one hand, and *prudential norms*, on the other. The impact of accounting on financial stability should not be underestimated. It is widely recognized that differences in valuation methodologies can have first-order effects on measures of net worth and income. They can be as important as the specification of the capital standards that should apply to them. And accounting conventions can have a major impact on firms' internal risk management practices.[58] Deficiencies in accounting practices, for instance, have played a role in many of the financial crises seen over the last two decades. Even so, for a number of objective reasons, valuation issues had, until recently, received less attention.

A number of developments have brought such issues into the limelight. First, the New Basel Accord has forced a reconsideration of the link between expected and unexpected losses, loan provisioning, capital, and pricing. Second, the debate on appropriate loan provisioning has come to the fore. There is a fairly broad consensus that more forward-looking provisioning could help to bring accounting valuations closer into line with economic valuations and could eliminate a source of artificial procyclicality. In particular, waiting for default to be highly probable before a provision can be made fails to recognize deteriorations in credit quality short of probable default.[59] But there is no agreement on how best to strengthen the forward-looking element. Finally, and more generally, proposals for fair value accounting have stirred a heated debate.[60]

A key question is whether cushions against risk and uncertainties should be built through "conservative," as opposed to "true and fair," valuations or through other means, such as specific prudential norms like minimum capital requirements. In the past, reliance on conservative valuations has been quite common. More recently, the shift toward "true and fair" valuations has reduced the scope of such mechanisms. Looking forward, one concern with fair value accounting is precisely that greater reliance on market values could have destabilizing effects whenever asset price misalignments are at the origin of financial instability. In the process, it might also increase the procyclicality of the financial system.

The issue of the relationship and roles of accounting and prudential norms will have to be addressed. On the one hand, conservative valuations may be a simple and effective means of introducing cushions into the system. On the other hand, it might be argued that a sharper distinction between the roles of accounting and prudential norms would increase transparency and clarify the relationship between the different goals and means to attain them. This could help reduce the tension between the two perspectives and also speed up progress toward convergence on agreed accounting principles. Clearly, this is an underresearched area that deserves greater attention.[61]

5. Conclusion

Tennyson once said: "Words, like nature, half reveal and half conceal the soul within." But, one could add, while we *cannot* choose what nature is like, we can choose what words mean.

This essay has argued that two sharp, intentionally polarized definitions of the "macroprudential" and "microprudential" perspectives are helpful in bringing out the two souls that inevitably coexist in the current regulatory and supervisory arrangements. And that they are useful in highlighting the complementarities, as well as tensions, between the two approaches to securing financial stability. The key thesis developed is that strengthening further the macroprudential orientation of the framework could promote the achievement of this goal.[62]

Strengthening the macroprudential orientation would, in some respects, bring the framework closer to its origin, when the main concern was the disruption to the economic life of a country brought about by *generalized* financial distress. It would take it somewhat away from the pursuit of narrowly interpreted depositor protection objectives while at the same time helping to achieve them in a more meaningful way. And it holds the promise of bringing realistic objectives into closer alignment with the means to attain them.

If this diagnosis is shared, then there is still plenty of work ahead. The agenda is a full one, both for researchers and policymakers. For researchers, there is quite a lot to be done analytically and empirically to sharpen the macroprudential perspective, to better understand what it can tell us about the dynamics of risk and financial instability, and to help develop the tools to address them. For policymakers, the task is to turn the desirable into the feasible, to distinguish the feasible from the impracticable, and to make progress in implementing the shift. Success will also depend on the ability and willingness of market participants to incorporate more meaningfully the lessons of a macroprudential perspective into their own assessment of risk.

In some respects, the search for appropriate policy responses to financial instability resembles the state of monetary policy in the early 1970s. Now, as then, both researchers and policymakers are beginning to sharpen their understanding of the "enemy." Now, as then, they are groping for solutions. Now, as then, there is no reason to believe that, eventually, their endeavors will not be successful.

In fact, strengthening the macroprudential orientation of the policy framework will put a premium on closer cooperation between supervisory authorities and central banks.[63] This is true regardless of the specific allocation of supervisory responsibilities. It reflects the processes that generate financial instability and its consequences for the macroeconomy. As argued elsewhere, the relationship between the monetary and financial regimes deserves particular attention.[64]

There is still a lot we need to learn about how monetary policy interacts with prudential policies and how best to make the two mutually supportive. We need much more research in this area too. But this, as they say, is another story.

Notes

1　This article was originally published in *CESifo Economic Studies*, 49, 2003. It is reprinted with permission of the original publisher with only minor alternations to adhere to the style of Oxford University Press. This paper is a revised version of an invited lecture at the CESifo Summer Institute Workshop "Banking Regulation and Financial Stability" that took place in Venice, Italy, on July 17–18, 2002. I would like to thank Philip Lowe, Bengt Mettinger, Hyun Shin, Kostas Tsatsaronis, and two anonymous referees for their helpful comments, and Janet Plancherel for the patience and efficiency with which she put the lecture together under heavy time pressure. This essay reflects personal views and not necessarily those of the BIS. Any remaining errors are my sole responsibility.

2　Quoted in Samuelson (1973).

3　Previous statements of the distinction between the macro and microprudential perspectives can be found in Crockett (2000a) and (2001a). Borio et al. (2001) apply the distinction to the analysis of capital standards. Tsatsaronis (2002) provides a more in-depth, complementary analysis of these issues.

4　This view of prudential policy is formalized in Dewatripont and Tirole (1993).

5　The term "correlation" is used loosely here. For the purpose at hand, tail interdependence is more suitable. When returns cannot be accurately described by multivariate normal distributions, the difference can be important, as correlations are too restrictive. See Embrechts et al. (1999).

6　Obviously, this analogy has its limitations. In particular, the monotonic relationship assumes that the marginal contribution of each financial institution to the macro risk of distress (losses) is the same, regardless of its specific characteristics. For instance, there is no distinction between banks and nonbanks at this level of abstraction. And the analogy glosses over the distinction between institutions and markets. Clearly, any rigorous theoretical analysis would need to address these issues. For this reason, taking the analysis one step further, Tsatsaronis (2002) prefers to focus on the more basic notion of "intermediation capacity." He sees this as reflecting the ability of financial arrangements to channel funds from savers to investors, overcoming the problems arising from asymmetric information, and to allocate and absorb risk. Borio (2000) argues that the functional distinction between markets and institutions can easily be overstated.

7 Put differently, a microprudential researcher would focus on games against nature. Nature throws the dice and determines the risk characteristics of an economy. The only issue is how this risk is sliced and distributed. Moreover, strictly speaking, he would be concerned only with single-player games. A macroprudential researcher would focus on games among economic agents. The outcome would determine the level of aggregate risk.

8 See, for instance, Hoggarth and Saporta (2001), who measure costs in terms of output forgone, and the references therein.

9 For instance, if ill-designed, a safety net can address one cause of instability, generalized liquidity crises, by generating another, namely slower-moving solvency crises.

10 Note that this rationalization of deposit insurance schemes is rather different from the one normally found in the literature. It recognizes that, in modern economies, it is "runs" by *sophisticated* creditors, typically exempt from insurance, that can precipitate a crisis, especially through the interbank market. And it sees discretionary emergency liquidity assistance as a better instrument than deposit insurance to deal with liquidity crises, since it does not afford *unconditional* protection in the case of failure to achieve that goal. At the same time, deposit protection schemes can be useful precisely in cases of *insolvency*, by shielding supervisors from public pressure to bail out institutions, thereby lending credibility to the threat of a more discriminating resolution of the insolvency.

11 This view, in fact, is a mixture of various elements stressed by somewhat different strands of thought. It is supposed to capture a general intellectual atmosphere that has permeated much of the thinking on systemic risk.

12 Santos (2000) reviews part of this literature and its relationship to bank regulation and minimum capital requirements in particular. De Bandt and Hartmann (2000) provide a more general survey of systemic risk and Davis (1995) a broader overview of the literature on financial instability.

13 See, for instance, ECSC (1992).

14 For the link between systemic risk and the interbank market, see in particular Rochet and Tirole (1996a). For a review of systemic risk in payment and settlement systems, see, for instance, Borio and Van den Bergh (1993) and references therein, as well as the many publications of the Committee on Payment and Settlement Systems on the BIS website. In the same spirit, Furfine (1999) examines the scope for contagion through Fedwire in the United States. See also Rochet and Tirole (1996b).

15 The relationship between credit and asset prices is investigated econometrically in, for instance, Borio et al. (1994) and Hofmann (2001); its theoretical underpinnings have received renewed attention in recent years (e.g., Bernanke et al. 1999, Kiyotaki and Moore 1997, and, in a different vein, Allen and Gale 2000). More generally, the role of credit booms in the buildup of financial crises is widely recognized (e.g., Honohan 1997, Gourinchas et al. 2001, and Eichengreen and Arteta 2000). Of course, the roles of credit and asset prices in the context of boom-bust financial cycles have a long tradition (e.g., Kindleberger 1996 and Minsky 1982) and history (e.g., Goodhart and De Largy 1999 and Kent and D'Arcy 2001).

16 Mechanisms of this sort are also at work in episodes of market stress, which may or may not have serious macroeconomic consequences (e.g., Borio 2000).

17 Note that, for any given set of institutions, common exposures to risk factors arise from two sources. First, directly, from the exposure of these institutions to economic agents outside this set. Second, indirectly, from exposures to each other (the interlocking aspect). In practice, it is arguably the former that has played the main role in widespread crises with macroeconomic consequences. See Elsinger et al. (2002) for an interesting approach that can be used to shed evidence on this question and for some corroborating evidence in the case of the Austrian banking system.

18 There is a strand of the literature on financial crises in open economies that can be seen as a natural extension of the contrasting paradigms discussed here. Thus, a number of authors have stressed the role of external liabilities and self-fulfilling runs (e.g., Chang and Velasco 1998 and Sachs and Radelet 1998), while others have stressed fundamental vulnerabilities. Among the latter, and in contrast to the analysis developed here, ex ante distortions associated with implicit government guarantees have tended to play a key role (e.g., Corsetti et al. 1999). Corsetti (1998) reviews some of the recent literature on this.

19 A number of academics have recently been developing notions of systemic risk that are closer to the one put forward in this essay. What might be called the emerging "LSE school" stresses the endogeneity of risk (e.g., Danielsson et al. 2001, Danielsson et al. 2002) and the time dimension of risk (Goodhart and Danielsson 2001). Acharya (2001) focuses on common exposures and the asset side of balance sheets. Hellwig (1995, 1998) has for a long time emphasized the need for a system-wide, general equilibrium approach, but within a static framework and a focus on interest rate risk as the key driver of credit risk too. Work that extends the Diamond and Dybvig–type models to link bank run equilibria to economic fundamentals, not least in the context of differential information, can also be seen as a step in the direction of a more macroprudential notion of systemic risk, as defined here (e.g., Morris and Shin 1998, Zhu 2001). And for some time now, a number of authors have noted the importance of deteriorating fundamentals as a cause of financial crises; see e.g., Gorton (1988) and Calomiris and Gorton (1991).

20 There are a number of ways in which this statement can be rationalized or made more precise. The most intuitive states that the signs of possible financial imbalances in the upswing lead to a rise in the uncertainty regarding future outcomes. The boom might indeed be sustainable, but "tail losses" are also higher. See Lowe (2002) in particular. More formal rationalizations are also suggested in Borio et al. (2001).

21 See, initially, Crockett (2000b) or Borio and Crockett (2000) and BIS (2001a). A detailed discussion of this point can be found in Borio et al. (2001). See also Goodhart and Danielsson (2001).

22 See Cantor (2002).

23 A careful reading of the well-known survey article on market discipline by Flannery (1998) makes this abundantly clear.

24 Borio et al. (2001) provide a discussion of these issues. See also Goodhart and Danielsson (2001) for an elaboration closely linked to the problems of risk measurement.

25 See, e.g., Allen and Gale (2000), Allen et al. (2003), and Abreu and Brunnermeier (2003). See also Froot et al. (1992) for an example of the implications of short horizons for asset pricing in the context of rational speculation.

26 See, e.g., Carey (1990).

27 It is well known that asymmetric information (including ex post nonverifiability by a third party) is essential to explain financing frictions of the kind relevant here; see, e.g., Hart and Holmström (1988), Gertler (1988), Hart (1995), and Bernanke et al. (1999) for surveys of various aspects of what has become a rather fragmented field of inquiry. See also Schleifer and Vishny (1997) on the limits of arbitrage more generally.

28 See Bordo et al. (2001).

29 One implication of the presence of safety nets is that, by comparison with the historical period when they were less extensive, banking crises may take somewhat longer to emerge, as liquidity constraints would be less binding. This is especially likely where external considerations are less of an issue, as is typically the case in industrial countries. This conjecture seems to be broadly consistent with the evidence in Gorton (1988), who finds that in the pre-Depression era in the United States, crises tended to occur close to the peak of the business cycle, rather than once the downturn was already well under way.

30 For a discussion of analogies between the two, see, for instance, Borio (2000).

31 See, for instance, Borio and Filosa (1994).

32 Interestingly, the weights in the proposed New Capital Accord have been derived from a conceptual model that, for each bank portfolio, assumes a single systematic risk factor, full diversification of the idiosyncratic component of risk, and a common correlation across all exposures.

33 See, for instance, De Nicolo and Kwast (2001) for an attempt to estimate the impact of financial consolidation on systematic risk based on stock price information.

34 See also the discussion of the implications of mergers on system-wide risk in Tsatsaronis (2002). BIS (2001b) provides a broader analysis of the impact of financial sector consolidation on systemic risk.

35 Some supervisory authorities have indeed called for such a treatment on systemic grounds. The Swiss banking supervisory agency is a case in point.

36 Of course, this should be subject to some absolute minimum, so as to avoid the risk of undue forbearance and limit the scope for "betting-for-survival" behavior.

37 Here and in what follows, a variable or type of behavior is said to be procyclical if its movement is such as to *amplify* financial and business cycles.

38 This is the view expressed, for instance, by Goodhart and Danielsson (2001).

39 See Fernández de Lis et al. (2001) and Borio and Lowe (2001).

40 Of course, this depends on the characteristics of the measures. The Spanish rule for loan provisioning, for instance, seems to have been quite successful so far.

41 See Borio and Lowe (2002a) for details of the approach. Borio and Lowe (2002b) extend the analysis further.

42 Other improvements could be considered, quite apart from refinements in the statistical methodology. For example, our studies to date could not use real estate prices, because the information available for emerging market countries is too limited. Similarly, the definition of "financial stress" could be refined to capture better the type of episodes that are consistent with macro stress. And, following similar principles, further indicators could be developed tailored to types of financial crises other than those considered here.

43 Rigorous statistical analysis has largely focused on currency, rather than banking crises; see, for instance, IMF (2002a) for a review, as well as Hawkins and Klau (2000). Likewise, banking supervisors have tended to concentrate their efforts on indicators of individual bank, rather than systemic, failure (Van den Bergh and Sahajwala 2000). More generally, considerable work has been done trying to lay out a broad set of so-called "macroprudential" indicators. See, for instance, IMF (2002b) and references therein.

44 Goodhart and Danielsson 2001, while sharing many of the concerns expressed here about the difficulties of measuring risk over time, reaches more pessimistic conclusions. Its evidence, however, is based on the predictability of business cycle fluctuations *on the basis of their duration only*. The point here is that this approach is unnecessarily restrictive. Judgments can be conditioned on a broader information set.

45 Will the indicators continue to perform satisfactorily in the future? As always, there is no such guarantee. For example, efforts made in recent years to improve the infrastructure of the financial systems might reduce the likelihood of distress for any given threshold level. Moreover, learning from postliberalization mistakes could well reduce the incidence of crises. At the same time, the historiography of financial crises suggests that the core regularities on which the indicators are based have been so common in the past that they may prove comparatively robust in the future.

46 The IMF and national central banks have been quite active in this area.

47 For a more detailed treatment, see, in particular, Lowe (2002), Borio et al. (2001), and Allen and Saunders (2003) and references therein. See also Berger and Udell (2003) for possible reasons for, and some evidence of, excessive procyclicality in risk assessments.

48 This is the formalization found in Carey (2000). Rating agencies' risk assessments are sometimes characterized as "through-the-cycle" and contrasted with the "point-in-time" nature of banks' internal credit rating systems or model-based measures; see in particular, Amato and Furfine (2003) for an empirical examination of the degree of procyclicality in ratings. See also Cantor (2002), who provides a somewhat different characterization of rating agencies' ratings.

49 Note that, strictly speaking, there is a distinction between the horizon for the *assessment* of risk and that for its *quantification*. The former includes the period ahead considered in the evaluation of the risk, the latter the period used for the risk metric. The distinction is clearest if one considers an instrument that is marked to market. Events that might occur over

the residual maturity of the instrument affect its current value and its future variability (the assessment horizon). But the holder might just be interested in potential changes in this value over a possibly shorter horizon over which it plans to hold the instrument. This determines the quantification horizon for risk. These issues are further discussed below.

50 This positive correlation in the time dimension has recently been documented by Altman et al. (2002).

51 See, for instance, Danielsson et al. (2001) and ECB (2001). For the provisions of the Accord, see BCBS (2001a) and (2001b). See also BIS (2001a). Note that concerns with the procyclicality of capital standards had already been expressed in relation to the current Accord (Goodhart 1995; Blum and Hellwig 1995). These, however, had little to do with time-varying risk perceptions. They related simply to the fact that higher losses in recessions would make capital require-ments more binding. The evidence on whether such minimum requirements have led to "credit crunches" is reviewed in BCBS (1999).

52 See, in addition, Jordan et al. (2002) and Catarineu-Rabell et al. (2002). Note that in November 2001 the Basel Committee decided to reduce the steepness of the risk curve linking the capital requirement weights to the probability of default partly with a view to dampening the cyclical variability in minimum requirements. This response deals with a time dimension issue through changes in cross-sectional calibration BCBS (2001b).

53 See, in particular, the discussion in BIS (2002a) and Greenspan (2002).

54 Fama and French (1988).

55 This issue is explored more thoroughly in Borio et al. (2001).

56 These issues are discussed in Lowe (2002).

57 See Barakova and Carey (2002).

58 Enron's internal risk management manual is quite telling here: "Reported earnings follow the rules and principles of accounting. The results do not always create measures consistent with underlying economics. However, corporate management's performance is generally measured by accounting income, not underlying economics. *Risk management strategies are therefore directed at accounting rather than economic performance*" (italics added). See Crockett (2002) for an elaboration on these issues.

59 The changes incorporated in IAS39 go in this direction.

60 These issues are discussed in Borio et al. (2001), Borio and Lowe (2001), BIS (2002a), and Crockett (2002).

61 Aspects of these issues are discussed in Borio and Lowe (2001) and Crockett (2002).

62 Recently, Padoa-Schioppa (2002) too has emphasized the importance of the macroprudential dimension.

63 For a focused elaboration on this point, see Crockett (2001b).

64 Borio and Crockett (2000), Borio and Lowe (2002a), and Borio et al. (2003). See also BIS (2001a) and (2002b).

References

Abreu, D., and M. K. Brunnermeier. 2003. "Bubbles and Crashes." *Econometrica* 71, 173–204.

Acharya, V. 2001. "A Theory of Systemic Risk and Design of Prudential Bank Regulation." Mimeo.

Allen, F. and D. Gale. 2000. "Bubbles and Crises." *Economic Journal* 110, 236–256.

Allen, F., S. Morris, and H. Shin. 2003. "Beauty Contests, Bubbles and Iterated Expectations in Asset Markets." Mimeo.

Allen, L., and A. Saunders. 2003. "A Survey of Cyclical Effects in Credit Risk Measurement Mod-els." Paper presented at the BIS Conference "Changes in Risk through Time: Measurement and Policy Options," Basel, BIS Working Paper No. 126, January.

Altman, E. I., A. Resti, and A. Sironi. 2002. "The Link between Default and Recovery Rates: Effects on the Procyclicality of Regulatory Capital Ratios." Paper presented at the BIS

Conference "Changes in Risk through Time: Measurement and Policy Options," Basel, BIS Working Paper No. 113, July.

Amato, J., and C. Furfine. 2003. "Are Credit Ratings Procyclical?" BIS Working Paper No. 129, February.

Bank for International Settlements. 2001a. "Cycles and the Financial System." In *71st Annual Report*, June.

————— 2001b. "Consolidation in the Financial Sector." In *Report by the Group of Ten Working Party on Financial Sector Consolidation*, January.

—————. 2002a. "The Interaction between the Financial Sector and the Real Economy." In *72nd Annual Report*, June.

—————. 2002b. "Monetary Policy in the Advanced Industrial Economies." In *72nd Annual Report*, June.

Barakova, I., and M. Carey. 2002. "How Quickly Do Troubled US Banks Recapitalize? With Implications for Portfolio VaR Credit Loss Horizons." Mimeo.

Basel Committee on Banking Supervision. 1999. "Capital Requirements and Bank Behaviour: The Impact of the Basel Accord." BCBS Working Paper No. 1, April.

—————. 2001a. *The New Basel Capital Accord*. Consultative document, January.

—————. 2001b. "Potential Modifications to the Committee's Proposals." November 5.

Berger, A. N., and G. F. Udell. 2003. "The Institutional Memory Hypothesis and the Procyclicality of Bank Lending Behaviour." Paper presented at the BIS Conference "Changes in Risk through Time: Measurement and Policy Options," Basel, BIS Working Paper No. 125, January.

Bernanke, B. S., M. Gertler, and S. Gilchrist. 1999. "The Financial Accelerator in a Quantitative Business Cycle Framework." In J. B. Taylor and M. Woodford, eds., *Handbook of Macroeconomics*. Amsterdam: North-Holland.

Blum, J., and M. Hellwig. 1995. "The Macroeconomic Implications of Capital Adequacy Requirements for Banks." *European Economic Review* 39, 739–749.

Bordo, M. D., M. J. Dueker, and D. C. Wheelock. (2001). "Aggregate Price Shocks and Financial Stability," Federal Reserve Bank of St. Louis Working Paper No. 2001–018A, November.

Borio, C. 2000. "Market Liquidity and Stress: Selected Issues and Policy Implications." *BIS Quarterly Review*, November, 38–48.

Borio, C., and A. D. Crockett. 2000. "In Search of Anchors for Financial and Monetary Stability." *Greek Economic Review* 20(2), 1–14.

Borio, C., B. English, and A. Filardo. 2003. "A Tale of Two Perspectives: Old or New Challenges for Monetary Policy?" BIS Working Paper no. 127, February.

Borio, C., and R. Filosa. 1994. "The Changing Borders of Banking: Trends and Implications." BIS Economic Paper No. 43, December.

Borio, C., C. Furfine, and P. Lowe. 2001. "Procyclicality of the Financial System and Financial Stability: Issues and Policy Options." *BIS Papers* 1, 1–57.

Borio, C., N. Kennedy, and S. Prowse. 1994. "Exploring Aggregate Asset Price Fluctuations across Countries: Measurement, Determinants and Monetary Policy Implications." BIS Economic Paper No. 40, April.

Borio, C., and P. Lowe. 2001. "To Provision or Not to Provision." *BIS Quarterly Review*, June, 36–48.

—————. 2002a. "Asset Prices, Financial and Monetary Stability: Exploring the Nexus." Paper presented at the BIS Conference "Changes in Risk through Time: Measurement and Policy Options," Basel, BIS Working Paper No. 114, July.

—————. 2002b. "Assessing the Risk of Banking Crises." *BIS Quarterly Review*, December, 43–54.

Borio, C., and P. Van den Bergh. 1993. "The Nature and Management of Payment System Risks: An International Perspective." BIS Economic Paper No. 36, February.

Calomiris, C., and G. Gorton. 1991. "The Origins of Banking Panics: Models, Facts and Bank Regulation." In R. Hubbard, ed., *Financial Markets and Financial Crises*. Chicago: University of Chicago Press for NBER.

Cantor, R. 2002. "Through-the-Cycle vs Point-in-Time Ratings." Presentation at the BIS Conference "Changes in Risk through Time: Measurement and Policy Options," Basel, March.

Carey, M. 1990. "Feeding the Fad: The Federal Land Banks, Land Market Efficiency and the Farm Credit Crisis." Ph.D. dissertation, University of California, Berkeley.

———. 2000. "Dimensions of Credit Risk and Their Relationship to Economic Capital Requirements." In F. Mishkin, ed., *Prudential Supervision: What Works and What Doesn't*. Chicago: University of Chicago Press.

Catarineu-Rabell, E., P. Jackson, and D. P. Tsomocos. 2002. "Procyclicality and the New Basel Accord—Banks' Choice of Loan Rating System." May. Mimeo.

Chang R., and A. Velasco. 1998. "Financial Crises in Emerging Markets: A Canonical Model." National Bureau of Economic Research Working Paper No. 6606.

Corsetti, G. 1998. "Interpreting the Asian Financial Crisis: Open Issues in Theory and Policy." *Asian Development Review* 16(2), 18–63.

Corsetti, G., P. Pesenti, and N. Roubini. 1999. "Paper Tigers, a Model of the Asian Crisis." *European Economic Review* 43, 1211–1236.

Crockett, A. 2000a. "Marrying the Micro- and Macroprudential Dimensions of Financial Stability." *BIS Speeches*, September 21.

———. 2000b. "In Search of Anchors for Financial and Monetary Stability." *BIS Speeches*, April 27.

———. 2001a. "Market Discipline and Financial Stability." *BIS Speeches*, May 23. Reprinted in *Bank of England Financial Stability Review* 10, Article 6, 166–173.

———. 2001b. "Monetary Policy and Financial Stability." *BIS Speeches*, February 13.

———. 2002. "Financial Reporting: From Shadows to Limelight." Keynote speech at the joint BIS / Bocconi University Centennial conference "Risk and Stability in the Financial System: What Roles for Regulators, Management and Market Discipline?" Milan, June.

Danielsson, J., P. Embrechts, C. Goodhart, C. Keating, F. Muennich, O. Renault, and H. S. Shin. 2001. "An Academic Response to Basel II." Special Paper No. 130, London School of Economics Financial Markets Group.

Danielsson, J., H. S. Shin, and J.P. Zigrand. 2002. "The Impact of Risk Regulation on Price Dynamics." Financial Markets Group, London School of Economics. Mimeo.

Davis, E. P. 1995. *Debt Financial Fragility and Systemic Risk*. Rev. ed. Oxford: Clarendon Press.

De Bandt, O., and P. Hartmann. 2000. "Systemic Risk: A Survey." ECB Working Paper No. 35.

De Nicolo, G., and M. Kwast. 2001. "Systematic Risk and Financial Consolidation: Are They Related?" Board of Governors of the Federal Reserve System, Finance and Economics Discussion Series no. 2001–2033, August.

Dewatripont, M., and J. Tirole. 1993. *The Prudential Regulation of Banks*. Cambridge, MA: MIT Press.

Diamond, D. W., and P. H. Dybvig. 1983. "Bank Runs, Deposit Insurance and Liquidity." *Journal of Political Economy* 91, 401–419.

Eichengreen, B., and C. Arteta. 2000. "Banking Crises in Emerging Markets: Presumptions and Evidence." Center for International and Development Economics Research Working Paper C00–115, August.

Elsinger, H., A. Lehar, and M. Summer. 2002. "Risk Assessment for Banking Systems." Paper presented at the CESifo Venice Summer Institute 2002 workshop, July 13–20, Austrian National Bank Working Paper No. 79, October.

Embrechts, P., A. McNeil, and D. Straumann. 1999. "Correlation and Dependence in Risk Management: Properties and Pitfalls." ETH. Mimeo.

Euro-currency Standing Committee. 1992. "Recent Developments in International Interbank Relations." *Promisel Report* no. 2, October.

European Central Bank. 2001. *The New Basel Capital Accord: Comments of the European Central Bank*.

Fama, E., and K. French. 1988. "Permanent and Temporary Components of Stock Prices." *Journal of Political Economy* 96, 246–273.

Fernández de Lis, S. J. Martinez Pagés, and S. Saurina. 2001. "Credit Growth, Problem Loans and Credit Risk Provisioning in Spain." Presented at a Bank for International Settlements conference: , 331–353. Available at http://www.bis.org/publ/bppdf/bispap01.htm

Flannery, M. 1998. "Using Market Information in Prudential Bank Supervision: A Review of the U.S. Empirical Evidence." *Journal of Money, Credit and Banking* 30, 273–305.

Frankel, J., and K. Froot. 1990. "Chartists, Fundamentalists and Trading in the Foreign Exchange Market." *American Economic Review* 80, 181–185.

Froot, K. A., D. S. Sharfstein, and J. C. Stein. 1992. "Herd on the Street: Informational Efficiencies in a Market with Short-Term Speculation." *Journal of Finance* 47, 1461–1484.

Furfine, C. 1999. "Interbank Exposures: Quantifying the Risk of Contagion." BIS Working Paper No. 70, June.

Gertler, M. 1988. "Financial Structure and Aggregate Economic Activity." *Journal of Money, Credit and Banking* 20, 559–588.

Goodhart, C. 1995. "Price Stability and Financial Fragility." In K. Kawamoto, Z. Nakajima, and H. Taguchi eds., *Financial Stability in a Changing Environment*. London: Macmillan.

Goodhart, C., and J. Danielsson. 2001. "The Inter-temporal Nature of Risk." 23rd SUERF Colloquium on "Technology and Finance: Challenges for Financial Markets, Business Strategies and Policy Makers." Brussels, October.

Goodhart, C., and P. J. R. De Largy. 1999. "Financial Crises: Plus ça change, plus c'est la meme chose." LSE Financial Markets Group Special Paper No. 108.

Gorton, G. 1988. "Banking Panics and Business Cycles." *Oxford Economic Papers* 40, 751–781.

Gourinchas, P., R. Valdes and O. Landerretche. 2001. "Lending Booms: Latin America and the World." National Bureau of Economic Research Working Paper No. 8249.

Greenspan, A. 2002. "Cyclicality and Banking Regulation." Remarks given at the conference "Bank Structure and Competition," Federal Reserve Bank of Chicago, May 10.

Hart, O. 1995. *Firms, Contracts and Financial Structure*. Oxford: Oxford University Press.

Hart, O., and B. Holmström. 1988. "The Theory of Contracts." In T. Bewley, ed., *Advances in Economic Theory*. Cambridge: Cambridge University Press.

Hawkins, J., and M. Klau. 2000. "Measuring Potential Vulnerabilities in Emerging Market Economies." BIS Working Paper No. 91, October.

Hellwig, M. 1995. "Systemic Aspects of Risk Management in Banking and Finance." *Schweizerische Zeitschrift für Volkswirtschaft and Statistik* 131, 723–737.

Hellwig, M. 1998. "Banks, Markets and the Allocation of Risks in an Economy." *Journal of Institutional and Theoretical Economics* 154, 328–345.

Hofmann, B. 2001. "The Determinants of Bank Credit to the Private Sector in Industrialised Countries." BIS Working Paper No. 108, December.

Hoggarth, G., and V. Saporta. 2001. "Costs of Banking System Instability: Some Empirical Evidence." *Bank of England Financial Stability Review* 10, Article 5, June, 148–165.

Honohan, P. 1997. "Banking System Failures in Developing and Transition Economies: Diagnosis and Prediction." BIS Working Paper No. 39, January.

International Monetary Fund. 2002a. *Global Financial Stability Report*, March 13.

———. 2002b. "Financial Soundness Indicators: Analytical Aspects and Country Practices." Occasional Paper No. 212, April 8.

Jordan, J., J. Peek, and E. Rosengren. 2002. "Credit Risk Modeling and the Cyclicality of Capital." Paper presented at the BIS Conference "Changes in Risk through Time: Measurement and Policy Options," *BIS Working Paper*, Basel, March 6.

Kaminsky, G., and C. Reinhart. 1999. "The Twin Crises: The Causes of Banking and Balance-of-Payments Problems." *American Economic Review* 89, 473–500.

Kaufman, G. 1994. "Bank Contagion: A Review of the Theory and Evidence," *Journal of Financial Services Research 8*, April, 123–150.

Kent, C., and P. D'Arcy. 2001. "Cyclical Prudence—Credit Cycles in Australia." *BIS Papers* 1, 58–90.

Kindleberger, C. 1996. *Manias, Panics and Crashes*. 3rd ed. Cambridge: Cambridge University Press.

Kiyotaki, N., and J. Moore. 1997. "Credit Cycles." *Journal of Political Economy* 105, 211–248.

Lowe, P. 2002. "Credit Risk Measurement and procyclicality." Paper presented at the Conference "Banking Supervision at the Crossroads" on the occasion of the 50th Anniversary of the Dutch Act on the supervision on credit systems, BIS Working Paper No. 116, August.

Minsky, H. P. 1982. "Can 'It' Happen Again?" In *Essays on Instability and Finance*. Armonk, NY: M. E. Sharpe.

Morris, S., and H. Shin. 1998. "Unique Equilibrium in a Model of Self-Fulfilling Currency Attacks." *American Economic Review* 88, 587–597.

Padoa-Schioppa, T. 2002. "Central Banks and Financial Stability." Paper presented at the second biennial ECB conference "The Transformation of the European Financial System," Frankfurt am Main, October24–25.

Rochet, J.C., and J. Tirole. 1996a. "Interbank Lending and Systemic Risk." *Journal of Money, Credit and Banking* 28, 733–762.

———. 1996b. "Controlling Risk in Payment Systems." *Journal of Money, Credit and Banking* 28, 832–862.

Sachs, J., and S. Radelet. 1998. "The East Asian Financial Crisis: Diagnosis, Remedies, Prospects." *Brookings Papers on Economic Activity* 1, 1–74.

Samuelson, P. 1973. *Economics*. 9th ed. Tokyo: McGraw-Hill.

Santos, J. A. C. 2000. "Bank Capital Regulation in Contemporary Banking Theory: A Review of the Literature." BIS Working Paper No. 90, September.

Segoviano, M. A., and P. Lowe. 2002. "Internal Ratings, the Business Cycle and Capital Requirements: Some Evidence from an Emerging Market Economy." Paper presented at the Federal Reserve Bank of Boston Conference "The Impact of Economic Slowdowns on Financial Institutions and Their Regulators," BIS Working Paper No. 117, August.

Shleifer, A., and R. Vishny. 1997. "The Limits of Arbitrage." *Journal of Finance* 52, 33–55.

Tsatsaronis, K. 2002. "Systemic Financial Risk and Macroprudential Supervision." Paper presented at the Bocconi University Centennial conference "Risk and Stability in the Financial System: What Roles for Regulators, Management and Market Discipline?

Van den Bergh, P., and R. Sahajwala. 2000. "Supervisory Risk Assessment and Early Warning Systems." Basel Committee on Banking Supervision Working Paper No. 4, December.

Zhu, H. 2001. "Bank Runs without Self-Fulfilling Prophecies." BIS Working Paper No. 106, December.

CHAPTER 9

Bank Liquidity and Bubbles

WHY CENTRAL BANKS SHOULD LEAN AGAINST LIQUIDITY

■

Viral V. Acharya and Hassan Naqvi

What caused the tremendous worldwide asset growth in the period 2003–2007, especially in the housing sector, and its subsequent puncture, is likely to intrigue economists for years. However, it was likely not a coincidence that the phase of remarkable asset growth started at the turn of the global recession of 2001–2002 and the preceding Southeast Asian crisis. In response to the unprecedented rate of corporate defaults, investors looked increasingly to park their wealth in the perceived safety of financial sectors. Loose monetary policy adopted by the Federal Reserve further enhanced the liquidity of financial intermediaries. A period of abundant availability of liquidity to the financial sector ensued, large bank balance-sheets grew twofold within four years, and when the "bubble burst," a number of agency problems within banks in those years came to the fore. These agency problems were primarily concentrated in centers that were in charge of underwriting loans and positions in securitized assets. Loan officers and risk-takers received huge bonuses based on the volume of assets they originated and purchased rather than on (long-term) profits these assets generated. Moreover, in many cases, it was a conscious choice of senior management to silence the risk management groups that had spotted weaknesses in the portfolio of building risks.[1]

Rajan (2005, 2008) called this bank-level principal-agent problem the "fake alpha" problem—wherein performance is measured based on short-term returns but risks are long term, or in other words in the "tail." An earlier report by the Office of the Comptroller of the Currency in the United States (OCC 1988) had also found that "Management-driven weaknesses played a significant role in the decline of 90 percent of the failed and problem banks the OCC evaluated . . . directors' or managements' overly aggressive behavior resulted in imprudent lending practices and excessive loan growth." They also found that 73% of the failed banks had indulged in overlending. This suggests that principal-agent problems within banks have been one of the key reasons for bank failures and that bank managers often tend to engage in "overly aggressive risk-taking behavior."[2] And recently Reinhart and Rogoff (2008, 2009), among others, have documented that this lending boom-and-bust cycle has in fact been typical for several centuries, usually (but not always) associated with bank lending and real estate, and also often coincident with abundant liquidity in the form of capital inflows.

Why does access to abundant liquidity aggravate the risk-taking incentives at banks, giving rise to excess lending and asset price bubbles? A simple explanation is that easy access to liquidity gives bankers insurance against meeting their future losses. In response, they underprice the downside risk of loans they make and assets they fund. Somewhat paradoxically, seeds of the crisis are thus sown precisely at the turn of the previous crisis or recession, unless central banks rein in the abundance of liquidity at the right time.

Consider this argument informally (formal treatment is provided in Acharya and Naqvi 2011). The representative bank collects deposits from savers in the economy and then allocates a fraction of these deposits to houses and investment projects in the form of mortgages and corporate loans. The bank runs the risk of facing interim deposit withdrawals. Alternately, it needs to meet drawdowns on home equity and corporate lines of credit. In case the bank is unable to meet its liquidity shortfalls, it may have to sell its assets at short notice or raise equity in markets, suffering in the process some liquidation or issuance costs. In order to avoid such costs, the bank has an incentive to set aside some reserves (say, cash and marketable assets or other forms of ready liquidity). The key question is whether the bank sets interest rates on mortgages and corporate loans at a level that appropriately reflects the underlying risk of houses and corporate assets.

In practice, bankers and loan officers often have incentives to give out excessive loans since their payoffs are increasing in the amount of loans advanced. For instance, the Bureau of Labor Statistics reports that "Most (loan officers) are paid a commission based on the number of loans they originate."[3] It is not hard to see why such incentives arise as part of an optimal contracting outcome of a principal-agent problem. Put simply, if bankers are asked to bear almost all of the risk of loans, then they would be too risk-averse to originate any assets. Risk-averse bank officers need to be compensated for the effort induced in marketing loans. The upside from originating more assets gives bankers incentives to exert effort in seeking more customers and expanding financial intermediation.

However, such upside is usually also combined with performance evaluation of bankers. In particular, the bank's board (or its risk management function) can conduct an audit to verify whether or not the bankers acted prudently while originating assets, or instead acted overaggressively by lowering the lending rate and sanctioning excessive loans. Suppose that subsequent to such an audit, it is inferred that bankers had indeed acted overaggressively; then they can be penalized for some (possibly all) of the costs the bank incurs from meeting liquidity shortfalls when the excessive loans go bad. In principle, the threat of such an audit and penalty, if sufficiently stringent, could ensure that bankers take appropriate account of the downside risk of assets while extending credit.

The problem, however, is that while commission- or volume-based compensation schemes are precommitted to bankers, their audits, risk management, and subsequent penalties, if any, are necessarily ex post. This leads to a time-consistency problem inside banks. While the bank board may want to commit ex ante to a tough audit policy, such audits and risk management are costly, so that it is ex post optimal for the bank to conduct them seriously only if the bank suffers a liquidity shortfall that is large enough.[4]

This commitment to upside in bankers' payoff but uncertainty about the downside creates an interesting incentive trade-off for bankers. Bankers can increase their payoffs by underpricing the inherent risk of loans and consequently setting a low interest rate for mortgages and loans. This effectively elicits greater demand for borrowing from households and corporations. But an increase in credit volume can trigger a liquidity shortfall for the bank, subsequent to which the manager faces the risk of being audited and penalized. The level of bank liquidity, which on a day-to-day basis is readily observed by bank insiders but not as visible to the bank board, becomes a crucial determinant of whether bankers will underprice loan risk in the interest rates. In particular, bankers underprice loan risk only when bank liquidity is sufficiently high.

Intuitively, even though bankers face some downside risk, in the presence of excessive liquidity, the probability that the bank will ex post experience a liquidity shortage is low. In case of no liquidity shortfalls or only a low liquidity shortage, it will not be ex post efficient for the bank to incur costly audits of lending practices. Anticipation of this lax audit policy encourages bankers to engage in excessive lending. Put another way, high bank liquidity has an "insurance effect" on bankers: it makes banker compensation more sensitive to loan volume—and less sensitive to the downside risk of loans. In turn, this incentivizes bankers to lend below the efficient rate and make more and excessively risky loans. Conversely, for low enough bank liquidity, the perceived risk of audits by bankers is high, the agency problem is not actuated, and bankers do not sanction excessive loans.

This dark side of bank liquidity in inducing excessive lending behavior by bankers ultimately has an impact on asset prices. Suppose that the demand for loans arises from investments by the household sector in real assets of the economy. Then, we can define the "fundamental" asset prices as those that arise in the absence of any agency frictions within banks. If the bank lending rate underprices risks, then there is an increase in aggregate borrowing by the household sector from banks. This in turn fuels an excessive demand for assets in the real sector, which in absence of a perfectly elastic supply, leads to prices rising above their fundamental values. This asset price inflation constitutes a "bubble." Importantly, such bubbles are formed only when bank liquidity is high enough, as only then do bank managers underprice risk.

To better understand the mechanics behind the formation of a bubble, the four-quadrant diagram in Figure 9.1 is useful. Quadrant I in the figure depicts the relationship between the downside risk of project failure, and the loan rate charged by the bank. In general, the higher the downside risk of assets, the higher would be the equilibrium lending rate as is captured by the line AA. The loan rate in turn determines the demand for loans and the volume of credit in the economy. The lower the loan rate the higher is the amount of expected investment in the economy, as captured by the line NN in quadrant II. The increase in investment pushes up the asset demand, which in turn pushes up asset prices. This relationship between the demand for the asset and the asset price is captured by the line YY in quadrant III. Finally quadrant IV derives the relationship between the asset price and risk. In general, the higher is the underlying risk the lower will be the asset price as is depicted by the line ZZ.

However, the equilibrium relationship between asset price and risk is derived by tracing the effect of risk on the loan rate, which in turn has an effect on the amount of investment, which subsequently determines the asset price. Let the line AA represent the fundamental relationship between risk and the bank loan rate, that is, the relationship that would be obtained in the absence of agency issues. Then for any given level of risk, the fundamental asset price would be represented by the line ZZ. However, the bank agency problem is actuated for sufficiently high bank liquidity levels whereby the bank loan rate is lowered for any given level of risk. This in turn shifts the AA line to A^1A^1. From quadrant II we

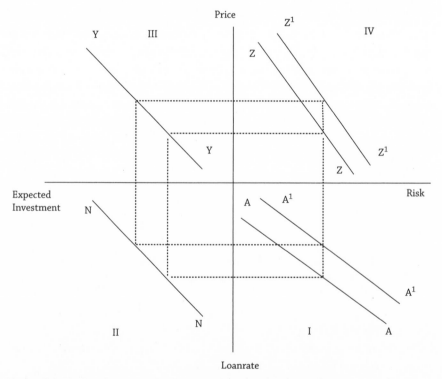

Figure 9.1 The mechanics of the formation of asset price bubbles.

know that the volume of credit in the economy increases following lower loan rates. Consequently asset prices increase as is shown in quadrant III. The final relationship between asset prices and risk is shown in quadrant IV and the actuation of the principal-agent problem shifts the ZZ line to Z^1Z^1. In the end, the asset price is higher for the same level of risk once the agency problem is actuated, leading to the formation of a bubble. This is different from restricting attention to quadrant IV alone in relating risk to asset price, which ignores the role of the banking sector in affecting asset prices.

Given asset price bubbles are formed when bank liquidity is substantially high, the question that arises is when are banks most likely to be flushed with liquidity? In an empirical study, Gatev and Strahan (2006) find that as spreads in the commercial paper market increase, bank deposits increase and bank asset (loan) growth also increases. The spreads on commercial paper are a measure of the investors' perception of risk in the real economy. Intuitively, when investors are apprehensive of the risk in the corporate sector they are more likely to deposit their investments in banks rather than make direct investments.[5] More generally, as macroeconomic risk increases, there is a flight to quality whereby investors prefer to invest in bank deposits rather than engage in direct lending. Subsequently, banks find themselves flushed with liquidity, which encourages bankers to increase the volume of credit in the economy by mispricing downside risk of assets and fueling a bubble in asset prices.

What are the implications of this link between bank liquidity and asset prices for optimal monetary policy? If the central bank adopts a contractionary monetary policy in times of excessive bank liquidity, then it can counter the perverse incentive effect on bankers of flight to quality by drawing out the increases in bank liquidity and avoiding the emergence of bubbles. On the contrary, if the central bank adopts an expansionary monetary policy in such times, then this accentuates the formation of bubbles. Intuitively, an increase in the money supply only serves to increase bank liquidity further when there is already a flight to quality of deposits. In contrast, in times of scarce bank liquidity, banks raise lending rates, which can adversely affect aggregate investment. If the central bank adopts an expansionary monetary policy in such times, then it can boost aggregate investment by effectively injecting liquidity into the banking system.

Proponents of the "Greenspan camp" often argue that the central bank may not be aware where we are in the business cycle and hence whether bank liquidity is increasing or decreasing in macroeconomic risk. Nevertheless, a much simpler policy recommendation is to lean against bank liquidity regardless of where we are in the business cycle. The "Greenspan put" should be employed in times of falling bank liquidity. However, in times when banks are flush with liquidity, a loose monetary policy only enhances the liquidity insurance enjoyed by banks, and thus aggravates their risk-taking incentives. This in turn increases the likelihood of bubbles in asset prices. Thus, the optimal monetary policy involves a "leaning against liquidity" approach, and "leaning against macroeconomic risk" is not necessarily the desirable policy.

One implicit assumption in the analysis is that the central bank can observe aggregate liquidity with a good degree of precision. But this assumption is justified along the following lines: individual bank-level liquidity is hard to verify because the presence of the interbank market implies that liquidity moves around among banks and hence it is difficult to ascertain an individual bank's liquidity. But this then implies that aggregate liquidity should be more precisely observable (by the central bank) vis-à-vis individual bank level liquidity (by its owners or the board).

In terms of historical evidence on the effect of monetary policy on asset prices, Allen and Gale in their book *Understanding Financial Crises* document the following: "In Finland an expansionary budget in 1987 resulted in massive credit expansion. The ratio of bank loans to nominal GDP increased from 55 percent in 1984 to 90 percent in 1990. Housing prices rose by a total of 68 percent in 1987 and 1988.... In Sweden a steady credit expansion through the late 1980's led to a property boom" (2007, 236). These observations are perfectly in line with the link between bank liquidity and asset bubbles proposed above. Further, this proposed link is also consistent with the generally held view that lax monetary policy in Japan during the mid-1980s led to asset price inflation. Bank of Japan (BOJ) reduced the official discount rate five times between January 1986 and February 1987, leaving it finally at 2.5%. It is widely accepted that the easy credit policies adopted by BOJ created excess liquidity in the Japanese economy, as also acknowledged by Goyal and Yamada (2004). The sequence of events started with the Plaza Accord (1985), in which the G5 countries agreed on a stronger yen so as to lower the U.S. trade deficit. However, BOJ's intervention in foreign exchange markets appreciated the yen rapidly. Responding to the strengthening yen and seeking to avert deflationary effects in the domestic economy, Bank of Japan lowered interest rates and consequently increased liquidity in the economy. In the subsequent years a large real estate bubble was formed.

One of the suggested causes of the recently witnessed subprime crisis is the loose monetary policy adopted by the Federal Reserve in the United States. In 2003, the Fed lowered the federal funds rate to 1%—a level that at that time was last seen in 1958. Subsequently banks mispriced risk and engaged in overlending, which culminated in the subprime crisis. In fact the world was awash with liquidity prior to the crisis, creating incentives to disregard the downside risk of housing markets. In their counterfactual exercise, Bean et al. (2010) show (in their Table 3) that an interest rate scenario of 2.5% greater than the Federal Reserve policy rates in 2005 and 2006 would have reduced annual real house price growth by 7%, and 10%, respectively. Geanakoplos (2010) also documents that banks progressively made worse loans from 2003 to 2006; the down payment for mortgages fell from 10%, on average, to a low of 2%, while the Case Shiller House Price Index climbed from 145 to 190.

The issue of when a central bank should tighten monetary policy following a crisis has resurfaced in the aftermath of the rescue packages administered to recover from the crisis of 2007–2009. For instance, the Federal Reserve in the United States has discussed raising the interest paid to banks on their reserves holdings and selling its inventory of mortgage-backed assets as potential tools. The Federal Reserve chairman, Ben Bernanke, has, however, argued that "The economy continues to require the support of accommodative monetary policies. However, we have been working to ensure that we have the tools to reverse, at the appropriate time, the currently very high degree of monetary stimulus."[6]

In contrast, some other countries have already started the monetary tightening process. China, in particular, has "ordered its commercial banks to increase the reserves (by 50 basis points from February 25) they hold, as an effort to control rapid lending, rather than significantly tighten monetary policy."[7] The Chinese economy expanded by 10.7& in the fourth quarter of 2009 and Chinese banks issued a record Rmb9,600bn in new loans in 2009, about double the amount from the previous year, which fueled a rapid increase in asset prices, especially in Chinese stock markets. House prices in China had increased by 7.8% in December 2009 from the same month a year earlier.[8] Not surprisingly, the liquidity of Chinese banks also soared during this period. In fact, household and corporate deposits in the Chinese banking system are now equivalent to a record 150% of gross domestic product.[9]

Both of these examples get at the heart of our policy discussion, that the key parameter to examine is the extent of bank liquidity and lending in the economy, as in the discussion about Chinese lending and asset prices above. The risk of the Federal Reserve not tightening monetary policy sufficiently soon is precisely that lending may take off by several multiples given the high levels of bank liquidity (reserves) and force the Fed to either tighten excessively ex post or be mopping up after the asset prices have been inflated too high.

In summary, the seeds of a crisis may be sown when banks are flush with liquidity. In particular, (*a*) bank managers behave in an overly aggressive manner by mispricing risk when bank liquidity is sufficiently high; (*b*) asset price bubbles are formed for high enough bank liquidity; (*c*) bubbles are more likely to be formed when the underlying macroeconomic risk is high, as it induces investors to save with banks rather than make direct entrepreneurial investments; and, finally, (*d*) bubbles are more likely to be formed following loose monetary policies adopted by the central bank.

Optimal monetary policy involves a "leaning against liquidity" approach, that is, a central bank should adopt a contractionary monetary policy at times when banks are awash with liquidity so as to draw out their reserves; and it should adopt an expansionary monetary policy at times when banks have scarce liquidity so as to boost investment.

Some, most notably Alan Greenspan, have argued that we are never certain "where we are in the cycle"[10] and hence monetary policy should not be used to target asset prices. Even if this is the case, a "leaning against liquidity" policy can be rationalized. This is because our argument does not rely on the central bank's ability to observe macroeconomic risk. Our policy recommendations are relevant as long as the central bank can reasonably monitor aggregate liquidity. As argued earlier this is a plausible assumption. We thus argue that monetary policy should target not just interest rates and employment but also asset prices, as they are reflections of the risk appetite of the financial intermediation sector (as also stressed by Adrian and Shin 2009).

It should be noted that an increase in global macroeconomic risk can also increase bank liquidity of developed economies due to "global imbalances." For instance, Caballero (2010) argues that as a result of the Southeast Asian crisis and the NASDAQ crash there was an increased global demand for safe securities, and the U.S. financial system catered to this demand by creating collateralized debt obligations (CDOs). This in turn was conducive to global imbalances whereby there was an influx of liquidity in the U.S. financial system from emerging economies. Inevitably this increased the liquidity of the U.S. banking system.

More broadly speaking, the rise in bank deposits in our model could also be interpreted as capital inflows which find their way into an economy's financial system. For instance, similarly to Caballero (2009), Jagannathan et al. (2009) argue that after the stock market crash of 2000, savings from China flowed into the United States debt market. The flow of money into securitized mortgage pools drove down the cost of borrowing by banks, inducing them to relax credit standards, resulting in a housing bubble. The presence of explicit or implicit government guarantees, such as deposit insurance, and the too-big-to-fail problem (as considered by Allen and Gale 2000), accentuate the agency problems inside banks induced by access to abundant liquidity, and accelerate the formation of asset-pricing bubbles.

Notes

1 See chapter 8 of Acharya and Richardson (2009b), which contains a detailed account of governance and management failures at a number of financial institutions. The most detailed evidence is for UBS based on its "Shareholder Report on UBS's Write Downs" prepared in 2008 for the Swiss Federal Banking Commission.

2 The OCC's study was based on an analysis of banks that failed, became problems, and recovered, or remained healthy during the period 1979–1987. The study analyzed 171 failed banks to identify characteristics and conditions present when the banks deteriorated.

3 See the Bureau of Labor Statistics' *Occupational Outlook Handbook*, 2008–2009 edition, available at http://www.bls.gov/oco/ocos018.htm\#earnings.

4 Tirole (2006) refers to this as the topsy-turvy problem of corporate governance: The principal would like to commit to tougher governance standards, but since implementing them is costly, will do so ex post only if it is desirable at that point of time.

5 The flight of depositors to banks may be due to banks having greater expertise in screening borrowers during stress times, inducing a natural negative correlation between the usage of lines of credit and deposit withdrawals, as argued by Kashyap, Rajan, and Stein (2002).

Alternatively, the flight may simply be due to the fact that bank deposits are insured (up to a threshold) by the Federal Deposit Insurance Corporation (FDIC) whereas commercial paper and money market funds are uninsured, at least until the extraordinary actions taken by the Federal Reserve during 2008 and 2009. Pennacchi (2006) finds evidence supportive of this latter hypothesis by examining lending behavior of banks during crises prior to the creation of the FDIC.

6 *Financial Times*, February 11, 2010.
7 *Financial Times*, February 13, 2010.
8 *Financial Times*, January 14, 2010.
9 *Financial Times*, March 3, 2010.
10 Alan Greenspan, *Financial Times*, May 27, 2008.

References

Acharya, Viral V., and Hassan Naqvi. 2011. "The Seeds of a Crisis: A Theory of Bank Liquidity and Risk-Taking over the Business Cycle." Working paper, New York University Stern School of Business.

Acharya, Viral V., and Matthew Richardson. 2009a. "Causes of the Financial Crisis." *Critical Review* 21(2–3), 195–210.

———, eds. 2009b. *Restoring Financial Stability: How to Repair a Failed System*. Hoboken, NJ: Wiley.

Acharya, Viral V., and Tanju Yorulmazer. 2007. "Too-Many-to-Fail: An Analysis of Time-Inconsistency in Bank Closure Policies." *Journal of Financial Intermediation* 16(1), 1–31.

Adrian, Tobias, and Hyun-Song Shin. 2009. "Money, Liquidity and Monetary Policy." *American Economic Review* 99, 600–605.

Allen, Franklin, and Douglas Gale. 2000. "Bubbles and Crises." *Economic Journal* 110, 236–255.

———. 2007. *Understanding Financial Crises*. New York: Oxford University Press.

Bean, Charles, Matthias Paustian, Adrian Penalver, and Tim Taylor. 2010. "Monetary Policy after the Fall." Paper presented at the Federal Reserve Bank of Kansas City Economic Symposium, Jackson Hole, Wyoming.

Bureau of Labor Statistics. *Occupational Outlook Handbook*. 2008–2009 ed. http://www.bls.gov/oco/ocos018.htm\#earnings.

Caballero, Ricardo J. 2010. "The 'Other' Imbalance and the Financial Crisis." National Bureau of Economic Research Working Paper No. 15636.

Farhi, Emmanuel, and Jean Tirole. 2009. "Collective Moral Hazard, Maturity Mismatch and Systemic Bailouts." National Bureau of Economic Research Working Paper No. 15138.

Friedman, Milton, and Anna J. Schwartz. 1963. *A Monetary History of the United States, 1867–1960*. Princeton, NJ: Princeton University Press.

Gatev, Evan, and Philip E. Strahan. 2006. "Banks' Advantage in Hedging Liquidity Risk: Theory and Evidence from the Commercial Paper Market." *Journal of Finance* 61, 867–892.

Geanakoplos, John. 2010. "Managing the Leverage Cycle." Presentation at the Federal Reserve Bank of Kansas City Economic Symposium, Jackson Hole, Wyoming.

Goyal, Vidhan K., and Takeshi Yamada. 2004. "Asset Price Shocks, Financial Constraints, and Investment: Evidence from Japan." *Journal of Business* 77(1), 175–199.

Jagannathan, Ravi, Mudit Kapoor, and Ernst Schaumburg. 2009. "Why Are We in a Recession? The Financial Crisis Is the Symptom Not the Disease!" National Bureau of Economic Research Working Paper No. 15404.

Kashyap, Anil K., Raghuram G. Rajan, and Jeremy C. Stein. 2002. "Banks as Liquidity Providers: An Explanation for the Co-existence of Lending and Deposit-Taking. *Journal of Finance* 57, 33–74.

Kindleberger, Charles P. 2005. *Manias, Panics, and Crashes: A History of Financial Crises*. 5th ed. Hoboken, NJ: Wiley.

Office of the Comptroller of the Currency (OCC). 1988. *Bank Failure: An Evaluation of the Factors Contributing to the Failure of National Banks*. Washington, DC: OCC.

Pennacchi, George. 2006. "Deposit Insurance, Bank Regulation, and Financial System Risks." *Journal of Monetary Economics* 53, 1–30.

Rajan, Raghuram G. 2005. "Has Financial Development Made the World Riskier?" *Proceedings, Federal Reserve Bank of Kansas City*, August, 313–369.

———. 2008. "Bankers' Pay Is Deeply Flawed." *Financial Times*, January 9.

Reinhart, Carmen M., and Kenneth S. Rogoff. 2008. "Is the 2007 US Sub-prime Financial Crisis So Different? An International Historical Comparison." *American Economic Review* 98, 339–344.

———. 2009. *This Time Is Different: Eight Centuries of Financial Folly*. Princeton, NJ: Princeton University Press.

Tirole, Jean. 2006. *The Theory of Corporate Finance*. Princeton, NJ: Princeton University Press.

BUBBLES: BEHAVIORAL EXPLANATIONS

CHAPTER 10

Overconfidence and Speculative Bubbles

José A. Scheinkman and Wei Xiong

1. Introduction

The behavior of market prices and trading volumes of assets during historical episodes of price bubbles presents a challenge to asset pricing theories. A common feature of these episodes, including the recent Internet stock boom, is the coexistence of high prices and high trading volume.[1] In addition, high price volatility is frequently observed.[2]

In this paper, we propose a model of asset trading, based on heterogeneous beliefs generated by agents' overconfidence, with equilibria that broadly fit these observations. We also provide explicit links between parameter values in the model, such as trading cost and information, and the behavior of equilibrium prices and trading volume. More generally, our model provides a flexible framework to study speculative trading that can be used to analyze links between asset prices, trading volume, and price volatility.

In the model, the ownership of a share of stock provides an opportunity (option) to profit from other investors' overvaluation. For this option to have value, it is necessary that some restrictions apply to short selling. In reality, these restrictions arise from many distinct sources. First, in many markets, short selling requires borrowing a security, and this mechanism is costly.[3] In particular, the default risk if the asset price goes up is priced by lenders of the security. Second, the risk associated with short selling may deter risk-averse investors. Third, limitations to the availability of capital to potential arbitrageurs may also limit short selling.[4] For technical reasons, we do not deal with short-sale costs or risk aversion. Instead we rule out short sales, although our qualitative results would survive the presence of costly short sales as long as the asset owners can expect to make a profit when others have higher valuations.

Our model follows the basic insight of Harrison and Kreps (1978) that when agents agree to disagree and short selling is not possible, asset prices may exceed their fundamental value. In their model, agents disagree about the probability distributions of dividend streams—the reason for the disagreement is not made explicit. We study overconfidence, the belief of an agent that his information is more accurate than it is, as a source of disagreement. Although overconfidence is only one of the many ways by which disagreement among investors may arise,[5] it is suggested by some experimental studies of human behavior and generates a mathematical framework that is relatively simple. Our model has an explicit solution, which allows us to derive several comparative statics results and restrictions on the dynamics of observables. The model may also be regarded as a fully worked out example of the Harrison-Kreps framework in continuous time, where computations and comparison of solutions are particularly tractable.

We study a market for a single risky asset with limited supply and many risk-neutral agents in a continuous-time model with an infinite horizon. The current dividend of the asset is a noisy observation of a fundamental variable that will determine future dividends. In addition to the dividends, there are two other sets of signals available at each instant. The information is available to all agents; however, agents are divided into two groups, and they differ in the interpretation of the signals. Each group overestimates the informativeness of a different signal and, as a consequence, has distinct forecasts of future dividends.[6] Agents in our model know that their forecasts differ from the forecasts of agents in the other group, but behavioral limitations lead them to agree to disagree. As information flows, the forecasts by agents of the two groups oscillate, and the group of agents that is at one instant relatively more optimistic may become at a future date less optimistic than the agents in the other group. These fluctuations in relative beliefs generate trade.

When evaluating an asset, agents consider their own view of fundamentals and the fact that the owner of the asset has an option to sell the asset in the future to agents in the other group. This option can be exercised at any time by the current owner, and the new owner gets, in turn, another option to sell the asset. These characteristics make the option "American" and give it a recursive structure. The value of the option is the value function of an optimal stopping problem. Since the buyer's willingness to pay is a function of the value of the option that he acquires, the payoff from stopping is, in turn, related to the value of the option. This gives us a fixed-point problem that the option value must satisfy. This difference between the current owner's demand price and his fundamental valuation, which is exactly the resale option value, can be reasonably called a bubble.[7] Fluctuations in the value of the bubble contribute an extra component to price volatility. We emphasize that the bubble in our model is a consequence of the divergence of opinions generated by the overestimation of informativeness of the distinct signals. On average, our agents are neither optimists nor pessimists.

In equilibrium, an asset owner will sell the asset to agents in the other group whenever his view of the fundamental is surpassed by the view of agents in the other group by a critical amount. Passages through this critical point determine turnover. When there are no trading costs, we show that the critical point is zero: it is optimal to sell the asset immediately after the valuation of fundamentals is "crossed" by the valuation of agents in the other group. Our agents' beliefs satisfy simple stochastic differential equations, and it is a consequence of properties of Brownian motion that once the beliefs of agents cross, they will cross infinitely many times in any finite period of time right afterward. This results in a trading frenzy, in which the unconditional average volume in any time interval is infinite. Since the equilibria display continuity with respect to the trading cost c, our model with small trading costs is able to capture the excessive trading observed in bubbles.

When trading costs are small, the value of the bubble and the extra volatility component are maximized. We show that increases in some parameter values, such as the degree of overconfidence or the information content of the signals, increase these three key variables. In this way, our model provides an explanation for the cross-sectional correlation between price, volume, and volatility that has been observed in bubbles. However, to obtain more realistic time-series dynamics, it may be necessary to allow the parameter values to change over time. In Section 7.5, we discuss how to accommodate fluctuations in parameter values, though we do not provide a theory that explains these oscillations.

In the model, increases in trading costs reduce the trading frequency, asset price volatility, and option value. For small trading costs, the effect on trading frequency is very significant. The impact on price volatility and on the size of the bubble is much more modest. As the trading cost increases, the increase in the critical point also raises the profit of the asset owner from each trade, thus partially offsetting the decrease in the value of the resale option caused by the reduction in trading frequency. Our analysis suggests that a transaction tax, as proposed by Tobin (1978), would, in fact, substantially reduce the amount of speculative trading in markets with small transaction costs but would have a limited effect on the size of the bubble or on price volatility. Since a Tobin tax will no doubt also deter trading generated by fundamental causes that are absent from our model, the limited impact of the tax on the size of the bubble and on price volatility cannot serve as an endorsement of the Tobin tax. The limited effect of transaction costs on the size of the bubble is also compatible with the observation of Shiller (2000) that bubbles have occurred in the real estate market, where transaction costs are high.[8]

The existence of the option component in the asset price creates potential violations to the law of one price. Through a simple example, we illustrate that the bubble may cause the price of a subsidiary to be larger than that of its parent firm. The intuition behind the example is that if a firm has two subsidiaries with fundamentals that are perfectly negatively correlated, there will be no differences in opinion, and hence no option component on the value of the parent firm, but possibly strong differences of opinion about the value of a subsidiary. In this example, our model also predicts that trading volume on the subsidiaries would be much larger than on the parent firm. This nonlinearity of the option value may help explain the "mispricing" of carve-outs that occurred in the late 1990s such as the 3Com-Palm case.

The paper is structured as follows. In Section 2, we present a brief literature review. Section 3 describes the structure of the model. Section 4 derives the evolution of agents' beliefs. In Section 5, we discuss the optimal stopping time problem and derive the equation for equilibrium option values. In Section 6, we solve for the equilibrium. Section 7 discusses several properties of the equilibrium when trading costs are small. In Section 8, we focus on the effect of trading costs. In Section 9, we construct an example in which the price of a subsidiary is larger than that of its parent firm. Section 10 concludes the paper with some discussion of implications for corporate finance. All proofs are in the appendix.

2. Related Literature

There is a large literature on the effects of heterogeneous beliefs. In a static framework, Miller (1977) and Chen, Hong, and Stein (2002) analyze the over-valuation generated by heterogeneous beliefs. This static framework cannot generate an option value or the dynamics of trading. Harris and Raviv (1993), Kandel and Pearson (1995), and Kyle and Lin (2002) study models in which trading is generated by heterogeneous beliefs. However, in all these models there is no speculative component in prices.

Psychology studies suggest that people overestimate the precision of their knowledge in some circumstances, especially for challenging judgment tasks (see Alpert and Raiffa 1982; Lichtenstein, Fischhoff, and Phillips 1982). Camerer (1995) argues that even experts can display overconfidence. A similar phenomenon is *illusion of knowledge*, the fact that persons who do not agree become more polarized when given arguments that serve both sides (Lord, Ross, and Lepper 1979) (see Barber and Odean 2001 and Hirshleifer 2001 for reviews of this literature). In finance, researchers have developed theoretical models to analyze the implications of overconfidence on financial markets (see, e.g., Kyle and Wang 1997; Daniel, Hirshleifer, and Subrahmanyam 1998; Odean 1998; Bernardo and Welch 2001). In these papers, overconfidence is typically modeled as an overestimation of the precision of one's information. We follow a similar approach but emphasize the speculative motive generated by overconfidence.

The bubble in our model, based on the recursive expectations of traders to take advantage of mistakes by others, is quite different from "rational bubbles" (see Blanchard and Watson 1982; Santos and Woodford 1997). In contrast to our setup, rational bubble models are incapable of connecting bubbles with turnover. In addition, in these models, assets must have (potentially) infinite maturity to generate bubbles. Although, for mathematical simplicity, we treat the infinite horizon case, the bubble in our model does not require infinite maturity. If an asset has a finite maturity, the bubble will tend to diminish as maturity approaches, but it would nonetheless exist in equilibrium.

Other mechanisms have been proposed to generate asset price bubbles (e.g., Allen and Gorton 1993; Allen, Morris, and Postlewaite 1993; Horst 2001; Duffie et al. 2002). None of these models emphasize the joint properties of bubble and trading volume observed in historical episodes.

3. The Model

There exists a single risky asset with a dividend process that is the sum of two components. The first component is a fundamental variable that determines future dividends. The second is "noise." The cumulative dividend process D_t satisfies

$$dD_t = f_t dt + \sigma_D dZ_t^D, \tag{1}$$

where Z^D is a standard Brownian motion and σ_D is a constant volatility parameter. The fundamental variable f is not observable. However, it satisfies

$$df_t = -\lambda\left(f_t - \bar{f}\right)dt + \sigma_f dZ_t^f, \tag{2}$$

where $\lambda \geq 0$ is the mean reversion parameter, $\bar{f}$ is the long-run mean of f, $\sigma_f > 0$ is a constant volatility parameter, and Z^f is a standard Brownian motion. The asset is in finite supply, and we normalize the total supply to unity.

There are two sets of risk-neutral agents. The assumption of risk neutrality not only simplifies many calculations but also serves to highlight the role of information in the model. Since our agents are risk-neutral, the dividend noise in equation (1) has no direct impact in the valuation of the asset. However, the presence of dividend noise makes it impossible to infer f perfectly from observations of the cumulative dividend process. Agents use the observations of D and any other signals that are correlated with f to infer current f and to value the asset. In addition to the cumulative dividend process, all agents observe a vector of signals s^A and s^B that satisfy

$$ds_t^A = f_t dt + \sigma_s dZ_t^A \tag{3}$$

and

$$ds_t^B = f_t dt + \sigma_s dZ_t^B, \tag{4}$$

where Z^A and Z^B are standard Brownian motions, and $\sigma_s > 0$ is the common volatility of the signals. We assume that all four processes Z^D, Z^f, Z^A, and Z^B are mutually independent.

Agents in group A (B) think of s^A (s^B) as their own signal, although they can also observe s^B (s^A). Heterogeneous beliefs arise because each agent believes that the informativeness of his own signal is larger than its true informativeness. Agents of group A (B) believe that innovations dZ^A (dZ^B) in the signal s^A (s^B) are correlated with the innovations dZ^f in the fundamental process, with ϕ ($0 < \phi < 1$) as the correlation parameter. Specifically, agents in group A believe that the process for s^A is

$$ds_t^A = f_t dt + \sigma_s \phi dZ_t^f + \sigma_s \sqrt{1 - \phi^2} dZ_t^A.$$

Although agents in group A perceive the correct unconditional volatility of the signal s^A, the correlation that they attribute to innovations causes them to overreact to signal s^A. Similarly, agents in group B believe that the process for s^B is

$$ds_t^B = f_t dt + \sigma_s \phi dZ_t^f + \sigma_s \sqrt{1 - \phi^2} dZ_t^B.$$

On the other hand, agents in group A (B) believe (correctly) that innovations to $s^B(s^A)$ are uncorrelated with innovations to Z^B (Z^A). We assume that the joint dynamics of the processes D, f, s^A, and s^B in the mind of agents of each group are public information.

Lemma 1 below shows that a larger ϕ increases the precision that agents attribute to their own forecast of the current level of fundamentals. For this reason, we shall refer to ϕ as the overconfidence parameter.[9]

Each group is large, and there is no short selling of the risky asset. To value future cash flows, we may assume either that every agent can borrow and lend at the same rate of interest r or, equivalently, that agents discount all future payoffs using rate r and that each group has infinite total wealth. These assumptions will facilitate the calculation of equilibrium prices.

4. Evolution of Beliefs

The model described in the previous section implies a particularly simple structure for the evolution of the difference in beliefs between the groups of traders. We show that this difference is a diffusion with volatility proportional to ϕ.

Since all variables are Gaussian, the filtering problem of the agents is standard. With Gaussian initial conditions, the conditional beliefs of agents in group $C \in \{A, B\}$ are Gaussian with mean $\hat{f}^c$ and variance γ^c. We shall characterize the stationary solution. Standard arguments (e.g., Rogers and Williams 1987, sec. 6.9; Liptser and Shiryaev 1977, Theorem 12.7) allow us to compute the variance of the stationary solution and the evolution of the conditional mean of beliefs. The variance of this stationary solution is the same for both groups of agents and equals

$$\gamma \equiv \frac{\sqrt{\left[\lambda + \left(\phi\sigma_f / \sigma_s\right)\right]^2 + \left(1 - \phi^2\right)\left[\left(2\sigma_f^2 / \sigma_s^2\right) + \left(\sigma_f^2 / \sigma_D^2\right)\right]} - \left[\lambda + \left(\phi\sigma_f / \sigma_s\right)\right]}{\left(1/\sigma_D^2\right) + \left(2/\sigma_s^2\right)}.$$

The following lemma justifies associating the parameter ϕ to "overconfidence."

Lemma 1. The stationary variance γ decreases with ϕ.

In addition, the conditional mean of the beliefs of agents in group A satisfies

$$d\hat{f}^A = -\lambda\left(\hat{f}^A - \bar{f}\right)dt + \frac{\phi\sigma_s\sigma_f + \gamma}{\sigma_s^2}\left(ds^A - \hat{f}^A dt\right)$$
$$+ \frac{\gamma}{\sigma_s^2}\left(ds^B - \hat{f}^A dt\right) + \frac{\gamma}{\sigma_D^2}\left(dD - \hat{f}^A dt\right). \tag{5}$$

Since f mean-reverts, the conditional beliefs also mean-revert. The other three terms represent the effects of "surprises." These surprises can be represented as standard mutually independent Brownian motions for agents in group A:

$$dW_A^A = \frac{1}{\sigma_s}\left(ds^A - \hat{f}^A dt\right), \tag{6}$$

$$dW_B^A = \frac{1}{\sigma_s}\left(ds^B - \hat{f}^A dt\right), \tag{7}$$

and

$$dW_D^A = \frac{1}{\sigma_D}\left(dD - \hat{f}^A dt\right). \tag{8}$$

Note that these processes are only Wiener processes in the mind of group A agents. Because of overconfidence ($\phi > 0$), agents in group A overreact to surprises in s^A. Similarly, the conditional mean of the beliefs of agents in group B satisfies

$$d\hat{f}^B = -\lambda\left(\hat{f}^B - \bar{f}\right)dt + \frac{\gamma}{\sigma_s^2}\left(ds^A - \hat{f}^B dt\right) + \frac{\phi\sigma_s\sigma_f + \gamma}{\sigma_s^2}\left(ds^B - \hat{f}^B dt\right)$$
$$+ \frac{\gamma}{\sigma_D^2}\left(dD - \hat{f}^B dt\right), \tag{9}$$

and the surprise terms can be represented as mutually independent Wiener processes:

$$dW_A^B = \frac{1}{\sigma_s}\left(ds^A - \hat{f}^B dt\right),$$

$$dW_B^B = \frac{1}{\sigma_s}\left(ds^B - \hat{f}^B dt\right),$$

$$dW_D^B = \frac{1}{\sigma_D}\left(dD - \hat{f}^B dt\right).$$

These processes are a standard three-dimensional Brownian motion only for agents in group B.

Since the beliefs of all agents have constant variance, we shall refer to the conditional mean of the beliefs as their *beliefs*. We let g^A and g^B denote the differences in beliefs:

$$g^A = \hat{f}^B - \hat{f}^A, \quad g^B = \hat{f}^A - \hat{f}^B.$$

The next proposition describes the evolution of these differences in beliefs.

Proposition 1.

$$dg^A = -\rho g^A dt + \sigma_g dW_g^A,$$

where

$$\rho = \sqrt{\left(\lambda + \phi\frac{\sigma_f}{\sigma_s}\right)^2 + \left(1 - \phi^2\right)\sigma_f^2\left(\frac{2}{\sigma_s^2} + \frac{1}{\sigma_D^2}\right)},$$

$$\sigma_g = \sqrt{2}\phi\sigma_f,$$

and W_g^A is a standard Wiener process for agents in group A, with innovations that are orthogonal to the innovations of $\hat{f}^A$.

Proposition 1 implies that the difference in beliefs g^A follows a simple mean-reverting diffusion process in the mind of group A agents. In particular, the volatility of the difference in beliefs is zero in the absence of overconfidence. A larger ϕ leads to greater volatility. In addition, $-\rho/2\sigma_g^2$ measures the pull toward the origin. A simple calculation shows that this *mean reversion*[10] decreases with ϕ. A higher ϕ causes an increase in fluctuations of opinions and a slower mean reversion.

In an analogous fashion, for agents in group B, g^B satisfies

$$dg^B = -\rho g^B dt + \sigma_g dW_g^B,$$

where W_g^B is a standard Wiener process, and it is independent of innovations to $\hat{f}^B$.

5. Trading

Fluctuations in the difference of beliefs across agents will induce trading. It is natural to expect that investors that are more optimistic about the prospects of future dividends will bid up the price of the asset and eventually hold the total (finite) supply. We shall allow for costs of trading: a seller pays $c \geq 0$ per unit of the asset sold. This cost may represent an actual cost of transaction or a tax.

At each t, agents in group $C \in \{A, B\}$ are willing to pay p_t^C for a unit of the asset. The presence of the short-sale constraint, a finite supply of the asset, and an infinite number of prospective buyers guarantee that any successful bidder will pay his reservation price.[11] The amount that an agent is willing to pay reflects the agent's fundamental valuation and the fact that he may be able to sell his holdings for a profit at a later date at the demand price of agents in the other group. If we let $o \in \{A, B\}$ denote the group of the current owner, $\bar{o}$ be the other group, and E_t^o be the expectation of members of group o, conditional on the information they have at t, then

$$p_t^o = \sup_{\tau \geq 0} E_t^o \left[\int_t^{t+\tau} e^{-r(s-t)} dD_s + e^{-r\tau} \left(p_{t+\tau}^{\bar{o}} - c \right) \right],$$

where τ is a stopping time, and $p_{t+\tau}^{\bar{o}}$ is the reservation value of the buyer at the time of transaction $t + \tau$.

Since $dD = \hat{f}_t^o dt + \sigma_D dW_D^o$, using the equations for the evolution of the conditional mean of beliefs (eqq. 5 and 9 above), we have that

$$\int_t^{t+\tau} e^{-r(s-t)} dD_s = \int_t^{t+\tau} e^{-r(s-t)} \left[\bar{f} + e^{-\lambda(s-t)} \left(\hat{f}_t^o - \bar{f} \right) \right] ds + M_{t+\tau}, \tag{10}$$

where $E_t^o M_{t+\tau} = 0$. Hence, we may rewrite equation (10) as

$$p_t^o = \max_{\tau \geq 0} E_t^o \left\{ \int_\tau^{t+\tau} e^{-r(s-t)} \left[\bar{f} + e^{-\lambda(s-t)} \left(\hat{f}_t^o - \bar{f} \right) \right] ds + e^{-r\tau} \left(p_{t+\tau}^{\bar{o}} - c \right) \right\}. \tag{11}$$

We shall start by postulating a particular form for the equilibrium price function, equation (12) below. Proceeding in a heuristic fashion, we derive properties that our candidate equilibrium price function should satisfy. We then construct a function that satisfies these properties and verify that we have produced an equilibrium.[12]

Since all the relevant stochastic processes are Markovian and time-homogeneous and traders are risk-neutral, it is natural to look for an equilibrium in which the demand price of the current owner satisfies

$$p_t^o = p^o \left(\hat{f}_t^o, g_t^o \right) = \frac{\bar{f}}{r} + \frac{\hat{f}_t^o - \bar{f}}{r + \lambda} + q\left(g_t^o \right), \tag{12}$$

with $q > 0$ and $q' > 0$. This equation states that prices are the sum of two components. The first part, $\left(\bar{f}/r \right) + \left[\left(\hat{f}_t^o - \bar{f} \right) \middle/ (r + \lambda) \right]$, is the expected present value of future dividends from the viewpoint of the current owner. The second is the value of the resale option, $q\left(g_t^o \right)$, which depends on the current difference between the beliefs of the other group's agents and the beliefs of the current owner. We call the first quantity the owner's fundamental valuation and the second the value of the resale option. Using (12) in equation (11) and collecting terms, we obtain

$$p_t^o = p^o \left(\hat{f}_t^o, g_t^o \right) = \frac{\bar{f}}{r} + \frac{\hat{f}_t^o - \bar{f}}{r + \lambda} + \sup_{\tau \geq 0} E_t^o \left\{ \left[\frac{g_{t+\tau}^{\bar{o}}}{r + \lambda} + q\left(g_{t+\tau}^{\bar{o}} \right) - c \right] e^{-r\tau} \right\}.$$

Equivalently, the resale option value satisfies

$$q\left(g_t^o\right)=\sup_{\tau\geq0} E_t^o\left\{\left[\frac{g_{t+\tau}^o}{\tau+\lambda}+q\left(g_{t+\tau}^{\bar{o}}\right)-c\right]e^{-r\tau}\right\}. \tag{13}$$

Hence to show that an equilibrium of the form (12) exists, it is necessary and sufficient to construct an option value function q that satisfies equation (13). This equation is similar to a Bellman equation. The current asset owner chooses an optimal stopping time to exercise his resale option. Upon the exercise of the option, the owner gets the "strike price" $\left[g_{t+\tau}^o/(r+\lambda)\right]+q\left(g_{t+\tau}^{\bar{o}}\right)$, the amount of excess optimism that the buyer has about the asset's fundamental value and the value of the resale option to the buyer, minus the cost c. In contrast to the optimal exercise problem of American options, the strike price in our problem depends on the resale option value function itself.

It is apparent from the analysis in this section that one could, in principle, treat an asset with a finite life. Equations (10) and (11) would apply with the obvious changes to account for the finite horizon. However, the option value q will now depend on the remaining life of the asset, introducing another dimension to the optimal exercise problem. The infinite horizon problem is stationary, greatly reducing the mathematical difficulty.

6. Equilibrium

In this section, we derive the equilibrium option value, duration between trades, and contribution of the option value to price volatility.

6.1. RESALE OPTION VALUE

The value of the option $q(x)$ should be at least as large as the gains realized from an immediate sale. The region in which the value of the option equals that of an immediate sale is the stopping region. The complement is the continuation region. In the mind of the risk-neutral asset holder, the discounted value of the option $e^{-rt}q\left(g_t^o\right)$ should be a martingale in the continuation region and a supermartingale in the stopping region. Using Ito's lemma and the evolution equation for g^o, we can state these conditions as

$$q(x)\geq\frac{x}{r+\lambda}+q(-x)-c \tag{14}$$

and

$$\frac{1}{2}\sigma_g^2q''-\rho xq'-rq\leq0, \tag{15}$$

with equality if (14) holds strictly. In addition, the function q should be continuously differentiable (smooth pasting). We shall derive a smooth function q that satisfies equations (14) and (15) and then use these properties and a growth condition on q to show that in fact the function q solves (13).

To construct the function q, we guess that the continuation region will be an interval $(-\infty, k^*)$, with $k^* > 0$. The variable k^* is the minimum amount of difference in opinions that generates a trade. As usual, we begin by examining the second-order ordinary differential equation that q must satisfy, albeit only in the continuation region:

$$\frac{1}{2}\sigma_g^2 u'' - \rho x u' - r u = 0. \tag{16}$$

The following proposition helps us construct an "explicit" solution to equation (16).

Proposition 2.
Let

$$h(x) = \begin{cases} U\left(\dfrac{r}{2\rho}, \dfrac{1}{2}, \dfrac{\rho}{\sigma_g^2} x^2\right) & \text{if } x \leq 0 \\[2em] \dfrac{2\pi}{\Gamma\left(\dfrac{1}{2}+(r/2\rho)\right)\Gamma\left(\dfrac{1}{2}\right)} M\left(\dfrac{r}{2\rho}, \dfrac{1}{2}, \dfrac{\rho}{\sigma_g^2} x^2\right) - U\left(\dfrac{r}{2\rho}, \dfrac{1}{2}, \dfrac{\rho}{\sigma_g^2} x^2\right) & \text{if } x > 0, \end{cases} \tag{17}$$

where $\Gamma(\cdot)$ is the gamma function, and $M: R^3 \to R$ and $U: R^3 \to R$ are two Kummer functions described in the appendix. The function $h(x)$ is positive and increasing in $(-\infty, 0)$. In addition, h solves equation (16) with

$$h(0) = \frac{\pi}{\Gamma\left(\dfrac{1}{2}+(r/2\rho)\right)\Gamma\left(\dfrac{1}{2}\right)}.$$

Any solution $u(x)$ to equation (16) that is strictly positive and increasing in $(-\infty, 0)$ must satisfy $u(x) = \beta_1 h(x)$ with $\beta_1 > 0$.

We shall also need properties of the function h that are summarized in the following lemma.

Lemma 2. For each
$x \in R, h(x) > 0,\ h'(x) > 0,\ h''(x) > 0,\ h'''(x) > 0, \lim_{x \to -\infty} h(x) = 0,$
and $\lim_{x \to -\infty} h'(x) = 0$.

Since q must be positive and increasing in $(-\infty, k^*)$, we know from Proposition 2 that

$$q(x) = \begin{cases} \beta_1 h(x) & \text{for } x < k^* \\[1em] \dfrac{x}{r+\lambda} + \beta_1 h(-x) - c & \text{for } x \geq k^*. \end{cases} \tag{18}$$

Since q is continuous and continuously differentiable at k^*,

$$\beta_1 h(k^*) - \frac{k^*}{r+\lambda} - \beta_1 h(-k^*) + c = 0,$$

$$\beta_1 h'(k^*) + \beta_1 h'(-k^*) - \frac{1}{r+\lambda} = 0.$$

These equations imply that

$$\beta_1 = \frac{1}{\left[h'(k^*) + h'(-k^*)\right](r+\lambda)}, \tag{19}$$

and k^* satisfies

$$\left[k^* - c(r+\lambda)\right]\left[h'(k^*) + h'(-k^*)\right] - h(k^*) + h(-k^*) = 0. \tag{20}$$

The next theorem shows that, for each c, there exists a unique pair (k^*, β_1) that solves equations (19) and (20). The smooth pasting conditions are sufficient to determine the function q and the "trading point" k^*.

THEOREM 1. For each trading cost $c \geq 0$, there exists a unique k^* that solves (20). If

$$c = 0, \text{ then } k^* = 0. \text{ If } c > 0, k^* > c(r+\lambda).$$

The next theorem establishes that the function q described by equation (18), with β_1 and k^* given by (19) and (20), solves (13). The proof consists of two parts. First, we show that (14) and (15) hold and that q' is bounded. We then use a standard argument to show that in fact q solves equation (13) (see, e.g., Kobila 1993 or Scheinkman and Zariphopoulou 2001 for similar arguments).

THEOREM 2. The function q constructed above is an equilibrium option value function. The optimal policy consists of exercising immediately if $g^o > k^*$; otherwise wait until the first time in which $g^o \geq k^*$.

It is a consequence of Theorem 2 that the process g^o will have values in $(-\infty, k^*)$. The value k^* acts as a barrier, and when g^o reaches k^*, a trade occurs, the owner's group switches, and the process is restarted at $-k^*$. The function $q(g^o)$ is the difference between the current owner's demand price and his fundamental valuation and can be legitimately called a bubble. When a trade occurs, this difference is

$$b \equiv q(-k^*) = \frac{1}{r+\lambda} \frac{h(-k^*)}{h'(k^*) + h'(-k^*)}. \tag{21}$$

Using equation (21), we can write the value of the resale option as

$$q(x) = \begin{cases} \dfrac{b}{h(-k^*)} h(x) & \text{for } x < k^* \\[4mm] \dfrac{x}{r+\lambda} + \dfrac{b}{h(-k^*)} h(-x) - c & \text{for } x \geq k^*. \end{cases} \tag{22}$$

6.2. DURATION BETWEEN TRADES

We let $w(x, k, r) = E^o[e^{-r\tau(x, k)}|x]$, with $\tau(x,k) = \inf\{s : g_{t+s}^0 > k\}$ given $g_t^0 = x \leq k$. The term $w(x, k, r)$ is the discount factor applied to cash flows received the first time the difference in beliefs reaches the level of k given that the current difference in beliefs is x. Standard arguments (e.g., Karlin and Taylor 1981, 243) show that w is a nonnegative and strictly monotone solution to

$$\frac{1}{2}\sigma_g^2 w_{xx} - \rho x w_x = rw, w(k,k,r) = 1.$$

Therefore, Proposition 2 implies that

$$w(x,k,r) = \frac{h(x)}{h(k)}. \tag{23}$$

Note that the free parameter β_1 does not affect w.

If $c > 0$, trading occurs the first time $t > s$ when $g_t^0 = k^*$ given that $g_s^0 = -k^*$. The expected duration between trades provides a useful measure of trading frequency. Since w is the moment-generating function of τ,

$$E\left[\tau(-k^*,k^*)\right] = -\frac{\partial w(-k^*,k^*,r)}{\partial r}\bigg|_{r=0}.$$

When $c = 0$, the expected duration between trades is zero. This is a consequence of Brownian local time, as we discuss below.

6.3. AN EXTRA VOLATILITY COMPONENT

The option component introduces an extra source of price volatility. Proposition 1 states that the innovations in the asset owner's beliefs f^o and the innovations in the difference of beliefs g^o are orthogonal. Therefore, the total price volatility is the sum of the volatility of the fundamental value in the asset owner's mind, $(\bar{f}/r) + \left[(\hat{f}_t^0 - \bar{f})/(r+\lambda)\right]$, and the volatility of the option component.

Proposition 3. The volatility from the option value component is

$$\eta(x) = \frac{\sqrt{2}\phi\sigma_f}{r+\lambda}\frac{h'(x)}{h'(k^*)+h'(-k^*)}\forall x < k^*. \tag{24}$$

Since $h' > 0$, the volatility of the option value is monotone.

The variance of an agent's valuation of the discounted dividends is

$$
\frac{1}{(r+\lambda)^2}\left[\left(\frac{\phi\sigma_s\sigma_f+\gamma}{\sigma_s}\right)^2+\left(\frac{\gamma}{\sigma_s}\right)^2+\left(\frac{\gamma}{\sigma_D}\right)^2\right]=
$$

$$
\left(\frac{2}{\sigma_s^2}+\frac{1}{\sigma_D^2}\right)^{-1}(r+\lambda)^{-2}\left\{\begin{bmatrix}2\lambda^2+\dfrac{2\lambda\phi\sigma_f}{\sigma_s}+\dfrac{2\sigma_f^2}{\sigma_s^2}+\dfrac{\sigma_f^2}{\sigma_D^2}\\[2ex]-2\lambda\left[\lambda^2+\dfrac{2\lambda\phi\sigma_f}{\sigma_s}+\left(2-\phi^2\right)\dfrac{\sigma_f^2}{\sigma_s^2}+\left(1-\phi^2\right)\dfrac{\sigma_f^2}{\sigma_D^2}\right]^{1/2}\end{bmatrix}\right\},
$$

which increases with ϕ if $\lambda > 0$ and equals $\sigma_f^2/(r+\lambda)^2$ if $\lambda = 0$. Therefore, an increase in overconfidence increases the volatility of the agent's valuation of discounted dividends. In the remainder of the paper, we ignore this effect, which vanishes when $\lambda = 0$, to focus on the extra volatility component caused by the option value.

7. Properties of Equilibria for Small Trading Costs

In this section, we discuss several of the characteristics of the equilibrium for small trading costs, including the volume of trade and the magnitudes of the bubble and of the extra volatility component. We also provide some comparative statics and show how parameter changes co-move price, volatility, and turnover.

7.1. TRADING VOLUME

It is a property of Brownian motion that if it hits the origin at t, it will hit the origin at an infinite number of times in any nonempty interval $[t, t + \Delta t)$. In our limit case of $c = 0$, this implies an infinite amount of trade in any nonempty interval that contains a single trade. When the cost of trade $c = 0$, in any time interval, turnover is either zero or infinity, and the unconditional average volume in any time interval is infinity.[13] The expected time between trades depends continuously on c, so it is possible to calibrate the model to obtain any average daily volume. However, a serious calibration would require accounting for other sources of trading, such as shocks to liquidity, and should match several moments of volume, volatility, and prices.

7.2. MAGNITUDE OF THE BUBBLE

When $c = 0$, a trade occurs each time traders' fundamental beliefs "cross." Nonetheless, the bubble at this trading point is strictly positive since

$$b = \frac{1}{2(r+\lambda)}\frac{h(0)}{h'(0)}.$$

Owners do not expect to sell the asset at a price above their own valuation, but the option has a positive value. This result may seem counterintuitive. To clarify it, it is worthwhile to examine the value of the option when trades occur whenever the absolute value of the differences in fundamental valuations equals an $\epsilon > 0$. An asset owner in group A (B) expects to sell the asset when agents in group B (A) have a fundamental valuation that exceeds the fundamental valuation of agents in group A (B) by ϵ, that is, $g^A = \epsilon$ $(g^A = -\epsilon)$. If we write b_0 for the value of the option for an agent in group A that buys the asset when $g^A = -\epsilon$ and b_1 for the value of the option for an agent of group B that buys the asset when $g^A = \epsilon$, then

$$b_0 = \left(\frac{\epsilon}{r+\lambda} + b_1\right)\frac{h(-\epsilon)}{h(\epsilon)}$$

where $h(-\epsilon)/h(\epsilon)$ is the discount factor from equation (23). Symmetry requires that $b_0 = b_1$ and hence

$$b_0 = \frac{\epsilon}{r+\lambda}\frac{h(-\epsilon)}{h(\epsilon)-h(-\epsilon)}.$$

As $\epsilon \to 0$,

$$b_0 \to \frac{1}{2(r+\lambda)}\frac{h(0)}{h'(0)} = b.$$

In this illustration, as $\epsilon \to 0$, trading occurs with higher frequency and the waiting time goes to zero. In the limit, traders will trade infinitely often and the small gains in each trade compound to a significant bubble. This situation is similar to the cost from hedging an option using a stop-loss strategy studied in Carr and Jarrow (1990).

It is intuitive that when σ_g becomes larger, there is more difference of beliefs, resulting in a larger bubble. Also, when ρ becomes larger, for a given level of difference in beliefs, the resale option is expected to be exercised quicker, and therefore there is also a larger bubble. In fact we can show that the following lemma is true.

Lemma 3. If c is small, b increases with σ_g and ρ and decreases with r and θ. For all $x < k^*$, $q(x) = b[h(x)/h(-k^*)]$ increases with σ_g and ρ and decreases with r and θ.

The proof of Lemma 3 actually shows that whenever c is small, the effect of a change in a parameter on the barrier is second-order.

Proposition 1 allows us to write σ_g and ρ using the parameters ϕ, λ, σ_f, $i_s = \sigma_f/\sigma_s$, and $i_D = \sigma_f/\sigma_D$, where i_s and i_D measure the information in each of the two signals and the dividend flow, respectively. To simplify calculations, we set $\lambda = 0$. Then

$$\sigma_g = \sqrt{2}\phi\sigma_f,$$

$$\rho = \sqrt{\left(2 - \phi^2\right)i_s^2 + \left(1 - \phi^2\right)i_D^2}.$$

Differentiating these equations, one can show the following: (1) As σ_f increases, σ_g increases and ρ is unchanged. Therefore, b and $q(x)$, for $x < k^*$, increase. The bubble increases with the volatility of the fundamental process. (2) As i_s or i_D increases, σ_g is unchanged and ρ increases since $0 < \phi < 1$. Therefore, b and $q(x)$, for $x < k^*$, increase. The bubble increases with the amount of information in the signals and the dividend flow. (3) As ϕ increases, σ_g increases and ρ decreases. Thus an increase in ϕ has offsetting effects on the size of the bubble. However, numerical exercises indicate that the size of the bubble always increases with ϕ.

7.3. MAGNITUDE OF THE EXTRA VOLATILITY COMPONENT

As the difference of opinions x approaches the trading point, the volatility of the option value approaches

$$\frac{\sqrt{2}\phi\sigma_f}{r + \lambda} \frac{h'\left(k^*\right)}{h'\left(k^*\right) + h'\left(-k^*\right)}.$$

We have the following lemma.

Lemma 4. If c is small, $\eta(k^*)$ decreases with the interest rate r and the degree of mean reversion λ and increases with the overconfidence parameter ϕ and the fundamental volatility σ_f.

This lemma implies that an increase in the volatility of fundamentals has an additional effect on price volatility at trading points, through an increase in the volatility of the option component.

7.4. PRICE, VOLATILITY, AND TURNOVER

Our model provides a link between asset prices, price volatility, and share turnover. Since these are endogenous variables, their relationship will typically depend on which exogenous variable is shifted. In this subsection, we illustrate this link using numerical examples with a small trading cost.

Figure 10.1 shows the effect of changes in ϕ on the equilibrium when there is a small transaction cost on the trading barrier k^*, expected duration between

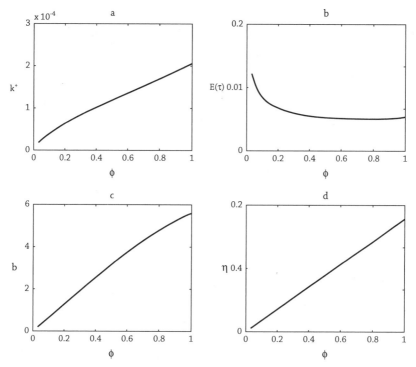

Figure 10.1 EFFECT OF OVERCONFIDENCE LEVEL

a, trading barrier; *b*, duration between trades; *c*, bubble; *d*, extra volatility component. Here, $r = 5$ percent, $\lambda = 0$, $\theta = 0.1$, $i_s = 2.0$, $i_D = 0$, and $c = 10^{-6}$. The values of the bubble and the extra volatility component are computed at the trading point. The trading barrier, the bubble, and the extra volatility component are measured as multiples of $\sigma_f/(r + \lambda)$, the fundamental volatility of the asset.

trades, the bubble at the trading point *b*, and the volatility of the bubble at the trading point, $\eta(k^*)$. The expected duration between trades is measured in years. The terms k^*, $\eta(k^*)$, and *b* are measured in multiples of the fundamental volatility $\sigma_f/(r + \lambda)$.[14] Recall that, as ϕ increases, the volatility parameter σ_g in the difference of beliefs increases, whereas the mean reversion parameter ρ decreases. As a result, the resale option becomes more valuable to the asset owner, the bubble and the extra volatility component become larger, and the optimal trading barrier becomes higher. The duration between trades is determined by two offsetting effects as ϕ increases. On the one hand, the trading barrier becomes higher, making the duration between trades longer. On the other hand, the volatility σ_g of the difference in beliefs increases, causing the duration to be shorter. As we stated, the proof of Lemma 3 shows that, when *c* is small, the change in the trading barrier k^* is second-order. Thus the duration between trades typically decreases, as illustrated in Figure 10.1b.

Figure 10.2 shows the effect of changes in the volatility of the noise in signals σ_s on the equilibrium, again with a small transaction cost. We measure the changes of σ_s in terms of the ratio $i_s = \sigma_f/\sigma_s$. As i_s increases, the mean reversion

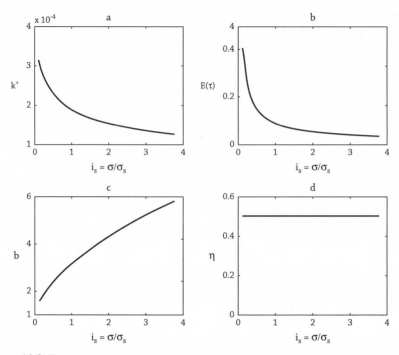

Figure 10.2 EFFECT OF INFORMATION IN SIGNALS

a, trading barrier; *b*, duration between trades; *c*, bubble; *d*, extra volatility component. Here, $r = 5$ percent, $\lambda = 0$, $\theta = 0.1$, $\phi = 0.7$, $i_D = 0$, and $c = 10^{-6}$. The values of the bubble and the extra volatility component are computed at the trading point. The trading barrier, the bubble, and the extra volatility component are measured as multiples of $\sigma_f/(r + \lambda)$, the fundamental volatility of the asset.

parameter ρ of the difference in beliefs increases, and the volatility parameter σ_g is unchanged. Intuitively, the increase in ρ causes the trading barrier and the duration between trades to drop. Nevertheless, the bubble at the trading point becomes larger because of the increase in trading frequency. The extra volatility component η is almost independent of i_s since it is essentially determined by ϕ and σ_f as shown in equation (24).

In both cases, there is a monotonically increasing relationship between the size of the bubble at the trading point and duration between trades. In addition, the extra price volatility either increases or does not decrease. We have also verified that this qualitative relationship holds for many other parameter values. In our risk-neutral world, we may consider several assets and analyze the equilibrium in each market independently. In this way our comparative statics properties can be translated into results about correlations among equilibrium variables in the different markets. Thus our model is potentially capable of explaining the observed cross-sectional correlation between log market/book and log turnover for U.S. stocks in the period 1996–2000 as documented by Cochrane (2002) and a similar cross-sectional correlation between the price ratio of China's A shares to B shares and turnover (see Mei, Scheinkman, and Xiong 2003).

7.5. CRASHES AND FLUCTUATIONS IN PARAMETERS

There are several ways in which we can imagine a change in equilibrium that brings the bubble to zero. The fundamental of the asset may become observable. The overconfident agents may correct their overconfidence. The fundamental volatility of the asset may disappear. For concreteness, imagine that agents in both groups believe that the asset fundamental will become observable at a date determined by a Poisson process that has a parameter θ and is independent of the four Brownian motions described earlier in the model. Once the fundamental becomes observable, agents in each group believe that the beliefs of agents in the other group will collapse to their own. In this case, it is easy to see that the option value

$$q\left(g_t^0\right) = \sup_{\tau \geq 0} \mathrm{E}_t^0 \left\{ \left[\frac{g_{t+\tau}^0}{r+\lambda} + q\left(g_{t+\tau}^0\right) - c \right] e^{-(r+\theta)\tau} \right\}.$$

Effectively, a higher discount rate $r + \theta$ is used for the profits from exercising the option.

Cochrane (2002) shows that there was a (time-series) correlation between the New York Stock Exchange index and NYSE volume through the 1929 boom and crash and between the NASDAQ index and NASDAQ volume throughout the Internet bubble. To reproduce such a correlation in a nontrivial manner, we would have to generalize our model to account for parameter changes, in the same spirit as our discussion of crashes. For concreteness, imagine that the overconfidence parameter ϕ or the informativeness of signals i_s can assume a finite number of values and that the value of the parameter follows a Markov process with Poisson times that are independent of all the other relevant uncertainty. The model will then produce results that are qualitatively similar to the case in which these parameters are constant, except that the average size of the bubble at any time will depend on the current value of the parameter. In this way, we can admit fluctuations on the size of the bubble and turnover rates, although a more interesting discussion should account for reasons for the parameter fluctuations.

8. Effect of Trading Costs

Using the results established in Section 6.1, we can show that increasing the trading cost c raises the trading barrier k^* and reduces b, $q(x)$, and $\eta(x)$. In fact, we have the following proposition.

Proposition 4. If c increases, the optimal trading barrier k^* increases. Furthermore, the bubble $q(x)$ and the extra volatility component $\eta(x)$ decrease for all $x < k^*(c)$. As $c \to 0$, $dk^*/dc \to \infty$, but the derivatives of b, $q(x)$, and $\eta(x)$ are always finite.

In order to illustrate the effects of trading costs, we use the following parameter values from our previous numerical exercise: $r = 5\%$, $\phi = 0.7$, $\lambda = 0$, $\theta = 0.1$, $i_s = 2.0$, and $i_D = 0$. Figure 10.3 shows the effect of trading costs on the trading barrier k^*, expected duration between trades, the bubble at the trading point b, and the volatility of the bubble at the trading point, $\eta(k^*)$.

Figure 10.3a shows the equilibrium trading barrier k^*. For comparison, we also graph the amount $c(r + \lambda)$, which corresponds to the difference in beliefs that would justify trade if the option value was ignored. The difference between these two quantities represents the "profits" that the asset owner thinks he is obtaining when he exercises the option to sell. When the trading cost is zero, the asset owner sells the asset immediately when it is profitable, and these profits are infinitely small. As the trading cost increases, the optimal trading barrier increases, and the rate of increase near $c = 0$ is dramatic since the derivative dk^*/dc is infinite at the origin. As a result, the trading frequency is greatly reduced by the increasing trading cost as shown in Figure 10.3b.

Figures 10.3c and 10.3d show that trading costs also reduce the bubble and the extra volatility component, but, as guaranteed by Proposition 4, at a limited rate even near $c = 0$. Although one could expect that the strong reduction in trading

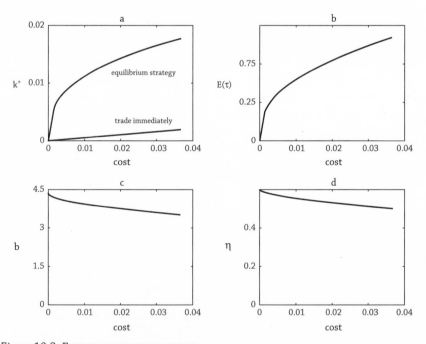

Figure 10.3 EFFECT OF TRADING COSTS

a, trading barrier; b, duration between trades; c, bubble; d, extra volatility component. Here, $r = 5$ percent, $\phi = 0.7$, $\lambda = 0$, $\theta = 0.1$, $i_s = 2.0$, and $i_D = 0$. The values of the bubble and the extra volatility component are computed at the trading point. The trading barrier, the bubble, the extra volatility component, and trading cost are measured as multiples of $\sigma_f/(r + \lambda)$, the fundamental volatility of the asset.

frequency should greatly reduce the bubble, this effect is partially offset by the increase in profits in each trade.[15] Similar intuition applies to the effect of the trading cost on the extra volatility component.

To estimate the impact of an increase in trading costs, measured as a proportion of price, as opposed to a multiple of fundamental volatility, we must take a stand concerning the relationship between price and volatility of fundamentals. For the parameter values used in our example, Figure 10.3c shows that the bubble at the trading point, for $c \sim 0$, is close to four times the fundamental volatility parameter $\sigma_f/(r + \lambda)$. The drop in prices of Internet stocks from the late 1990s until today exceeds 80%. If we take this variation as a measure of the size of the bubble in the late 1990s, then the size of the fundamental volatility also must have been approximately 20% of trading prices. In this way, we can reinterpret the values in the figures as multiples of prices. The numerical results indicate that in this case a tax of 1% of prices would have caused a reduction of less than 20% to the magnitudes of both the bubble and the extra volatility component.

The effectiveness of a trading tax in reducing speculative trading has been hotly debated since Tobin's (1978) initial proposal for a transaction tax in foreign currency markets. Shiller (2000, 225–228) provides an overview of the current status of this debate. Our model implies that for small trading costs, increases in trading costs have a much larger impact in trading frequency than in excess volatility or the magnitude of the price bubble. In reality, trading also occurs for other reasons, such as liquidity shocks or changes in risk-bearing capacity, that are not considered in our analysis; for this reason, the limited impact of transaction costs on volatility and price bubbles cannot serve as an endorsement of a tax on trading. Our numerical exercise can also answer a question raised by Shiller of why bubbles can exist in real estate markets, where the transaction costs are typically high.

9. Can the Price of a Subsidiary Be Larger Than That of Its Parent Firm?

The existence of the option value component in asset prices can potentially create violations to the law of one price and even make the price of a subsidiary exceed that of a parent company. In this section, we use a simple example to illustrate this phenomenon.

There are two firms, indexed by 1 and 2. For simplicity, we assume that the dividend processes of both assets follow the process in equation (1) with the same parameter σ_D, but with independent innovations and with different fundamental variables f_1 and f_2, respectively. The fundamental variables f_1 and f_2 are unobservable, and both follow the mean-reverting process in equation (2) with the same parameters $\lambda = 0$, $\overline{f}$, and σ_f.

There is a third firm, and the dividend flow of firm 3 is exactly the sum of the dividend flows of firms 1 and 2. In this sense, firms 1 and 2 are both subsidiaries of firm 3. In addition, it is known to all participants that $(f_1)_t + (f_2)_t = f_3$, a constant. This implies that innovations to f_1 and f_2 are perfectly negatively correlated. In particular, the price of a share of firm 3 is f_3/r.

However, according to our analysis, a speculative component exists in the prices of the shares of firms 1 and 2. Since $\hat{f}_1^c + f_2^c = f_3$ for $C \in \{A, B\}$, when agents in group A are holding firm 1, agents in group B must be holding firm 2, and the option components in the prices of these two firms are exactly the same.

The numerical exercise in Section 7.4 shows that the magnitude of the option component can equal four or five times fundamental volatility. If fundamental volatility is large relative to the discounted value of fundamentals, the value of one of the subsidiaries will exceed the value of firm 3, even though all prices are nonnegative.[16] Although highly stylized, this analysis may help clarify the episodes such as 3Com's equity carve-out of Palm and its subsequent spinoff.[17] In early 2000, for a period of over two months, the total market capitalization of 3Com was significantly less than the market value of its holding in Palm, a subsidiary of 3Com. Other examples of this kind are discussed in Schill and Zhou (2001), Mitchell, Pulvino, and Stafford (2002), and Lamont and Thaler (2003). Our model also predicts that trading in the subsidiary would be much higher than trading in the parent company because of the higher fluctuation in beliefs about the value of the subsidiary. In fact, Lamont and Thaler show that the turnover rate of the subsidiaries' stocks was, on average, six times higher than that of the parent firms' stocks.

This example also indicates that the diversification of a firm reduces the bubble component in the firm's stock price because diversification reduces the fundamental uncertainty of the firm, therefore reducing the potential disagreements among investors. This result is consistent with the diversification discount "puzzle"—the fact that the stocks of diversified firms appear to trade at a discount compared to the stocks of undiversified firms (see, e.g., Lang and Stulz 1994; Berger and Ofek 1995).

10. Conclusion and Further Discussions

In this paper, we provide a simple model to study bubbles and trading volume that result from speculative trading among agents with heterogeneous beliefs. Heterogeneous beliefs arise from the presence of overconfident agents. With a short-sale constraint, an asset owner has an option to sell the asset to other agents with more optimistic beliefs. Agents value this option and consequently pay prices that exceed their own valuation of future dividends because they believe that in the future they will find a buyer willing to pay even more. We solve the optimal exercise problem of an asset owner and derive, in an almost analytic form, many of the equilibrium variables of interest. This allows us to characterize properties of the magnitude of the bubble, trading frequency, and asset price volatility and to show that the model is consistent with the observation that in actual historical bubbles, volatility and turnover are also inordinate. Theoretical results and numerical exercises suggest that a small trading tax may be effective in reducing speculative trading, but it may not be very effective in reducing price volatility or the size of the bubble. Through a simple example, we also illustrate that the bubble can cause the price of a subsidiary to be larger than that of its parent firm, a violation of the law of one price.

It is natural to conjecture that the existence of a speculative component in asset prices has implications for corporate strategies. Firm managers may be able to profit by adopting strategies that boost the speculative component.

The underpricing of a firm's initial public offering (IPO) has been puzzling. Rajan and Servaes (1997) show that higher initial returns on an IPO lead to more analysts and media coverage. Since investors may disagree about the precision of information provided by the media, the increase in this coverage could increase the option component of the stock. Therefore, IPO underpricing could be a strategy used by firm managers to boost the price of their stocks. If this mechanism is operative, underpricing is more likely to occur when managers hold a larger share of the firm. This agrees with the empirical results in Aggarwal, Krigman, and Womack (2002). According to our model, a bigger underpricing should be associated with a larger trading volume. In fact, Reese (2000) finds that the higher initial IPO returns are associated with larger trading volume for more than three years after issuance. In a similar fashion, our framework may also be useful for understanding returns and volume on name changes (adding "dot-com").

In addition, if prices contain a large nonfundamental component, many standard views in both corporate finance and asset pricing that use stock prices as a measure of fundamental value will be substantially altered. For example, Bolton, Scheinkman, and Xiong (2002) analyze managerial contracts in such a model. The paper shows that the presence of overconfidence on the part of potential stock buyers could induce incumbent shareholders to use short-term stock compensation to motivate managerial behavior that increases short-term prices at the expense of long-term performance. This provides an alternative to the common view that the recent corporate scandals were caused by a lack of adequate board supervision.

Appendix:

PROOFS

Proof of Lemma 1

Let $\vartheta(\phi) = \lambda + \phi(\sigma_f/\sigma_s)$ and $i(\phi) = (1 - \phi^2)\left[(2\sigma_f^2/\sigma_s^2) + (\sigma_f^2/\sigma_D^2)\right]$. Then

$$\frac{d\gamma}{d\phi} \sim \frac{1}{2} \frac{2\vartheta(d\vartheta/d\phi) + (d_l/d\phi)}{\sqrt{(\vartheta^2 + l)}} - \frac{d\vartheta}{d\phi}$$

$$= \left(\frac{\vartheta}{\sqrt{\vartheta^2 + 1}} - 1 \right) \frac{d\vartheta}{d\phi} + \frac{1}{2\sqrt{\vartheta^2 + l}} \frac{d_l}{d\phi} \leq 0.$$

Proof of Proposition 1

The process for g^A can be derived from equations (5) and (9):

$$dg^A = d\hat{f}^B - d\hat{f}^A = -\left(\lambda + \frac{2\gamma + \phi\sigma_s\sigma_f}{\sigma_s^2} + \frac{\gamma}{\sigma_D^2} \right) g^A dt + \frac{\phi\sigma_f}{\sigma_s} \left(ds^B - ds^A \right).$$

Using the formula for γ, we may write the mean-reversion parameter as

$$\rho = \sqrt{\left(\lambda + \phi \frac{\sigma_f}{\sigma_s} \right)^2 + (1 - \phi^2)\sigma_f^2 \left(\frac{2}{\sigma_s^2} + \frac{1}{\sigma_D^2} \right)}.$$

Using equations (6) and (7), we get

$$dg^A = -\rho g^A dt + \frac{\phi\sigma_f}{\sigma_s} \left(\sigma_s dW_B^A - \sigma_s dW_A^A \right).$$

The result follows by writing

$$W_g^A = \frac{1}{\sqrt{2}} \left(W_B^A - W_A^A \right).$$

It is easy to verify that innovations to W_g^A are orthogonal to innovations to $\hat{f}^A$ in the mind of agents in group A.

Proof of Proposition 2

Let $\upsilon(y)$ be a solution to the differential equation

$$y\upsilon''(y) + \left(\frac{1}{2} - y \right) \upsilon'(y) - \frac{r}{2\rho} \upsilon(y) = 0. \tag{A1}$$

It is straightforward to verify that $u(x) = \upsilon((\rho/\sigma_g^2)x^2)$ satisfies equation (16). The general solution of equation (A1) is (see Abramowitz and Stegun 1964, chap. 13)

$$\upsilon(y) = \alpha M\left(\frac{r}{2\rho}, \frac{1}{2}, y \right) + \beta U\left(\frac{r}{2\rho}, \frac{1}{2}, y \right),$$

where $M(\cdot, \cdot, \cdot)$ and $U(\cdot, \cdot, \cdot)$ are Kummer functions defined as

$$M(a, b, y) = 1 + \frac{ay}{b} + \frac{(a)_2 y^2}{(b)_2 2!} + \dots + \frac{(a)_n y^n}{(b)_n n!} + \dots,$$

with $(a)_n = a(a + 1)(a + 2) \dots (a + n - 1)$ and $(a)_0 = 1$; and

$$U(a,b,y) = \frac{\pi}{\sin \pi b}\left[\frac{M(a,b,y)}{\Gamma(1+a-b)\Gamma(b)} - y^{1-b}\frac{M(1+a-b,2-b,y)}{\Gamma(a)\Gamma(2-b)}\right].$$

Furthermore, $M_y(a, b, y) > 0$, for all $y > 0$, $M(a, b, y) \to \infty$, and $U(a, b, y) \to 0$ as $y \to +\infty$.

Given a solution u to equation (16), we can construct two solutions v to equation (A1) by using the values of the function for $x < 0$ and for $x > 0$. We shall denote the corresponding linear combinations of M and U by $\alpha_1 M + \beta_1 U$ and $\alpha_2 M + \beta_2 U$. If these combinations are constructed from the same u, their values and first derivatives must have the same limit as $x \to 0$. To guarantee that $u(x)$ is positive and increasing for $x \to 0$, α_1 must be zero. Therefore,

$$u(x) = \beta_1 U\left(\frac{r}{2\rho}, \frac{1}{2}, \frac{\rho}{\sigma_g^2}x^2\right) \quad \text{if } x \le 0.$$

The solution must be continuously differentiable at $x = 0$. From the definition of the two Kummer functions, we can show that

$$x \to 0-, u(x) \to \frac{\beta_1 \pi}{\Gamma\left(\frac{1}{2}+(r/2\rho)\right)\Gamma\left(\frac{1}{2}\right)}, \qquad u'(x) \to \frac{\beta_1 \pi\sqrt{\rho}}{\sigma_g\Gamma(r/2\rho)\Gamma\left(\frac{3}{2}\right)},$$

$$x \to 0+, u(x) \to \alpha_2 + \frac{\beta_2 \pi}{\Gamma\left(\frac{1}{2}+(r/2\rho)\right)\Gamma\left(\frac{1}{2}\right)}, \qquad u'(x) \to -\frac{\beta_2 \pi\sqrt{\rho}}{\sigma_g\Gamma(r/2\rho)\Gamma\left(\frac{3}{2}\right)}.$$

By matching the values and first-order derivatives of $u(x)$ from the two sides of $x = 0$, we have

$$\beta_2 = -\beta_1, \quad \alpha_2 = \frac{2\beta_1 \pi}{\Gamma\left(\frac{1}{2}+(r/2\rho)\Gamma\left(\frac{1}{2}\right)\right)} > 0.$$

The function h is a solution to equation (16) that satisfies

$$h(0) = \frac{\pi}{\Gamma\left(\frac{1}{2}+(r/2\rho)\right)\Gamma\left(\frac{1}{2}\right)} > 0,$$

and $h(\infty) = 0$. Equation (16) guarantees that at any critical point at which $h < 0$, h has a maximum, and at any critical point at which $h > 0$, it has a minimum. Hence h is strictly positive and increasing in $(-\infty, 0)$.

Proof of Lemma 2

Write $\alpha = \sigma_g^2/2\rho > 0$ and $\beta = \eta/\rho > 0$. The function $h(x)$ is a positive, and increasing in $(-\infty, 0)$, solution to $\alpha h'' xh' - \beta h = 0$.

If $x^* \in R$ with $h(x^*) > 0$ and $h'(x^*) = 0$, then $h''(x^*) = \beta h(x^*)/\alpha > 0$. Hence h has no local maximum while it is positive, and as a consequence, it is always positive and has no local maxima. In particular, h is monotonically increasing. Since $h' > 0$ for $x \leq 0$ and $h'' \geq 0$ for $x \geq 0$, $h'(x) > 0$ for all x. From the solution constructed in Proposition 2, $\lim_{x \to \infty} h(x) = 0$.

Note that any solution to the differential equation is infinitely differentiable. Next, we show that h is convex. For $x > 0$, $h''(x) = [xh'(x)/\alpha] + [\beta h(x)/\alpha] > 0$. To prove that h is also convex for $x < 0$, let us assume that there exists $x^* < 0$ such that $h''(x^*) \leq 0$. Then

$$h'''(x^*) = \frac{x^* h''(x^*)}{\alpha} + \frac{(\beta+1)h'(x^*)}{\alpha} > 0.$$

This directly implies that $h''(x) < 0$ for $x < x^*$. Then $\lim_{x \to \infty} h'(x) = \infty$. In this situation the boundary condition $h(-\infty) = 0$ cannot be satisfied. In this way, we get a contradiction.

Let $v(x) = h'(x)$. The function $v(x)$ is positive and increasing. Also, v satisfies $\alpha v''(x) xv'(x) (\beta + 1)v(x) = 0$. By repeating the proof that we use for h, we can show that $v(x)$ is convex and $\lim_{x \to -\infty} v(x) = 0$. In fact, one can show that any higher-order derivative of $h(x)$ is positive, increasing, and convex.

Proof of Theorem 1

Let

$$l(k) = \left[k - c(r + \lambda)\right]\left[h'(k) + h'(-k)\right] - h(k) + h(-k).$$

We first show that there exists a unique k^* that solves $l(k) = 0$.

If $c = 0$, then $l(0) = 0$ and $l'(k) = k[h''(k) \, h''(k)] > 0$ for all $k \neq 0$. Therefore, $k^* = 0$ is the only root of $l(k) = 0$.

If $c > 0$, then $l(k) < 0$ for all $k \in [0, c(r + \lambda)]$. Since h'' and h''' are increasing (Lemma 2), for all $k > c(r + \lambda)$,

$$l'(k) = \left[k - c(r + \lambda)\right]\left[h''(-k)\right] > 0,$$
$$l''(k) = h''(k) - h''(-k) + \left[k - c(r + \lambda)\right]\left[h'''(k) - h'''(-k)\right] > 0.$$

Therefore, $l(k) = 0$ has a unique solution $k^* > c(r + \lambda)$.

Proof of Theorem 2

First we show that q satisfies equation (14). Using the notation introduced in equations (21) and (22), we have

$$q(-x) = \begin{cases} \dfrac{b}{h(-k^*)} h(-x) & \text{for } x > -k^* \\[4mm] \dfrac{-x}{r+\lambda} + \dfrac{b}{h(-k^*)} h(x) - c & \text{for } x \leq -k^*. \end{cases}$$

We must establish that

$$U(x) = q(x) - \frac{x}{r+\lambda} - q(-x) + c \geq 0.$$

A simple calculation shows that

$$U(x) = \begin{cases} 2c & \text{for } x < -k^* \\[4mm] \dfrac{-x}{r+\lambda} + \dfrac{b}{h(-k^*)}\left[h(x) - h(-x)\right] + c & \text{for } x - k^* \leq x \leq k^* \\[4mm] 0 & \text{for } x > k^*. \end{cases}$$

Thus

$$U''(x) = \frac{b}{h(-k^*)}\left[h''(-x)\right], \; -k^* \leq x \leq k^*.$$

From Lemma 2 we know that $U''(x) > 0$ for $0 < x < k^*$ and $U''(x) < 0$ for $-k^* < x < 0$. Since $U'(k^*) = 0$, $U'(x) < 0$ for $0 < x < k^*$. On the other hand, $U'(k^*) = 0$, so $U'(x) < 0$ for $-k^* < x < 0$. Therefore, $U(x)$ is monotonically decreasing for $-k^* < x < k^*$. Since $U(k^*) = 2c > 0$ and $U(k^*) = 0$, $U(x) > 0$ for $-k^* < x < k^*$.

We now show that equation (15) holds. By construction, it holds in the region $x \leq k^*$. Therefore, we need only to show that equation (15) is valid for $x \geq k^*$. In this region,

$$q(x) = \frac{x}{r+\lambda} + \frac{b}{h(-k^*)} h(-x) - c;$$

thus

$$q'(x) = \frac{1}{r+\lambda} - \frac{b}{h(-k^*)} h'(-x)$$

and

$$q''(x) = \frac{b}{h(-k^*)} h''(-x).$$

Hence,

$$\frac{1}{2}\sigma_g^2 q''(x) - \rho x q'(x) - rq(x) = \frac{b}{h(-k^*)}\left[\frac{1}{2}\sigma_g^2 h''(-x) + \rho x h'(-x) - rh(-x)\right]$$

$$- \frac{r+\rho}{r+\lambda}x + rc$$

$$= -\frac{r+\rho}{r+\lambda}x + rc \le -(r+\rho)c + rc$$

$$= -\rho c < 0,$$

where the inequality comes from the fact that $x \ge k^* > (r + \lambda)c$ from Theorem 1. Also, q has an increasing derivative in $(-\infty, k^*)$ and has a derivative bounded in absolute value by $1/(r + \lambda)$ in (k^*, ∞). Hence q' is bounded.

If τ is any stopping time, the version of Ito's lemma for twice-differentiable functions with absolutely continuous first derivatives (e.g., Revuz and Yor 1999, chap. 6) implies that

$$e^{-r\tau}q(g_\tau^0) = q(g_0^0) + \int_0^\tau \left[\frac{1}{2}\sigma_g^2 q''(g_s^0) - \rho g_s^0 q'(g_s^0) rq(g_s^0)\right]ds$$

$$+ \int_0^\tau \sigma_g q'(g_s^0) dW_s.$$

Equation (15) states that the first integral is nonpositive, and the bound on q' guarantees that the second integral is a martingale. Using equation (14), we obtain

$$E^0\left\{e^{-r\tau}\left[\frac{g_\tau^0}{r+\lambda} + q(-g_\tau^0) - c\right]\right\} \le E^0\left[e^{-r\tau}q(g_\tau^0)\right] \le q(g_0^0).$$

This shows that no policy can yield more than $q(x)$.

Now consider the stopping time $\tau = \inf\{t : g_t^0 \ge k^*\}$. Such a τ is finite with probability one, and g_s^0 is in the continuation region for $s < \tau$. Using exactly the same reasoning as above, but recalling that in the continuation region (15) holds with equality, we obtain

$$q(g^0) = E^0\left\{e^{-r\tau}\left[\frac{g_\tau^0}{r+\lambda} + q(-g_\tau^0) - c\right]\right\}.$$

Proof of Proposition 3

Since

$$q(x) = \frac{1}{r+\lambda}\frac{h(x)}{h'(k) + h'(-k)},$$

the volatility of $q(g_t^0)$ is given by

$$\frac{1}{r+\lambda}\frac{h'(g_t^0)}{h'(k)+h'(-k)}$$

multiplied by the volatility of g_t^o. From the proof of Proposition 1,

$$dg_t^o = -\rho g_t^o dt + \frac{\phi\sigma_f}{\sigma_s}(ds^{\bar{o}} - ds^o).$$

From equations (3) and (4), the volatility of $s^{\bar{o}} - s^o$ is $\sqrt{2\sigma_s}$ in an objective measure.

Hence the volatility of g^o is $\sqrt{2}\phi\sigma_f$.

Proof of Lemma 3

When $c = 0$, the magnitude of the bubble at the trading point is

$$b_o = \frac{\sigma_g}{2\sqrt{2\rho}(r+\lambda)}\frac{\Gamma\big((r+\theta)/2\rho\big)}{\Gamma\Big(\frac{1}{2}+\big[(r+\theta)/2\rho\big]\Big)}.$$

It is obvious that b_0 increases with σ_g. We can directly show that b_0 increases with ρ and decreases with r and θ by plotting it.

When $c = 0$, the bubble is $q_0(x) = b_0\big[h(x)/h(0)\big]$, where $h(x)$ is a positive and increasing solution to

$$\frac{1}{2}\sigma_g^2 h''(x) - \rho x h'(x) - (r+\theta)h(x) = 0,$$

$$h(0) = \frac{\pi}{\Gamma\Big(\frac{1}{2}+\big[(r+\theta)/2\rho\big]\Big)\Gamma\Big(\frac{1}{2}\Big)}.$$

Note that $q_0(x)$ is not affected by letting $h(0) = 1$.

Assume $\tilde{\sigma}_g > \sigma_g$, let $\tilde{h}(x)$ solve $\frac{1}{2}\tilde{\sigma}_g^2 \tilde{h}''(x) - \rho x \tilde{h}'(x) - (r+\theta)\tilde{h}(x) = 0$, $\tilde{h}(-\infty) = 0$,

and

$$\tilde{h}(0) = \frac{\pi}{\Gamma\Big(\frac{1}{2}+\big[(r+\theta)/2\rho\big]\Big)\Gamma\Big(\frac{1}{2}\Big)}.$$

We show that $\tilde{h}(x) > h(x)$ for all $x < 0$. Let $f(x) = \tilde{h}(x) - h(x)$. Then from Lemma 2, $f(-\infty) = f(0) = 0$. Suppose that f has a local minimum x^* with $f(x^*) < 0$. If such a local minimum exists, $f'(x^*)=0$ and $f''(x^*)\geq 0$. On the other hand, from the equations satisfied by $\tilde{h}(x)$ and $h(x)$, we have

$$\frac{1}{2}\left[\tilde{\sigma}_g^2\tilde{h}''(x)-\sigma_g^2 h''(x)\right]-\rho x\left[\tilde{h}'(x)-h'(x)\right]-(r+\theta)\left[\tilde{h}(x)-h(x)\right]=0.$$

This implies that $\tilde{\sigma}_g^2\tilde{h}''(x^*)<\sigma_g^2 h''(x^*)$. Since $\tilde{\sigma}_g^2>\sigma_g^2$, this in turn implies that $\tilde{h}''(x^*)<h''(x^*)$. This is equivalent to $f''(x^*)<0$, which contradicts with x^* as a local minimum. Therefore, $f(x)$ cannot have a local minimum with its value less than zero. Since $f(-\infty)=f(0)=0$, $f(x)$ must stay above zero for $x\in(-\infty,0)$. Therefore, $\tilde{h}(x)>h(x)$ for all $x<0$. This implies that the bubble $q_0(x)$ increases with σ_g for all $x<0$.

Assume $\bar{\rho}>\rho$, and let $\bar{h}(x)$ solve

$$\frac{1}{2}\sigma_g^2\bar{h}''(x)-\bar{\rho}x\bar{h}'(x)-(r+\theta)\bar{h}(x)=0,$$

$$\bar{h}(-\infty)=0\text{, and}$$

$$\bar{h}(0)=\frac{\pi}{\Gamma\left(\frac{1}{2}+\left[(r+\theta)/2\rho\right]\right)\Gamma\left(\frac{1}{2}\right)}.$$

We can show that $\bar{h}(x)<h(x)$ for all $x<0$. Again let $f(x)=\bar{h}(x)-h(x)$. We first establish that $f(x)$ has no local minimum x^* with $f(x^*)<0$. If such a local minimum exists, $f'(x^*)=0$ and $f''(x^*)\geq 0$. On the other hand, taking differences, we obtain

$$\frac{1}{2}\sigma_g^2\left[\bar{h}''(x)-h''(x)\right]-\rho x\left[\bar{h}'(x)-h'(x)\right]-(r+\theta)\left[\bar{h}(x)-h(x)\right]=(\bar{\rho}-\rho)x\bar{h}'(x).$$

This last equation implies that $\bar{h}'(x^*)<0$, which contradicts the fact that $\bar{h}(x)$ is an increasing function. Therefore, $f(x)$ cannot have a local minimum below zero. Since $f(-\infty)=f(0)=0$, $f(x)$ must stay above zero for $x<0$. This directly implies that $\bar{h}(x)>h(x)$ for all $x<0$, and $q_0(x)$ increases with ρ for all $x<0$.

Similarly, we can prove that $q_0(x)$ decreases with r and θ for all $x<0$.

One can extend the comparative statics we established for $c=0$ for the case of c small. Let $\zeta\in\{\sigma_g,\rho,\theta\}$. From equation (21) it follows that if $\partial k^*(\zeta,c)/\partial\zeta=o(k^*)$, then the comparative statics of b with respect to ζ is preserved for small c.

Using the definition of function h in equation (17), we write h as $h(x, \zeta)$. From equation (20),

$$\frac{\partial k^{*}(\zeta,c)}{\partial \zeta} =$$

$$\frac{\left[\dfrac{\partial h\!\left(k^{*},\zeta\right)}{\partial \zeta}-\dfrac{\partial h\!\left(-k^{*},\zeta\right)}{\partial \zeta}\right]-\left[k^{*}-c(r+\lambda)\right]\left[\dfrac{\partial^{2}h\!\left(k^{*},\zeta\right)}{\partial x\partial \zeta}+\dfrac{\partial^{2}h\!\left(-k^{*},\zeta\right)}{\partial x\partial \zeta}\right]}{\left[k^{*}-c(r+\lambda)\right]\left[\dfrac{\partial^{2}h\!\left(k^{*},\zeta\right)}{\partial x^{2}}-\dfrac{\partial^{2}h\!\left(-k^{*},\zeta\right)}{\partial x^{2}}\right]}. \qquad (A2)$$

As $c \to 0$, $k^{*} \to 0$ and the numerator and denominator go to zero. To find the limit behavior, we use the explicit form of h given in the proof of Proposition 2 and write

$$h(x,\zeta)=C_{0}+C_{1}x+C_{2}x^{2}+C_{3}x^{3}+o\!\left(x^{4}\right),$$

with

$$C_{0}=\frac{\pi}{\Gamma\!\left(\left(r/2\rho\right)+\dfrac{1}{2}\right)\Gamma\!\left(\dfrac{1}{2}\right)},\quad C_{1}=\frac{\pi\sqrt{\rho}}{\Gamma\!\left(r/2\rho\right)\Gamma\!\left(\dfrac{3}{2}\right)\sigma_{g}},$$

$$C_{2}=\frac{\pi r}{4\Gamma\!\left(\left(r/2\rho\right)+\dfrac{1}{2}\right)\Gamma\!\left(\dfrac{1}{2}\right)\sigma_{g}^{2}},\quad C_{3}=\frac{\pi\sqrt{\rho}(r+\rho)}{3\Gamma\!\left(r/2\rho\right)\Gamma\!\left(\dfrac{3}{2}\right)\sigma_{g}^{3}}.$$

We use equation (20) to replace the term $k^{*}-c(r+\lambda)$ on the right-hand side of equation (A2) by

$$\frac{h\!\left(k^{*},\zeta\right)-h\!\left(-k^{*},\zeta\right)}{\left[\partial h\!\left(k^{*},\zeta\right)/\partial x\right]+\left[\partial h-\!\left(-k^{*},\zeta\right)/\partial x\right]}.$$

Taking limits as $k^{*} \boxtimes 0$, we obtain

$$\frac{\partial k^{*}(\zeta,c)}{\partial \zeta}\sim o\!\left(k^{*}\right),\quad \zeta\in\left\{\sigma_{g},\rho,\theta\right\}.$$

A small variation establishes the same result for $\partial k^{*}(r,c)/\partial r$. Hence, for small c, b increases with σ_{g} and ρ and decreases with r and θ. In addition, we can show that $q(x)$ for $x < k^{*}$ increases with σ_{g} and ρ and decreases with r and θ.

Proof of Lemma 4

This is analogous to the proof of Lemma 3.

Proof of Proposition 4

Let

$$l(k,c) = \left[k - c(r+\lambda)\right]\left[h'(k) + h'(-k)\right] - h(k) + h(-k).$$

The function $k^*(c)$ is the root of $l(k, c) = 0$. If $c > 0$,

$$\frac{dk^*}{dc} = \frac{r+\lambda}{k^* - c(r+\lambda)} \frac{h'(k^*) + h'(-k^*)}{h''(k^*) - h''(-k^*)} > 0.$$

Hence $k^*(c)$ is differentiable in $(0, \infty)$. Now suppose that $c_n \to 0$. The sequence k^* (c_n) is bounded, and every limit point $\bar{k}^*$ must solve $l(\bar{k}^*, 0) = 0$. Hence, as we argued in the proof of Theorem 1, $\bar{k}^* = 0$ and the function $k^*(c)$ is continuous.

Hence $dk^*/dc \to \infty$ as $c \to 0$. The claims on b and $q(x)$ follow from equations (21) and (22) and Lemma 2. The derivative of $\eta(x)$ with respect to c is

$$\frac{d\eta(x)}{dc} = \frac{\sqrt{2}\phi\sigma_f h'(x)\left[h''(k^*) - h''(-k^*)\right]}{r+\lambda \; \left[h'(k^*) + h'(-k^*)\right]^2}\left(-\frac{dk^*}{dc}\right)$$

$$= -\frac{\sqrt{2}\phi\sigma_f h'(x)}{\left[k^* - c(r+\lambda)\right]\left[h'(k^*) + h'(-k^*)\right]} < 0.$$

Therefore, $\eta(x)$ decreases with c. However, note that $d\eta(x)/dc$ is finite as $c \to 0$, although $dk^*/dc \to \infty$ as $c \to 0$.

Notes

This article was originally published in the Journal of Political Economy, volume 111, 2003, pp. 1183–1220. It is reprinted with permission of the original publisher, the University of Chicago Press, with only minor alternations to adhere to the style of Oxford University Press. We thank the authors and the original publisher for permission to reprint this article.

1. See Lamont and Thaler (2003) and Ofek and Richardson (2003) for the Internet boom. Cochrane (2002) emphasizes the significant correlation between high prices and high turnover rates as a key characteristic of the 1929 boom and crash and of the Internet episode. Ofek and Richardson (2003) point out that between early 1998 and February 2000, pure Internet firms represented as much as 20% of the dollar volume in the public equity market, even though their market capitalization never exceeded 6%.
2. Cochrane (2002, p. 6) commented on the much-discussed Palm case: "Palm stock was also tremendously volatile during this period, with ... 15.4% standard deviation of 5 day returns, [which] is about the same as the volatility of the S&P500 index over an entire *year*."
3. Duffie, Garleanu, and Pedersen (2002) provide a search model to analyze the actual short-sale process and its implication for asset prices. D'Avolio (2002), Geczy, Musto, and Reed (2002), and Jones and Lamont (2002) contain empirical analyses of the relevance of short-sale costs.

4. Shleifer and Vishny (1997) argue that agency problems limit the capital available to arbitrageurs and may cause arbitrage to fail. See also Kyle and Xiong (2001), Xiong (2001), and Gromb and Vayanos (2002) for studies linking the dynamics of arbitrageurs' capital with asset price dynamics.

5. For example, Morris (1996) assumes noncommon priors, and Biais and Bossaerts (1998) examine the role of higher-order beliefs.

6. "We all have the same information, and we're just making different conclusions about what the future will hold" (Henry Blodget, the former star analyst at Merrill Lynch, quoted in Lewis [2002]).

7. An alternative would be to measure the bubble as the difference between the asset price and the fundamental valuation of the dividends by an agent that correctly weights the signals. We opted for our definition because it highlights the difference between beliefs about fundamentals and trading price.

8. In contrast, Federal Reserve Chairman Alan Greenspan seems to believe that the low turnover induced by the high costs of transactions in the housing market are an impediment to real estate bubbles: "While stock market turnover is more than 100 per cent annually, the turnover of home ownership is less than 10 per cent annually—scarcely tinder for speculative conflagration" (quoted in *Financial Times* [April 22, 2002]). The results in this paper suggest otherwise.

9. In an earlier draft, we assumed that agents overestimate the precision of their signal. We thank Chris Rogers for suggesting that we examine this alternative framework. The advantage of the present setup is that every agent attributes the same volatility to the signals.

10. Conley et al. (1997) argue that this is the correct measure of mean reversion.

11. This observation simplifies our calculations but is not crucial for what follows. We could partially relax the short-sale constraints or the division of gains from trade, provided that it is still true that the asset owner expects to make speculative profits from other investors.

12. The argument that follows will also imply that our equilibrium is the only one within a certain class. However, there are other equilibria. In fact, given any equilibrium price p_t^0 and a process M_t that is a martingale for both groups of agents, $\tilde{p}_t^0 = p_t^0 e^{rt} M_t$ is also an equilibrium.

13. The unconditional probability that it is zero depends on the volatility and mean reversion of the process of the difference of opinions and on the length of the interval. As the length of the interval goes to infinity, the probability of no trade goes to zero.

14. Since the bubble is generated through an option value, it is natural to normalize it by the volatility of the underlying fundamental value, i.e., the price volatility that would prevail if fundamentals were observable.

15. Vayanos (1998) makes a similar point in a different context when analyzing the effects of transaction costs on asset prices in a life cycle model. He shows that an increase in transaction costs can reduce the trading frequency but may even increase asset prices.

16. Duffie et al. (2002) provide another mechanism to explain this phenomenon based on the lending fee that the asset owner can expect to collect.

17. The missing link is to demonstrate that the divergence of beliefs on the combined entity was smaller than the divergence of beliefs on the Palm spinoff

References

Abramowitz, Milton, and Irene A. Stegun, eds. 1964. *Handbook of Mathematical Functions, with Formulas, Graphs, and Mathematical Tables*. New York: Dover.

Aggarwal, Rajesh K., Laurie Krigman, and Kent L. Womack. 2002. "Strategic IPO Underpricing, Information Momentum, and Lockup Expiration Selling." *Journal of Financial Economics* 66, 105–137.

Allen, Franklin, and Gary Gorton. 1993. "Churning Bubbles." *Review of Economic Studies* 60, 813–836.

Allen, Franklin, Stephen Morris, and Andrew Postlewaite. 1993. "Finite Bubbles with Short Sale Constraints and Asymmetric Information." *Journal of Economic Theory* 61, 206–229.

Alpert, Marc, and Howard Raiffa. 1982. "A Progress Report on the Training of Probability Assessors." In Daniel Kahneman, Paul Slovic, and Amos Tversky, eds., *Judgment under Uncertainty: Heuristics and Biases*. Cambridge: Cambridge University Press.

Barber, Brad M., and Terrance Odean. 2001. "The Internet and the Investor." *Journal of Economic Perspectives* 15, 41–54.

Berger, Philip G., and Eli Ofek. 1995. "Diversification's Effect on Firm Value." *Journal of Financial Economics* 37, 39–65.

Bernardo, Antonio E., and Ivo Welch. 2001. "On the Evolution of Overconfidence and Entrepreneurs." *Journal of Economics and Management Strategy* 10, 301–330.

Biais, Bruno, and Peter Bossaerts. 1998. "Asset Prices and Trading Volume in a Beauty Contest." *Review of Economic Studies* 65, 307–340.

Blanchard, Olivier J., and Mark W. Watson. 1982. "Bubbles, Rational Expectations, and Financial Markets." In Paul Wachtel, ed., *Crises in the Economic and Financial Structure*. Lexington, MA: Lexington Press.

Bolton, Patrick, José A. Scheinkman, and Wei Xiong. 2002. "Executive Compensation and Short-Termist Behavior in Speculative Markets." Working paper, Princeton University.

Camerer, Colin. 1995. "Individual Decision Making." In John H. Kagel and Alvin E. Roth, *The Handbook of Experimental Economics*. Princeton, NJ: Princeton University Press.

Carr, Peter P., and Robert A. Jarrow. 1990. "The Stop-Loss Start-Gain Paradox and Option Valuation: A New Decomposition into Intrinsic and Time Value." *Review of Financial Studies* 3, 469–492.

Chen, Joseph, Harrison Hong, and Jeremy C. Stein. 2002. "Breadth of Ownership and Stock Returns." *Journal of Financial Economics* 66, 171–205.

Cochrane, John H. 2002. "Stocks as Money: Convenience Yield and the Tech-Stock Bubble." National Bureau of Economic Research Working Paper No. 8987.

Conley, Timothy G., Lars Peter Hansen, Erzo G. J. Luttmer, and José A Scheinkman. 1997. "Short-Term Interest Rates as Subordinated Diffusions." *Review of Financial Studies* 10, 525–577.

Daniel, Kent, David Hirshleifer, and Avanidhar Subrahmanyam. 1998. "Investor Psychology and Security Market Under- and Overreactions." *Journal of Finance* 53, 1839–1885.

D'Avolio, Gene. 2002. "The Market for Borrowing Stock." *Journal of Financial Economics* 66, 271–306.

Duffie, Darrell, Nicolae Garleanu, and Lasse Heje Pedersen. 2002. "Securities Lending, Shorting, and Pricing." *Journal of Financial Economics* 66, 307–339.

Geczy, Christopher C., David K. Musto, and, Adam V. Reed. 2002. "Stocks Are Special Too: An Analysis of the Equity Lending Market." *Journal of Financial Economics* 66, 241–269.

Gromb, Dennis, and Dimitri Vayanos. 2002. "Equilibrium and Welfare in Markets with Financially Constrained Arbitrageurs." *Journal of Financial Economics* 66, 361–407.

Harris, Milton, and Artur Raviv. 1993. "Differences of Opinion Make a Horse Race." *Review of Financial Studies* 6, 473–506.

Harrison, J. Michael, and David M. Kreps. 1978. "Speculative Investor Behavior in a Stock Market with Heterogeneous Expectations." *Quarterly Journal of Economics* 92, 323–336.

Hirshleifer, David. 2001. "Investor Psychology and Asset Pricing." *Journal of Finance* 56, 1533–1597.

Horst, Ulrich. 2001. "Financial Price Fluctuations in a Stock Market Model with Many Interacting Agents." In *ISE Finance Award Series*, vol. 2. Istanbul: Istanbul Stock Exchange.

Jones, Charles M., and Owen A. Lamont. 2002. "Short-Sale Constraints and Stock Returns." *Journal of Financial Economics* 66, 207–239.

Kandel, Eugene, and Neil D. Pearson. 1995. "Differential Interpretation of Public Signals and Trade in Speculative Markets." *Journal of Political Economy* 103, 831–872.

Karlin, Samuel, and Howard M. Taylor. 1981. *A Second Course in Stochastic Processes*. New York: Academic Press.

Kobila, T. O. 1993. "A Class of Solvable Stochastic Investment Problems Involving Singular Controls." *Stochastics and Stochastics Reports* 43, 29–63.

Kyle, Albert S., and Tao Lin. 2002. "Continuous Speculation with Overconfident Competitors." Working paper, Duke University.

Kyle, Albert S., and F. Albert Wang. 1997. "Speculation Duopoly with Agreement to Disagree: Can Overconfidence Survive the Market Test?" *Journal of Finance* 52, 2073–2090.

Kyle, Albert S., and Wei Xiong. "Contagion as a Wealth Effect." *Journal of Finance* 56, 1401–1440.

Lamont, Owen A., and Richard H. Thaler. 2003. "Can the Market Add and Subtract? Mispricing in Tech Stock Carve-outs." *Journal of Political Economy* 111, 227–268.

Lang, Larry H. P., and Rene M. Stulz. 1994. "Tobin's *q*, Corporate Diversification, and Firm Performance." *Journal of Political Economy* 102, 1248–1280.

Lewis, Michael. 2002. "In Defense of the Boom." *New York Times Magazine,* October 27.

Lichtenstein, Sarah, Baruch Fischhoff, and Lawrence D. Phillips. 1982. "Calibration of Probabilities: The State of the Art to 1980." In Daniel Kahneman, Paul Slovic, and Amos Tversky, eds., *Judgment under Uncertainty: Heuristics and Biases.* Cambridge: Cambridge University Press.

Liptser, R. S., and A. N. Shiryaev. 1977. *Statistics of Random Processes.* 2 vols. New York: Springer-Verlag.

Lord, Charles G., Lee Ross, and Mark R. Lepper. 1979. "Biased Assimilation and Attitude Polarization: The Effects of Prior Theories on Subsequently Considered Evidence." *Journal of Personality and Social Psychology* 37, 2098–2109.

Mei, Jianping, José A. Scheinkman, and Wei Xiong. 2003. "Speculative Trading and Stock Prices: An Analysis of Chinese A-B Share Premia." Working paper, Princeton University.

Miller, Edward M. 1977. "Risk, Uncertainty, and Divergence of Opinion." *Journal of Finance* 32, 1151–1168.

Mitchell, Mark, Todd Pulvino, and Erik Stafford. 2002. "Limited Arbitrage in Equity Markets." *Journal of Finance* 57, 551–584.

Morris, Stephen. 1996. "Speculative Investor Behavior and Learning." *Quarterly Journal of Economics* 111, 1111–1133.

Odean, Terrance. 1998. "Volume, Volatility, Price, and Profit When All Traders Are Above Average." *Journal of Finance* 53, 1887–1934.

Ofek, Eli, and Matthew Richardson. 2003. "DotCom Mania: The Rise and Fall of Internet Stock Prices." *Journal of Finance* 58, 1113–1137.

Rajan, Raghuram, and Henri Servaes. 1997. "Analyst Following of Initial Public Offerings." *Journal of Finance* 52, 507–529.

Reese, William. 2000. "IPO Underpricing, Trading Volume, and Investor Interest." Working paper, Tulane University.

Revuz, Daniel, and Marc Yor. 1999. *Continuous Martingales and Brownian Motion.* 3rd ed. New York: Springer.

Rogers, L. C. G., and David Williams. 1987. *Diffusions, Markov Processes, and Martingales.* Vol. 2, *Ito Calculus.* New York: Wiley.

Santos, Manuel S., and Michael Woodford. 1997. "Rational Asset Pricing Bubbles." *Econometrica* 65, 19–57.

Scheinkman, José A., and Thaleia Zariphopoulou. 2001. "Optimal Environmental Management in the Presence of Irreversibilities." *Journal of Economic Theory* 96, 180–207.

Schill, Michael J., and Chunsheng Zhou. 2001. "Pricing an Emerging Industry: Evidence from Internet Subsidiary Carve-outs." *Financial Management* 30, 5–33.

Shiller, Robert J. 2000. *Irrational Exuberance.* Princeton, NJ: Princeton University Press.

Shleifer, Andrei, and Robert W. Vishny. 1997. "The Limits of Arbitrage." *Journal of Finance* 52, 35–55.

Tobin, James. 1978. "A Proposal for International Monetary Reform." *Eastern Economic Journal* 4, 153–159.

Vayanos, Dimitri. 1998. "Transaction Costs and Asset Prices: A Dynamic Equilibrium Model." *Review of Financial Studies* 11, 1–58.

Xiong, Wei. 2001 "Convergence Trading with Wealth Effects: An Amplification Mechanism in Financial Markets." *Journal of Financial Economics* 62, 247–292.

CHAPTER 11

Asset Bubbles

INSIGHTS FROM BEHAVIORAL FINANCE

Werner De Bondt

A decade ago most economists paid almost no attention to the complex cognitive and motivational factors that shape financial decision-making. Economic psychology and behavioral finance were ignored. The meltdown of the Internet bubble and the world financial crisis that followed the housing crash in the United States have made this conventional way of thinking untenable. In these remarks, I comment on (1) the current malaise in the United States and elsewhere; (2) past research on speculative asset price bubbles and overconfidence, in particular, the 2003 article authored by Jose Scheinkman and Wei Xiong; and (3) financial reform and bubble control.

1. The Current Malaise

Many people believed until a few years back that better monetary policy, improvements in risk management, and deregulation had permanently lessened macroeconomic volatility. Soon, the business cycle would be a relic of the past.

The crash in U.S. housing followed by the banking crisis and the global economic downturn changed all that. Early in 2011, the U.S. economy shows new signs of strain. The economic recovery is sluggish, to say the least, and we may well slide back into recession. A big problem is the downward spiral in real estate. Its severity is comparable to what happened during the Great Depression. Housing prices are hitting new lows.[1] With the 2012 presidential election in sight, the Obama administration has a stake in accentuating the positive, of course, but rising oil and food prices and high joblessness squeeze consumer spending. Both fiscal and monetary policy are tapped out. The stalemate between Democrats and Republicans over taxes and social spending may lead to a government debt crisis. (How much longer can we "stay the course" and close our eyes to the mountain of debt?) Though some investments in infra-structure are sorely needed and would pay for themselves, there is little appetite for another fiscal stimulus package. At the same time, interest rates are already very low by historical standards. As it looks now, the Federal Reserve may keep them low for many months to come.[2]

The world economy is also faltering. While the euro zone was a relative anchor of stability until mid-2011, several nations on the periphery of the European Union struggle with budget deficits and rising government debt. The austerity measures designed to bring back investor confidence are contractionary, surely in the short run. Governments in Ireland, Portugal, Spain, and Greece are weak. There are mass protests and riots in Athens. Some top officials in France and Germany seek a deeper political union in exchange for economic rescue (Trichet 2011). Outside of Europe, the Japanese economy remains feeble—even more so after the earthquake, tsunami, and nuclear catastrophe in March 2011. Hikes in interest rates intended to cool inflation are also moderating growth in China. On top of intense economic uncertainty, the Arab awakening, the continuing violence in a long list of Islamic countries (Afghanistan, Bahrain, Iraq, Libya, Pakistan, Syria, and Yemen), and the drug wars in Mexico and Central America add significant geopolitical risk.

Global imbalances and political conflict wrecked the international economy between the world wars. We should never fail to remember that with globalization the interests of nations are intertwined. Today, de facto, no single nation has absolute control of its destiny. Many countries are in crisis because of the unsound policies of others. Successful economic coordination, however, requires a degree of policy consensus that does not exist at the moment.[3]

In sum, we live in exceptionally uncertain and unhappy times. From the viewpoint of academic study, however, the bursting of the latest asset price bubble unlocks unusual opportunities for research on public opinion and sentiment. We can examine consumer, investor, worker, business, and voter sentiment. That is only a start. The potential is huge. An important aspect of opinion research has to do with understanding people's hopes and fears, and the confidence expressed in intuitive forecasts. Naïve forecasts, and the confidence in forecasts, are key variables for many economic models. Above all, spontaneous optimism ("animal spirits") and uncertainty play a major role in Keynesian economics.[4] What differentiates *behavioral* from other economic research is that it is not automatically assumed that agents' expectations are "rational." Instead, this conjecture is empirically investigated and refined.

Needless to say, the range of mental processes that economic psychologists look at extends far beyond prediction. It includes how people look at today's social and economic environment. Voters are "cynical" and "angry," we are told. They are "tired" of the squabbling and posturing in Washington. Less than 25% think that the country is moving in the right direction. There is an "erosion" of trust. Gretchen Morgenson and Joshua Rosner (2011) declare that "the American people realize that they've been robbed. They're just not sure by whom." A lot of hostility is directed against Wall Street. Bankers are seen as innately greedy and dishonest. (These emotions tie in with the resentment about the bailout, the revolving door between corporate boardrooms and government agencies, and bankers' pay.) For instance, Goldman Sachs is accused of "massively" shorting the mortgage market while selling securities based on home loans. Some Europeans think that Goldman was also disloyal to Greece. Note that in the beginning bankers were accused of recklessness. Now they are held to be excessively cautious. Likewise, the legend of Alan Greenspan, the maestro who was in the public eye for decades, has been tarnished. In hindsight, Greenspan's "blunders" in terms of monetary and regulatory policy are thought to be self-evident. More gravely, some charge Greenspan with looking out for the wealthy and leaving workers' interests behind.

From a societal perspective, the factor that perhaps deserves most attention is the suffering associated with long-term unemployment. By now, the crisis has irrevocably ruined the lives of many middle-aged blue-collar workers. Their anguish is genuine and seems justified by past events. Since 1980, rising labor productivity no longer translates into rising real wages. Frank Levy and Thomas Kochan (2011) document that the average high-school-educated, middle-aged man earns about 10% less than his counterpart did in 1980. (High-school-educated minority men have experienced even slower wage growth.) It is important to take note of the fact that whites who did not finish college remain the backbone of the labor market. College-educated whites total one-fifth of the workforce, while minorities account for one-third. A March 2011 survey released by the Pew Charitable Trusts' Economic Mobility Project clearly shows that blue-collar whites are gloomy about the future. For example, asked whether they expect to be better off financially in 10 years than they are today, 55% of college-educated whites and two-thirds of blacks and Hispanics say yes, but only 44% of noncollege whites agree. One-third of noncollege whites say that their children will live better than they do. (A comparable number think their kids will not match their standard of living.)[5]

A related concern is high youth unemployment. In a tough labor market, people look for a secure bet and many trust that a university education (or other added training) is one of the best ways "to win the future." This orthodox position, I believe, is largely correct. Yet it may well be that we expect too much and that our present enthusiasm for more education and training, like our past obsession with housing, is exaggerated. Peter Thiel, a high-tech billionaire with large investments in PayPal and Facebook, definitely thinks so. He has mounted a hard-hitting public relations campaign arguing that university education in the United States is wildly overpriced. Thiel predicts that the "education bubble" will pop (Sarah Lacy 2011). (He encourages young people to self-educate and to become entrepreneurs.) Over the last 30 years, college tuition has risen ten times faster than inflation and three times faster than health-care costs (James Altucher 2011). As a result, a university education has become in essence unaffordable for large segments of the population. Various studies suggest that income and wealth, not brainpower, are the key factor in the decision to attend college. Still, most people go ahead and pay up. The statistics are frightening. Perhaps as many as 40% of college students do not graduate in six years. Nearly half of 2009 graduates are either unemployed or hold jobs that do not require a university degree. For the first time ever, total student debt in the United States exceeds credit-card debt. Tens of thousands of young people are holding over

$100,000 in debt. According to Thiel, we are graduating "a generation of indentured servants." Then again, it is also true that the jobless rate for college graduates is a fraction what it is for high-school educated workers.[6]

Richard Taffler (2011) analyzes investment frenzies in terms of "phantastic objects." Modern research in neurobiology, he argues, is beginning to validate insights that go back to Sigmund Freud. According to Taffler, a phantasm is an idea which fulfills an individual's deepest desires. The ultimate phantasm has magical attributes such as exclusive access, originality, technical complexity, a larger-than-life identity, or the promise of exceptionally high returns. Even though investors may not be fully aware of it, many are in perpetual pursuit of phantastic objects. This never-ending chase, Taffler believes, accounts for the mystique of gold, technology stocks, London real estate, or hedge funds run by celebrities like John Paulson, James Simons, and Bernard Madoff.

Taffler's theory strikes a chord. We do not have to agree with everything he says to imagine that right now the phantastic object for America's middle class is education. For the wealthy it may be investments in high-tech social media or frontier emerging markets (see, e.g., Robert Farzad 2010).

2. Past Research on Asset Bubbles and Overconfidence

It is important to see beyond the current troubles and to keep a historical perspective. The past has often witnessed asset bubbles. Indeed, episodes of rampant market speculation followed by collapse are almost the norm. As everyone knows, famous "first" bubbles include the tulip mania (The Netherlands, 1637), the South Sea bubble (England, 1711), the railway mania (Britain, 1845), and the stock market crash of 1929 followed by the Great Depression. Charles Kindleberger (1978) and Carmen Reinhart and Kenneth Rogoff (2009) review this evidence and much more.

Nonetheless, a generation ago, most financial economists were in agreement that capital markets are extremely efficient and that news is immediately and accurately incorporated into asset prices. Theorists had developed the efficient market hypothesis in order to make sense of the "random walk." If prices quickly reflect all available information, then tomorrow's price change would only echo the part of tomorrow's news that is unpredictable today. Eugene Fama (1970) spoke candidly about this. Research, he said, "did not begin with the development of a theory of price formation which was then subjected to empirical tests. Rather, the impetus...came from the accumulation of evidence...that the behavior...of speculative prices could be well approximated by a random walk. Faced with the evidence, economists felt compelled to offer some rationalization. In short, there existed a large body of experimental results in search of a rigorous theory."

Beginning in the 1980s, however, new empirical research discovered a series of stock market anomalies including (1) predictable reversals in stock prices over two-year to five-year horizons; (2) predictable trends as far as one year into the future; (3) predictable momentum reversals. All three price patterns are seen in my 1985 paper coauthored with Richard Thaler. Our paper emphasized the reversals since they agreed with what we were looking for based on a psychological theory of market overreaction, itself suggested by the experimental work of Daniel Kahneman, Paul Slovic, and Amos Tversky (1982) on heuristics and biases.[7]

A further novelty of our work was that we interpreted *extreme* past price movements in the cross-section of stocks as noisy measures of investor sentiment, not necessarily indicators of changes in fundamental value. Thus, from the start, we assumed the uncoupling of price from value which is the defining characteristic of a price bubble. It would take a separate paper to review all noteworthy findings in this area gathered since 1985 but I am fond of the words of William Stanley Jevons, who said in *The Theory of Political Economy* (1871) that "as a general rule, it is foolish to do just what other people are doing, because there are almost sure to be too many people doing the same thing." This quote nicely captures the initial momentum, likely caused by investor herding, as well as the subsequent price reversals, and it recommends that investors go against the crowd.[8]

BEHAVIORAL FINANCE

How do behavioral scientists think about the study of financial decision-making? While many activities are routine or conventional, behavioral finance agrees with standard finance that by and large people think before they act—especially when they face a new decision problem of some consequence for the first time. People reason and they make an effort to be sensible in what they do. However, their actions do not meet the ideal of *homo economicus*. The rationality of judgment and choice is bounded; for example, it is a struggle for most of us to manage several decision problems at the same time; and we may not pay attention when we really ought to, or we forget things. In addition, emotions and sociopsychological factors (e.g., a concern with how one is perceived by others) may hinder the quality of decisions.

Three elemental building blocks of behavioral theories are the concepts of (1) mental frames, (2) loss aversion, and (3) heuristics. If you want to understand, predict, or influence a decision taken by another individual, your first aim should be to get a glimpse of how that person thinks about the issue. What is his or her mental frame? Frames organize our thinking. They matter in countless ways. For example, frames suggest reference points that affect how people experience outcomes. Because of our strong dislike of below-target results, people choose as if they are risk-averse in the domain of attainable gains (relative to a reference point) and risk-loving in the domain of losses. This is one of the key insights of prospect theory (Kahneman and Tversky 1979). Thus, minor alterations in the decision environment often have a big impact on performance.[9] Judgment under uncertainty also depends on a small number of heuristics, that is, short-cuts in the brain that influence the formation of beliefs. Heuristics are effective most of the time but they may lead us astray. In a classic article, Tversky and Kahneman (1974) describe three heuristics: (1) *representativeness* or judgment by similarity; (2) judgment based on the *availability* of instances and scenarios; and (3) judgment based on *anchoring and adjustment*. In every case, easily accessible information has a lopsided impact on our beliefs—either because it fits a stereotype, or because it is vivid or readily imagined, or because it already left a first impression.

On the whole, mental frames, loss aversion, and heuristics are psychological mechanisms that cause behavior to systematically and predictably deviate from the axioms of rationality. These core concepts also explain everyday decision traps such as overconfidence, unrealistic optimism, or hindsight bias, and they are tied to widespread biases in financial judgment and choice such as the naïve extrapolation of past stock price trends or lack of diversification in retirement portfolios.

The behavioral approach is mostly inductive. Its chief method is to generate financial decision-making "facts" and to arrange these pieces of evidence so that enlightening patterns emerge. The initial facts themselves are inferred from data obtained at three levels: (1) in a controlled laboratory environment and therefore subject to replication; (2) in a natural environment but based on the behavior of individual actors, for example, survey data or trading records; and (3) in a market environment, for example, price and volume data. It is methodological triangulation, also referred to as cross-examination, that makes a behavioral theory truly convincing. For instance, much past research indicates that investors are painfully slow to sell assets that are going down in price. (This is the so-called disposition effect.) Its primary cause, loss aversion, is easily demonstrated in the laboratory. Surveys and trading records confirm that investors detest turning "paper losses" into permanent losses. Lastly, the disposition effect is linked to price momentum and related stock market anomalies.[10]

BEHAVIORAL ASSET PRICING

Since its emergence, behavioral finance has produced three central insights.

1. Intuition is fragile. To repeat, human decision errors are systematic and predictable. Many individuals do not learn basic financial principles from everyday experience.[11]
2. Decision process matters. The secret to high-quality decision-making is a structured, disciplined framework.[12]
3. Market prices are chronically distorted by widely shared, self-reinforcing misconceptions. The delusions are intelligible and to some extent predictable, however. This is all important. Fluctuations in investor sentiment produce risk but they are also a profit opportunity for sophisticated traders.

Behavioral asset pricing theory is based on two major assumptions. First, it is assumed that false beliefs about future cash flows, mistakes in risk perception, or unsteadiness in risk attitudes have an effect on market prices. Second, it is assumed that betting against investor sentiment is costly and risky. As a result, what rational arbitrage can achieve is limited. (Indeed, such arbitrage may be destabilizing.)

The psychological sources of bias may be cognitive, emotional, or sociopsychological. Bernard Baruch said that "what is important in market fluctuations are not the events themselves, but the human reactions to those events." Especially in uncertain times, experts may find it less problematic to forecast the "state of the market" (i.e., the behavior of the crowd) than "the state of the economy." Kindleberger (1978) and others believe that a speculative price bubble usually starts with irrational enthusiasm about the business prospects of an asset or asset class.[13] The bubble expands with the use of leverage and with the entry into the market of less informed newcomers. Besides, many actors have a rational motive (self-interest!) to pump up the market.[14] One challenging aspect of predicting the crowd, stressed by Keynes, is that mass opinion is influenced by what people think others accept as true. For example, individuals who become aware that their personal view is spreading will speak with more confidence than individuals who notice the opposite. This creates a spiral effect.[15] In due course, the bubble becomes unsustainable. For example, in the recent housing bubble, "many people could afford the high prices [of housing] only on the premise that prices would continue to rise" (Posner 2010, 29). When the crash arrives, the sudden and sharp discontinuity in prices is surprising to many traders, and it may cause panic.[16]

SCHEINKMAN-XIONG (2003)

There are many ways to rationalize speculative bubbles.[17] Jose Scheinkman and Wei Xiong (2003) go back to some old, venerable ideas to find the origins of market mispricing. Their elegant continuous-time model takes differences in beliefs among traders and short-sales constraints as starting points. Scheinkman and Xiong develop a "marginal opinion theory" of asset prices that is in line with the initial chapters in The Theory of Investment Value of John Burr Williams (1938). (A much-quoted paper by Edward Miller, 1977, later extended Williams.)

The early models of Williams and Miller are static but produce results that are analogous to Scheinkman-Xiong. For instance, Williams and Miller show that, among all traders, the investors who are most optimistic about the prospects of an asset will be the ones who own it. So, divergence of opinion tends to cause overpricing and the subsequent return earned by the asset is likely to be inferior. The limits-to-arbitrage assumption is essential, of course. Tangible short-sales constraints or other frictions (for example, the psychological discomfort of trading against majority opinion) prevent that prices fully assimilate negative information.

In Scheinkman-Xiong, fluctuations in heterogeneous beliefs generate trade and people willingly pay a premium (over and above their private appraisal of future dividends) in exchange for the option to resell the asset to investors who are more optimistic than they are themselves. Hence, there exists a speculative component in prices. This interesting result reminds us of the illustrious greater fool theory: *Res tantum valet quantum vendi potest.*

The main contribution of Scheinkman-Xiong is that the authors succeed in rationalizing high prices, high trading volume, and high price volatility within one dynamic framework. The model captures three unmistakable stylized facts of financial history. (In contrast, the static models of Williams and Miller cannot explain high volume since investors never rebalance their positions. There is no trading.) With "overconfidence" in the title of their article, though, Scheinkman and Xiong also leave the impression that there is a strong behavioral aspect to their work. That is not true since the authors only introduce overconfidence to motivate a specific dynamic structure of disagreement among investors.[18]

THE PSYCHOLOGY OF CONFIDENCE

What do we know about confidence in judgment? Excessive confidence and over-optimism are aspects of human nature that philosophers and social scientists have commented upon for centuries. In *The Wealth of Nations* (1776), Adam Smith writes that "the overweening conceit which the greater part of men have of their own abilities, is an ancient evil remarked by the philosophers and moralists of all ages. Their absurd presumption of their own good fortune has been less taken notice of. It is, however, if possible, more universal. There is no man living who, when in tolerable health and spirits, has not some share of it. The chance of gain is by every man more or less overvalued, and the chance of loss is by most men undervalued."

It is not easy to sum up past research on overconfidence in a few paragraphs. A 2010 survey by Markus Glaser and Martin Weber that I recommend finds that since the year 2000 possibly as many as 1,500 research papers have been published on this topic in peer-reviewed journals. The survey itself lists 90 references; about 25 of these articles focus specifically on financial decision-making. Many psychologists look upon overconfidence as the judgment bias that is the most common departure from rationality.

In fact, overconfidence refers to a whole range of phenomena. The main finding is that people often overestimate the precision of their private beliefs. This is called miscalibration. For instance, when they are asked to state 90% confidence intervals for predictions of the Dow Jones one year from today, subjects' hit rates will typically be much lower than 90%, perhaps less than 50%. Overconfidence is widespread but not omnipresent. It depends on (1) task domain and task difficulty (the bias intensifies if people attempt to answer harder questions, for example, if the forecast horizon is extended); (2) the amount of available information (with more data, confidence rises but accuracy does not); (3) individual differences, for example, gender (men are more confident than women) and cultural heritage; (4) the exact measurement method that is used. The evidence is overwhelming that overconfidence applies to acknowledged "experts" (weather forecasters excluded) as well as amateurs. Alas, we still need more study on the dynamics of overconfidence and the impact of outcome feedback and monetary incentives. Current work indicates that these factors curb but do not smother overconfidence.[19]

Finance theory links investor overconfidence to high trading volume, stock price momentum, excess volatility, and speculative bubbles. Much research develops the conditions under which highly self-confident traders are likely to "survive" in competitive markets. Empirical research broadly confirms that more confident traders (e.g., men) trade more and earn lower returns. The overconfidence of CEOs and CFOs also influences corporate investment decisions.[20]

RISK, UNCERTAINTY, DISAGREEMENT, AND STOCK RETURNS

I conclude my discussion of Scheinkman-Xiong (2003) with some pertinent empirical evidence. Because the results of time-series studies are often fragile, I focus on a few studies that inspect the cross-section of stock returns.[21]

In life risk, uncertainty, and disagreement usually go together. Maybe for this reason, the marginal opinion theory of stock prices is frequently used to make sense of anomalies that have competing explanations, for example, (1) the poor performance of high-beta and volatile stocks; (2) the apparent short-term underpricing and long-term overpricing of IPOs (since disagreement often lessens over time); (3) the finding that "anything that increases investor awareness of a stock will increase its price" (since a security will not be purchased unless it is being noticed).

Guohua Jiang et al. (2005) study the link between information uncertainty (which the authors also refer to as "value ambiguity") and stock returns directly. They use four measures of uncertainty. In general, higher value ambiguity is associated with lower returns. This may be because uncertainty is tied to differences of opinion, or because uncertainty makes it more costly to short the stock, or both.

Do the data support asset mispricing by optimists? On balance, the answer appears to be yes. In a prominent paper, Karl Diether, Christopher Malloy, and Anna Scherbina (2002) study the returns of portfolios of stocks sorted by dispersion of analyst one-year earnings forecasts. (This dispersion is interpreted as a measure of disagreement among expert investors.) High-dispersion stocks underperform. Much of the profit of an arbitrage trading strategy based on this notion is generated around earnings announcements. (See also Henk Berkman et al. 2009.) Diether et al. believe that the profit is less in periods when the short-selling constraints are less binding. Recent work by Jialin Yu (2011) shows that the underperformance of high-disagreement stocks is stronger among growth stocks. This is as we would expect since growth stock investors are generally thought to be overly optimistic. Further, Doron Avramov et al. (2009) find that the negative relationship between dispersion and returns is concentrated in highly speculative firms with poor credit ratings, especially in periods of financial distress. It may be that high cross-sectional and increasing time-series uncertainty is systematically mispriced by equity markets. Lastly, Mesrop Janunts (2011) also performs an array of further tests. One troubling finding is that the dispersion trading strategy performed well until the late 1990s but has failed since that time.

3. Behavioral Aspects of Financial Reform

Speculative asset price bubbles misallocate capital and hurt innocent people. The financial instability of the last decade, as well as the economic stagnation, are the principal reasons why there is outward agreement in favor of financial reform and bubble control (see, e.g., De Bondt 2010).

In the United States, there is a continuing conflict of visions, however.[22] One vision of reform says that Washington should get out of the way. Government adds to the climate of uncertainty. It imposes regulatory costs. It is captured by special interests. (Only bureaucrats who want more power to justify their own salaries and positions benefit.) Most significantly, government regulation is no match for self-regulation. Alan Greenspan (1998) said that "the primary source of regulatory effectiveness has always been private traders being knowledgeable of their counterparties. Government regulation can only act as a backup."[23]

The other vision of reform finds unfettered capitalism unacceptable. It says that the increased power of finance, for example, the worship of the goal of shareholder wealth maximization, has led to the breakdown of the social contract. Wall Street governs by panic, it says, and we face a choice between finance and democracy (Robert Skidelsky 2011).[24] This vision seeks a new beginning. It wants public policymakers who do not have reservations about the legitimacy of government intervention; who make full employment their top priority; and who believe that corporations should add to social welfare as well as to shareholder wealth.[25]

Is a compromise solution possible? Is there a third way? Jean-Paul Fitoussi (2011), Raghuram Rajan (2010), and others believe that democracy and capitalism are in fact symbiotic. I agree. On the one hand, democratic government helps to legitimize capitalism by providing a safety net and by avoiding excessive market-based exclusion. On the other hand, the market supports democracy by limiting political control over people's lives. We should not pretend that economics is value-free. If we admit that market outcomes are not natural phenomena but political choices, we can build the society that we want.

What can psychology contribute to this effort? I have three comments. First, it should be clear that behavioral research finds suboptimality in public as well as private decision-making (see, e.g., Jonathan Baron et al. 2006, on the psychology of poor legislation). No one has a monopoly on wisdom.

Second, research shows in a decisive way that *homo economicus* does not exist. While I do not question that education and learning may boost rational decision-making, it is doubtful that financial literacy programs will ever be very effective in guaranteeing financial security, let alone in preventing future bubbles. It seems better to put our efforts into making financial systems less dependent on the professional capabilities of individual agents and into making financial products consumer-friendly and safe.[26]

My final comment is that, at this critical juncture, we should encourage dialogue even if the conflict of visions that I described earlier is likely to delay decision-making on various controversial aspects of financial reform. Consider consumer financial protection. Thaler and Sunstein (2008) argue persuasively that it is feasible to design helpful default solutions to common decision problems such as saving for retirement or choosing the right mortgage. The crux of their so-called libertarian paternalism is to reflexively "nudge" people toward solutions that a choice architect regards either as socially *desirable* or privately *optimal*. The approach is libertarian in the sense that it avoids direct government coercion. (If people are clearheaded and understand what is happening, they are still able to overrule the default solution. In that sense, they do as they want.) I do not oppose all social engineering on principle, but I do believe specific government interventions in consumer decision processes should always be preceded by comprehensive democratic debate. Much behavioral research indicates that dialogue brings about legitimacy, and that the perception of legitimacy produces trust. No one will dispute, I imagine, that in this era of cynicism and mistrust, trust is more important than ever.

Acknowledgements

I thank Jim Booth, Bill Higbee, Mesrop Janunts, Stephen Malpezzi, Robert Krainer, and Richard Taffler for useful discussions. Some of the ideas that I put forward here were also outlined at forums organized by the American Association of Individual Investors (Milwaukee Chapter), the CFA Society of Chicago, the Katholieke Universiteit Leuven (Conference in honor of Paul de Grauwe), and DePaul University. I thank event participants for their comments. All errors that remain are my own.

Notes

1 This creates the risk of a vicious circle. Alan Greenspan (1995) describes the danger as follows: "Consumers are not willing to buy a house unless they are confident they will retain their jobs and that the value of the home will not decline."

2 The policy debate is causing a great deal of ill feeling and bitterness. Consider, for instance, how David Stockman (2011) or Paul Krugman (2011) play the blame game.

3 See, e.g., Raghuram Rajan (2010), chapter 10.

4 See, e.g., David Blanchflower (2010) or Richard Posner (2010). Posner's narrative of the economic crisis is fascinating. His latest thinking builds on John Maynard Keynes—but not new

Keynesian economics. Inadequate financial regulation, loose monetary policy, and today's policy failures are summarized as "forgetfulness of Keynes" (8). However, "if one idea had to be picked out as central to *The General Theory*, it is the idea of uncertainty," Posner says (288). He discusses "irreducible" Keynesian uncertainty and the role of confidence in shaping the business cycle. Posner disapproves of behavioral as well as real business cycle economics. A bit ominously, he asks whether U.S. political institutions "are adapted to the challenges [of the] crisis" (6).

5   For a general discussion of what is happening in the American workplace, see Steven Greenhouse (2008). In a recent *Wall Street Journal* article that caused a stir, Damian Paletta (2011) reports that Social Security Disability Insurance, which was intended to help people who cannot work, is increasingly becoming an "early retirement plan." Paletta suggests that costs are exploding and bankrupting the system.

6   The student debt problem may escalate over time since President George W. Bush signed a law by which that type of debt is no longer expungeable in bankruptcy. The related quandary of unemployed youth with college degrees is already acute in Portugal, Spain, Italy, and Greece. (Young people are camping out in central Madrid.) One reason is that in these countries university education is heavily subsidized by the state. Finally, many commentators also link the chaos in North Africa and the Middle East to young people with high aspirations but without work.

7   Thus, the evidence agrees with the perspective of Benjamin Graham and David Dodd (1934): "What goes up, must come down." For a summary of contemporary research on heuristics and biases, see Thomas Gilovich et al. (2002).

8   For a collection of recent papers on this topic, see De Bondt (2005).

9   Interestingly, the variations may affect decision processes and outcomes without modifying the underlying "true" preferences (if they exist!). Indeed, this is what choice architecture, a term used by Richard Thaler and Cass Sunstein (2008), is all about.

10   For a comprehensive survey of the disposition effect, see Markku Kaustia (2010).

11   To avoid misreading, I emphasize that fragile means "easily breakable." It does not mean "broken."

12   For an introduction to this literature, see, e.g., Jay Russo and Paul Schoemaker (2002) as well as Thaler and Sunstein (2008).

13   Or, in the words of Alan Greenspan (2002), "bubbles are often precipitated by perceptions of real improvements in the productivity and underlying profitability of the corporate economy. But as history attests, investors then too often exaggerate the extent of the improvement in economic fundamentals" (10).

14   Consider, e.g., misleading accounting practices. This is often linked to the market's obsession with earnings targets. The pressure can be ruinous. Over the last decade, three celebrated winners of CFO Magazine Excellence Awards—Mark Swartz of Tyco, Scott Sullivan of WorldCom, and Andrew Fastow of Enron—faced criminal charges.

15   See, e.g., Elisabeth Noelle-Neumann (1977). Carroll Glynn et al. (2004) and John Zaller (1992) survey the literature on the dynamics of public opinion.

16   Or, in the words of Alan Greenspan (1998), "the history of large swings in investor confidence...counsels caution....[J]ust as a bull stock market feels unending and secure as an economy and stock market move forward, so it can feel when markets contract that recovery is inconceivable. Both, of course, are wrong. But because of the difficulty of imagining a turnabout when such emotions take hold, periods of euphoria and distress tend to feed on themselves."

17   For an introduction to the theoretical literature and further references, see Gadi Barlevy (2007).

18   There are a series of other mechanisms that may plausibly generate disagreement, e.g., some investors may be slow to react to information because they do not pay close attention. This creates a divergence of opinion with traders who do pay attention.

19   Evidently, this evidence on the dynamics of overconfidence is also what we need in order to evaluate the realism of the detailed modeling assumptions in Scheinkman and Xiong (2003).

20 Useful references include Kent Daniel, David Hirshleifer, and Avanidhar Subrahmanyam (1998), Pete Kyle and Albert Wang (1997), Markus Glaser and Martin Weber (2007), and Ulrike Malmendier and Geoffrey Tate (2005).

21 For a much longer survey and more references, see Hong and Stein (2007).

22 An illustration of the ideological split is the contrast between the majority report of the Financial Crisis Inquiry Commission (2011) and the dissent formulated by Peter Wallison (2011).

23 A somewhat longer Greenspan (1997) quote is as follows: "[N]o market is ever truly unregulated in that the self-interest of participants generates private market regulation....Thus, the real question is not whether a market should be regulated. Rather, it is whether government intervention strengthens or weakens private regulation. Regulation by government unavoidably involves some element of perverse incentives, that is, moral hazard. If...market participants believe that government is protecting their interests, their own efforts to do so will diminish".

24 Robert Fishman (2011) develops this idea with respect to the Portuguese bailout. Helena Smith and Jill Treanor (2011) describe the frustrations of Prime Minister George Papandreou in the battle between the bond rating agencies and Greece.

25 In January 2010, President Nicholas Sarkozy of France said in Davos (Switzerland) that the G20 "symbolizes the return of politics whose legitimacy was denied by unregulated globalization." For more discussion, see also Thomas Palley (2009) and Anatole Kaletsky (2010).

26 For more discussion, see Oren Bar-Gill (2009) and Robert Shiller's proposal to humanize and democratize finance (Randall Kroszner and Shiller, 2011). The efforts to build a consumer financial protection agency seem justified. (Jean Monnet said that "nothing is possible without men and women, but nothing is lasting without institutions.")

References

Altucher, James. 2011. "College Is a Scam. So Let's Make Money Off It." *MarketWatch*, May 27.

Avramov, Doron, et al. 2009. "Dispersion in Analysts' Earnings forecasts and Credit Rating." *Journal of Financial Economics* 91, 83–101.

Bar-Gill, Oren. 2009. "The Law, Economics and Psychology of Subprime Mortgage Contracts." *Cornell Law Review* 94, 1074–1151.

Barlevy, Gadi. 2007. "Economic Theory and Asset Bubbles." *Federal Reserve Bank of Chicago Economic Perspectives*, Third Quarter, 44–59.

Baron, Jonathan, Max H. Bazerman, and Katherine Shonk. 2006. "Enlarging the Societal Pie through Wise Legislation: A Psychological Perspective." *Perspectives on Psychological Science* 1(2), 123–132.

Berkman, Henk, et al. 2009. "Sell on the News: Differences of Opinion, Short-Sales Constraints, and Returns around Earnings Announcements." *Journal of Financial Economics* 92, 376–399.

Blanchflower, David G. 2010. "Models Miss Risk of Falling Confidence." *Bloomberg*, July 28.

Daniel, Kent, David Hirshleifer, and Avanidhar Subrahmanyam. 1998. "Investor Psychology and Security Market Under- and Overreactions." *Journal of Finance* 53, 1839–1885.

De Bondt, Werner, ed. 2005. *The Psychology of World Equity Markets*. Northampton, MA: Edward Elgar.

De Bondt, Werner. 2010. "The Crisis of 2008 and Financial Reform." *Qualitative Research in Financial Markets* 2(3), 137-156.

De Bondt, Werner, and Richard Thaler. 1985. "Does the Stock Market Overreact?" *Journal of Finance* 40, 793–805.

Diether, Karl B., Christopher J. Malloy, and Anna Scherbina. 2002. "Differences of Opinion and the Cross Section of Stock Returns." *Journal of Finance* 57, 2113–2141.

Fama, Eugene F. 1970. "Efficient Capital Markets: A Review of Theory and Empirical work." *Journal of Finance* 25, 383–417.

Farzad, Roben. 2010. "Investing in Frontier Emerging Markets: Your Next Money-Making Opportunity Is in the Last Place You'd Think to Look." *Bloomberg Businessweek*, October 14.

Financial Crisis Inquiry Commission. 2011. *The Financial Crisis Inquiry Report: Final Report of the National Commission on the Causes of the Financial and Economic Crisis in the United States.* Washington, DC: Financial Crisis Inquiry Commission.

Fishman, Robert M. 2011. "Portugal's Unnecessary Bailout." *New York Times*, April 12.

Fitoussi, Jean-Paul. 2011. "Capitalism, Socialism and Democracy, Once Again." Working paper, Institute for New Economic Thinking.

Gilovich, Thomas, Dale Griffin, and Daniel Kahneman. 2002. *Heuristics and Biases: The Psychology of Intuitive Judgment.* New York: Cambridge University Press.

Glaser, Markus, and Martin Weber. 2007. "Overconfidence and Trading Volume." *Geneva Risk and Insurance Review* 32(1), 1–36.

———. 2010. "Overconfidence." In H. Kent Baker and John R. Nofsinger, eds., *Behavioral Finance: Investors, Corporations, and Markets.* Hoboken, NJ: John Wiley & Sons, Inc.

Glynn, Carroll J., et al. 2004. *Public Opinion.* Boulder, CO: Westview Press.

Graham, Benjamin, and David Dodd. 1934. *Security Analysis.* New York: McGraw-Hill.

Greenhouse, Steven. 2008. *The Big Squeeze: Tough Times for the American Worker.* New York: Alfred A. Knopf.

Greenspan, Alan. 1995. "U.S. Economic Outlook." Testimony before the Senate Budget Committee, U.S. Senate. Washington, D.C., Jan 26.

Greenspan, Alan. 1997. "Remarks to the G-7 economic summit meeting. Presentation at the Spring Meeting of the Institute of International Finance. Washington, D.C. April 29.

Greenspan, Alan. 1998. "The Regulation of OTC Derivatives." Testimony before the Committee on Banking and Financial Services, U.S. House of Representatives. Washington, D.C. July 24.

Greenspan, Alan. 2002. "Opening Remarks at the Bank's 2002 Economic Policy Symposium." *Federal Reserve Bank of Kansas City Economic Review* 87, 4.

Hong, Harrison, and Jeremy C. Stein. 2007. "Disagreement and the Stock Market." *Journal of Economic Perspectives* 21, 109–128.

Janunts, Mesrop. 2010. "Differences of Opinion and Stock Returns." Ph.D. dissertation, Department of Economics, University of Neuchatel, Switzerland.

Jiang, Guohua, Charles M. C. Lee, and Yi Zhang. 2005. "Information Uncertainty and Expected Returns." *Review of Accounting Studies* 10, 185–221.

Kahneman, Daniel, Paul Slovic, and Amos Tversky. 1982. *Judgment under Uncertainty: Heuristics and Biases.* New York: Cambridge University Press.

Kahneman, Daniel, and Amos Tversky. 1979. "Prospect Theory: An Analysis of Decision under Risk." *Econometrica* 47, 263–292.

Kaletsky, Anatole, 2010, *Capitalism 4.0: The Birth of a New Economy in the Aftermath of Crisis.* New York: Public Affairs.

Kaustia, Markku. 2010. "Disposition Effect." In H. Kent Baker and John R. Nofsinger, eds., *Behavioral Finance: Investors, Corporations, and Markets.* Hoboken, NJ: John Wiley & Sons, Inc.

Kindleberger, Charles P. 1978. *Manias, Panics and Crashes: A History of Financial Crises.* New York: Basic Books.

Kroszner, Randall S., and Robert J. Shiller. 2011. *Reforming U.S. Financial Markets: Reflections before and beyond Dodd-Frank.* Cambridge, MA: MIT Press.

Krugman, Paul. 2011. "The Mistake of 2010." *New York Times*, June 2.

Kyle, Albert S., and F. Albert Wang. 1997. "Speculation Duopoly with Agreement to Disagree: Can Overconfidence Survive the Market Test?" *Journal of Finance* 52, 2073–2090.

Lacy, Sarah. 2011. "Peter Thiel. We're in a Bubble and It's Not the Internet. It's Higher Education." *TechCrunch*, April 10.

Levy, Frank, and Thomas Kochan. 2011. "Addressing the Problem of Stagnant Wages." Working paper, Massachusetts Institute of Technology.

Malmendier, Ulrike, and Geoffrey Tate. 2005. "CEO Overconfidence and Corporate Investment Decisions." *Journal of Finance* 60, 2661–2700.

Miller, Edward M. 1977. "Risk, Uncertainty, and Divergence of Opinion." *Journal of Finance* 32, 1151–1168.

Morgenson, Gretchen, and Joshua Rosner. 2011. *Reckless Endangerment: How Outsized Ambition, Greed, and Corruption Led to Economic Armageddon*. New York: Times Books.

Noelle-Neumann, Elisabeth. 1977. "Turbulences in the Climate of Opinion: Methodological Applications of the Spiral of Silence." *Public Opinion Quarterly* 41, 143–158.

Paletta, Damian. 2011. "Disability-Claim Judge Has Trouble Saying 'No.' Near-Perfect Approval Record. Social-Security Program Strained." *Wall Street Journal*, May 19.

Palley, Thomas. 2009. "America's Exhausted Paradigm: Macroeconomic Causes of the Financial Crisis and Great Recession." Working paper, New America Foundation, July.

Posner, Richard A. 2010. *The Crisis of Capitalist Democracy*. Cambridge, MA: Harvard University Press.

Rajan, Raghuram G. 2010. *Fault Lines: How Hidden Fractures Still Threaten the World Economy*. Princeton, NJ: Princeton University Press.

Reinhart, Carmen M., and Kenneth S. Rogoff. 2009. *This Time Is Different: Eight Centuries of Financial Folly*. Princeton, NJ: Princeton University Press.

Russo, J. Edward, and Paul J. H. Schoemaker. 2002. *Winning Decisions: Getting It Right the First Time*. New York: Currency Doubleday, Random House.

Scheinkman, José A., and Wei Xiong. 2003. "Overconfidence and Speculative Bubbles." *Journal of Political Economy* 111, 1183–1219.

Smith, Helena, and Jill Treanor. 2011. "Papandreou Slams Rating Agencies 'Trying to Shape Greece's Future.'" *The Guardian*, April 22.

Skidelsky, Robert. 2011. "Democracy or Finance?" April 21. www.project-syndicate.org/commentary.

Stockman, David. 2011. "The End of Sound Money and the Triumph of Crony Capitalism." Henry Hazlitt Memorial Lecture, Austrian Scholar's Conference, March 12.

Taffler, Richard. 2011. "Mortgage Fraud, Consumer Protection, Financial Literacy, and Behavioral Finance." Talk presented at the Annual Meeting of the Midwest Finance Association, Chicago, March 3.

Thaler, Richard H., and Cass R. Sunstein. 2008. *Nudge: Improving Decisions about Health, Wealth and Happiness*. New Haven: Yale University Press.

Trichet, Jean-Claude. 2011. "Building Europe, Building Institutions." Speech by the President of the European Central Bank on receiving the Karlspreis 2011, Aachen, June 2.

Tversky, Amos, and Daniel Kahneman. 1974. "Judgment under Uncertainty: Heuristics and Biases." *Science* 185(4157), 1124–1131.

Wallison, Peter J. 2011. *Dissent from the Majority Report of the Financial Crisis Inquiry Commission*. Washington, DC: American Enterprise Institute.

Williams, John Burr. 1938. *The Theory of Investment Value*. Cambridge, MA: Harvard University Press.

Yu, Jialin. 2011. "Disagreement and Return Predictability of Stock Portfolios." *Journal of Financial Economics* 99, 162–183.

Zaller, John R. 1992. *The Nature and Origins of Mass Opinion*. New York: Cambridge University Press.

BUBBLES: KEYNOTE PRESENTATIONS

CHAPTER 12

An Old Perspective on Asset Price Bubbles Policy

■

William Poole

There must be ten thousand speeches and papers, at least, on bubbles. With regard to policy, what I find missing is a clear statement applying control theory from the 1960s and rational expectations macroeconomics from the 1970s. Based on this work, I want to convince you that it would be a mistake for the government to attempt to influence, through direct market intervention, an asset price suspected of displaying a bubble. Somewhat in passing, I will also argue that the problem with a bubble is not the bubble per se but the accumulation of bubble-related assets in leveraged portfolios. From this observation, I outline three key reforms to strengthen the banking system.

Everyone agrees that the housing and mortgage bubbles of the first decade of this century turned out to be incredibly costly. There is no need to review the data. Many observe the enormous costs and conclude that there just must be a way, or we must invent a way, to prevent a recurrence of a bubble in the housing market or any other significant market. So, I want to go back to basics. Just because something is incredibly costly does not necessarily mean that there are solutions that will leave us better off. I intend my argument to be general but actual policy might well depend on the market involved. I am thinking primarily about a monetary policy device of some sort. But the argument holds also for a fiscal device such as a tax that might go on and off depending on efforts to control the bubble.

From work in the 1950s and 1960s—Tinbergen, Theil, Brainard, and others—we settled certain things. We need at least as many policy instruments as goals. If we are going to control a bubble by using an aggregate monetary policy instrument—ordinarily, the federal funds rate—we will have to accept unpleasant trade-offs because tighter policy may push the economy below full employment. So, let us use the economist's favorite can-opener device—assume there exists policy lever Z that has no unwanted side effects. There just has to be a Z out there somewhere.

We also want our policy levers to have predictable effects. A policy lever Z that would control a targeted asset price only within a range of plus or minus 20% would not be a good lever. Well, as a longtime economist, I know how to solve that problem, too—let there be policy lever ZZ that controls the target asset price with no error.

I will talk about regulation later, but beyond that hope, everyone knows that there is no ZZ. Many reach the same point as I have in this analysis but say that we must be prepared to use some policy instrument anyway because failure to do so has been so ghastly. This reaction is altogether wrong. Assume we really could find instrument ZZ, which would be better than what we actually have. From work in the 1970s—Lucas, Sargent, Taylor, and others—we know that we cannot analyze the application of instrument ZZ without analyzing asset pricing and decisions that depend on asset prices.

How is the market going to trade an asset knowing that the government has ZZ in operation? Asset prices are not exogenous. How will trading in other assets be affected? How will the market make investment decisions that depend on asset prices knowing that ZZ is in operation? We know that we cannot understand how a policy is going to work without analyzing private behavior based on expectations of what the policymaker is going to do. I do not know of even the simplest toy model illustrating how private agents would behave in the market for houses, or equities, or any other asset in the face of policymakers wielding instrument ZZ. If we do not understand how the market would work with an ideal instrument ZZ, how can we possibly know what will happen using the federal funds rate or a variable tax or some other instrument?

Actually, my claim that we do not have an example of a closed model is a bit of an overstatement, as we do know something about how the foreign exchange market works with government intervention. In an open-economy macro model, we can understand government intervention defined in terms of international capital flows. But there is no accepted model of government policy in the foreign exchange market of the sort we actually observe, such as the G7 intervention in the yen market on March 18, 2011. That makes it impossible to model private expectations of government behavior. In contrast, a Taylor-type rule of monetary policy allows a macroeconomic model to be closed with a defined monetary policy.

We also have experience in a related problem: that of employing a variable investment tax credit for economic stabilization. The interaction of policymakers' uncertainty and of market expectations created an unsatisfactory outcome in the 1960s. Adjustments in the ITC were almost perfectly mistimed from a stabilization perspective. We gave up on the idea of active use of the ITC for very good reason.

But I want to drive this argument further. Would we really want a government agency setting an asset price? Asset pricing is one of the most fundamental characteristics of a market economy. I can almost hear the objection to this conclusion: "You have taken logic too far. The government should *influence* when appropriate but not *set* asset prices." This fuzzy argument ignores what we learned from control theory and the rational expectations revolution. And I can also hear Milton Friedman's delightful and gleeful reply, which I heard on a number of occasions. Milton would put it this way: "As far as possible is the only place you *can* take logic." The bottom line is that once the government makes an effort to influence an asset price on a systematic basis we really do not know what may happen.

To avoid misunderstanding, of course the central bank should take account of the behavior of asset prices in setting monetary policy. Asset prices often contain valuable information as the central bank pursues policy to maintain aggregate price stability and does what it can to cushion disturbances to employment and output. Using information in asset prices is completely different from targeting asset prices.

The Mirage of Better Regulation

An asset price bubble creates a problem when the asset is held in highly leveraged accounts, such as bank portfolios. The dot-com bust, which took the NASDAQ average down by 70%, did not yield a financial crisis because the stocks were mostly held in unleveraged portfolios. A much smaller decline in house prices did create a crisis because homeowners had too much mortgage debt and highly leveraged commercial and investment banks held that debt in highly leveraged portfolios.

I am skeptical that tighter safety and soundness regulation can solve the problem of banking instability. Right now, everyone is cautious. But caution will fade. After all, the most recent crisis occurred with lots of regulators around and less than two decades after the S&Ls were shut down.

Regulation is a political animal. The old saw about the making of sausage and of legislation is true. I don't like that process. But, worse than that, the process assures that regulation will not at the end of the day be effective. Over time, lobbyists wielding campaign contributions and the promise of votes will persuade powerful congressmen to insert obscure provisions in obscure legislation. Dodd-Frank leaves us worse off than before because it institutionalizes too-big-to-fail and, potentially, adds large nonbanks to the protected list.

The so-called Volcker Rule institutionalizes a permanent game over the permissible activities of banks. Banks with lobbying power will work endlessly to carve out special provisions. To me, the logic of the Volcker Rule is flawed from the beginning. Risk is very hard to measure, but it would seem almost impossible for regulators to take account of the covariance of returns across different activities. Banning banks from certain activities may actually increase risk in a bank portfolio.

Structural Reforms

Are we doomed, then, to suffer asset price bubbles from time to time and their damage to the general economy through banking instability? To a degree, perhaps, but not to the degree of the recent disaster. Three reforms would help: fair-value accounting, higher capital requirements, and elimination of the deductibility of interest on all tax returns. These reforms do not raise control-theoretic issues.

Fair-value accounting is an issue like standards for weights and measures, though obviously much more complicated to implement. Nevertheless, implementation is not impossible—we have been doing it with mutual funds for over a half century. Within a few minutes of the market close every day, I can find the net asset value of my mutual fund shares on the Internet. By "fair-value accounting," I mean the use in accounting statements of market values for actively traded instruments—sometimes called "marked-to-market"—and best estimates of value when market values are not available.

Current accounting practice under Generally Accepted Accounting Principles—GAAP—is not much better than allowing a grocery store to sell breakfast cereal by the box without disclosing weight. GAAP is equivalent to being very careful about when a cereal box was manufactured without insisting that the weight of the cereal in the box be disclosed. Under GAAP, banks can hold securities in a portfolio labeled "held-to-maturity" and report them at prices that can be substantially different from observed market prices. The standard banker argument is that fair-value accounting would make earnings too volatile. The argument is specious; original-cost accounting does not make earnings less volatile but simply hides the volatility that exists.

Examples abound. Firms just do not want to recognize losses. The *Wall Street Journal* reported just a few days ago, on March 28, 2011, that the SEC required Berkshire Hathaway, a firm revered for its high standards, to restate some asset values to reflect market values. Berkshire's chief financial officer complained that current stock prices did not reflect the true value of the shares. That might be, but the place to make the argument is in the letter to shareholders and not in a falsely stated balance sheet. A well-capitalized firm can ride out periods of depressed asset prices. That is what capital is for.

Besides resistance to recognizing losses, I have another hypothesis as to what is going on. Consider an example from the current situation in which the cost of overnight money to a large bank—one too big to fail—is the current federal funds rate of about 15 basis points. Suppose the bank borrows in the funds market and invests the proceeds in five-year treasuries at 2.25%. The bank plans to keep rolling over its fed funds borrowings for five years. Using original-cost accounting, this position will yield positive carry as long as the funds rate remains below 2.25%. However, using fair-value accounting this position might quickly lose money if market expectations about the future federal funds rate rise and the five-year bond drops below par. Using original-cost accounting, employees getting bonuses from reported profits will continue to get their bonuses even if the position quickly creates a capital loss. The loss will not show up until the federal funds rate exceeds 2.25%.

Original-cost accounting does not change the ultimate size of a gain or loss but does change its timing. Fair-value accounting would do more than report financial information more accurately—it would change management incentives. Knowing that a bad bet on the direction of the five-year T-bond might yield an immediate reported loss for the bank, the incentive to put on the trade would change. Fair-value accounting is a powerful incentive for good risk management and an inducement to hold adequate capital.

In fact, fair-value accounting may be the most powerful incentive for sound risk management we can find. The S&L disaster would never have happened if S&Ls had been required to use fair-value accounting. The whole world would have observed the deteriorating financial position of these firms in the mid to late 1960s. Moreover, a decade of federal government policies to prop up the industry would probably have been untenable politically with the losses out there for all to see. Thus, the policies pursued by both the S&Ls and the federal government would have been different. The incentive effects of fair-value accounting do not garner enough attention.

As for the recent crisis, I suspect that the potential for deterioration in the fair value of a subprime mortgage portfolio would have made banks more cautious from the outset. I realize that putting a fair-value estimate on the complicated CDOs backed by subprime mortgages might have been difficult, but that problem arose anyway and would have been faced earlier. Fair-value accounting would have forced the Countrywides of the world to slow down. The transparency that more accurate accounting can bring should not be underestimated as a way to address the bubble problem.

Stiffer capital requirements for banks also deserve attention. The Dodd-Frank legislation did not solve the problem; capital requirements for the largest banks remain too low. The current situation is reminiscent of Fanny and Freddie before they were conserved in September 2008. Eventually, a big bank will get into trouble. The competitive pressures on banks will encourage one or more to accept risks that the banks and we do not understand today. The most powerful incentive effects would come from a system in which banks were required to issue long-term subordinated notes. That idea has been thoroughly vetted in the literature. Capital requirements are a nonintrusive regulation, unlike regulations that substitute examiner judgment for management judgment with regard to asset quality, adequacy of liquidity, compensation practices, and a host of other management responsibilities.

Another powerful structural reform would be to reduce or eliminate the deductibility of interest on all tax returns. Public finance experts have recommended such a reform for years. Given the instability that flows from excessive leverage, it makes no sense to provide a tax incentive for debt. Interestingly, the *Wall Street Journal* reported just a few days ago, on April 4, 2011, that a congressional study of this issue is under way.

In terms of reform, fair-value accounting ranks above higher capital requirements. The reason is simple. Capital is the difference between assets and liabilities and therefore cannot be measured accurately without measuring assets accurately.

Concluding Comment

The objections to macroeconomic policies to deal with bubbles are decisive: the case against even trying is clear. However, microeconomic policies to change incentives and improve bank strategy are available and should be implemented.

A banking crisis of the magnitude of the recent one is not inevitable. We know how to construct a more robust banking system. Unfortunately, it seems that large banks have won the debate for now. They operate under federal protection, or think they do, as did Fannie and Freddie and the S&Ls before them. Bubbles can occur, run on, or pop, reflecting the market's efforts to price assets appropriately and the enthusiasms of an innovative market economy. Without banking instability, bubbles are interesting but do not pose great risks to the macroeconomy.

CHAPTER 13

Struggling to Escape from "Assumption 14"

■

Benjamin M. Friedman

At least four hypotheses, none mutually exclusive, have emerged to explain the origins of the financial crisis that began in the United States in 2007: (1) Managers of financial institutions, or their employees, may have engaged in criminal activity. (2) Principal/agent conflicts may have given the managers of financial institutions incentives to undertake activities that, though legal, nonetheless exposed their institutions and their institutions' shareholders to excessive risk that the shareholders would not have chosen. (3) The operation of government in a variety of ways—ranging from specific lender-of-last-resort actions and policies fostering homebuilding and home ownership to matters as general as limited liability—may have given both managers and shareholders incentives to put their institutions, and ultimately the taxpayers and the economy, at excessive risk. (4) Participants in the relevant financial markets, especially including mortgage borrowers, originators, securitizers, and investors, may not have understood the risks inherent in the positions they and their institutions were taking. Any or all of these influences may have been at work in creating the worst financial crisis since the depression of the 1930s, and the work needed to sort out the relative importance of each will no doubt occupy economists and other empirical researchers for some time to come.

Hypothesis (4), however—that key market participants failed to understand the relevant risks—lies outside the bounds of today's conventionally accepted modes of economic analysis. The very first of the seminal papers under retrospective review in this book, for example, the 1993 classic by Franklin Allen and Gary Gorton, specifies a lengthy series of assumptions underlying the authors' analysis. The crucial one for this purpose is Assumption 14: "All agents know the structure of the model and the distributions of the random variables, but do not observe the particular realizations of random variables."[1] The notion that some realizations are unobserved is hardly restrictive. By contrast, the assumption that all agents (act as if they) know the processes that govern those realizations, including the structural relations among them as well as the distributions of the underlying random influences—in other words, the standard "rational expectations" assumption that has governed most economic analysis for the past four decades—is the heart of the matter.

Although economists have long been aware of evidence, in part from psychology and other fields, that contradicts the standard full-rationality assumption (hence the burgeoning field of "behavioral finance"),[2] the convention nonetheless has been to maintain the assumption that whatever departures exist do not matter for macroeconomic outcomes. But the recent financial crisis clearly had macroeconomic consequences. In the United States the subsequent downturn in real economic activity was the steepest since the 1930s. The loss of wealth, in the value of both houses and equity claims to the stock of corporate capital, also set a post–World War II record. The real dislocations in many markets, beginning with but not limited to residential construction, remain readily apparent. If expectations by market participants that violated Allen and Gorton's Assumption 14 were a significant factor underlying the crisis, they certainly did have macroeconomic implications. The further implication that follows is that attempting to analyze the crisis while maintaining this assumption—or, perhaps more important, assessing potential new policy measures and regimes while doing so—is a highly limited endeavor and may ultimately prove fruitless.

Although it is too soon to evaluate the evidence systematically, by now there has been a steady accumulation of indications that during the run-up to the crisis many key market participants, including not just individuals of modest wealth but highly paid professionals working at major financial institutions, indeed did not understand the risks they were facing. At the broadest level, the evaluations that the major credit rating agencies applied to securities backed by home mortgages, especially subprime mortgages and especially those issued in 2006 and 2007, were strikingly at variance with the subsequent default experience of the underlying loans.[3] Many forms of derivative contracts priced against these and similar securities also appear, in retrospect, to have been widely mispriced. At a more technical level, recent research has shown that the "copula" models many firms used to price these and other related securities had serious analytical flaws.[4] To be clear, the question at issue is not what was, or should have been, the market's best estimate of any given future outcome; it is the assessment, and hence the pricing, of the *risk* associated with those outcomes.

Accumulating anecdotal evidence further drives home that it was often the largest firms—the ones whose managers and employees should be most likely to think and behave as the standard rationality assumption indicates—that made the biggest mistakes. The losses on derivatives contracts incurred by insurance giant AIG, which in September 2008 forced U.S. taxpayers to put $182 billion into rescuing the firm, represent one well-known example. Another is Merrill Lynch, which in December 2007 sold off its portfolio of mortgage-backed securities at a loss of $18 billion. (In September 2008 the firm was taken over by Bank of America, which was apparently acting under pressure from the U.S. Treasury Department.) Merrill's internal estimate of the value at risk on this portfolio was $92 *million*—smaller by more than two orders of magnitude.[5]

Other large, well-known firms made similar errors, often with similar resulting need for rescue. Royal Bank of Scotland, which the British government took over in October 2008, incurred losses of $15 billion on its portfolio; the firm's internally estimated VaR was $22 million—nearly three orders of magnitude smaller. Zurich-based UBS, which the Swiss government had to rescue that same month by setting up a classic "bad bank" called the StabFund, lost $38 billion; the VaR that UBS had estimated was $636 million.[6] U.S. investment bank Morgan Stanley, which survived intact (albeit with substantial loan support from the Federal Reserve System after the firm hurriedly converted itself to bank form), lost $14 billion on its portfolio; its estimated VaR was $83 million.

Was the decline in house prices and the consequent sequence of events that precipitated the crisis simply an extraordinary event that could not, and therefore should not, have been factored into the risk structure market participants saw themselves facing? To repeat, the issue here is not what market participants should have *expected*, but what *risk* they should have attached to their expectations. Perhaps what happened in the U.S. mortgage market was the proverbial "six-sigma," or even "ten-sigma," event. No one goes out of his or her way to avoid being struck by lightning on a clear day, or being crushed by an unseen piano falling to the sidewalk from an upper-story window.

But the history of financial crises that have occurred just within recent decades has thrown up too many supposed six- (or ten-) sigma events to be credible. Many people made the same claim when Long-Term Capital Management had to be rescued in 1998, in the midst of the "Asian financial crisis" and the turmoil surrounding Russia's debt obligations. Before that the same notion emerged after a series of problems involving real estate and leveraged buyout transactions impaired many of the country's banks in the late 1980s and early 1990s, and before that in the "Latin American debt crisis" of the early 1980s. When six-sigma events occur with this frequency, they are not six-sigma events.

One of the most senior officials at Citigroup, which was involved in each of these episodes, has publicly expressed a similar view. In the early stages of the most recent crisis, Citi took losses totaling $55 billion, more than any other bank. It was also centrally involved, with losses that at times became institution-threatening, in each of the prior crises. Looking back over this decades-long series of mishaps, and referring not just to Citi but to other banks as well, William Rhodes, the chairman of Citibank and senior vice chairman of Citigroup at the time of the most recent crisis, subsequently referred to "flawed analyses" and wrote, "Clearly, time and time again, economic and market trends were not accurately assessed." Referring more specifically to Citi's real estate losses in the early 1990s, Rhodes quoted the bank's then-CEO John Reed as saying, "we did not understand the risks in the financial environment or the work that Citibank was undertaking within it."[7]

At a more formal level, we also have both evidence and models for the kind of systematic error that many of these episodes, including the most recent crisis, appear to represent. Another of the seminal contributions under review in this book, José Scheinkman and Wei Xiong's 1993 paper, today looks prescient in exactly this regard. Sheinkman and Xiong based their analysis on "heterogeneous beliefs generated by agents' overconfidence." And they referred in turn to Michael Harrison and David Kreps's earlier (1978) insight that "when agents agree to disagree and short selling is not possible, asset prices may exceed their fundamental value."[8] (One could readily extend the result to cases in which short selling is merely restricted, or expensive.) As they acknowledged, today there is ample evidence, again much of it from the psychology and behavioral literatures, of systematic overconfidence in a wide variety of settings.

Why, then, has the economics profession—especially the profession's macroeconomics wing—been so reluctant to abandon Assumption 14? I believe two forces are at work.

First, abandoning or even seriously weakening the full-rationality assumption would be deeply subversive of the all-important role of markets in allocating scarce resources, including, most importantly for purposes of this book, the role of the financial markets in allocating capital investment. As is often the case, most of the attention in the wake of the recent crisis has focused on the financial losses that investors, banks, and other institutions took on the assets they held that declined in value. But the essential role of the financial markets in a capitalist economy is to allocate the economy's scarce investment capital. (The financial markets serve other functions as well, such as operating the payments mechanism and providing liquidity and various forms of insurance; but in notable contrast to the allocation of capital, there are well-established public utility models for each of these.) Mispricing of assets and subsequent losses to their holders matter in themselves, but they are also—and more fundamentally—the financial reflection of an underlying misallocation of real resources.

In the most recent crisis, for example, the greatest amount of discussion has focused on the losses investors incurred on their holdings of mortgages, mortgage-backed securities, and related derivative instruments. But the fact that the mortgages were overpriced means that the corresponding interest rate was too low, with the result that Americans built and bought far too many houses— millions of which are now empty or unpaid for, or financed with unserviced debt and facing potential foreclosure. Similarly, in the aftermath of the "dot-com" bubble of the late 1990s, most of the attention focused on the losses investors incurred on their positions in telecom stocks. But the fact that the stock prices were too high meant that the cost of capital to the firms issuing them was too low, with the result that firms in the industry laid hundreds of millions of miles of fiber-optic cable that have never been lit and probably never will be.

Second, abandoning the full-rationality assumption poses a major analytical challenge. A familiar maxim holds that you can't beat something with nothing. The full-rationality assumption provides a way of disciplining analysis in which forward-looking behavior is of the essence—as is inevitably the case when the economic setting of interest encompasses speculative securities markets. For all the debate over "rational" expectations since the introduction of this methodology into macroeconomics nearly four decades ago, and even despite substantial research into models of "limited" (or "bounded") rationality, there is today no readily evident alternative to provide a comparable discipline on such lines of research.

Here again, the literature following from one of the seminal papers under review in this book serves as an example. Implicit in Ben Bernanke and Mark Gertler's 1999 paper (although they did not emphasize the point in just this way) was the idea that a decline in the net worth of *either* banks *or* their borrowers would diminish banks' willingness to lend, all else equal, and hence would trigger both a decline in lending volume and an increase in lending rates, and via both of those mechanisms would depress real economic activity. (The effect stemming from a decline in borrowers' net worth reflects the role of collateral in loan arrangements.) The idea is important for purposes of this book's inquiry in that it provides a way of understanding the positive feedback running from rising/declining asset prices to rising/declining economic activity and net worth, and on to further rising/declining asset prices. Much work since then—for example, the pair of now-classic 1997 papers by Bengt Holmstrom and Jean Tirole and by Nobuhiro Kiyotaki and John Moore—has fleshed out the microfoundations of this mechanism. More recent work—for example, the 2011 paper by Mark Gertler and Peter Karadi, and the 2010 paper by Andrea Gerali and coauthors on the euro area—has brought this line of analysis to bear more directly on pertinent issues of monetary policy, including policy in a crisis like the recent one.

But all of this analysis—the original idea from Bernanke and Gertler, the subsequent microfoundations, and the more recent applications to monetary policy in the crisis—rests on the full-rationality assumption. To the extent that market participants' failure to understand the risks they were incurring, either personally or on behalf of the financial institutions for which they worked, was central to what happened in the crisis, therefore, this entire line of research, and others like it too, are unlikely to get at the essence of the matter. They are, in effect, handcuffed by Assumption 14.

Macroeconomics sorely needs a disciplined alternative to the full-rationality assumption, and when one emerges it will represent a fundamental revolution in economic methodology comparable to the rational expectations revolution of four decades ago. As was the case then, economists will look back at the years of accumulating evidence and wonder that the full-rationality assumption ever held sway—just as people four decades ago remarked that the prerational expectations literature seemed to imply that policymakers could "fool all the people all the time," or that economic agents regularly "left $50 bills lying on the sidewalk." But the profession is not there yet.

What kind of progress, then, can we make while we wait for this analytical lacuna to be remedied? Several new directions, at both the positive and the normative levels, seem possible despite this overarching impediment to more fundamental progress.

To begin, it is important to recognize that while price stability (a low mean and small variance for whatever measure of an economy's inflation is taken to be most relevant) is an important policy objective in itself, it is not sufficient to guarantee favorable, or even acceptable, macroeconomic outcomes more generally. As James Tobin often said, there are worse things than 3% inflation. The American economy has just experienced some of them. Second, in the wake of the worst financial crisis since the 1930s—involving the collapse of major financial firms, large-scale declines in asset values and the consequent destruction of citizens' wealth, the interruption of credit flows, the loss of confidence both in firms and in credit market instruments, the widespread fear of default by counterparties, and ultimately the need for extraordinary (in both scale and scope) intervention by central banks and other governmental institutions—it is also important to acknowledge that "market discipline" enforced by creditors is not sufficient to prevent financial institutions from taking actions that, collectively, prove publicly harmful. There is therefore a need for regulation and/or supervision of financial institutions to prevent what amounts to a straightforward externality. Indeed, the importance of just this externality and the consequent need for regulatory measures to contain it have a distinguished pedigree in economics. Adam Smith, writing the *Wealth of Nations* in the aftermath of Scotland's worst banking crisis in two generations, favored not only restrictions on how banks could fund themselves but also limits on the interest rates they could charge on loans. Smith explained that he favored these measures for the same reasons he favored laws requiring firewalls between houses in Edinburgh.

The experience of the crisis and the subsequent downturn in real economic activity made clear the limited capacity of monetary policy, even including the "unconventional" measures that many central banks have taken in this episode, to correct such a situation once it is in progress and especially once short-term interest rates have reached the zero lower bound. Further, a growing body of research casts doubt on the usefulness of potential rules that would relate the central bank's interest rate setting to levels of asset prices with an eye toward arresting the crisis while it is still developing. The resulting danger for economic thinking is analogous to what led macroeconomics to focus on "real" business cycle theories. The logic there was that (*a*) everyone knows that monetary shocks are the only demand shocks worth considering, but (*b*) the evidence increasingly indicated that fluctuations in the money stock, however measured, are not systematically related to fluctuations in economic activity, and therefore (*c*) demand shocks as a category must be irrelevant for economic fluctuations. Today an all-too-familiar presumption in macroeconomics is that monetary policy is the only policy worth considering; if monetary policy cannot do much about asset price bubbles and their consequences, the analogous logic would imply, then no policy is worth considering. Smith knew better. So should we.

What policy measures do we then require? With the 2010 Dodd-Frank legislation now behind us, the most pressing need is to move forward with stricter capital requirements on leveraged financial institutions, especially including those that, on account of size or "interconnectedness" or both, pose potential systemic risks. Importantly, however, effective reform of capital requirements is not merely a matter of specifying higher stated capital ratios or even more finely tuned capital ratios pegged to the riskiness of the assets on an institution's balance sheet. Two more elements are needed. One is accounting reform. As the experience of some of the largest U.S. institutions in the crisis revealed, often what matters for capital adequacy is not the numerical ratio but the quantity to which it applies. Assets hidden off the balance sheet are, in effect, subject to zero capital requirement regardless of the stated required ratio.

The other missing element is clearly specified resolution procedures. The Dodd-Frank legislation usefully expanded the government's resolution *authority* to include endangered financial institutions other than banks (for example, bank holding companies, broker/dealers, and insurance companies), but it did not lay out what procedures the relevant agencies would use, within that authority, if such an institution becomes undercapitalized. In general, requirements are effective only if some consequence follows on the failure to meet them. Capital requirements are no different. It is precisely the awareness of the consequences of failing to do so that should keep institutions in compliance.

As the crisis has also made clear, however, there is, in addition, a deeper principle of *political economy* at work. In a democracy like America's, if the voters elect to public office individuals who do not believe in regulation, and those officeholders appoint people of like mind to head the principal agencies that constitute the nation's regulatory apparatus, then there will not be effective regulation regardless of the prevailing statutes and rules. The public may or may not get the regulation it deserves, but it does get the regulation it chooses.

Finally, in the wake of the recent crisis it is worth asking a yet more fundamental question that is also implicit in the entire subject of asset price "bubbles," and that is likewise intimately connected to the implications of the full-rationality assumption in economics: Is our financial system serving us well, as judged by both the way it does its job and what it costs us to do that?[9]

As much recent literature has emphasized, especially in the United States the financial system has always been large and in recent years it has gotten substantially larger. To recall, the essential function of the financial system in a capitalist economy is to allocate scarce investment capital. Seen in this perspective, the U.S. economy's mechanism for allocating its capital has been getting more expensive not just absolutely but compared to the total returns earned on the capital being allocated. From the 1950s through the 1980s, profits earned by financial firms (not counting insurance companies and firms in the real estate business) represented 10% of all profits earned in the U.S. economy. In the 1990s financial firms' share of total profits rose to 22%. And in the first half of the last decade—that is, until just before the crisis—these firms' share of all U.S. profits reached 34%.[10]

Further, this significant share of the profits earned by U.S. business is far from the total cost of running the economy's financial system. That cost also includes the salaries financial firms pay to their workforce and the rents they pay for their office space (including the rental equivalent for firms that own their own buildings), as well as more mundane elements like all the associated utility bills, travel tickets, and advertising budgets. Like its share of economy-wide profits earned, the finance industry's share of all U.S. wages and salaries paid has also been rising in recent decades. Fifty years ago it was 3%; more recently it has been 7%.[11] The standard argument is that these high salaries (including the eight-figure bonuses for those at the top) are necessary to attract the talent that enables these firms to do their job. If this is true, it means that the economy's capital allocation mechanism is inherently all the more expensive to operate. The same principle applies to the financial sector's other expenses. It may be true that without lavishly furnished offices in choice locations, or lots of prime-time television advertising, the capital allocation mechanism would not be able to serve its function. But if so, this means that the necessary cost of running it is all the greater.

And, here as elsewhere, the basic principle of a market economy holds: expenses paid are the counterpart of resources used. At my university, for example, more than one-fourth of the graduates in recent classes have gone to work at investment banks, hedge funds, private equity firms, and the like. These talented and energetic young people could be doing something else. If they are not really needed in the financial firms that employ so many of them—if what they do there actually adds little or no economic value—then something is seriously wrong with yet another market that allocates our economy's resources (in particular, the labor market). But if the financial sector *is* the best place to use their talents and energies, that need is yet another part of what makes our economy's capital allocation mechanism so expensive to run.

At the same time that the financial sector has been growing ever more expensive to operate—absorbing a larger fraction of the economy's total profits, claiming a larger share of the most talented workers, and so on—the economy's performance has been disappointing. Wholly apart from the recent housing bubble and all of the economic costs associated with its demise (costs which must be subtracted from the economic benefits the financial sector delivers), there is less about which to cheer in the aggregate gains accruing to capital investment either. How much of the disappointing performance of U.S. productivity growth in recent experience is due to poor allocation of capital? The truth is that no one knows.

An important task for the economic profession, therefore, is to gain some well-grounded quantitative understanding both of how good a job the financial sector is doing at allocating our economy's investment capital and of what it is costing on an all-in basis. Neither is the focus of this book—at least not directly—but any measure of the overall cost must include the risk of the occasional meltdowns to which asset price bubbles expose us. And the answers we find may turn out to bear on how much longer we will be willing to continue to constrain our analysis within the confines of Assumption 14.

Notes

1 Allen and Gorton (1993), 817.
2 See, for example, Thaler (1993–2005).
3 See, for example, Foote et al. (2008) and Gerardi et al. (2009).
4 See Jarrow et al. (2008) and Jarrow and van Deventer (2008).
5 Here and below, figures on losses incurred and firms' internal estimates of value at risk are from *The Economist*, "Hall of Shame," August 7, 2008, and van Deventer (2011), in both cases taken from the respective firms' annual reports and other filings.
6 See Zimmermann and Szelyes (2011) and the 2009 and 2010 *Accountability Reports* of the Swiss National Bank (2009 report, section 6.5; 2010 report, section 6.7). The amount that the SNB transferred to the StabFund was $40 billion.
7 Rhodes (2011), xxviii, 31.
8 Sheinkman and Xiong (1993), 1184.
9 See Friedman (2010) for a fuller development of this line of argument.
10 Data are from the U.S. Department of Commerce.
11 See Philippon and Reshef (2007).

References

Allen, Franklin, and Gary Gorton. 1993. "Churning Bubbles." *Review of Economic Studies* 60, 813–836. Reprinted in this volume.

Bernanke, Ben, and Mark Gertler. 1999. "Monetary Policy and Asset Price Volatility." In *New Challenges for Monetary Policy: A Symposium*. Kansas City, MO: Federal Reserve Bank of Kansas City. Reprinted in this volume.

Foote, Christopher L., Kristopher Gerardi, Lorenz Goette, and Paul S. Willen. 2008. "Just the Facts: An Initial Analysis of Subprime's Role in the Housing Crisis." *Journal of Housing Economics* 17, 291–305.

Friedman, Benjamin M. 2010. "Is Our Financial System Serving Us Well?" *Daedalus* 139, 9–21.

Gerali, Andrea, Stefano Neri, Luca Sessa, and Federico M. Signoretti. 2010. "Credit and Banking in a DSGE Model of the Euro Area." *Journal of Money, Credit and Banking* 42, Supplement, 107–141.

Gerardi, Kristopher S., Andreas Lehnert, Shane M. Sherlund, and Paul S. Willen. 2009. "Making Sense of the Subprime Crisis." *Brookings Papers on Economic Activity* 39(2), 69–159.

Gertler, Mark, and Peter Karadi. 2011. "A Model of Unconventional Monetary Policy." *Journal of Monetary Economics* 58, 17–34.

Harrison, J. Michael, and David M. Kreps. 1978. "Speculative Investor Behavior in a Stock Market with Heterogeneous Expectations." *Quarterly Journal of Economics* 92, 323–336.

Holmstrom, Bengt, and Jean Tirole. 1997. "Financial Intermediation, Loanable Funds, and the Real Sector." *Quarterly Journal of Economics* 112, 663–691.

Jarrow, Robert A., Li Li, Mark Mesler, and Donald R. van Deventer. 2008. "CDO Valuation: Fact and Ficton." In Gunter Meissner, ed., *The Definitive Guide to CDOs: Market, Application, Valuation, and Hedging*. London: Risk Publications.

Jarrow, Robert A., and Donald R. van Deventer. 2008. "Synthetic CDO Equity: Short or Long Correlation Risk?" *Journal of Fixed Income* 17, 1–11.

Kiyotaki, Nobuhiro, and John Moore. 1997. "Credit Cycles." *Journal of Political Economy* 105, 211–248.

Philippon, Thomas, and Ariell Reshef. 2007. "Skill Biased Financial Development: Education, Wages and Occupations in the US Financial Sector." National Bureau of Economic Research Working Paper No. 13437.

Rhodes, William R. 2011. *Banker to the World: Leadership Lessons from the Front Lines of Global Finance*. New York: McGraw-Hill.

Scheinkman, José A., and Wei Xiong. 2003. "Overconfidence and Speculative Bubbles." *Journal of Political Economy* 111, 1183–1219. Reprinted in this volume.

Thaler, Richard H., ed. 1993–2005. *Advances in Behavioral Finance*. 2 vols. New York: Russell Sage Foundation.

van Deventer, Donald R. 2011. "Value at Risk as an Index of Financial Institutions Risk in the Credit Crisis." Kamakura Corporation, May 2.

Zimmermann, Marcel, and Zoltan Szelyes. 2011. "The StabFund: A Look at the Inner Workings of a 'Bad Bank.'" *Central Banking* 21, 47–53.

NEW IDEAS ON ASSET PRICE BUBBLES

CHAPTER 14

Monetary Policy and Stock Market Booms

Lawrence J. Christiano, Cosmin Ilut, Roberto Motto, and Massimo Rostagno

1. Introduction and Summary

The interaction between monetary policy and asset price volatility has been a matter of increased concern since the collapse of stock market booms in 2000 and 2007. Are booms like these suboptimal? Is monetary policy partially responsible for stock market booms? Should monetary policy actively seek to stabilize stock market booms? These classic questions have been put back on the table by the experience of the past two decades.

1.1. THE CONVENTIONAL WISDOM

There is, we believe, a conventional wisdom on the answers to these questions. Booms arise for reasons largely unrelated to the conduct of monetary policy. Some booms are indeed excessive. But it is unwise to identify which booms are excessive and to actively resist them using interest rate policy. The conventional wisdom is that, in any case, a strategy of raising the policy interest rate when the inflation forecast is high and reducing it when the inflation forecast is low should help to dampen excessive volatility. The notion is that booms which are excessive involve a rise in stock prices above levels justified by fundamentals. Such a boom represents a surge in demand because there is nothing currently on the supply side of the economy to justify it. In a demand boom, however, one expects inflation to be high. The policy of inflation forecast targeting using an interest rate rule "leans against the boom" at precisely the right time. This conventional wisdom was given an intellectually coherent foundation in two very influential papers (Bernanke and Gertler 1999, 2001).

1.2. DATA

We explore an alternative perspective on the relationship between monetary policy and booms. We are motivated to consider this alternative by the historical record of U.S. stock market booms as well as by the Japanese stock market boom of the 1980s. We find that inflation was relatively low in each of the 18 U.S. stock market boom episodes that occurred in the past two centuries.[1] The Japanese case is particularly striking, with inflation slowing sharply during the boom from its preboom level. The notion that stock market booms are not periods of high inflation, and that they are if anything periods of low inflation, is not new to this paper. The recent work of Adalid and Detken (2007), Bordo and Wheelock (2004, 2007), and White (2009) also draws attention to this observation. Here we stress the implications for monetary policy. The historical record suggests that, at least at an informal level, a monetary policy which implements inflation forecast targeting using an interest rate rule would actually destabilize asset markets. The lower-than-average inflation of the boom would induce a fall in the interest rate and thus amplify the rise in stock prices in the boom.

A noticeable feature of stock market booms is that, with the exception of only two of the 18 booms in our U.S. data set, credit growth is always stronger during a boom than outside a boom. On average, credit growth is twice as high in booms than it is in nonboom periods. Casual reasoning suggests that volatility would be reduced if credit growth were tightened as booms get underway. In practice, this tightening in response to credit growth would not be justifiable based on the inflation outlook alone because booms are not in fact periods of elevated inflation. The idea that credit growth should be assigned an independent role in monetary policy has been advocated in several papers. We have advocated this position in work that we build on here (Christiano et al. 2008).[2]

According to the conventional wisdom, it is only the "excessive" booms that are inflationary. Assuming at least some of the booms considered in this paper are excessive, our results contradict the conventional wisdom that inflation accelerates during such booms. Indeed, the results raise the possibility that monetary policy is in part responsible for at least some booms, by responding to the fall in inflation with interest rate cuts.

1.3. INTERPRETING THE DATA WITH A NEW KEYNESIAN MODEL

Our empirical results raise an important question. How could it be that a stock market boom based purely on expectations about the future, which is therefore driven purely by demand, *not* raise inflation? At first glance, the apparent finding that inflation is low during such booms may appear simply odd. Without a coherent framework to make sense out of it, one is reluctant to make an apparent anomaly the foundation for constructing a monetary policy strategy. This is why we turn to model simulations.

We show that the standard New Keynesian model provides an intellectual foundation for the notion that inflation is relatively weak in a boom. This is so, even in a boom that is only based on optimistic (possibly ill-founded) expectations about the future, and not on real current developments. Our simulations provide support for the notion that a monetary policy which focuses heavily on inflation can exacerbate booms. No doubt there exist improvements to banking supervision and credit market regulations that can moderate asset price volatili-ty.[3] However, it seems inefficient to use supervision and regulation to remove volatility injected by monetary policy. That source of volatility could instead be removed by an adjustment to monetary policy.

We begin with the simplest possible New Keynesian model, the one analyzed in Clarida, Gali, and Gertler (1999) and Woodford (2003). Because this model does not have capital in it, we cannot use it to think about a stock market boom. Still, we can use the model to think about booms driven only by optimism about the future, why inflation might be low at such a time, and how an inflation forecast targeting interest rate rule might be destabilizing under these circumstances.[4] This analysis gets at the core of the issue—how inflation could be low in a demand-driven boom—and creates the basic intuitive foundation for understanding the later results based on models that do incorporate asset prices.

We assume that people receive a signal which leads them to expect that a cost-saving technology will become available in the future. In the model, prices are set as a function of current marginal costs as well as future marginal costs. The expectation that marginal costs in the future will be lower dampens the current rise in prices. The inflation forecast targeting interest rate rule leads the mon-etary authority to cut the interest rate, stimulating the demand for goods. Output expands to meet the additional demand, raising current marginal costs. The expected future reduction in marginal cost exceeds the current rise, so that prices actually fall during the boom.[5]

That prices are set in part as a function of future marginal costs is essential to our analysis. In the model, forward-looking price setting reflects the presence of price adjustment frictions. However, it is easy to think of other reasons why price setters might be forward looking. For example, firms may be motivated to seek greater market share in order to be in a better position in the future to profit from anticipated new future technologies. The drive for greater market share may lead to a pattern of price cutting. This particular strategy for responding to anticipa-tions of improved technology is one that has, for example, been stressed by Jeff Bezos, the CEO of Amazon.[6]

1.4. WHY AN INFLATION FORECAST TARGETING INTEREST RATE RULE MAY DESTABILIZE A BOOM

The boom that occurs in the wake of a signal about future technology in our model simulation is excessive in a social welfare sense. Its magnitude reflects the suboptimality of the inflation forecast targeting interest rate rule. The monetary policy that maximizes social welfare responds to the optimistic expectations by raising the real interest rate sharply (we refer to the socially optimal interest rate as "the natural rate of interest"). The reason for the sharp rise in the natural rate of interest is simple. The expectation of higher future consumption opportunities creates the temptation to increase consumption right away. But such an increase is inefficient because the basis for it—improved technology—is not yet in place. In a world where markets operate smoothly the efficient outcome—a delay in the urge to consume—is automatically brought about by a rise in the real interest rate. In such a world, the natural and actual rates of interest coincide. In the world of our model, the smooth operation of markets is hampered by price and wage frictions, and the monetary authority's control over the nominal rate of interest gives it control over the real interest rate. This control can be used for good or ill: the monetary authority has the power to make the real rate of interest close to or far from the natural rate of interest. The monetary authority using an inflation forecast targeting interest rate rule responds to the signal about future productivity in exactly the wrong way. The monetary authority observes downward pressure on inflation in the wake of the signal, and responds by reducing the interest rate. The difference between the high interest rate that is optimal and the low interest rate that actually occurs represents a substantial and socially suboptimal monetary stimulus. The boom that occurs in the wake of a signal of improved future technology is largely a phenomenon of loose monetary policy, in our model.

One way to characterize the problem with the inflation forecast targeting interest rate rule is that the rule does not assign any weight to the natural rate of interest or to any variable that is well correlated with it. Traditionally, the absence of the natural rate of interest from interest rate rules is motivated on two grounds. First, in practice this variable is hard to measure because it depends on hard-to-determine details about the structure of the economy. Second, in much of the model analysis that appears in the existing literature, the natural rate of interest fluctuates relatively little and so approximating it by a constant does not represent a very severe mistake. Regarding the first consideration, we argue that credit growth may be a good proxy for the natural rate.

Consider the second motivation for ignoring the natural rate of interest in an interest rate rule. Until recently, builders of models have assumed that shocks to the demographic factors which influence labor supply, to government spending, and to the technology for producing goods and services occur without advance warning. We confirm that the natural rate of interest fluctuates relatively little in response to shocks that occur without warning. However, recently there has been increased attention to the possibility that people receive advance signals about shocks.[7] Consider the case of shocks to government spending and to technology. The major government spending shocks are associated with wars. When that kind of spending jumps—the troops are on the move and the bullets are flying—it does so after a lengthy period of increased tensions and political maneuvering. These events prior to actual increases in war spending represent the early signals about government spending.[8] Disturbances in technology work in the same way. Signals that the information technology revolution would transform virtually everything about how business is done existed decades ago.[9] We show below that the natural rate of interest fluctuates a lot more in response to a signal about a future shock than it does to a shock that occurs without any advance warning.[10] That is, when we take seriously that many disturbances occur with advance warning, the assumption of a constant natural rate of interest in an interest rate rule is no longer tenable.

So, the problem with the inflation forecast interest rate targeting rule is that it reduces the interest rate in a boom triggered by optimistic expectations, while the efficient monetary policy would increase the interest rate.[11] Paradoxically, we first develop this finding below in a model with only price frictions, in which the optimal monetary policy (i.e., the policy that sets the interest rate equal to the natural rate) completely stabilizes inflation. That is, our analysis does not necessarily challenge the wisdom of inflation targeting per se, only the effectiveness of doing so with an inflation forecast interest rate targeting rule that is principally driven by the inflation forecast.[12]

1.5. WHY ADDING CREDIT GROWTH TO THE INTEREST RATE RULE MAY HELP

Up to this point, the analysis has focused on models that are sufficiently simple that they can be analyzed with pen and paper. We then verify the robustness of the analysis by redoing it in a medium-sized new Keynesian DSGE model that incorporates capital and various frictions necessary for it to fit business cycle data well. In this model, optimism about the future triggers a fall in inflation and a rise in output, the stock market, consumption, investment, and employment. The boom is primarily an artifact of the empirically estimated interest rate policy rule, in which the forecast of inflation is assigned an important role. Under the optimal monetary policy the boom would involve only a modest rise in output and this would be accomplished by a sharp rise in the rate of interest.

We use the medium-sized model to investigate the possibility, suggested by the historical data record, that assigning a role—beyond its role in forecasting inflation—to credit growth may help to stabilize booms. First, however, we must modify the model to incorporate an economically interesting role for credit. We do so by introducing financial frictions along the lines suggested in the celebrated contribution by Bernanke, Gertler and Gilchrist (1999) (BGG). We obtain the same results in this model that we found in our simple model and in the model with capital. The inflation forecast interest rate targeting rule causes the economy to overreact to the optimism about the future, though inflation during the boom is low. The natural rate of interest rises sharply in the model. When we assign a separate role for credit growth in the interest rate rule, then the response of the economy is more nearly optimal. We interpret this as signifying that credit growth is a reasonable proxy for the natural rate of interest.

1.6. ORGANIZATION OF THE PAPER

The paper is organized as follows. The first section below describes the data. The following section describes the analysis of our simple model. Our analysis features a baseline parameterization, but also examines the robustness of the argument to perturbations. We consider, for example, interest rate rules which look at inflation forecasts as well as at current inflation. We also consider the case where price stickiness arises because of frictions in the setting of wages rather than because of frictions in price setting per se. This is an important perturbation to consider because empirical analyses typically find that it is crucial to include wage stickiness if one is to fit the data well. The next section considers the analysis of the expanded model with credit and asset markets. We offer concluding remarks at the end.[13]

2. Inflation and Credit Growth in Stock Market Booms: The Evidence

This section displays data on stock market boom-bust episodes. We find that in all cases, inflation is relatively low during the boom phase in these episodes. Real credit growth was relatively high in all but two episodes. We also examine data on the Japanese stock market boom in the 1980s. As in all U.S. stock market booms, this Japanese boom is associated with a drop in inflation. Presumably, the boom was fueled in part by the accommodative Japanese monetary policy of the time, which cut short-term interest rates substantially. We show that if the Bank of Japan had followed a standard interest rate rule that assigns weight to inflation and also the output gap, then its interest rate would have been cut even more sharply. The Japanese experience of the 1980s presents perhaps the most compelling empirical case for the proposition that an interest rate rule which focuses on the forecast of inflation exacerbates stock market volatility.[14]

We split our U.S. data-set into two parts. The first part covers 12 episodes in the nineteenth and early twentieth centuries and the second considers four episodes beginning with the Great Depression. We divide out data set in this way because we have annual observations for the first part and quarterly observations for the second part. In addition, data availability considerations require that our concepts of credit differ slightly between the two periods.

Consider the first part of our data, which are displayed in Figure 14.1. The stock market index is the log of Schwert's (1990) index of common stock, after deflating by the consumer price index.[15] The real output measure is the logarithm of real gross national product.[16] Our measure of real credit is the quantity of bank loans, scaled by the consumer price index.[17] We define a stock market boom-bust episode as follows. We start with 12 financial panics in the nineteenth century and the pre–World War I portion of the twentieth century.[18] These are indicated by a solid circle in Figure 14.1 and they are listed in Table 14.3. Although each panic is associated with a drop in the stock market, Figure 14.1 indicates that in all but three cases the stock market had already begun to drop before. We define the peak associated with a particular financial panic as the year before the panic when the stock market reached a local maximum. We define the trough before the peak as the year when the stock market reached a local minimum. The period bracketed by the trough and the peak associated with a financial panic is indicated in Figure 14.1 by a shaded area. In addition, we block from our analysis the period of the Civil War, which is indicated by its own shaded area.

We can see from Figure 14.1 that in virtually every stock market boom, the price level actually declined. Moreover, in no case did the price level rise more than its average in the nonboom, non–Civil War periods. In addition, we see that stock market booms are typical periods of accelerated credit growth. Table 14.1 quantifies the findings in Figure 14.1. According to that table, consumer price (CPI) inflation averaged −2.5% during stock market booms, substantially less than the 0.7% inflation that occurred on average over nonboom periods. In addition, credit grew twice as fast, on average, during a stock market boom as during other periods. Table 14.1 shows just how volatile the stock market was over this period. It grew at a 10% pace during boom periods and shrank at a

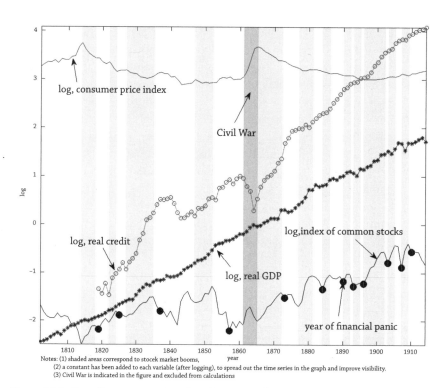

Notes: (1) shaded areas correspond to stock market booms,
(2) a constant has been added to each variable (after logging), to spread out the time series in the graph and improve visibility.
(3) Civil War is indicated in the figure and excluded from calculations

Figure 14.1 Data for nineteenth and early twentieth centuries.

Table 14.1 **Variables over Various Subperiods, 1803–1914**

Periods	CPI	Credit	GDP	Stock Price
Boom	−2.5	9.5	4.6	10.2
Other	0.7	4.0	3.1	−6.3
Non–Civil War	−0.7	6.5	3.7	0.8

Note: (1) Number presented 100 times average of log first difference of indicated variable over indicated period. (2) Boom periods are the union of the trough to the peak periods enumerated in Table 14.2. (3) Other are periods that are not booms and that fall outside of 1861–1865. (4) Results for credit data based on period, 1819–1914, due to data availability.

6.3% rate in nonbooms. Table 14.2 provides a breakdown of the data across individual boom periods. The table documents the fact, evident in Figure 14.1, that there is little variation in the general pattern. Inflation is lower in every stock market boom than its average value outside of booms. In the case of credit, there is only one episode in which credit growth was slower in a stock market boom than its average outside of booms. That is the boom associated with the 1884 panic.

We now turn to the data for the post–World War I period.[19] The data are displayed in Figure 14.2. We exclude the World War II period from our analysis, and this period is indicated by the shaded area. The other shaded areas indicate six stock market booms in the twentieth and early twenty-first centuries. As in the earlier data set, each boom episode is a time of nonaccelerating inflation. In several cases, inflation actually slowed noticeably from the earlier period. Note, too, that stock market booms are a time of a noticeable increase in the growth rate of credit. These results in Figure 14.2 are quantified in Tables 14.3 and 14.4. According to Table 14.3, CPI inflation in stock market booms is half its value in other (non–World War II) times. Credit growth, as in the nineteenth century, is twice as rapid in boom times as in other times. According to the results in Table 14.4, inflation in each of the six boom episodes considered is below its average in nonboom times. With one exception, credit growth is at least twice as fast in booms as in other periods. The exception was the boom that peaked in 1937. This started in the trough of the Great Depression.

Figure 14.3 displays a real index of Japanese stock prices, as well as the Japanese CPI.[20] The trough and peak of the 1980s boom corresponds to 1982Q3 and 1989Q4, respectively. The time of the boom is highlighted in both Figure 14.3 and Figure 14.4. What is notable about Figure 14.3 is that CPI inflation is significantly positive before the start of the 1980s stock market boom, and it then slows significantly as the boom proceeds. Inflation even falls below zero a few times in the second half of the 1980s. We ask what a monetary authority that follows a standard inflation targeting interest rate rule would have done in

Table 14.2 **Variables in Stock Market Boom Episodes**

		A. Nonboom, non–Civil War, 1803–1914			
	CPI	Credit	GDP	Stock Price	
	0.7	4.0	3.1	−6.3	
		B. Boom episodes			
Panic	Trough-peak	CPI	Credit	GDP	Stock price
1819	1814–1818	−8.0	na	1.8	9.8
1825	1822–1824	−9.8	21.9	3.7	12.1
1837	1827–1835	−1.5	14.6	4.9	5.2
1857	1847–1852	−1.3	7.6	5.4	6.9
1873	1865–1872	−4.1	11.9	4.8	8.5
1884	1877–1881	−0.6	3.5	7.5	16.0
1890	1884–1886	−2.2	4.9	5.9	15.2
1893	1890–1892	0.0	5.6	4.5	7.9
1896	1893–1895	−3.3	4.2	4.4	3.9
1903	1896–1902	0.3	8.6	5.3	11.1
1907	1903–1905	0.0	7.6	2.3	18.3
1910	1907–1909	−1.8	4.0	0.6	25.1

Note: (1) Numbers represent 100 times average of log first difference of indicated variable over indicated perio d. (2) Panel A: data averaged over period 1802–1914, skipping 1861–1865 years and trough-to-peak years. (3) Panel B: data averaged only over the indicated trough-peak years. (4) Panics occur after stock market peak. (5) na signifies not available; observations on credit begin in 1819

the 1980s. In particular, we posit the following policy rule for setting Japanese call money rate, R_t:

$$R_t = 0.7R_{t-1} + (1-0.7)\left[R + 1.5\left(\pi_t - \pi\right) + 0.5 gap_t\right], \tag{1}$$

where t denotes quarters, gap_t denotes the output gap, and π_t denotes the actual, year-over-year rate of inflation. For R and π we used the sample average of the call money rate and the inflation rate in the period immediately preceding the boom, 1979Q1–1982Q3. Also, we used the gap estimates produced by the International Monetary Fund in the process of preparing the "World Economic Outlook."[21] The

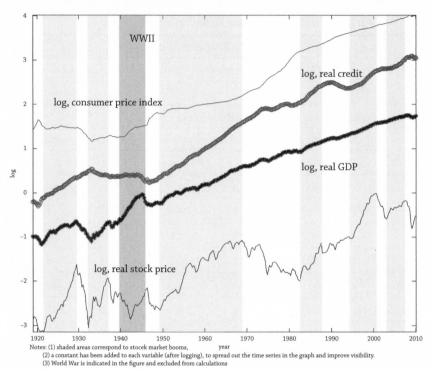

Notes: (1) shaded areas correspond to stoceck market booms,   year
(2) a constant has been added to each variable (after logging), to spread out the time series in the graph and improve visibility.
(3) World War is indicated in the figure and excluded from calculations

Figure 14.2 Data for twentieth and early twenty-first centuries.

Table 14.3 **Variables over Various Subperiods, 1919Q1–2010Q1**

Periods	CPI	Credit	GDP	Stock price
Boom	1.8	5.3	4.6	13.8
Other	4.0	2.3	0.2	−11.7
Whole period	2.7	4.0	2.7	2.7

Note: (1) Numbers represent 100 times average of log first difference of indicated variable over indicated period. (2) Boom periods are the union of the trough-to-peak periods enumerated in Table 14.2. (3).Others are periods that are not booms and that exclude World War II (1939Q4–1945Q4). Whole period corresponds to the full sample, excluding World War II.

results are displayed in Figure 14.4.[22] The starred line displays the actual call money rate, while the solid line displays the values of R_t that solve (1) over the period 1979Q1–1989Q4. Note that the Bank of Japan loosened policy very significantly during the boom, bringing the interest rate down on the order of 300 basis points. That action by the Bank of Japan is thought by many to have been a mistake, and to have contributed to a stock market boom that in retrospect appears to have definitely been "excessive" (see, e.g., Shirakawa 2010). But, note that if

Table 14.4 **Variables in Stock Market Boom Episodes**

A. Nonboom, non–World War II, 1919Q1–2010Q1

	CPI	Credit	GDP	Stock price	
	4.0	2.3	0.2	−11.7	

B. Boom episodes

trough-peak	CPI	Credit	GDP	Stock Price
1921Q3–1929Q3	−0.2	5.7	5.9	19.3
1932Q2–1937Q2	0.6	−2.1	6.5	24.2
1949Q2–1968Q2	−2.0	6.3	4.2	8.1
1982Q3–1987Q3	3.2	7.5	4.3	17.5
1994Q2–2000Q2	2.5	6.1	3.9	16.4
2003Q1–2007Q1	3.0	4.6	3.0	10.1

Note: (1) Numbers represent 100 times average of log first difference of indicated variable over indicated period. (2) Panel A: data averaged over period 1919Q1–2010Q1, skipping 1939Q4–1945Q4 and trough-to-peak years. (3) Panel B: data averaged only over the indicated trough-peak years. (4) Panics occur after stock market peak.

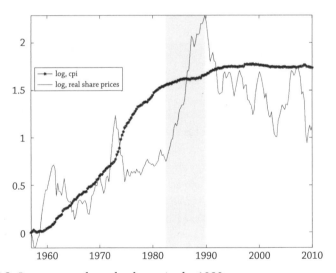

Figure 14.3 Japanese stock market boom in the 1980s.

the Bank of Japan had implemented the policy rule, (1), they would have reduced the interest rate an additional 200 basis points over what they actually did do. One has to suppose that this would only have further destabilized an already volatile market. We hasten to add a caveat because we are conjecturing what would have happened under the counterfactual monetary policy rule, (1). Such

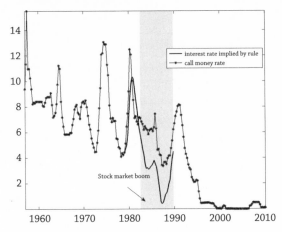

Figure 14.4 Japan, actual rate and rate implied by simple interest rate rule

a counterfactual experiment would have a host of general equilibrium consequences that might have changed the realized data in profound ways. This is why we now leave the informal analysis of data and turn to the analysis of models next.

3. A Simple Model for Interpreting the Evidence

We begin our analysis in a model that is simple enough that the core results can be obtained analytically, without the distraction of all the frictions required to fit aggregate data well. The model is a version of the workhorse model used in Clarida, Gali and Gertler (1999) (CGG) and Woodford (2003).

We posit that the driving disturbance is a "news shock," a disturbance to information about next period's innovation in technology.[23] News that technology will improve in the future creates the expectation that future inflation will be low and this leads an inflation forecast targeting monetary authority to reduce the nominal rate of interest. This policy creates an immediate expansion in the economy. Although the expansion is associated with higher current marginal cost, inflation nevertheless drops in response to the lower future expected marginal costs.

We obtain our results in this section under two specifications for why there are frictions in prices. In one scenario ("pure sticky prices"), there are frictions directly in the setting of prices. In this scenario, wages are set flexibly in a competitive labor market. In the second scenario ("pure sticky wages"), prices are set flexibly, but are influenced by frictions in the setting of wages. Our model of wage frictions is the one proposed in Erceg, Henderson, and Levin (2000) (EHL). The inefficient boom with low inflation occurs in both scenarios, though it does so across a wider range of parameter values under sticky wages.

The action of the monetary authority in reducing the nominal rate of interest in response to a news shock is exactly the wrong one in this model. Under the efficient monetary policy, the nominal rate of interest should not be decreased. Indeed, under pure sticky prices the nominal rate of interest should be increased substantially in response to a news shock. In the model, it is efficient for employment to be constant in each period, and for consumption to track the current realization of technology. The news shock triggers an expectation of higher future consumption, and the efficient rate of interest rises in order to offset the intertemporal substitution effects associated with an expectation of higher future consumption.

Household preferences in the model are:

$$E_t \sum_{l=0}^{\infty} \beta^l \left[\log(C_{t+l}) - \frac{L_{t+l}^{1+\sigma_L}}{1+\sigma_L} \right],$$

where C_t denotes consumption and L_t denotes employment. The household budget constraint is:

$$P_t C_t + B_{t+1} \le W_t L_t + R_{t-1} B_t + T_t,$$

where T_t denotes lump sum income from profits and government transfers, R_t denotes the nominal rate of interest, and P_t, W_t denote the price level and wage rate, respectively.

Final goods, Y_t, are produced as a linear homogeneous function of Y_{it}, $i \in (0,1)$ using the following Dixit-Stiglitz aggregator:

$$Y_t = \left[\int_0^1 Y_{lt}^{\frac{1}{\lambda_f}} dl \right]^{\lambda_f}.$$

A representative, competitive final good producer buys the ith intermediate input at price, P_{it}. The ith input is produced by a monopolist, with production function

$$Y_{it} = \exp(a_t) L_{it}.$$

Here L_{it} denotes labor employed by the ith intermediate good producer. The ith producer is committed to sell whatever demand there is from the final good producers at the producer's price, P_{it}. The producer receives a tax subsidy on wages in the amount, $(1-v)W_t$, where v is set to extinguish the monopoly distortion in steady state. The subsidy is financed by lump sum taxes on households.

In the pure sticky price version of the model, wages are set flexibly in competitive markets and prices are set by the intermediate good monopolists, subject to Calvo-style frictions. In particular, with probability ξ_p the ith producer, $i \in (0,1)$, must keep its price unchanged from its value in the previous period and with the complementary probability the producer can set its price optimally. In the pure sticky wage version of the model, intermediate good producers set prices flexibly, as a fixed markup over marginal cost. Following EHL, we adopt a slight change in the specification of household utility in which households are monopolists in the supply-differentiated labor services indexed by j, $j \in (0,1)$, and they set wages subject to Calvo-style frictions. With probability ξ_w the wage of the jth type of specialized labor service cannot be changed from its value in the previous period. With the complementary probability the wage rate of the jth specialized labor service is set optimally.

We consider these two extreme specifications of price/wage setting frictions, because their simplicity allows us to derive results analytically. We consider the case with both sticky wages and prices, as well as other features useful for fitting aggregate data well, in the next section.

In our baseline analysis, we adopt the following law of motion for a_t:

$$a_t = \rho a_{t-1} + u_t, u_t \equiv \xi_t^0 + \xi_{t-1}^1. \tag{2}$$

Here, u_t represents the white noise one-step-ahead error in forecasting a_t based on its own past. We posit that this error is the sum of two mean-zero, white noise terms, ξ_t^0 and ξ_{t-1}^1, where

$$E\xi_t^0 a_{t-s} = E\xi_{t-1}^1 a_{t-s} = 0, s > 0.$$

The subscript on ξ_t^j indicates the date when this variable is revealed to agents in the model, $j = 0,1$. Thus, at time t agents become aware of ξ_t^0 and ξ_t^1. Here, ξ_t^0 represents the last piece of information received by agents about u_t and ξ_t^1 represents the first piece of information about u_{t+1}. We refer to ξ_t^1 as "news."

As is now standard, we express the household's log-linearized intertemporal Euler equation in deviation from what it is in the first-best equilibrium—in which the inflation rate is always zero and the interest rate is R_t^*—as follows:

$$\hat{x}_t = -E_t\left[\hat{R}_t - \tilde{\pi}_{t+1} - R_t^*\right] + E_t\hat{x}_{t+1}. \tag{3}$$

Here, $\hat{x}$ denotes the output gap, the percent deviation between the actual and efficient levels of output. Also, $\hat{R}_t$ and $\hat{\pi}_t$ denote the percent deviation of the gross nominal interest rate and of the gross inflation rate, respectively, from their values in steady state. Similarly, R_t^* denotes the percent deviation of the gross nominal interest rate in the efficient equilibrium from its steady state.

As noted above, employment is constant in the efficient equilibrium and consumption is proportional to $\exp(a_t)$. In addition, inflation is zero. These properties, together with the assumption of unit intertemporal elasticity of substitution, imply that, after linearization, R_t^* corresponds to the expected change in a_t:[24]

$$R_t^* = E_t a_{t+1} - a_t = (\rho - 1)a_t + \xi_t^1. \tag{4}$$

The shock to current productivity, ξ_t^0, enters via a_t with a coefficient of $\rho - 1$. In standard empirical applications which do not incorporate news shocks, the values of autoregressive coefficients like ρ are estimated to be large (in a neighborhood of 0.9), and as a result R_t^* is not very volatile. At the same time, note how the signal shock, ξ_t^1, appears with a unit coefficient in R_t^*. Evidently, the introduction of news shocks may increase the volatility of R_t^* by an order of magnitude. The intuition is simple. A persistent shock that arrives without advance warning creates little incentive for intertemporal substitution. Such a shock creates only a small need to change the interest rate. By contrast, a signal that a persistent shock will occur in the future creates a strong intertemporal substitution motive which requires a correspondingly strong interest rate response.

The simplest representation of an interest rate rule that focuses on inflation is the following:

$$\hat{R}_t = a_\pi E_t \hat{x}_{t+1}. \tag{5}$$

This specification of the monetary policy rule, together with a particular labor market subsidy, is structured so that the steady states of the efficient and actual equilibria coincide.[25]

Completing the model requires an additional equation, a Phillips curve. We discuss the Phillips curve corresponding to pure sticky prices and pure sticky wages, respectively, in the following two sections. The derivation of the equilibrium conditions is tedious, but well known.[26]

3.1. PURE STICKY PRICES

The equilibrium condition associated with price setting is, after linearization,

$$\hat{\pi}_t = \gamma \hat{x}_t + \beta E_t \hat{\pi}_{t+1}. \tag{6}$$

The slope of the Phillips curve with respect to the output gap, γ, is related to structural parameters as follows:

$$\gamma = \frac{\left(1 - \xi_p\right)\left(1 - \beta \xi_p\right)}{\xi_p}\left(1 + \sigma_L\right), \tag{7}$$

where ξ_p is the probability that a firm cannot change its price. Also, $1 + \sigma_L$ represents the elasticity of firm marginal cost with respect to the output gap.

The price Phillips curve, (6), and IS relation, (3), after substituting out for $\hat{R}_t$ and R_t^*, represent two equations in two unknowns, $\hat{\pi}_t$ and $\hat{x}_t$. We posit the following solution,

$$\hat{\pi}_t = \eta_\pi a_t + \varphi_\pi \xi_t^1 \tag{8}$$

$$\hat{x}_t = \eta_x a_t + \varphi_x \xi_t^1, \tag{9}$$

where $\eta_\pi, \varphi_\pi, \eta_x, \varphi_x$ are undetermined coefficients.[27] In the case of the response to a_t (hence, ξ_t^0):

$$\eta_x = -\frac{\psi(1-\rho\beta)(1-\rho)}{\gamma}, \quad \eta_\pi = \frac{\gamma}{1-\rho\beta}\eta_x.$$

Here,

$$\psi = \frac{\gamma}{(1-\rho\beta)(1-\rho)+(a_\pi-1)\gamma\rho} > 0.$$

It is evident that

Proposition 1. $\eta_x, \eta_\pi < 0$ for all admissible parameter values.

Simple substitution implies the following solution for the interest rate:

$$\hat{R}_t = a_\pi \psi (\rho-1)\rho a_t + a_\pi \psi (\rho-1)\xi_t^1, \tag{10}$$

It is interesting to compare the actual interest rate response, $\hat{R}_t$ in (10), with the efficient interest rate response, R_t^* in (4). We can see that if a_π is sufficiently large, then $a_\pi \psi(\rho-1)\rho \to \rho-1$ and the interest rate response to a_t (and, hence, to ξ_t^0) is efficient. For more moderate values of a_π the interest rate at least has the right sign response to a_t, though the magnitude of that response is inefficiently weak. By contrast, the response of R_t to ξ_t^1 is perverse. As noted above, the efficient interest rate displays a strong and positive response to ξ_t^1, while R_t remains unchanged for $\rho=1$ and actually declines for $\rho<1$. To understand the perverse response of the interest rate to a news shock, we need to first discuss the reduced form parameters, $\eta_x, \eta_\pi, \varphi_\pi, \varphi_x$.

Consider η_x, η_π. Proposition 1 implies that ξ_t^0 drives both the output gap and inflation down. The intuition for this result is straightforward. Given the assumed time-series representation for a_t, a positive shock to ξ_t^0 raises a_t and creates the expectation that a_t will be smaller in later periods. Relative to the efficient intertemporal consumption path in which $c_t = a_t$, households wish to reallocate consumption into the future. The monetary policy rule offsets the relative weakness in period t demand by reducing the interest rate, R_t, but the response is not strong enough. As a result, period t spending expands by less than the rise in a_t, accounting for the fall in the output gap in period t. The fall in the output gap implies weak labor demand and, hence, low labor costs. The reduction in costs accounts for the drop in inflation.

The fact, $\eta_\pi < 0$, explains why R_t drops in response to ξ_t^1. The news shock creates the expectation that technology will be launched on a temporary high in the next period, creating the expectation that inflation in the next period will be low. This is evident by evaluating (8) in $t+1$ and taking the period t conditional expectation:

$$E_t \hat{\pi}_{t+1} = \eta_\pi \left(\rho a_t + \xi_t^1 \right).$$

Because a positive disturbance to ξ_t^1 reduces anticipated inflation, and because our assumed monetary policy rule reacts to the inflation forecast, it follows that R_t drops in response to a positive innovation in ξ_t^1.

The remaining reduced form parameters, φ_π and φ_x, control the response of inflation and the output gap to a news shock, ξ_t^1. These parameters are given by:

$$\varphi_x = \psi(a_\pi - 1), \; \varphi_\pi = \psi\left[-\beta(1-\rho) + (a_\pi - 1)\gamma\right]. \tag{11}[28]$$

From the first expression, we see that $\varphi_x > 0$, so that the output gap always jumps with a positive signal about future productivity, ξ_t^1. The consumption smoothing motive and the rise in expected future consumption create a desire to increase current spending. In the efficient equilibrium the interest rate, R_t^*, increases sharply in order to keep spending equal to the unchanged current value of a_t. But, as discussed earlier, R_t either does not respond at all in the limiting case, $\rho = 1$, or it actually falls.

Turning to φ_π, the impact of ξ_t^1 on $\hat{\pi}_t$ operates by way of its effects on current and future marginal cost. These effects can best be seen by solving the Phillips curve forward and making use of (9) and the law of motion for a_t:[29]

$$\hat{\pi}_t = \gamma\left[\check{x}_t + \beta E_t \check{x}_{t+1} + \beta^2 E_t \check{x}_{t+2} + \beta^3 E_t \check{x}_{t+3} + \dots\right] \tag{12}$$

$$= \gamma\eta_\pi \frac{1}{1-\beta\rho} a_t + \gamma\varphi_x \xi_t^1 + \gamma\frac{\beta\eta_\pi}{1-\beta\rho}\xi_t^1.$$

The first term involving ξ_t^1, $\gamma\varphi_x$, pertains to the impact of a news shock on date t marginal cost. This term is definitely positive because a positive period t news shock raises the period t output gap (recall, $\varphi_x > 0$). Thus, the impact of the news shock on $\hat{\pi}_t$ is positive if we only take into account period t marginal cost (i.e., if $\beta = 0$). Note that the second term involving ξ_t^1 is definitely negative (recall, $\eta_\pi < 0$). This term reflects that a positive realization of ξ_t^1 signals a fall in future marginal costs. Thus, the net effect on current inflation of ξ_t^1 is ambiguous and so we must turn to a numerical example.

The intuition sketched in this section suggests that the sign of the period t inflation and output response to ξ_t^1 is likely to be sensitive to the assumptions about the time-series representation of a_t. Suppose, for example, that $a_{t+1} > a_t$ after a positive shock to ξ_t^0. In this case, the shock to ξ_t^0 is likely to trigger a surge in the demand for goods, making η_x and η_π positive.[30] This in turn suggests that in the period of a jump in ξ_t^1, firms would anticipate a rise in marginal cost not only in the current period but in future periods as well, so that π_t would increase. We explore the robustness of our results to the assumptions about a_t in the numerical experiments below.

3.2. PURE STICKY WAGES

We now consider the case in which prices are flexible, but there are frictions in the setting of wages, as spelled out in EHL. They derive the following equilibrium condition:

$$\hat{\pi}_{w,t} = \frac{\left(1 - \xi_w\right)\left(1 - \beta\xi_w\right)}{\xi_w \left(1 + \sigma_L \frac{\lambda_w}{\lambda_w - 1}\right)} \Big[\left(1 + \sigma_L\right)\hat{x}_t - \hat{\bar{w}}_t \Big] + \beta\hat{\pi}_{w,t+1}, \tag{13}$$

where $\pi_{w,t}$ denotes the gross growth rate of the nominal wage rate and $\bar{w}_t$ denotes the real wage, divided by technology, $\exp(a_t)$. As before, a hat over a variable indicates percent deviation from steady state. The intuition for (13) is straightforward. The first object in the square brackets is the real marginal cost of work scaled by the technology shock, expressed in percent deviation from steady state.[31] It is perhaps not surprising that when this object is higher than the scaled real wage, nominal wage growth is high. The growth rate of the scaled real wage, $\bar{w}_t$, the price level, the nominal wage rate, and the state of technology are related by the following identity:

$$\hat{w}_t = \hat{w}_{t-1} + \hat{\pi}_{w,t} - \hat{\pi}_t - \left(a_t - a_{t-1}\right). \tag{14}$$

With flexible prices, (6) drops from the system. In addition, the fact that price setters set prices as a fixed markup over marginal cost implies $\hat{w}_t = 0$ for all t. Imposing this condition and rearranging, we find, using (4):

$$E_t \hat{\pi}_{w,t+1} = E_t \hat{\pi}_{t+1} + R_t^*. \tag{15}$$

Rewriting (13) taking $\hat{w}_t = 0$ into account, we obtain:

$$\hat{\pi}_{w,t} = \gamma_w \hat{x}_t + \beta\hat{\pi}_{w,t+1}, \tag{16}$$

where

$$\gamma_w = \frac{\left(1 - \xi_w\right)\left(1 - \beta\xi_w\right)}{\xi_w \left(1 + \sigma_L \frac{\lambda_w}{\lambda_w - 1}\right)}\left(1 + \sigma_L\right). \tag{17}$$

We see an important distinction here between sticky wages and sticky prices. For a given degree of stickiness in wages and prices, that is, $\xi_p = \xi_w$, slope of the wage Phillips curve, (16), is smaller than the slope of the price Phillips curve, (6). The intuition for this is simple. Because of constant returns to scale, firms in this economy have constant marginal costs. The marginal cost of supplying labor, by contrast, is increasing in labor and is steeper for larger σ_L. The price set by a monopolist with a steep marginal cost curve reacts less to a cost shock than does the price set by a monopolist with flat marginal cost. This effect on the monopolist's price response is magnified when demand is highly elastic and explains the presence of the elasticity of demand for labor in (17), $\lambda_w/(\lambda_w - 1)$.[32]

Using (15) to replace price inflation with wage inflation in the policy rule and the IS equation (see (5) and (3)),

$$\hat{R}_t = a_\pi E_t \left[\hat{\pi}_{w,t+1} - R_t^* \right] \tag{18}$$

$$\hat{\pi}_t = -E_t \left(\hat{R}_t - \hat{\pi}_{w,t+1} \right) + E_t \hat{x}_{t+1}. \tag{19}$$

The three equilibrium conditions associated with the pure sticky wage model are the wage Phillips curve, (16), the policy rule, (18), and the IS equation, (19). This system can be solved for $\hat{\pi}_t$, $\hat{\pi}_{w,t}$, and $\hat{R}_t$. The implications for price inflation can then be deduced using (14) and $\hat{w}_t = 0$.

The solution of the system can be represented as follows:

$$\hat{\pi}_{w,t} = \eta_\pi^w a_t + \varphi_\pi^w \xi_t^1, \ \hat{x}_t = \eta_x^w a_t + \varphi_x^w \xi_t^1, \tag{20}$$

as in (11), with

$$\hat{\pi}_t = \hat{\pi}_{w,t} - \left(a_t - a_{t-1} \right), \tag{21}$$

according to (14). By this last expression, the impact of ξ_t^1 on $\hat{\pi}_t$ is simply φ_π^w. It can be shown that:[33]

$$\eta_\pi^w = \frac{\gamma_w}{1 - \beta\rho} \eta_x^w, \ \eta_x^w = \frac{-a_\pi (1-\rho)(1-\beta\rho)}{(1-\rho)(1-\beta\rho) + (a_\pi - 1)\rho\gamma_w} = -a_\pi \frac{\psi_w}{\gamma_w}(1-\rho)(1-\beta\rho).$$

Evidently, the analogue of Proposition 1 holds for sticky wages:

Proposition 2. η_π^w, $\eta_x^w < 0$ for all admissible parameter values.

In addition, it can be shown that:[34]

$$\varphi_x^w = a_\pi \left(a_\pi - 1 \right) \psi_w, \ \varphi_\pi^w = a_\pi \psi_w \left[-\beta(1-\rho) + \left(a_\pi - 1 \right) \gamma_w \right], \tag{22}$$

where

$$\psi_w = \frac{\gamma_w}{(1-\rho\beta)(1-\rho) + \left(a_\pi - 1 \right)\gamma_w\rho}.$$

According to (22), the sign of φ_x^w is definitely negative. To see why, consider a scenario in which the period t state of technology, a_t, is fixed and a signal arrives that a_{t+1} will jump. That this can be expected to create expected deflation can be seen by considering the extreme case in which the nominal wage rate is literally fixed. In this case, constancy of $\bar{w}_t$ and $\bar{w}_{t+1}$ requires that an $x\%$ increase in technology be accompanied by an $x\%$ decrease in the contemporaneous price level. This implies that the current price level remains fixed after a 1% shock to ξ_t^1, while the period $t+1$ price level falls by 1%, that is, $\pi_{t+1} < 0$. This anticipated deflation, under a price inflation targeting rule with $a_\pi > 1$, is met in a fall in R_t sufficiently large so that the real interest rate also falls. This expansionary monetary reaction raises the period t output gap by stimulating period t spending. The wealth effect associated with the anticipated future rise in technology also helps to drive up spending.

By (21), the impact on period t price inflation, π_t, of a signal, ξ_t^1, about future technology corresponds to φ_π^w. As in the case of sticky prices, the sign of φ_π^w is ambiguous (see (22)). Present considerations alone (i.e., $\beta = 0$) make it positive. This is because the monetary expansion described in the previous paragraph increases the current marginal cost of working and this places upward pressure on $\pi_{w,t}$ according to the wage Phillips curve (16). Considerations of the future alone make φ_π^w negative. Intuitively, wage inflation in the next period, $\pi_{w,t+1}$, can be expected to fall with the anticipated jump in a_{t+1} because of the negative sign of η_π^w (see Proposition 2). The nature of the Calvo-style wage frictions suggest that $\pi_{w,t}$ should fall in anticipation of the fall in $\pi_{w,t+1}$ (see (16)). To determine the sign of φ_π^w for interesting values of the parameters requires numerical simulation.

Departing momentarily from our main theme, we note that in the pure sticky wage model, a monetary policy that relates the nominal rate of interest to price inflation does not optimize social welfare. As emphasized by EHL, the efficient allocations can be supported by a rule which replaces price inflation in the interest rate targeting rule with wage inflation. To see this, note that in this case the equilibrium conditions formed by the wage-targeting interest rate rule, (16) and (19), do not include the natural rate of interest. As a result the variables, $\hat{x}_t$, $\hat{R}_t$, and $\hat{\pi}_{w,t}$, determined by those equations evolve independently of the technology shock. In particular, the first best outcomes,

$$\hat{x}_t = \hat{\pi}_{w,t} = 0$$

and $\hat{R}_t = 0$ satisfy the equilibrium conditions with wage targeting. According to (21), the rate of price inflation, $\hat{\pi}_t$, is the negative of technology growth under a wage-targeting monetary policy. Because the nominal wage rate is constant under this monetary policy, while the real wage must fluctuate with technology, it follows that optimal policy does not stabilize the high-frequency movements in inflation in the pure sticky wage case.

3.3. NUMERICAL RESULTS

In this section, we report numerical simulations of the period t impact on inflation and output of a signal, ξ_t^1, that technology will expand by 1% in the next
period. To investigate robustness of the analysis, we embed the time series representation of a_t in (2) in the following more general representation:

$$a_t = (\rho + \lambda)a_{t-1} - \rho\lambda + u_t, u_t \equiv \xi_t^0 + \xi_{t-1}^1, |\rho|, |\lambda| \le 1. \tag{23}$$

The representation in (2) corresponds to (23) with $\lambda = 0$. When $\rho + \lambda > 1$,
then (23) implies that a_t follows a "hump-shape" pattern after an innovation
to a_t. As indicated in our discussion of sticky prices, with λ sufficiently large the
model is expected to predict a rise in inflation in the wake of a positive signal, ξ_t^1.
Numerical results are reported in Table 14.5, and the value of λ is indicated in
the first column. Results for the forward-looking rule, (5), are reported in Panel A
of the table. As a further check on robustness, we also report results for the case
where the interest rate responds to the contemporaneous rate of inflation, rather
than to its expected value in the next period. Results for this case are presented
in Panel B.

We adopt the following baseline parameterization of the model:

$$\beta = 1.03^{-1/4}, a_\pi = 1.50, \xi_w = \xi_p = 0.75, \lambda_1 = 0.9, \lambda_2 = 0, \sigma_L = 1, \lambda_w = 1.20.$$

In the pure sticky price version of the model, $\xi_w = 0$ and $\xi_p = 0.75$, while in
the pure sticky wage version, $\xi_w = 0.75$ and $\xi_p = 0$.

Consider first the results for sticky prices in Panel A. Note that in the case
stressed in the text, $\lambda = 0$, inflation falls 2.8 basis points in the period that ξ_t^1
jumps by 0.01, or 1%. At the same time, employment jumps by nearly 1% and
the nominal rate of interest falls by 29 basis points. Under the efficient monetary policy, the interest rate jumps a full 100 basis points, employment does not
change, and inflation remains at zero. Evidently, the interest rate targeting rule
that feeds back on expected inflation produces very inefficient results. It creates a
boom where there should be none, and it does not stabilize inflation.

Note that as λ increases, the interest rate targeting rule becomes more inefficient. For the largest value of λ considered, employment increases 2.5% in
the period of the signal shock. However, the case ceases to be relevant from an
empirical standpoint because inflation now increases in response to the signal
shock.

Motivated by the fact that equilibrium models which do well empirically also
incorporate sticky wages, we now consider the sticky wage case in Table 14.5.
Note that with sticky wages, inflation is predicted to fall and output rise, for all
the values of λ reported. Thus while the model with sticky prices is not robust to
a hump-shape representation of a_t, one which also incorporates sticky wages can

Table 14.5 Period t Response to News, ξ_t^1 that Period t + 1 Technology Innovation Will be 1% Higher

In all cases, the natural rate, R_t^*, jumps 100 basis points $a_t = (0.9 + \lambda)a_{t-1} - 0.9\lambda a_{t-2} + \xi_t^o + \xi_t + \xi_{t-1}^1$

Panel A: Policy rule – $\hat{R}_t = a_\pi E_t \hat{\pi}_{t+1} R_t^*$

λ	π_t		h_t		R_t		$E_t R_t / \pi_{t+1}$	
	Sticky P	Sticky W	Sticky P	Sticky W	Sticky P	Sticky W	Sticky P	Sticky W
0	-2.8	-15	0.98	0.84	-29	-175	-9.8	-58
0.125	-0.42	-16	1.1	0.98	-29	-178	-9.8	-59
0.2	1.7	-18	1.2	1.1	-29	-181	-9.6	-60
0.6	42	-28	2.1	2.3	8.2	-200	2.8	-67
0.8	117	-25	2.5	4.7	111	-206	37	-69

Panel B: Policy rule $\hat{R}_t = a_\pi \hat{\pi}_t R_t^*$

λ	π_t		h_t		R_t		$E_t R_t / \pi_{t+1}$	
	Sticky P	Sticky W	Sticky P	Sticky W	Sticky P	Sticky W	Sticky P	Sticky W
0	-1.7	-10	0.78	0.93	-2.5	-15	13	97
0.125	-0.25	-11	0.87	1.1	-0.4	-16	15	97
0.2	1.0	-12	0.93	1.2	1.5	-17	16	97
0.6	22	-16	1.4	2.3	33	-24	35	98
0.8	61	-8.7	1.6	4.2	92	-13	58	106

Note: (1) Inflation and rates of return, π_t, R_t, $E_t R_t / \pi_{t+1}$ expressed in deviations, in units of quarterly basis points, from steady state. (2) Hours worked, h_t is expressed in percent deviation from steady state. (3) For parameter values, see text.

be expected to predict more robustly that inflation falls and the output gap rises, in response to a signal shock.

Now consider Panel B, which reports results for the contemporaneous specification of the interest rate rule. The results for π_t, h_t, R_t are qualitatively similar to the results in Panel A. Figure 14.5 reports the period t impact on the output gap (φ_x) and inflation (φ_π) of a 1% news shock under perturbations to our baseline model parameterization. In each case, we fix $\lambda = 0$ and use the policy rule in (23). In addition, the parameter perturbations reported change only the value of the parameter indicated and hold the other parameters at their baseline value. As in Table 14.5, the sticky wage model is more robust in predicting $\varphi_\pi < 0$. For example, if the price stickiness parameter, ξ_p, falls substantially below the benchmark value, then $\varphi_\pi > 0$. However, $\varphi_\pi < 0$ for all values of ξ_w reported. Similarly, if a_π is substantially above its value in the benchmark parameterization, then $\varphi_\pi > 0$ with pure sticky prices, but $\varphi_\pi < 0$ with pure sticky wages. Finally, $\varphi_x > 0$ for all parameterizations considered.

In summary, our benchmark sticky price model predicts that inflation drops and employment rises in the period that a signal about a future technology expansion arrives. This resembles the pattern observed for stock market booms. When

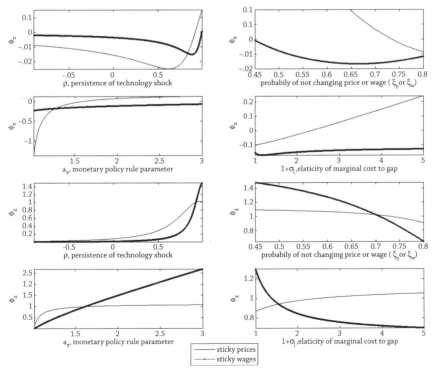

Figure 14.5 Contemporaneous effect on output gap (φ_x) and inflation (φ_π) of a 1% signal shock

we depart substantially from the benchmark parameterization the model predicts a rise in inflation after a news shock. However, a model with pure sticky wages predicts much more robustly that inflation drops and the output gap rises in response to a signal shock. We conclude that models with sticky wages and sticky prices are likely to robustly predict that inflation falls and output rises in response to a signal shock. Models which simultaneously incorporate both sticky wages and sticky prices have a state variable and are not so easy to solve analytically as the case of pure sticky wages and pure sticky prices considered here. We turn to the model that incorporates both sticky wages and prices in the next section.

4. Analysis in a Medium-Sized Model

In this section, we consider a medium-sized new Keynesian model fit to U.S. post-war data by Bayesian methods.[35] Relative to the material in the previous section, the analysis here has the disadvantage that it cannot be done analytically. On the other hand, the results may perhaps be taken more seriously because they are produced in a model which generates time-series data that more closely resemble actual U.S. data. In addition, in this model we are able to consider the impact of optimistic expectations about the future on the stock market (however, the model shares the shortcoming of most models in that it understates the magnitude of volatility in the stock market). The stock market is a variable that is missing in the analysis of the previous section. Finally, by adding the financial frictions proposed in BGG to our estimated model, we are able to consider interesting modifications to the inflation forecast targeting interest rate rule. We find that when we allow credit growth to play an independent role in that rule, one that goes beyond its role in forecasting inflation, then the interest rate targeting rule's tendency to produce excessive volatility in response to optimistic expectations about the future is reduced. We interpret this as evidence that credit growth is correlated with the natural rate of interest. The natural rate of interest is what one really wants in the interest rate targeting rule, and credit growth appears to be a good proxy, at least relative to shocks to expectations about the future.

4.1. A MEDIUM-SIZED MODEL

The estimated model incorporates Calvo-style sticky prices and wages, habit persistence in preferences, variable capital utilization, and adjustment costs in the change in investment. We do not display the shocks that were used in the estimation of the model. This section presents simulations of the model analogous to the simulations performed in the previous section. Our presentation of the model is limited to what is relevant for those simulations. As in EHL, we suppose that households supply a differentiated labor service, $l_{t,j}$, $j \in (0,1)$. Preferences of the household supplying the jth type of labor services are given by:

$$E_t^j \sum_{l=0}^{\infty} \beta^l \left\{ \log(C_{t+l} - 0.75 C_{t+l-1}) - 110 \frac{l_{t+l,j}^2}{2} \right\}, \beta = 1.03^{-1/4},$$

where C_t denotes consumption. The household is a monopoly supplier of its type of labor service and sets the wage rate, W_{jt}, subject to the demand for $l_{t,j}$ and to the following friction. With probability, $\xi_w = 0.80$ the household cannot reoptimize its wage and with the complementary probability it can set the wage optimally. In case it cannot reoptimize its wage, W_{jt} is set as follows:

$$W_{jt} = \bar{\pi} \mu_z W_{jt-1},$$

where $\mu_z = 1.0038$ is the steady-state growth rate of the underlying shock to technology and $\bar{\pi} = 1.006$ is the steady-state rate of inflation. The household accumulates capital subject to the following technology:

$$\bar{K}_{t+1} = (1 - \delta) \bar{K}_t + \left(1 - S\left(\frac{I_t}{I_{t-1}}\right)\right) I_t,$$

where $\bar{K}_t$ is the beginning of period t physical stock of capital, and I_t is period t investment. The function S is convex, with $S(\mu_z) = S'(\mu_z) = 0$ and $S''(\mu_z) = 2.2$. The physical stock of capital is owned by the household and it rents capital services, K_t, to a competitive capital market:

$$K_t = u_t \bar{K}_t,$$

where u_t denotes the capital utilization rate. Increased utilization requires increased maintenance costs in terms of investment goods according to the function

$$a(u_t) \bar{K}_t,$$

where a is increasing and convex, $a(1) = a'(1) = 0$, $a''(1) = 0.02$, and u_t is unity in nonstochastic steady state.

The households' specialized labor inputs are aggregated into a homogeneous labor service according to the following function

$$L_t = \left[\int_0^1 (l_{t,i})^{\frac{1}{\lambda_w}} di \right]^{\lambda_w}, \lambda_w = 1.05.$$

A final good, Y_t, is produced by a representative, competitive firm according to the following technology:

$$Y_t = \left[\int_0^1 Y_{lt}^{\frac{1}{\lambda_f}} dl \right]^{\lambda_f}, \lambda_f = 1.20.$$

Here, Y_{lt} is the lth intermediate good produced by a monopolist using the following technology:

$$Y_{lt} = \left(z_t A_t L_{lt} \right)^{1-\alpha} \left(K_{lt}^\alpha \right), z_t = \exp(\mu_z t), \alpha = 0.4,$$

where K_{lt}, L_{lt} denote the capital and labor services used by the lth monopolist. Also, $a_t = \log(A_t)$ and has law of motion analogous to the one in (2):

$$a_t = 0.9 a_{t-1} + \xi_t^0 + \xi_{t-8}^8,$$

where ξ_t^0, ξ_{t-8}^8 are i.i.d. shocks which are uncorrelated with each other at all leads and lags, and with a_{t-j}, $j > 0$. The shock, ξ_{t-i}^i, is observed by agents at date $t-i$. We refer to ξ_{t-8}^8 as a "signal" about a_t that arrives eight quarters in advance.

The monopoly supplier of the intermediate good can reset its price optimally with probability $1 - \xi_p$, $\xi_p = 0.77$ and with probability ξ_p it follows the following simple rule:

$$P_{lt} = \bar{\pi} P_{l,t-1}.$$

Monetary policy is governed by the following interest rate rule:

$$\log\left(\frac{R_t}{R} \right) = \tilde{\rho} \log\left(\frac{R_{t-1}}{R} \right) + (1 - \tilde{\rho}) \bar{R}_t, \tag{24}$$

where R_t denotes the gross nominal rate of interest and

$$\bar{R}_t = a_\pi E_t \log\left(\frac{\bar{\pi}_{t+1}}{\pi} \right) + \frac{a_y}{4} \log\left(\frac{y_t}{y} \right), \tag{25}$$

where $a_\pi = 2.25$, $a_y = 0.32$. Here, y_t denotes gross domestic product (scaled by z_t) and y denotes the corresponding steady state value. Also, $\tilde{\rho} = 0.57$.

4.2. SIMULATION

Figure 14.6 presents the results of simulating a particular stock market boom-bust episode. In the first period a signal, $\xi_t^8 > 0$, arrives which creates the expectation that a_t two years later will jump. However, that expectation is ultimately disappointed, because $\xi_{t+8}^0 = -\xi_t^8$. Thus, in fact, nothing real ever happens. The dynamics of the economy are completely driven by an optimistic expectation about future productivity, an expectation that is never realized. This experiment has a variety of interpretations. One is that people receive actual evidence that things will improve in the future, evidence that ultimately turns out to be false. Another is that they are irrationally optimistic about the future and they realize their error when the thing they expected does not happen.

In interpreting the results it is important to recognize that whether or not the signal is realized is irrelevant for the analysis in the periods before the anticipated

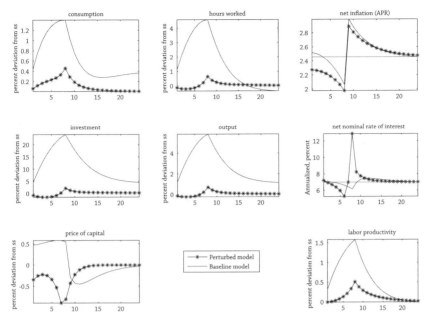

Figure 14.6 Response of baseline and perturbed model to signal shock (signal not realized); perturbation = Ramsey

event is supposed to occur. This is true whether we consider optimal policy, or policy that sets the interest rate according to a particular rule. This is because neither actual policy nor the policymaker implementing the optimal policy makes use of any information beyond what private agents know.

We simulate the dynamic response of the economy under two circumstances. The thin line in Figure 14.6 corresponds to the response of the baseline model, the one defined in the previous subsection. The starred line corresponds to the response in the Ramsey-efficient equilibrium corresponding to the baseline model. To obtain the Ramsey equilibrium, we drop the monetary policy rule. The system is now undetermined, there being many constellations of stochastic processes that satisfy the remaining equilibrium conditions. The Ramsey equilibrium is the stochastic process for all the variables that optimizes a social welfare criterion constructed by integrating the utility of each type j household, $j \in (0,1)$. The Ramsey equilibrium roughly corresponds to the equilibrium associated with the real business cycle model obtained by shutting down the wage and price setting frictions and by imposing that all intermediate good firms produce at the same level and each type j worker works the same amount. We say "roughly" here because deleting only one equation (i.e., the interest rate rule) does not provide enough degrees of freedom for the Ramsey equilibrium to literally extinguish all the frictions in the model. The Ramsey equilibrium forms a natural benchmark because it corresponds to the equilibrium with optimal monetary policy.

Note how the rise in investment, consumption, output, and hours worked in the baseline equilibrium exceeds the corresponding rise in Ramsey equilibrium by a very substantial amount. This excess entirely reflects the suboptimality of the monetary policy rule, (24). Interestingly, the inflation rate in the boom is below its steady-state value of roughly 2.5% annually, as in the examples of the previous section and as in the data. At the end of the boom, inflation rises a bit. According to the evidence in Adalid and Detken (2007) this is what typically happens in boom-bust episodes: inflation is low in the boom phase and then rises a little at the end.

The 3,1 panel in the figure displays the response of the price of capital in terms of consumption goods in the model. We interpret this as the price of equity in the model. Note that in the baseline model, the price of capital rises during the boom. In the Ramsey equilibrium, the price of capital actually falls. One way to understand this fall in the price of capital is that the real interest rate in the Ramsey equilibrium (the "natural rate of interest," in the language of the previous section) rises sharply with the signal shock. The increased discounting of future payments to capital explains the fall in the price of capital.[36] Monetary policy in the baseline equilibrium prevents the sharp rise in the interest rate. This is the heart of the problem with the monetary policy rule. The interest rate should be raised, as in the Ramsey equilibrium, but there is nothing in the monetary policy rule that produces this outcome. The most important variable in the interest rate targeting rule, inflation, actually drives the interest rate in the wrong direction. In effect, monetary policy is overly expansionary in the boom. This is what makes the stock market boom (actually, it is not a very strong boom) and what makes indicators of aggregate activity boom too. As Figure 14.6 indicates, only a small part of the boom reflects the operation of optimistic expectations. The boom is primarily a phenomenon of loose monetary policy. Again, it bears repeating that the nature of the boom is independent of whether the signal is ultimately realized or not.

Interestingly, an outside observer might be tempted to interpret the rise in labor productivity during the boom as indicating that an actual improvement in technology is under way. In fact, the rise in productivity reflects a sharp rise in capital utilization. This phenomenon would be even greater if the model also incorporated variations in labor utilization.

In sum, an interest rate targeting rule that assigns substantial weight to inflation transforms what should be a modest expansion into a significant boom. The reason is that the monetary policy does not raise the interest rate sharply with the rise in the natural rate of interest. This problem can be fixed by setting the interest rate to the natural rate or, if that is deemed too difficult to measure, to some variable that is correlated with the natural rate. We explored the latter option. We added the financial frictions sketched by BGG to the baseline model, in order to obtain a model in which credit growth plays an important economic role. We found that when we simulate the resulting model's response to a signal shock, the equilibrium more closely approximates the corresponding Ramsey equilibrium if credit growth is introduced into the interest rate targeting rule, (24). In particular, we replace $\bar{R}_t$ in (25) with:

$$\bar{R}_t = \alpha_\pi \left[E_t \left(\pi_{t+1} \right) - \bar{\pi} \right] + \alpha_y \frac{1}{4} \log \left(\frac{y_t}{y} \right) + \alpha_c \times \text{nominal credit growth}_t, \alpha_c = 2.5,$$

where credit is the quantity of loans obtained in the BGG model by entrepreneurs for the purpose of financing the purchase of capital. We find that in the baseline model, with $\alpha_c = 0$, households would pay 0.23% of consumption forever to switch to the Ramsey equilibrium. We also find that households would pay 0.19% of consumption forever to switch to the equilibrium in which $\alpha_c = 2.5$. We interpret this as evidence that including credit growth in the interest rate rule moves the economy a long way in the direction of the Ramsey equilibrium, in which monetary policy sets the interest rate to the natural rate of interest. These calculations have been done relative to signal shocks. A full evaluation of the policy of including credit in the interest rate targeting rule would evaluate the performance of this change when other shocks are present as well.

5. Conclusion

We have reviewed evidence which suggests that inflation is typically low in stock market booms and credit growth is high. The observation that inflation is low suggests that an interest rate targeting rule which focuses heavily on anticipated inflation may destabilize asset markets and perhaps the broader economy as well. The observation that credit growth is high in booms suggests that if credit growth is added to interest rate targeting rules, the resulting modified rule would moderate volatility in the real economy and in asset prices.

These inferences based on examination of the historical data constitute conjectures about the operating characteristics of counterfactual policies. To fully evaluate conjectures like these requires constructing and simulating a model economy. This is why we devoted substantial space to model analysis. The model simulations reported in the paper lend support to our conjectures.

Notes

This article was originally prepared for the Federal Reserve Bank of Kansas City's conference "Macroeconomic Challenges: The Decade Ahead," and was presented at Jackson Hole, Wyoming, August 26–28, 2010. The editors are grateful to the Kansas City Federal Reserve Bank for allowing it to be reproduced for this volume. The article is also accessible on the Bank's website at www.kc.frb.org. In the original text the author's affiliations and acknowledgments were as follows: Christiano is affiliated with Northwestern University and National Bureau of Economic Research, Ilut is affiliated with Duke University, and Motto and Rostagno are affiliated with the European Central Bank. The views expressed in this paper are those of the authors and do not necessarily reflect those of the ECB or the Eurosystem. The authors are grateful for discussions with David Altig, Gadi Barlevy, Martin Eichenbaum, Ippei Fujiwara, and Jean-Marc Natal, and for comments from John Geanakoplos. The authors also benefited from the advice and assistance of Daisuke Ikeda and Patrick Higgins.

1. We exclude the Civil War and World War I and II from our data set.

2. See also Christiano, Motto, and Rostagno (2007). The position is often labeled "the BIS view" (see Eichengreen 2009, White 2009 and the references therein). For an application of the Christiano et al. (2008) analysis to the Japanese economy, see Christiano and Fujiwara (2006). In related work, Cecchetti et al. (2000) argue that monetary policy should also react to movements in the stock market.

3. We are sympathetic to the idea (see, for example, Hirtle, Schuermann, and Stiroh 2009) that a macroprudential perspective ought to be brought to bear on the supervision and regulation of financial firms. See, for example, Barlevy (2008), Evans (2010), and Geanakoplos (2009).

4. In developing the intuition for our model results, we stress the case where the interest rate rule is a function of expected future inflation. However, we show that the results are robust to the assumption that the interest rate rule is a function of current, actual inflation.

5. Barsky and Sims (2010) provide vector autoregression evidence using postwar U.S. data which suggests that a news shock much like the one considered here drives stock prices and economic activity up, and inflation down. We view this as support for our news-shock interpretation of a stock market booms.

6. For example, according to one biography, "from the beginning, Bezos sought to increase market share as quickly as possible, at the expense of profits" (see http://www.achievement.org/autodoc/page/bez0bio-1).

7. Recent work has been stimulated by the papers of Beaudry and Portier (2004, 2006).

8. Valerie Ramey (2009, forthcoming) has done important recent work fleshing out the idea that government spending shocks are heralded by early signals.

9. See Michelle Alexopoulos (2007) for a discussion of how the publishing industry broadcasts signals about future technology changes.

10. The intuition for this finding is simple. The natural rate of interest corresponds roughly to the expected growth rate of consumption from the present to the future. In new Keynesian models fit to the data, one estimates that shocks are highly persistent. For example, an unexpected jump in technology today creates the expectation of a roughly equal jump in technology in the future. The absence of substantial internal persistence in models then implies a similar pattern for consumption. This means that the expected growth rate of consumption—and, hence, the natural rate—is relatively insensitive to the shocks incorporated in standard econometric analyses. But note how very different a shock to expectations about the future is. Nothing happens in the present. Something only happens in the future. Such a shock has the potential to have a big impact on the intertemporal slope of consumption.

11. Here, we are implicitly assuming that price frictions play a more important role than wage frictions. If there were only wage frictions, then optimal monetary policy would simply not reduce the interest rate. We elaborate on these observations in the following subsection.

12. Again, we implicitly assume that the key frictions are price frictions. The case for price stabilization weakens if there are significant wage frictions. With only wage frictions, it is desirable to stabilize wages, not prices (Erceg, Henderson, and Levin 2000).

13. Technical details are relegated to an appendix, which is accessible in the version of the paper available on the Kansas City Federal Reserve Bank's web page.

14. This is a theme also developed by Shirakawa (2010), governor of the Bank of Japan.

15. Schwert (1990)'s annual index of common stock prices is available for the period 1802–1999 as series Cj797 in the Millennial Online Edition of Historical Statistics of the United States. The consumer price index is series Cc1 in the same source.

16. These are series Ca9 in Historical Statistics of the United States, Millennial Edition Online. We also considered the annual industrial production index constructed in Davis (2004), which spans the period 1790 to 1915. Using this variable instead of GDP has very little impact on the results. The mean logarithmic growth rate of industrial production in the nonboom, non–Civil War part of the period 1802–1914 is 4.0%. The corresponding mean growth rate in each of our nine stock market boom periods is 1.2, 7.2, 6.8, 5.3, 11.8, 4.3, 8.5, 4.9, and –0.2 percent, respectively. These results are very similar to those reported for GDP in Table 14.2.

17. Our measure of credit splices together three time series. For the years 1819–1834 we add series Cj148 (loans and discounts, state banks) and Cj189 (loans and discounts, Second Bank of the United States) from Historical Statistics of the United States, Millennial Edition Online. For the period 1834 to 1896 we use "total loans of all banks," series X582 in chapter 10 ("Banking"), page 1019 of Bicentennial Edition: Historical Statistics of the United States, Colonial Times to 1970, part 2 (HSUS). For the period 1896 to 1914, we use series X582 in the table on page 1020 in HSUS. Though the latter two series have the same name, the coverage of the first series is incomplete, by comparison with that of the second series (see page 1011 of HSUS for details). To explain how we spliced the data, let x_t denote the first data series, y_t the second and z_t the third. Let $t = t_1$ and $t = t_2$ denote the (unique) date when the first two and the second two series overlap, respectively. We let $a = y_{t_1}/x_{t_1}$ and set $\tilde{x}_t = ax_t$. We let $b = z_{t_2}/y_{t_2}$ and set $\hat{x}_t = b\tilde{x}_t$, $\hat{y}_t = by_t$. Our data series is then $\left(\hat{x}_t, \hat{y}_t, z_t\right)$. Our measure of credit differs from the one used in Bordo and Wheelock (2004) (see http://research.stlouisfed.org/publications/review/04/11/0411dwd.xls). First, in constructing y_t they compute the sum of series X582 (i.e., the only series we use) plus series X583 ("total investments of all banks"). We did not include series X583 because, according to page 1011 in HSUS, X583 is composed primarily of government debt, while we seek a measure of nonfinancial business borrowing. In any case, our results are not sensitive to the inclusion of X583. We also differ from Bordo and Wheelock in that we use data from before 1834.

18. We identified these as follows. Using Google in Windows Internet Explorer (32-bit or 64-bit versions), we typed "panic of 18" and Google completed the phrase with 10 panics. To select the episodes in the pre–World War I portion of the twentieth century, we performed the same Windows Explorer exercise. We used all the panics identified in this way except the panic of 1901, which was too small to show up as a drop in the stock market in our annual data set.

19. Our data on the CPI and the real value of the S&P composite price index were taken from Robert Shiller's web page. Data on pre–World War II U.S. real, quarterly seasonally adjusted GNP were taken from the online data appendix to Bordo and Wheelock (2004). The latter data were spliced with analogous GNP data for the post–World War II period taken from the Federal Reserve Bank of St. Louis' online database. For the period after 1946, we measured credit with the flow of funds data, "credit market instruments," taken from Haver Analytics (mnemonic, AL14TCR5). For the period, 1946–1951, these data are stocks pertaining to the fourth quarter of each year. We used log-linear interpolation to estimate observations for the first, second, and third quarters in the period 1946–1951. For the period before 1945, credit market data are observations on corporate debt, which corresponds to variable cj876, taken from Historical Statistics of the United States Millennial Edition Online. The pre-1945 data were log-linearly interpolated and spliced with the post-1945 data. The credit data were converted into real terms by dividing by the CPI.

20. Both series were obtained from the IMF's International Financial Statistics data set. The share prices correspond to series code 15862…ZF…and the CPI corresponds to series code 15864…ZF… The real share prices displayed in Figure 14.3 have been converted to real terms by dividing by the CPI.

21. The call money rate was obtained from International Financial Statistics. The International Monetary Fund's gap data were found at http://www.imf.org/external/pubs/ft/weo/2010/01/weodata/weoselser.aspx?c=158&t=1.

22. The results are qualitatively similar for a range of values of the coefficients on inflation and the gap, and the smoothing parameter.

23. The empirical model of the next section includes news about periods further into the future than just one period. We work with one-period-ahead news in this section because our objective is to keep things sufficiently simple that the basic ideas are apparent.

24. It can be shown that the "efficient" equilibrium is the Ramsey optimal equilibrium, in the case that there is no initial price dispersion. The Ramsey equilibrium considers just the private-sector optimality and market-clearing conditions, and leaves out a specification of the monetary policy rule. In addition, there is a subsidy on the employment of labor, designed to address the distortions associated with monopoly power. The endogenous variables, including the tax subsidy, are now underdetermined, as there are two more variables than equations. The Ramsey

optimal equilibrium is the configuration of variables that satisfies the private-sector equilibrium conditions and maximizes social welfare.

25. Additional details are available in a technical appendix to this publication that is available on the Kansas City Federal Reserve Bank's web page.

26. For completeness, we include them in a technical appendix that is accessible in the version of this paper available on the Kansas City Federal Reserve Bank's web page.

27. In a technical appendix we use straightforward, though tedious, algebra to solve for these objects. Details are available in the version of this paper available on the Kansas City Federal Reserve Bank's web page.

28. Technical details are relegated to an appendix which is accessible in the version of this paper available on the Kansas City Federal Reserve Bank's web page.

29. The law of motion for a_t implies $E_t a_{t+j} = \rho^j a_t + \rho^{j-1} \xi_t^1$.

30. For an extensive discussion of the relationship between the time-series representation of a_t and the sign of the contemporaneous inflation and output response to ξ_t^0, see Christiano, Trabandt, and Walentin (2010).

31. For completeness, (13) is derived in a technical appendix that is accessible in the version of this paper available on the Kansas City Federal Reserve Bank's web page. Let C_t denote consumption, scaled by $\exp(a_t)$ and let H_t denote hours worked. The appendix shows that $\hat{c}_t = \hat{H}_t = \hat{x}_t$. Then, $(1 + \sigma_L)\hat{x}_t = \hat{c}_t + \sigma_L \hat{H}_t$, which is the log-linear expansion of the (scaled) marginal rate of substitution between consumption and leisure when utility is logarithmic in consumption, and constant elasticity in labor.

32. These results can be verified by considering the usual static monopoly diagram with price on the vertical axis and quantity on the horizontal, depicting demand, marginal revenue, and marginal cost. Then, examine the effects of a given upward shift in marginal cost under two scenarios: one in which the marginal cost curve is flat and another in which the marginal cost curve is steep.

The impact of increasing marginal costs on the slope of the price Phillips curve has received a lot of attention in the literature on firm-specific capital. To our knowledge, the effect was first noted in Sbordonne (2002), and also discussed in Altig et al. (2005) and de Walque, Smets, and Wouters (2005).

33. This is established in the technical appendix to this paper that is accessible in the version available on the Kansas City Federal Reserve Bank's web page.

34. This is established in the technical appendix to the paper that is accessible in the version available on the Kansas City Federal Reserve Bank's web page.

35. The model is a version of the one in Christiano, Eichenbaum, and Evans (2005) and Smets and Wouters (2007).

36. There is a second equilibrium condition that the price of capital must satisfy, in addition to the present discounted value relation. The second condition is the requirement that in competitive markets the price of capital must equal its marginal cost (i.e., the "Tobin's q" relation). The signal shock creates the expectation that technology will be high in the future, and that investment will be strong in response. Given the adjustment cost specification, there is a gain to having increased investment in advance. This gain manifests itself in the form of a reduction in the current marginal cost of producing capital. Given our assumption that capital is traded in competitive markets, the reduction in cost is passed on in the form of a reduction in price.

References

Adalid, Ramon, and Carsten Detken. 2007. "Liquidity Shocks and Asset Price Boom/Bust Cycles." European Central Bank Working Paper No. 732.

Altig, David, Larry J. Christiano, Martin Eichenbaum, and Jesper Linde. 2005. "Firm-Specific Capital, Nominal Rigidities and the Business Cycle." NBER Working Paper No. 11034.

Alexopoulos, Michelle and J. Cohen. 2009. "Measuring our Ignorance, one Book at a Time: New Indicators of Technological Change, 1909–1949." *Journal of Monetary Economics*, 56, 450–470..

Barlevy, Gadi. 2008. "A Leverage-Based Model of Speculative Bubbles." Federal Reserve Bank of Chicago Working Paper No. 2008-01.

Barsky, Robert B., and Eric R. Sims. 2010. "News Shocks and Business Cycles." Manuscript, University of Notre Dame, July 22.

Beaudry, Paul, and Franck Portier. 2004. "An Exploration into Pigou's Theory of Cycles." *Journal of Monetary Economics* 51, 1183–1216.

———. 2006. "News, Stock Prices and Economic Fluctuations." *American Economic Review* 96, 1293–1307.

Bernanke, Ben S., and Mark Gertler. 1999. "Monetary Policy and Asset Volatility." *Federal Reserve Bank of Kansas City Economic Review* 84(4), 17–52.

———. 2001. "Should Central Banks Respond to Movements in Asset Prices?" *American Economic Review* 91(2), Papers and Proceedings of the Hundred Thirteenth Annual Meeting of the American Economic Association, 253–257.

Bernanke, Ben, Mark Gertler, and Simon Gilchrist. 1999. "The Financial Accelerator in a Quantitative Business Cycle Framework." In John B. Taylor and Michael Woodford, eds., *Handbook of Macroeconomics*. Amsterdam: North-Holland.

Bordo, Michael D., and David C. Wheelock. 2004. "Monetary Policy and Asset Prices: A Look Back at Past U.S. Stock Market Booms." *Federal Reserve Bank of St. Louis Review* 86(6), 19–44.

———. 2007. "Stock Market Booms and Monetary Policy in the Twentieth Century." *Federal Reserve Bank of St. Louis Review* 89(2), 90–122.

Cecchetti, Stephen G., Hans Genberg, John Lipsky, and Sushil Wadhwani. 2000. *Asset Prices and Central Bank Policy*. Geneva: International Center for Monetary and Banking Studies.

Christiano, Lawrence J., Martin Eichenbaum, and Charles L. Evans. 2005. "Nominal Rigidities and the Dynamic Effects of a Shock to Monetary Policy." *Journal of Political Economy* 113, 1–45.

Christiano, Lawrence J., and Ippei Fujiwara. 2006. "The Bubble, Overinvestment, Reduction in Working Hours, and the Lost Decade" (in Japanese). Bank of Japan Working Papers Series 06-J-8.

Christiano, Lawrence, Cosmin Ilut, Roberto Motto, and Massimo Rostagno. 2008. "Monetary Policy and Stock Market Boom-Bust Cycles." European Central Bank Working Paper No. 955, October.

Christiano, Lawrence J., Roberto Motto, and Massimo Rostagno. 2007. "Two Reasons Why Money and Credit May Be Useful in Monetary Policy." National Bureau of Economic Research Working Paper No. 13502.

Christiano, Lawrence, Mathias Trabandt, and Karl Walentin. 2010. "DSGE Models for Monetary Policy." In Benjamin M. Friedman and Michael Woodford, eds., *Handbook of Monetary Economics*. New York: North-Holland.

Clarida, Richard, Jordi Gali, and Mark Gertler. 1999. "The Science of Monetary Policy: A New Keynesian Perspective." *Journal of Economic Literature* 37, 1661–1707.

Davis, Joseph H. 2004. "An Annual Index of U.S. Industrial Production, 1790–1915." *Quarterly Journal of Economics* 119, 1177–1215.

de Walque, G., F. Smets, and R. Wouters. 2005. "Price Setting in General Equilibrium: Alternative Specifications." Computing in Economics and Finance 370, Society for Computational Economics.

Eichengreen, Barry. 2009. "The Financial Crisis and Global Policy Reforms." Prepared for the Federal Reserve Bank of San Francisco's conference "Asia and the Financial Crisis," Santa Barbara, California, October 19–21.

Erceg, Christopher J., Dale W. Henderson, and Andrew T. Levin. 2000. "Optimal Monetary Policy with Staggered Wage and Price Contracts." *Journal of Monetary Economics* 46, 281–313.

Evans, Charles. 2010. "Letter to 10 Senators Discussing Financial Reform." http://www.chicago-fed.org/webpages/utilities/newsroom/news_releases/ 010/03.04_ce_letter_release.cfm.

Geanakoplos, John. 2009. "The Leverage Cycle." In Daron Acemoglu, Kenneth Rogoff, and Michael Woodford, eds., *NBER Macroeconomic Annual 2009*. Chicago: University of Chicago Press.

Hirtle, Beverly, Til Schuermann, and Kevin Stiroh. 2009. "Macroprudential Supervision of Financial Institutions: Lessons from the SCAP." Federal Reserve Bank of New York Staff Report No. 409, November.

Ramey, Valerie. 2009. "Defense News Shocks, 1939–2008: Estimates Based on News Sources." October, manuscript.

———. 2011. "Identifying Government Spending Shocks: It's All in the Timing." *Quarterly Journal of Economics*, 125, 1–50.

Schwert, G. William. 1990. "Indexes of United States Stock Prices from 1802 to 1987." *Journal of Business* 63, 399–426.

Shirakawa, Masaaki. 2010. "Revisiting the Philosophy behind Central Bank Policy." Speech at the Economic Club of New York, April 22. http://www.boj.or.jp/en/type/press/koen07/ko1004e.htm.

Smets, Frank, and Raf Wouters. 2007. "Shocks and Frictions in US Business Cycles." *American Economic Review* 97, 586–606.

White, William R. 2009. "Should Monetary Policy Lean or Clean?" BIS Working Paper No. 205, April.

Woodford, Michael. 2003. *Interest and Prices: Foundations of a Theory of Monetary Policy*. Princeton, NJ: Princeton University Press.

CHAPTER 15

Leverage and Bubbles

THE NEED TO MANAGE THE LEVERAGE CYCLE

John Geanakoplos

1. Introduction[1]

In my view the fundamental missing ingredients in quantifiable macro models used by the Federal Reserve and the ECB are endogenous default and endogenous lending terms distinct from the interest rate. The models do not recognize that changes in the perception of potential defaults can radically alter lending conditions and therefore economic activity. This failure has prevented policymakers from recognizing asset bubbles, from understanding the source of debt crashes, and from accurately gauging the severity and duration of their aftermath. It led to policy errors in ignoring the dangerous buildup of debt before this last crisis and to further policy errors after the crisis in not acting to restructure unpayable debts. In short, it has led to a faulty understanding of the nature of the debtor-creditor relationship and its impact on the macroeconomy.

For a long time now, maybe since Irving Fisher, we have come to believe that managing interest rates is the way to regulate lending and borrowing in the macroeconomy. Whenever anything goes wrong, people say change the interest rate. Similarly, we have developed a phobia about forgiving debt. My view is that neither of these prejudices can be unambiguously derived from a proper general equilibrium model with endogenous default and lending. Collateral rates or leverage can be more important to economic activity and prices than interest rates, and more important to manage. And the only expeditious way out of a severe leverage cycle crash is to move quickly in writing down debts. The fact that we do not presently know how to compute the optimal leverage ratios, or the optimal amount of debt forgiveness, is not an argument against taking such actions, but rather further proof that we have been developing the wrong models.

The nature of promises and debt has been a preoccupation of philosophers for thousands of years. Keeping promises was Plato's first proposed definition of justice in the Republic (it was shown not to be always just). Nietzsche, in the *Genealogy of Morals*, says the emergence of Conscience came from the repeated punishing of people who failed to honor their debts and the subsequent internalization of that punishment. (Thus *schuld* is the root of the German word for debt and also for one version of Conscience.) The subtlest literary analysis of keeping promises can be found in Shakespeare's *Merchant of Venice*.

The plot of the *Merchant of Venice* turns on the contract negotiated by Antonio to borrow money from Shylock to finance his friend Bassanio's courtship of the beautiful and rich Portia. In the central scene in the play, Antonio and Shylock argue over the rate of interest on the loan. But Shakespeare understood the primary importance of collateral. How many of you can remember the interest rate Shylock charged Antonio and Bassanio? Yet, all of you remember the collateral agreed on in the contract—the pound of flesh. Obviously, Shakespeare thought the collateral was more important. When all the boats apparently sink and Antonio is unable to repay the loan, the Court alters the collateral, saying it should have been a pound of flesh, but not a drop of blood.

The theme of borrowing and default is repeated several times in the play with the story of the rings. Portia and her assistant lend Bassanio and his assistant their rings in exchange for the promise that they will never be taken off their fingers. Shylock has earlier made it clear that he would never break his promise about the ring his wife Leah gave him. Yet when faced with an urgent need, Bassanio and his assistant do give up their rings, and they expect forgiveness. "To do a great right, do a little wrong" is Bassanio's philosophy. Or as Portia describes forgiveness of debts, "The quality of mercy is not strain'd; . . . It blesseth him that gives and him that takes."

Following Shakespeare's lead, I discuss models of collateral and debt forgiveness (or punishment for default). In the next section I argue for the necessity of collateral and leverage in macro models. I point out that, at present, leverage is absent from those models, even if lip service is paid to it now. I illustrate my view by describing the kinds of effects I have obtained in my models of leverage that cannot be reproduced by the more carefully calibrated macro models that guide central bank action. Next, I show that only by taking collateral seriously can one properly assess the effect on asset prices of new derivatives like credit default swaps. Finally, I talk about the optimal punishment for default and the current deplorable conditions of debt overhang much of the world finds itself in.

2. Leverage and Asset Pricing

Just as with Shakespeare's Court, I believe today that the regulatory authority ought to be managing collateral rates in addition to interest rates. I have worked on the leverage cycle, as I call it, for over 10 years—not quite as long as Shakespeare and with somewhat less attention than Shakespeare received. My oldest published papers on the subject are "Promises, Promises" in 1997, about collateral general equilibrium, "Liquidity Default and Crashes" in 2003, about the leverage cycle, and "Leverage Cycles and the Anxious Economy" in 2008 with

Ana Fostel, about the spread of leverage cycles across markets. In those papers I showed that when leverage is high, asset prices tend to rise, and when leverage declines, asset prices fall, sometimes in a violent crash.

There have been other early papers on collateral. In fact, Ben Bernanke was one of the pioneers in emphasizing collateral. However, he did not really write very much about leverage or changes in leverage. Instead he emphasized that when collateral goes down in value, the amount that can be borrowed goes down (as would be the case with a constant loan-to-value lending rule). What I emphasized is that the loan-to-value can change dramatically and it is the rapid change in loan-to-value that is a crucial source of crashes. And as I shall argue, loan-to-value is a variable that can be regulated.

The modern calibrated macro models that pay any attention to collateral, such as those presented by Christiano at the American Federal Reserve meetings in Jackson Hole last August (Christiano et al. 2010) and by Smets at the current ECB meetings in Frankfurt (Fahr et al. 2010), derive from the foundational work of Bernanke, Gertler and Gilchrist (1999), and Kiyotaki and Moore (1997). In the foundational work, leverage is barely mentioned and changes in leverage play no significant role. In Kiyotaki and Moore, for example, leverage actually rises after a bad shock, dampening any crisis. In the papers of Christiano and Smets, leverage is duly noted, though it is not clearly distinguished from credit, but again it does not play a central role. Both those models suggest the possibility of calibrating what happened in the current crisis. In the Smets paper, mysterious shocks started the crisis. No effort is made to identify what the shocks are or what they correspond to in reality; their existence is inferred from the fact that we had a crisis. Not even their properties are identified. In the leverage story I told in 2003 (and which is also told in Brunnermeier and Pedersen in 2009), it is crucial that the shocks are not only negative, but that they increase in volatility, as they did in reality. Moreover, I identify the first shocks as increases in mortgage delinquencies. In the Smets paper, there is no reason why his shocks should cause leverage to decrease rather than increase. In Christiano, the shocks are explicitly identified as changes in future productivity. But again there is no reason why such shocks should lower leverage. It is quite clear that in these models, leverage is not needed and changes in leverage do not play a vital role.

The foundational work of Bernanke, Gertler, and Gilchrist (1999), Kiyotaki and Moore (1997), and Holmstrom and Tirole (1997) is about credit cycles, not leverage cycles. In those papers, a drop in asset values or the wealth of entrepreneurs makes it more difficult to borrow, which in turn hampers productivity, which then lowers asset values, making it harder to borrow, and so on. Their story is about levels of credit, not ratios. It could be told as if the ratio of loans to asset values were constant. The leverage cycle differs from the credit cycle insofar as it is about ratios of credit to asset values. In my view it is these ratios which played the crucial dynamic role.

What I mean by leverage is loan-to-value on *new* loans. If the loan-to-value is 80%, USD 20 down gets you a USD 100 house. The leverage is five because your cash down payment of USD 20 has been multiplied by five in the USD 100 value of the asset. Loan-to-value and leverage describe the same thing. But let me emphasize it is on new loans. Debt-to-equity is essentially loan-to-value on old loans. Debt-to-equity is also an important ratio, but different from what I mean by leverage. And the two ratios often go in different directions. Historically, debt-to-equity typically increases for two or three years after a crisis and then starts a long slow decline stretching over years. But leverage on new loans drops abruptly *before* a crash. It is a cause, not a lagging result. How well things are going in the economy usually depends more on the leverage on new loans, than on what is happening to old loans, which often goes in the opposite direction. Of course, as we shall see, the duration of a crisis depends critically on the debt overhang, that is, on the loan-to-value on old loans.

The point of my equilibrium theory of leverage is that supply and demand determine not just the interest rate, but leverage as well. Supply equals demand for a loan is apparently just one equation, which gives rise to a puzzle. How can one equation determine two variables: interest and leverage? That is part of the reason why leverage has received so little attention in economics. It is just awkward for economic theory. That is why, as an economic theorist, I began to think about the subject. I wanted an equilibrium theory of what influences leverage and what role leverage plays in the economy.

In my theory, supply and demand do determine both the interest rate and leverage. (The trick is that there is more than one supply-equals-demand equation, but I do not have space to discuss that here.) What ends up influencing the interest rate in equilibrium is impatience; what influences leverage in equilibrium is volatility in the short run and, in the long run, innovation (because the economy is always looking for innovative ways to stretch scarce collateral).

Why are people now saying leverage is important? Every trader knows, if you are leveraged five to one and the asset goes up or down 1%, your wealth goes up or down 5%. You are more sensitive to changes. And the second thing they say is that since collateralized loans often turn out to be no-recourse loans, people can walk away from their debts. "If we had only limited leverage, these banks would not have lost so much money when prices started to go down. And homeowners would not be walking away from their homes."

Of course, I believe those two things are very important and they played a crucial role in my theory. But there was a third aspect of leverage in my theory which I think is far more important. The real significance of leverage is it allows fewer people to buy more assets and therefore raises the price of assets. Leverage causes bubbles.

In the leverage cycle, periods of high leverage produce higher asset prices, while periods of low leverage produce lower asset prices, provided there is no

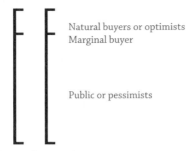

Figure 15.1 Marginal buyer theory of price.

short selling. In Figure 15.1, you can see why that is. Imagine a continuum of people from top to bottom, who have different views about the value of assets. The people at the top think the assets are worth a lot. The people at the bottom do not think they are worth very much. This heterogeneity is of crucial importance. Whatever the price is, there are going to be people at the top who think the price is cheap and they will be the buyers. The people lower down are going to think the price is too much and they will be sellers. The guy who thinks the price is just right, his valuation is equal to the price. You might say his valuation is determining the price.

When leverage goes up, the people at the top can borrow more. Fewer of them are required to hold all the assets, so the marginal buyer goes up and the price rises, not because there is any fundamental change in the economy, but because the marginal buyer is someone who has a higher opinion of the value of the asset. More leverage causes higher asset prices because it changes the marginal buyer. Most of modern finance basically assumes this heterogeneity away. I am not aware of a single finance or macro textbook that mentions endogenous leverage and its effect on asset pricing.

There are many reasons why agents in reality have heterogeneous valuations of assets. For example there are real differences in risk tolerance—risk-averse people value the assets less, even with the same information. There are also real differences in how people can use assets for production. There are also differences in utility from owning assets, like living in a house, for example. And some people maybe are just more optimistic about the assets than others.

3. The Leverage Cycle in Theory

Over the leverage cycle, leverage gradually rises, as I said earlier, because of technological innovation stretching the available collateral and because volatility is low. After a big, bad shock that increases volatility, leverage abruptly plummets. The fall in asset prices can be much bigger than anybody thinks is justified by the news alone because it is coupled with a crash in leverage and the bankruptcy of the most optimistic buyers. There is too much leverage in normal times and therefore too-high asset prices, and too little leverage in bad times and therefore too-low asset prices.

Leverage cycle crashes always happen in exactly the same way. First, there is a period in which leverage becomes very high and the assets are concentrated in the hands of the natural buyers (optimists for short) who have borrowed large sums of money to get them, setting the stage for the crisis. Then there is bad news that causes asset prices to fall because every investor values the assets less. This price fall forces the leveraged natural buyers or optimists to sell assets to meet their margin calls, thus realizing their losses. In Figure 15.2, I assume they all go bankrupt. Their departure causes asset prices to fall more because the assets fall into less optimistic hands. If the bad news is "scary," then lenders demand more collateral. This means that the remaining, less ebullient optimists each buy less, requiring more of them to hold all the assets. The new marginal buyer must be much further down the continuum and so much more pessimistic, and prices drop even further, reflecting the opinion of the lower marginal buyer.

Now what is "scary bad news"? It is not just bad news, but it is the kind that creates more uncertainty, more volatility. You are at an airport and they say the plane is going to be 10 minutes late. That is bad, but 10 minutes is really nothing. However, once you hear it is 10 minutes late, you think, "My gosh, maybe it is going to be an hour late." That could be really bad.

It is the *uncertainty* the news creates that is critical, not how bad it is. Another example is subprime delinquencies going from 2% to 5% in January 2007. Now 5% is not catastrophic. However, once it has reached 5% and broken the old pattern, investors think maybe it will go to 30% or 40%. That is what causes people to get nervous. When the lenders get nervous, they ask for more collateral and they force deleveraging. That is the beginning of the crisis.

The leverage cycle would occur even with completely rational agents; it gets much worse with irrationality. For example, if, in the boom, irrational lenders thought prices could only go up, leverage would get absurdly high, or if, as bad times approached, panicked investors sold everything, prices would fall much faster.

X – Bankrupt old optimists

New optimists

New marginal buyer

Public or pessimists

Figure 15.2 Leverage cycle theory of crashes

4. Leverage Cycles in History

I believe our financial history is full of recurring leverage cycles, during which leverage gradually builds up, creating a huge asset bubble, and then leverage and asset prices suddenly come crashing down. That is what happened in the tulip mania of 1637 in Holland, in the great Florida land boom and bust just before the Great Depression, in the 1980s land bubble in Japan, in the Asian crisis of 1998, and in the subprime crisis of 2007–2009. Of course, the data on historical collateral rates is spotty and needs assembling. There is a lot more work that could be done about this. We need to develop macro models that could calibrate the waste in the overbuilding that inevitably takes place in the ebullient stage when asset prices are too high and, even more importantly, that could calibrate the loss from the crisis stage and its aftermath.

The current crisis, I believe, is a clear example of a leverage cycle crash after a long leverage boom. And for this we do have some data. In Figure 15.3, the green line is Shiller's famous housing index. In 2000, it is at 100 on the right-hand scale. By the second quarter of 2006, it hits 190, a 90% increase in six years. Then it

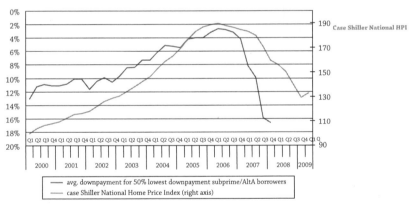

Figure 15.3 Housing leverage cycle: Margins offered (down payments required) and housing prices.

Notes: Observe that the down payment axis has been reversed, because lower down payment requirements are correlated with higher home prices. For every Alt-A or subprime first loan originated from Q1 2000 to Q1 2008, the down payment percentage was calculated as appraised value (or sale price if available) minus total mortgage debt, divided by appraised value. For each quarter, the down payment percentages were ranked from highest to lowest, and the average of the bottom half of the list is shown in the figure. This number is an indicator of the down payment required: clearly, many homeowners put down more than they had to, and that is why the top half is dropped from the average. A 13% down payment in Q1 2000 corresponds to leverage of about 7.7, and a 2.7% down payment in Q2 2006 corresponds to leverage of about 37. Subprime/AltA issuance stopped in Q1 2008.

goes down by 30% or so from there. Shiller famously said that it was irrational exuberance driving prices up. And when the narrative changed because people decided things cannot go up forever, they started telling bad stories, so everyone got depressed and the prices went down.

I believe the housing boom and bust was more a matter of leverage than of irrational exuberance. The pink line above gives the average loan-to-value for securitized subprime and Alt-A loans among the top 50% leveraged homeowners. The left vertical axis measures loan-to-value from 0% at the bottom to 100% at the top, or equivalently, the down payment measured from 0% at the top to 100% at the bottom. You can see that the average down payment goes from 14% (that is 86% loan-to-value) in 2000 to 2.7% in the second quarter of 2006. In exactly the same quarter that leverage hits its maximum—the second quarter of 2006–so do home prices. It is not irrational exuberance, I say, but leverage that caused housing prices to go up and then go down.

In Figure 15.4, you see the analogous leverage-price diagram for prime mortgage-backed security bond prices. Measured along the right vertical axis, the prices in the red curve stay close to 100 until the beginning of 2008, when they start to fall, eventually declining all the way to 70. Leverage is measured as in Figure 15.3 on the left vertical axis, and is given by the blue curve. These repo down payments (margins) are data the Federal Reserve should be keeping, but apparently the Federal Reserve did not closely monitor repo margins before the crisis. The hedge fund Ellington Capital Management that I work with gave me the history of margins they were offered, averaged over a large portfolio of prime mortgages. You see that down payments were at 10% in 1998, then in the 1998 leverage cycle crisis they jumped to 40%, then went back to 10% very quickly when the crisis subsided. Margins eventually went down to 5% in 2006—so a 20-to-1 leverage. Then in 2007 leverage began to collapse, and afterward you see prices and leverage collapsing together. Leverage on these AAA bonds, measured properly as loan-to-value on new loans, starts to collapse before prices and is part of the reason for the collapse of prices. The deleveraging comes before the fact, not two years after the fact. Of course, much of the deleveraging in the diagram (and in other time series of security prices) comes simultaneously with the fall in prices. Falling prices make rational lenders demand more collateral, which in turn lowers prices, making lenders ask for still more collateral, and so on.

What caused prices and leverage to go down? What was the scary bad news? To listen to the conventional accounts, the crisis began with housing prices suddenly plummeting, completely unexpectedly, out of the blue. In Figure 15.3, you see housing went down slowly. It is a nice slow curve. It goes up, it stops going up, and then it comes down slowly. That housing prices stopped going up is not really a surprise from the leverage cycle vantage point. Down payments cannot go below 0%, so as housing down payments approach their minimum, one would expect housing prices to stop increasing. What is surprising is how fast leverage

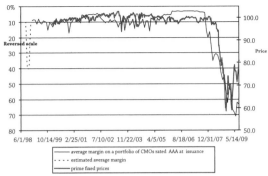

Figure 15.4 Securities leverage cycle: Margins offered and AAA securities prices.
Margin % (down payment required to purchase securities) Note: The figure represents the
average margin required by dealers on a hypothetical portfolio of bonds subject to certain
adjustments noted below. Observe that the margin % axis has been reversed, since lower
margins are correlated with higher prices. The portfolio evolved over time, and changes in
average margin reflect changes in composition as well as changes in margins of particular
securities. In the period following August 2008, a substantial part of the increase in margins
is due to bonds that could no longer be used as collateral after being downgraded, or for other
reasons, and hence count as 100% margin.

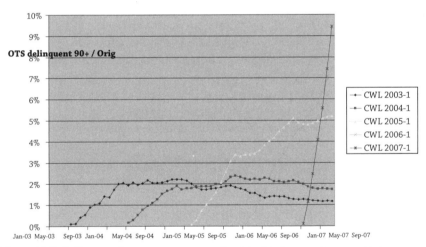

Figure 15.5 Delinquencies as a percentage of original balances–Countrywide loans
(CWL) more than 90 days delinquent divided by the original loans.
Note: The result was that the subprime BBB ABX index collapsed in January and Feburary
2007, as we see in Figure 15.6.

comes down just after the second quarter of 2006. What happened? What was the
scary bad news?

The scary bad news was that delinquencies on subprime loans started going
up in 2006 and by the beginning of 2007 it was clear a dangerous trend was

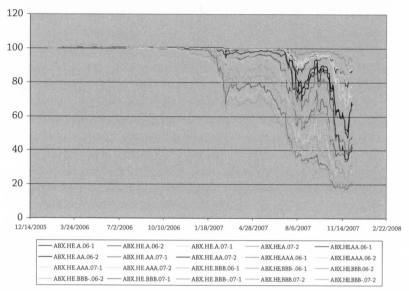

Figure 15.6   BBB subprime bond prices crash before big drop in housing.

materializing. In Figure 15.5 we see that historical delinquencies as a percentage of original balances for Countrywide deals asymptote at 2%. But in January 2007 the delinquencies on 2005 and 2006 loans were already approaching 5%.

The result was that the subprime BBB ABX index collapsed in January and February 2007, as we see in Figure 15.6.

It may seem surprising that an increase in delinquencies from 2% to 5% could cause such a drop in the subprime security index. I argued earlier this should not be surprising because of a sharp decline in leverage on subprime securities as nervous lenders ask for more collateral. I do not have the data on subprime security collateral, but I have the next best thing. As buyers of subprime securities get more nervous, one would expect them to prefer pools with subprime loans that have bigger down payments. And that is just what we see in Figure 15.2. Leverage on subprime loans collapses just after January 2007. And I believe that is what led to the housing price collapse.

5. The Leverage Cycle and Derivatives

The role of derivatives in the financial crisis has not been well understood. In my opinion the introduction of credit default swaps (CDSs) played a vital role in the subprime crash. Before their introduction, a pessimist could not leverage his views. CDSs did not become standardized for mortgages until the end of 2005. Only then could you could easily leverage your position as a pessimist. All those guys at the bottom of the continuum in Figure 15.1, who earlier just had to stand by and shake their heads at the high subprime prices, could thereafter

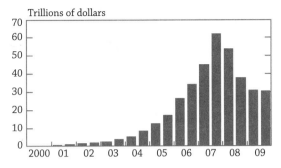

Figure 15.7 Volume of credit default swaps.
Source: ISDA market survey: historical data.

weigh in with money behind their opinion. This was bound to push the marginal buyer lower and to have a big effect on asset prices. Figure 15.7 shows the dramatic increase in CDSs in general (data is not available for mortgage CDSs in particular).

But this raises an interesting puzzle. The growth of derivatives, for example, as tranches in the collateralized mortgage obligation market or as separate bonds in subprime securitizations, long predated the spectacular expansion of the CDS market. In this prior stage, the growth in derivatives seemed to raise asset prices. Indeed, one of the major reasons the government sponsored securitization and encouraged tranching was because it was believed to raise the underlying mortgage price, thereby making it cheaper for homeowners to borrow money to buy homes. But why should the creation of a derivative inside a mortgage securitization increase the value of the mortgage, whereas the creation of a similar derivative like a CDS outside the tranche reduces the value of the mortgage?

The answer that Ana Fostel and I gave in a recent paper (2011) is that the collateralized mortgage obligation tranches obviously make the underlying mortgage more valuable relative to cash because the mortgage payoffs can be divided in ways that appeal to heterogeneous investors. The mortgage acts as collateral for the tranches (and in fact is literally called collateral in the deal). On the other hand, when trading a CDS one has to put up cash as collateral to guarantee the payment. In effect, the CDS tranches the cash, making the cash more valuable relative to the mortgage.

6. Managing the Leverage Cycle

Let me conclude my discussion of the 2000–2010 leverage cycle by briefly mentioning four reasons why this last leverage cycle was worse than its predecessor cycles. First, leverage reached levels never seen before in previous cycles. There is a variety of reasons for this, including the great and long moderation in volatility. Another is the aforementioned securitization and tranching. Yet another is that the government effectively guaranteed the debt of Fannie and Freddie, and perhaps even implicitly for the big banks, letting them all leverage with no market discipline. Still another reason is that the banks hid their leverage from regulators who might have turned a blind eye to them anyway. Lastly, low rates might have encouraged more leverage from investors searching for yield. The second reason this last leverage cycle was so bad is that it was really a double leverage cycle—in securities on the repo market and on homes in the mortgage market. These cycles fed off each other and, as we saw, as security prices fell and leverage collapsed there, leverage then went down in the housing mortgage market. Third, CDSs played a huge role and had been absent from previous cycles. CDSs helped optimists leverage at the end of the boom, making them more vulnerable, but most importantly, they provided an opportunity for pessimists to leverage and so made the crash much faster than it would have been without them. Lastly, because leverage got so high and then prices fell so far, a huge number of people and businesses ended up underwater, including 14 million homeowners. This debt overhang is playing a big role in our current malaise.

What should be done about the leverage cycle? Something to prevent it from getting too high, and then something to get out of the acute crisis once there is a crash, and, lastly, something to shorten the costly aftermath.

To prevent leverage from building up, we have to monitor it by collecting not only debt-to-equity ratios on a large variety of institutions, but also loan-to-value leverage data on all kinds of securities and assets. We have to put derivatives like CDSs on an exchange or something similar. I do not have space to explain it, but CDSs are just another way of leveraging. So you have to monitor the leverage of derivatives just like you would monitor the leverage of asset purchases. During normal times, loan-to-value leverage should be regulated. The Federal Reserve or another body that is given the authority should simply say, "You cannot loan at 2% down on houses. You cannot make repo loans with 0.5% down. You cannot write CDS insurance unless your initial margin is comparable to the margin on buying the security. And if you want to buy CDS insurance, you also have to put comparable margins down."

Allow me to mention four of the six reasons I have given elsewhere why monitoring and regulating leverage should be based at least partly on loan-to-value ratios on new loans (asset-based leverage) for all borrowers and lenders, rather than solely according to debt-equity ratios of entire institutions (investor leverage). First, leverage in the system can move away from regulated institutions. Second, limiting the overall leverage of an institution can sometimes incentivize it to choose riskier investments that are leveraged less. Third, as we have seen, investor leverage and asset leverage often move in the opposite direction. Fourth, it is harder to lie about asset-based leverage because separate reports will be obtained from both the borrower and the lender.

If, despite efforts to curtail leverage, the crisis begins anyway, the only way to get out is to reverse the three standard causes of leverage cycle crises: reduce the uncertainty, releverage the system (to moderate levels), and inject optimistic capital to make up for the lost demand from the suddenly bankrupt or insolvent optimists. In the acute stage of the crisis we always see the same thing. There are a huge number of people who have gone bankrupt, but a much bigger group is teetering on the edge of bankruptcy. Partly because of counterparty worries, a number of markets freeze up and liquidity disappears. Regulatory controls may suddenly be triggered. So there is a new kind of uncertainty, quite distinct from the volatile shock that triggered the crisis. The government must step in to quell this uncertainty and to keep markets transparent.

During the crisis and its aftermath, what looks like a demand problem—no one is borrowing at the going low interest rate—is really a collateral problem. Lenders are asking for so much collateral that investors cannot borrow because they do not have the collateral. What the Federal Reserve has to do is to go around the banks and lend directly on less collateral, not at lower interest rates. In fact, that is one of the things the Federal Reserve and the Treasury did (in the TALF and PPIP programs) that helped get the United States out of the depths of the crisis. It could have been done on a much broader scale. But the bravery to do something that had never been done before played a critical role in helping avoid a worse catastrophe.

Let me close this section by challenging the false separation between interest and collateral that has been maintained by some monetary authorities. It has been suggested that the Federal Reserve or the ECB should deal exclusively with interest in normal times, perhaps managing collateral in crises as "nonstandard" policies. Of course, it has now been recognized that leverage must be systemically curtailed. But the idea is that in normal times the central bank worries about interest, while collateral management is left to the macroprudential regulator. This reminds me of the old Soviet separation: one bureau was put in charge of prices, another in charge of quantities. A crisis is a window into the soul of the economy, as Plato's Republic was the soul writ large. If nonstandard policies saved the economy during the crisis, they surely should play a role in normal times.

7. The Aftermath: Getting Out from Underwater

After a major crisis has stabilized, the most important uncertainty becomes who else will go bankrupt and how they will behave while they are underwater. The depth and length of the crisis and its aftermath depend on how much leverage there was to begin with and on how effective government policy is in reducing value-destroying bankruptcies and debt overhang.

Debt overhang causes terrible deadweight losses. Once a homeowner is far enough underwater, he is not going to spend money to fix his house in order to raise its value when he knows he will probably lose it eventually anyway. Even if he wanted to fix his house, nobody would lend him the money to finance the repairs anyway. The underwater homeowner might continue to make his mortgage payments if he feels it would be more expensive to move and rent another house and live with a diminished credit rating, or if he thinks there is a chance his house might eventually recover enough value to be worth more than the debt. However, once he becomes far enough underwater it becomes too expensive *not* to default.

A major reason many homeowners stopped paying in this crisis has been that they are underwater. Figure 15.8 indicates that homeowners with current loan-to-values well below 100% rarely default, whereas subprime borrowers with loan-to-value at 160% were defaulting at the rate of 8% per month in 2009. Default rates are steeply monotonic in how far underwater the homeowner is.

Throwing a homeowner out of the house for defaulting also incurs huge costs. Subprime lenders on average recover less than 25% of their loan from foreclosing. It takes 18 months to three years nowadays to throw somebody out of his house, during which time the mortgage is not paid, taxes are not paid, the house is not fixed, the house is often vandalized, and realtor expenses are incurred.

By writing down principal on subprime loans so that the homeowners are above water, lenders and borrowers can both gain. For example, the lender can expect less than USD 40 back on a USD 160 loan if the house has a market value of USD 100 at the time of the default. If the lender cut the principal to USD 80, the homeowner would probably pay. If not, he would fix up the house and sell it. Either way the lender would get USD 80 instead of USD 40. The biggest policy mistake of the Obama administration in the current crisis was entrusting mortgage modifications to the servicers and the banks. The servicers do not own the mortgages and thus do not have the same incentives as the bondholders or the homeowners to write down principal. On the contrary, their incentives lie in not writing down principal. And the big bank lenders are afraid of taking an immediate loss on their books, even though they will incur a bigger loss down the road by foreclosing. I wrote about this over two years ago in two op-ed pieces

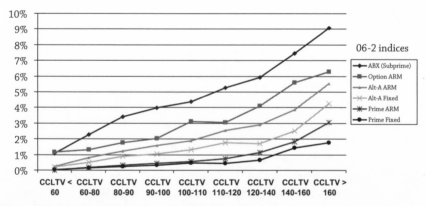

Figure 15.8 Loan-to-value ratios and default frequency.
Note: Net monthly flow (excluding mods) from <60 days to ≥60 days delinquent: six-month average as of Jan 2009. CCLTV=current combined loan-to-value.

with Susan Koniak in the *New York Times*, predicting a foreclosure fiasco if the government did not act.

The same logic can be applied to the many underwater businesses in America today. What appears to be a lack of demand for investment may instead be an inability to borrow either because of debt hangover (as Myers pointed out in 1977) or because lenders now require too much collateral. Macro models that do not capture such effects cannot possibly predict the effect of a stimulus or the period of time until normal employment levels are restored. Reducing interest, which in the conventional historical times used to calibrate the standard macro models can be relied on to generate more activity, may be completely ineffective in the aftermath of a leverage cycle crash.

What applies to homeowners and businesses applies even more to sovereign debts. After every leverage cycle crash, the government assumes some private debts and borrows to stimulate the economy. If the government debt was large before the crisis, it can become almost unmanageable after the crisis. In the United States, cities and states are beginning to cut back on vital services like policemen, firemen, and teachers because they feel they can no longer increase their debt. When we add on top all the pension and medical obligations many Western governments took on before the crisis, it is difficult to honestly maintain that any of them are solvent. This brief discussion is surely not the place to document my claim, but in my opinion many Western governments will be obliged to scale down their promises, that is, they will have to find ways to write down their debts or default on them.

One of the standard methods for governments to write down their nominal debt is to inflate it away. A 20% inflation over four years would reduce U.S. government debt by 20% and bring millions of homeowners out from underwater. As the need for debt reduction becomes more acute and as the money supply created by the government to stimulate demand via low interest becomes larger, the private sector will begin to expect inflation. Central bankers will declare that they will not allow inflation to start, presumably for fear that once started it may spiral out of control. However, such protestations will not stop the private sector from hedging by moving money into commodities, which will be where inflation begins. With unemployment high and activity low, central bankers will be reluctant to put on the brakes and the inflation will start to spread. The surest way for inflation to spiral out of control is if the central bankers vow it will never start and it does. Then people will really believe it is out of control.

8. Default, Punishment, and Forgiveness

It is generally believed that forgiving debt might start a chain reaction of defaults because the lender might then be unable to keep his promises, or that a default in one sector will lead lenders to expect a default in another sector and so kill lending there, or that debt forgiveness will create a moral hazard, encouraging future borrowers to take on too much debt and to strategically default. Most importantly, it is believed that default is immoral, that the defaulter deserves blame and that if one man's debt is forgiven, everyone's should be.

I believe that much of this viewpoint derives from the primitive creation of Conscience described by Nietzsche following centuries of punishment. Collateral is a much more sophisticated guarantor of delivery than punishment. It should spread the stigma of default to the lender. If the collateral falls so far in value that it no longer covers the loan, who is more to blame—the borrower or the lender? If a grocer goes bankrupt because he sells below cost (like the lender who asked for too little collateral), is the buyer to blame for purchasing on such absurd terms?

The law recognizes the difference between deception before the fact and default. A tort case and a contract case are treated differently. It may, in fact, be more blameworthy of governments to claim that all debts will be paid, say by entities they are bailing out or by programs started many years before during boom times, even after they realize they will not than it was to make those promises in the first place when it was thought they could be paid. As Plato said, it is not always just to keep promises when unexpected or unusual circumstances arise.

My point, of course, is not that ancient philosophers understood default better than modern economists, but that we must change our models to incorporate default and lending terms in order to understand the macroeconomy in ways the ancient philosophers could not dream of doing.

Consider for a moment an example presented in Dubey, Geanakoplos, and Shubik (2005). Each investor would like to borrow money because he is almost always much richer in the future, but each has a state in the future in which he will be quite poor. Suppose the government can set ex ante a penalty per dollar of default (say how long one goes to jail, or how long one's credit rating is destroyed). One might also think of the penalty as a pang of Conscience. How high should the penalty be set?

If the penalty is infinite, nobody will default and lenders can be sure to get their money back and so will lend at low interest. If the penalty is set lower, even for some people, then people will start to default, especially in the state when they are poor. Lenders will then want a higher interest rate and even the borrowers who do not plan to default (but who cannot be distinguished from the low-conscience borrowers by the lender) will face high interest rates. Moreover, the people who default will pay the penalty, which is a pure deadweight loss for society. There seem to be several compelling reasons to eliminate default by setting high penalties.

Yet it is Pareto superior to set an intermediate level of penalty, allowing for some defaults, the resulting higher interest rates, and the deadweight losses of paying the penalties. An infinite default would force people to repay even in their bad state, which, with diminishing marginal utility, would be extremely painful. Foreseeing this, they would not borrow much, even at low interest rates, and everyone would be worse off. Notice that the optimal default penalty allows agents in bad circumstances to default (in exchange for paying the penalty) not because they cannot repay, for in fact they could, but because it would be so painful to repay.

This story includes almost all the elements of default that are so scary to central bankers: lenders demand higher interest rates, even completely reliable borrowers must pay the higher rates, defaults occur, and the defaults are messy and incur deadweight losses. Yet it is socially optimal to have them!

Moreover, if the government could intervene and declare a situation a crisis ex post and mandate debt forgiveness, then there would be yet another Pareto gain because the messy losses from default would be reduced. Ex ante, the lenders would of course anticipate that they would be forced to forgive debt in some circumstances. But the point is that they would not have been paid in those circumstances with the ex ante optimal default penalty either.

One could ask a further question. Can the market set the default penalties? The answer, as shown in Dubey, Geanakoplos, and Shubik, is yes, just as the market sets leverage ratios. In some circumstances, the market will set the correct levels of penalties, in some not. But these penalties will have a profound effect on the levels of aggregate borrowing and lending and therefore on macroeconomic activity.

To the best of my knowledge, these kinds of considerations are completely absent from the calibrated models that guide macroeconomic policy. The ECB needs a macroeconomic model in which the anticipation of some sovereign default raises interest rates and then works out all the likely direct and indirect effects of an actual default. My guess is that the specter of such an event makes modelers shrink from doing the labor to create the models.

9. Pension Plan Default

One of the principal sources of default is pension obligations. Firms, cities, and states alike seem to promise more for future retirees than they can actually deliver. One important reason for this is the lack of regulatory guidelines. There does not appear to be a consensus on how much money should be required in the trust fund to back those promises, or how it should be invested, or even on how to compute the present value of the pension obligations. Discounting expected benefits at the risk-free rate gives astronomical numbers that would put most pension funds deeply underwater. Discounting at an equity return makes the liabilities seem manageable. I believe the reason for the lack of models and clear guidelines for pension plans is that regulators do not want to think seriously about default. If they got rigorous about default and wanted to ensure that it never happened, they would need to force pension managers to cut all the risk out of their portfolios. But regulators and managers alike seem to agree that it is sensible to hold a large stake in equities because their expected returns are so much higher. Inevitably, that leads to scenarios where the pension fund defaults. This probability must be quantified and the consequences of default systematically investigated.

Note

1. This article is reprinted with permission from the European Central Bank. It was originally presented at the 6th ECB Central Banking Conference November 18–19, 2011. It was summarized as "Endogenous Leverage and Default," in *Approaches to Monetary Policy Revisited—Lessons from the Crisis*, edited by Marek Jarociński, Frank Smets, and Christian Thimann (Frankfurt am Main: 2011).

References

Bernanke, B., M. Gertler, and S. Gilchrist. 1999. "The Financial Accelerator in a Quantitative Business Cycle Framework." In J. B. Taylor and M. Woodford, eds., *Handbook of Maroeconomics*. Amsterdam: North-Holland.

Brunnermeier, M., and L. Pedersen. 2009. "Market Liquidity and Funding Liquidity." *Review of Financial Studies* 22, 2201–2238.

Christiano, L., C. Ilut, R. Motto, and M. Rostagno. 2010. "Monetary Policy and Stock Market Booms." In *Macroeconomic Challenges: The Decade Ahead*. Kansas City, MO: Federal Reserve Bank of Kansas City. Reprinted in this volume.

Dubey, P., J. Geanakoplos, and M. Shubik. 2005. "Default and Punishment in General Equilibrium." *Econometrica* 73, 1–37.

Fahr, S., R. Motto, M. Rostagno, F. Smets, and O. Tristani. 2010. "Lessons for Monetary Policy Strategy from the Recent Past." Presentation to the Sixth European Central Bank Central Banking Conference, Frankfurt am Main.

Fostel, A., and J. Geanakoplos. 2008. "Leverage Cycles and the Anxious Economy." *American Economic Review* 98, 1211–1244.

———. 2011. "Do Derivatives Make Asset Prices Go Up or Down: The Case of Securitized Tranches vs CDS." Working Paper Series, Yale University .

Geanakoplos, J. 1997. "Promises, Promises." In W. B. Arthur, S. Durlauf, and D. Lane, eds., *The Economy as an Evolving Complex System II*. Reading, MA: Addison-Wesley.

———. 2003. "Liquidity, Default, and Crashes: Endogenous Contracts in General Equilibrium." In M., Dewatripont, L. P. Hansen, and S. J. Turnovsky, eds., *Advances in Economics and Econometrics: Theory and Applications*. New York: Cambridge University Press.

Geanakoplos, J., and S. Koniak. 2008. "Mortgage Justice is Blind." Op-ed, *New York Times*, October 30.

———. 2009. "Principal Matters." Op-ed, *New York Times*, March 5.

Holmstrom, B., and J. Tirole. 1997. "Financial Intermediation, Loanable Funds, and the Real Sector." *Quarterly Journal of Economics* 112, 663–692.

Kiyotaki, N., and J. Moore. 1997. "Credit Cycles." *Journal of Political Economy* 105, 211–48.

Minsky, H. 1986. *Stabilizing an Unstable Economy*. New Haven: Yale University Press.

Myers, S. 1977. "Determinants of Corporate Borrowing." *Journal of Financial Economics* 5, 147–176.

ASSET BUBBLES, CENTRAL BANKS AND INVESTMENTS

CHAPTER 16

Asset Price Bubbles and Central Bank Policies

THE CRASH OF THE "JACKSON HOLE CONSENSUS"

A. G. Malliaris

Introduction

The global financial crisis that began in mid-2007 progressed to become the most severe economic recession since the Great Depression of the 1930s. In the United States, the recession officially lasted for about 19 months, from December 2007 to June 2009, with a decline in real GDP by more than 4% and a loss of over 8 million jobs. The unemployment rate doubled from about 5% to 10% during this period. The household sector lost more than $13 trillion in wealth because of substantial declines in both equities and housing.

Economists, journalists, political panels, and commissions, among others, have investigated this global financial crisis in detail and will, in all probability, continue doing so for some time in the future. There is no shortage of likely causes. Candidate causes can be organized in certain groups such as macroeconomic, microeconomic, global, government, institutional, ethical, and even psychological. Within each of these groups there is a list of specific factors that may have contributed, propagated, or amplified the crisis. Macroeconomic factors include an overly easy monetary policy from 2002 to 2005 and the development of a real estate bubble. This real estate bubble burst in early 2007, when significant declines in real estate prices that continue to this date took place. This bursting caused macroeconomic financial instability. The microeconomic list is longer and contains subprime lending, opaque derivative securities, underestimation of risk leading to excessive risk-taking, failed risk management techniques, insufficiently capitalized banks and shadow banking institutions, too much leverage, and a shortage of liquidity. Global considerations cited mention the global savings glut, fixed exchange rates for certain countries with undervalued currencies like China, global imbalances, and an unstable global monetary system.

Government policies promoting affordable housing, insufficient regulation of the shadow banking sector, and deficient implementation of existing regulations for financial institutions have also been mentioned. Institutional elements such as the model of originate-to-distribute, the role of credit rating agencies, and suboptimal management compensation incentives that encouraged excessive risk-taking, have received attention along with ethical dimensions such as greed and corruption. Finally, psychological factors such as animal spirits, exuberance, and panic are introduced to convey the density of the crisis. Kolb (2010, 2011), Paulson (2010), the Financial Crisis Inquiry Commission (2011), and Sorkin (2010), among numerous other studies, provide academic, government, and journalistic perspectives on the crisis.

With the exception of a handful of analysts, the global financial crisis was not anticipated. The main reason for this failure was the prevailing consensus prior to the crisis that the successful pursuit of price stability over the previous three decades had produced macroeconomic stability, called the Great Moderation, for the United States and other industrial economies with steady economic growth, low GDP volatility, and low inflation. The Great Moderation paradigm did not focus on financial instability. It was widely accepted that price stability also contributed to financial stability.

In pursuing price stability during the Great Moderation period from the mid-1980s to the onset of the global financial crisis, both the Fed and other central banks around the world were challenged by the emergence of asset bubbles in general and the Internet bubble in particular. Alan Greenspan (1996, 6), then Federal Reserve chairman, reminded us, "How do we know when irrational exuberance has unduly escalated asset values, which then become subject to unexpected and prolonged contractions as they have in Japan over the past decade? And how do we factor that assessment into monetary policy? We as central bankers need not be concerned if a collapsing financial asset bubble does not threaten to impair the real economy, its production, jobs, and price stability. Indeed, the sharp stock market break of 1987 had few negative consequences for the economy. But we should not underestimate or become complacent about the complexity of the interactions of asset markets and the economy."

Because Chairman Greenspan raised this important question in the midst of celebrating the accomplishments of both monetary research and central bank policies that were credited with producing the Great Moderation, a spirited debate erupted on how monetary policy should respond to asset bubbles. It is acknowledged now that the profession's initial Hamletian ambivalence toward a central bank "responding to" or "not responding to" an asset bubble was resolved by the formation of a consensus in the United States to follow the asymmetric approach to bubbles. This asymmetric approach supported no or little Fed action against an asset bubble, while it was developing, but aggressive cuts in Fed funds when the bubble burst to minimize its potential destabilizing effects on the real economy. This was articulated in Greenspan (2002) during that year's Jackson Hole Conference and further solidified in subsequent meetings such as in Blinder and Reis (2005).

It is the purpose of this article to reexamine the main arguments of the two methodological lines: monetary policy should respond versus monetary policy should not respond to asset bubbles. The initial question of how the central bank should respond to an asset bubble can be reformulated in two ways. First, how does the central bank respond to an asset bubble while it is growing, and second, how does it respond after the bubble bursts? There has been strong agreement among economists that a central bank should respond to the bursting of a bubble by aggressively decreasing the Fed funds rate to minimize the impact of financial instability on the real economy. Achieving maximum employment is one of the Fed's mandates. However, there is no clear answer to the question of how should the central bank respond to an asset bubble before it bursts. If there is evidence that the bubble is contributing to inflation, then the Fed will respond; but what if prices remain stable? Some economists argue that the central bank should not respond to the bubble prior to its bursting, while others believe that it should try to target it or at least lean against the bubble to avoid future financial instability. Thus, we have two broad responses: the asymmetric approach, mentioned earlier, that advocates no response prior to the bursting and the symmetric approach that argues that the central bank should respond to an asset bubble both before and after it bursts. Within the choice of the symmetric response there are various degrees of intensity: burst the bubble, target the bubble, or lean against it. Targeting the bubble during its growth elevates the importance of bubbles to the goal of inflation targeting. Leaning against an asset bubble is a weaker strategy. Kohn (2006, 2008) uses the terminology of "conventional strategy," focusing on the Fed's mandate to describe the asymmetric approach, versus "extra action" for the symmetric response when the Fed takes steps against an asset bubble. These questions were debated for several years before the 2002 "Jackson Hole Consensus," supporting the asymmetric approach to asset bubbles, was reached.

This paper concludes that the 2007–2009 global financial crisis undermined the Jackson Hole Consensus and the new central bank policy paradigm has shifted toward "leaning against bubbles." Such an examination necessitates framing the discussion in the broader context of asset bubbles and financial instabilities. Another way to state the intention of this paper is to say that financial instabilities created by the bursting of asset bubbles can be extremely disruptive to the real economy, and that the policy of "leaning against" potential bubbles appears to dominate central bank neutrality.

While my focus is anchored on asset price bubbles and the shifting paradigm of central bank policies, I contribute toward an integrative approach between the real and financial sectors of an economy by presenting first a general overview of asset bubbles that supports their existence. Then, I discuss how the bursting of asset price bubbles may cause financial instability that often impacts the real sector of an economy adversely. This analysis guides us to reexamine how central banks should respond to asset price bubbles. I make a distinction between normative and positive responses of a central bank to asset price bubbles. I also introduce the concept of macroprudential regulation, originally advocated by Borio (2003) and reprinted in this volume, as an approach for leaning against asset bubbles. This leads me to draw three main conclusions at the close of the paper. I also follow a balanced approach in that all the pieces highlighted in this overview are important. This enables us to avoid the methodological selectivity that prevailed during the Jackson Hole Consensus.

Risk Management by Central Banks

Central banks around the world have mandates to promote price stability. In the United States the Fed by congressional mandate also seeks to achieve stable economic growth. Clearly, targeting stable asset prices is not an explicitly mandated goal of the Fed. Why then is the Fed concerned with asset price bubbles?

In 1996, Alan Greenspan raised concerns about an asset bubble as quoted earlier. Reviewing a half-century of changes in monetary policy, Taylor (2002) does not mention concerns about asset bubbles. According to Taylor, the big and dramatic changes in monetary policy occurred as a result of five episodes: the famous accord reached between the Treasury and the Federal Reserve in 1951, the end of the Bretton Woods fixed exchange rate system, the significant rise in inflation during the 1970s to the early 1980s, the dramatic success of disinflation in the early 1980s, and the Great Moderation. While Taylor celebrates the great successes of monetary policy during the Great Moderation, both in the United States and in numerous other countries, Greenspan (2004, 35) contemplates that

> "perhaps the greatest irony of the past decade is that the gradually unfolding success against inflation may well have contributed to the stock price bubble of the latter part of the 1990s. Looking back on those years, it is evident that technology-driven increases in productivity growth imparted significant upward momentum to expectations of earnings growth and, accordingly, to stock prices. At the same time, an environment of increasing macroeconomic stability reduced perceptions of risk. In any event, Fed policymakers were confronted with forces that none of us had previously encountered.

This quotation from Greenspan clearly answers the question of why monetary policy may be concerned with asset bubbles. To paraphrase Greenspan, during normal times, monetary policy focuses on price stability and maximum employment. However, when irrational exuberance drives asset prices to unsustainable levels and the risk of a bubble bursting increases the likelihood of financial instability, monetary policy is expected to address these issues. Greenspan (2004, 37) has clearly stated that the conduct of monetary policy in the United States has come to involve, at its core, crucial elements of risk management. This conceptual framework emphasizes understanding as much as possible the many sources of risk and uncertainty that policymakers face, quantifying those risks when possible, and assessing the costs associated with each of the risks. In essence, the risk management approach to monetary policymaking is an application of Bayesian decision making.

Greenspan is clearly advocating an activist discretionary central bank policy. Friedman (2006) describes this nonmechanistic flexibility of the Greenspan Fed. Such discretion offers broader latitude to central bankers in considering the risks of an asset bubble bursting and the costs of mopping up afterward. In contrast a "rules only"-driven price stability policy is not distracted by asset bubbles unless asset price increases foster inflationary expectations as consumers choose to spend a portion of their appreciated wealth.

Asset Price Bubbles

The risk management approach to monetary policy may call for a judgment about the existence of an asset bubble, the stage of its development, and the risks associated with its bursting. Asset bubbles are just one among many developments that the risk management approach to monetary policy considers. The stock market crash of October 19, 1987, the bursting of the Internet bubble in March 2000, and the collapse of the real estate market in 2007 are representative asset bubbles. The Fed however, has also addressed, during the last 20 years, many other economic and political developments. For purposes of illustration, a representative sample might include the Asian financial crisis of 1997–1998, the Russian debt default of August 1998, the collapse of the Long-Term Capital Management hedge fund in September 1998, the potential Y2K problem on January 1, 2000, the September 11, 2001 terrorist attacks, and the deflation fears in 2004.

Of course, in addition to these events, the central bank is continuously assessing in its risk management approach, the risks of inflation and the risks of a recession. Thus, asset bubbles are only a subset of the central bank's concerns, yet asset bubbles are very critical in view of the adverse financial consequences of the bursting of a bubble. Furthermore, among various asset bubbles that may develop in an economy, the Fed has identified only stock market bubbles and housing bubbles as financial developments that may cause serious instabilities. Commodity bubbles, like oil and gold, or exchange rate crashes as in the Asian financial crisis, have not explicitly been addressed by the Fed.

What is an asset price bubble in general? Do asset bubbles exist in financial markets? We hypothesize that if the price of an asset exceeds its "fundamentals," there is a bubble. The implication is that the asset price exceeds fundamentals by a significant amount and this persists for some time. If the price of an asset exceeds its fundamentals by a very small amount, we can call this amount noise. Also, if the deviation from fundamentals lasts for a very short trading interval, this may be called a temporary mispricing. When, however, the price of an asset exceeds its fundamentals by a large amount, say 30% above its fundamental value, for several months or even years, we can call it a bubble.

Kindleberger (1978) describes a bubble as an upward price movement over an extended range that then implodes. He also says that an asset bubble occurs when the purchase of an asset is not made because of the rate of return on the investment, but in anticipation that the asset can be sold to a "greater fool" at an even higher price. He lists and discusses numerous episodes of financial bubbles. Brunnermeier (2008) adopts Kindleberger's definition and says that a bubble refers to an asset price that exceeds the asset's fundamental value because the trader who buys it high believes he can resell it at an even higher price in the future.

Definitions of bubbles depend on a model of valuating fundamentals. Furthermore such fundamentals usually involve a long stream of future earnings appropriately discounted. Both the expected earnings and the discounting factor are uncertain and thus the fundamental value is also uncertain. By definition, efficient markets that continuously reevaluate the arrival of new information contribute to the discovery of the fundamental value of a particular asset. However, for new innovations whose future earnings are very uncertain, the pricing of fundamentals has a very large margin of error. In the past, bubbles have developed and then crashed in stocks of railroad, electricity, aviation, automobiles, radio, pharmaceutical, Internet, and biotechnology firms when they were new technologies. Do we currently have bubbles in stocks of firms in search-engine and social network technologies?

Asset price bubbles are often accompanied by increases in trading volume and also by high price volatility. As price bubbles develop, they encourage increases in the supply of similar assets. After the crash, the valuation of most firms in the bubble sector decreases. This was experienced during the Internet bubble. In contrast to loud bubbles with high price volatility, there are also quiet bubbles with substantial price increases but with low volatility, as discussed in Hong and Sraer (2011).

In general, the common underlying characteristic of mispricing is the high degree of uncertainty that surrounds the future profitability of the asset. The theory of market efficiency does not recognize the existence of asset bubbles. It accommodates the high degree of uncertainty that may surround new technologies and views the high volatility as evidence of a continuous reassessment of the fundamental value by market participants. It claims that if a price of an asset significantly exceeds its fundamentals value, arbitrage activities will exploit such discrepancies and return the asset price to its fundamental value. However, if arbitrage is limited, behavioral finance believes that bubbles may persist.

There are a large number of theoretical papers that study asset price bubbles. Useful surveys include Bhattacharya and Yu (2008), Brunnermeier (2008), Vogel (2010), and, in this book, Barlevy (2012). Brunnermeier (2008) offers an excellent brief survey by organizing the bubbles literature into four categories. Here, I cite some representative results to illustrate that there is theoretical support for the existence of asset bubbles. The first group of papers assumes that all investors are rational and have identical information. In this case, finite bubbles cannot arise but infinite ones can develop under certain conditions and with a precise rate of growth. The second group of papers maintains the assumption of rational expectations, but investors now have asymmetric information. In this group, bubbles develop a little easier. The third group of papers allows traders to be either rational or behavioral and bubbles may last for a long period since rational and behavioral investors struggle to influence the evolution of prices. The final group allows traders to have heterogeneous beliefs. Reprinted in this book, Scheinkman and Xiong (2003) combines heterogeneous beliefs with a short-sale constraint to show that speculative bubbles can emerge. The mechanism that generates bubbles with high trading volume and price volatility relies on optimistic or overconfident traders willing to buy an asset at a higher price, while pessimistic traders are unable to moderate the bubble because of short-sale constraints. Barlevy (2012) focuses on the important issue of the welfare implications of central banks choosing to burst a bubble. He argues effectively that the recent crisis has highlighted that most models of asset bubbles do not address the critical question of whether bursting a bubble by the central bank is welfare improving or not.

Beyond the theoretical literature that offers conditions for the existence of asset bubbles, there is extensive evidence in experimental economics about the emergence of bubbles in the laboratory. The classic reference is Smith, Suchanek, and Williams (1988), and more recently Hussam, Porter, and Smith (2008). Also, behavioral economists such as Shiller (2002) have argued in favor of the existence of bubbles. Shiller argues that the key idea for the formation of bubbles is the feedback mechanism. A price increase for an asset leads to investor enthusiasm, which further causes increased demand and additional price increases. The high demand is supported by the public's memory of high past returns or by optimism that this new asset will generate very high future earnings. Various bubbles have different positive feedback mechanisms, but because non-fundamentally driven price increases cannot be sustained indefinitely, a negative feedback pattern will eventually replace the positive one. Usually, the initial increases are slow, and it takes a long time for the bubble to grow. In contrast, bubble crashes take place during a relatively short period.

Kindleberger (1978) describes the feedback mechanism in detail and gives numerous illustrations of specific bubbles. Keynes (1936), in his famous chapter 12, clearly states that an investor's

> knowledge of the factors which will govern the yield of an investment some years hence is usually very slight and often negligible. (149)

This description leads Keynes to talk about his famous "beauty contest" since there are no readily available concrete valuation benchmarks. He adds that

> most, probably, of our decisions to do something positive, the full consequences of which will be drawn out over many days to come, can only be taken as a result of animal spirits—of spontaneous urge to action rather than inaction, and not as the outcome of a weighted average of quantitative benefits multiplied by quantitative probabilities. (161)

Akerlof and Shiller (2009) elaborate in detail on Keynes's idea of animal spirits and demonstrate its importance in several areas of economics.

The successful speculator Soros (1987, 2010) introduces the idea of "reflexivity" to explain the development of asset bubbles. Soros's point of departure is philosopher Karl Popper's claim that empirical truth cannot be known with absolute certainty. If this is correct, Soros argues that financial markets cannot be exactly correct moment by moment in their valuation of all assets. If prices generated by market participants are not exactly correct, they are biased contrary to the claim of market efficiency. The degree of distortion or fallibility usually ranges from the negligible, called a random error, to the significant, called an asset bubble. Next, this principle of fallibility interacts with the principle of reflexivity that says that the prices generated by market forces are a reflection of fundamentals. So if market participants are euphoric about a certain asset and its price increases, this price now has an impact on the assessment of the asset's fundamentals. As the price increases, the value of the fundamentals increases and various financial decisions that depend on fundamentals such as leverage, both debt and equity, are influenced. Soros then proceeds to develop several steps that an asset bubble goes through from its inception to its collapse.

Gisler and Sornette (2010) generalize the idea of a bubble, from a phenomenon related to asset pricing, to social bubbles that describe reinforcing feedback mechanisms for social projects such as the Apollo space project. Malliaris (2005) discusses asset bubbles across countries and globally. Finally, Tuckett and Taffler (2008) and Tuckett (2009) apply psychoanalytic techniques to explain the development of asset bubbles. They argue that financial assets have the power to generate both excitement and anxiety, causing risk and reward judgments to become uneven. When the utility of potential gain is detached from the disutility of potential loss, critical reasoning is disturbed, and the emergence of an erroneous consensus may lead to the development of asset bubbles.

The theoretical literature about bubbles does not address the extensive narratives related to booms and busts, bubbles and crashes, animal spirits and panics, and exuberance and contraction discussed in Kindelberger (1978), Minsky (1986), Soros (1987), Akerlof and Shiller (2009), and others. This is surprising because financial booms and busts and business cycles appeared joined together in various theories even before Keynes. For example, Haberler's (1960) original version of *Prosperity and Depression* was completed in the summer of 1936 and contains several expositions of the role of financial instabilities as a source of recessions. Laidler (2003) gives a detailed account of the interwar debate on financial and economic stability and shows that the recent bursting of the stock and housing bubbles and their impact on the real economy "do bear more than a passing resemblance to earlier episodes" (17). Today's reader will find these descriptive theories perhaps limited in their explanatory scope. Modern mixed capitalist economies with sophisticated financial markets and global financial integration have little in common with pre–World War II economies. Besides, the Keynesian revolution has overshadowed this old literature, primarily by advocating the use of fiscal and monetary policies to combat recessions and financial instabilities.

Thus the literature, both academic and popular, recent as well as pre-Keynesian, attests to the existence of asset bubbles as a financial phenomenon in contrast to advocates of market efficiency who reject their presence. Prior to bursting, the existence of an asset bubble is only a probable event and only after it bursts is there certainty that it has occurred. To give some quantitative evidence of past stock market and housing bubbles I reproduce a table from the IMF (2002) in Table 16.1.

This table does not include the recent global financial crisis. It clearly illustrates that stock market and housing bubbles and crashes, or busts and bear markets, are not rare financial events. No wonder the Fed was concerned ex ante with the

Table 16.1 **Equity and Housing Price Bear Markets in Industrial Countries**

	(Median over all episodes)			
	Real equity prices		*Real housing prices*	
	Contraction[a] *(percent)*	*Duration[b]* *(quarters)*	*Contraction[a]* *(percent)*	*Duration[b]* *(quarters)*
Bear markets[c]	−24.4	5	−5.7	5
Busts[d]	−45.5	10	−27.3	16
1960s	−40.5	11	–	–
1970s	−49.5	10	−27.3	19
1980s	−47.6	10	−28.5	16
1973[e]	−60.1	10	–	–
2000[f]	−43.6	10	–	–

Source: International Monetary Fund 2003, Table 2.1.

[a] Contraction from peak to trough in real equity and housing prices, respectively.

[b] Time from peak to trough (excluding the peak quarters).

[c] All bear markets, including busts.

[d] All bear markets in the bottom quartile (see text).

[e] Busts beginning during 1972–74.

[f] Busts beginning at the peaks recorded in 2000 and ending in 02:Q3 (end of sample).

Internet bubble. With this discussion as a guide, let us assume that at any given time period there may be one or more asset bubbles in an economy. The central bank need not be concerned with a potential bubble in the price of individual assets, such as Google or Facebook or even a bubble in gold or oil. The central bank, however, is concerned with the aggregate stock market or the real estate market. Sometimes overvaluations may self-correct or deflate. Other times the bubble in the stock market or the real estate market may continue to grow until some triggering event causes a crash, as in Japan in 1989. Crashes usually desta-bilize financial markets, but in certain cases, as in the October 1987 crash, there is no spillover to the real economy. The bursting of the Internet bubble in 2000, despite an almost 80% crash in the NASDAQ, had only a small impact on the real economy, with a short and mild recession. Unfortunately, both in Japan and the United States, the joint crashes of the stock and real estate bubbles had serious real effects: the lost decade in Japan and the financial crisis of 2007–2009 in the United States. At the present time there are no theoretical models about bubbles that can direct central banks to choose confidently the symmetric or asymmet-ric approach to bubbles. Thus, we continue the descriptive analysis by asking the critical question: how does the bursting of an asset bubble destabilize the finan-cial system?

Financial Instability

Asset bubbles are an inherent part of the financial system and the financial sys-tem is part of the total economy. A theoretical challenge remains to eventually integrate the real and financial sectors with sufficient quantitative details so that answers can be provided to the following questions: under what conditions is the financial sector stable or unstable? What are the causes of financial insta-bility? What role do asset bubbles and crashes play in causing financial instabili-ties? What are the relationships between asset bubbles and crashes, booms and busts, exuberance and panic, jubilant animal spirits and depressions, manias and financial crises? Under what conditions do financial crises impact the real economy by reducing GDP and employment? And, of course, what can monetary and fiscal policies do, if anything, to stabilize both the financial system and the real economy?

Minsky (1975, 1986) unwearyingly opined that financial crises have been coupled with capitalism throughout history. He has also argued that Keynes's principal contribution was his hypothesis that capitalism is inherently unstable. Furthermore, such instability originates in the financial sector that allocates capi-tal to investment decisions driven by animal spirits. Minsky (1986) develops these Keynesian ideas into his famous financial instability hypothesis. He argues that in a modern capitalist economy with expensive capital assets and a complex and sophisticated financial system, actual economic activity is greatly influenced by firms' expectations of future profits and financing decisions by banks and other financial institutions. Minsky proposes a credit cycle model of five stages: displacement, boom, euphoria, profit taking, and panic. There is an active interplay between the real economy and the financial sector in this process. Minsky (1968) describes how asset managers become optimistic with a new technology, such as the Internet, and are willing to finance it. Gradually, this sector grows and an asset boom develops. As the sector attracts new funding further technologies are developed and the financial and technological euphoria grows. Certain triggering events, such as disappointing earnings, lead to profit taking. Further deterioration in fundamentals translates into a panic. The bursting of an asset bubble leads to financial instability that causes real sector instability.

In spite of Minsky's concerns about the inherent financial instability of capitalism, the Great Moderation doctrine, supported by empirical evidence, led to the conclusion that "this time is different." Reinhart and Rogoff (2009) document that this assessment is a recurring theme. They offer comprehensive narratives and analysis of the connections between the financial and real sectors of an economy, how financial crises impact both sectors and how financial crises appear idiosyncratic. Details may differ because of the rapidly evolving financial sector, but the essential mechanisms of positive feedback initially, followed by negative feedback later, persist.

The financial sector includes the central bank, commercial and investment banks, nonbank financial institutions such as insurance companies, managed money flowing through financial markets for equity, debt, real estate, commodities, currency, and other derivative instruments traded over the counter or on established exchanges. Alternatively, and perhaps an easier definition, the financial sector is the one that allocates financial resources efficiently in the domestic and global economies. Financial sectors may have their roots in a given country, but nowadays they extend globally. The concept of a financial sector is dynamic, global, and evolving. As the recent crisis demonstrated, even the very best financial experts may not have a comprehensive understanding of all its financial and legal intricacies.

In the United States and in many advanced economies, the financial sector has total financial assets equivalent to several times the size of the country's GDP. Adrian and Shin (2009) discuss the current financial system in the United States and its stability with emphasis on security brokers and dealers. Kaufman (2004) gives a detailed analysis of macroeconomic stability and links it to bank soundness. The Federal Reserve Flow of Funds accounts describe how the share of assets of commercial banking as a percentage of total financial assets in the financial sector has been declining for several decades, while the share of assets held by other financial institutions and money managers has been growing.

When is a financial sector stable? Defining financial stability or instability is challenging. Financial stability can broadly be distinguished between "microstability," which involves conditions of individual financial institutions, and "macro-stability," which focuses on the efficient functioning of the financial system as a whole. In a more intuitive sense, financial stability means the avoidance of financial shocks that are large enough to cause economic loss to the real economy. Here we view macroeconomic financial stability as influenced not only by banks and other financial institutions, but also by the volatility of asset prices. Spotton (1996) identifies financial instability with dramatic swings in the price of financial assets. Schinasi (2004) discusses the concept of financial stability in detail and proposes the following definition:

> A financial system is in a range of stability whenever it is capable of facilitating (rather than impeding) the performance of an economy, and of dissipating financial imbalances that arise endogenously or as a result of significant and unanticipated events. (8)

Mishkin (2007) describes a financial system as stable, if it performs the function of efficiently channelling funds to optimal investment opportunities. Friedman and Laibson (1989) focus on the role of stock markets with their extreme movements as part of the financial system allocating scarce capital resources. Malliaris and Yan (2010) argue that even in stable markets capital allocation may be slow, and they give a behavioural explanation. Bernanke (2011a) addresses domestic financial stability as it relates to global imbalances in capital flows, currency devaluations, or even country defaults.

Suppose that financial stability means that the financial system allocates capital efficiently. Then, if the system becomes unstable, there are dramatic swings in asset prices, and as a result the financial system does not allocate capital efficiently. When the system is unstable, two types of interrelated risks emerge. First, the system experiences valuation risk because the financial instability has increased uncertainty and traders have difficulty correctly measuring fundamental values of assets. Second, there is macroeconomic risk. This means that traders also need to assess the likelihood of a recession as a result of financial disruptions in investment and consumer spending. Thus, financial instability creates uncertainty, asset price volatility, and misallocation of capital, all of which negatively impact the real economy. It is logical to ask, "What economic policies may contribute to financial stability?"

One important expectation of monetary policy during the 1970s and 1980s was that price stability would also bring financial stability. When inflation was high during the 1970s, asset prices were distorted. It was debated whether the stock market was a hedge against inflation. Housing prices increased in response to inflation in the late 1970s. The financial sector during this period of high inflation performed poorly. A monetary policy targeting inflation was believed to lead to financial stability. Taylor (2002) documents the long journey of monetary policy from inflation and financial instability to price stability and the Great Moderation. He discusses how low and stable inflation rates reduce uncertainty and promote sound economic decisions. Price stability removes market distortions in price signals and, by anchoring inflation expectations, reduces risk premia in interest rates, along with the likelihood of misperceptions about future asset returns.

In a seminal paper, Bernanke and Gertler (1999), also reprinted in this book, develop a macroeconomic model and obtain the result that price stability and financial stability are complementary and mutually consistent objectives. Kuttner (2012), in this book, discusses price and financial stability and several other results of the Bernanke and Gertler (1999) paper in detail. Ferguson (2002), Papademos (2006), and Plosser (2008) examine the interplay between price stability and financial stability. Often, an economy simultaneously experiences price and financial stabilities, as during most of the 1990s. However, there have been periods of price inflation and financial stability, as during the 1970s. Between 2000 and 2004 there was price stability with financial instability. Currently we have price stability but markets remain financially unstable. Borio and White (2003) tell us that episodes of financial instabilities with serious macroeconomic costs have taken place with greater frequency in the last 30 years than earlier in the midst of price stability, in both developed and emerging markets.

In other words, in the presence of price stability, financial markets have become more volatile recently than in the past. Once inflation was conquered, the challenge of financial instability arose again. Greenspan (2004, 2005) reflects on this issue of price stability producing a decrease in real volatility but paradoxically an increase in financial volatility. Rajan (2005) articulates in detail how the financial system has increased risk. Most of the times, central banks pursue their mandated price stability goal; however, during periods of financial crises, central banks give priority to stabilizing the financial sector in order to contain losses to the real sector. Thus, price stability is neither necessary nor sufficient for financial stability.

Borio and White explore this paradox and argue that, in order to resolve it, one needs to examine carefully the procyclicality of the financial sector. In an economic environment of economic growth, with a credible monetary policy that is achieving its primary objective of price stability, the financial sector may expand rapidly, and asset prices may increase. Confidence based on sound economic performance tends to drive up both the amount of credit and asset prices. If monetary policy continues to pursue price stability only, the eventual decline in asset prices may destabilize the financial system and the economy.

Issing (2002) argues that, as market-based financing has expanded during the last decade, asset prices have gradually gained in importance, and monetary policy transmission mechanisms have become more diversified and complex. As a result, a change in asset prices might have a huge impact on financial system stability and economic activity in general and hinder the effectiveness of monetary policy.

If a successful monetary policy, as the one during the Great Moderation, cannot produce long-term financial stability, can financial instability impact monetary policy? Yes. Papademos (2006) argues that a reduction of interest rates, for example, may have weaker effects than under normal conditions if the financial system is unstable, because increasing risk premia may prevent most lending rates from falling, or because of credit rationing arising from a general unwillingness on the part of banks to lend. A striking example of this sort has been the asset price bubble in Japan in the late 1980s. Plummeting asset prices and rising nonperforming loans have undermined the solvency position of banks, making them unwilling to lend, or perhaps incapable of lending. The extremely accommodating policy stance, with interest rates close to 0%, did not reopen the bank lending channel. Currently, the United States has used an essentially zero Fed funds rate to address the serious unemployment problem that resulted from the financial crisis. The very slow improvement in the job market is evidence that financial instability constrains the effectiveness of monetary policy.

Domestic financial stability is also closely interrelated to the global monetary system. Mishkin (1999, 6) carefully develops a conceptual framework for global monetary instability and concludes by proposing the following definition: Financial instability occurs when shocks to the financial system interfere with information flows so that the system can no longer do its job of channeling funds to those countries with productive investment opportunities.

Beyond the definitions of stability given above, Brock and Malliaris (1989) present a comprehensive exposition of the technical concept of stability and its applications to economics. They define stability as a special property of an economic system that allows it to return quickly to its original state after an exogenous or endogenous shock. These authors view an economic system as a group of relationships between endogenous variables represented as a vector X, exogenous variables as I, and random shocks as U. Furthermore, one can decompose the vector X into real variables R and financial variables F, so that $X = R + F$. Suppose that GDP is one key real endogenous variable that is used to monitor the stability of the system. Disturbances in such a system may occur because of shocks to X, real or financial, or I or U. One may wish to characterize the source(s) of instability arising endogenously (drop in productivity, technology) or exogenously (decline in foreign trade or foreign currencies) or from random shocks (terrorist attacks, wars, natural disasters). What we are interested in is disturbances in the financial sector F or in any other variable that immediately involves F.

A system $f(X, I, U)$ is stable if such shocks to any of the variables R, F, I, or U do not translate to deviations from trend GDP. If such shocks cause deviations from trend GDP (say a recession) then we say the system is unstable. In particular the system is financially unstable if a shock in some financial variable F causes a recession and prevents the economy's GDP from recovering quickly. It remains a formidable analytical challenge to develop a sufficiently complete macroeconomic model that is capable of addressing factors contributing to macroeconomic instability. Such a model needs to distinguish between instability caused endogenously by real or financial factors and exogenously by random shocks. Asset price bubbles straddle the real and financial sectors, with their fundamentals driven by the real sector and the bubble component by the financial sector. If the fundamentals disappoint, the bubbles burst. When the bubble bursts, the financial sector, because of excessive credit and leverage, becomes unstable and transmits this instability to the real sector. How can a theorist decompose these interrelated feedback mechanisms?

This brief bibliographical discussion leads to the observation that, when asset price bubbles burst, they often cause financial instability. This instability in turn diminishes the effectiveness of the financial sector to allocate capital efficiently and it may also reduce the effectiveness of monetary policy. Furthermore, it is not known how long such instability could last, or to put it differently, it is not known how quickly both the financial and real sectors can recover. The lost decade in Japan and the loss of the last four years in the United States demonstrate the great risks associated with asset bubbles bursting. This leads us to the next question. How should monetary policy respond to asset price bubbles?

Asset Prices and Monetary Policy

When Greenspan (1996) reported that the stock market appeared to be driven by irrational exuberance and wondered how this should factor into the conduct of monetary policy, a lively debate erupted. Bordo and Wheelock (2004, 2007) studied stock market booms and monetary policy both in the United States and in nine other industrialized countries. They identified several episodes of sustained price increases in stock prices in the nineteenth and twentieth centuries and then examined the growth of real output, productivity, the price level, and credit during each episode. They concluded that most asset price bubbles occurred during periods of relatively rapid real economic growth with increases in productivity and credit. Also, most asset bubbles during the twentieth century developed during periods of price stability, but there were bubbles during the nineteenth century that developed during periods of inflation or deflation. Booms often ended within a few months of an increase in inflation and consequent monetary policy tightening.

Cogley (1999), Bullard and Schaling (2002), and Goodfriend (2002) study how monetary policy should respond to asset prices. They conclude that using monetary policy to attempt to burst asset price bubbles is likely to result in greater economic instability than waiting for bubbles to burst on their own. In particular Bullard and Schaling (2002) study the macroeconomic consequences of a Taylor-type monetary policy rule that targets the level of equity prices in addition to inflation and output growth. They find, in extreme cases, that a policy that explicitly targets equity prices can lead to an indeterminate rational expectations equilibrium.

Rigobon and Sack (2003) acknowledge that it is difficult to estimate the response of asset prices to changes in monetary policy because both stock prices and interest rates react to numerous other variables. They develop a new estimator and conclude that an increase in short-term interest rates results in a decline in stock prices. Bernanke and Kuttner (2005) also analyze the impact of changes in monetary policy on equity prices. They find that, on average, a hypothetical unanticipated 100-basis point increase in the Fed funds rate is associated with about a 5% decline in broad stock indices. Their results imply that a series of modest Fed funds increases may not moderate asset bubbles effectively. Kuttner (2012) in this book reconfirms the empirical evidence that marginal interest rates adjustments cannot effectively dampen asset price bubbles.

Filardo (2000, 2001) explores the role of monetary policy in an economy with asset bubbles by developing a small-scale macroeconomic model and running various simulations. He finds that if there is no uncertainty about the role of asset prices in determining output and inflation then monetary policy should respond to asset prices. In a later paper, Filardo (2004) suggests that, in dealing with asset price bubbles, the use of both fiscal policy and financial regulation policies should be considered along with monetary policy.

Blanchard (2000) and Bordo and Jeanne (2002) use a dynamic new Keynesian framework in which asset price bubbles lead to excessive capital or debt accumulation which result in a prolonged slump when the asset price bubble bursts. Bordo and Jeanne argue that more restrictive monetary policy will dampen an asset price bubble at a cost of lower output during the bubble. The benefit of such a monetary policy is higher output than otherwise would have been the case when the bubble bursts. However, Bordo and Jeanne are skeptical about whether, in the real world, central bankers can actually identify bubbles accurately and assess the intertemporal trade-offs involved in attempting to dampen an asset price bubble.

In an influential paper cited earlier and reprinted in this book, Bernanke and Gertler (1999) apply the Bernanke, Gertler, and Gilchrist (1999) financial accelerator model by incorporating exogenous bubbles in asset prices. The asset bubble affects real activity via the wealth effect on consumption and firms' financial decisions via appreciations of their assets in the balance sheet. Stochastic simulations lead Bernanke and Gertler to conclude that central banks should view price stability and financial stability as highly complementary and central bank policies should not respond to changes in asset prices, except insofar as they signal changes in expected inflation. Bernanke and Gertler (2001) use the same model to perform stochastic simulations to evaluate the expected performance of alternative policy rules. Their findings are complementary to their earlier study. An aggressive inflation-targeting rule stabilizes output and inflation when asset prices are volatile and there is no significant additional benefit to responding to asset prices. Bean (2003, 2004) is supportive of the Bernanke and Gertler results. He reasons that flexible inflation targeting essentially considers the entire future path of expected inflation and growth and, thus, there is no further reason to consider asset prices. Kuttner (2012) offers a detailed assessment of the Bernanke and Gertler results in view of the financial crisis.

Cecchetti et al. (2000) and Cecchetti, Genberg, and Wadhwani (2002) critique the Bernanke and Gertler results, and argue for a central bank that pursues both inflation targeting at a given time horizon and achieves a smooth path for inflation. These policies will most likely achieve better results by considering asset prices along with inflation forecasts and output gaps. Their logic is based on the fact that reacting to asset prices during normal times will reduce the probability of asset bubbles forming and growing to the point that their bursting may destabilize the economy.

Chairman Greenspan (2002) participated in this debate and articulated the asymmetric approach to asset bubbles. He claimed that

> the notion that a well-timed incremental tightening could have been calibrated to prevent the late 1990s bubble is almost surely an illusion. Instead, we . . . need to focus on policies to mitigate the fallout when it occurs and, ease the transition to the next expansion. (5)

Blinder and Reis (2005) strongly support the asymmetric approach. They state,

> "Regarding Greenspan's legacy, then, we pose a simple rhetorical question. If the mopping up strategy worked this well after the mega-bubble burst in 2000, shouldn't we assume that it will also work well after other, presumably smaller, bubbles burst in the future? Our suggested answer is apparent. (68)

This position was also articulated by Kohn (2006, 2008), Mishkin (2008), Evans (2009), and others. Issing (2009) was the first to call this position the "Jackson Hole Consensus." As already discussed earlier, this consensus proposes that central banks should ignore an asset bubble while it is growing and follow a "mop-up" strategy after a bubble bursts. This involves supplying sufficient liquidity to the financial system following the bursting of the bubble to avoid a macroeconomic collapse. Issing (2009, 2011) carefully argues that the European Central Bank did not adopt the Jackson Hole Consensus and instead followed a strategy of leaning against bubbles. Thus, the initial considerations of central banks targeting asset price bubbles or trying to puncture bubbles were quickly dismissed as viable strategies both in the United States and in Europe.

Instead of asking the normative question about how monetary policy should respond to asset bubbles, Hayford and Malliaris (2001, 2004, and 2005) take a positive approach. They use a forward-looking Taylor rule model to examine, if monetary policy since 1987 has been influenced by the valuation of the stock market. They search for empirical evidence that the Fed is stock market neutral while the bubble is emerging, as suggested by the Jackson Hole Consensus. They develop several models and use different inputs and find empirical evidence that during the 1994–1999 period, the Fed not only avoided neutralizing the asset bubble, as expected, but also, perhaps, unintentionally may have contributed to the bubble's growth.

Roubini (2006) argues that central banks can deflate asset price booms without an adverse impact on economic activity. To support his argument he cites the cases of the real estate markets of the United Kingdom during 2003–2004, Australia during 2003–2005, and New Zealand during 2004–2005 as empirical evidence that

> prove[s] that monetary policy can if used wisely and moderately, be very effective in pricking asset and housing bubbles without leading to significant economic or financial damage. (99)

In the case of the UK and Australia the central banks increased short-term interest rates by relatively modest amounts starting from low initial levels. For example for the UK, rates went up by 125 basis points starting from 3.50%, an increase that arguably was from slightly below, up to a neutral short-term interest rate. The Reserve Bank of New Zealand increased the official cash rate, its primary instrument of monetary policy, from about 5.0% in January 2004 to 6.75% in summer 2005. According to Roubini this was done both to cool inflationary pressures and to deflate the housing bubble. As a result of this tightening, economic growth decreased from 4.8% to 2.3%, which Roubini states "is hardly an economic or financial meltdown." In all three of these cases economic growth slowed in response to the tightening of monetary policy.

Taylor (2007) acknowledges that the Fed had

> good reasons stated at the time for the prolonged period of low interest rates, most importantly the risk of deflation following the experience of Japan in the mid-1990s.(471)

However Taylor (2007) argues that the Fed could have prevented the housing bubble that ended up bursting in 2007 if the Fed had stuck to the Taylor rule and increased the Federal funds rate at the beginning of 2002. Taylor's argument seems to depend entirely on whether or not the risk from causing a housing boom and bust was greater than the risk of deflation. When the Fed did start to increase the Federal funds rate in 2004, long-term interest rates, such as the 30-year fixed mortgage rate, did not increase.

The cause of this "bond market conundrum," that is, the lack of response of long-term interest rates to monetary tightening has not been resolved. At least two explanations have been proposed: Ben Bernanke (2005) has suggested the cause was a global saving glut, while Smith and Taylor (2007) argue it was due to U.S. monetary policy deviating from the Taylor rule by not increasing the Federal funds rate sooner. However the fact that inflation did not accelerate as a consequence of the Fed deviating from the Taylor rule from 2002–2004 provides partial evidence that the risk of deflation was real and was dealt with. If the Fed had increased the Federal funds rate as in Taylor's counterfactual, deflation may have occurred along with a stop to the boom in housing starts. This episode points out the difficulty central bankers face in balancing multiple risks to the economy while having only one monetary policy instrument. One way to deal with the risk of deflation and the housing boom would have been to use monetary policy as was done, but also to additionally regulate real estate lending more closely. Since the Fed followed an easy monetary policy during 2002–2004, Taylor's argument that the Fed contributed to the housing bubble appears to have some validity. Bernanke (2010) reviews Taylor's evidence on the link between monetary policy during 2002–2006 and the rapid increases in housing prices during this period and concludes that the direct links are weak.

Jalilvand and Malliaris (2010) ponder a possible link between the Internet bubble crashing and the housing bubble. They reason that the asymmetric approach to bubbles may have contributed to the Internet bubble. When the bubble burst in 2000, the easy monetary policy that followed, due to the recession and also to deflationary worries, may have fueled the housing bubble. This link between the Internet and housing bubbles can be called a sequence of bubbles. One may further argue that the remarkably easy monetary policy during the 2008–2011 years, also motivated by the Jackson Hole Consensus, may currently be contributing to the emergence of new bubbles in the sequence.

Yellen (2009) gives an overview of the lessons she learned from the current financial crisis about financial bubbles and monetary policy. She acknowledges that there are several difficult issues for monetary policymakers that prevent them from taking action. Among these issues are the following: (1) Do we know that a bubble exists? (2) What is the optimal timing to lean against the bubble? (3) How can we assess the risk-and-reward characteristics of the bubble? (4) How much risk is too much? (5) How can we estimate or evaluate the consequences of the bursting of the bubble? (6) What tools do we have to manage or target the bubble? She concludes that the current crisis challenges economists to provide answers to such questions instead of advocating the asymmetric approach. She answers the question we have been discussing:Should central banks attempt to deflate asset price bubbles before they get big enough to cause big problems? Until recently, most central bankers would have said no. They would have argued that policy should focus solely on inflation, employment, and output goals—even in the midst of an apparent asset-price bubble. That was the view that prevailed during the tech stock bubble and I myself have supported this approach in the past. However, now that we face the tangible and tragic consequences of the bursting of the house price bubble, I think it is time to take another look. (Yellen 2009, 8)

She concludes that "monetary policy that leans against bubble expansion may also enhance financial stability by slowing credit booms and lowering overall leverage" (10).

Dudley (2010) also argues that the financial crisis of 2007–2009 necessitates the need for central banks to reexamine the asymmetric approach to bubbles because it has been demonstrated very clearly that the cost of waiting to respond to an asset bubble until after it has burst can be very high. He argues in favor of a policy that leans against the bubble. Such a policy may use three broad sets of tools: first, the bully pulpit where the policymakers speak out about the dangers associated with an incipient bubble; second, the use of macroprudential tools, and third, a tighter monetary policy that may reduce desired leverage in the financial system by flattening the yield curve.

In a noteworthy paper Christiano et al. (2010) use historical data and model simulations containing 18 booms in the United States to show that, if inflation is low during stock market bubbles, an interest rate rule that narrowly targets inflation actually destabilizes asset markets and the whole economy. The authors remark that economic historians like Bordo and Wheelock (2004, 2007), mentioned earlier, and White (2009) have documented that in every stock market bubble in the last 200 years excluding the Civil War and World War I and II, asset price bubbles occurred during years of low inflation. A logical consequence of this empirical fact is that by setting interest rates to target low inflation, the central bank is induced to set real rates below the natural rate, thus fueling a bubble. This is consistent with Hayford and Malliaris (2001, 2004, 2005). Thus one can make the argument that a central bank that follows an asymmetric response to asset bubbles actually encourages a bubble in its growing phase. This challenges the conventional wisdom of the Jackson Hole Consensus. To correct this problem, Christiano et al. (2010) propose targeting credit growth as a good proxy for the natural rate.

Also, it is important to recognize several contributions of Geanakoplos on leverage and asset bubbles and how central banks should respond. They are briefly discussed in Geanakoplos (2012) in this book. The author argues that leverage causes asset price bubbles and such leverage cannot be stopped by increasing interest rates, nor can it be boosted by lowering interest rates. Leverage must be managed directly. Geanakoplos suggests that central banks manage both interest rates and the leverage cycle. Acharya and Naqvi (2012), in this book, argue that asset bubbles are formed only when bank liquidity is high enough because such high liquidity leads bank managers to underprice risk. Therefore the authors suggest that leaning against a bubble by a central bank takes the specific form of leaning against liquidity.

Lastly, Bernanke (2011b) without directly discussing the bursting of the housing bubble and the seriousness of the recent financial crisis, outlines what are the important sources of systemic risks for both national and global financial and real stability. He advocates the macroprudential approach that supplements the traditional supervision and regulation of individual banks with an explicit deliberation of risks undermining the stability of the entire financial system.

Conclusions

There are three conclusions that follow from my detailed exposition. The first and most important is that the Jackson Hole Consensus, favoring the asymmetric approach to responding to asset price bubbles, has lost its commanding power among central bankers. The Jackson Hole Consensus proposed that asset bubbles take a long time to develop, often with numerous corrections and reassessments along the slow climb to the top, only to crash very quickly and dramatically in a fraction of the time it took to reach the peak. Central bankers cannot agonize for several years about what to do with asset bubbles while they are growing. Increasing Fed funds rates gradually and continuously if the bubble persists over an extended period of time entails very high risks of the central bank itself causing a recession, without sufficient evidence of the effectiveness of such marginal Fed funds increases. It is less risky to ignore the bubble and decrease interest rates rapidly after its bursting. Thus, the asymmetry of asset bubbles translates into an asymmetry of central bank policy. While the bursting of the Internet bubble should have challenged this consensus, it actually solidified the consensus. Had the consensus been weakened by the Internet bubble bursting, the housing bubble may have been avoided all together. It took the great recession of 2007–2009 to educate central bankers that the consensus had crashed and needed to be replaced by leaning against asset bubbles. However, leaning against an asset bubble while it is developing, often over several years, is currently only a guiding principle and much remains to be articulated before central banks can implement it.

The second conclusion is that the pursuit of price stability does not always deliver financial stability. The triumph of price stability as a strategy that produced the Great Moderation is now being reconsidered as new research documents that a central bank pursuing inflation targeting during low inflation environments may drive the real interest rate below its natural rate and thus fuel asset bubbles. Could it be that, instead of central bankers asking how to respond to asset price bubbles, they should be asking, "How may central banks be causing asset bubbles?" Alternatively, with each bursting of an asset bubble, as with the Internet bubble in 2000 and the housing bubble in 2007–2009, the fear of deflation causes the Fed to ease aggressively in order to avoid an experience similar to the lost decade of Japan. How does the Fed know whether or not the degree of stimulative excess may be planting the seeds of the next bubble? How does the Fed avoid moral hazard that leads to financial instability? How does the Fed conduct monetary policy in the presence of several financial institutions that are too big to fail? The Dodd-Frank Wall Street Reform and Consumer Act created a new Financial Stability Oversight Council to address these issues, among numerous other threats to the stability of the financial system of the United States. Will it work where others have failed? Will financial stability remain the responsibility of the Fed or will it be transferred to the Financial Stability oversight Council?

Will the Council recommend appropriate monetary policies to promote financial stability or will the Council use macroprudential policies?

The third conclusion is that the asset bubble literature has made great progress in determining what drives the feedback mechanisms, but much more is needed. When it comes to macro bubbles such as the entire stock market or housing, we need to know more about the conditions that give rise to such bubbles as well as the mechanisms that propel them to grow and then crash. The research of economic historians has been very useful in identifying the emergence of bubbles with the development of new technologies, solid economic growth with high productivity, and stable monetary conditions as characterized by low inflation and low interest rates. Naturally there is a paradox. All these conditions are those for which central banks typically strive. How can central banks avoid this Promethean penalty? The Dodd-Frank Act has established, within the Treasury Department, the Office of Financial Research, which may choose to collect data to evaluate conditions conducive to the emergence and development of asset bubbles, their growth, and eventual crash. The approach is similar to the way national income accounting data has contributed to identifying business cycles. Such new data on asset booms and busts may help in the formulation and testing of new hypotheses about bubbles and the appropriate policies to moderate them. Moving forward, economists have an opportunity to respond to the challenge of developing theoretical models of asset price bubbles, and assessing the risks and benefits in terms of the welfare of both the symmetric and asymmetric approaches. Central banks need to respond to an asset bubble ex ante rather than fighting a new bubble using the lessons learned from the bursting of the last bubble.

Note

1. The author is thankful to Gadi Barlevy, Andrew Filardo, Ken Kuttner, Viral Acharya, Ben Friedman, and Werner De Bondt for many useful ideas that clarified issues discussed in this paper. He is also thankful to Doug Evanoff, George Kaufman, and Mary Malliaris, who read carefully an earlier draft and offered numerous insightful comments that improved the exposition of the ideas presented. Marc Hayford and the author have coauthored several papers on similar topics and his support is much appreciated. Finally, the author also thanks the graduate scholar April Heitz for her bibliographical assistance.

References

Acharya, V. V., and H. Naqvi. 2012. "Bank Liquidity and Bubbles: Why Central Banks Should Lean against Liquidity." In this volume.

Adrian, T., and H. S. Shin. 2009. "Financial Intermediaries, Financial Stability, and Monetary Policy." In *Maintaining Stability in a Changing Financial System: A Symposium*. Kansas City, MO: Federal Reserve Bank of Kansas City. 287–334.

Akerlof, G. A., and R. J. Shiller. 2009. *Animal Spirits: How Human Psychology Drives the Economy, and Why It Matters for Global Capitalism*. Princeton, NJ: Princeton University Press.

Barlevy, G. 2012. "Rethinking Theoretical Models of Bubbles: Reflections Inspired by the Financial Crisis and Allen and Gorton's Paper 'Churning Bubbles.'" In this volume.

Bean, C. 2003. "Asset Prices, Financial Imbalances and Monetary Policy: Are Inflation Targets Enough?" In A. Richards and T. Robinson, eds., *Asset Prices and Monetary Policy*. Sydney: Reserve Bank of Australia.

———. 2004. "Asset Prices, Financial Instability, and Monetary Policy." *American Economic Review* 94, 14–18.

Bernanke, B. 2005. "The Global Saving Glut and the U.S. Current Account Deficit." Speech given at the Homer Jones Lecture, St. Louis, MO, April 14.

———. 2010. "Monetary Policy and the Housing Bubble." Speech given at the Annual Meeting of the American Economic Association, Atlanta, January 3.

———. 2011a. "Global Imbalances: Links to Economic and Financial Stability." Speech given at the Banque de France Financial Stability Review Launch Event, Paris, February 18.

———. 2011b. "Implementing a Macroprudential Approach to Supervision and Regulation." Speech delivered at the 47th Annual Conference on Bank Structure and Competition, Chicago, May 5.

Bernanke, B., and M. Gertler. 1999. "Monetary Policy and Asset Price Volatility." In *New Challenges for Monetary Policy: A Symposium*. Kansas City, MO: Federal Reserve Bank of Kansas City. Reprinted in this volume.

———. 2001. "Should Central Banks Respond to Movements in Asset Prices?" *American Economic Review* 91, 253–257.

Bernanke, B., M. Gertler, and S. Gilchrist. 1999. "The Financial Accelerator in a Quantitative Business Cycle Framework." In J. B. Taylor and M. Woodford, eds., *Handbook of Macroeconomics*. Amsterdam: North-Holland.

Bernanke, B., and K. Kuttner. 2005. "What Explains the Stock Market's Reaction to Federal Reserve Policy?" *Journal of Finance* 60, 1221–1257.

Bhattacharya, U., and X Yu. 2008. "The Causes and Consequences of Recent Financial Market Bubbles: An Introduction." *Review of Financial Studies* 21, 8–10.

Blanchard, O. J. 2000. "Bubbles, Liquidity Traps, and Monetary Policy: Comments on Jinushi et al, and on Bernanke." In Ryoichi Mikitani and Adam S. Posen, eds., *Japan's Financial Crisis and Its Parallels to U.S. Experience*. Washington, DC: Institute for International Economics.

Blinder, A. S., and R. Reis. 2005. "Understanding the Greenspan Standard." In *The Greenspan Era: Lessons for the Future*. Kansas City, MO: Federal Reserve Bank of Kansas City.

Bordo, M. D., and O. Jeanne. 2002. "Boom-Busts in Asset Prices, Economic Instability and Monetary Policy." CEPR Discussion Paper No. 3398.

Bordo, M. D., and D. C. Wheelock. 2004. "Monetary Policy and Asset Prices: A Look Back at Past U.S. Stock Market Booms." *Federal Reserve Bank of St. Louis Review* 86, 19–44.

———. 2007. "Stock Market Booms and Monetary Policy in the Twentieth Century." *Federal Reserve Bank of St. Louis Review* 89, 90–122.

Borio, C. 2003. "Towards a Macro-prudential Framework for Financial Supervision and Regulation?" *CESifo Economic Studies* 49, 181–216. Reprinted in this volume.

Borio, C., and W. White. 2003. "Whither Monetary and Financial Stability? The Implications of Evolving Policy Regimes." In *Monetary Policy and Uncertainty: Adapting to a Changing Economy*. Kansas City, MO: Federal Reserve Bank of Kansas City.

Brock, W. A., and A. G. Malliaris. 1989. *Differential Equations, Stability and Chaos in Dynamic Economics*. Amsterdam: North-Holland.

Brunnermeier, M. K. 2008. "Bubbles." In Steven N. Durlauf and L. E. Blume, eds., *The New Palgrave Dictionary of Economics*. 2nd ed. New York: Palgrave Macmillan.

Bullard, J. B., and E. Schaling. 2002. "Why the Fed Should Ignore the Stock Market." *Federal Reserve Bank of St. Louis Review* 84, 35–41.

Cecchetti, S. G., H. Genburg, J. Lipshy, and S. Wadhwani. 2000. *Asset Prices and Central Bank Policy*. Geneva: International Center for Monetary and Banking Studies.

Cecchetti, S. G., H. Genberg, and S. Wadhwani. 2002. "Asset Prices in a Flexible Inflation Targeting Framework." In W. Hunter, G. Kaufman, and M. Pomerleano, eds., *Asset Price*

Bubbles: The Implications for Monetary, Regulatory and International Policies. Cambridge, MA: MIT Press.

Christiano, L. J., C. Ilut, R. Motto, and M. Rostagno.2010. "Monetary Policy and Stock Market Booms." In *Macroeconomic Challenges: The Decade Ahead.* Kansas City, MO: Federal Reserve Bank of Kansas City. Reprinted in this volume.

Cogley, T. 1999. "Should the Fed Take Deliberate Steps to Deflate Asset Price Bubbles?" *Federal Reserve Bank of San Francisco Economic Review,* 42–52.

Dudley, W. C. 2010. "Asset Bubbles and the Implications for Central Bank Policy." Remarks given at the Economic Club of New York, April 7.

Evans, C. L. 2009. "The International Financial Crisis: Asset Price Exuberance and Macroprudential Regulation." Remarks given at the International Banking Conference, Chicago, September 24.

Ferguson, R. W. 2002. "Should Financial Stability Be an Explicit Central Bank Objective?" In Piero C. Ugolini, Andrea Schaechter, and Mark R. Stone, eds., *Challenges to Central Banking from Globalized Financial Systems: Papers Presented at the Ninth Conference on Central Banking, Washington, D.C., September 16–17, 2002.* Washington, DC: International Monetary Fund.

Filardo, A. J. 2000. "Monetary Policy and Asset Prices." *Federal Reserve Bank of Kansas City Economic Review* 85, 11–37.

———. 2001. "Should Monetary Policy Respond to Asset Price Bubbles? Some Experimental Results." In G. Kaufman, ed., *Asset Price Bubbles: Implications for Monetary and Regulatory Policies.* New York: Elsevier Science, JAI.

———. 2004. "Monetary Policy and Asset Price Bubbles: Calibrating the Monetary Policy Trade-Offs." BIS Working Paper No. 155.

Financial Crisis Inquiry Commission. 2011. *The Financial Crisis Inquiry Report: Final Report of the National Commission on the Causes of the Financial and Economic Crisis in the United States.* Washington, DC: Financial Crisis Inquiry Commission.

Friedman, B. 2006. "The Greenspan Era: Discretion, Rather Than Rules." *American Economic Review* 96, 174–177.

Friedman, B., and D. Laibson. 1989. "Economic Implications of Extraordinary Movements in Stock Prices." *Brookings Papers on Economic Activity,* 137–189.

Geanakoplos, J. 2012. "Leverage and Bubbles: The Need to Manage the Leverage Cycle." In this volume.

Gisler, M., and D. Sornette. 2010. "Bubbles Everywhere in Human Affairs." In L. Kajfez-Bogataj, K. H. Mueller, I. Svetlik, and N. Tos, eds., *Modern RISC-Societies: Towards a New Framework for Social Evolution.* Vienna: Edition Echoraum.

Goodfriend, M. 2002. "Interest Rate Policy Should Not React Directly to Asset Prices." In W. Hunter, G. Kaufman, and M. Pomerleano, eds., *Asset Price Bubbles: The Implications for Monetary, Regulatory and International Policies.* Cambridge, MA: MIT Press.

Greenspan, A. 1996. "The Challenge of Central Banking in a Democratic Society." Remarks delivered at the Annual Dinner and Francis Boyer Lecture of the American Enterprise Institute for Public Policy Research, Washington, DC, December 5.

———. 2002. "Opening Remarks." In *Rethinking Stabilization Policy: A Symposium.* Kansas City, MO: Federal Reserve Bank of Kansas City. 1–10.

———. 2004. "Risk and Uncertainty in Monetary Policy." *American Economic Review* 94, 33–40.

———. 2005. "Risk Transfer and Financial Stability." Speech delivered at the Federal Reserve Bank of Chicago's 41st Annual Conference on Bank Structure, Chicago, May 5.

Haberler, G. 1960. *Prosperity and Depression: A Theoretical Analysis of Cyclical Movements.* 4th ed. London: Bradford and Dickens.

Hayford, M. D., and A. G. Malliaris. 2001. "Is the Federal Reserve Stock Market Bubble-Neutral?" In G. Kaufman, ed., *Asset Price Bubbles: Implications for Monetary and Regulatory Policies.* Oxford: Elsevier Science.

———. 2004. "Monetary Policy and the U.S. Stock Market." *Economic Inquiry* 42, 387–401.

———. 2005. "How Did the Fed React to the 1990s Stock Market Bubble? Evidence From an Extended Taylor Rule." *European Journal of Operational Research* 163, 20–29.

Hong, H., and S. Sraer. 2011. "Quiet Bubbles." Working paper. http://ssrn.com/abstract=1767453.

Hussam, R. N., D. Porter, and V. L. Smith. 2008. "Thar She Blows: Can Bubbles Be Rekindled With Experienced Subjects?" *American Economic Review* 98, 924–937.

International Monetary Fund. 2003. *World Economic Outlook, April 2003.* Washington, DC: International Monetary Fund.

Issing, O. 2002. "Monetary Policy in an Environment of Global Financial Markets." Launching Workshop of the ECB-CFS Research Network on Capital Markets and Financial Integration in Europe, Frankfurt am Main.

———. 2009. "In Search of Monetary Stability: The Evolution of Monetary Policy." Bank for International Settlements Working Paper No. 273.

———. 2011. "Lessons for Monetary Policy: What Should the Consensus Be?" IMF Working Paper No. Wp/11/97.

Jalilvand, A., and A. G. Malliaris. 2010. "Sequence of Asset Bubbles and the Global Financial Crisis." In R. W. Kolb, Ed., *Lessons from the Financial Crisis.* Hoboken, NJ: John Wiley and Sons.

Kaufman, G. 2004. "Macroeconomic Stability, Bank Soundness and Designing Optimum Regulatory Structures." *Multinational Finance* 8, 141–171.

Keynes, J. M. 1936. *The General Theory of Employment, Interest and Money.* London: Macmillan.

Kindleberger, C. P. 1978. *Manias, Panics, and Crashes: A History of Financial Crises.* Hoboken, NJ: John Wiley and Sons.

Kohn, D. L. 2006. "Monetary Policy and Asset Prices." Speech given at "Monetary Policy: A Journey from Theory to Practice," European Central Bank Colloquium in honor of Otmar Issing, Frankfurt am Main.

———. 2008. "Monetary Policy and Asset Prices Revisited." *Cato Journal* 29, 31–44.

Kolb, R. W., ed. 2010. *Lessons from the Financial Crisis, Causes, Consequences, and Our Economic Future.* Hoboken, NJ: John Wiley and Sons.

———. 2011. *The Financial Crisis of Our Time.* New York: Oxford University Press.

Kuttner, K. 2012. "Monetary Policy and Asset Price Volatility: Should We Refill the Bernanke-Gertler Prescription?" In this volume.

Laidler, D. 2003. "The Price Level, Relative Prices, and Economic Stability: Aspects of the Interwar Debate." Prepared for the Bank for International Settlements Conference "Monetary Stability, Financial Stability, and the Business Cycle," Basel.

Malliaris, A. G. 2005. *Economic Uncertainty, Instabilities & Asset Bubbles.* Hackensack, NJ: World Scientific Publishing.

Malliaris, S., and H. Yan. 2010. "Reputation Concerns and Slow-Moving Capital." Yale International Center for Finance, working paper.

Minsky, H. P. 1968. "Private Sector Asset Management and the Effectiveness of Monetary Policy: Theory and Practice." *Journal of Finance* 24, 223–238.

———. 1975. *John Maynard Keynes.* New York: Columbia University Press.

———. 1986. *Stabilizing and Unstable Economy.* New York: Columbia University Press.

Mishkin, F. S. 1999. "Global Financial Instability: Framework, Events, Issues." *Journal of Economic Perspectives* 13, 3–20.

———. 2007. "Financial Instability and Monetary Policy." Speech at the Risk USA 2007 Conference, New York, November 5.

———. 2008. "How Should We Respond to Asset Price Bubbles?" Speech at the Wharton Financial Institutions Center and Oliver Wyman Institute's Annual Financial Risk Roundtable, Philadelphia, May 15.

Papademos, L. 2006. "Price Stability, Financial Stability and Efficiency and Monetary Policy." Speech at the Third Conference of the Monetary Stability Foundation, "Challenges to the Financial System-Ageing and Low Growth," Frankfurt am Main.

Paulson, H. M. 2010. *On the Brink: Inside the Race to Stop the Collapse of the Global Financial System.* New York: Business Plus.

Plosser, C. I. 2008. "Two Pillars of Central Banking: Monetary Policy and Financial Stability." Opening remarks for the Pennsylvania Association of Community Bankers 130th Annual Convention, Federal Reserve Bank of Philadelphia, Waikoloa, H, HI, April 18.

Rajan, R. G. 2005. "Has Financial Development Made the World Riskier?" In *The Greenspan Era: Lessons for the Future*. Kansas City, MO: Federal Bank of Kansas City.

Reinhart, C. M., and K. S. Rogoff. 2009. *This Time Is Different: Eight Centuries of Financial Folly*. Princeton, NJ: Princeton University Press.

Rigobon, R., and B. Sack. 2003. "Measuring the Reaction of Monetary Policy to the Stock Market." *Quarterly Journal of Economics* 118, 639–669.

Roubini, N. 2006. "Why Central Banks Should Burst Bubbles." *International Finance* 9, 87–107.

Schinasi, G. J. 2004. "Defining Financial Stability." IMF Working Paper. No. Wp/04/187.

Scheinkman, J., and W. Xiong. 2003. "Overconfidence and Speculative Bubbles." *Journal of Political Economy* 111, 1183–1219. Reprinted in this volume.

Shiller, R. J. 2002. "Bubbles, Human Judgment, and Expert Opinion." *Financial Analysts Journal* 58, 18–26.

Smith, A., and J. Taylor. 2007. "Monetary Policy Rules." Presented at the Taylor Rule Conference at the Dallas Federal Reserve.

Smith, V. L., G. L. Suchanek, and A. W. William. 1988. "Bubbles, Crashes, and Endogenous Expectations in Experimental Spot Asset Markets." *Econometrica* 56, 1119–1151.

Sorkin, A. R. 2010. *Too Big to Fail: The Inside Story of How Wall Street and Washington Fought to Save the Financial System—and Themselves*. New York: Penguin.

Soros, G. 1987. *The Alchemy of Finance*. Hoboken, NJ: John Wiley and Sons.

———. 2010. *The Soros Lectures at the Central European University*. New York: Public Affairs.

Spotton, B. L. 1996. "Financial Instability: Some Stylized Facts." *Canadian Journal of Economics* 29, S202–S206.

Taylor, J. B. 2002. "A Half Century of Changes in Monetary Policy." Remarks delivered at the Conference in Honor of Milton Friedman at the University of Chicago, November 8. http://www.stanford.edu/~johntayl/Onlinepaperscombinedbyyear/2002/A_Half-Century_of_Changes_in_Monetary_Policy.pdf.

———. 2007. "Housing and Monetary Policy." *National Bureau of Economic Research, Inc, Working Paper*: 13682.

Tuckett, D. 2009. "Addressing the Psychology of Financial Markets." *Economics: The Open-Access, Open-Assessment E-Journal*, 3, 2009–2040. doi:10.5018/economics-ejournal.ja.2009–40.

Tuckett, D., and R. Taffler. 2008. "Phantastic Objects and the Financial Market's Sense of Reality: A Psychoanalytic Contribution to the Understanding of Stock Market Instability." *International Journal of Psychoanalysis* 89, 389–412.

Vogel, H. L. 2010. *Financial Market Bubbles and Crashes*. New York: Cambridge University Press.

White, W. R. 2009. "Should Monetary Policy Lean or Clean?" BIS Working Paper No. 205, April.

Yellen, J. 2009. "A Minsky Meltdown: Lessons for Central Bankers." Presented at the 18th Annual Hyman Minsky Conference on the State of the U.S. and World Economies, April 16.

CHAPTER 17

Do Bubbles Lead to Overinvestment?
A Revealed Preference Approach

Robert S. Chirinko and Huntley Schaller*

Are bubbles just a zero-sum game among financial market participants, or do they have real effects on investments, consumption, and employment? ... This, in our view, is the most important question. ... Many more such papers are needed.
—Bhattacharya and Yu 2008, 8–9

1. Introduction

Many economists believe that market prices do a good job of allocating resources. In particular, the stock market is seen as playing an important role in efficiently allocating capital to its most productive uses. The stock market price of a firm represents the expected present value of future dividends—the "fundamental" price. Increases in the stock market price provide incentives for managers to issue equity and attract capital to their firms.

This standard view of the stock market was called into question by events in the late 1990s. Scores of commentators—including many economists—claim that there was stock market overvaluation in the late 1990s. Moreover, there is a widespread belief that stock market overvaluation—or a bubble—led to overinvestment, especially in ".com" companies and internet-related firms, such as those in telecommunications.[1] A bubble might affect investment if investors become unduly excited about particular firms and, in their excitement, they bid up the prices of these firms (Shiller 2001; Shleifer 2000). Overvalued shares lower the perceived cost of equity capital. If managers act on this lower perceived cost, they issue new shares, lower the discount rate used in evaluating investment projects, and increase investment spending.[2]

The central core of the standard story of capital allocation involves rates of return and discount rates. Favorable shocks—an increase in demand or a technical improvement—raise returns to capital for the fortunate firm (Cochrane 2001; Fama 1976). A firm earning high returns (relative to its cost of capital or discount rate) increases its capital stock until the return on the marginal unit of capital again equals the discount rate. Absent externalities, capital is being allocated optimally.

The central core of the overinvestment story also involves rates of return and discount rates. A bubble lowers the discount rate, leading to higher investment. If managers use a discount rate below the market rate, they would invest too much, the rate of return on their investment would be too low, and capital would be misallocated.

This paper focuses on the central core of these two stories by examining the discount rates used by firms in making their investment decisions. One possible way to measure discount rates would be to survey managers. This approach has many advantages but, for our purposes, it has two key disadvantages. First, we cannot reach back in time to find out the discount rate used by managers at a time when their firm might have been overvalued. Second, there are potential issues of selection bias due to differential response rates across firms with different characteristics. Instead, we use a revealed preference approach that relies on the investment decisions of firms—combined with investment theory—to estimate the discount rates actually used by managers of U.S. firms.

To assess the potential role of bubbles, we focus on a class of firms—high-price firms—that financial economists have identified as possibly overvalued. The high-price portfolio comprises firms with high stock market prices relative to a simple accounting measure of fundamentals. This class of firms is frequently referred to as "growth" firms. Such a label would be inconsistent with the perspective taken in this paper. Firms facing fundamental shocks and whose behavior is described by the standard story could be considered growth firms. However, this label is inappropriate for those firms whose high stock price is due to bubbles and whose behavior is described by the overinvestment story.

The standard story in economics holds that firms may enter the high-price portfolio as a result of favorable shocks that provide the firms with good investment opportunities and thus increase their stock market price. The overinvestment story claims that the high stock price of high-price firms is based on investor sentiment, not good investment opportunities. We therefore divide the firms in the high-price portfolio into those with good or poor investment opportunities. If the standard story applies to all high-price firms, firms with both good and poor investment opportunities should have discount rates equal to the market rate (suitably adjusted for risk).[3] If the overinvestment story applies to all high-price firms, both subclasses of firms should have discount rates that are lower than the market rate. Our econometric work suggests something in between. The estimated discount rate is approximately equal to the market rate for firms with good investment opportunities. For firms with poor investment opportunities, the discount rate is below the market rate. The difference in discount rates (relative to risk-adjusted market rates) is economically and statistically significant. Thus the standard story describes high-price firms with good investment opportunities and the overinvestment story high-price firms with poor investment opportunities.

We then undertake three robustness checks. First, the benchmark results are based on using demand shocks as a measure of investment opportunities. We examine cost shocks as an alternative way to identify recent news about investment opportunities. Firms with favorable cost shocks should have relatively good investment opportunities. Using cost shocks as a measure of investment opportunities, we confirm the benchmark results—the estimated discount rate for high-price firms with poor investment opportunities is below the market rate. It is significantly lower than the discount rate used by high-price firms with good investment opportunities. Second, insofar as investment opportunities may be difficult to measure, we also examine the discount rate wedge for high-price firms whose shareholders have long horizons. We would not expect firms described by these two characteristics to have a discount rate wedge that differs systematically from zero. This prediction is borne out by the empirical results. Third, we take a different but complementary approach that evaluates a series of restricted econometric models in terms of J tests. These misspecified models are useful in evaluating the standard and overinvestment stories, and the test results are consistent with the above findings.

The paper proceeds as follows. Section 2 derives the Euler equation from a formal optimization problem that is the basis for the econometric analysis. Section 3 discusses the panel data-set (details are provided in the Data Appendix in Chirinko and Schaller (2011))and the summary statistics that describe various subsets of firms. Section 4 presents our benchmark results with this Euler equation and uncovers strong evidence for the empirical relevance of both the standard and overinvestment stories for appropriate subsets of firms. Section 5 contains several robustness checks. Section 6 concludes.

2. Model

Our estimation strategy exploits the intertemporal pattern of investment spending to "reveal" the discount rate guiding investment decisions. The Euler investment equation has been a workhorse model in the investment literature and has been used by, among others, Shapiro (1986), Whited (1992), Hubbard and Kashyap (1992), and Chirinko and Schaller (2001, 2004) to study investment spending. Being a first-order condition for profit-maximization, the Euler equation is closely tied to optimal firm behavior. Moreover, investment and discount rate variables enter explicitly (unlike, for example, the equally popular Brainard-Tobin Q equation), and thus it is straightforward to introduce a parameter representing the discount rate wedge.

The Euler equation that is the basis for our estimates can be obtained through informal and formal derivations.[4] The informal derivation begins with the net present value relation that links the stream of future benefits from an incremental capital project to its cost,

$$\sum_{j=0}^{\infty} R^{j+1} MPK_{t+j} = MIC_t, \tag{1}$$

where R is the real discount factor equal to $(1+r+\delta)^{-1}$ in the absence of bubbles (where r is the real risk-adjusted discount rate and δ is the economic rate of depreciation), MPK_{t+j} is the marginal product of capital associated with this incremental capital project, and MIC_t is the marginal investment cost. The latter term is composed of two parts, the purchase cost of the capital project relative to the price of output $((p^I / p^Y)_t)$ and the marginal adjustment cost (MAC_t). Equation (1) is based on the timing assumptions that revenues accrue at the end of the period, while investment costs are paid at the beginning of the period. It proves convenient to rewrite equation (1) as follows:

$$R\, MPK_t + \sum_{j=1}^{\infty} R^{j+1} MPK_{t+j} = MIC_t. \tag{2}$$

The companion net present value relation to equation (1) for period $t + 1$ is written as follows:

$$R\sum_{j=0}^{\infty} R^{j+1} MPK_{t+1+j} = R\, MIC_{t+1}, \tag{3}$$

where both sides of the equation have been multiplied by an extra R. Equation (3) can be rewritten as follows:

$$\sum_{j=1}^{\infty} R^{j+1} MPK_{t+j} = R\, MIC_{t+1}. \tag{4}$$

The difficulty with using any of these equations in estimation is that they contain an infinite number of future variables. This problem is overcome by a suitable transformation (akin to a Koyck transformation in distributed lag models). In this case, we subtract equation (4) from (2) and thus obtain the following Euler equation,

$$R\, MPK_t - (MIC_t - R\, MIC_{t+1}) = 0,$$
$$- (1+r+\delta)\, MIC_t + (MPK_t + MIC_{t+1}) = 0. \tag{5}$$

The Euler equation (5) can also be obtained as a first-order condition in a formal optimization problem. We assume that the firm chooses labor and capital inputs to maximize its market value. The firm is constrained by three technologies. The production technology $(F[L_t, K_t])$ relates output (Y_t) to the labor (L_t) and capital (K_t) inputs and to a stochastic technology shock. The adjustment cost technology $(G[I_t, K_t]$, where I_t is investment) affects the acquisition of capital (though not labor). Adjustment costs are valued by the price of foregone output, are affected by a stochastic shock, and are convex in investment. The latter is a critical assumption, as it forces the firm to consider its future plans when making current decisions. The accumulation technology determines the existing capital stock as a weighted sum of past investments, where the weights follow a declining exponential or geometric pattern. Moreover, the firm is a price-taker in its input market, though not necessarily in its output market. With the value maximization objective and these four constraints, optimal behavior for a forward-looking firm is determined by variational, optimal control, or dynamic programming methods.

In order to implement the Euler equation, we need to specify the MIC, MPK, and R variables. The MIC is specified as follows:

$$MIC_t = (p^I / p^Y)_t + MAC_t,$$ (6)

$$MAC_t = \alpha_0 + \alpha_1 (I/K)_t + \alpha_2 (I/K)_t^2,$$ (7)

where MAC_t is a second-order Taylor approximation to the marginal adjustment cost function, $G_I[I_t, K_t]$.

The MPK is determined by an application of Euler's Theorem of Homogeneous Functions to the following relation between output and the production and adjustment cost technologies:

$$Y_t = F[L_t, K_t] - G[I_t, K_t],$$ (8)

to yield the following expression for the MPK,

$$MPK_t = \zeta(SALES/K)_t - (COST/K)_t + (I/K)_t MAC_t,$$ (9)

where SALES is net nominal sales, COST is the nominal cost of goods sold and selling, general, and administrative expenses, and ζ is a parameter capturing the combined effects of imperfect competition and nonconstant returns to scale in production. When the firm is a price-taker in its output market and $F[L_t, K_t]$ exhibits constant returns to scale, ζ equals 1. Deviations from these characteristics results in deviations of ζ from unity.

The discount factor, R, is generalized in two ways from the specification reported for equation (1). We recognize the possibility that our specification of the discount rate, r, may not be complete and may include a parameter, Θ, common to all firms. Of most importance to this study is the discount rate wedge, μ, that enters the specification only for subsets of firms and is multiplied by an indicator variable, Ω. This indicator variable varies by firm and over time, takes a value of 1 when firm i enters either the high-price PIO or high-price GIO portfolios, and leads to the following specification of the discount factor:

$$R_{i,t} = (1 + r_{i(s),t} + \delta_{i(s),t} + \Theta + \Omega_{i,t}^{PIO} \mu^{PIO} + \Omega_{i,t}^{GIO} \mu^{GIO})^{-1},$$ (10)

where the firm (i), time (t), and sector (s) subscripts are explicit and $i(s)$ indicates that the variable is available at the sector level for firm i.

The Euler equation is estimated by GMM with instruments that are lags of the variables appearing in the Euler equation,

$$W_{i,t} = \begin{Bmatrix} \left(1-\tau_{t-1}\right)(SALES_{i,t-1}/p^{Y}_{i(s)})/K_{i,t-2}, \ \left(1-\tau_{t-1}\right)\left(1+r_{i(s),t-1}+\delta_{i(s),t-1}\right), \\ \left(1-\tau_{t-1}\right)(I_{i,t-1}/K_{i,t-2}), \ \left(1-\tau_{t-1}\right)(I_{i,t-1}/K_{i,t-2})^{2}, \ \left(1-z_{t-1}-u_{t-1}\right)(p^{I}_{i(s),t-1}/p^{Y}_{i(s),t-1}), \\ \Omega^{PIO}_{i,t-1}, \ \Omega^{GIO}_{i,t-1} \end{Bmatrix}$$

(11)

where τ_{t-1} is the corporate income tax rate, u_{t-1} is the investment tax credit rate, and z_{t-1} is the present value of depreciation allowances.

3. Data Set

We examine U.S. firms for two reasons. First, the United States has the most richly developed capital markets in the world and is therefore less likely to suffer from overvaluation and overinvestment. Second, the maximum amount of firm-level data is available for the United States. This latter factor is important to obtain a sufficient number of firms in the high-price portfolio, which contains only the top two deciles in a given year. This portfolio is further reduced by sorting by investment opportunities. Most of the empirical work is based on more than 50,000 firm-year observations. The panel data consists of a representative sample of U.S. publicly traded firms for the period 1980–2004. In fact, the sample approaches the universe of U.S. publicly traded firms. The primary data source is CompuStat with additional information obtained from CRSP and various sources of industry and aggregate data. Data sources and variable construction are described in the Data Appendix in Chirinko and Schaller (2011).

We maximize the size of the data set used in estimation in three ways. First, we use an unbalanced panel, and thus avoid the severe data restrictions imposed by a balanced panel. This choice has the further advantage of attenuating survivorship bias. Second, even in an unbalanced panel, some methods of constructing the replacement value of the capital stock require long strings of contiguous data to implement the perpetual inventory formula. We partly avoid this problem by tailoring our algorithm to preserve observations when there are gaps in the data and to use data that are more frequently available in CompuStat (e.g., when we find evidence of substantial acquisitions and divestitures, we use data on property, plant, and equipment in addition to the capital expenditure data). An additional problem posed by the perpetual inventory formula is its dependence on an initial or seed value of the capital stock drawn from financial statements. This initial value can be a particularly poor measure of capital's replacement cost that distorts the computed capital stock (K) until the impact of the initial value is largely depreciated. One solution to this problem is to compute the capital stock for many years before using these data in estimation, but this approach discards a substantial number of observations. As an alternative, we adopt the procedure discussed in detail in Chirinko and Schaller (2005) that computes an adjustment factor for the initial value taken from financial statements. Third, the Euler equation and the instruments we have chosen require only three years of contiguous data. All of the estimates reported below are based on sample sizes that exceed 50,000 firm-year observations.

The real risk-adjusted market discount rate $(r_{i(s),t})$ is constructed in several steps. We begin with a weighted-average of the nominal returns to debt and equity, where the weights vary by sector. The nominal return to debt is adjusted for the tax deductibility of interest payments. The nominal return to equity is based on the CAPM and thus accounts for systematic risk. The nominal weighted-average is converted to a real return with an inflation adjustment that varies across sectors and over time.

The other variables used in this study are constructed as follows. Gross nominal investment is capital expenditures computed in a two-step procedure. We begin with the data on capital expenditures (CompuStat item 128). CompuStat does not always have reliable data for the changes to the capital stock associated with large acquisitions or divestitures, and we modify the algorithm of Chirinko, Fazzari, and Meyer (1999) to adjust the reported investment data. If the financial statement data indicate a substantial acquisition or divestiture, we use accounting identities to derive a more accurate measure of investment that replaces the data from item 128. Net Sales is CompuStat item 12. This nominal investment series is converted to a real investment series (I) by dividing by a sector-specific price deflator. Sales growth (SG) is the annual growth rate in nominal net sales divided by a sector-specific price deflator. Variable cost is the sum of the Cost of Goods Sold (CompuStat item 41) and Selling, General, and Administrative Expense (CompuStat item 189; when this item is not reported, it is set to zero). The depreciation rate is taken from the BEA and is allowed to vary across industries and over time. The relative price of investment is the ratio of the price of investment to the price of output. These industry-specific, implicit price deflators are taken from the BEA; the relative price series is adjusted for corporate income taxes. New share issues (NSI) are measured as the ratio of the proceeds from equity issues relative to nominal investment spending. The marginal product of capital (MPK) is computed as described in equation (9).

We determine whether a firm is in the high-price portfolio in a given year using the Sales/Price ratio, the ratio of net nominal sales to the nominal value of common equity. The Sales/Price ratio has several key advantages: sales is a relatively straightforward accounting concept, rarely extremely small, and never negative.[5] Portfolios are formed by sorting all the firms for which the necessary data are available in a given year by the Sales/Price ratio. The two deciles with the lowest

Sales/Price ratio—equivalently, the highest equity value (relative to sales)—in a given year are classified as high-price firms. The portfolio formation procedure allows a firm to be a high-price firm this year but not in a subsequent year. In fact, it is common for firms to move in and out of the high-price portfolio.

Firms that enter the high-price portfolio are further classified by investment opportunities (IO), which are measured by real sales growth over the prior three years. Firms with poor investment opportunities (PIO) or good investment opportunities (GIO) are those firms with sales growth in the bottom and top quartiles of high-price firms, respectively. Thus, in a given year, firms that are in the high-price, poor investment opportunity portfolio represent approximately 5% of the firms with serviceable data for that year.

When analyzing investment, we use the capital stock to control for size, which is frequently measured by the equity value of the firm (especially in finance research). In the current study concerned with stock market bubbles, this approach would be clearly inappropriate. Instead, we use the capital stock calculated using a standard perpetual inventory algorithm. The primary variable we analyze is the ratio of investment to the capital stock (I/K). There are a few extreme outliers for I/K. This is a common issue in panel data studies involving I/K. We address this issue by deleting the 1% tails of the I/K distribution.

Summary statistics are presented in three separate panels in Table 17.1. Panel A contains the Sales/Price ratio defining high-price portfolios and SG and the Cost/Sales ratio (the latter used as a robustness check) defining firms with poor or good investment opportunities. Panel B contains variables describing these portfolios. As measured by the capital stock, the median high-price firm is less than half as large as the median firm in the sample. The median high-price firm expands more rapidly than the median firm; the respective I/K ratios are 0.135 and 0.087. Among the high-price firms, those with good investment opportunities (I/K equal to 0.151) are expanding at nearly twice the rate as firms with poor investment opportunities (I/K equal to 0.077). Consistent with this expansion, NSI (new share issues normalized by I) is very large for GIO firms. Moreover, high-price firms with poor investment opportunities have higher NSI than the median firm in the full sample (which includes all firms, not just those with high stock prices). The NSI is 0.381 for PIO firms, compared with 0.187 for the median firm. This active participation in equity markets by PIO firms resonates with the possibility that they are exploiting the availability of cheap equity finance due to a bubble in their share price.

Panel C contains variables other than I/K entering the estimating equation. Consistent with the robust investment opportunities available to high-price GIO firms, their median MPK of 0.310 is much larger than that for the median high-price PIO firm (0.092) or the median firm (0.231). The values of the remaining variables—the real risk-adjusted market rate and the relative price of investment goods—are similar across subsets of firms.[6] Taken together, these results suggest that investment opportunities and MPKs are the key differences

Table 17.1 **Summary Statistics**

A. Variables determining portfolios

	N	Mean	25%	50%	75%	Std. Dev.	Skewness	Kurtosis
Sales/Price								
All	55,021	77.777	0.691	1.477	3.086	6459.91	117.120	15191.56
High price	6,019	0.340	0.137	0.249	0.403	0.770	42.373	2332.31
High price & PIO	1,162	0.385	0.120	0.252	0.416	1.434	28.829	917.257
High price & GIO	962	0.322	0.097	0.213	0.398	0.448	7.010	87.483
SG								
All	55,021	0.137	-0.046	0.061	0.199	1.241	71.092	6734.88
High price	6,019	0.522	-0.0001	0.175	0.444	3.606	26.090	849.660
High price & PIO	1,162	0.958	-0.059	0.118	0.482	6.678	16.274	312.515
High price & GIO	962	0.663	-0.009	0.261	0.609	3.577	20.900	528.662
Cost/Sales								
All	55,021	0.988	0.842	0.903	0.959	3.606	199.842	43914.78
High price	6,019	1.574	0.707	0.841	1.216	10.862	66.700	4863.65
High price & PIO	1,162	2.617	0.751	0.977	1.599	23.962	31.962	1060.24
High price & GIO	962	2.119	0.827	1.083	1.760	4.275	8.943	100.892

Table 17.1 (Continued)

B. Variables describing portfolios

	N	Mean	25%	50%	75%	Std. Dev.	Skewness	Kurtosis
K								
All	55,021	1463.20	16.293	78.871	427.381	12632.77	86.369	12394.70
High price	6,019	789.291	7.265	35.520	276.902	3049.90	9.983	160.613
High price & PIO	1,162	648.392	3.944	17.817	183.375	3073.55	12.049	200.205
High price & GIO	962	269.783	4.314	14.148	53.328	1428.99	8.919	91.768
I								
All	55,021	122.878	1.086	6.561	37.890	780.978	32.571	1757.34
High price	6,019	104.235	0.636	4.546	34.066	493.473	14.032	279.405
High price & PIO	1,162	53.035	0.219	1.270	12.633	207.757	6.926	58.972
High price & GIO	962	41.806	0.311	1.529	9.407	217.249	9.679	115.579
I/K								
All	55,021	0.130	0.041	0.087	0.165	0.140	2.334	6.834
High price	6,019	0.199	0.052	0.135	0.283	0.196	1.461	1.800
High price & PIO	1,162	0.122	0.030	0.077	0.157	0.141	2.286	6.642
High price & GIO	962	0.223	0.055	0.151	0.338	0.215	1.210	0.792

Table 17.1 (Continued)

B. Variables describing portfolios (Continued)

NSI

All	48,725	15.425	0.000	0.187	2.845	118.503	37.817	2388.67
High price	4,969	26.791	0.057	1.195	8.310	150.421	20.263	566.958
High price & PIO	978	19.506	0.000	0.381	4.270	178.792	21.783	535.091
High price & GIO	771	27.634	0.188	1.592	6.523	173.688	15.414	305.096

C. Other variables entering the estimating equation

MPK

All	55,021	0.870	0.041	0.231	0.760	2.126	4.686	28.095
High price	6,019	1.749	0.028	0.509	2.020	3.474	2.621	8.151
High price & PIO	1,162	0.519	-0.051	0.092	0.623	2.095	4.092	29.637
High price & GIO	962	1.857	-0.112	0.310	2.529	3.980	2.124	5.087

r

All	55,021	0.120	0.093	0.120	0.146	0.037	0.429	2.829
High price	6,019	0.116	0.085	0.111	0.146	0.047	1.277	5.274
High price & PIO	1,162	0.121	0.085	0.112	0.148	0.056	1.695	5.526
High price & GIO	962	0.116	0.088	0.113	0.139	0.043	1.503	6.882

Table 17.1 (Continued)

C. Other variables entering the estimating equation (Continued)

	N	Mean	25%	50%	75%	Std. Dev.	Skewness	Kurtosis
p^I/p^Y								
All	55,021	1.032	0.871	1.000	1.123	0.287	1.718	5.704
High price	6,019	1.035	0.807	1.000	1.147	0.331	1.541	3.242
High price & PIO	1,162	0.994	0.767	1.000	1.121	0.298	1.349	3.772
High price & GIO	962	1.050	0.767	0.998	1.156	0.379	1.431	2.066

Note: The variables are computed for the period 1980 to 2004 and are defined as follows: Sales/Price is the ratio of nominal sales to nominal common equity value; SG is real sales growth; Cost/Sales is the ratio of nominal costs of goods sold to nominal sales; K is the real replacement cost of the stock of capital in property, plant, and equipment in millions of 1996 dollars; I is real investment in property, plant, and equipment in millions of 1996 dollars; NSI is the ratio of new share issues to nominal investment spending; MPK is the marginal product of capital; r is the real risk-adjusted market discount rate; p^I/p^Y is the ratio of the price of investment goods to the price of output. Firms with poor investment opportunities (PIO) [good investment opportunities (GIO)] are those firms in the high-price portfolio with sales growth in the bottom [top] quartile Details concerning the definitions, construction, and sources of the data are discussed in Section 3 and the Data Appendix in Chirinko and Schaller (2011).

between high-price PIO and GIO firms, and hence will play an important role for our estimates of the discount rate wedge.

4. Benchmark Empirical Results

This section presents estimates of the discount rate wedge based on the Euler equation (5) and the investment behavior of high-price firms at the time of portfolio formation. To attempt to differentiate between the standard and overinvestment stories, we divide the high-price portfolio by the investment opportunities available to firms. If the standard story applies to all firms in the high-price portfolio, firms with either PIO or GIO should use discount rates that do not differ systematically from their risk-adjusted market rates. However, if the overinvestment story is relevant for a subset of firms in the high-price portfolio, their actual discount rate should be below their risk-adjusted market rate. This situation is most likely to occur for high-price PIO firms. Thus, the discount rate wedge, represented by μ and defined as the difference between the actual discount rate used by the firm and its risk-adjusted market rate, will allow us to discriminate between the standard and overinvestment stories.

We use the Euler equation to estimate the discount rate wedge for the high-price firms with poor (μ^{PIO}) and good (μ^{GIO}) investment opportunities, respectively. In the first column of Table 17.2, μ^{PIO} is –0.195, a result that is both economically and statistically significant and consistent with the overinvestment story. By contrast, μ^{GIO} is very close to zero, which is consistent with the standard story. The Wald test reported in the second row evaluates the hypothesis that $\mu^{PIO} = \mu^{GIO}$ and is computed by the delta method. The null hypothesis of equal discount rate wedges is rejected with a p-value of 0.021. These results provide strong evidence for the importance of differentiating between classes of firms and for the empirical relevance of both the standard and overinvestment stories.

Three additional results presented in column (1) are worth noting. First, the ζ parameter, which captures deviations from constant returns to scale or perfect competition, is less than 1. While the difference from unity is statistically significant, it would not appear to be economically important. Second, marginal adjustment costs are positive and increasing, and thus the adjustment cost function is convex. This property is required by the optimization problem presented in Section 2 that underlies the Euler equation. Third, the Hansen-Sargan J test evaluating the overidentifying restrictions fails to reject the model, thus providing some assurance of the reasonableness of our empirical specification.

The point estimate of $\mu^{PIO} = -0.195$ indicates a substantial misallocation of capital. In order to draw the implications of bubbles for capital formation, we need to assess the impact of μ^{PIO} on the incentive to accumulate capital and then the impact of this enhanced incentive on capital accumulation. Recall that our

Table 17.2 **Estimates of the Discount Rate Wedge: Baseline Model**

	High-price firms		
	Investment opportunities measured by demand shocks	Investment opportunities measured by cost shocks	Long Horizons
	(1)	(2)	(3)
μ^{PIO}	-0.195** (0.097)	-0.224** (0.133)	
μ^{GIO}	-0.004 (0.060)	0.051 (0.059)	
μ^{LH}			0.055 (0.046)
Wald	5.337** [0.021]	4.202** [0.040]	1.431 [0.232]
ζ	0.931*** (0.013)	0.939*** (0.012)	0.919*** (0.016)
α_0	0.593 (0.648)	0.365 (0.599)	1.009 (0.815)
α_1	35.132*** (10.713)	30.609*** (3.695)	45.695*** (15.424)
$G_I[I_t, K_t : \alpha_0, \alpha_1]$	3.657	3.016	5.023
$G_{II}[I_t, K_t : \alpha_0, \alpha_1]$	0.445	0.366	0.589

Table 17.2 Estimates of the Discount Rate Wedge: Baseline Model (Continued)

J	0.685 [0.408]	1.241 [0.265]	0.087 [0.926]
N	55021	53038	55486

Note: GMM estimates are based on equation (5) and on panel data for the period 1980 to 2004. Firms are placed in the high-price portfolio if their Sales/Price ratio is in the lowest two deciles. The μ^{PIO}, μ^{GIO}, and μ^{LH} parameters are the discount rate wedges for high-price firms with poor investment opportunities (PIO), with good investment opportunities (GIO), and with long horizons (LH), respectively. Investment opportunities are measured in column (1) by sales growth, defined as real sales growth over the prior three years, and in column (2) by the change in the cost ratio, defined as the change in the ratio of nominal costs to nominal sales over the previous three years. Firms with poor investment opportunities are those firms in the high-price portfolio with sales growth in the bottom quartile or the cost ratio in the top quartile. The portfolio for good investment opportunities is formed in a similar way for the top quartile for sales growth and the bottom quartile for the cost ratio. Horizons are measured by share turnover, defined as the mean (over the year) of the daily ratio of the volume of shares traded to shares outstanding at the end of the day. Firms with long horizons are those with share turnover in the prior year below the median for all observations in the prior year. All portfolios are formed based on beginning-of-period values and are reevaluated every year. The Wald statistic is computed by the delta method and evaluates the hypothesis that $\mu^{PIO} = \mu^{GIO}$ in columns (1) and (2) and the hypothesis that $\mu^{LH} = 0$ in column (3); p-values are in brackets. The ζ parameter captures deviations from constant returns to scale or perfect competition; a value of ζ less than unity is consistent with either decreasing returns to scale regardless of the degree of competition in the output market or increasing returns to scale and a sufficient degree of imperfect competition to force the marginal return to capital below its average return. In either case, the firm is earning positive economic rents. The $G_I[I_t, K_t : \alpha_0, \alpha_1] = MAC_t$ statistic is the marginal adjustment cost function; the α parameters are from the marginal adjustment cost function defined in equation (7). The $G_I[I_t, K_t : \alpha_0, \alpha_1] = MAC_t$ statistic is the marginal adjustment cost function. Both adjustment cost statistics depend on the estimated α parameters and are evaluated at the median values of I_t and K_t. The J statistic is the Hansen-Sargan statistic for overidentification; p-values are in brackets. N is the number of firm/year observations. The instruments are discussed in Section 2. Details concerning the definitions, construction, and sources of the data are discussed in Section 3 and the Data Appendix in Chirinko and Schaller (2011). Standard errors are in parentheses, and ***, **, and * indicate statistical significance at the 1%, 5%, and 10% levels, respectively.

estimates of μ^{PIO} and μ^{GIO} apply to the lowest and highest quartile of high-price firms, respectively, sorted by investment opportunities. We assume that this wedge would decline evenly between these two extremes, and hence the average value for the change in the discount rate wedge for all high-price firms is $\Delta\mu = -0.100$. Lowering the discount rate by -0.100 leads to a 37.7% decline in the user cost of capital: (see the Appendix for the computation). The impact of these enhanced incentives on capital formation depends on the degree to which capital substitutes for other factors in the production function. Estimates of this elasticity of substitution have varied widely from 0.40 (Chirinko, Fazzari, and Mayer, 2011) to 1.00 (the value implied by a Cobb-Douglas production function) to 1.20 (Schaller 2006). Given this range of elasticities, high-price firms accumulate between 15.1% and 45.2% too much capital. While high-price firms comprise 20% of the sample, their mean capital stock is approximately half as large as that for the mean firm (see Table 17.1B.). Taken together, these figures roughly imply a reduction of 1.5% to 4.5% of the capital stock for publicly traded firms. It takes a substantial period of time for these excesses to be reversed by the depreciation of capital (though the adjustment process could be accelerated by a reduction in planned investment spending). Five years after a bubble, nearly one-half of the misallocated capital would remain. The effects of bubbles on misallocating capital are substantial and may be long-lasting.

5. Robustness Checks

This section presents a series of robustness checks on the Euler equation and the core result that both the standard and overinvestment stories are empirically relevant.

5.1. COST SHOCKS

The results discussed so far have been based on demand shocks as a measure of investment opportunities. In this subsection, we turn instead to cost shocks. Specifically, we use low (or perhaps negative) recent growth in the Cost/Sales ratio to identify firms with good investment opportunities. Favorable cost shock observations are defined as those with a change in the ratio of nominal costs to nominal sales over the previous three years in the bottom quartile.

The results based on cost shocks are presented the column (2) of Table 17.2, and the results strongly parallel those with demand shocks. In particular, μ^{PIO} is negative and statistically and economically significant, and μ^{GIO} is not statistically far from zero. The difference between these two discount rate wedges is somewhat smaller than in column (1); nonetheless, the Wald statistic confirms that this difference is statistically significant.

5.2. LONG HORIZONS

Stein (1996) develops a theoretical model in which a bubble induces a firm to use a discount rate lower than the risk-adjusted rate if the manager has short horizons or the financing constraint is binding. In the former case, a bubble presents short-horizon managers with an opportunity in the form of cheap equity without the attending costs when a bubble becomes widely known. In the latter case, a bubble presents financially constrained managers with an opportunity to relax a binding constraint. According to the Stein model, the discount rates of firms with long horizons and without a financing constraint at the time of portfolio formation will be unaffected by a bubble.

To test this latter prediction, we need to identify a class of firms that is financially unconstrained and whose managers have short horizons. High-price firms are unlikely to have binding finance constraints. We identify firms with short horizons on the basis of their share turnover. The intuition is simple. Investors care about the performance of the firm until when they sell their shares. When turnover is high—and the expected duration of share ownership is therefore low— the median shareholder will tend to care less about the firm's performance in the more distant future. As a result, managers may behave as if they have a short horizon. Horizons are measured by share turnover, defined as the mean (over the year) of the daily ratio of the volume of shares traded to shares outstanding at the end of the day. Firms with long horizons are those with share turnover in the prior year below the median for all observations in the prior year.

Euler equation estimates of the discount rate wedge for firms with high prices and low share turnover are presented in column (3) of Table 17.2. The model delivers sensible results for the adjustment cost function and the J statistic. More importantly, these results document that the prediction of the Stein model is consistent with the data. The estimated discount rate wedge for high-price firms with long horizons is small and statistically insignificant.

5.3. RESTRICTED MODELS

The results presented in Table 17.2 have defined discount rate wedges in order to evaluate hypotheses suggested by the theory. This subsection takes a different but complementary approach and estimates a series of restricted models. These misspecified models are useful in assessing the standard and overinvestment stories and are evaluated by the J statistic.

Table 17.3 contains estimates of several restricted models. We begin with our benchmark model presented in column (1) of Table 17.2 (with investment opportunities measured by demand shocks) and constrain the discount rate wedge for firms with good investment opportunities (μ^{GIO}) to zero. The estimates are extremely similar to those for the benchmark model; for example, the coefficient

Table 17.3 **Estimates of the Discount Rate Wedge: Restricted Models**

	Investment opportunities measured by demand shocks			Investment opportunities measured by cost shocks		
	$\mu^{GIO}=0$	$\mu^{PIO}=0$	$\mu^{GIO}=0$ $\mu^{PIO}=0$	$\mu^{GIO}=0$	$\mu^{PIO}=0$	$\mu^{GIO}=0$ $\mu^{PIO}=0$
	(1)	(2)	(3)	(4)	(5)	(6)
μ^{PIO}	−0.192** (0.082)	0	0	−0.270** (0.137)	0	0
μ^{GIO}	0	0.003 (0.058)	0	0	0.041 (0.058)	0
Wald	5.459** [0.019]	0.003 [0.958]		3.865** [0.049]	0.504 [0.478]	
ζ	0.931*** (0.011)	0.923*** (0.014)	0.924*** (0.011)	0.943*** (0.009)	0.925*** (0.015)	0.930*** (0.011)
α_0	0.628 (0.440)	0.673 (0.703)	0.645 (0.468)	0.079** (0.040)	1.034 (0.739)	0.717 (0.477)
α_1	35.712*** (7.295)	38.513*** (11.528)	38.058*** (7.681)	26.005*** (6.505)	42.294*** (11.663)	37.245*** (7.508)
$G_I[I_t,K_t:\alpha_0,\alpha_1]$	3.743	4.032	3.964	2.331	4.696	3.942
$G_{II}[I_t,K_t:\alpha_0,\alpha_1]$	0.453	0.488	0.483	0.311	0.506	0.446
J	0.620 [0.733]	7.839** [0.020]	7.861** [0.049]	2.620 [0.270]	4.505 [0.105]	6.859* [0.077]
N	55021	55021	55021	53038	53038	53038

Note: See the note to Table 17.2.

on μ^{PIO} changes by less than 2%. Specification issues arise, however, when μ^{PIO} is constrained to zero in column (2). In this case, the J statistic rises sharply and has a p-value of 0.020 that indicates model misspecification. Given these results, it is not surprising that when both discount rate wedges are constrained to zero, the J statistic indicates that the model remains misspecified.

These results are confirmed in columns (4) through (6) when investment opportunities are measured by cost shocks. The only difference is that when μ^{PIO} is constrained to zero in column (5), the p-value of 0.105 is slightly above the conventional cutoff of 0.100.

Taken together, the results in Table 17.3 confirm the findings that both the standard and overinvestment stories describe subsets of high-price firms.

6. Conclusions

This paper considers the possibility that the stock market occasionally overvalues firms and these bubbles lead to overinvestment. If stock prices rise above fundamental values (a possibility suggested by much recent academic literature), firms would have access to a relatively cheap source of finance that results in an increase in investment. For these overvalued firms, the added investment represents a misallocation of capital, and thus financial market bubbles have real effects. This overinvestment story contrasts with the standard story of stock markets efficiently allocating capital to its best uses.

We present empirical evidence to differentiate between the standard and overinvestment stories. Our primary tests rely on the discount rates guiding investment decisions. The standard story predicts that high-price firms with good investment opportunities should have discount rates that do not differ systematically from the risk-adjusted market rate. (The Stein model also predicts that the pattern of discount rates used by firms that are financially unconstrained and owned by shareholders with long horizons should be similar to the standard story.) The overinvestment story predicts that high-price firms with poor investment opportunities should have discount rates consistently below the market rate. The discount rates guiding investment decisions are unobservable but are revealed by examining the intertemporal pattern of investment implied by the Euler equation for investment and variation in panel data.

Based on a panel data-set of over 50,000 firm-year observations, we find support for both stories. The investment behavior of high-price firms with good investment opportunities is consistent with the standard story. However, the overinvestment story best describes the behavior of high-price firms with poor investment opportunities. Our estimates indicate that high-price firms (with both poor and good investment opportunities) accumulate between 15.1% and 45.2% too much capital as a result of a stock market bubble. Even before they burst, bubbles adversely affect economic activity by misallocating capital. The overinvestment story is further supported by a series of robustness checks on the Euler equation. Our overall conclusion is that, for an important subset of firms, stock market bubbles lead to capital misallocation.

Notes

*   University of Illinois at Chicago, CESifo, and the Federal Reserve Bank of San Francisco, and Carleton University, respectively. The authors thank Mark Blanchette for excellent research assistance and participants at the American Economic Association, Banque de France, European Econometric Society, and the University of Illinois at Chicago, Gadi Barlevy, and the editors for comments and suggestions. Chirinko gratefully acknowledges financial support from The International Center for Futures and Derivatives at the University of Illinois at Chicago. All errors and omissions remain the sole responsibility of the authors, and the conclusions do not necessarily reflect the views of the institutions with which they are associated.

1. We are aware of the controversies that surround the use of the term "bubble" (see, for example, O'Hara 2008). In this paper, bubble is merely shorthand for stock market overvaluation.
2. Baker (2009) reviews studies that have focused on the role of the supply of finance for investment spending.
3. The discount rate will be above the market rate if finance constraints prevent firms from equating the discount rate to the market rate on a period-by-period basis
4. The formal derivation can be found in any of the Euler equation studies cited above. The informal derivation was presented in Chirinko and Schaller (2004), which also contains an intuitive discussion of the Euler equation (185).
5. The book/market ratio is also used in the literature, but it has many disadvantages. See, for example, the discussion of book/market in Lakonishok, Shleifer, and Vishny (1994).
6. The median and mean value of r is approximately 0.120. This figure is consistent with survey evidence. Poterba and Summers (1995) report estimates of the average real hurdle rate indicating that r is 0.122. This estimate has been confirmed in a study by Meier and Tarhan (2007), who report a comparable financial cost of capital of between 0.119 and 0.141.

References

Baker, Malcolm, 2009. "Capital Market-Driven Corporate Finance." *Annual Review of Financial Economics* 1, 181–205.

Bhattacharya, Utpal, and Yu Xiaoyun. 2008. "The Causes and Consequences of Recent Financial Market Bubbles: An Introduction." *Review of Financial Studies* 21, 3–10.

Chirinko, Robert S., Steven M. Fazzari, and Andrew P. Meyer. 1999. "How Responsive Is Business Capital Formation To Its User Cost? An Exploration with Micro Data." *Journal of Public Economics* 74, 53–80.

———. 2011. "A New Approach to Estimating Production Function Parameters: The Elusive Capital-Labor Substitution Elasticity." *Journal of Business & Economic Statistics* 29, 587–594.

Chirinko, Robert S., and Huntley Schaller. 2001. "Business Fixed Investment and 'Bubbles': The Japanese Case." *American Economic Review* 91, 663–680.

———. 2004. "A Revealed Preference Approach to Understanding Corporate Governance Problems: Evidence from Canada." *Journal of Financial Economics* 74, 181–206.

———. 2005. "The Initial Value Problem: Identifying and Correcting a Bias with Constructing the Firm-Level Capital Stock in Panel Data." Carleton University and Emory University, March.

———. 2011. "Do Bubbles Lead to Overinvestment? A Revealed Preference Approach." CESifo, working paper, June

Cochrane, John H. 2001. *Asset Pricing*. Princeton, NJ: Princeton University Press.

Fama, Eugene F. 1976. *Foundations of Finance*. New York: Basic Books.

Hubbard, R. Glenn, and Anil Kashyap. 1992. "Internal Net Worth and the Investment Process: An Application to U.S. Agriculture, 1910–1987." *Journal of Political Economy* 100, 506–534.

Lakonishok, Joseph, Andrei Shleifer, and Robert W. Vishny. 1994. "Contrarian Investment, Extrapolation and Risk." *Journal of Finance* 49, 1541–1578.

Meier, Iwan, and Vefa Tarhan. 2007. "Corporate Investment Decision Practices and the Hurdle Rate Premium Puzzle." HEC Montreal, working paper.

O'Hara, Maureen. 2008. "Bubbles: Some Perspectives (and Loose Talk) from History." *Review of Financial Studies* 21, 11–17.

Poterba, James M., and Lawrence H. Summers. 1995. "A Survey of U.S. Companies, Time Horizons, and Hurdle Rates." *Sloan Management Review* 37, 43–53.

Schaller, Huntley. 2006. "Estimating the Long-Run User Cost Elasticity." *Journal of Monetary Economics* 53, 725–736.

Shapiro, Matthew D. 1986. "The Dynamic Demand for Labor and Capital." *Quarterly Journal of Economics* 101, 513–542.

Shiller, Robert J. 2001. *Irrational Exuberance*. Princeton, NJ: Princeton University PressPaperback edition.

Shleifer, Andrei. 2000. *Inefficient Markets: An Introduction to Behavioral Finance*. Oxford: Oxford University Press.

Stein, J. 1996. "Rational Capital Budgeting in an Irrational World." *Journal of Business* 69, 429–55.

Whited, Toni M. 1992. "Debt, Liquidity Constraints, and Corporate Investment: Evidence from Panel Data." *Journal of Finance* 47, 1425–1460.

Appendix

This appendix provides the details underlying the calculations reported in Section 4. Three steps are required to translate the discount rate wedge of $\mu^{PIO} = -0.195$ into the amount of misallocated capital for high-price firms.

First, we translate the estimate of the discount rate wedges that apply to the lowest and highest quartile (measured by investment opportunities) of high-price firms to all high-price firms. We know that the discount rate wedges are $\mu^{PIO} = -0.195$ and $\mu^{GIO} = -0.004$ for the lowest and highest quartile of high-price firms, respectively. We assume that this wedge declines evenly between these two extremes, and hence the discount rate wedges for all four quartiles are -0.195, -0.131, -0.068, and -0.004. (This procedure is numerically equivalent to averaging the estimates of μ^{PIO} and μ^{GIO}.) The average value for the change in the discount rate wedge for all high-price firms is $\Delta\mu = -0.100$.

Second, the user cost of capital can be represented as follows,

$$UC = (r + \mu + \delta) * RP * TAX \tag{A1}$$

where r is the real risk-adjusted discount rate, μ is the discount rate wedge, δ is the economic rate of capital depreciation, RP is the relative price of investment goods, and TAX represents a collection of tax variables (income tax and investment credit rates; value of tax depreciation). The percentage change in the user cost (evaluated at $\mu = 0$) is computed as follows,

$$\%\Delta UC = \Delta\mu / (r + \delta). \tag{A2}$$

Based on the dataset, the mean value of r is 0.120 and δ is 0.145, and the percentage change in the user cost equals,

$$\%\Delta UC = \Delta\mu / (r + \delta) = -0.100 / (0.120 + 0.145) = -0.377. \tag{A3}$$

Third, per the discussion in Section 4, we assume that the elasticity of substitution between capital and other factors (σ) is between 0.40 and 1.20. Thus, the lower and upper bounds of the percentage change in the capital stock is computed according to the following formula,

$$\%\Delta K = -\sigma * (\%\Delta UC) = \{0.151, 0.452\}. \tag{A4}$$

INDEX